A Genealogy of 'Japanese' Self-images

JAPANESE SOCIETY SERIES

General Editor: Yoshio Sugimoto

Lives of Young Koreans in Japan
Yasunori Fukuoka

Globalization and Social Change in Contemporary Japan
J.S. Eades Tom Gill Harumi Befu

Coming Out in Japan: The Story of Satoru and Ryuta
Satoru Ito and Ryuta Yanase

Japan and Its Others:
Globalization, Difference and the Critique of Modernity
John Clammer

Hegemony of Homogeneity:
An Anthropological Analysis of *Nihonjinron*
Harumi Befu

Foreign Migrants in Contemporary Japan
Hiroshi Komai

A Social History of Science and Technology in
Contempory Japan, Volume 1
Shigeru Nakayama

Farewell to Nippon: Japanese Lifestyle Migrants in Australia
Machiko Sato

The Peripheral Centre:
Essays on Japanese History and Civilization
Johann P. Arnason

A Genealogy of 'Japanese' Self-images
Eiji Oguma

A Genealogy of 'Japanese' Self-images

Eiji Oguma

Translated by David Askew

Trans Pacific Press
Melbourne

This English edition first published in 2002 by
Trans Pacific Press, PO Box 120, Rosanna, Melbourne, Victoria 3084, Australia
Telephone: +61 3 9459 3021 Fax: +61 3 9457 5923
Email: enquiries@transpacificpress.com
Web: http://www.transpacificpress.com

Copyright © Trans Pacific Press 2002

Designed and set by digital environs Melbourne. enquiries@digitalenvirons.com

Printed in India by Thomson Press (India) Ltd.

Distributors

USA and Canada
International Specialized Book
Services (ISBS)
920 NE 58th Avenue, Suite 300
Portland, Oregon 97213-3786
USA
Telephone: (800) 944-6190
Fax: (503) 280-8832
Email: orders@isbs.com
Web: http://www.isbs.com

Japan
Kyoto University Press
Kyodai Kaikan
15-9 Yoshida Kawara-cho
Sakyo-ku, Kyoto 606-8305
Telephone: (075) 761-6182
Fax: (075) 761-6190
Email: sales@kyoto-up.gr.jp
Web: http://www.kyoto-up.gr.jp

All rights reserved. No production of any part of this book may take place without the written permission of Trans Pacific Press.

ISSN 1443–9670 (Japanese Society Series)
ISBN 1-8768-4383-7 (Hardback)
ISBN 1-8768-43 04-7 (Paperback)

National Library of Australia Cataloging in Publication Data

Oguma, Eiji, 1962–.
   A genealogy of 'Japanese' self-images.
   Bibliography.
   Includes index.
   ISBN 1 876843 04 7(pbk.)
   ISBN 1 876843 83 7.

   1. Ethonology – Japan. 2. Japanese – Ethnic identity. 3.
   Japan – Ethnic relations. 4. Japan – Colonies – East Asia.
   I. Title. (Series : Japanese society series).

305.8956

Contents

Translator's Commentary	vii
Chronology	xvi
Central Terms in the Kiki Myths	xvii
An Introduction to the English-Language Edition	xviii
Introduction	xxvi

Part One: The Thought of an 'Open Country'

1 The Birth of Theories of the Japanese Nation	3
2 The Debate on Mixed Residence in the Interior	16
3 The Theory of the National Polity and Japanese Christianity	31
4 The Anthropologists	53
5 The Theory that the 'Japanese' and Koreans share a Common Ancestor	64
6 The Japanese Annexation of Korea	81

Part Two: The Thought of 'Empire'

7 History and the 'Abolition of Discrimination'	95
8 The Reformation of the National Polity Theory	110
9 National Self-Determination and National Borders	125
10 The Japanese as Caucasians	143
11 'The Return to Blood'	156

Part Three: The Thought of an 'Island Nation'

12 The Birth of an Island Nation's Folklore	175
13 Japanisation versus Eugenics	203
14 The Revival of the Kiki Myths	237
15 From 'Blood' to 'Climate'	260
16 The Collapse of Empire	285
17 The Myth Takes Root	298

Conclusion	321
Notes	350
References	395
Index	428

Japan, showing principal places mentioned in the text. Broad districts are in large type, prefectures in medium type and cities in small type.

Translator's Commentary

I first read the original Japanese version of this book, *Tan'itsu minzoku shinwa no kigen – 'Nihonjin' no jigazō no keifu*, in late 1995. At the time, I quickly skipped through it, cursed Oguma for his age (born in 1962, he is of my own generation), and filed it away in my mind as an interesting read. It was perhaps two years or so later, when I was asked if I was interested in translating it, that I dug it up again and read it through carefully. After writing a long article on it – an article I was later asked to expand by including Oguma's second work, *'Nihonjin' no kyōkai – Okinawa· Ainu·Taiwan·Chōsen shokuminchi shihai kara fukki undō made* (The Boundaries of the 'Japanese': Okinawa, the *Ainu*, Taiwan and Korea. From Colonial Domination to the Return Movement) (Oguma 1998) – and giving the matter far too little thought, I agreed.[1] Although I have some minor quibbles with Oguma, his work is, I thought then and still think now, both interesting and important.

It is interesting because it challenges a major assumption frequently seen in works, both in English and in Japanese, about the Japanese self-image: that the myth of ethnic homogeneity was a product of prewar Japan. This assumption can perhaps be partly explained by the unfortunate habit many Japanese have of viewing the prewar years – and in fact the entire history of modern Japan from 1868 to 1945 – as a dark age, and thus to tend to believe that all the negative aspects of modern Japanese intellectual life must have their roots in this period. As Oguma also implies, this assumption is also the result of a lack of historical research – after all, as this work shows, to read the pre-1945 literature is to realise that the dominant myth of the Great Japanese Empire was not one of ethnic homogeneity. Moreover, it is perhaps a sign of how dramatic the paradigm shift was, from a self-image of the Japanese nation as consisting of a plurality of ethnic groups to one of the

1 See David Askew, 'Review Essay: Oguma Eiji and the Construction of the Modern Japanese National Identity', *Social Science Japan Journal*, vol. 4, no. 1, April 2001, pp. 111–6.

Japanese as consisting of a single ethnicity, that this assumption has not previously been challenged. Oguma has, however, exposed it as false, and it is difficult to believe that it could ever be taken seriously again.

This work also argues that the size of the Japan of the day heavily influenced the dominant self-image. As Japan grew with imperial expansion, the notion that the Japanese were the product of a melting pot of many different ethnic groups strengthened but, as Japan's borders contracted with military defeat, this notion was replaced with a belief in ethnic homogeneity. Although I have my doubts about this argument, it is without question both interesting and a plausible explanation for the changes in the discourse on the Japanese nation.

The major theme tackled here is the discourse on modern Japanese national identity. This is examined through an analysis of a number of debates in imperial Japan, including those between assimilation and racism, imperialism and national self-determination, nationalism (in the sense of ethnocentricity) and Pan-Asianism, and pure blood and Japanisation. This work examines the location of various minorities within the Japanese intellectual landscape. It encompasses the relationship between the Japanese nation and the ethnic minorities of the empire – the *burakumin* (seen to be an alien people), the *Ainu*, the peoples of Okinawa, Taiwan, Korea and the South Seas (Japanese Micronesia) – and, within the Japanese nation itself, the role and status of women and Christians. A strong sub-text of this work is the process (analysed in further detail in Oguma's second work) by which lines, borders and boundaries are drawn between individuals and groups in establishing self-identity, and the accompanying discourse on acceptance and rejection (or racism, or discrimination).

This book will appeal to readers with an interest in the relationship between empire and national identity, nationalism, and the Japanese orientalist discourse, as well as specialists in modern Japanese history and Japanese colonialism. It examines the discourse on ethnic and other minorities within Japan, and provides an intellectual history of one key concept in modern Japan – Japanese national identity. It sheds light on several aspects of the intellectual landscape of postwar Japan, such as the Symbolic Emperor System, and the importance of rice in at least one approach to constructing the Japanese.

***

Translator's Commentary

Although I have been involved in a number of projects to translate monographs from English into Japanese, and have translated a few book chapters into English, this is my first book-length translation from Japanese into English.

I have always enjoyed translating. The first project I was involved in, as an undergraduate, was a joint translation over the summer holidays of 1989 of Norman Barry, *On Classical Liberalism and Libertarianism* (subsequently published as *Jiyū no seitōsei – kotenteki jiyūshugi to ribatarianizumu*, Bokutakusha, 1990). Although it did not seem unusual at the time, I now realise in retrospect that the opportunity to participate in this kind of project could only have been possible in the very special environment that was Kyoto University. I was only to realise how lucky I was to have been a part of that intellectual environment, with its extremely liberal and tolerant character and its unfailing emphasis on academic and intellectual excellence, after I had experienced university life elsewhere. Japanese academics frequently translate at least one or two works into Japanese, and the prestige given to translators in Japan is far greater than in the English-speaking world, but to have been able to participate in this sort of project as an undergraduate student was unusual, even in Kyoto. My interest in translating and any success I have had owes much to Professor Adachi Yukio, his interest in writing styles, and his enormous generosity and kindness in mentoring me. I remain eternally in his debt. I was to do more translating as a postgraduate student and, after taking up a position in Australia, was happy to agree to try translating the other way around.

Although I had been trained in translating into Japanese by professors such as Adachi Yukio and Miyamoto Moritarō, when I agreed to translate Oguma into English, I had no role models, no one I could turn to for advice, and no one with both a real feel for language and experience in translating from Japanese into English at my home institution in Australia. However, the basic principles of translation are the same, whether translating into or from Japanese, and Oguma Eiji generously agreed to read my translation as it came out and offer comments on it. Since I had the luxury of being able to communicate on a very regular basis with the author – in the decade I have been involved in translating academic work, e-mail has revolutionised the way this is done – I decided to start with a draft translation of the entire work first, make sure that he was happy with it, and then polish the prose into something more sophisticated.

I made three early decisions that have influenced the final outcome. First, I decided that I would not reproduce Oguma's style. His work in Japanese is extremely easy to read, written in a colloquial style not often seen in academic works, and makes extensive use of the literary *taigen-dome* style (ending sentences with substantives). Although I have tried to keep the persistent murmur of the translator far in the background, I was not able to reproduce this style in English. For better or worse, therefore, the style of the translation is very different from the original. This stylistic decision has also influenced the structure: in a number of cases, for instance, paragraphs have been merged. Secondly, the original contains a large number of quotations from a variety of pre-1945 texts, a time when written Japanese was a very different language from the Japanese of today (Japanese students actually have to be taught how to read written texts that are only a hundred years old). When such texts are directly cited, Japanese academics often rephrase them in modern Japanese to save their readers from the need to use dictionaries. Oguma is no exception. For my own entertainment – I obviously have far too much time on my hands – I originally tried to translate some quotations into medieval English and follow them with modern English equivalents, but quickly decided that the final translation should be as straightforward and easy to read as possible. This meant that many of those sections where an original text was rephrased were cut out. Thirdly, rather than adding background information in translator's endnotes to make the meaning of certain passages clear, the author and I quickly decided to include this in the main body of the text. Some of this was limited to merely adding the first name of the author under discussion. Kita Sadakichi and Kita Ikki, for instance, are written in Japanese with different characters, so 'Kita said' in Japanese leaves no ambiguity about which Kita is meant, but this is clearly not the case in English. Short explanations about a large range of words and phrases in the original with which a Japanese audience would be very familiar, but about which an English-language audience might not be as knowledgeable, have been incorporated into the text. This information will, I hope, make the work more accessible.

Other decisions were made for me. First, the style used by Trans Pacific Press in citing sources is different from that used in the original text, so a bibliography was prepared and the in-text citation system was consistently used. This is straightforward, although since many of the works cited are from collected works, the citations are longer than is sometimes the case. Kita Sadakichi (1979–82: vol. 8, 8, 51, 59), for instance, cites pages 8, 51 and 59 from volume 8 of Kita's Collected Works. Moreover, some of the cited works are from long articles that appeared in a number of issues of a particular journal. Thus Kume Kunitake (1894: no. 223, 15–19, no. 224, 11, 13, no. 225, 12, 17, no. 226, 11, 14–15) cites pages 15–19 from the first part (no. 223) of an article published in *Kokumin no tomo*, in addition to pages 11 and 13 from another part (no. 224), pages 12 and 17 (no. 225), and finally pages 11 and 14–15 from the last part (no. 226). Second, after a rough first draft was completed, and in consultation with the author, it was decided to make a large number of additions, especially in the earlier chapters, to provide further background information that would make this work more accessible to readers without a deep knowledge of modern Japanese history. Much of this information is included in the endnotes. Third, part of the conclusion was removed and replaced with a new section.

Although the first draft was a very straightforward translation, with the author's agreement, I have made a number of changes in the interests of readability. For instance, the key concept of this work, *minzoku* (nation) can be extremely difficult to translate (as, in fact, translating 'nation' into Japanese can be), and while I have attempted to be consistent throughout, I have at times happily sacrificed consistency at the altar of readability. Moreover, in addition to adding a number of new sections, a much smaller number of sentences have been removed. As far as I am aware, I have not taken outrageous liberties in translating this work, except in the case of some of the titles of articles and books cited by the author. Here, in some cases at least, I have been happy to abandon the virtues of faithfulness to provide a better understanding of what these articles and books actually discuss.

Several housekeeping notes. First, as a basic rule of thumb, I have attempted to provide macrons for the long vowels of Japanese words not commonly known in English, but have refrained from doing so in those cases where I have decided words are reasonably well known. However, in citing titles of articles and books, and journal titles, I have consistently used macrons. This has led to a few cases where, for instance, Tokyo as a city remains Tokyo but in the title of a journal, the Tokyo Anthropological Society Magazine, becomes Tōkyō (*Tōkyō jinruigakkai zasshi*). Second, I have written all Japanese names in the Japanese format, with the surname first, with the one exception of our publisher, who writes and is well known in English as Yoshio Sugimoto. Many of the individual thinkers Oguma writes about here used pen-names, and some changed their names during their lifetimes. However, with only a few exceptions, I have followed the original text, which uses the names by which the various theorists are best known. Third, I have romanised the same characters for Japan as *Nippon* for the prewar era and *Nihon* for the postwar era, despite the fact that in the early postwar era *Nippon* remained the more common pronunciation. *Nippon* has a more nationalist feeling, and I have attempted to give some sense of the enormous watershed created by defeat by using two different romanisations. For the same reasons, in the original draft I used the feminine 'her' and 'she' when prewar nationalists referred to Japan, and the neutral 'it' for the voice of the author. This, however, did not work well and, after careful thought, I decided to use the feminine throughout as this seemed to best represent the voice of the Japanese discourse, and especially the prewar nationalist discourse, at the cost, perhaps, of misrepresenting the voice of the author. The attentive reader will note that Oguma speaks of the 'national polity' (*kokutai*), whereas national polity theorists refer to the 'National Polity'. On the other hand, however, the frequent use of phrases such as 'our country' (*wagakuni*) to refer to Japan, while natural in the original, do not translate well: 'our country' and 'we Japanese' have in many cases been quietly transformed into 'Japan' and 'the Japanese' in the interests of smooth reading. Fourth, I have given modern readings for many of the figures of the Kiki myths. Thus Ōkuninushi has not been given as the archaic Opo-Kuni-Nusi, nor the slightly less archaic Ohokuninushi. Fifth, the original text contained a number of terms that are now dated, if not offensive. Thus, for instance, China was known throughout much of the period covered in this work in Japanese as *Shina*, and Oguma at times uses this term in quotation marks to contextualise the intellectual framework of the authors he examines. However, in English translation, both the modern *Chūgoku* and the politically incorrect *Shina* are translated as China, and since including only some in quotation marks looked unnatural, the quotation marks were removed. Sixth, some of the works cited by Oguma have introductions written in Arabic numerals: the original text cited these as, for instance, Watsuji (1920: Introduction, p. 2, pp. 2–5). I have changed all such citations to roman numerals for introductions, and thus the above citation becomes Watsuji (1920: ii, 2–5). Seventh, in the list of references contained at the end of this volume, I have given translations for book and article titles except where the title consisted of a single name: I have not bothered to translate books entitled Watsuji Tetsurō, for instance. Moreover, the place of publication, which is not usually given in Japanese texts, has not been given here for Japanese language works either. The reader can safely assume that almost without exception the place will be Tokyo. Finally, the original text contained a number of photographs and pictures – such as photocopies of pages from prewar textbooks that require an ability to read Japanese if they are to make sense – that have not been reproduced here.

Although I have been as careful as possible to provide the correct readings for the names of the various individuals and the titles of their various works discussed here, this has proved difficult in some cases. In a very few cases, where it has proved impossible to clarify what the 'correct' reading of a name is, I have chosen what I believe must be the more probable of various options (Chinese characters, or *kanji*, usually have a number of possible readings in Japanese: the *kun-yomi*, or Japanese reading, and the *on-yomi*, or Chinese reading, and sometimes a number of each). In other cases, a choice has been made between two readings, both of which could be argued to be correct. The surname of the brilliant military strategist and thinker Ishiwara Kanji is usually given in Japanese works as Ishihara. Given the fact that he is known in English as Ishiwara (after the title of a monograph on his life and thought by Mark Peattie), I have followed this convention here (Peattie interviewed Ishiwara's younger brother, who informed him that the family pronounced their surname as Ishiwara). In other cases, where incorrect readings have become established (such as the name of Nakano Seigō, who eventually gave up trying to persuade other Japanese to read his name as he felt it should be read), I have followed the incorrect but established view. I have seen Minoda Kyōki given as Minoda Muneki in the past, and decided in this case to follow the on-line Japanese university catalogue, NACSIS, which gives him as Kyōki. Another example of two possible readings is provided by Tsuda Sōkichi's first work, *Kamiyoshi no atarashii kenkyū*, which could be read as *Jindaishi no atarashii kenkyū*. Indeed, during the Taishō Period when the work was published, many *kun-yomi* words (such as *kamiyo*) were pronounced in their *on-yomi* forms (*jindai* in this case) because this was believed to sound more authoritative. Tsuda, however, almost certainly would have resisted this trend, which is why I have given the title as he would (I suspect) have read it, rather than how many of his contemporaries would have. Oguma Eiji, with his willingness to engage in long discussions about possible readings, has proved invaluable here.

***

Although I first agreed to do this translation several years ago, various challenges posed by my workplace in Australia prevented me from taking it up seriously until 2001. I remain surprised that I managed to complete it at all: although the translation itself was relatively easy, it was produced during a time of enormous personal and professional stress.

I would like to express my deep gratitude to the author, Oguma Eiji, who must have despaired of ever seeing this translation published, but was always sympathetic when I explained each year that with a teaching load that eventually peaked at 20 class hours a week for the last two or three semesters that I taught in Australia, I was yet again going to be unable to finish it. When I finally was able to find the time to sit down and concentrate on the translation in 2001, he was unfailingly quick to respond to my many questions about his original text. Over the past few months, I have sent numerous drafts of each chapter to him, always with new questions – asking if I could cut words out, or add words, or take small liberties with his original – and, I am afraid, with jokes that I am certain I enjoyed far more than he did embedded into the text, to which he has always responded. Our publisher, Yoshio Sugimoto, who must also have wondered if he was ever going to see the final work, has also been an enormous asset. I am very grateful to him for originally asking me to translate this work at a time when I had not only translated nothing into English but had not even published any of my own work in English, to have refrained from replacing me after such a long silence, and to have remained confident in my ability to produce a polished translation. He has been highly professional and supportive, and, an outstanding academic himself in a field very close to Oguma Eiji, must be the single publisher most qualified to publish this book. Translating this work was always going to be fun, but both have made the task of producing a final version a hugely enjoyable experience for me. My students in Australia helped make life tolerable, and even at times enjoyable, despite the appalling nature of the workplace I was in.

I am also highly indebted to my chief proofreader, my father David Askew who, despite a very serious illness, agreed to read through the entire translation. He made numerous corrections and suggestions that have improved my original enormously. It is not the way I would have chosen to spend what in his case well may have proved to be the last months of his life – thankfully, he has survived the ordeal so far – and I am more grateful than I have words to express. I would therefore like to dedicate this translation to the man I can honestly say is the best father I have.

David Askew
Associate Professor
Ristumeikan Asia Pacific University

Chronology

Jōmon Period   –c. BC 400
Yayoi Period   BC 300–
Kofun Period   mid-3rd Century AD–
Asuka Period   late 6th Century–
Nara Period   710–
Heian Period   794–
Kamakura Period   1192–
The Southern and Northern Courts Period   1336–
Muromachi Period   1392–
Momoyama Period   1573–
Edo Period   1603–
Meiji Period   1868–
  Meiji Restoration   1868
  Annexation of Okinawa   1879
  Promulgation of the Meiji Constitution   1889
  Promulgation of the Imperial Rescript on Education   1890
  Opening of the National Diet   1890
  Sino-Japanese War   1894–95
  Annexation of Taiwan   1895
  Beginning of mixed residence in the interior of Japan   1899
  Hokkaido Former Aborigines Protection Act   1899
  Russo-Japanese War   1904–05
  Annexation of Korea   1910
Taishō Period   1911–
  Beginning of Japan's Mandated Rule of Japanese Micronesia   1921
Shōwa Period   1925–
  The Manchurian Incident   1931
  Japan leaves the League of Nations   1933
  Sino-Japanese War   1937–45
  Pacific War   1941–45
  Promulgation of the Japanese Constitution   1946
  San Francisco Treaty comes into effect (the end of the Occupation)   1952

Central Terms in the Kiki Myths

- Amaterasu, the Sun Goddess and supreme god in the Shintō system of beliefs.
- Izanagi and Izanami, a male and a female couple who gave birth to the land.
- Susano-O, Amaterasu's younger brother.

Peoples
- The Tenson (literally 'descendants of the gods'), or in other words the 'Japanese'.

Clans (either alien in culture or ethnicity) that were hostile to the Imperial Family
- The Emishi (who lived in the northeastern region of the archipelago).
- The Izumo, an alien clan that voluntarily ceded its territory to the Imperial Family (Izumo today refers to a region in Shimane). The chief of the Izumo who made the decision to recognise the authority of the Imperial Family was Ōkuninushi.
- The Kumaso (who lived in the south of the archipelago).
- The Tsuchigumo.

Others
- Yamato. The early Imperial Court (the Yamato Court), another word used by the 'Japanese' to refer to themselves, as in the Yamato nation, and which is also used today to refer to a geographical area in the Kinki region.
- The Emperor Jinmu, the first (mythical) Emperor who was said to have led an expedition to the east of the archipelago and conquered many of the alien nations mentioned above.
- The Empress Jingū, another mythical figure who was said to have led an invasion of the Korean peninsula.

An Introduction to the English-Language Edition

In lamenting the lack of interest foreigners have in Japan, a Japanese magazine recently quoted the comments of an European journalist – 'to be honest, I am not greatly interested in Japan, apart from traditional Japanese culture such as the ancient temples of Kyoto and *kabuki*, together with the secret to Japan's economic development, and the coexistence of traditional culture and modernisation, such as scenes of *geisha* using mobile telephones'.

This book, however, may perhaps prove of interest even to this journalist. It examines the genealogy of the 'self-image of the Japanese' through an analysis of the changes in the discourse on the origin of the Japanese nation in modern Japan. This is a history of how the imported Western methodologies of anthropology and ancient history have been used to reconstruct ancient Japanese myths in an effort to create a modern nationalism – effectively, the equivalent of *geisha* using a mobile telephone.

When this book was first published in Japan in 1995, I thought only of my Japanese readers. However, in recent years, I have become increasingly aware that the theme of my research is universal. One trigger for this new awareness was provided when I was invited to India in 2000 as a Visiting Professor to teach modern Japanese history. In talking to Indian scholars, it became clear that we shared a common problem consciousness. Parallel to modernisation and globalisation, we were aware of an increased interest in national origins and ancient history, and it was clear to us that the formation of a national self-identity was to a large extent related to the rise of fundamentalism and discrimination against minorities.

The formation of a national self-image is linked to a great extent to relationships with the Other. As demonstrated in this work, the discourse on the self-image of the 'Japanese' in modern Japan was inseparable from the discourse on the West and various Asian countries, and on the minorities within Japan herself. In modern

Japan, however, this issue cannot be understood simply within the framework of Orientalism, in which the representation of the East is created by the West. At the same time that Japan was subjected to the Orientalising gaze of the West, she was colonising various nations of Asia.

In 1853, a fleet of US warships, some powered by steam, arrived off the shores of Edo Period (1603–1867) Japan. That the people of Edo called these vessels the 'Black Ships' is an indication of their fear of them. The dispute about the best way to deal with the threat posed by the West was so acute that it led to a civil war, followed by the Meiji Restoration of 1868. Although the Meiji government began to implement a series of policies to modernise Japan, the inferiority complex felt by Japanese intellectuals towards the West was to last throughout the period discussed in this book. The phrase 'Black Ships' is still used today in Japan as a term for a foreign threat.

After she had modernised, Japan invaded Korea and China – the countries that were the advanced regions of East Asian civilisation and that had been the objects of pre-modern Japan's feelings of inferiority.

During the Edo Period, Confucianism was imported into Japan from China, and became the official ideology of the government of the day, the Bakufu (military government or Shogunate). In response to Confucianism, a philosophy known as *kokugaku* (nativism or National Learning) emerged in Japan in the eighteenth century. Nativist scholars lauded the ancient myths of Japan and depicted ancient Japan as a natural golden age that had been untarnished by the depravity of civilisation. This Japanese Romanticism viewed China, not the West, as the Other.

Thus Japanese nationalism after the Meiji Restoration was formed while Japan was not only interacting with the new ideologies imported from the West but also facing two distinct Others – the 'West' and the 'East'. Mainstream Japanese nationalism, however, did not combine with Republicanism (as in France) or with Rationalism and Secularism (as in India). Rather, in a similar fashion to Imperial Russia and Prussia, it developed as an official ideology with links to a specific court.

The Meiji government used the Imperial Family that had existed since the seventh century as the symbol of national unification. The Imperial Family had lost all real political power during the Edo Period, when Japan was ruled by the military *samurai* class, and was at the time an almost forgotten relic of an ancient royal court. In 1889, the Meiji government promulgated a Constitution modelled on the constitutional monarchy of Prussia. Japan had recreated herself as a modern state, and called herself the Great Japanese Empire until defeat in the Second World War in 1945.

At almost the same time, a new position emerged as the official government ideology – the national polity (*kokutai*) theory. This ideology idealised the monarchy centred on the Emperor as a system unique to Japan. Although the word '*kokutai*' was used by Edo Period scholars, as will be noted in chapter 3 of this work, the national polity theory of the Meiji Period was developed by Japanese intellectual elites who had studied in the West. They introduced to Japan the European concept of a 'national' unification where all nationals of a state were seen to be members of a common community that transcended feudal status and domains, as well as the theory of the social organism that justified a unity headed by a monarch, and merged these new ideas with the Edo Period nativism to produce the national polity theory.

This theory was also influenced by European ideas, beginning with Romanticism, that criticised modern rationality and modern civilisation. In 1890 – a time when modernisation was being pursued in Japan in the area of technology, and especially technology with military applications – democratisation was restrained and the *Kyōiku Chokugo* (Imperial Rescript on Education) that emphasised the Confucian ethics of loyalty and filial duty was promulgated. The mixture of Western technology and what were claimed to be the 'traditional' Japanese virtues was described as '*Wakon Yōsai*' (Japanese Spirit and Western Knowledge). The importation of European ideas critical of modern Western civilisation proved to be greatly beneficial in justifying the 'Japanese Spirit'. A large number of Japanese intellectuals, such as the scholar of ethics, Watsuji Tetsurō (1889–1960, see chapter 15), and others discussed in this work, imported criticism of modernism and cultural relativism from Europe and used it in an idealisation of Japan.

The ancient Japanese mythology – the Kiki myths, which were contained in two texts, the *Kojiki* (The Record of Ancient Matters, compiled in 712) and *Nihon shoki* (The Chronicles of Japan, compiled in 720) – had been lauded by the nativist scholars of the Edo Period and was now taught to Japanese school children in the compulsory education system Meiji Japan had imported from the

An Introduction to the English-Language Edition

West. These myths had been edited by scholars in the early eighth century on the orders of the Imperial Family, and claimed that the founder of the Imperial Family had descended from the heavens in 660 BC. In a reflection of the realities of the policies of 'Japanese Spirit and Western Knowledge', the Japanese Emperor wore a Western-style military uniform, and both the Kiki myths and the Imperial Rescript were propagated in state textbooks printed with modern printing technology imported from the West. The Emperor was said to be God Incarnate (*arahitogami*), his photograph was distributed to all schools, and school children were forced to pay their respects to it. Japanese nationalism was thus formed through this type of marriage between the ancient Imperial Court and modern Western technology.

This complicated form of nationalism was also reflected in the various social movements Japan was to experience. For instance, chapter 11 of this work examines a feminist thinker, Takamure Itsue (1894–1964), who was dissatisfied with 'traditional' Japanese culture because she believed that it restricted women. At the same time, however, she did not believe that the feminism imported from the West was well fitted to address the issue of the *status quo* of women in Japan. In facing this dilemma, she argued that contemporary Japanese culture was heavily influenced by Chinese culture and especially Confucianism, and therefore was not the true 'traditional' culture of Japan. Claiming that discrimination against women had not existed in ancient Japan, she moved into the nativist (*kokugaku*) camp that lauded ancient Japan and came out in favour of an invasion of China.

In a private discussion in Calcutta with a researcher in subaltern studies, I mentioned the case of Takamure and was informed that similar examples existed in India. In India today, alongside the issue of the reform of a 'traditional culture' that restricts women, the dramatic penetration of Western culture as a result of globalisation is also producing an increased sense of social unease. The dilemma of not being able to approve of 'traditional culture', while simultaneously feeling uneasy about the uncritical acceptance of Western thought, was the same as that faced by Takamure in the 1930s. What has emerged in some circles in India is a view of history that claims that discrimination against women did not exist in ancient Hindu civilisation, and that it was only after the influx of Islam that discrimination against women worsened. This view of history has linked up with a Hindu nationalism that lauds the spirit of ancient Hinduism and that shows an enmity towards Pakistan and minorities in India such as Muslims.

Chapter 12 of this work focuses on the founder of Japanese folklore studies, Yanagita Kunio (1875–1962). Originally a bureaucrat involved in agricultural policies, Yanagita himself was from a poor farming background. Aiming to bridge the gap between city and country and between rich and poor, he founded a folklore studies that researched the culture of the common people as a way of deepening the understanding of rural farmers and of unifying the nation around Japan's native culture. To his despair, however, the culture of the common people was split into many different regional cultures and was incapable of providing a foundation for the unification of the entire country. Moreover, urban culture had in the past been influenced by China and in his own day by the West, and was monopolised by the rich. He thus turned to agricultural rites centred on rice cultivation as a culture that was both rural in nature and common to all Japan. This type of response again was not unique to Yanagita or Japan: I recently learned that it has similarities to the emphasis on taro cultivation as an important element in the cultural movement of the indigenous peoples of Hawaii.

In the Japan before the defeat in the Second World War, a position that I call in this book the 'mixed nation theory' flourished. This argued that a number of different peoples from Korea, China, the Malay Peninsula and the South Seas migrated to the ancient Japanese archipelago and intermarried to form the Japanese nation, which was therefore the product of a mixture of many nations. As I will argue here, the mixed nation theory lent itself to the claim that the Japanese nation embodied the unification of Asia, and that the peoples of neighbouring regions could be assimilated into the Japanese nation and their lands annexed by the Great Japanese Empire.

Needless to say, the view that a mixture of various nations lies at the core of national identity appears in other cultures. The mixed nation theory has similarities to the American idea of a melting pot. Indeed, as I note in this book, many authors in Japan described Japan as a melting pot and claimed that the Japanese experience was similar to that of the USA.

As noted in chapter 1, the prototype of the mixed nation theory in modern Japan was created in the nineteenth century by Western scholars who had travelled to Japan. Their ideas were similar to the self-image of the French put forward by Comte de Boulainvilliers – that the 'French' were a mixture of the conquering Franks and the conquered Gauls. These Western scholars argued that the Japanese nation was produced after a conquering people that came from the Korean peninsula mingled with the conquered indigenous people.

Japanese intellectuals initially viewed this position with distaste as one that defined the 'Japanese' as a 'mongrel nation', but eventually came to accept it reluctantly as part of the process of Westernisation and modernisation on which Japan had embarked. As time passed, this self-image, initially forced on Japan as a stigma by the West, was reconceptualised as an integral element of Japanese nationalism, and was used to justify invasion in the name of Asian unity. This is one example of an indigenous reconstruction of a Western representation of a people. In this case, it was not only reconstructed but also actively developed to justify Japanese aggression against neighbouring regions.

Another form of reconceptualisation is discussed in this work – the re-reading of history and mythology. Politicians and intellectuals used ancient Japanese history and myths to justify the policies of the day. The names of the heroes of Japanese history and the gods that appear in the myths of ancient Japan are thus sprinkled throughout this book in a reflection of this discourse. Although some readers may have trouble with these names, the Japanese discourse can perhaps be compared to American discourses that use names such as Jefferson and Pocahontas in discussing contemporary politics, or to the India that tested a nuclear weapon using a word from Hindu mythology.

Just as the world of the Bible forms the basis for a common discourse in the Christian world, the 'Japanese' throughout the period covered in this work used the Kiki texts as the basis for a common understanding of the world. The ancient myths were taught to all students in the compulsory education system of Japan, and were used in discussions of contemporary politics. In the process of reconstructing these texts, Japanese scholars who had mastered modern archaeology and anthropology became involved in fierce debates that can be compared to theological debates about the Bible.

One of the greatest contradictions faced by the nationalism of modern Japan was the fact that, as Japanese territory expanded, there emerged peoples – such as the Koreans and Taiwanese who were turned into Japanese subjects as Korea and Taiwan were incorporated into Japan – who could be described as 'non-Japanese "Japanese"'. The Japanese government had produced the national polity theory that emphasised Japanese uniqueness as a counter to the threat posed by the West and China. However, the theory now faced the contradiction posed by the existence of Koreans and Taiwanese within Japan. In an attempt to resolve this dilemma, Japanese intellectuals began to reconstruct Japanese myths.

At the same time, there was a reconstruction of the concept of the 'Japanese' that redefined 'non-Japanese' as 'Japanese'. A strange alliance formed between those who wanted to fight discrimination by arguing that Koreans should be treated as 'Japanese' and those imperialists who wanted to secure the territory of Korea, with both groups agreeing on the desirability of expanding the concept of 'Japanese'. At the same time, eugenicists who discriminated against Koreans, and cultural isolationists who were opposed to the territorial expansion of Japan, were in agreement about the necessity of limiting the concept of the 'Japanese'.

This work first attempts to cover the historical changes in this concept. It is still relevant in Japan today because Japan has to deal with ethnic minorities such as the indigenous *Ainu*, the large numbers of Koreans who live in Japan, and foreign workers. In dealing with minorities, the myth of the homogeneous nation – the ideology that claims the 'Japanese' consist of a single pure nation – can be countered by a broader concept of what is meant by the term 'Japanese'. After Japan was defeated in the Second World War in 1945, she was stripped of Korea and Taiwan. As a result, as this work will argue, the postwar concept of the 'Japanese' was based on a narrower definition than had been the case before 1945.

Although I am critical of Japan's imperialistic expansion, I wanted to revisit the issue of the modern concept of the 'Japanese' through an examination of the changes in the concept at a time when Japan was clearly a multi-national empire.

At the same time, this work is also a case study of universal issues, such as nationalism and the reconstruction of texts shared in common by all members of a nation. I hope that my work will appeal both to those with an interest in Japan and to those concerned with these broader, universal themes. I am convinced that readers will find that many of the issues tackled by the various intellectuals discussed here are echoed outside Japan. I have added some endnotes to the first few chapters to provide the background information that will help in an understanding of modern Japan.

Finally, I would like to express my deepest gratitude to my translator, David Askew. Without his dedication, his broad knowledge and wonderful language ability, this long and intricate work could not have been translated. I would also like to thank Yoshio Sugimoto of Trans Pacific Press. It is only because of individuals like David and Yoshio that research published in non-European languages, and that remains unnoticed because of the language barrier, can be introduced to the English-speaking world.

Introduction

The Great Japanese Empire is neither a state based on an homogeneous nation, nor a country based on nationalism (*minzokushugi*). Indeed, from the day she was founded, Japan has never been a country based purely on nationalism. All scholars agree that our distant ancestors were Tungus, Mongolians, Indonesians and Negritos...The number of people who became naturalised as Japanese is large indeed. Japan took these various peoples in, and they intermarried and merged. In this fashion, what scholars call the 'modern Japanese nation' was formed.

The Japanese nation did not originally emerge as an homogeneous nation. Rather, it was formed in ancient times through a fusion and assimilation into the Japanese nation of aboriginal peoples and those who came from the continent, and was formed through the cultivation of a strong belief that all were members of the same nation under the Imperial Family.

These two excerpts are both from Japanese works published in 1942 during the Pacific War (1941–45). The first is from the opening editorial notes of a general opinion magazine, the second from a book published by the Social Education Department of the Ministry of Education.[1]

From the second half of the 1970s, many Japanese authors have argued as follows. 'From the Meiji Period (1868–1911), during which a modern state was built in Japan, the Japanese have been ruled by the myth of the homogeneous nation, which argues that the Japanese are an homogeneous nation with pure blood-lines. This myth is the source of Japanese ethnocentrism, of imperialistic aggression in the 1930s and 40s and Japanese colonial rule in Korea and Taiwan, of discrimination against the various peoples of Asia, and of the discrimination against minorities and the ostracism of foreign workers that we see today'. If this is so, how can the two quotations above that were written during the Pacific War at a time of heightened ethnocentrism be explained?

The Issue

I would here like to establish two facts. The first is that the prewar Great Japanese Empire was a multi-national empire. Although this is sometimes forgotten today, after the empire expanded by including Taiwan in 1895 and annexing Korea in 1910, 30 per cent of its population came to consist of non-Japanese subjects. The 'one hundred million' in the well-known Japanese government slogan of the Second World War, 'onwards, one hundred million balls of fire', refers to the total population of the empire, including Korea and Taiwan. At the time, the population of Japan Proper (*naichi*) was only 70 million. As will be discussed in chapter 9, textbooks compiled by the state clearly stated that 30 per cent of the population of the empire consisted of peoples other than the Yamato (Japanese) nation. Needless to say, the empire was not a state in which various nations coexisted equally, but the fact remains that Japan was not an homogeneous nation-state.

It is perhaps understandable that the myth of the homogeneous nation was accepted in a postwar Japan that had lost Korea and Taiwan, and in which the size of the non-Japanese population had plummeted, but the question that has to be asked is, how could this myth have taken root in the prewar multi-national empire?

The second fact that I would like to establish is that, although a large number of criticisms of the myth of ethnic homogeneity have been developed by Japanese intellectuals to date, there has been very little research on how and when it emerged and took root.

It is understandable that human-rights activists, legal scholars and sociologists, among others, do not engage in historical research. Criticism of the myth of the homogeneous nation by Japanese historians is not uncommon, but almost all these criticisms are based on research that demonstrates how many different ethnic peoples and cultures existed in the past on the Japanese archipelago or within the borders of the Japanese state. These historians have tacitly accepted the premise that the myth of ethnic homogeneity was established during the Meiji Period as a state ideology, and so have felt no need to substantiate the claim.

However, is this premise correct? Was the multi-national Great Japanese Empire really dominated by arguments that Japan consisted solely of a Japanese nation with a single, pure and homogeneous origin? If so, how was the issue of non-Japanese subjects such as the peoples of Korea and Taiwan dealt with?

This book begins with these questions. It will examine historically when and how the myth of the homogeneous nation that is said to have been the dominant self-image of the 'Japanese' from the age of the Great Japanese Empire through to the postwar period emerged, and to provide a sociological analysis of the myth's function.

Exactly when did the 'Japanese' begin to depict themselves as a single and homogeneous nation? Under what circumstances, and with what motives, was this done? Research that focuses on these questions is important not just to shed light on Japanese history, but also to examine larger issues of today's international society, such as the national consciousness of pure blood based on historical narratives, the drive for homogeneous nation-states, and discrimination against and ostracism of alien peoples.[2]

This work will not, however, examine the so-called 'theories of the Japanese' (*Nihonjinron*) – arguments that first assume the existence of an homogeneous people called the 'Japanese' and then debate their unique characteristics. What will be discussed here are the concepts that are premised by 'theories of the Japanese' – namely, an homogeneous 'Japanese people' and nation.

To be more specific, the theme of this work is the genealogy of the consciousness of identity held by the people who call themselves the 'Japanese', as revealed in discourses of the nation. When a people sees itself as a single nation, what sort of self-image do they develop? How does this self-image change as their circumstances change? Such questions are not necessarily limited only to the 'Japanese'.

The Definition of the 'Myth of the Homogeneous Nation'

Readers not interested in research methodology may wish to omit the rest of the introduction. I would first like to define the object of this research – the myth of the homogeneous nation – since it is difficult to say that a clear definition has been provided in many of the criticisms of the myth that have appeared to date. How have representative criticisms of the myth of ethnic homogeneity been developed in Japan?

In the work by the scholar of international law, Ōnuma Yasuaki, *Tan'intsu minzoku shakai no shinwa o koete* (Moving Beyond the Myth of the Homogeneous Nation Society), the notion that the Japanese are an homogeneous nation is criticised from two directions. First, people in the pre-modern Edo Period viewed themselves as members of feudal domains (*han*) and villages, and until the Meiji Period did not think of themselves as 'Japanese'. Second, 'the origin of the so-called Japanese nation lies in the movement, intermarriage, and mingling of the peoples of the Eurasian continent and the islands of the south, and even when it comes to the birth of the first unified state in Japanese history, there is much evidence that points to the importance of the relationship with Korea'.[3]

The sociologist Fukuoka Yasunori gives examples of various border-line cases such as Japanese migrants (Nikkei), returnee school children (*kikoku shijo*), naturalised people, Japanese orphans left behind and raised in China (*zanryū koji*),[4] the indigenous *Ainu*, and *zainichi* Koreans, in addition to the 'pure Japanese' who have 'Japanese' lineage, culture, and nationality.[5] Fukuoka also emphasises the fact that one-third of the families listed in the early ninth century family name register, the *Shinsen shōjiroku* (A Newly Compiled Record of Aristocratic Families), came from overseas. This demonstrates that a 'pure Japanese nation' does not exist in terms of lineage, but that in ancient times various people came to Japan from the Chinese continent and the south, while in historical times, too, large numbers continued to arrive from overseas. Fukuoka thus criticises the 'myth that Japan is an "homogeneous society"'.[6]

The historian, Amino Yoshihiko, describes his 'questions about the theory of the homogeneous nation' as follows. Firstly, people within the Japanese nation itself are not homogeneous: there are regional differences in both language and culture. Secondly, 'the idea that the Japanese are a hybrid mixture' is supported by the fact that there are Japanese with facial features similar to the people of the south, north (China and Siberia) and Korea, and is also corroborated by Egami Namio's (1906–) theory of the arrival in Japan of a horse-riding people from Mongolia. According to our current understanding of history, Amino says, the people of the Jōmon period (10,000–400BC) are the direct ancestors of the modern 'Japanese', but there must have been large-scale migrations from the Korean peninsula in the Yayoi (300BC–300AD) and Kofun (mid 3rd century –700AD) periods.[7]

From such criticisms offered by legal scholars, sociologists and historians, it can be said that the myth of the homogeneous nation is assumed to take the following form.

One aspect is an understanding of the *status quo* of the nation-state, namely that 'the Japanese nation-state is formed only from the Japanese nation which shares the same language and culture'. A second aspect is an understanding of the history of the nation, namely that 'only the Japanese nation, which shares a single, pure blood-line, has lived on the Japanese archipelago since time immemorial'. Of course, the two aspects cannot be strictly separated, and it can be said that both advocates and critics of the myth of ethnic homogeneity mix the two in constructing their arguments.

In this book, the myth of the homogeneous nation will be defined as encompassing both aspects. In other words, the myth is the belief that 'the Japanese nation has consisted, and today still consists, of only the Japanese nation, which shares a single, pure origin, and a common culture and lineage'.

Some may be dissatisfied with this definition. It is possible to define the myth as a conviction that so long as all aim for an homogeneous Japan, then it is irrelevant if the origin of the Japanese nation is not pure or if alien nations reside in Japan. However, I have decided on a narrow definition. The push to homogeneity is not limited to the state, but is also seen in other organisations, and the use of national education to promote a degree of homogeneity is not limited just to Japan, but can be found in all modern nation-states. With a broader definition, it will become more difficult to draw distinctions and there will be little merit in researching the myth.

Given this definition of the myth, where did it originate and what was its function? The concrete object of this research will be limited to printed materials. It will not deal with any consciousness which has not been written down and so has not survived, nor with the realities of discrimination. Although I recognise the importance of these issues in any discussion of how national consciousness and the realities of discrimination are related, I will not deal with the over-hasty criticism that claims that where there is discrimination there is a myth of an homogeneous nation, but will instead explore the national consciousness of the Japanese. The focus of examination will therefore be the theory of the Japanese nation as it emerges from the dominant majority. I have discussed the policies of colonial rule and the thinking of the minorities elsewhere.[8]

Of the two aspects of the myth of the homogeneous nation, emphasis will be placed on the second – historical consciousness and the debate on the origins of the Japanese nation. There are three reasons for this. First, as this book will demonstrate, the understanding of the *status quo* and the views of Japanese history were almost completely fused. Secondly, as will also be shown in this work, after Taiwan and Korea were incorporated into the Great Japanese Empire, the idea that it consisted only of the Japanese nation almost completely disappeared from the printed media, and debate centred almost exclusively on whether or not the origin of the Japanese nation was one of pure blood. Thirdly, unlike the understanding of the *status quo* which changed as the *status quo* changed, historical views continued to wield an influence in the postwar era.

Sociology and History

I believe that the unique properties of the focus of this research require both a sociological approach and a history of ideas approach when exploring the origins of the myth of the homogeneous nation.

The self-image of any group of people, including the myth of ethnic homogeneity, is not the product of any particular individual, but is something shared by the majority. Using Max Weber's *The Protestant Ethic and the Spirit of Capitalism* as an example of research into the consciousness of the majority, I would like to describe the differences between the sociological and historical approaches.

Although Weber's work has many different aspects, an important one is his argument that the ethics of Puritanism, which were antagonistic to the pursuit of profits, contributed to the birth of modern capitalism. To make this argument, he examined the ideas of Calvinism, the Lutherans and Benjamin Franklin, and compared them with Chinese and Indian thought. This sort of approach is well known in sociology, but not in historiography.

Historical research in Japan usually places an emphasis on limiting the focus of research. Weber's book, by contrast, placed no limits on either time or place. Calvin was a sixteenth century Swiss intellectual, while Franklin was an eighteenth century American thinker. The starting point was the consciousness of German labourers in the east of Germany in the late nineteenth century, and India was used as a comparison. In historiography, on the other hand, researchers specialise and research narrower topics such as 'The Intellectual History of Economic Ethics in Benjamin Franklin' and 'The Concept of Economics in Lutheran Thought'.

If a historiographic argument were to be made that these philosophies influenced the emergence of capitalism, the historian would have, for instance, to look at the number of copies of Franklin's work that were printed and at the response to Franklin, as well as examining how deeply his ideas penetrated the thought of the people in general and of entrepreneurs in particular. Moreover, the historian would have to choose a policy-maker in the American government who had been influenced by Franklin's thought and determine how, and to what degree, that influence affected the policy-making process. The result would be research into 'The Influence of Franklin's Economic Philosophy on the Development of Capitalism in the USA and on Modernisation Policies in the Second Half of the Eighteenth Century'. However, to relate this to the consciousness of German labourers in the late nineteenth century, or to compare it with countries like China and India and to describe it as a common social phenomenon, would be virtually impossible using only the historiographical approach.

The macro view and the micro view are contained in all areas of the social sciences, either in confrontation with, or mutually supportive of, each another. The first aims to cover a large area, while the second focuses on a narrower area in more detail. To generalise, it could be said that sociology tends to be macro and history micro in approach. In sociology, phrases such as 'modern consciousness in the nineteenth century' are often used. The Japanese historian, however, would narrow the focus to a decade in the nineteenth century, ask whether the place is England or India or Japan and, if Japan, ask which village in which prefecture, and argue that even in a single village the consciousness of intellectuals, bureaucrats, wealthy farmers and poor farmers would all differ.

The debate about whether society is the sum of all its parts or something greater is also one that exists in all areas of the social sciences. The idea that society is larger than the sum of its parts was seen in the thought of Auguste Comte and Emile Durkheim, and has been influential from the origins of sociology. In sociology, individual phenomena are seen as ripples on the surface of the great sea that is society. Sociologists believe that these ripples are not independent of the whole. Surface phenomena are not themselves important, but the common logic and structure of the whole that exists in the background is. Therefore, what is important is whether or not the abstracted model is persuasive, and there is a tendency to ignore the problems inherent in cases where there is a great distance in time or place between the phenomena examined, or where a concrete proof of the mutual relationship is postponed. (There are of course many exceptions to this in sociology.)

In history, facts are seen as being of the greatest importance. Whether a universal model can be abstracted or not is of secondary importance. Moreover, the enemy of historiography has frequently been the argument that society is something that transcends the individual. In the case of prewar Japanese historians, the major antagonist was the officially sanctioned Imperial View of History (*Kōkoku shikan*). This lauded the superiority of Japan through meaningless comparisons with the West and Asia, and lauded manifestations of the timeless Japanese spirit from the medieval *samurai* until the era of modern war. The conscientious position for Japanese historians to take in both the prewar and postwar eras was to use detailed empirical research to undermine this grand-scale story. Moreover, in the postwar period, Marxism for a long time provided the broad framework, so they only had to work on the details of their research projects.

Needless to say, the macro approach of sociology also has its limits. There is a tendency for researchers to flesh out their work with facts chosen because they fit a preconceived hypothesis. The micro approach of historiography is supported by a belief in an unsparing devotion to accumulating individual research in order to see the whole. However, to grasp the entire world with this approach without using some sort of rough sketch would require an investigation into and reconstruction of the relations between all thinkers of all ages, and all villages, all factories and all policy-making processes. Needless to say, that would be impossible.

In the light of sociological and historical approaches, the methodology required to deal with the myth of the homogeneous nation is now clear.

The fundamental approach of this work is sociological, and derives especially from the sociology of ideas and discourses. As already noted, the myth of ethnic homogeneity is a consciousness supported by the majority, and not the product of individual thinkers or newspaper companies. This is a theme ill-suited to historiography with its emphasis on limiting the focus of research.

Ethnic research carried out by American sociologists is of help here. For instance, Milton Gordon's classic piece of research, *Assimilation in American Life*, distinguishes between three types of ideals for uniting the multi-national state in the USA: Anglo-Conformity, the Melting Pot, and Cultural Pluralism.[9] These are also fundamental concepts in Japanese ethnic research.

I would like to focus here on Gordon's approach. He examines the work of the playwright Israel Zangwill and the philosopher John Dewey as authors who developed the ideals of the Melting Pot and Cultural Pluralism. A historian might ask how many copies of their works were published during their lifetimes, and what concrete influence their ideas had on the policy-making process in the area of immigration. A historian of ideas might focus on the place of cultural pluralism in Dewey's pragmatism. However, Gordon's theme was to abstract ideas from each of these individual thinkers and examine how they function in society. His goal was to develop a model that could be applied in many directions rather than to look at specific times and thinkers. This book will examine the discourses of many individuals, but the purpose is to analyse the whole, with the individuals as case studies.

In many cases, sociologists draw sketches based on the results of historiography. However, since systematic empirical research on Japanese theories of the nation does not exist at present, a historical investigation is required before an analysis can be begun. Here, I have attempted to adopt the strength of history – scrupulousness. Using the methodology of the history of ideas, albeit with some sacrifices in the shape of limiting the target, the target of investigation in this work was established in the following way.

The myth of the homogeneous nation will be defined as a form of self-perception of the 'Japanese'. If historical views are central to this myth, one must examine how the history of the Japanese nation has been discussed. To this end, an analysis needs to be conducted in chronological order of the arguments of (1) those historians of the ancient Japanese archipelago, anthropologists and linguists who provided the basis for the various theories of the Japanese nation, (2) those who influenced postwar theories of the Japanese nation and culture, and (3) the 'national polity' (*kokutai*) theorists and eugenicists who were so enthusiastic about developing theories of the Japanese nation.[10] Next, (4) the debate during periods when the size of the Japanese state changed, such as when Japan annexed Korea and during the Pacific War, needs to be chronologically examined. Finally, (5) these areas need to be supplemented with articles about the Japanese nation from a chronological survey of major journals.

The history of the schools of thought in the fields of ancient history and anthropology will be of use in examining (1), while the arguments of the founder of folklore in Japan, Yanagita Kunio, and the scholar of ethics, Watsuji Tetsurō, have been used for (2). Although there has been little research done on (3) to date, since there were not many major authors and media organisations to examine, I believe that I have covered this area. The debates referred to in historical research conducted so far on colonial history were used in the survey of the theories of the nation developed in newspapers and magazines for (4). Finally, I looked up the table of contents in as many major journals as possible to identify articles related to nationality for (5).

Focussing on these five aspects, this work will examine how the origins and composition of the Japanese nation were discussed and how ethnic minorities within Japan were treated in these arguments. Historical changes are tracked chronologically from parts 1 to 3. Part 1 examines the debate from the mid-Meiji Period and through the process of Japan becoming a multi-national empire as Taiwan was ceded to Japan and Korea was annexed. Part 2 follows the process of the completion of the theory of nationality as the ideology of imperial rule. Finally, part 3 examines the origins of the postwar myth of the homogeneous nation. Although part 1 matches the Meiji Period, I would like to stress that this is coincidental, and I have not used the Japanese names of eras in dividing up the major periods.[11] In the conclusion, I will analyse sociologically the perceptions of self and Other as seen in the various discussions of the Japanese nation.

In this work, I have endeavoured to use the methodology of the history of ideas where possible in each individual examination. However, the fundamental approach is sociological. The history of Japanese political thought was also used, as was, where appropriate, research in the areas of cultural anthropology and social psychology. In a sense, then, the methodology can be described as an attempt to draw a sketch by linking miniatures in a correlated approach.

It is possible that sociologists may see this work as too detailed, while historians and historians of ideas may see the brush strokes as being too broad and sweeping. However, there are many works that have been readily accepted despite the boundaries imposed by academic divisions, such as the work of Michel Foucault, and Edward Said's *Orientalism*. Among Japanese sociologists, there is the research of Mita Minesuke who has examined the 'ideology of rising in the world' (*risshin-shusse shugi*) of modern Japan as a Japanese version of Weber's Protestant ethic, and of Yamanaka Hayato who has examined the policies of assimilation regarding Korea in the age of the Great Japanese Empire from the point of view of sociological ethnic research.[12] Moreover, in the area of Japanese intellectual history, Kano Masanao has attempted to analyse such difficult topics as the change in consciousness from the 1930s to the 1980s triggered by defeat in the Second World War.[13] In this sense, my approach is not an uncommon one.

Finally, I would like to mention the definition of the nation. I do not believe that the Japanese nation is an entity that actually exists. The target of research in this book is, to be exact, 'the various discourses discussed by individual thinkers as the identity of the Japanese nation'. In the following pages, the way that a large number of 'Japanese' depicted themselves on meeting with Others in Asia or the West will be discussed.[14]

I would also like to note that historical terms that are no longer considered appropriate have been used in this work when citing historical texts.

Part One
The Thought of an 'Open Country'

1 The Birth of Theories of the Japanese Nation

It is difficult to determine when discussion on the origins of human beings living on the Japanese archipelago began. As long ago as the eighth century, the *Hitachi-no-kuni fudoki* (The Hitachi-no-kuni Domain: Records of Wind and Earth) mentioned shell mounds, and there is also the Edo Period Confucian scholar Arai Hakuseki's (1657–1725) theory of stone tools of 1725. However, the first theory of the origin of the Japanese nation based on a modern scientific discourse must be dated from the excavation of the Ōmori shell mounds by Edward S. Morse (1838–1925) in 1877.[1]

Western Academics' Theories of the Japanese Nation

During the Edo Period, Japan strictly limited all interaction with Western countries. However, after the Edo Bakufu was overthrown through the Meiji Restoration, the Meiji government introduced policies to modernise Japan and invited a large number of Western advisers and teachers to the country.

Morse had been a research assistant in biology at Harvard University in the USA, but fell out with his professor over the acceptance of evolutionary theory and resigned. He travelled to Japan to research *Brachiopoda*. Arriving in the port city of Yokohama in 1877, he was invited by the Japanese Ministry of Education to become a professor at Tokyo Imperial University, and began his investigation of the Ōmori shell mounds in that year.[2] While giving lectures at the university and speeches to enlighten the Japanese about evolutionary theory, Morse unearthed a large amount of earthenware. His publication of the results of his excavations was the first academic paper to emerge from a Japanese university.

As to Morse's theory of the Japanese nation, he concluded that the ancient people of the Japanese archipelago had cannibalistic customs. This conclusion was drawn from the discovery of damaged human bones in the shell mounds. Although this was a mistake, what is of importance is that he did not believe that this ancient people were the direct ancestors of the modern Japanese nation. The ethnic group that lives in the archipelago today other than the Japanese nation is the indigenous *Ainu*. However, based on the fact that the *Ainu* did not practise cannibalism and had not developed pottery, Morse hypothesised that the people who had formed the shell mounds were the direct ancestors of neither the *Ainu* nor the contemporary Japanese nation, but an earlier indigenous people, the *pre-Ainu*. Furthermore, based on Japanese legends, he argued that the present inhabitants of the archipelago, the Japanese nation, had come from the south, and had gained their present position after conquering the earlier inhabitants.

Morse was not the first to argue that an aboriginal people had earlier inhabited the archipelago and that the 'Japanese' were conquerors who arrived later. Phillip Franz von Siebold (1796–1866), who came to Japan as early as 1823, had suggested in *Nippon*, a work that was published after he returned home to Germany, that the stone tools discovered in various parts of the archipelago had been left behind by the *Ainu*, an aboriginal people, and that a Tartar nation had later fought these earlier inhabitants and occupied their land.

The idea that the stone tools unearthed in various parts of Japan had been crafted by a people other than the 'Japanese' was also shared by some scholars of the Edo Period. The best known example is Arai Hakuseki, who developed the *Shukushin* theory. In 1725, he argued that the stone tools which had been thought to have been created by Buddhist and Shintōist deities and goblins were in fact left behind by a nation called the Shukushin which had entered the Tōhoku and Hokuriku regions of northern Japan from the Asian continent. Another Edo Period researcher of stone tools, Kiuchi Sekitei (1724–1808) advanced the theory that the Shukushin were the *Ezo* (in other words, the *Ainu*). Siebold was shown Kiuchi's collection of stone tools and adopted his theory.[3]

The Japanese legends that Morse consulted were the so-called Kiki myths, which were contained in the *Kojiki* and *Nihon shoki*. These ancient Japanese myths include the story of the 'descent to earth of the descendants of the gods' (*Tenson Kōrin*), which described the ancestors of the Japanese Emperor descending from the Heavens (or 'Takamagahara'), the story of the 'Eastern Expedition of the Emperor Jinmu', which depicted the conquest by the Emperor Jinmu – the first (mythological) Emperor and founder of the Yamato Dynasty – of those who had not submitted to the authority of the Imperial Household, and the story of the conquest of a people known as the *Kumaso* by Prince Yamato Takeru-no-Mikoto. Peoples with different customs that were not ruled by the Imperial Household were described in terms such as *Emishi* (a clan that lived in northeast Japan: according to one theory, now dated, the ancient term for the *Ainu*) and *Tsuchigumo*.

Arai Hakuseki had already argued that 'god is a man' and that the 'descent to earth of the descendants of the gods' therefore described a movement from a place called Takamagahara, and that the legend that two gods, Izanagi and Izanami, had given birth to the archipelago was in fact a description of the conquest of various areas of Japan by warships. Western scholars took this idea one step further, and argued that the 'descent to earth of the descendants of the gods' was a legend that depicted the migration of a conquering people to the archipelago and that the conquered Kumaso and Emishi were earlier aboriginal peoples.[4]

Siebold's second son, Heinrich Phillipp von Siebold (1852–1908), who arrived in Japan several years before Morse, collected a large amount of pottery and numerous stone tools, and reinforced his father's theory. There are two types of ancient earthenware in Japan: the earlier Jōmon pottery and the Yayoi pottery (the oldest periods in Japanese prehistory are known after this pottery as the Jōmon and Yayoi eras). According to Heinrich, the Jōmon pottery had been created by the *Ainu* who had once lived throughout the archipelago as far south as Shikoku and Kyūshū, but were later pushed northwards towards Hokkaido by a conquering people. Furthermore, John Milne (1850–1913), an English *Oyatoi* (foreign employee) who taught geology, also advanced the idea that the *Ainu* were Japan's aboriginal people.

Alongside this thesis of the existence of an earlier aboriginal people and the immigration of a conquering nation to the archipelago, another thesis that was very influential among Western theories of the Japanese nation was that the contemporary Japanese nation consisted of a mix of various Asian nations.

For instance, in 1875, W. Denitz, a Professor at the Tokyo Medical School (this was merged with the Kaisei Gakkō in 1877 to form what later became Tokyo Imperial University), argued that the Japanese nation was a mixture of two types of the Mongolian race, including the *Ainu*, in addition to the Malaysian race. Furthermore, in 1883, the typology of the German, Erwin von Bälz (1849–1913, another Professor at the Tokyo Medical School), which is still known today in Japan, was made public. According to Bälz, leaving aside the *Ainu*, the 'Japanese' could be divided into two large groups, the 'Chōshū type', with long heads and thin bodies, a type which he argued was often seen in upper class Japanese, and the 'Satsuma type', with short heads and thickset bodies, which was often seen in lower class Japanese (both Chōshū and Satsuma were feudal domains that played a dominant role in the Meiji government). The first group, Bälz continued, was similar to Chinese and Koreans, and had arrived in south-western Honshū from the Asian continent through Korea, whereas the later was similar to the Malays, and had arrived in Kyūshū by a sea-route and had then moved northwards through the archipelago (see the map of Japan at p. vi). This 'mixture' theory became part of the theory of a conquered aboriginal nation through the idea that contemporary 'Japanese' consisted of a mixture of a ruling nation which came to the archipelago from overseas and conquered aboriginal peoples.

It seems that the 'Japanese' of this time appeared to those Westerners who advocated the mixed nation theory as a people with a vast range of personal features. Although this contradicts the notion that the 'Japanese' were frequently seen as an homogeneous group, at the time this seems not to have been an unusual impression. For instance, *Around the World in Eighty Days*, which Jules Verne wrote in the form of a compilation of information obtained from Western travel diaries of the time, stated that whereas all Chinese had the same 'yellow' faces, the 'Japanese' had many different facial colours and features. Much later, in 1934, Bruno Taut (1880–1938) also wrote in his diary that the 'Japanese' had a large range of features.[5]

It cannot possibly be the case that Meiji Period 'Japanese' were much more diverse in their features than is the case today. One possible conjecture is that differences in individual 'Japanese' features that people are not usually conscious of today tended then to be seen by travellers who had experience, and were conscious, of multi-national regions which contained national differences. The view seen in Bälz that classes were directly linked to national differences, while quite baffling to many Japanese today, was an idea that may well have occurred naturally to Germans of the time.

Since this work will not investigate the origins of the 'Japanese', but rather focus on the discourse about these origins, it will not examine whether or not the Japanese nation was a conquering nation or a mixed nation. However, the theory that the 'Japanese' were a mixed nation and an immigrant/conquering nation was almost uniform in Western academic theories. In the early Meiji Period, these theories were the only ones seen as scientific views of the Japanese nation. It was not until after the second half of the 1880s that the 'Japanese' themselves began to develop theories of the Japanese nation based on Western anthropological methodology.

Japanese Anthropology and the Revolt against Western Scholars

In 1884, a number of students, including Tsuboi Shōgorō (1863–1913), a young student of 20 who was studying biology at the Imperial University College of Science (this later became the Faculty of Science at the Tokyo Imperial University) called a meeting to research ancient Japanese history. A total of ten science students and staff members answered this call, and the research group that borrowed a classroom and opened proceedings is said to be the predecessor of Japan's Anthropological Society.

Tsuboi was the grandson of a Japanese *rangakusha* (scholar of Dutch studies) and the son of a doctor in the service of the Shōgun (*bakushin'i*). From his days as a student at preparatory school, he had published a number of handwritten circulating newspapers, including *Kore demo shinbun* (It May Not Look Like One, But This is a Newspaper), *Tonchinkan* (Irrelevancy), *Negoto hanbun* (Half Nonsense), and was an active and brilliant student.[6] The official title of the research group was first 'Jinruigaku no Tomo' (Friends of Anthropology),[7] but was later changed to the 'Jinruigaku Kenkūkai' (Anthropology Research Association) and then the 'Tōkyō Jinruigakkai' (Tokyo Anthropological Society) in 1886. In 1931, it became the 'Nippon Jinruigakkai' (Anthropological Society of Nippon).[8] At first, this group was nothing more than a gathering of young students in a classroom who discussed the *Ainu* and earthenware. However, in 1886, an official journal, the *Jinruigakkai hōkoku* (Anthropological Society Bulletin) was issued at the same time as the title of the association changed from Association to Society. The title of the journal was changed again the next year to the *Tōkyō jinruigakkai zasshi* (Tokyo Anthropological Society Magazine), and later to the *Jinruigaku zasshi* (Journal for the Anthropological Society of Nippon) in 1911. This publication became the central academic magazine for anthropology in Japan.

For these budding anthropologists, the origin of the Japanese nation was an area of great interest from the start. Japanese anthropologists, like Western anthropologists, would later engage in fieldwork in various areas of Asia, but Japan at this time was the focus of research by the Western Powers. Japanese anthropologists thus struggled to shoulder the burden of studying their own country, though anthropology in Japan eventually emerged from the situation where the overpowering influence was the Western mixed nation theory. Although many talented individuals, such as Torii Ryūzō (1870–1951), a student of Tsuboi's who was to become the leading spirit behind the surveys of areas to which the Great Japanese Empire had expanded, and Koganei Yoshikiyo (1859–1944), who was to become the father of Japanese physical anthropology, participated in the Anthropological Society, almost all adopted the mixed nation theory. There was a debate between the vast majority, including Torii and Koganei, who believed that the *Ainu* were the aboriginal inhabitants of the Japanese archipelago, and Tsuboi, who claimed that the original inhabitants were an extinct race, the *Koropok-guru* or *Korobokkuru*, mentioned in legends. However, this can be seen as a rehash of the debate between the Siebolds, who claimed that the *Ainu* were the original inhabitants, and Morse, who claimed that it was the *pre-Ainu* who were the first inhabitants.

This was true of others apart from these young anthropologists. For instance, the nativist (*kokugaku*) scholar, Yokoyama Yoshikiyo (1826–1879), argued that the Japanese nation was a mixture of 'the earlier native inhabitants, the race descended from the Sun Goddess [the Tenson], and later arrivals from China and Korea'. According to Yokoyama, 'the earlier native inhabitants' were the same race as the *Ainu*. Ono Azusa (1852–1886), one of the intellectuals of the Meiji enlightenment, in his introduction of Yokoyama's theory accepted the theory advanced by Morse, stating that 'a cannibal race once inhabited Japan'.[9]

It was natural for there to have been an adverse reaction to this mixed nation theory. One example is Kurokawa Mayori (1829–1906), the author of *Kōgei shiryō* (A History of Japanese Arts and Crafts), a pathfinding work on fine arts and crafts, who wrote a number of papers on ancient Japanese peoples from about 1879 when Morse's theory began to emerge, and much earlier than scholars such as Tsuboi.

In 'Emishi jinshu ron' (On the Emishi Race) published in 1892, Kurokawa argued against the theory that the *Ainu* were the original inhabitants of the Japanese archipelago and were the mythical Emishi.[10] According to Kurokawa, the word *Emishi* originally came from a term that referred to all rebels who refused to obey the orders of the Imperial Family and was not a term for an alien nation. Moreover, he stated that the '*Ainu* of today [in Hokkaido] are descendants of Japanese who stopped evolving because they moved to the far frontiers of the state'. In other words, no alien peoples existed on the archipelago and, from time immemorial, the only inhabitants had been the 'Japanese'. He argued that those who claimed that the *Ainu* were an aboriginal people conquered by migrants led by the Imperial Family who arrived at a later stage were 'rogues giving vent to delusions' who 'are in contempt of the Imperial Court', or in other words were themselves Emishi in revolt against the Imperial Household.

Naitō Chisō (1823–1900), a Mito (a school influenced by nativist thought) scholar who became a professor at Tokyo Imperial University, stated in 1888 in his 'Kokutai hakki' (Manifesting the National Polity) that 'there is not a single person in this land who is not descended from the gods'. He criticised the theory that the 'Eastern Expedition of the Emperor Jinmu' and the 'descent to earth of the descendants of the gods' merely depicted the experience of an immigrant conquering nation, as 'viewing the Japanese national polity (*kokutai*) as equivalent to that of other violent and brutal countries.[11] According to Naitō, this sort of heresy committed the 'heinous crime of casting a slur on the national polity and the authority of the Emperor', and anyone who blindly followed Western scholars ought to be immediately put to death.

Two Forms of Nationalism

This reaction seems an irrational and narrow-minded form of ethnocentricity. However, when passing judgment on it, one point needs to be taken into account: the Japan of the 1880s was not the military or economic superpower of later years, but a small and weak country.

Although the shock of Western military strength, as symbolised by the so-called 'Black Ships', was a large one, during the early

Meiji Period there was a temporary lull in the competition between the Western Powers to acquire new colonies, and the 'Japanese' felt admiration for, rather than fear of, the West. However, during the 1880s, the colonisation and carving up of Asia and Africa by the Western Powers proceeded at a furious pace and, in response, a growing sense of crisis and a heightened sense of nationalism emerged even among Japan's intelligentsia who favoured modernisation. The fact that countries such as the USA, Great Britain and France – the very models of Japan's Civilisation and Enlightenment (*bunmei kaika*) Movement and the Liberty and People's Rights (*jiyū-minken*) Movement – were engaged in subjugating and ruling large parts of Asia and Africa must have forced the intellectuals of the Meiji enlightenment to re-examine their views of the world.

The 'Black Ships' were warships of the US Navy that arrived off the shores of Japan in 1853. The Edo Bakufu had refused to establish relations with most Western countries but, faced with the military threat posed by the Black Ships, was forced in a classic case of gunboat diplomacy to establish relations with the USA. This triggered a political crisis in Japan that was only resolved by the eventual collapse of the Edo Bakufu in the Meiji Restoration of 1868.

Following the Restoration, the Meiji government opened Japan's doors to Western civilisation, although the political regime remained one that stressed a government-led development. From the second half of the 1870s, a Liberty and People's Rights Movement emerged that was influenced by Western ideals of human rights and freedom. This declined towards the end of the 1880s, mainly because of government suppression, but also because of a growing sense of disillusionment with the West among the Japanese intelligentsia, a disillusionment caused by a new Western push to colonise parts of Asia and Africa.

The main aims of the Liberty and People's Rights Movement were democracy and the overthrow of the *hanbatsu* (cliques formed by members of the same feudal domains). The Meiji Restoration was led by powerful southern domains, namely Satsuma and Chōshū, and members of these domains dominated the Meiji government. Those from other regions criticised this as a '*hanbatsu* (domain-dominated) government'. The main demand of the Liberty and People's Rights Movement was to open a national parliament and to ensure that the opinions of all regions were reflected in national policy making. The movement was thus a democratic one, and at the same time had elements of a nationalistic movement that aimed for national unification.

Faced with this movement, the Meiji government promised in 1881 to open a national parliament – the Imperial Diet – and enact a Constitution within a decade. While making approaches to the right-wing of the movement, the government suppressed the left. In 1889, the Constitution of the Great Japanese Empire was promulgated – this was modelled on the Prussian model and defined sovereignty as residing with the Emperor – and the Diet was convened. By this time, some of those active in the Liberty and People's Rights Movement had come to place a greater emphasis on nationalism than democratisation in order to combat the threat posed by the colonisation of Asia by the Western Powers.

Moreover, because of the unequal treaties forced onto Japan when the country was opened up, the Japan of the day did not enjoy tariff autonomy, and Western nationals in Japan were granted extraterritoriality. From the second half of the 1880s, until Japan was victorious in the Sino-Japanese War of 1894–95, obtained a revision of the treaties, and gained confidence as a powerful country, Japanese intellectuals shared a broad consciousness of the problem of how, as a small and weak country on the outskirts of Asia, Japan was going to maintain her independence.

If we take Kurokawa as an example, his *Kōgei shiryō*, now seen as a history of Japanese arts and crafts, was not written for academic reasons or because of some personal interest, but rather was based on a catalogue of traditional craftwork that Japan had exhibited at the Paris Exhibition of 1878.

At the time, Japan's status at the Exhibition was simply that of a small, quaint, Oriental country. The decision to participate in the Exhibition was necessary to maintain her prestige as an independent country. However, since any exhibition of the products of the Civilisation and Enlightenment Movement would have served only to expose Japan's backwardness, she had no choice but to submit traditional craftwork and content herself with satisfying the curiosity of those interested in *Japonisme*. This could be said to be the limit of Japan's ability to assert herself. As a small and weak Asian nation, well aware that she could not compete with the Western Powers in the area of modern civilisation, Japan chose to assert herself by accepting the indignity of placing herself within the Orientalist framework of the West.

Although there is no doubt that Kurokawa was a nationalist who worshipped the Emperor, in a paper titled 'Kun-Shin setsu' (On the Relationship Between the Sovereign and His Subjects), in which he forcefully argued that the 'Japanese' had from time immemorial been united under the Emperor, he wrote as follows.[12]

> Compared to various foreign countries, it must be said that Japan is not their equal in literature, nor in military strength, nor in architecture, nor in transport, nor in traditional crafts, nor in commerce. In fact, the only area where they are not equal to us is the ethic of [i.e. loyalty between] sovereign and subject, and here we can receive their respect as their superior.

Japan could not compete with the West in literature, military strength, architecture, technology, economic strength, or even in the craftwork of which Kurokawa himself had such high expectations. Once he realised this, the only option open to him was to proclaim the powerful solidarity of the Japanese people (that is, the nation) gathered around the Emperor. To accept the anthropological views of Western scholars that the Japanese nation consisted of a conquering people and an indigenous people was to relinquish this last form of identity. It is not excessively unreasonable to see here the obsessive notion that to give up this view of national identity would have meant to destroy the solidarity of the Japanese people that was essential to maintain Japan's independence, and to pave the way for its partition and colonisation by the Western Powers. To see this as the equivalent of the later military aggression of the Great Japanese Empire or the arrogance of the even later economic superpower is not a judgement that can be made without reservations.

Even Tsuboi Shōgorō, who accepted the mixed nation theory, was no different to individuals such as Kurokawa in that he, too, was an ardent nationalist. Despite the undoubted fact that Japanese anthropologists were influenced by Bälz and Morse, Tsuboi deliberately emphasised the fact that the Anthropological Society was not related to Bälz, and stated that 'it is mortifying for me that it is said that I am a disciple of Morse and that Morse is the father of Japanese anthropology'. Tsuboi was later to study in England, where he neither attended lectures at university nor interacted with British scholars, but spent all his time studying by himself in museums and libraries. It is said that he wrote in reply to a letter of reprimand from the Japanese government that if there were anyone whom he could respect as a teacher of anthropology, then he wanted to know who this was.

An active individual, in later years Tsuboi was to display his energy in a series of lectures in various parts of Europe and America in which he attempted to demonstrate the progress that Japanese anthropology had made. It is therefore not true that some personality trait meant that he could not exchange views with scholars in England. Nor was he a conservative, anti-Western individual. According to Torii Ryūzō, 'of all the students who studied overseas at the time, none returned [to Japan] with as many books as Tsuboi'. Indeed, these books became the core of the Tokyo Imperial University anthropology collection. This suggests the psychology of a young student from a developing nation who burned with a strong feeling of opposition to the West, but at the same time believed that to compete, it was necessary to absorb modern Western sciences as quickly as possible and build an independent Japanese scholarship and civilisation.

Again, according to Torii, Tsuboi later removed from the setting board on which it had been exhibited at Tokyo Imperial University the entire Morse collection of archaeological findings from the Ōmori shell mounds, saying that since Japanese archaeologists had put together a better collection themselves than 'these miserable specimens', it was no longer necessary to treat them with respect. The idea that the roots of the 'Japanese' should be clarified by the 'Japanese' themselves, and not by Westerners, can be seen here. As was always the case when scholars from the Western Powers excavated sites in Asia, Morse's excavation of the Ōmori shell mounds was supported by enormous sums of money that were paid, for instance, to the labourers employed at the site and the landowners. In years to come, anthropologists from the Great Japanese Empire were to march into Korea, Taiwan and Manchuria as the empire expanded, and the specimens gathered in these countries by Tsuboi's students were in their turn to be 'removed' by the native peoples after the Second World War. This, however, is a much later story.

It can be said that the reason early Japanese anthropologists, beginning with Tsuboi, accepted the mixed nation theory despite being nationalists themselves was that it was almost the only theory at the time that was clothed in the costume of modern Western science. At a time when the only choices were between the mixed nation theory of modern science and the homogeneous nation theory of Japanese nativism (*kokugaku*), options were linked directly to the issue of whether Japan's independence could best be protected by returning to native traditions or by assimilating modern civilisation.

This was the case, for instance, with Ono Azusa as well. In 1879, in an essay entitled 'Tada Nippon ari' (Japan and Japan Alone), he criticised both those who idolised Western civilisation without moderation, and those who remained wedded to the old, feudalistic ways of the past and saw themselves not as 'Japanese' but as nationals of individual feudal domains.[13] Japan's independence could not be maintained through an unlimited importing of culture if this led to the destruction of the unique Japanese way of life, nor could it be maintained by an adherence to out-dated traditions and an internal division into various regional districts. In this paper, Ono argued that Japan should chose the path of strengthening the country by adopting Western civilisation, while maintaining Japan's uniqueness, and criticised the domain-dominated (*hanbatsu*) government which was oppressing the Japanese people through domain networks. In the paper on the Japanese nation mentioned above, Ono wrote that although some might think that to describe Japan as once being a country of 'cannibals' was a 'national disgrace', it was in fact a matter of pride that the 'Japanese' had developed a civilisation from such a primitive state.

It is noteworthy that, when Tsuboi opened the anthropological research group in 1884 at the age of 20, Kurokawa was 54 and Naitō 61. It was only natural that, as opposed to Kurokawa and Naitō who had reached a certain age and tended to depend on an outdated understanding of the world, members of the younger generation like Tsuboi chose instead to assimilate modern civilisation. For the later group, even if the homogeneity of the Japanese nation was denied, it was possible to create a new identity in its place by adopting modern civilisation.

In a certain sense, the arguments of Kurokawa and others who shared his views were pessimistic in that they suggested that Japan could not compete with the West in modern civilisation. Individuals like Tsuboi were much more optimistic. However, although they might seem superficially to be totally opposed to one another, both sides could be said to differ only in how their nationalism was manifested. The 1880s were a time in which Westernisation, as represented by the Rokumeikan, the Western-style building built with the backing of and operated by the Japanese government as a place for social gatherings with Westerners, and the patriotic *kokusui* movement, which emerged as a backlash against Westernisation, interacted with one another – a fact reflected in the various theories of the Japanese nation that were developed during this period.[14] The interaction between the two types of nationalism becomes clearer if one remembers that it was Katō Hiroyuki (1836–1916) (see chapter 3), then President of Tokyo Imperial University, and an advocate in his youth of both civilisation and enlightenment and liberty and people's rights, and later an influential public theorist of the national polity and the homogeneous nation, who made it possible for Morse's paper to be published and who provided facilities for Tsuboi's research association.

The theories of the Japanese nation had thus developed into two currents by the 1880s. One was the mixed nation theory which argued that the Japanese nation consisted of a mixture between a conquering people and a previous aboriginal people and others, while the second was the homogeneous nation theory, which argued that the Japanese nation had lived in Japan since time immemorial and that their lineage had been handed down to contemporary 'Japanese'. It is no exaggeration to say that theories of the origin of the Japanese nation from that time to today have scarcely moved a step beyond a number of variations on this framework. As was the case then, so today the two currents sometimes oppose and sometimes support one another, and have reflected the international status of Japan and the state of Japanese nationalism in each of the major periods from the 1880s to the present.

2 The Debate on Mixed Residence in the Interior

The debate on mixed residence in the interior occurred as Japan revised the unequal treaties concluded in the 1850s in the closing days of Tokugawa Shogunate.[1] In the Japan before the treaties were revised, foreigners lived only in extraterritorial settlements such as the port city of Yokohama. After they were revised, these foreigners were allowed to reside anywhere within Japan and to purchase real estate. This triggered a debate for and against what was called 'mixed residence'.

It is difficult to give a succinct explanation of the character of this debate, which lasted until 1899 when the settlements were abolished. It can be seen as a conflict between the members of the Japanese enlightenment who played a leading role in the new age, and the conservatives who consisted of the remnants of the xenophobic 'expel the barbarians' school of thought. The leading philosopher of the Japanese enlightenment, Fukuzawa Yukichi (1834–1901), viewed the situation in these terms. Today, some researchers regard this debate about the acceptance of foreigners as the origin of the contemporary debate about foreign labourers in Japan.[2]

However, although it is true that some of the opponents of mixed residence were clearly conservative, others cannot be schematised in this fashion. For example, some opponents, such as the journalist, Yokoyama Gennosuke (1870–1915), who is known for having tried to bring the position of Japan's lower strata of society to public attention, argued from the standpoint of protecting the people.

In his *Naichi zakkyogo no Nippon* (Japan After Mixed Residence), Yokoyama argued that if mixed residence were allowed, powerful Western capital would flow into Japan, annihilate Japan's national capital, and force Japanese workers, overwhelmed by Western machines, to become low-wage labourers employed by the Western enterprises that would invade Japan. While noting the menace posed by Western capital, Yokoyama emphasised that 'they

[Westerners] are a different race', and that 'they will not treat our workers, who are from their point of view an alien race, humanely'.³

Although this position included the element of the exclusion of 'different races', it differed in tone from the arguments seen in the economic superpower that is Japan today. It reflected a sense of crisis in a developing Asian country that feared the threat of colonisation. If it is to be compared to anything in the Japan of today, it should be compared to the discussion about opening the domestic market to rice imports rather than to the problem of foreign workers.

The debate on mixed residence embraced complicated opposing schema: opening the market versus domestic protection on the one hand, and enlightenment versus xenophobia on the other. Among the many debates on mixed residence in the interior, I will focus on that between the historian and economist Taguchi Ukichi (1855–1905) and the philosopher Inoue Tetsujirō (1856–1944) as an example of a debate that developed into an exchange of arguments about the origin of the Japanese nation. Taguchi is known as a liberal theorist of the enlightenment, while Inoue is known as a 'national polity' (*kokutai*) theorist who wrote the official commentary for the Imperial Rescript on Education (*Kyōiku Chokugo*).⁴ Taguchi was for, and Inoue against, mixed residence, but the debate had an aspect that cannot be schematised simply as a conflict between members of the enlightenment and conservatives.

The United States of America as a Model

After retiring from the Ministry of Finance, Taguchi Ukichi edited the *Tōkyō keizai zasshi* (Tokyo Economic Magazine) and enjoyed a reputation as a celebrated economist that was comparable at the time to that of Fukuzawa Yukichi. He also had a firm grasp of history, authoring *Nippon kaika shōshi* (A Short History of Japanese Modernisation), a work that examined the social evolution of Japan from ancient times, and editing a magazine *Shikai* (The Ocean of History). His economic philosophy was greatly influenced by the British laissez-faire economists. He was therefore opposed to government regulation and intervention and advocated a further opening of the country. At the same time, he was unenthusiastic about measures such as the enactment of labour laws.

On the other hand, Inoue Tetsujirō was a member of the intellectual elite. He graduated from the Department of Philosophy at Tokyo Imperial University, took a post there as assistant professor of philosophy at the age of 27 and become a professor on his return from further study in Germany. Unlike the older Buddhist and Japanese nativist (*kokugaku*) scholars such as Naitō Chisō (see chapter 1) who were opposed to mixed residence, Inoue was well versed in theories of social organism and evolution, and was the same age as Taguchi. This debate therefore was a dispute between members of the new generation who had acquired some knowledge of Western philosophy.

Taguchi's proposal that mixed residence be permitted appeared as early as 1879 in an article titled 'Naichi zakkyoron' (On Mixed Residence in the Interior).[5] Taguchi was then 24 years old, and had just published his *Nippon kaika shōshi*. This paper clearly shows his economic thought and his view of social unity.

According to Taguchi, people are united not by belonging to the 'same race' or because of differences in wealth – Taguchi denied the idea of a class consciousness – but by reason of common interests through mutual trade. From this point of view, the system of extraterritorial settlements served to separate Japanese and foreigners and prevent them from trading with one another, and thus 'breeds discord between Japanese and foreigners'. During the Edo Period, he continued, people of the various feudal domains were separated from and hostile to one another. With the abolition of the feudal domains and the formation of a modern unified state, however, people from different areas came to 'live together in the same towns' and were united as a single nation. Therefore, he concluded, 'the establishment of the extraterritorial settlements is, I believe, a revival of the feudal system'.

The question that Taguchi asked was whether the influx of Western capital would 'exploit the poor of Japan and deprive us of Japan's wealth'. His answer was that this was a 'groundless worry', 'empty speculation', and the product of a mind that 'knows nothing of the logic of capital'. Workers are dependent on capital to provide jobs, and therefore the idea that an increase in the number of capitalists will damage labourers is a 'fallacious superstition'. According to Taguchi, even the working class in England, whose wretched state had been reported in Japan, would 'starve to death' without capitalists. Western capital would not only provide jobs but also 'shore up mines and bring new land under cultivation'.

Even Taguchi, however, was conscious of the threat of colonisation posed by the Western Powers. Nevertheless, he insisted that it was precisely because of this threat that it was even more necessary to implement a policy of mixed residence. This was due to the segregation and hostility caused by the extraterritorial settlements, where 'Japanese' and foreigners sat in opposing camps and watched one another for an unguarded moment. Moreover, it was certain that the number of foreigners would increase in future. If this issue were not addressed, the foreigners gathered together in the extraterritorial settlements might become the vanguard of the Western Powers, and Japan would then suffer the same fate as the East Indies (India). It was therefore necessary for mixed residence to be realised as soon as possible in order to abolish the extraterritorial settlements. Taguchi stated:

> In my opinion, people are united and establish close relations with one another when and only when they share common interests, and never because they belong to the same race, or because of a lack of differences in wealth or talent. Some insist that the Japanese are united because they are homogeneous, but the reality is very different. In ancient times, we had the immigrants from Korea and China and, in the modern era, we had the descendants of Dutch immigrants.

In other words, looking to the Korean and Chinese immigrants in ancient times, and to the Dutch in the Edo Period, as precedents for an influx of foreign peoples into Japan, Taguchi insisted that the 'Japanese' were not homogeneous even before mixed residence.[6]

Taguchi's views of mixed residence did not change fundamentally later. A new argument added in 1884 focused on Chinese immigrants, in addition to Westerners, as foreigners who were coming to Japan.[7] In response to the position that held that an influx of low-wage Chinese workers would cause unemployment among Japanese workers, Taguchi said that he welcomed the influx, even though he clearly revealed his prejudices when he wrote that 'it is most detestable that Chinese are engaged in monkey business without any sense of shame'. From the point of view of an economic liberal, the existence of low-wage workers was 'in the interests of the capitalist' and 'in the interests of the consumer', and 'competition was in the interests of our country'. Needless to say, the notion that the low wages of the Chinese workers might be the result of exploitation was not a part of Taguchi's thinking.

Taguchi viewed the USA as one of the models for a future Japan. In a paper published in 1889, he held it up as an example of a country that had enjoyed rapid development because of an influx of capital and labour from overseas.[8] Noting that the USA was a country composed of immigrants from various nations, and insisting that Japan too had received many immigrants in the past, he wrote:

> ...In ancient times, many Korean people migrated to our country. Some gained official positions in the bureaucracy, other became peers, and many established villages in some parts of the countryside. Afterwards Japan began to associate with China, and many Chinese immigrants were naturalised as Japanese. At that time, Korea and China undoubtedly possessed a higher civilisation than Japan, and it was beneficial for Japan to have immigrants from those countries. Once they became naturalised and joined our nation, they became no different from our fellow countrymen.

According to Taguchi, in ancient times, large numbers of Korean and Chinese immigrants had come to the Japanese archipelago, bringing civilisation with them, and among the modern 'Japanese' there existed a large number of their descendants. There was thus no need to fear mixed residence. Once foreigners resident in Japan became naturalised Japanese citizens, they would become 'loyal fellow countrymen' as was the case with past immigrants. Furthermore, Taguchi declared:

> Why do we debate the difference in bloodlines? I want foreigners to live freely among us, and contribute both to an increase in the Japanese population and to our material prosperity. This is what has happened in the USA. There is nothing to fear from this. What I worry about is that the extraterritorial settlements might expand (at the expense of Japanese territory) in step with trade, and that the foreigners will join together and deprive us of political power as happened in the East Indies.

Taguchi was thus of the opinion that Japan faced a choice of either repeating the tragedy of the East Indies which did not abolish foreign settlements and was colonised as a result, or following the example set by the USA and uniting Japanese and foreigners through mixed residence.

Furthermore, Taguchi insisted that naturalised foreigners were no longer foreigners, and therefore should be granted 'the same rights as Japanese nationals'.[9] What was an issue was that 'those who suffer losses due to the acts of foreigners are compelled to bear those losses silently' because of the extraterritoriality of the foreign concessions. In exchange for recognising the foreigners' rights as 'Japanese' through mixed residence, he argued, they must be made to obey Japanese law. His approval of mixed residency was therefore accompanied by the demand that the privileges of extraterritoriality be abolished and those areas placed under the control of Japanese law.

It is Impossible to Advance Abroad

Inoue Tetsujirō who debated the issue of mixed residence with Taguchi developed his opposition to mixed residence in *Naichi zakkyoron* (On Mixed Residence in the Interior) published in 1889.[10] According to the preface, although he was still studying in Berlin at that time, he was persuaded of the importance of this issue by the Buddhist scholar, Inoue Enryō (1858–1919), who visited him in Berlin, and 'on that very day I started writing and completed the book in several days'.

Naichi zakkyoron is a pedantic work, and makes full use of Inoue's knowledge of European thought. One can hardly read through a single page without encountering the names of European thinkers such as Machiavelli, Montesquieu, Spencer, Rousseau and Hegel. Inoue Tetsujirō's argument was based especially on the theory of social evolution that stresses the survival of the fittest and the superiority or inferiority of races. What is notable about his argument, however, is that it did not assume the racial superiority of the 'Japanese', but rather the opposite.

According to Inoue, mixed residence would force 'all Japanese people, young and old, rich and poor...to compete with Western people'. However, 'most Japanese people are inferior to Western people in intelligence, wealth, physical constitution and in all other things, so it is inevitable that they will always lose any competition'. Mentioning the results of a measurement of bodies of the 'Japanese', Inoue stated that the 'Japanese are smaller and shorter than Chinese and Koreans', let alone Europeans. They are like 'women and children', and mixed residence would be similar to a fight between a 'feeble child' and a 'desperado' (Inoue 1889: 10–15).

Inoue also insisted that the strength of a country depends on the homogeneity of its nationals. Therefore, when 'several races dwell together in a country, and accordingly several customs, religions and languages coexist, it is harmful to the unity of that country and makes it extremely difficult to rule and control'. Moreover, if those foreigners residing in Japan were naturalised, according to Taguchi's position, they 'would gain the same qualifications as Japanese, and once they began to compete with Japanese in politics...they would surely make good use of their superior intelligence and eventually win power' (Inoue 1889: 16–17).

Besides, according to Inoue, in areas of the south into which Europeans had advanced and where they lived with native peoples, such as Tonga, Tahiti, Fiji and Tasmania, the native peoples had been overwhelmed by the Europeans in the struggle for survival, and their numbers were steadily declining. In the Sandwich Islands (today's Hawaii) of the South Pacific 'discovered' by Captain Cook, the islanders had 'imitated Western customs...adopted Christianity, and become the prominent civilised country in the South Seas'. This was 'very similar to the situation in Japan'. However, even on these islands, the number of islanders had decreased over a period of 100 years to one sixth of what it had been. The cause of this decrease was the same as the decline of 'the Aborigines of America' and 'the Ezo [*Ainu*] of Japan'. That is 'when an inferior race resides together with a superior race, a tendency for their population to decrease emerges, and they are eventually overcome by the superior race' (Inoue 1889: 33–8).

Here Inoue defined the 'Japanese' as an inferior race, and argued that exclusionism and national unity were essential to maintain Japan's independence. He also rejected the argument that the 'Japanese' were a 'civilised race', and stated that the importing of Western civilisation into Japan was undertaken by the government and had nothing to do with the progress of the people. He insisted that 'the law which applies to other inferior races also applies to the Japanese' (Inoue 1889: 49–51).

However, Inoue was, from first to last, a member of the new generation which tried to absorb the knowledge of the West. He emphasised the difference between his arguments and those of the Edo Period 'expel the barbarians' school of thought. According to Inoue, the latter school was for those who 'are ignorant of international conditions' and who 'regard Western people as a savage and inferior race'. Inoue, however, did not look down with contempt on the West. 'I do not regard Western people as savages, but feel respect and affection for them as members of a superior race'. He mentioned the fact that 'America prohibited the immigration of Chinese' as one of the many examples of the restriction of the immigration of alien peoples whose migration ran counter to the national interest (Inoue 1889: 53–5).

Inoue at this time could not have foreseen that this exclusion of Chinese immigrants in the USA would develop in the 1910s into the exclusion of Japanese migrants that became a large issue between Japan and America.[11] He did not think that the 'Japanese', an inferior race, would ever be able to move out into the world. With the Japanese Empire's aggressiveness in later years in mind, his following words deserve consideration (Inoue 1889: 6).

> The only place in the whole world where the Japanese can live is Japan and Japan alone. We have to be aware of the fact that our home is limited to the area within this country. From the way things are today, it is difficult to believe that the Japanese will ever progress, become an advanced, powerful nation and go out into the world and migrate abroad. Therefore, the Japanese for a while will have to be content to regard this small island-country, Japan, as the only place to live. Under these circumstances, if we allow foreigners to live with us, the people of Europe and America will enter Japan and will take possession of our land.

Here, there is no sign whatsoever of an argument in favour of territorial expansion or a movement overseas. The 'Japanese' described by Inoue in his argument opposing mixed residence were a people inferior to Koreans and Chinese, let alone Westerners, with no prospects of becoming a 'powerful nation' in the foreseeable future. Japan was seen as a small, weak and peaceful state, like 'women and children', a state that, thrust into the maelstrom of the threat posed by the Western Powers, was trying to maintain the national homogeneity of a small island-country, while at the same time maintaining friendly relations with the West. This is very different to the theory of advancing into the world, which emerged in later years during the age of the Great Japanese Empire. Inoue was thus opposed to mixed residence, and advocated postponing the treaty revision until Japan had made enough progress in her push towards civilisation and enlightenment.

'The Assimilative Ability of the Japanese People'

The month after the publication of Inoue's *Naichi zakkyoron* (On Mixed Residence in the Interior), Taguchi's *Jōyaku kaiseiron* (On the Revision of the Treaties) was published. In this collection of lectures, to which an introduction by the famous journalist and Christian, Tokutomi Sohō (1863–1957), was added, Taguchi referred to 'those who most vigorously oppose' mixed residence, namely Shiga Shigetaka, Miyake Setsurei, Tani Tateki, Hayashi Hōmei and Inoue Kakugorō, and advanced a strange counter-argument, saying 'all these gentlemen are foreigners'.

This claim was based on the origin of their family names, which Taguchi looked up in the *Shinsen shōjiroku*. As noted in the introduction, the *Shinsen shōjiroku* is a list of family names recorded in the ninth century during the early Heian Period. The contents are divided into three sections: 'Kōbetsu', which deals with the Imperial Family and those related to it, 'Shinbetsu', which deals with other Japanese natives, and 'Banbetsu', which deals with foreign immigrants. *Shinsen shōjiroku* can thus be used to identify which family names are those of the foreign migrants of that time. According to Taguchi, Shiga, Miyake, Tani, Hayashi and Inoue were all originally surnames that indicated Chinese or Korean lineage. In other words, he said, those who were opposed to mixed residence were themselves the descendants of foreign immigrants.

Furthermore, with reference to the names of leading figures of the government, together with aristocratic members of society and others, Taguchi stated that 'even if Chinese or Korean immigrants come to settle in Japan, there is no need for worry or fear as long as they turn into upright members of society such as Lord Shimazu, or Viscount Soejima, or Lieutenant-General Tani, or Mr. Shiga Shigetaka, or Mr. Hayashi Hōmei, or Mr. Inoue Kakugorō – for, indeed, the immigrants will also become reliable members of this state'.[12] This provoked boisterous laughter and applause from his audience. Taguchi next referred to his pet opinion that 'what we do have to fear are the extraterritorial settlements'. The lecture ended amid thunderous applause. Taguchi sent a copy of his work to Inoue Tetsujirō, who had just arrived home from abroad, with a letter noting that the family name Inoue is that of the descendants of Chinese immigrants.

Inoue could hardly ignore this challenge. In his *Naichi zakkyo zokuron* (Revisiting the Issue of Mixed Residence in the Interior), published two years later in 1891, Inoue savaged Taguchi's position as 'a completely worthless argument'.[13] Bringing out a name list edited a thousand years ago, he claimed, was pointless because the family names of today differed from those of the past, since they had undergone changes because of adoption or for other reasons. In fact, Inoue continued, his own surname had changed three times since his childhood.[14] To base any claim that someone was descended from immigrants on the surnames of today was 'nonsense that even suckling babes would refrain from giving vent to'. Even if he was to accept, for the sake of argument, that he was truly the descendant of foreign immigrants, their migration occurred over a thousand years ago and, moreover, 'the immigrants never came in groups large enough to radically change the Japanese state, but instead came only in small groups, and were assimilated as Japanese'. Therefore, the issue of ancient immigration could not be put in the same category as mixed residence.

According to Inoue, the immigrants came to Japan during a period before the contemporary 'invincible National Polity' was formed. At the time, the mixed residence of alien peoples may have been permitted. However, once the 'invincible National Polity had been formed', it became the 'primary duty of Japanese nationals' to endeavour 'heart and soul' to thoroughly 'protect' it. If mixed residence were to be permitted, not only Westerners, but also Indians, Chinese and Koreans, or, in his words, 'foreigners of all colours, yellow, white, red and black', would 'suddenly flood into Japan from all directions'. To 'assimilate them into Japan' would be an impossible task for the inferior 'Japanese'.

Furthermore, in an appendix to his *Naichi zakkyo zokuron*, Inoue advanced the idea that 'the ancestors of the Japanese came from the South Seas' in support of his belief that the 'Japanese' were an inferior race. According to him, although 'continental races, such as the Mongolians, Koreans and Chinese' had probably migrated to Japan, their influence was only minor. Inoue barely mentions the grounds for this position, but there is no doubt that the theory of a South Seas origin for the Japanese nation was convenient for his argument against mixed residency, since such a theory shored up two points. First, the Chinese and Koreans, who together with

Westerners were expected to pour into Japan if mixed residence was to be permitted, have 'different racial origins' from the 'Japanese'. Secondly, the 'Japanese' are of the same race and share a great deal with the people of the South Seas whom Inoue also thought to be an inferior race. As will be explained in chapter 6, Inoue later became an advocate of the northern origin theory (the position that the Japanese nation originated in the north – the Chinese continent and Korea), but attention should be paid to the fact that he had an inferiority complex to the West at this time and agreed with the theory of a southern origin (the position that the origin of the Japanese nation lay in Southeast Asia).

Taguchi, to whom Inoue sent a copy of *Naichi zakkyo zokuron*, immediately responded with a short paper, 'Inoue Tetsujirō ni tadasu' (Querying Inoue Tetsujirō), in which he wrote that 'Mr. Inoue's argument is also utterly worthless, and has no more effect on me than a louse in hysterics'.[15]

According to Taguchi, if Inoue's family name had indeed undergone three changes, then it was also possible that past immigrants had changed their names to Japanese ones. Moreover, Inoue on one hand insisted that Japan was not yet civilised enough to allow mixed residence, but on the other hand also claimed that Japan enjoyed such an invincible national polity today that it was impossible for her to accept foreigners. This, Taguchi noted, was a contradiction. In the ancient era, when Japan had accepted foreign immigrants, the 'Japanese' were uncivilised, and accepting civilised foreign immigrants at this stage, according to Inoue's law of the survival of the fittest, should have been vigorously rejected. In short, 'there is no stable standard in his so-called theory of the survival of the fittest', which was simply opportunistic.

However, the following section of Taguchi's counter-argument demands attention.

> I believe in the theory of evolution. However, I cannot agree that the Japanese are inferior animals. Remember, if we cannot succeed in mixed residence, we will never be able to succeed in establishing colonies abroad.

Here, Taguchi opposed Inoue's opinion that the 'Japanese' were an inferior race, saying that the Japanese would never be able to establish colonies overseas and move out into the world unless they first succeeded in implementing mixed residence. Conversely,

Taguchi advocated mixed residence precisely because he believed that the 'Japanese' were a superior race capable of moving out into the world.

This aspect of Taguchi's thought became even clearer in his *Kyoryūchi seido to naichi zakkyo* (Extraterritorial Settlements and Mixed Residence in the Interior), published two years later in 1893. Here he again explained the ability of mixed residence to contribute to smooth economic relations, and criticised the evil effects of foreign concessions. He also came to grips with the question that most interested the opponents of mixed residency, how Japan could maintain her independence.

Taguchi wrote that 'it is an enormous mistake to believe that the way for the Japanese race to maintain its independence is to confine itself to these isolated islands', saying that to do so would be like a turtle retreating into its shell. Contrary to Inoue, Taguchi claimed that 'the Japanese race has no reason to be fearful of the Aryan race in technology, the sciences, or industry and agriculture'. Saying there would have been no British Empire if the British had locked themselves up in their isles, he claimed 'the Japanese race should actively spread our race over the globe'. According to Taguchi, there were only two ways to do this.

> Firstly, to spread pure blooded brethren all over the world, and increase their numbers. Secondly, to spread all over the world those who, even if not always of pure blood, share our language and have the same customs as us.

Taguchi argued that this 'first hope' was an impossibility. Japanese migrants would be assimilated into the places to which they had emigrated, and 'if those overseas Japanese emigrants lose their language and customs, they will yield no profit to Japan'. On the other hand, if Japan 'assimilates' those foreign immigrants who had come to Japan together with children of mixed parentage, this would be 'profitable' and would strengthen Japan. There was no need to worry about whether or not this would ruin the pure blood of the 'Japanese'. Many foreign immigrants had come to the archipelago from ancient times, and it was their culture that had strengthened Japan. There was also no need to fear that non-Japanese subjects would lack in patriotic sentiment in the future. Although the USA was a collection of many peoples, 'the strong patriotic sentiment of Americans is widely acknowledged'. In times of war, he noted, Americans even fight against their countries of origin.

Here, Taguchi mentioned two members of the Imperial Family. The Empress Jingū, according to the Kiki myths, directed the invasion of Korea in ancient times, while the Emperor Kanmu (737–806) dispatched the general Sakanoue-no-Tamuramaro (758–811) to northern Japan to quell the Emishi, a people who were resisting the Imperial Family (see chapter 3, endnote 17). These members were mentioned as past examples of intermarriage with foreign immigrants.

> These two are remarkable examples. Empress Jingū's mother was a descendant of a King of Silla, and Emperor Kanmu's mother was a descendant of the Royal family of Pekche.[16]

Refuting the opinion that non-Japanese subjects lacked patriotic feelings, Taguchi noted that these two members of the Imperial Family, who conquered alien nations both inside and outside Japan, were descendants of Korean immigrants. Mentioning this example to demonstrate that mixed residence could change alien peoples into 'loyal brethren', he claimed that if mixed residence were allowed, Japan, 'as time goes by, will without a doubt accept, digest and assimilate these foreigners, who will eventually become our brethren. If we mix with each other by marriage, nobody will bother about the differences in language and customs'.

In the same year, an anonymous article, 'Nippon kokumin no dōkaryoku' (The Assimilative Ability of the Japanese), appeared in *Kokumin no tomo*, a magazine edited by Tokutomi Sohō (the writer who contributed the preface to Taguchi's *Jōyaku kaiseiron*).[17] The argument developed in this article closely resembles that of Taguchi. Like Taguchi, the author spoke with pride about 'the assimilative ability of the Japanese', mentioning the existence of foreign migrants and the lineage of the Empress Jingū. In the article, the author wrote that foreigners and theorists who argued against mixed residence claimed that Japan was as backward as South Sea island nations such as Fiji and Hawaii. However, in reply to this, the author emphasised the Japanese achievement in assimilating foreign migrants from 'superior races', and ended the article with the words 'do not trouble yourselves, you theorists opposing mixed residence: the Japanese are not Hawaiians'.

In this way, support for mixed residence increased, the unequal treaties were revised and, from 1899, mixed residence was realised. In that year, Taguchi wrote a critique entitled 'Kyoryūchi o shite sumiyaka ni naichi ni dōka seshimu beshi' (The Extraterritorial Settlements should be Quickly Returned to Japan). Here he said 'we should drink a hearty toast in celebration when we can finally abolish the settlements, something which is in the interest of the state', and suggested 'depriving [the foreigners living in the foreign concessions of their] privileges' and absorbing the settlements into the Japanese homeland. From his point of view, mixed residence was the memorable first step for Japan to become a great power able to move out into the world, and to 'assimilate' into Japan regions not currently under the authority of the Japanese government.

The debate over mixed residence thus ended with the victory of those who favoured it. As can be seen in the debate between Taguchi and Inoue, this was not merely a confrontation between conservatives and members of the enlightenment. It was a conflict between two conceptions of the state, or two types of nationalism – about whether the best way of maintaining the independence of Japan would be to give precedence to maintaining the homogeneity of the Japanese nation by confining the Japanese to their home islands, or to go out into the world and assimilate alien nations.

However, unlike the arguments of Kurokawa or Naitō in the past, Inoue as well as Taguchi accepted the theory that the Japanese nation came from abroad. The difference was that while Taguchi emphasised the mixed blood of the 'Japanese' in the debate, Inoue tried to ignore it as much as possible. In his heart of hearts, Inoue probably wanted to adopt the homogeneous nation theory. However, he needed above all to avoid being labelled as a theorist of the old 'expel the barbarians' school of thought, and therefore had no choice but to accept the mixed nation theory, since there was no anthropological support for the homogeneous nation theory which by this time had become unacceptable even to those theorists who wanted to maintain national homogeneity.

For half a century after this, the homogeneous nation theory was pushed aside in the press, and the mixed nation theory moved into the mainstream discourse. This is not only because there existed no academic research to support the theory of ethnic homogeneity, but also because the people of the Great Japanese Empire began to define themselves as a superior nation capable of moving out into the world, rather than as an inferior race whose sphere of activity was limited to the Japanese archipelago. Although neither Taguchi nor Inoue was aware of it, the framework of ideas they developed in their debate on mixed residence laid the foundation for the arguments advanced in the following period. This framework survived them, and came to rule the consciousness of the age when Japan became a multi-national empire.

3 The Theory of the National Polity and Japanese Christianity

The national polity (*kokutai*) theory, the ruling ideology of the empire, saw the Great Japanese Empire as a large Family State presided over by the Imperial Family. As already noted (see introduction, endnote 10), the word *kokutai* (national polity) had existed from the Edo Period, but re-emerged in the late nineteenth century as a term for a monarchy centred on the Emperor. Having seized power from the Edo Period Bakufu in 1868, the Meiji government embarked on a policy of modernisation under the slogan 'Wealthy Country and Strong Military' (*fukoku kyōhei*), and in 1872 introduced a Western system of compulsory education. At first, much of this relied on translated Western textbooks. However, in order to combat the Liberty and People's Rights Movement of the 1880s, it became necessary to promote an education that emphasised loyalty to the Emperor and government.

The anti-government movements, beginning with the Liberty and People's Rights Movement, were an alliance between an intelligentsia that had imbibed the imported Western notion of human rights, and a populace that felt threatened by the radical policies of modernisation. The two were united by their opposition to the government. In order to combat this movement, the Meiji government began to propagate the importance of loyalty to the Emperor, and at the same time attempted to pacify the populace by appealing to traditional morals.

The national polity theory, which viewed the Japanese state as a family and the Emperor as the patriarch, succeeded in both these aims. That is, by extending the Confucian ethic of 'respecting one's parents' to include 'loyalty to the Emperor', it was possible both to pacify the populace and rural power-brokers who were anxious about the collapse of their traditional status, and at the same time to channel their loyalties towards the state. Therefore, state education, with the help of the Kiki myths, taught that the ancestors of the Imperial Household who had descended from Heaven were the ancestors of all 'Japanese' nationals.

In the 1880s, a new course of 'morals' (*shūshin*) was established as a major part of compulsory education. It used the ancient myths to teach this ethic, and ensured that all students memorised the *Kyōiku Chokugo* (Imperial Rescript on Education) (see chapter 2, endnote 4), which glorified the national polity and argued that the unity of the family parallelled the unity of the state. A portrait of the Emperor in a Western-style military uniform was distributed to primary schools, and students were made to worship it. (This education was to continue until 1945, when the Great Japanese Empire was defeated in the Second World War.)

The patriarchs of influential families, especially in rural areas, welcomed this approach because it meant that the state would help maintain their status by urging those subordinate to them in traditional communities to remain subordinate. This combination of Western modernisation with what were claimed to be 'traditional' Japanese morals was known as '*Wakon Yōsai*' (Japanese Spirit and Western Knowledge).

However, there was one problem with the national polity theory. Since it argued that imperial subjects were all members of a large family who shared the first, ancient Emperor as a common ancestor, it depended on a claim that all those subjects were members of a single nation who shared pure and homogeneous origins. How, then, did the national polity theorists manage to maintain the logic of their position after the alien peoples of Korea and Taiwan were incorporated into the Great Japanese Empire?

This chapter will examine the debate over this issue from the cession of Taiwan in 1895 to immediately before the annexation of Korea in 1910. In a word, for the national polity theory of this period, the existence of other ethnic groups within the empire was an Achilles' heel. The targets of the criticism of the national polity theorists, most notably Japanese Christian intellectuals, realised that the existence of Taiwan was a weak point in the theory, and used it, together with the anthropological mixed nation theory, as a launching pad for a counter-attack. Ironically, however, as a result of this process, Christian intellectuals prepared the grounds for a new justification of external aggression.[1]

The Rise of the National Polity Theory

The origin of the theory of the national polity can be traced back to the Edo Period.[2] However, the rise of the theory in the modern age dates from the 1890s, the decade that began with the issue of the Imperial Rescript on Education in 1890.

The feudalistic system of the Edo Period did not rest on the notion that all 'Japanese', regardless of social status or region, were members of a single large family. If anything, the idea that the Shōgun, the *samurai*, and the peasants – or the people of both the anti-Tokugawa Satsuma clan and the pro-Tokugawa Mito clan – were all the same 'Japanese' with a common ancestor was a philosophy that the Establishment would not have approved. It was only after the feudalistic system was overthrown and a nation-state formed that it was possible for the national polity theory to become an officially sanctioned ideology. Furthermore, as the integrating idea for a modern state, it was also necessary for national polity theorists to adopt a modern face to distinguish themselves from the 'Respect the Emperor and Expel the Barbarians' xenophobia of the narrow-minded Japanese nativist scholars. The theory therefore had to be reconciled with the need to adopt Western civilisation in accordance with the Meiji Period government-sponsored slogans 'Wealthy Country and Strong Military' and 'Japanese Spirit and Western Technology'.

Representative national polity theorists who did adopt a modern face were individuals such as one of the central members of the Japanese enlightenment, Katō Hiroyuki (1836–1916), the constitutional scholar Hozumi Yatsuka (1860–1912), and the philosopher Inoue Tetsujirō (1856–1944). All three were intellectuals who, in their different ways, digested Western thought and had had the experience of studying overseas.

In 1891, Inoue Tetsujirō published *Chokugo engi* (On the Imperial Rescript), an explanatory introduction to the Imperial Rescript on Education.[3] This was an officially sanctioned commentary that the Minister of Education asked Inoue to draft, in accordance with a Cabinet council decision. When he wrote it, Inoue referred to the opinions of individuals such as Katō Hiroyuki and the elite bureaucrat Inoue Kowashi (1844–1895), and the work was viewed by the Emperor before publication. It was published two years after his *Naichi zakkyoron* (On Mixed Residence in the Interior), and was written with a very similar perception of Japan – the belief that the 'Japanese' were far inferior to Western people, and a crisis-driven sense that, unless national unity were maintained, the 'Japanese' would soon lose any competition with the West and then their independence.

Inoue Tetsujirō began his introduction to this book: 'When I see the present situation of my mother country with eyes that have become used to the high civilisation of Europe [Inoue had just returned from Europe], I cannot but acknowledge the great difference between them and us, and I am deeply hurt'. He thus found the weakness of Japan, which was a developing Asian country, unbearable.

Inoue next wrote about his perception of the international state of affairs. Although a little long, this too deserves quotation.

> When I look at the situation of the World Powers, it is clear that not only the Western nations, but also those countries established and settled by Europeans, are prospering. Eastern nations are the only ones that can compete in progress with the West, but countries such as India, Egypt, Burma and Vietnam have already lost their independence, while others, such as Siam [Thailand], Tibet and Korea are extremely weak and will struggle to maintain their independence. Therefore, in the East of today, only China and Japan remain independent and are able to compete for their national interests with the [Western] Powers. However, China's eyes are fixed firmly on her past, and she shows few signs of a progressive spirit. Only Japan is making progress day and night, and will produce a glorious culture in the future if she plays her cards correctly. However, Japan is a very small country, and surrounded by rapacious enemies on all sides. It is important to maintain a friendly intercourse with the Powers, but also understand that, if they ever see a weakness in us, we will have nothing to depend on but our 40 million compatriots. Therefore, all Japanese should always be ready courageously to sacrifice their lives for the state.

According to Inoue, in the competitive jungle of international society, almost all Asian and African countries, with the exception of Japan, had lost their independence and had either been colonised by the Western Powers or fallen behind in the race towards civilisation and enlightenment. In this environment, the people of the 'very small country', Japan, must be aware that they were 'surrounded by...enemies on all sides', that all they could 'depend on...[are] our 40 million compatriots', and that everyone needed to be ready to sacrifice their lives to maintain the independence of the state. Inoue emphasised that 'as a general rule, the strength of a country is mainly determined by the degree to which public sentiment is united', and claimed that that the Emperor and the Imperial Rescript on Education lay at the centre of Japan's solidarity.

It cannot be said that this emphasis on crisis was a mere expedient to force people to accept the Emperor and the Imperial Rescript. As noted in chapter 2, Inoue at this time regarded Japan as a small and weak country, and thought Japan would not be able to march out into the world. Inoue's views after the Sino-Japanese War (1894–95) and the Russo-Japanese War (1904–05) will be examined in chapter 6. Before these wars, however, this sentiment was genuine.

After this, he wrote about the Family State, a concept based on the idea that the 'Japanese' were a family that consisted of the Emperor as the parent and the people as the children. Needless to say, as was emphasised in the debate on mixed residence, outsiders who threatened national solidarity were not tolerated. In the enlarged edition of this work, *Zōtei chokugo engi* (On the Imperial Rescript, Revised Edition), published in 1899, Inoue added the following passage. 'Since the time of the old legends, the Japanese nation has shared the same lineage and since the founding of the country, has lived in the same land and shared the same language, customs, habits, and history. Since it has never been conquered by another nation, the Japanese who reside in every corner of the archipelago are all kinsfolk'.[4] This was the year that the Hokkaido Former Aborigines Protection Act was enacted, and that mixed residence in the interior began.[5] This new section totally ignores the existence of alien peoples within the empire and might be seen as Inoue's response to the issue of mixed residence.

In the same year – 1891 – that Inoue published *Chokugo engi*, Hozumi Yatsuka, a leading national polity theorist and legal scholar, took part in a debate on the Civil Law. Hozumi was also an elite professor who, in his youth, was sent to Germany from Tokyo Imperial University. He was opposed to the proposed civil laws which were about to be enacted with the help of French foreign advisers to the Meiji government, claiming that 'the civil laws will mean an end to loyalty and filial duty'. In a critical article with the same title, 'Minpō idete, chūkō horobu' (The Civil Laws Will Mean an End to Loyalty and Filial Duty), Hozumi emphasised that 'Japan is a country of ancestor worship', and criticised the French-influenced proposal for civil laws that 'will harm national kinship by emphasising ideals of equality and fraternity'.[6] (As a result of Hozumi's protests, the Civil Law did not come into force until 1898, and the sections dealing with Family Law were completely rewritten.)

According to Hozumi's article, Europe also used to be a society based on a German community that worshipped its ancestors. However, the influence of Roman legal thought, and especially the concepts of contracts and rights, destroyed this ancestor worship. Rome came to include many colonies within its territory, grew into a multi-national empire and, in order to unite the alien nations under its rule, gradually abandoned its character as a city-state based on the Latin nation. As a result, Rome came to depend on the universalism of Christianity and of Roman laws. This was the view of history Hozumi learnt from his study in Germany and, as a result, he abhorred Christianity. As will be discussed later in this work, the Roman Empire was repeatedly mentioned throughout the period of the Great Japanese Empire as an example of an empire that collapsed as a result of changing into a multi-national state.

Like Inoue, Hozumi, too, accepted the view of international relations as a struggle for the survival of the fittest. According to Hozumi, it was important to resist the spell of 'humanism and benevolence' and the 'coexistence of all mankind' as advocated by Christians. For, in the age of imperialism, 'if we allow ourselves to become intoxicated with the idea of world peace, and disarm, we will be defenceless and inevitably become the prey of the strong if and when the world is not unified as promised...Given the state of things in the world today, it is clear that now is not the time to criticise patriotism as narrow-minded intolerance, nor to weaken our power of solidarity'.

In 1897, Hozumi published a book entitled *Kokumin kyōiku aikokushin* (National Education: Patriotism) where he emphasised that 'the ancestor of the Emperor is the earliest ancestor of all Japanese, and the Imperial Household is the head family of the Japanese people. Just as we should respect our parents, we should also respect the ancestor of the nation'. He stressed that 'the Japanese Empire consists of a great nation of one race that shares the same history and the same pure blood'. According to Hozumi, integrating the nation-state through shared interests or artificial contracts was inferior to kinship in generating solidarity. This was because interests change from situation to situation, and artificial contracts could be artificially rescinded, but 'for kinsmen to rely upon one another is a natural form of solidarity'. Moreover, while 'obedience based on a contract is not respected unless enforced with brute strength', 'obedience based on ancestor worship springs from the natural respect that children have for their fathers'. In other words, 'in enforced unity based on contracts, there may be loyalty, but no respect, and in relations based on human equality, there might be fraternity, but no loyalty', but 'it is a characteristic of kinship groups' that they enjoy both order (obedience) and loyalty.[7]

This is a view of the world far removed from the concept of multinational unity based on shared interests as advocated by Taguchi, or the theory of a social contract. In the first place, if Hobbes, who destroyed the premise of a natural affinity between king and subject and insisted that the essence of the state is rule through power, marks the beginning of modern thought, then Hozumi's thought was not modern. It should be noted here that the national polity theorists regarded rule by the Emperor in the Meiji state as a natural unity of a single nation, and not as rule through power.

It goes without saying that the national polity theory was easily reconciled with the myth of the homogeneous nation. However, in 1895, after winning the Sino-Japanese War of 1894–95 and gaining Taiwan, Japan came to incorporate as imperial subjects roughly 2.5 million Chinese, together with Taiwanese aboriginal peoples known in Japanese as the 'Banjin' or the 'Seiban'. This meant the emergence of a potential threat to the understanding that the 'Japanese' were an homogeneous kinsfolk.

The Counter-Argument of the Christian Intellectuals

It was Fukuzawa Yukichi who, in one sense, suggested the simplest solution to the problem of Taiwan. Immediately after its cession, when the resistance of the native inhabitants proved to be a thorn in the side of the Japanese military, Fukuzawa argued that 'we ought to aim only for the land [of Taiwan], and so mop up the whole island, ignoring the natives, and concentrate the management of all enterprises and industries in Japanese hands so as to develop the sources of wealth'. According to Fukuzawa, it was necessary for the Japanese 'to brace themselves to clean up mercilessly the whole island with military strength, to root up thoroughly all evil, to confiscate all land and turn the whole island into public land'.[8] From this point of view, what was needed was only the land of Taiwan, and not policies for the natives.

However, in the central Japanese press circles of the day, few people shared such primitive opinions. The great majority of writers understood the need to start any discussion from the premise that the 'Japanese' must somehow coexist with the native people of Taiwan, whether on an equal footing or an oppressive one. This made inevitable a re-examination of the national polity theory that claimed the Great Japanese Empire was an homogeneous nation-state. Those who first realised this were the Christian intellectuals who feared the threat posed by the rise of the national polity theory.

The conflict between the Christian intellectuals of Japan and the national polity theorists can be traced back to the debate known as the 'clash between education and religion' (*kyōiku to shūkyō no shōtotsu*), which erupted immediately after the issue of the Imperial Rescript on Education.[9] In January 1891, a little over two months after the Imperial Rescript was issued, a reading ceremony was held at the Imperial First High School (Daiichi Kōtō Gakkō), which later became the Department of Liberal Arts of Tokyo University, and teachers and students were made to pay reverence to a photograph of the imperial portrait that had been sent to the school with the rescript. At this time, the Christian intellectual, Uchimura Kanzō (1861–1930), a teacher at the school and a Christian, refused to engage in what he regarded as idolatry, and was criticised for the decision.

This incident occurred at a time when Inoue Tetsujirō was criticising Christianity. According to Inoue, the Imperial Rescript embodied the unique morals of Japan, while Christianity claimed that all human beings are the children of god and made no distinction between either nations or states. It followed, he said, that Christianity could not coexist with spirit of the Imperial Rescript, and was harmful to the state. This claim triggered a counter-argument from the Christians and developed into a major debate that lasted for two years and involved a large number of intellectuals.

Since the debate took place before the cession of Taiwan, it did not focus on the existence of alien peoples within the Great Japanese Empire. However, it should be noted that the arguments of individuals such as Inoue who attacked Christian intellectuals, emphasised the threat of the Western Powers that lay behind Christianity, and examples such as the compulsory propagation and colonisation carried out in Latin America and the South Seas were cited as proof of this. On the other hand, in reply to these arguments, many Christian intellectuals insisted on their ability to be worthy patriots despite their religious beliefs, and claimed that they did not deny the Japanese state itself. It was perhaps no coincidence that, at the time of the Sino-Japanese War, when the mood of the dispute was still lingering, Uchimura defended Japan.

After Japan's victory in this war, anxiety about the threat of colonisation by the West was almost completely laid to rest. Immediately after the victory, however, the so-called Triple Intervention occurred, with three European Powers – Russia, Germany and France – urging Japan to return to China the Liangtung Peninsula that Japan had won in the war. Following the Triple Intervention, Japanese intellectuals were forced to accept the fact that Japan could only bow to the demands of the Powers, and a fierce anti-Western nationalism erupted.

In May 1897, Inoue Tetsujirō and Kimura Takatarō (1870–1931), among others, established the Great Japan Society (Dai Nippon Kyōkai) and founded a magazine, *Nippon shugi* (Japanism). The first article of the Constitution of the Great Japan Society stated that 'we worship the founder of our country'. The prospectus of *Nippon shugi*, printed in the first issue, also emphasised the crucial importance of national unity for the maintenance of independence, and the magazine was to publish many articles critical of Christianity. In the third issue published in July 1897, a chapter on ancestor worship was extracted from Hozumi's *Kokumin kyōiku aikokushin*, and the intellectuals of that age joined the Great Japan Society one after another.

Christian intellectuals responded sensitively to this movement. The article published in their major central magazine, *Rikugō zasshi*, after the publication of *Nippon shugi* was announced, was 'Waga kokuze to shūkyōteki shinnen' (Japan's National Policy and Religious Belief) by Watase Tsunekichi who later became the manager (*rijichō*) of the Japanese Congregational Church (Nippon Kumiai Kyōkai).[10] In the article, Watase claimed that the 'enterprising spirit of opening the country' had been the ideal of Japan since its foundation, and insisted at the same time that 'we must realise the principles of independence and self-government'. At this stage, Watase was arguing only for independence through civilisation and enlightenment rather than through exclusivism. However, what is special about this article is that it mentioned the existence of many alien peoples in Taiwan, Japan's new territory, and insisted that 'at this time, when the empire is vigorously expanding, and Japan is accepting people of different nations as compatriots, to define narrowly the Japanese by unreasonably insisting on the theory that the sovereign and all his subjects share the same ancestor (*kunmin dōso*)' was not in the enterprising spirit of an open country.

According to Watase, large numbers of foreign immigrants had settled in Japan throughout Japanese history, but 'through their policy [of openness and enterprise], our ancestors assimilated many alien races'. Moreover 'today, those who vainly attempt to exclude alien races are in effect opposing the idea of the expansion of Japan'. Although he did not deny the worship of the Emperor, he did insist that the power of a religion that transcended the nation was required to assimilate alien peoples. Watase believed that 'to include different nations and to continue to expand' was a reflection of the 'spirit of opening the country', but that, in doing so, it would be impossible 'to stamp out all religions and convert all to worship of the Emperor'.

Thus Watase developed a defence of Christianity based on the position that Japan required a universal religion that transcended ethnicity in order to expand her territory. The argument that Christianity was not only not harmful to the state, but would actually contribute to its development, had already been advanced by Christian intellectuals in the 'clash between education and religion' debate. In order to put these ideas into practice, Watase in later years came to play a central role in the movement by Japanese Christians to cooperate with the Government-General of Korea and to propagate Christianity in Korea in competition with Western missionaries after it was annexed by Japan.

Furthermore, the September issue of the *Rikugō zasshi* of the same year included a commentary on current events by the philosopher and Christian liberal thinker Ōnishi Hajime (1864–1900) entitled 'Sosenkyō wa yoku sekyō no kiso taru bekika' (Can Ancestor Worship Become the Foundation for a World Religion?) that was critical of Hozumi.[11] He also criticised the theory of the national polity, stating that 'I doubt whether Mr. Hozumi's emphasis on the theory that the sovereign and all his subjects share the same ancestor is compatible with the Japanese national policy of expansion. How on earth are the people of our new territories to be viewed?'

This criticism touched on the essential weakness of the national polity theory. It advocated the solidarity of a pure and homogeneous kinsfolk, the 'Japanese people', headed by the Emperor, and denounced Christianity as an agent of the Western Powers. However, although excluding the universal and retiring into one's shell is effective in shutting out external influences, it also makes it impossible to move out into the world. To close the door firmly in order to defend oneself from the outside becomes an obstacle when one decides to go outside oneself.

Assimilation or Maintenance of Pure Blood?

The individual who countered the criticism of the Christian intellectuals was the literary critic Takayama Rinjirō (Chogyū) (1871–1902). A member of the Great Japan Society, Takayama was then 26, a young writer who had studied under Inoue Tetsujirō in the Department of Philosophy at Tokyo Imperial University, and the editor of the literary section of *Taiyō* (The Sun), a leading magazine of the time. In November 1897, immediately after the criticism of Watase and others appeared, he published 'Waga kokutai to shinhanto' (The Japanese National Polity and Our New Territories) in *Taiyō*.[12]

According to this article, Japan's 'unparalleled National Polity' was based on 'a special relationship between sovereign and subject'. That is, 'Japanese nationals are in most cases descendants of the sacred Imperial Family', and so the situation in Japan 'is completely different from the situation in other countries, which have gathered many alien races together, have based the relationship between sovereign and subjects on contract or force, and have thereby built the state'.

There were many Christians who believed in the 'vulgar view' that this consciousness would prove to be an obstacle to any expansion of the empire. According to Takayama, however, this was wrong. For 'if a country wishes to profit from its territories, it must rely mainly on relationships of power', while the theory of the national polity would produce 'a strong and rigorous power based on the ideals of the mother country'. In other words, alien nations should be ruled by power, and the national polity theory would serve as the source of such power. Moreover, since spiritual enlightenment is also ultimately produced through the power of the state, the consciousness of a kinship between sovereign and subject 'is not only not harmful to the expansion of Japan, despite the anxiety of the Christians, but actually the most important condition for it'.

Furthermore, Takayama mentioned the fall of the Roman Empire that Hozumi had also cited as a historical example of a failure in ruling alien nations. According to Takayama, the Roman Empire prospered as long as the Latin nation on which it was centred maintained their pure blood and kept aloof from alien nations. However, it collapsed when, poisoned by the egalitarianism of Christianity, the Roman belief in the racial supremacy of the Latin nation was abandoned and intermarriage with other nations occurred.

Thus Takayama appealed to his readers, saying 'do you not know that there are among us those who advocate abandoning the National Polity in order to unite the newly obtained territories?' He concluded his paper by urging Japanese Christians to feel grateful to the Imperial Constitution, which included an article guaranteeing the freedom of belief. Very soon, in the editorial comments of the seventh issue of *Nippon shugi*, excerpts from this article were included with the addition of the following triumphant comments: 'once Christians carefully peruse Mr Takayama's thesis, they will quickly realise that their own views are mistaken'.

However, the *Nippon shugi* writers were not aware of the potential problem contained in this counter-argument. Takayama advocated a power-based rule of the alien nations of Japan's new territories, but the national polity theorists, including Takayama, also insisted that the Emperor's rule was not an artificial power relationship, but rather based on natural emotions such as those between parents and children. Unintentionally, Takayama revealed the fact that the theory of the national polity, which hid rule through power in emotions such as those between parents and children, could not be applied to the new territories as long as it insisted the 'Japanese' were an homogeneous kinsfolk. The mask of the Emperor as the merciful father of the nation (*kokumin*) was torn away, and the underlying power relationship exposed. If this naked power rule continued, there would be no possibility that the love between parent and child could ever form between the Emperor and the Taiwanese. If so, Japan, like those foreign countries that Takayama had mocked as a 'collection of many alien races' with 'the relationship between sovereign and subject established by force', would also continue to be saddled with alien peoples who would look for the opportunity to overthrow their rulers.

There was also a larger problem. Learning from the lesson of the Roman Empire, Takayama insisted on avoiding intermarriage with the alien nations of Japan's new territories and maintaining the pure blood of the Japanese nation. As for the much later case of the apartheid system in South Africa, an effective way to realise this would be to forbid strictly inter-racial marriage, segregate residential areas and schools, and so cut off all opportunities for interaction. In South Africa under apartheid, the principle of segregation was applied to the army, and so conscription was mainly limited to the whites. In Nazi Germany, intermarriage with Jews was strictly prohibited, and Jews were removed from workplaces, schools and the military, and sent to ghettos and concentration camps.

The later rule of Taiwan and Korea by the Great Japanese Empire was different. As will be discussed in chapter 13, inter-racial marriage was encouraged in the Great Japanese Empire under slogans such as, for instance, 'Marriage Between Japanese and Koreans' (*naisen kekkon*), and Taiwanese and Koreans were conscripted into the army during the Second World War. This does not mean that the policies of the Great Japanese Empire were better than those of the Nazis, but these assimilationist policies were certainly ill suited to the maintenance of the pure blood of the nation. (I will discuss the characteristics of Japan's rule in the conclusion.)

In fact, in 'Teikokushugi to shokumin' (Imperialism and Colonisation), published two years later, Takayama mentioned not just the lesson of the Roman Empire, but also that of the Saracen Empire, which had lost its 'national consciousness' by enlisting slaves from alien nations into the army, and had consequently collapsed.[13] By contrast, Takayama praised British colonial rule, which was thoroughgoing in avoiding mixing British blood with that of the 'inferior races', the indigenous people of Britain's colonies. British colonial policy was frequently cited in criticisms of Japanese assimilative policies from this time on. Where the rule of Taiwan was concerned, Takayama argued in favour of 'following the Anglo-Saxon form of imperialism'. The policies of South Africa, which strictly prohibited racial intermarriage, were in a sense a vestige of the British colonial system, and if the promotion of inter-racial marriage in the Great Japanese Empire is viewed as a policy of assimilation, then Takayama was, without doubt, a critic of such a policy.

However, *Nippon shugi*, which had sung the praises of Takayama, insisted that Japan should implement policies of assimilation with regard to Taiwan. For example, in the editorial commentary of the first issue of *Nippon shugi*, Kimura Takatarō stated that 'we should educate the people of this land [Taiwan], mould them into a people with the Japanese spirit, and instil in them feelings exactly the same as those of the people of mainland Japan'.[14] However, it was a contradiction for the 'people of mainland Japan' to regard themselves, on the one hand, as an exclusive homogeneous kinsfolk, while at the same time attempting to educate and mould the Taiwanese into a people with 'feelings exactly the same as those of the people of mainland Japan'. This is like advocating the teaching of white supremacy to those identified as 'Black' people. How could a people not admitted as kinsfolk ever come to share the same feelings?

On the other hand, the theorists of *Nippon shugi* actively developed the argument that Japan was gifted with 'the power of assimilation'. In the 'statement of intention' issued on the launch of the magazine and published in the first issue, *Nippon shugi* stated that Japan had 'assimilated' foreign civilisations successfully, while extolling the virtues of 'the spirit of autonomy and independence'. In the same issue, the well-known educator, Yumoto Takehiko (1857–1925), insisted that 'the Japanese state first consisted only of the Yamato nation, and although it later came to include alien peoples, these were all Japanised and have not retained their identity and morals as aliens'. In his 'Waga kokutai to shinhanto' (The Japanese National Polity and Our New Territories), Takayama also stated that '2,500 years of our national history have melted foreign elements together and assimilated them into the leading minds of our national community'.

The paradox for these authors was that they had to cite historical examples where Japan had embraced alien nations and cultures in order to prove Japan's rich 'powers of assimilation'. This contradicted the Japan of the day which advocated tradition and nationalism while pursuing modernisation by assimilating Western civilisation. Takayama's metaphor of a 'melting pot' is the cliche used to refer to the USA, a multi-national state. It was impossible for even the national polity theorists to persist in their advocacy of a pure, homogeneous kinsfolk as long as they also argued in favour of assimilationist policies.

There were also other problems. Another factor that restrained the myth of the homogeneous nation was the existence of anthropology. Since national polity theorists believed in the importance of accepting Western civilisation and moving down the path towards becoming a rich and powerful country, they felt that it was impossible to completely deny research carried out in the name of science.

In addition to this, the perception gradually emerged in the Japan that had proved victorious in the Sino-Japanese War that the 'Japanese' were a superior nation. Kimura wrote an article titled 'Nipponjin wa yūshōteki minzoku nari' (The Japanese are a Superior Nation) for the third issue of *Nippon shugi* in 1897, and even Inoue Tetsujirō published a paper in 1898 titled 'Shinshu no kishō o jochō suru no shugi' (On Fostering an Enterprising Spirit) in the tenth issue of *Nippon shugi* in which he stated that the victory in the Sino-Japanese War was proof of the superiority of the Japanese national spirit.

Furthermore, the editorial comments of *Nippon shugi* regarded the movement to exclude Japanese immigrants in Canada, Hawaii, Australia and the USA as a racial war, and took up this problem in almost every issue. The exclusion of immigrants that Inoue had previously used as grounds for his opposition to mixed residence was now applied against the 'Japanese' themselves.

Thus, when the national polity theorists could no longer remain indifferent to the racial and national location of the 'Japanese', help from anthropology became indispensable. Indeed, in the fifth issue of *Nippon shugi*, in an editorial commentary titled 'Eeru Daigaku kyōju Nipponjin o sekai no yūshō jinshu to nasu' (A Professor of Yale University Regards the Japanese as a Superior Race), research by an American anthropologist (the very type of individual they used to detest) that used a comparison of brain sizes to demonstrate that the 'Japanese' were a superior nation was introduced at length. The thirst for such research can also be recognised from the fact that, from the first issue, Tsuboi Shōgorō was already included among the contributors.

Anthropology and the theory that the sovereign and all his subjects shared the same ancestor (*kunmin dōso*) seem to be contradictory and, as will be shown in the next chapter, Tsuboi was, if anything, a member of the camp opposing the national polity theorists. Tsuboi's contribution to the first issue of *Nippon shugi* was a paper, 'Tanshin oshoku hatashite hazubekika?' (Should we Really be Ashamed of our Short Stature and Yellow Skin?). In this paper, Tsuboi calmly argued that the characteristics of the nations of the world were all relative, and that none was superior or inferior to the others. This contrasted with the bombastic tone seen in other articles. In volume 10 of *Nippon shugi*, the anthropologist Yagi Shōzaburō (1863–1938) published a paper titled 'Nisennen mae no Nipponjin' (The Japanese 2,000 Years Ago). This completely accepted the view that the 'Japanese' had arrived in the archipelago from overseas and were a mixture of various nations, and branded those who believed the 'oral tradition that Japan was the location where the world was created' as 'old-fashioned bigots', saying this was similar to the Christian belief in the myth that god created heaven and earth.

The difficulties faced by the national polity theory were exposed when the theorists were forced to use the anthropologists' mixed nation theory to promote the superiority of the Japanese nation. In 1899, Takayama began to advocate the theory that the Japanese nation came over the seas from the south,[15] and, two years later, dropped out of the national polity camp, saying that his thinking in the 'Japanism' period was only a superficial part of his true philosophy.

The National Polity Theory in a Tight Corner

Shortly after the debate with the Christian intellectuals, a book criticising the national polity theory was published, which again drew on the existence of Taiwan. This was the debut work of the national socialist Kita Terujirō (Ikki) (1883–1937), *Kokutairon oyobi junsei shakaishugi* (The National Polity and Pure Socialism), published in 1906.[16] In it, Kita wrote that 'we will show who is the most formidable destroyer of the national polity theory'.

> It is none other than today's Emperor…He has used his power to bring foreign countries into Japan's sphere…The inclusion of Chinese as a result of the Sino-Japanese War was the precursor of the destruction of the theory that the sovereign and his subjects are members of the same family (*kunshin ikkaron*), and the notion of the concurrence of loyalty and

filial piety. To accept Russian nationals as Japanese following the Russo-Japanese War was to destroy the idols of bigoted priests. In the name of the Emperor of the Great Japanese Empire, the bigoted national polity theorists were rejected as primitive barbarians, and the treaty of mixed residence was concluded.

Kita claimed that the insistence of the national polity theorists that the Emperor was the father of all 'Japanese' was meaningless. Today, he continued, mixed residence has made it possible for 'red-haired and blue-eyed Western people' and 'negroids' to obtain Japanese nationality. 'Would the Emperor be happy to be called the parent of a black man?'

Furthermore, he emphasised the existence of foreign immigrants, and attacked Hozumi Yatsuka, saying 'Dr. Hozumi calls Empress Jingū, the heroine of Japanese history, a destroyer of the national polity because she was a descendant of naturalised Koreans. He views Sakanoue-no-Tamuramaro, the most popular hero among schoolboys in Japan, a traitor who damaged the national polity because of his mixed parentage'. He noted that, 'judging from linguistics, anatomy and racial studies, the Japanese nation is a mixture of the Malay, the Ezo [*Ainu*], and the Chinese races'. Finally, Kita stated that Takamagahara was located overseas, and rejected the theory that the sovereign and all his subjects shared the same ancestor, saying 'it is a superstition of Shintō, and has no basis'.[17]

Although this book was barred from circulation because of its extreme language, the theory of the mixed nation was unstoppable. In writing the book, Kita referred to the then best-seller, *Nisen gohyakunenshi* (A History of 2,500 Years of Japanese Civilisation), by Takegoshi Yosaburō (1865–1950). As will be explained in chapter 5, Takegoshi's work also adopted the viewpoint of the mixed nation theory, citing the arguments of Tsuboi Shōgorō and Koganei Yoshikiyo, and mentioned the birth of the Emperor Kanmu and the Empress Jingū. Materials that cast doubt on the theory of the national polity which insisted that the 'Japanese' were a pure homogeneous kinsfolk were thus already in general circulation.

This fact was underlined on a much larger scale by the debate triggered by Katō Hiroyuki's *Waga kokutai to Kirisutokyō* (The Japanese National Polity and Christianity) published in 1907.

Katō was one of the leading national polity theorists in Japan, comparable in status to Hozumi and Inoue. In this book, Katō defined rule by the Emperor as 'constitutional rule by the Father of the nation', and said: 'although there are some naturalised foreigners and conquered peoples among the Japanese, they are only a minority. The vast majority are the original Japanese nation. Therefore, the relationship between the Japanese Emperor and his subjects is in fact like that between a father and a son'. He admitted that the 'Japanese' were inferior to Westerners in many areas, but claimed they were superior in loyalty because of this paternalistic rule, and criticised Christianity, referring to the historic example of 'global religion destroying national religion'. During the debate over mixed residence, Katō had criticised Christianity because of fear that Japan would lose in the struggle for existence.[18]

Once the gilding of evolutionary theory is removed, Katō's criticism of Christianity is exposed as a conflict between a universal religion and the unique Japanese patriotism, and is almost exactly the same as Inoue Tetsujirō's line of argument 15 years previously. However, contrary to Katō's criticism, which was stuck in a changeless rut, Christian intellectuals were armed with new counter theories – the existence of Taiwan and the mixed nation theory. Immediately after the publication of Katō's book, the Christian pastor and later Chancellor of Dōshisha University, Ebina Danjō (1856–1938), Watase's mentor and a member of the Japanese Congregational Church, rebutted Katō in a paper titled 'Katō Hakase no *Waga kokutai to Kirisutokyō* o yomu' (Reading Dr Katō's *The Japanese National Polity and Christianity*), saying 'it is a historical fact that the Japanese nation includes the Malay, *Ainu*, Chinese and Tartar races, and was thus created through a mixture of many races'.[19] Ebina continued as follows.

> It can therefore be said that it is a great mistake to regard today's Japanese as a single race. Moreover, not only will it be very difficult to expand into the world in the name of single-race homogeneity, but this is a path that promises little in the future. If anything, Japan should actively assimilate the Chinese, the people of Manchuria, and other races after the old tradition of conquering, assimilating and mixing with other nations. Without this open attitude, the Japanese Empire will never grow into a Great Empire.

Ebina argued that 'the Japanese Empire has already transcended the age of national religion and is evolving towards an age of world religion'. Just glancing at the economy will demonstrate that 'Japan used to live on Japanese rice only, but today we have to eat the world's rice'. In fact, the Great Japanese Empire had already begun to import rice at this time, and later was to implement a large-scale importation from and exploitation of Korea, the continent and Southeast Asia.

Ukita Kazutami (1859–1946), a Christian intellectual famous as the editor-in-chief of *Taiyō* (The Sun) and as a political scientist, argued as follows.[20]

> ...The Japan of today consists of various alien nations. Although the majority consists of the Yamato nation, Japan includes the indigenous Taiwanese, the *Ainu* and eventually, as she develops, will perhaps come to include the peoples of Korea and Manchuria as Japanese subjects. To argue that the national polity is based on patriarchal rule is unsuitable for the national polity of today and also inconvenient for the future development of Japan's national polity.

It is difficult to judge to what degree these arguments reflect the general tendency of Christian intellectuals. In fact, it may be a little improper to regard Ebina, who, together with Watase, later promoted the propagation of Christianity in Korea at the request of the Japanese Government-General of Korea, or Ukita, who advocated an 'ethical imperialism', as representative Christian intellectuals.

However, even Uchimura Kanzō, who – regretting his support for Japan during the Sino-Japanese War – had argued in favour of absolute pacifism at the time of the Russo-Japanese War, wrote in the middle of this debate in 1908 (although he did not mention Katō by name, the criticism is implied): 'A patriotic spirit serves well enough in defence of one's own country, but falls short in governing other countries. To govern foreign countries requires a universal spirit, or a humanistic ideal'.[21] In 1896, in a paper which criticised 'the small Japan and the small Japanese', Uchimura had already said that 'there is no world-scale hero in Japan except Taikō [Toyotomi] Hideyoshi' (1537–1598), the Shōgun who had invaded Korea in the sixteenth century, and grieved over the 'insular mentality' that emphasised only the idiosyncrasies of Japan.

The gist of these essays by Uchimura was that Japan lacked a spirit of openness to the world, and not that Japan needed to invade countries overseas. However, it cannot be denied that Uchimura's form of logic resembled that of Ebina and others. To contribute to Japan with Christian universality, or, to use Uchimura's famous phrase, the coexistence of the love for the two 'Js', Jesus and Japan, was a common idea among most Christian intellectuals of that age, and something they emphasised in the 1891 debate with Inoue Tetsujirō. It is understandable that it was easy for the logic that argued that the universal spirit of religion could contribute to the development of the empire to emerge from this idea. The transformation of 'development' into 'expansion' was a crucial step, but only a very short one. The arguments of Watase, Ebina and Ukita may not be representative of the views of the Christian intellectuals, but were not totally unrelated to their general state of mind.

Katō was placed in difficult position in replying to these arguments. One response, for instance, was the following: 'As I said in my book, the Japanese nation includes [the descendants of] naturalised foreigners and conquered peoples. However, there is no doubt that a nation originally subject to the Emperor forms the nucleus of the Japanese, and therefore we can use the term the Japanese nation', or 'in the future, large numbers of foreigners may well become naturalised Japanese, and Japan may gain new territories. Even so, as long as the Japanese nation remains the nucleus and in charge, Japanese nationals will remain completely different from a collection of different peoples'. This is a weak counter-argument. The only sensible point Katō made was that 'the attempt to assimilate other races and nations into the Japanese nation can be called a nationalistic spirit because it aims at the development and expansion of the national character and customs of Japan'.[22] However, as became clear with Takayama's counter-argument, it was logically impossible not to abandon any consciousness that the 'Japanese' were a pure and homogeneous kinsfolk if Japan was to implement policies that aimed to assimilate 'other nations'.

Moreover, those individuals involved in ruling Taiwan began to abandon the idea that Japan was a single, pure, homogeneous kinsfolk, looking askance at the national polity theorists.[23] As early as 1897, Izawa Shūji (1851–1917), the Chief of the Educational Bureau of the Government-General of Taiwan, made the following point in a lecture at an Imperial Educational Conference.

...According to the old nativist scholars, the populace of Japan consists of nothing but the so-called Yamato nation. However, this interpretation is totally mistaken. The awful benevolence of our Imperial Family is not limited to such a small range. It is in fact as great as the universe. It is the idea of universal brotherhood under the Emperor (*isshi dōjin*), the idea that people all over the world can become his majesty's subjects, if only they are obedient....Since ancient times, the number of naturalised foreigners has never been small.

In 1904, Mochiji Mutsusaburō, the Head of the Educational Section of the Government-General of Taiwan that had resulted from the reduction in size of the Educational Bureau, said at a Taiwan Education Conference:

...The Japanese are not an homogeneous people. Of our 45 million compatriots, there are *Ainu*, Malays, and members of the Takamagahara race who have mixed together, and are all moulded together into the Yamato spirit. It is therefore possible to assimilate Koreans and Chinese, who are the same race as the Japanese, into the Japanese people. And this is what we must do.

The issue was now clear. The options open to the Great Japanese Empire were limited. It could (1) abandon the idea of a single, homogeneous kinsfolk-state and continue to assimilate overseas territory, or (2) abandon the policy of assimilation, abandon the superficial idea that rule by the Emperor was a natural form of sentiment, and openly admit that the new territories would be ruled through power relations and a refusal to allow intermarriage, or (3) as Inoue had advocated and Taguchi and Ebina derided, close the door to the outside world and abandon the path that led out into the world by severing all interaction with alien peoples. These three were the only options open to Japan.

In 1909, when Katō and the Christian intellectuals were continuing their debate, it was not yet clear which option the empire was going to chose. Katō managed to prevent his position from completely collapsing by using the argument that the number of alien people within the empire was so small, compared to what he called the Japanese nation, that they could be ignored. However, this ambiguous period did not last long. The next year saw Japan moving to incorporate over 10 million Koreans by annexing Korea, after which about 30 per cent of the total population of the empire came to consist of alien peoples.

4 The Anthropologists

Before commenting on the dispute over the annexation of Korea, it is necessary to examine the mixed nation theory as developed separately from the debate between the national polity theorists and Christian intellectuals during the period from the Sino-Japanese War to the annexation. Much of the later development of the mixed nation theory was foreshadowed here.

During this period, anthropologists such as Tsuboi Shōgorō, professor at Tokyo Imperial University and head of the Tokyo Anthropological Society, created the foundations for the development of the mixed nation theory. Together with the Christian intellectuals, Tsuboi especially was opposed to the national polity theorists and he, too, came to construct a justification for external aggression.

The Criticism of the Concept of Pure Blood

At this time, almost all Japanese anthropologists based their theories of the origins of the Japanese nation on the mixed nation theory. According to them, the Japanese nation was a mixture of a continental people which had come from the continent via the Korean peninsula, Malays who had come from the south, and the indigenous *Ainu*.

However, Japan's anthropology was still in its infancy, and the research methodology of Japanese anthropologists was, by today's standards, rather amateurish. In developing their theories of the Japanese nation, researchers freely turned their hands to areas such as the excavation of historical sites, the measurement of excavated human bones, the conduct of field surveys in neighbouring nations, and the analysis of Japanese myths, including those of the *Kojiki* and *Nihon shoki* (the Kiki myths) – areas that are now divided into specialised fields such as physical anthropology, archaeology, cultural anthropology, folklore and ancient history. At the time, simple judgements of Japanese features were frequently used as the basis of academic theories. Thus it was said that the Japanese nation consisted of a mixture of the *Ainu*, Malays and a continental people because some 'Japanese' were hirsute, and some had pale complexions while others were darker.

For example, Torii Ryūzō asserted that the existence of curly haired people in Japan, a type not found on the Asian continent, was evidence of a past mixture of the 'Japanese' with Negritos from the south. Torii, a young researcher in Tsuboi's class, was dispatched to the Liaotung Peninsula at the age of 25. He followed this with field trips to Taiwan, Manchuria, the Kuriles, Mongolia, Korea and China.

The relationship between the anthropology and the colonies of Japan was an unusual one. Japanese rule of Korea and Taiwan emphasised assimilationist policies, and thus forced Japanese nationality on the peoples of these areas and taught them the Japanese language and Emperor worship (as I will note in the conclusion, these policies emphasised cultural assimilation, not an equality in the area of rights).

Under this policy of assimilation, Japan refused to adopt an indirect form of rule that would have made it possible to utilise the traditional power structures and local customs of the colonies. As a result, surveys of native customs were not emphasised in Japan's colonial rule. Japanese anthropologists were therefore not often asked to survey native customs by the Governments-General of Taiwan and Korea.[1] The work Japanese anthropologists immersed themselves in was not the survey of the customs of other peoples, but the search for the origins of the Japanese nation, or for the national identity of the 'Japanese'. This was also an endeavour to reclaim the task of searching for the roots of the 'Japanese' from the hands of Western researchers. One of the major reasons why Torii surveyed neighbouring Asian peoples was to clarify the relationship between these peoples and the Japanese nation. Because she was a late-developing and weak imperial power, Japan could only advance into neighbouring regions, and Japan's colonies thus proved to be the targets of efforts to identify the origin of the Japanese nation.

The army and the Governments-General, however, saw another value in the anthropologists. First, from the viewpoint of the Governments-General, surveys of the conditions in outlying areas which were not well understood were valuable. To clarify the relationship between the Japanese nation and the colonies was also important.

Many anthropologists, beginning with Torii and Tsuboi, searched for the origins of the Japanese nation from their own academic interests. However, Torii's fieldwork in the Liaotung Peninsula was carried out in 1895, the year the Sino-Japanese War ended; his work in Taiwan in 1897, immediately after Taiwan was annexed; in Manchuria in 1905, the year the Russo-Japanese War ended; and in Korea in 1910, the year that Japan annexed the country. It can thus be seen that his movements closely followed the expansion of the Great Japanese Empire. His connection with politics was deep, whatever his personal opinions may have been. He went to the Kuriles on a naval warship, investigated the mountain natives in Taiwan who were resisting the Japanese, and carried out excavation field work in Korea at the request of the Government-General of Korea.[2] This fieldwork in Korea was not a survey of Korean customs, but an attempt to identify the relationship between Korea and Japan by surveying Korean archaeological sites.

However, although Torii did most of the hands-on work, it was Tsuboi Shōgorō, more than anyone else, who played the most important role in propagating the mixed nation theory and in developing its political applications.

As is often the case with leaders of new fields of study, Tsuboi gave priority to activities that aimed to enlighten the general populace about, and seek their support for, anthropology. He was in a position where he had to struggle to obtain social understanding, human resources, and above all financial resources, in competition with other leading practical areas of study such as law and medicine, in a country that was still developing. He therefore had to emphasise not only to the youth of Japan how appealing anthropology was, but also to politicians how useful it was for national politics. In the press of the day, changes in international relations triggered an interest in the national and racial place of the 'Japanese'. In these circumstances, Tsuboi was regarded as a godsend, and he understandably produced a series of political applications of the mixed nation theory.

As well as being a mixed nation theorist, Tsuboi was also aware of the existence of non-Japanese minorities within the empire with whom he interacted during his fieldwork. Although, compared to Torii, the number of field trips Tsuboi made is not large, he did investigate Hokkaido with Koganei Yoshikiyo in 1888, where he met the *Ainu* and other northern ethnic groups.

Tsuboi's defence of the mixed nation theory became the target of criticism from the national polity theorists. During the Sino-Japanese War, Katō Hiroyuki wrote a critique which argued that multi-national China lacked unity, while the 'Japanese are all fraternal brethren who belong to one nation' and so were deeply patriotic. He continued in this vein.[3]

> ...According to the anthropologist, Dr. Tsuboi, there are five nations within Japan: the Japanese, the people of Ryūkyū (Okinawa), the *Ainu*, the Sahhalin *Ainu*, and the people of Shikotan. However, the last four are not only very small in number, but it is also too early to call them true Japanese ...When the ancient Japanese are studied from the viewpoint of anthropology and ethnology, it is possible that they did not form a single nation without any exceptions. However, it is impossible to establish this historically, so nothing prevents us from assuming that they were members of one homogeneous nation.

Katō admired the theory of evolution, and had attacked Christianity in the name of science. He therefore had no choice but to accept the findings of anthropology, which had also been advanced in the name of science. It is clear, however, that he tried to minimise the influence of these findings.

The same confrontation was rekindled during the Russo-Japanese War. At this time, Katō published a book, *Shinkagaku yori kansatsu shitaru Nichi-Ro no unmei* (The Destiny of Japan and Russia Viewed from the Theory of Evolution), and emphasised the unity of the Japanese subjects when compared to 'Russia, which includes the Polish people who are always on the lookout for a chance to rebel'.[4] Needless to say, Katō did not mention the resistance of the mountain natives of Taiwan against the Japanese army which was still continuing.

In a lecture, Inoue Tetsujirō also listed ancestor worship, the unbroken line of the Emperors, and the 'purity' and unity of the nation as the reasons for Japan's victory. Unlike Katō, however, Inoue, who had already developed his own theory of the origin of the Japanese nation, did admit that 'the Japanese nation does in fact consist of a mixture of different peoples'. Despite this, he continued, the mixture had occurred in the distant past and the 'Japanese' had maintained the purity of their blood since then, and so Japan was different from Russia which 'is full of people plotting rebellion', such as the Poles, Finns, Jews and Armenians. Inoue said 'there are *Ainu* and native Taiwanese within the borders of Japan, but we have no reason to fear them', declaring 'no other country has managed to maintain a racial purity like Japan'.[5]

Tsuboi made a frontal attack in reply to these arguments. At the time of the Russo-Japanese War, he gave a lecture in 1905, 'Jinruigakuteki chishiki no yō masumasu fukashi' (The Need for Anthropological Knowledge is Greater than Ever), and insisted that 'many people say the Japanese will win because of our racial homogeneity, but this is wrong. I would like to stress the opposite: Japan will win because of her heterogeneity'.[6]

Tsuboi argued as follows in this lecture. Contrary to the popular view, the Great Japanese Empire was more ethnically diverse than Russia. Russians could be divided roughly into only two racial branches: the European branch, beginning with the Slav people, and the Asian branch in the East. On the other hand, the Great Japanese Empire included four types: the Asian branch (the Japanese and Chinese Taiwanese peoples); the Malay branch (the native Taiwanese); the European branch (the European residents of the Ogasawara islands); and finally the *Ainu* who, according to Tsuboi, did not belong to any racial branch. Moreover, since the Japanese nation, the largest group by far, had various types of faces, Tsuboi insisted that it was a mixture of the *Ainu*, Malays and continental peoples.

After arguing that Japan was a multi-national state and that the Japanese nation was a mixed one, Tsuboi added: 'I would like to say that being a mixture is truly a blessing'. This was because the development and progress of civilisation is generated by competition and intercourse between different peoples. Noting, for example, that the exchange of different opinions at meetings often proved fruitful, he said: 'in the same way it is a good thing for different types of people to assemble and form a single country'.

As an example of a country where a mixture of peoples had led to development, Tsuboi cited Britain, then the most advanced country in the world, and one about which there was increasing familiarity in Japan as a result of the newly introduced Anglo-Japanese Alliance. He claimed that Britain consisted of a mixture of several nations, including the Angles, the Saxons and the Danes, and said that 'it would be even better if the blood of still more different peoples were to be mixed' to allow Britain to attain the same high degree of mixture as seen in Japan. Such a view provides an interesting contrast to the line of argument in Japan that viewed the pure blood of the Japanese nation as a positive advantage as a way of overcoming any inferiority complex towards the Western Powers, including Britain.

According to Tsuboi, Japan developed because it was a multinational state, and was able to beat Russia because Russia had a simpler national makeup. Further, he wrote:

> Those who believe that it would be better for the Japanese to be pure must then believe that the *Ainu* should be driven away. The same is true of the native Taiwanese: they also need to be driven off. If it is better to be pure, then we need to remove them in order to avoid any future intermarriage. However, a better option, I believe, is to be generous and to accept all those who wish to become Japanese. Once we share a history with other people, even if only a few days, we should try to progress and work together instead of rejecting them as strangers...It is a mistake to believe that a race should be pure and that complexity is bad.

Tsuboi thus argued that if pure blood were to be viewed as a positive characteristic, then alien nations would have to be segregated to prevent intermarriage. This system of apartheid, as will be explained in chapter 13, did actually come to be advocated by the Japanese eugenicists. Tsuboi, however, was opposed to such a system, and argued instead in favour of the coexistence of all as 'Japanese'.

However, the *Ainu* and the people of Taiwan had not volunteered, but rather were compelled, to become 'Japanese' when their lands were incorporated within the borders of the empire. To advocate tolerance and diversity was, in these circumstances, to recognise annexation. Tsuboi's limitations appear more clearly in his philanthropic work for the *Ainu*.

Moving Out Into the World

In 1900, the year after the conclusion of the Hokkaido Former Aborigines Protection Act (see chapter 3, endnote 5), the *Tōkyō jinruigakkai zasshi* (Tokyo Anthropological Society Magazine) published a document which set out the aims behind the Society for the Education of the Natives of Hokkaido. This anonymous text began with the words, 'The *Ainu*, the natives of Hokkaido, are also Japanese nationals', and appealed for contributions for their education, saying 'Let us teach the *Ainu*. Let us lead the *Ainu*. And let us make it possible for them to enjoy the same freedoms and happiness available to others'. From this time, Tsuboi actively gave lectures in various parts of Japan that advocated providing assistance to the *Ainu*, and also organised charity concerts and slide shows to raise funds for them.[7]

A lecture given in 1906, 'Hokkaidō kyūdojin kyūiki jigyō' (An Education Project for the Hokkaido Natives) provides a good summary of Tsuboi's thinking.[8] Here he strongly stressed the need for sympathy for the impoverished *Ainu*, and argued in favour of turning the *Ainu* into farmers through enlightenment and in favour of an education based on rational and systematic ideas. He went on to say:

> Gentlemen, just as Hokkaido is no longer a foreign country called Ezo, the *Ainu* are also no longer foreigners called the people of Ezo. They, too, are Japanese subjects, just as we are. Is it not shameful that some members of our nation are uneducated? To despise them is to despise ourselves. It is the duty of our leaders to teach the ignorant, and to turn those who are good for nothing into useful members of society.

From this lecture emerges a nationalistic side to Tsuboi that viewed the uneducated as an embarrassment to the state. Also present is the notion of a modernisation from above that turns 'those who are good for nothing into useful members of society' and 'puts them to productive work' through education. What is noticeable, however, is that Tsuboi viewed the *Ainu* as 'Japanese subjects, just as we are', and as brethren, and treated them as members of a multinational state.

Whether nationalists or benevolent altruists, there were very few people at that time who were as passionate in advocating saving the *Ainu* as Tsuboi. I mention this not to defend Tsuboi, but to do him justice. The anthropologist, Koganei Yoshikiyo, who carried out fieldwork in Hokkaido with Tsuboi, said, in spite of his knowledge of the wretched state of the *Ainu*, that 'the *Ainu* race is a sort of decadent race' and even asserted that, since it is natural for 'the savage races to be gradually conquered by civilised races and perish', 'the pure *Ainu* race will eventually perish'.[9]

However, Tsuboi said in the lecture mentioned above that 'some people apparently refer to the *Ainu* as a people destined to decline and perish, and think it pointless to help and educate them, but how can one refuse to give medicine to those with an incurable disease?' Tsuboi also insisted: 'I believe that it is possible to save them from their misfortune by education'. Such comments can be counted among the conscientious voices of this period.

Tsuboi's belief in education was partly related to his opposition to racial discrimination. Those who regarded the *Ainu* as an innately inferior and 'decadent race' saw education as useless since there would be no prospect of modernising the *Ainu* no matter how much they were educated. However, in a lecture given in 1903, Tsuboi emphasised that racial characteristics, beginning with the colour of skin, were almost all the product of environment, and that there was no superiority or inferiority between the races.[10] Today, he said, some 'Black' Americans had achieved success as scholars or statesmen, and thus explicitly denied the view that the *Ainu* were innately inferior, saying that 'though the *"Ainu"* are said to be inferior, there are some *Ainu* who are so successful that it is the majority Japanese (*naichijin*) who should feel inferior'.

Tsuboi added the following in the lecture.

> ...Whether a race becomes inferior or superior is determined by the environment, or by social development. It is not determined by fate...Here is a picture someone took of native Americans as they originally were, and a second picture taken after four months of education and a decent life. Compare these photographs and see how much their features have changed.

The photographs that were then shown to the audience were not published with the lecture. However, the photographs may well be identical with those published in 'Amerika Dojin no kyōiku' (The Education of Native Americans), written by the Christian intellectual discussed in chapter 3, Uchimura Kanzō in 1895.[11] This paper recalled a day in 1884 when Uchimura visited a philanthropist in Pennsylvania who advocated protecting and enlightening the native Americans. According to Uchimura, this individual's 'aim was to turn the 300,000 native Americans into civilised Christians' and 'therefore, when a group of native people were first sent to him, he immediately had their hair cut, provided them with civilised clothes, strictly prohibited them from using their native language, gave them suitable jobs and made them lead clean, orderly lives. These two photographs fully demonstrate how much their new environment civilised them'.

The mental stress suffered by people who were prohibited from using their own language and interned in an institution can easily be imagined. The photographs compare a group of Apache who had just arrived at an institution, and then again 'after breathing civilised air for four months'. Uchimura praised the change, saying 'their manners were gentlemanly and ladylike, and their eyes were bright and hopeful'. Uchimura records the fact that his philanthropist cried with sympathy when told about the impoverished state of the *Ainu*, and noted that the 'ignorant, pitiful *Ainu* have a friend [in America] who fully sympathises with them'.

A transparent modernisation does not exist. Education is carried out in a specific language, and job training is based on the premise that people live in a society with a specific culture. In educating native Americans to enable them to survive in the American society of that period, it may well have been a short cut to teach them English, cut their hair, and convert them to Christianity. In the case of Japan, similar policies would mean teaching the *Ainu* the Japanese language and the art of cultivation, as well as the morality of Japanese subjects, including the ethic of loyalty to the Emperor.

Furthermore, to fight discrimination by gaining an education, 'making oneself useful', and working in a 'productive job' is not always limited to economical or cultural activity. It also included enlisting in the army and distinguishing oneself in war. It is well known that native Americans, African-Americans and Japanese Nikkei immigrants enlisted in the American army as a way of fighting against discrimination and raising the status of their ethnic groups. In the lecture given at the time of the Russo-Japanese War, 'Jinruigakuteki chishiki no yō masumasu fukashi' (The Need for Anthropological Knowledge is Greater than Ever), Tsuboi argued as follows.

Some people say the Japanese race has its own unique history, which differs from the history of the native Taiwanese and the *Ainu*. However, since the Sino-Japanese War, the Japanese people, which is an amalgamation of these races, have fought together. That is, the Japanese, who include the *Ainu* and native Taiwanese, are fighting together in wars and creating a single history. We should therefore no longer treat them as parasites, adopted children or strangers.

In Taiwan, people had not yet been conscripted into the Japanese army, but in the Russo-Japanese War, the *Ainu*, who had been conscripted from 1896, took part as Japanese soldiers for the first time in a foreign campaign.[12] A total of 63 *Ainu* took to the field. Of these, three died in battle, five died of disease, and two became invalids. On the other hand, over 85 per cent were granted military decorations, including three who were granted the highest decoration given to Japanese soldiers by the military, the Order of the Golden Kite.[13] That they were decorated despite the discrimination within their units is something that is highly valued in the history of the *Ainu* as an example of a brave struggle to overcome discrimination. There is one reported case where, in an *Ainu* village, one father was 'delighted' when his son, the breadwinner of the family, was conscripted, saying 'now we are equal to the Japanese'. Newspapers and magazines at the time played up the bravery of the *Ainu* soldiers, especially a soldier named Kitakaze Isokichi.[14]

Underlying Tsuboi's statement that 'the Japanese, who include the *Ainu* and native Taiwanese, are fighting together' were *Ainu* such as these. There was even a case where, in a home village of an *Ainu* soldier who had returned from a victorious campaign, a 'delighted' prominent individual said 'this is the result of the education he received at school', and urged the need for education on other *Ainu* people. This was exactly what Tsuboi was hoping for. Applauding the activity of the *Ainu* soldiers, he must have thought that the positive press would raise the status of the *Ainu* within the Great Japanese Empire.

Moreover, in the same lecture, Tsuboi noted that the Japanese nation was a mixture of the *Ainu* and people from the south, and claimed 'some Japanese are descended from people who came from the tropics, while others are descendants of people from cold countries'.

Therefore, when the population of Japan gradually increases and it becomes time to spread this population to other areas, we do not have to be selective: we do not have to say that we can go here, but not there. To the tropical areas, we can send those Japanese tolerant of heat, and to cold regions, those tolerant of the cold. However, when a nation consists of people who share the same characteristics, they may be good at some things, but not at all at others...the complexity of the Japanese race is a blessing, and certainly nothing to grieve about.

For Tsuboi, the fact that the *Ainu* soldiers fought bravely on the severely cold battlefields of the Russo-Japanese War was a good example of this. Contrary to Inoue Tetsujirō's insistence that it was impossible for the Japanese to move out into the world, the 'Japanese' as depicted by Tsuboi could move out all over the globe because they were a mixture of many ethnic groups.

From what he believed to be a conscientious position, Tsuboi devoted himself to the salvation of the *Ainu*, and emphasised that the Japanese nation was a mixed one, and that the Great Japanese Empire was a multi-national state. The reason thinkers like Uchimura and Tsuboi, who were detested by the national polity theorists, took a positive attitude to the process of civilising through education was not that they were racists, but rather that they believed in benevolence and the equality of the various ethnic groups. However, this was also a logic that assimilated the culture of minorities into that of the majority in the name of civilisation and, moreover, that mobilised the minorities and sent them to war as a form of unification. The argument that the 'Japanese' were a mixture of many nations glorified the ability of the Great Japanese Empire to move out into the world.

Both the Christian intellectuals examined in the last chapter and Tsuboi emphasised that minorities such as Christians and the *Ainu* could contribute to the state to gain recognition. This was a logic that the national polity theorists, who were in favour of an overseas expansion, could not argue against. However, no matter how conscientious, the philosophy of unification meant, as long as the unified state operated on the logic of invasion, the mobilisation of the minorities as a part of overseas aggression.

After this, Tsuboi and some Christian intellectuals came to praise the annexation of Korea using the same logic of imperial expansion that had originally been created to protect the rights of Japanese minorities. As the Great Japanese Empire expanded, the logic they had created escaped from the individual theorists and began to develop independently, leaving the defence of minorities behind.

5 The Theory that the 'Japanese' and Koreans share a Common Ancestor

The so-called *'Nissen dōsoron'* argues that the 'Japanese' and Koreans share a common ancestor. Among contemporary researchers of modern Japanese history, this is viewed as one of the most odious of the various ideologies that justified the aggression of the Great Japanese Empire.[1]

Although it is true that the common ancestor theory was used to justify aggression, it has another aspect on which it is difficult to pass judgement. First of all, *'Nissen dōsoron'* was a generic term that stood for a number of positions that differed quite significantly from one another. For example, there is a difference between a theory of a common ancestor that argues that 'the Koreans are the ancestors of the Japanese' and one that argues that 'the Japanese are the ancestors of the Koreans'. Secondly, it was both a type of mixed nation theory and an enlarged version of the homogeneous nation theory that was applied to the entirety of the Great Japanese Empire. This is because it insisted not only that the Japanese nation shared a common ancestor with peoples who resided on the continent, but also that the Great Japanese Empire, including Korea, consisted of a single nation that shared a common ancestor. The idea of a shared ancestor was also seen in the national polity theory, which argued that the sovereign and all his subjects shared the same ancestor.

However, most of the various positions that adopted the common ancestor theory agreed that a mutual intercourse (including invasion) had existed between Japan and Korea from ancient times. There were a few extreme cases where it was argued that the flow had been one-way, that the 'Japanese' had invaded the Korean peninsula, but that not a single Korean had ever come to the Japanese archipelago. Although it is possible to see in the theory of a common ancestor 'an enlarged version of the theory of the homogeneous nation for the Great Japanese Empire', this was still very different from the argument that the 'Japanese' were an exceptionally pure blooded, homogeneous race. As this chapter will demonstrate, many theorists in the Meiji era who argued that a common ancestor existed were not interested in developing a theory of a pure blooded Japanese nation, but instead actively advocated the mixed nation theory.

The Theory that the Imperial Family came from Korea

The claim that the inhabitants of the archipelago are the descendants of people who originally came from the Korean peninsula has existed since the Edo Period.[2] For example, the Confucian scholar Arai Hakuseki mentioned in chapter 1 examined the possibility that 'our ancestors came from Chen-Fan [in ancient Korea]', and seems to have believed that the Kumaso, an alien people in the Kiki myths, and the ancient Korean Koryo may have been the same nation. In 1781, another Confucian scholar, Tō Teikan, argued that Susano-O – the younger brother of the Sun Goddess Amaterasu – in the Kiki myths was originally the chief of the Ch'en Han in ancient Korea, and that the Emperor Jinmu was a descendant of the head of the Chinese Wu Dynasty. According to Tō, in the age of Jinmu, the language and customs of the archipelago were Korean, but the family line of the Emperor Jinmu died away, and another family line started after the Emperor Ōjin. Contemporary Japanese nativist (*kokugaku*) scholars were furious at this, and Motoori Norinaga rejected Tō's hypothesis as 'the words of a mad man'.

Unlike the Royal Families of Europe, the Japanese Imperial Family has not practiced international marriages between royal dynasties at least since medieval times (from when documentary records other than myths exist). Confucian scholars identified at least to a certain extent with the advanced Confucian countries of China and Korea, while nativist scholars who had emerged in a backlash against Confucianism opposed the Bakufu, which recognised Confucianism as the official ideology, and praised the Emperor as unique to Japan. They were deeply reluctant to recognise that Korean and Chinese blood might flow in the veins of the Imperial Family.

In the Kiki myths, a relationship between the ancient Imperial Family of the archipelago and Royal Families of Korea was suggested (it was noted, for instance, that the Empress Jingū was a descendant of a Korean prince). This was, however, a suggestion contained in myths, the veracity of which cannot be determined. Confucian scholars tended to read the Kiki texts as ancient materials, while nativist scholars tended to read them as sacred mythological texts, and the two groups thus debated the correct interpretation of the Kiki myths.

The controversy between Edo Period scholars of Native Learning or nativism (*kokugaku*) and scholars of Chinese Learning (*kangaku*) or Confucianism was continued in the Meiji era in the debate between nativist scholars and scholars who adopted the methodology of modern history and argued for the shared national heritage of the people of the peninsula and those of the archipelago. The theory of a common ancestor based on the discourse of modern historiography stemmed from the work of Hoshino Hisashi (1839–1917) and Kume Kunitake (1839–1931), both of whom developed their ideas by about 1890.

Following the Meiji Restoration, Japan underwent a revolutionary change to create a modern state. At the same time, an effort to chronicle Japanese history began at the first modern university built in the new capital, Tokyo, the Tokyo Imperial University. Together with Shigeno Yasutsugu (1827–1910), Hoshino and Kume were the first professors who took charge of editing the chronicles at Tokyo Imperial University, and were members of the first generation of scholars who practised positive historiography in modern Japan. From the viewpoint of positive history, they did not see the Kiki myths as sacred, but attempted to research them as ancient historical materials, a position opposed to that of the nativist scholars. Hoshino noted that there are mistakes in the dates in *Nihon shoki*. Kume is known for having travelled to various Western countries with the Iwakura Mission – a mission led by ambassador plenipotentiary Iwakura Tomomi (1825–1883) that travelled around Europe and the USA from 1872 to 1873 to study modern Western civilisation, and with which half the Cabinet members of the day travelled – and for having edited the *Bei-Ō kairan jikki* (A True Account of the Observations of the Ambassadorial Mission to America and Europe). Kume was forced to resign from his post as a professor of the Imperial University for his article, 'Shintō wa saiten no kozoku' (Shintō is an Ancient Custom of Heaven Worship), published in 1891, in which he insisted that Shintō was nothing but a primitive belief that worshipped the heavens, and that Japan would fall behind in global development if she adhered to Shintō and the national polity.

The Theory that the 'Japanese' and Koreans share a Common Ancestor

What sort of view of ancient Japanese history did these historians draw from their analysis of the Kiki myths? As an example, I will begin with Hoshino's strangely titled thesis, 'Honpō no jinshu gengo ni tsuite hikō o nobete yo no shinshin aikokusha ni tadasu' (Questions from an Old Man to the True Patriots Regarding the Race and Language of Japan).[3] This was long enough to be serialised, but was published all at once lest a partial reading cause a negative reaction.

Here Hoshino made an allegation that at the time must have been shocking. The ancestors of the Imperial Family were 'originally the rulers of the ancient Korean Silla', who emigrated from the Korean peninsula on 'discovering the Japanese archipelago'.

According to Hoshino, the ancestors of the Imperial Family came from the peninsula, flourished in the 'Izumo region', today's Shimane Prefecture, and then extended their power into the Yamato region, today's Kinki region centred around Kyoto. This clan then conquered the indigenous people of the archipelago through Jinmu's Eastern Expedition, and established a peaceful kingdom under the reign of Amaterasu, the Sun Goddess in the Kiki myths. Her younger brother, Susano-O was the ruler of Silla and, following the conquest of the archipelago, continued to make trips between the peninsula and the archipelago. In other words, the archipelago and the peninsula were unified under the 'ancestors of the Imperial Family' who were encamped in the archipelago and, in ancient times, 'the race and the language of Japan and Korea were the same' and 'the two countries were originally a single, undivided region'.

However, this state of affairs in which the archipelago and peninsula were unified as a single kingdom did not last long. A dispute erupted between Amaterasu and Susano-O. The peninsula broke away from the archipelago, and engineered a rebellion by the Kumaso, the indigenous people of the archipelago. As a result, the Empress Jingū attacked the peninsula and suppressed the Kumaso, and 'Japan and Korea once more became one country'. However, Silla broke away again, joining the Chinese Tang Dynasty to defeat the allied armies of Japan and the Korean Pekche at the battle of Pekchongan in the seventh century. Eventually, the archipelago lost the peninsula. Afterwards, 'during the reign of Emperor Kanmu, old documents that noted that the peoples of Japan and Korea are of the same race were destroyed...and the fact that our Imperial ancestors were once the rulers of Silla' was deleted from history and forgotten.

Of course, Hoshino realised that his ideas would be criticised. He noted that, beginning with the nativist scholars who followed in the wake of the Edo Period Motoori Norinaga, many Japanese intellectuals believed that Korea was different from Japan, and expected that they would 'view any person who argued that Japan and Korea share the same race and language as someone who had defiled the national polity (*kokutai*) and who lacked patriotism'. In his opinion, however, since 'Japan and Korea used to be one region', the Imperial Family's arrival from the peninsula was little more than a domestic trip within a single country.

Furthermore, the title of this article was 'Questions...to the True Patriots'. Hoshino lamented the loss of the peninsula in the ancient era as a 'most grievous and unfortunate' matter, and 'highly praised the military feat of arms' of the Shōgun Toyotomi Hideyoshi in invading Korea in the sixteenth century. Hoshino's position is clearly shown in the following passage.

> Today, the Japanese people dislike being treated as the same race as the Koreans. All this shows is that they have forgotten that our imperial ancestors were originally the rulers of Korea. They do not feel angry about the division of the nation, and do not understand that this is a matter of the expansion and contraction of Japan's territory.

Hoshino's intention is clear. The archipelago and the peninsula used to be one country and were originally of the same race and shared the same language. The Imperial Family used to rule the peninsula. It was therefore natural for the peninsula to be embraced once again as the territory of the Imperial Family. Here, the duality of Hoshino's theory of a common ancestor emerges. Although it is clear that this is a justification of invasion, on the other hand Hoshino also argued that the Imperial Family came from overseas, which might be regarded as a defilement of the national polity and lack of patriotism. In fact, at the time of the Kume incident over Shintō, this article of Hoshino's also became the target of criticism.

At the beginning of the article, Hoshino referred to the confrontation between Tō Teikan and Motoori Norinaga, and criticised Motoori as an individual who 'fabricated ancient texts to suit his own theories'. Kume also despised Motoori. Although Hoshino and Kume belonged to the first generation of historians to follow Western positive historicism, their education was originally based on a Chinese-style historiography. The confrontation between Chinese Learning (*kangaku*) and Japanese National Learning or nativist studies (*kokugaku*), symbolised in the confrontation between Arai Hakuseki and Motoori Norinaga, thus re-emerged in the debate on the Japanese nation, while undergoing a number of transformations (this issue will be re-examined in chapters 11 and 14).

Furthermore, Hoshino wrote that 'my friend and colleague, Professor Kume, also believes that Japan and Korea used to be one country'. In fact, Kume published an article, 'Nippon fukuin no enkaku' (The History of Japanese Territory), one year before Hoshino published his, which argued that the territory of Japan once included the Korean peninsula.[4] Here, Kume mentioned the past mutual exchange of traffic, the Empress Jingū's conquest of the peninsula, and the conquest of the indigenous people of the archipelago, beginning with the Emishi. He also argued that the 'race' in the south of China was the same as the 'Japanese'.

The theory of a common ancestor in historiographical circles was further developed by Yoshida Tōgo (1864–1918) and others. Yoshida was strongly influenced by Kume and Hoshino, and had the manuscript of his work checked by Kume, so there is no large difference in their views.[5] The theory of a common ancestor was thus not generated by national polity theorists or fanatics, but from people totally opposed to them.

At almost the same time as these articles, Inoue Tetsujirō published *Naichi zakkyoron* (On Mixed Residence in the Interior), a work I examined in chapter 2, where he clearly stated that the Koreans were a different race from the 'Japanese'. For Inoue at this time, the opinion that the Koreans and the 'Japanese' were the same nation would not only destroy the national unity of the 'Japanese' in resisting the Western Powers but, at the extreme, might also provide an excuse for Korea to annex Japan. This, however, could be the case only when it was assumed that Japan was weak and incapable of moving out into the world. With its victory in the Sino-Japanese and the Russo-Japanese Wars, the confidence of the empire mounted, and it was natural that the part of the theory of a common ancestor that was useful for the enlargement of the empire came to be highlighted.

The 'Insular Spirit' (*shimaguni konjō*) and the 'Northern and Southern Races'

In the spring of 1894, the year the Sino-Japanese War began, Kume serialised an article 'Shimabito Konjō' (The Insular Spirit) in Tokutomi Sohō's *Kokumin no tomo*.[6] Tokutomi Sohō was a Christian, and originally supported liberalism, but later became a firebrand supporting Japan's invasion of Asia (although he would have defined it as Japan's liberation of Asia). *Kokumin no tomo* (Friend of the Nation) was a magazine that advocated the modern concept of the 'nation' (*kokumin*), a concept that was new at the time.

Kume's article was written immediately after he had been driven from the Imperial University and illustrates the process by which the openness that had led him to reject the old-fashioned ways of Shintō developed into a position that favoured imperial expansion. According to the article, there are two types of 'insular spirit'. One is an exclusivism that detests both foreigners and imported civilisation, that shuts its borders through a closed country policy, 'prohibits people from going overseas', and falls behind in the global competition in civilisation and overseas development. The second is a position that favours opening the borders, welcoming foreigners and imports from all over the world, and sailing to all regions overseas.

According to Kume, of the two, the latter embodied the essential nature of Japan, and the former was merely a temporary characteristic acquired through the closed country policy of the Edo Period. He based his argument on 'the scale of openness during the first experiment at an open country [in the ancient era]'. According to Kume, the creation of the country by Izanami and Izanagi as depicted in the Kiki myths indicated the conquest of the indigenous people of the archipelago by warships (as seen in chapter 1, this was Arai Hakuseki's position), and 'it is the peculiarity of the people of an island nation to be experienced in seamanship'. Moreover, the medieval Japanese pirates, the Wakō or the 'sea-bound pirate fighters', in fact 'represent the true nature of an island nation'. The Empress Jingū succeeded in implementing an 'overseas expedition despite her sex', and 'the intercourse between Japan, Korea and China was so firmly fixed' that 'nobody even dreamed of the ideology of a closed country'. In other words, 'the insular spirit of the Japanese people was displayed in its pure form in the beginning of the country'.

After that, however, 'the united county of Japan and Korea' lost the peninsula and, from the eighth century Heian Period on, began to isolate the country because of the lethargy of the aristocrats. Following this, 'the records that stated that the Japanese were the same race as the Koreans were destroyed' and while the country was closed during the Edo Period, 'the insular spirit increasingly turned to bigotry'. Japan 'relaxed because of the peace and became lazy in learning because of the lack of competition with foreign countries', and eventually shrank and degenerated.

Kume mentioned 'the confusion of the true nature of the people of the island nation by the mountain people' as the reason for the loss of the open-minded spirit of Japan. A self-sufficient and closed mountain people know nothing about sea-routes and sea-battles. The aristocracy in Nara and Kyoto were so 'relaxed in the imperial capital in the mountains' of the Kinki region that they too became languid.

Following the opening of the country and the Meiji Restoration, this situation was finally overcome, but a narrow-minded exclusivism and isolationism still remained. In reply to this, Kume argued that if people truly disliked foreign countries and imported goods so much, a 'true closed country' should be implemented, and the 'Japanese' should become self-supporting like the people in Arcadia once were. However, he continued, international society is based on the rule of the survival of the fittest, and if Japan remained a defenceless and uncivilised country, it would suffer the same fate as that imposed by the Western Powers on 'the indigenous people of the West Indies'.

According to Kume, the closed, insular spirit was a 'philosophy that will cause Japan to become isolated and backward and join the savage islands of the South Seas'. He cited the Great British Empire as an example of an open-minded island-country. With an enterprising spirit that accepted the importation of civilisation and with a strong navy, Japan would be 'fully qualified to become the Britain of the East'.

Kume's views of the South Seas contrasted with those of Inoue Tetsujirō. Inoue was opposed to mixed residence, saying the fate of the 'Japanese' would be the same as the people in the South Seas who were being conquered by the West. Kume took exactly the opposite view. This contrast in views about the South Seas and the notion that an evil insular spirit had been generated in the mountains are the keys to understanding Yanagita Kunio's theories of the mountain people and the South Islands that will be examined in chapter 12.

What kind of theory of the origin of the Japanese nation did Kume advocate? He worked at the private Waseda University after retiring from the Imperial University and in 1905, during the Russo-Japanese War, published *Nippon kodaishi* (A History of Ancient Japan).[7] From that time until the 1910s, early in the Taishō era, this book was a standard text of ancient Japanese history based on the theory of the mixed nation. Watsuji Tetsurō, who will be examined in chapter 15, began his study of ancient history by reading it, and Tsuda Sōkichi (chapter 14) seems to have had a sense of rivalry with Kume's theory of the Japanese nation.

The book begins with a declaration that 'the popular legend' that Japan was 'a unique country' whose land and people were produced by the gods 'has been destroyed by science' (Kume 1905: 9). After declaring his scientific and empirical approach to history, Kume used the achievements of the anthropology of the time and argued that two 'races' existed in ancient Asia. One was the 'northern race' which was distributed from central Asia to North China, and which included the Tungus. The other was the 'southern race' which sailed from India to Vietnam, the Philippines, and into south China. The northern part of the Korean peninsula was occupied by the northern race, and the southern part by the southern (Kume 1905: 25–9).

In the archipelago, the northern race entered through northern Japan and established a base in the northeast region, while the southern race moved into the interior from the coast. The southern race was a sea-faring nation, and imported advanced civilisation, including ironware from the peninsula, that enabled them to enjoy a superior position. The northern race was gradually driven into the mountain regions of the archipelago, and was described as indigenous peoples such as the Emishi or Tsuchigumo in *Kojiki* and *Nihon shoki* (Kume 1905: 33–7). This is the basis for his argument that the people in southern Korea and the main body of the Japanese nation were the same race. The idea that the defeated race was driven into the mountains and formed an alien nation seems to have also influenced Yanagita's theory of a mountain people.

The southern race that conquered the archipelago formed 'an alliance of three countries', with the capital in Japan, which included south China and the southern part of the peninsula. The basis of Kume's argument about the Japanese location of the capital is very fragile. He merely states that this was a people who moved in search of a better place to live, and the place they eventually stopped at, the archipelago, must have been the best place, and finally 'a superior group' must have lived there (Kume 1905: 65).

After this, interpretations of the Kiki myths common to the theory of a common ancestor were trotted out – including the argument that Susano-O was the ruler of the ancient Korean Silla, that the Empress Jingū invaded the peninsula, and that a Japanese colony existed in ancient Korea. He praised Arai Hakuseki's 'keen insight' into the myths that saw the creation of the country by Izanami and Izanagi as depicting the conquest of the archipelago by a sea-faring people (Kume 1905: 73). Furthermore, he stated that Izumo was occupied by a southern race of Korean origin (although a different clan from the one that ruled the archipelago), and noted that the mythical ruler of Izumo, Ōkuninushi (see chapter 1, endnote 4), handed territory over to the central government of the archipelago (Kume 1905: 84–5). This cession is referred to in the later literature as an example of an amiable settlement between Japan and Korea in which Japan had the advantage.

The above summarises Kume's common ancestor theory and his views of ancient history. As with Hoshino, the duality in both the resistance against nativist scholars with their closed minds and the mixed nation theory that acted as a justification for invasion can be seen. However, Hoshino's insistence that the Imperial Family came from overseas does not come to the fore in Kume's *Nippon kodaishi* (The Ancient History of Japan). It is clear from a close reading that since the conquerors, the southern race, came from overseas, the assumption is that the Imperial Family did as well. However, perhaps because of his experience in writing about Shintō, this point was not emphasised.

From this time on, the mixed nation theory took the form of emphasising only the precedents for assimilation and overseas development, while basing its arguments on this tacit premise and tacit taboo. It was not until the collapse of the Great Japanese Empire following defeat in the Second World War that there again emerged another theory that emphasised the foreign origin of the Imperial Family – the theory of the immigration of a horse-riding people (this theory will be discussed in chapter 17).

Moving into the 'Homeland'

At almost the same time as the common ancestor theory emerged among historians, a theory that argued for the linguistic similarity of Japanese and Korean also appeared.

As was the case in anthropology, this idea was heralded by Westerners. In William George Aston's (1841–1911) 'A Comparative Study of the Japanese and Korean Languages', published in 1879 two years after Morse's excavation of the Ōmori shell mound, the notion that an essential relationship between the Japanese and Korean languages undoubtedly existed could already be seen. A decade later, a number of papers were published on the topic, including 'Nippongo to Chōsengo to no ruiji' (The Similarities Between the Japanese and Korean Languages) by Ōya Tōru and 'Chōsen gengokō' (On the Korean Language) by Takahashi Jirō, both in 1889, 'Chōsengo' (The Korean Language) by Miyake Yonekichi in 1890, and 'Nikkan gengo no kankei' (The Relationship between the Japanese and the Korean Languages) by Akamine Seichirō in 1892.[8] These were published almost at the same time as the articles by Hoshino and Kume, and made it clear that Hoshino was not alone in insisting that the Japanese and Korean languages were the same.

The trend that emphasised the similarity between the languages culminated with the linguist Kanazawa Shōzaburō's (1872–1967) *Nikkan ryōkokugo dōkeiron* (On the Common Genealogy of the Japanese and Korean Languages), which was published immediately before the annexation of Korea.[9] The opening sentence of this book sheds a great deal of light on the conclusion.

> The language of Korea belongs to the same family as the language of the Great Japanese Empire. It is nothing but a branch dialect of the Japanese language, and the relationship between Japanese and Korean is the same as that between Japanese and the Ryūkyū dialect.

The Ryūkyū Kingdom (Okinawa) was annexed by Japan in 1879 and made a prefecture. The definition of the language of Korea in the same terms as that of Okinawa, as a dialect of Japanese, was also a prediction of the future political status of Korea. According to Kanazawa, the relationship between Japanese and

Korean was similar to that between German and Dutch, or French and Spanish. He claimed that a reading of the *Kojiki* and *Nihon shoki* demonstrated that there was a frequent interchange between Japan and Korea, and it was self-evident that there was no inconvenience in communication. He also cited the theory of Hoshino Hisashi who proved 'the unity of Japan and Korea' and the conquest of the peninsula by 'our imperial ancestors'. Kanazawa's theory became well known internationally, and effectively became the established theory in the academic circles of the period. The fact that the phrase '*Nissen dōsoron*', the theory that the 'Japanese' and Koreans shared a common ancestor, became popular from the title of one of his later works shows how great his influence was.

I will not discuss in detail the content of research in linguistics from Kanazawa onwards. At the beginning, the research listed words that were similar in both Japanese and Korean and analysed phonemes and usage, and was of too specialised a nature to be introduced here. Instead, I would like to state only that the argument that insisted on the similarities between Japan and Korea occupied the mainstream in linguistics. What is more important is how the theory of a common ancestor in history and linguistics moved into the public discourse.

In this non-specialised public sphere, the common ancestor theory was frequently used in association with the anthropological mixed nation theory. A typical example is Takegoshi Yosaburō's *Nisen gohyakunenshi* (2,500 Years of Japanese Civilisation).[10] Takegoshi Yosaburō, or Sansa (1865–1950) became a member of the Imperial Diet after working as a journalist for the Min'yūsha (Friend of the People, the publisher of *Kokumin no tomo*), a democratic press edited by Tokutomi Sohō, but is also known as a historian not affiliated with any university (*minkanshika*). His book was published in 1896 when he was 31, a year after the annexation of Taiwan, and was one of the best-selling general works of Japanese history in that period.

Referring to the anthropologist Koganei Yoshikiyo, Takegoshi argued that a large number of peoples had come to the archipelago, and that legends of the 'Malay race', 'the people of the South Seas', 'Mongolians', Chinese' and 'dwarfs' (what Tsuboi called the indigenous 'Koropok-guru') could be seen in the Kiki myths (Takegoshi 1896: 2–6). He also stated that in the ancient era, Japan and Korea used to be 'as good as a single country, and the peoples were almost exactly the same', and that the Empress Jingū's invasion of Korea was 'merely a regaining of old territory'. Takegoshi, however, insisted that the ruling nation, 'the Tenson race' (literally, the race of 'descendants of the gods'), was a southern people which came to Japan on ocean currents, and it was the conquered people of Japan such as the Izumo who were the same race as the people of Korea. Beside the Koreans there also existed indigenous peoples including the Emishi (*Ainu*), who were 'savage races' like 'the red American Indians', but the Tenson nation, a 'superior race', conquered them (Takegoshi 1896: 48).

Furthermore, he said, through mixed marriage and migration to Japan, the Imperial Family came to include 'the blood of the natives' and 'the blood of Koreans', and the Empress Jingū and the Emperor Kanmu were of Korean origin (Takegoshi 1896: 13, 25, 200). He also described the technical and cultural contribution made by the immigrants, beginning with the building of the great Buddha in Nara (Takegoshi 1896: 196). From the activities of the Empress Jingū, he noted that there were no andocentric customs in the ancient era (Takegoshi 1896: 33). This view of the ancient era resembles that of the feminist Takamure Itsue who will be discussed in chapter 11.

In *Nangokuki* (An Account of the Lands of the South), a bestseller that was also published on the eve of the annexation of Korea, Takegoshi deepened his commitment to the theory that the Tenson nation came to Japan from the south.[11] *Nangokuki* was an account of a journey he made to the South Seas, to Java (then a Dutch colony), and to Indochina. Listing the similarities between the customs of Japan and the South Seas, such as ships that used bamboo and duet songs, he insisted that the nucleus of the 'Japanese' was a Malay people which came from the south.

Opposing the theory of a movement into the continent – the northern advance which entailed an economic and military push into Korea, Manchuria, Siberia and China – which was then the dominant ideology in the Japan, Takegoshi supported a movement into the South Seas – a southern advance into Southeast Asia and the Pacific Islands – which he viewed as the motherland of the Tenson nation.

Within the school that argued for the mixed nation theory of that period, if Takegoshi was the leading advocate of a southern advance, the leading advocate of a northern advance was the historical writer and critic Yamaji Aizan (1864–1917), a journalist one year older than Takegoshi with whom he had worked in the Min'yūsha, and who was also known as an amateur historian. Yamaji was a Christian, and took part in the debate with Katō Hiroyuki, the national polity theorist mentioned in chapter 3.

In 1901, Yamaji published a short essay, 'Nipponjin shi no daiichi peiji' (The First Page of the History of the Japanese People), and argued that three races had resided in the ancient archipelago: the *Ainu*, the Hayato (a clan which lived in ancient southern Kyūshū) and the Yamato. According to Yamaji, the indigenous *Ainu* used to live in every part of the archipelago and were known as the Emishi. The Hayato were Malays. The Yamato, who conquered both the *Ainu* and the Hayato, were 'one branch of the "Churanian"' race that came to Japan from the north of China via the Korean peninsula.[12] Yamaji clearly stated that the intention of his essay was 'to prove historically that the stage on which the Japanese should play an active role is not limited to the Japanese islands'. He advocated moving out into the world, not only into the Asia continent, the motherland of the Yamato nation, but elsewhere too, saying, 'our motherland is the whole world, and our stage should therefore not be limited to Japan'.

Again immediately before the annexation of Korea, and just after the publication of Takegoshi's *Nangokuki* (An Account of the Lands of the South), Yamaji, though not clearly mentioning Takegoshi's name, argued against the theory that the 'Tenson race' was Malay. According to Yamaji, the nucleus of the people of ancient Japan were clearly 'of the same parent source' as the Koreans, and the common customs Japan shared with the people of the south were brought by the Hayato, the conquered Malays. Furthermore, the Malays had come to Japan from southern China via the west coast of the Korean peninsula, rather than riding on the Kuroshio (Black) Current of the Pacific as Takegoshi had argued.[13] Yamaji's theory is an extension of Kume's theory of a southern and northern race. The only difference is that Yamaji thought the northerners had conquered the southerners, while Kume took the opposite position.

This controversy resulted in harsh criticism from the anthropologist Torii Ryūzō in which he noted that for Takegoshi and Yamaji to argue that Malays lived in Vietnam and southern China was proof of their total lack of knowledge of the basics of anthropology.[14] Their arguments were academically worthless, but they clearly demonstrate how inseparable were the theory of advancing out into the world and the theory of the origin of the nation.

Tokutomi Sohō, the founder of Min'yūsha where they both worked, and the editor of the magazine, *Kokumin no tomo* for which both Kume and Taguchi Ukichi wrote, adopted the same line of argument. In his *Dai Nippon bōchōron* (The Expansion of Great Japan) published in 1894, Tokutomi wrote that 'the ancestors of the Tenson race came all the way across the oceans', and for their descendants to move out into the world was 'nothing but a repetition of what our ancestors did 3,000 years ago'.[15] As will be explained in chapter 16, Tokutomi became a leading figure in propagating to the masses the mixed nation theory linked to the theory of invasion, especially after the Sino-Japanese War that started in 1937.

Another example of a common ancestor theorist is Ōkuma Shigenobu (1838–1922), who is known as a statesman active as a moderate in the Liberty and People's Rights Movement and as a one-time Prime Minister in 1898. According to his ideas on Korean policy in 1906, 'Korea…enjoyed a higher civilisation than Japan, and exported that civilisation to Japan. The Japanese invited architects, religious figures, and scholars from Korea', and 'the Hōryūji Temple in Nara is built in the Korean style and by Korean builders'.[16] (The Hōryūji Temple is said to be the oldest temple in Japan. For the debate on whether the builders of the temple were 'Japanese' or not, see chapter 15).

According to Ōkuma, however, the Korea of his day was in decline. This 'is not because of anything in the nature of the Koreans, but is caused by bad politics'. Koreans have 'the same ancestors as we do' and 'physically Koreans and Japanese are the same'. Japan before the Meiji Restoration did not progress because of the feudal system, but 'as soon as feudalism was abolished and liberal politics came to rule, Japan developed immensely'. Therefore, 'if only politics are improved, Koreans are destined to develop just like the Japanese'.

Here we catch a glimpse of how the enlightened aspects of Ōkuma's thought and his theory of overseas aggression dovetailed logically. Koreans are the same 'race' as the 'Japanese', and if only 'liberal politics came to rule' under the guidance of the 'Japanese', Koreans too would surely enjoy a movement towards 'civilisation and enlightenment'. According to Ōkuma, 'since the Japanese have the intelligence, experience and wealth…the Koreans will have to work under Japanese orders' and 'the Japanese will, I think, have to become the landowners and capitalists, while the Koreans will have to become the clerks, shop assistants, factory workers and farm tenants'.

It is important to note here that Ōkuma did not regard the Koreans as inherently inferior. This is not to defend him. Ōkuma strongly argued in favour of assimilationist policies, saying that 'a country that lacks an assimilative ability' would not be able to compete in the international struggle for survival, and that 'Korea is in fact the very touchstone of the existence or non-existence of the assimilative ability of the Japanese nation'. At the root of his argument, however, lay the perception that assimilation would be easy because 'the Koreans and the Japanese are the same race'. Since Ōkuma's argument was based on Kume's theory, he thought the people of the south of the peninsula were the same as the Japanese nation, while those of the north of the peninsula were a little different. In any case, to assume that the Koreans were inherently inferior would be to assume that the 'Japanese', 'the same nation', were also inferior. The 'Japanese' could therefore discriminate against them, but not view them as inferior. If Koreans were to be seen as inferior, the difference between the two peoples would have to be emphasised, which would mean that the logic that 'Japanese' could assimilate Koreans because the two were the same race could not be sustained. As will be explained in chapter 13, this strange relationship was seen in the conflict between the eugenicists and the theorists of Japanisation.

Furthermore, in a work written for a general readership – *Kaikoku gojūnenshi* (A History of the Half Century of Open Japan) – that Ōkuma edited in the following year 1907, he developed a theory of the origin of the Japanese nation. This included the standard arguments seen in contemporary theories, such as the existence in the archipelago of a number of peoples – a continental people and Malays, in addition to the Emishi and Hayato. The book also included an article on linguistic genealogy by a linguist, and a translation of Bälz' mixed nation theory, which demonstrated Ōkuma's observant attitude. He praised the mixture that had occurred in ancient Japan, saying that 'there is no country apart from Japan which includes the blood of so many various nations', and expressing his pride in 'how the Japanese are blessed with such a powerful ability to assimilate'.

Moreover, in a popular book, *Kokumin dokuhon* (The National Reader), Ōkuma also stressed that 'since the ancient era, various nations have come to Japan and we have assimilated them...and formed the great Japanese nation'.[17] This shows that this type of argument was not an 'esoteric' one limited to a few intellectuals.

Takegoshi, Yamaji, Tokutomi and Ōkuma were not bigoted conservatives or national polity theorists, and were known, at least at one stage of their lives, as progressive democrats. The mixed nation theory in anthropology beginning with Tsuboi, the common ancestor theory developed by Hoshino and Kume, and the arguments of the Christian intellectuals examined in chapter 3, all emerged from opposition to the national polity theorists and the nativist scholars. While the national polity theory was captured by the idea of a pure and homogeneous bloodline of the Japanese nation, it was unable to open the closed door and break the deadlock. At the same time, the opponents of the national polity steadily completed a logic of moving out into the world. The annexation of Korea in 1910 was carried out after this process of preparation.

6　The Japanese Annexation of Korea

In August 1910, at the time of the Japanese annexation of Korea, mixed nation theorists praised the annexation in a wide range of newspapers and magazines, using the logic they had previously put together.[1] In the process, the theory established a dominant position in the mainstream discourse on nationality in the Great Japanese Empire. Almost all the articles that referred to the history of Japan and Korea or to racial theories while extolling the annexation can be categorised as adhering either to the theory that the 'Japanese' and Koreans shared a common ancestor (*Nissen dōsoron*), or to the mixed nation theory. Articles advocating the pure blood theory were not seen in leading Japanese newspapers and magazines during this period.

The Line of Argument in Newspapers

It is natural that the position advanced by mixed nation theorists at the time of the annexation should have frequently been an extension of the logic that has already been described. Indeed, little in the arguments was novel. However, it was unprecedented for so many articles on the Japanese nation, linked to arguments on international relationships, to appear in the media within the short period of several weeks. The significance of the annexation to the debate on the Japanese nation was not the appearance of a new line of argument, but the sudden explosion in the press of the rhetoric of the mixed nation theory that individual writers had developed independently of one another over a 20-year period since the debate on mixed residence in the interior.

Despite the obvious limits of the methodology, articles from the leading newspapers and magazines of the time will be introduced to demonstrate that the mixed nation theory had moved into the mainstream of public discourse. Since the annexation treaty was promulgated on 29 August 1910, a survey was made of articles on the origin of the Japanese nation published in the leading newspapers from the last weeks of August to the first weeks of September. As will be seen below, the opinions of many of those examined in the previous chapters of this work were published during this time in the Japanese media.

Firstly, a talk (*danwa*) by Ebina Danjō (see chapter 3), 'Chōsenjin wa Nippon ni dōka shiuru ka' (Can Koreans be Assimilated into Japan?), published in the *Tōkyō asahi shinbun* (Tokyo Asahi Newspaper) on 25 August claimed that the Koreans were also 'a mixed breed, just like the Japanese', and that the Izumo of the Kiki myths were Korean. His conclusion was that assimilation would be easy because of the similarities in race and language. According to Ebina, those Koreans who had denounced Japan were 'like those Japanese who were hostile to Westerners when Japan's doors were opened'. The next day, on 26 August, the linguist Kanazawa Shōzaburō (see chapter 5) argued in 'Nippongo to Chōsengo' (The Japanese and Korean Languages) that the two languages belonged to the same family: 'in ancient times, Japan and Korea were one united country, and our imperial ancestors ruled the Korean kingdom of Silla'. On 27 August, the anthropologist Tsuboi Shōgorō (see chapter 4) published 'Doki no Nikkan renraku' (The Links Between Japan and Korea seen in Earthenware), stated that 'many Koreans migrated to Japan' where they made pottery, and noted the similarities in archaeological sites. On 29 August, Nori Toshio in 'Bijitsushijō no Nikkan' (Japan and Korea in the History of Art) mentioned the racial similarities and the contribution to art made by Korean migrants, and praised 'the great digestive ability' Japan had demonstrated in assimilating imported culture.

In the *Ōsaka asahi shinbun* (Osaka Asahi Newspaper), Inoue Mitsuru's talk of 24 August emphasised the history of the Empress Jingū. On 26 August, the newspaper column 'Tensei jingo' (Vox Populi, Vox Dei) stated 'there are many descendants of Koreans' among the 'Japanese' and, after noting that 'to regard Koreans as inherently inferior is to insult the Japanese', insisted that the Koreans would progress if Japan improved the political system in Korea. The 'Vox Populi, Vox Dei' of 27 August stated:

> All ethnologists agree that the Japanese are a mixture of races from all over the world. The pride of the Japanese nation lies in the fact that it has adopted the strengths of many other races. Although Koreans lack any speciality that the Japanese might adopt, since they share the same myths, have a similar

language and are of the same race as us, they have the potential to become honest Japanese.

The 'Vox Populi, Vox Dei' on 29 August insisted that Korean names 'should be changed into Japanese names'. The editorial of the same day entitled 'Nikkan gappei wa shizen nari' (The Annexation of Korea is a Natural Course of Events) noted that, 'judging from history, anthropology and linguistics, there are no doubts' a close relationship existed between Japan and Korea. It also claimed that Kyūshū historically had deeper ties to Korea than to the 'main island' (*hondo*) of Japan and that, but for the Empress Jingū, it would have become Korean territory. On 31 August, the ex-Prime Minister mentioned in chapter 5, Ōkuma Shigenobu, published a talk that argued that assimilation would be easy because 'Japanese' and Koreans were 'of the same race', and Japan had a history of successfully assimilating immigrants.

Furthermore, the same newspaper issued special enlarged editions on Korea from 29 August to 4 September. On 29 August, 'Hogomae no Chōsen' (Korea Before the Annexation) stated that ancient Japanese such as Susano-O, the Emperor Nintoku, and the Empress Jingū had tried to colonise Korea. In the edition of 31 August, Ōkuma in 'Seikanron no Tamamono (ge)' (The Result of the 'Conquer Korea' Line, Part 2) argued that assimilation would be easy, repeating what he had said in his talk published in the same paper on the same day. In the editions from 1 September to 4 September, the leading Sinologist, Naitō Konan (1866–1934), published a serial entitled 'Chōsen no shōrai' (The Future of Korea), where he noted that, according to the *Shinsen shōjiroku*, Korean immigrants in Japan were treated as aristocrats, and stated 'if Koreans in the future are also successfully assimilated, about 10 million Koreans will mix with the 50 million Japanese, and will gradually improve under the benevolent influence of the Japanese'. According to Naitō, Korea was 'a country that still maintains the state of affairs seen in China and Japan 600 or 700 years, if not 1,500 or 1,600 years, ago'.[2]

The *Tōkyō nichinichi shinbun* (Tokyo Nichinichi Newspaper) of 27 August published a talk, 'Ishuzoku dōka senrei' (A Precedent for the Assimilation of Alien Races) by the historian Kita Sadakichi, who will be examined in the next chapter. This praised 'the Tenson race's skilful assimilation of and fusion with many other races', referring to the immigrants who came to Japan and 'the Hayato and

Emishi', and mentioned 'the belief of ethnologists that the Japanese are a mixed-breed'. On 30 August, another historian, Yoshida Tōgo (see chapter 5), in 'Chirijō no hantō to hontō' (The Peninsula and the Main Islands [Korea and Japan] from the Point of View of Geography) stated that Japan and Korea were 'completely the same race'. The same day, Ōkuma Shigenobu, in 'Kuma-haku no heigō kan' (My View of the Annexation), also emphasised that the Japanese and Koreans were the same race. On 31 August, the legal scholar, Tomizu Hirondo in 'Dōkashugi o tore' (Adopt a Policy of Assimilation!) argued that assimilation would be easy because the Japanese and Koreans were of the same race and shared a related language. On the same day, the historian Kume Kunitake (see chapter 5), in 'Gappei ni arazu fukko nari' (This is not an Annexation but a Restoration), claimed that the annexation was simply a return to the past state of affairs when the two used to be one country, stressing the existence of the 'Japanese Government in Korea known as Mimana' (a Japanese colony in Korea that was mentioned in *Nihon shoki* and which is said to have existed from about 400 to 600AD, although many doubt it ever existed in reality). The editorial on 1 September, 'Chōsenjin no kyōiku' (The Education of Koreans), stated that very large numbers of 'naturalised Koreans' and 'immigrants from the Asian Continent' resided in the ancient archipelago and that 'those alien peoples were all moulded into Japanese in a great national smelting furnace'. It encouraged the use of this 'national assimilative ability inherited from our ancestors' in the case of Korea.

In 'Chōsenjin o kangei seyo' (Welcome the Koreans) in the *Yomiuri shinbun* (Yomiuri Newspaper) on 25 August, Ōkuma noted that 'those who introduced civilisation to Japan in the ancient past were Koreans', and insisted on welcoming 'the new Japanese, the Koreans'. On 26 and 27 August, Kanazawa in 'Chōsen kyōiku konpon mondai' (The Basic Issue in the Education of Koreans) wrote that the two languages were affiliated. On 27 August, Ogino Yoshiyuki in 'Kankoku kikajin no rekishi' (The History of Naturalised Koreans) stressed the ancient ideal of 'universal brotherhood under the Emperor' (*isshi dōjin*), referred to the Korean roots of the Empress Jingū, Sakanoue-no-Tamuramaro, and the imperial consort of the Emperor Kanmu, and stated that 'the Japanese have Korean blood...and also have Chinese blood in their veins'. On 21 August, the historian, Uchida Ginzō (1872–1919) in 'Sakoku to wa nanzoya' (What was the Closed Country?) argued that large numbers of Koreans and Chinese had migrated to Japan.

On 31 August, the legal scholar, Yamada Saburō in 'Chōsen no keihatsu dōka' (The Enlightenment and Assimilation of Korea) wrote that the large numbers of immigrants had all become 'loyal subjects of his Majesty' and that 'the Japanese nation gradually came to include the blood of naturalised peoples', arguing that the experience of 'assimilating many immigrants' in the ancient past should be put to use in the annexation.

In 'Gengogakujō no Nikkan dōkei' (The Affiliation of the Japanese and Korean Languages from the Viewpoint of Philology) in the *Tōkyō mainichi shinbun* (Tokyo Mainichi Newspaper) of 25 August, Kindaichi Kyōsuke (1882–1971), a linguist who will be discussed in chapter 10, argued in favour of the theory of the affiliation of the Korean and Japanese languages, saying that 'anthropologists all agree with the academic theory that the earliest ancestors of the Japanese came from Korea', and concluded that the annexation was a restoration. On 26 August, Tsuboi in 'Nippon jinshu no seiritsu to Chōsenjin' (The Formation of the Japanese Race and the Koreans) said the 'Japanese' were a mixture of the *Ainu*, Malay and continental peoples and that, of these three, the *Ainu* and the Malays (the indigenous Taiwanese) had already been incorporated by the empire. He welcomed the fact that, with the annexation of Korea, the last group of continental peoples had also been incorporated, saying all three 'have now been put into a large cauldron'. On 27 and 28 August, Kanazawa argued in favour of the theory of the affiliation of the two languages in 'Gappeigo wa ika ni Nippongo o fukyū seshimu beki ka' (How Should Japanese Be Propagated After the Annexation?).

In an anonymous article, 'Chōsen no kako' (Korea's Past) published on 25 and 26 August, the newspaper *Yorozu chōhō* (Viewing the World) praised the invasion of Korea by 'the Empress Jingū who inherited the blood of Ame-no-hiboko', a prince of Silla. On 1 September, an editorial 'Dōjinshu no wagō' (Joining the Same Race Together) claimed that, in ancient times, Koreans frequently migrated to the archipelago, and welcomed the fact that 'today the same race has become a single nation through annexation', saying 'the fact that the Yamato nation of today mostly consists of Koreans is beyond doubt'.

At this time, the only newspaper article that did not adopt the theory that the 'Japanese' and Koreans shared a common ancestor was one authored by the anthropologist Torii Ryūzō (see chapter 4) and published on 4 September in the *Yomiuri shinbun*, 'Jinshugakujō

Chōsenjin wa nanihodo made kenkyū seraretaru ka' (To What Degree Have the Koreans Been Racially Studied?). Here Torii noted that it had not yet been proved that the Japanese and Koreans were the same race, and warned that 'although it may be a result of the annexation of Korea, first class scholars still should not be so careless as to state publicly that it has been shown that the two races are the same'. Since Torii was a student of Tsuboi, and was at the time only a lecturer, this was a brave statement to make. However, as will be shown in chapter 9, by the time of the March First Independence Movement a decade later, Torii emerged as the most important anthropological theorist of the view that the 'Japanese' and Koreans shared a common ancestor.

This summarises the entire discourse on nationality in the newspapers of this period, with the exception of a few editorials and articles that mentioned in passing that the 'Japanese' and Koreans were the same race.[3] In this discourse, there is no mention whatsoever of the theory that the Imperial Family arrived from abroad, although this idea was originally part of both the theory that the 'Japanese' and Koreans shared a common ancestor and the mixed nation theory. It can be assumed that the idea was regarded as taboo. At the same time, however, there were also almost no cases where it was argued that the 'Japanese' should invade the peninsula while maintaining purity of blood.

Of course, these articles praised the annexation as a restoration and argued that assimilation was going to be an easy task, but at the same time they clearly also stressed the existence of foreign immigrants and the mixed origin of the Japanese nation. It is noteworthy that the metaphor of a melting pot was often used, with phrases such as a 'large cauldron' or 'smelting furnace'. Since these expressions appeared so often, regular readers of Japanese newspapers at the time must have come across this line of argument at least once or twice.

The newspapers discussed above featured the leading figures of anthropology, history and linguistics in Japan. It is clear that almost all, in welcoming the annexation, adopted either the mixed nation theory or the theory that the 'Japanese' and Koreans shared a common ancestor, or both. It is symbolic that, in an extra edition of *Rekishi chiri* (History and Geography) entitled 'Chōsen gō' (The Korean Edition) issued in November, Hoshino Hisashi, Kume Kunitake, Yoshida Tōgo, Kita Sadakichi, Tsuboi Shōgorō and Kanazawa Shōzaburō all appeared, and all welcomed the annexation.

The Line of Argument in the Leading Magazines

Representative magazines of opinion of that era were the *Taiyō* (Sun), *Nippon oyobi Nipponjin* (Japan and the Japanese), and *Chūō kōron* (Public Opinion). From September to October 1910, *Nippon oyobi Nipponjin* published seven articles, and *Chūō Kōron* five, on the annexation of Korea, in addition to a number of short talks. Most of the articles, however, discussed Japanese policies or welcomed the annexation, and few are important from the viewpoint of the theory of the Japanese nation. However, Sasagawa Shigerō's 'Kankoku heigō to ko Izumo' (The Annexation of Korea and the Ancient Izumo) in the 15 September edition of *Nippon oyobi Nipponjin* stated that the Izumo were a Korean clan and argued that 'the Izumo were the origin of the union of Japan and Korea'. In the same edition, Kita Sadakichi's talk 'Heigōgo no kyōikukan' (Views of Education After the Annexation) emphasised that Japanese and Koreans were the same race. In addition, several other articles noted the similarities of race and language. Finally, Shiratori Kurakichi (1865–1942), an authority on Oriental history, wrote an article on the history of ancient Japan-Korea relations for the October edition of *Chūō kōron* which will be examined in chapter 14.

At this time, *Taiyō*, the most widely read monthly magazine among intellectuals, published almost 20 articles on Korea from September to December, and in November published an extra edition, *Nippon minzoku no bōchō* (The Expansion of the Japanese Nation). In these articles, the mixed nation theory was developed even more positively than in the newspapers, in the context of a glorification of the annexation. This may have been a reflection of the intentions of the then editor-in-chief, the Christian and political scientist Ukita Kazutami (see chapter 3). Apart from the talk of Unno Kōtoku, an eugenicist who will be examined in chapter 13, the line of argument can be roughly divided into three categories.

On the basis of the racial closeness with Korea and the other areas into which Japan was moving, the first argued that both rule and assimilation were going to be easy.

Ukita Kazutami claimed that assimilation would be easy: 'the Japanese and Koreans were originally a single nation, of the same race and with the same culture'. Ōkuma Shigenobu also said that it would be easy to govern Korea because Koreans were the same race and that 'many European countries expanded into countries with different races, different nations and different religions, unlike Japan which expanded into areas occupied by the same race and the same nation'. As will be mentioned in the conclusion, 'expansion to incorporate the same race' was a special characteristic of the Japanese rule of alien nations, and this reference demonstrates that people were aware of this at the time. For Ōkuma, the more the Japanese nation was a mixed breed, the more areas Japan was qualified to move into, absorb and assimilate.[4]

The second category insisted that the Japanese nation was superior because it was a mixed nation with great powers of assimilation.

Takegoshi Yosaburō (see chapter 5), for example, repeating what Tsuboi had argued in the past, said that 'the Japanese are a mixed-breed of southern and northern peoples, and are therefore capable of adapting to life in regions both in the south and the north'. Tomizu Hirondo praised the adaptability produced in the Japanese by the mixture of southern and northern races, writing that 'it must be said that, from this point of view, the Japanese are far better qualified as colonists than Westerners'. The one-time Vice-Minister of Education and later President of Kyoto Imperial University Sawayanagi Masatarō (1865–1927) recorded his pride in the fact that the Japanese people had 'assimilated' culture from Korea, China, India and Europe, and criticised 'xenophobic conservative thought', claiming that 'the Japanese people have always had the ability to take in the strengths of others and assimilate them. This is a special strength unique to the Japanese, and is one that the people of the Western Powers lack'. Here, the mixed nation theory was used to overcome the racial inferiority complex felt towards the Western Powers.[5]

However, Takegoshi argued for a southward advance, since the homeland of the Japanese nation lay in the south, while Tomizu criticised this view, noting that since the Japanese nation was a mixture between the north and the south, there was no reason for it to limit itself to a southward advance. Takegoshi welcomed the annexation of Korea, but emphasised that the Chinese Han nation was 'a completely alien race', and reiterated his pet opinion on the importance of a southward advance, saying that 'the advance into the continent and the Korean peninsula has gone far enough'.[6] Here, as with Ōkuma, the direction of Japan's advance was determined by a belief in the importance of 'moving towards the same race and same nation'.

Furthermore, Ukita argued against the claim that the Russo-Japanese War and the annexation of Korea were the products of a selfish Japanese expansionist policy. 'The Japanese are a mixture of the *Ainu* who are a Caucasian people, a continental race which is Mongolian, and the Malay race, and some people in the Kyūshū district are said to have Negroid blood in their veins'. For this reason, the victory of the Japanese nation was not an honour won by any specific nation, but rather a 'shining example of all men who have any patriotic sentiment'.[7] This is a logic that argued that the Japanese nation was a representative of the world, since it was a mixture of all races. In addition, Ōkuma and Ukita advocated the theory of a fusion of Eastern and Western civilisations in which Japan would have the role of synthesising both cultures.

The third category converted the acceptance of immigration and mixture into a theory of moving out into the world. Ebina Danjō wrote as follows:

> The Japanese are not a people who originally emerged in the Japanese islands of today, but migrated there from far abroad. The Japanese are therefore not a people dominated by the so-called native spirit...[The Japanese nation consists of a mixture between] the Malay, Korean and the so-called Tenson races, together with the *Ainu* and Chinese races. It is difficult to break the nation down into separate parts, but representatives of four or five races risked their lives travelling across the ocean from a land far away. The situation at that time was perhaps like that of the USA today.

After describing the Japanese nation in these terms, Ebina went on to say: 'this is the time for us to spread further into the world, using the spiritual strength that...our ancestors...showed in coming to the islands of Japan'. While claiming that 'Korea is actually the touchstone for Japan: if successful in assimilating Korea, it is clear that the Japanese will be able to develop on a global scale', he also argued for Christian enlightenment. According to Ebina, although hostility towards foreigners 'was necessary...in the Japan of the past...to maintain the independence of the state', 'the future Japan is no longer the old isolated Japan, but a new global Japan', and accordingly Japan had to reject forever xenophobia and the insular spirit (*shimaguni konjō*). He described An Chung Ken (1879–1910), the Korean who assassinated Itō Hirobumi (1841–1909) – Japan's first Prime Minster, and the first Resident-General of Korea when it was made a Japanese protectorate in 1905 – as a 'patriot', saying 'in Japan recently too, just before the Meiji Restoration, those like him who killed foreigners were regarded as patriots'.[8]

A similar view can be seen in the talk given by the novelist, Shimamura Hōgetsu (1871–1918). According to Shimamura, it used to be characteristic of Japanese culture to be 'weak, small and decadent rather than progressive, insular rather than global', but 'something stronger is wanted'. He welcomed colonisation and expansion because he believed that there would be no cultural development if the Japanese remained locked up in their islands, saying 'I remember that the Viscount Ōkuma once said that the forte of the Japanese lay in the collection of the strengths of several races from different areas, just as the blood of our ancestors was collected from diverse areas such as the South Seas and Mongolia'.[9]

As can be seen from this, the position of the press towards the mixed nation theory had changed by this period. It was no longer viewed as something that people were reluctant to accept, but had been actively developed into a positive view of the 'Japanese' in which the 'Japanese' themselves could take pride.

The Conversion of the National Polity Theorists

In an environment where the mixed nation theory which praised the annexation reigned supreme, a small minority opinion existed that was concerned that the purity of the 'Japanese' might be threatened by the incorporation of alien nations into the empire. The talk by Fujioka Katsuji, a linguist, in the September edition of *Shin kōron* (New Public Opinion), 'Chōsen gappei ni tsuite okoru kokugokai no daikiken' (The Great Danger to the Japanese Language Posed by the Annexation of Korea), is an example of this minority opinion. Fujioka insisted that, as a result of the annexation, the Japanese language faced a crisis in that it might become mixed with the Korean language.

However this line of argument was seen in only a very few cases. A search of the leading newspapers and magazines of the time shows that not a single national polity theorist, including writers such as Hozumi, Katō and Inoue, seems to have been asked to write for the press. The pure blood theorists were ignored completely at the time of annexation.

One event that symbolised this turnround in the current of thought was the conversion of Inoue Tetsujirō to the mixed nation theory. In October 1910, he published an article in *Tōa no hikari* (The Light of East Asia) in which he wrote:[10]

> Koreans are not very different from the Japanese. In a wide sense, they are the same race as the Japanese. However, they not completely the same race, since quite a number of Japanese came from the South Seas, while some – fewer than those of South Seas origin – intermarried with the *Ainu*. Having said that, however, the vast majority of Japanese came from the continent via the Korean peninsula.

At the time of the debate over mixed residence in the interior, Inoue had regarded the Koreans as an alien nation. Now, however, he claimed that 'Japanese and Koreans can be called relatives'. Regarding immigrants, too, he said that 'very large numbers of Koreans must have settled in Japan', and they established a great power as the 'Izumo nation'. He also claimed that 'the Korean peninsula served as the conduit for the introduction of civilisation'.

Inoue had once argued that the Japanese nation came from the south, and opposed mixed residence, saying that the law of racial competition seen in the South Seas could be applied to Japan. In this talk, however, he wrote that Japan, 'unlike the natives of the South Seas, could not remain idle, but developed herself, and ranks today among the greatest Powers in the world'. Furthermore, although he supported the mixed nation theory, Inoue differed from Takegoshi who believed that the Japanese came from the south and so argued for a southward advance. Instead, Inoue now insisted that the majority of the Japanese nation came from the continent. He thus converted to the theory that the Japanese were from the north (the Asian continent), and wrote as follows:

> Until the present, Japan has consisted of nothing but islands: not only Honshū, but also Shikoku, Kyūshū, Hokkaido, Sakhalin Island, Ryūkyū and Taiwan are all islands. Japan used to consist of a collection of many islands. However, now that the Korean peninsula has been annexed, things have changed completely. The Korean peninsula, although it looks like an island, projecting towards the north edge of Kyūshū, is still part of the continent....Once Korea is included as part of Japan, we can travel directly to Europe from Korea by train.

In the past, Inoue would perhaps have said 'if Korea is included as part of Japan, Europeans will travel by train to invade Japan'. There is no longer any trace in Inoue's argument of the idea that the 'Japanese', as mere 'women and children', had to confine themselves within the archipelago because of a fear of the West, nor any sense of crisis that Japan was surrounded by 'enemies on all sides'. Not only had such a sense of crisis disappeared, Inoue actually said that, through this annexation, 'the Japanese have accomplished a new development that will enable them in future to move out on to the great stage of the continent and thus the world. There is no doubt that this will evoke a great positive spirit in our nation'.

This perception was not limited to Inoue. Even before his critique, editorials in the *Yorozu chōhō* and *Tōkyō asahi shinbun* expressed the view that 'Japan has changed from a mere island empire into a continental empire through the annexation of Korea', and that 'Japan has become a great continental country through this annexation'. The Christian, agricultural economist, American specialist and, from 1920 to 1926, Assistant Director General of the League of Nations, Nitobe Inazō (1862–1933) also argued in favour of using the annexation to destroy Japan's insular spirit.[11] Inoue's opinion was merely a reflection of this general trend.

The Great Japanese Empire emerged from its status as an island-country. At the same time, 'the great, positive spirit' of jumping up on to 'the great stage' of the world filled people's minds. There, the 'insular spirit' – that is, the belief in maintaining an empire that consisted only of the Japanese nation – came to be regarded as something to be destroyed. Annexation was the turning point.

The door was now fully open. After this, the discourse in the Great Japanese Empire ran along the lines laid down during this period until Japanese expansionism reached its limits and imploded.

Part Two
The Thought of 'Empire'

7 History and the 'Abolition of Discrimination'

Later assessments of the historian Kita Sadakichi (1871–1939) have split into two completely different camps.[1] One has praised him highly as one of the rare few who emphasised the existence of victims of discrimination and who argued for the idea that the Japanese nation was a mixed one. The other camp has criticised him as one of the leading figures who used history to justify colonial rule.

As has already been shown, however, the mixed nation theory itself was not unique or special to Kita. Nevertheless, Kita is unusual in that he made the theme his life work.

To state my own conclusion first, Kita was the most important ideologue of the mixed nation theory in the Great Japanese Empire. It can even be said that the discourse of the Governor-General of Korea during the period of its Japanisation policy (this will be discussed in chapter 16) was based on Kita's studies. At the same time, however, Kita tried to use the mixed nation theory to fight racial discrimination. It is in him that the emotions and limitations of a conscientious mixed nation theorist in imperial Japan can most clearly be seen.

Sympathy for the Victims of Discrimination

The third son of a tenant farmer, Kita was born in 1871 in a farming village of the Tokushima Prefecture in Shikoku. A teacher at the local school who noticed Kita's talent persuaded his parents to let their son enter primary school. Good grades permitted him to proceed to junior high school, where, however, he was ridiculed as a 'peasant' and 'flat nose' by fellow students from *samurai* families. Kita recollected that experience as an 'intolerable humiliation' caused by his birth and the physical features over which he had no control. Many view this experience to be related to his later interest in the issue of discrimination.

Kita next proceeded to the Tokyo Imperial University, did postgraduate work in Japanese history, and obtained a position in the Ministry of Education, where he was involved in examining (*kentei*) primary and junior high school textbooks edited by private publishing firms. Corruption was ever present as publishers attempted to bribe the examiners and, although Kita remained an individual of strict morals, a scandal occurred in 1902 at his place of work. The government found a convenient excuse in this incident to enforce the use of state textbooks. In 1903, the use of state textbooks was enforced by means of a primary school regulation. Kita devoted himself to editing geography and history textbooks.

In 1910, however, another incident occurred. Known as the 'Southern-Northern Courts Issue' (*Nanbokuchō seijun mondai*), this controversy is one of the indicators that marked the rise of a chauvinistic nationalism in modern Japan. In the fourteenth century, two courts – the Southern and Northern Courts – both claimed legitimacy and the throne. Private history textbooks had regarded only the Southern Court as legitimate. In editing the state textbook, Kita was in two minds about how to deal with the conflict within an Imperial Family that was supposed to consist of an unbroken line of Emperors, and eventually described the coexistence of the two regimes as a historical fact. This, however, triggered criticism of Kita in newspapers and a great debate. A later Prime Minister, Inukai Tsuyoshi (1855–1932) made an impeachment address in the Diet and Kita was forced into retirement. This led to a revision of the textbooks, where the Southern Court was described as legitimate, and the names of the Emperors of the Northern Court were deleted.

After his retirement from the Ministry of Education, Kita devoted himself to the study of history while working as a lecturer at Kyoto Imperial University and Tōhoku Imperial University and, in 1919, founded a magazine, *Minzoku to rekishi* (Nation and History). This was also the year when the March First Independence Movement erupted in Korea (see chapter 9), and Kita was most full of energy at this time, publishing one of his representative works, 'Nissen ryōminzoku dōgenron' (The Common Origin of the Japanese and Korean Nations), and many other articles on the Japanese nation in his *Minzoku to rekishi* and other academic periodicals.

From his retirement from the Ministry of Education at the age of 39 to his death in 1939, Kita published a wide range of research on areas including archaeology, ancient history, folklore, religious history and cultural history. These can all be said to have focused on one theme, the 'abolition of discrimination'. Taking his 1921 publication 'Nippon minzoku no seiritsu' (The Formation of the Japanese Nation) as an example which clearly shows the connection between his studies of folklore, the history of the *burakumin* (the Japanese untouchables), and the origin of the Japanese nation, Kita's thought will next be examined.[2] Although his thinking varied slightly from time to time, there were no great changes in his main ideas.

Before turning to Kita's article, general views about the *burakumin* in Japan at the time need to be summarised. The *burakumin* consisted of a group that had formed in the Edo Period from those who were involved in slaughtering animals (mainly domestic animals) and processing skins. Although it is difficult to imagine today, it was a widely accepted idea in Kita's time that the people known as the *burakumin* were an alien race. For example, Yamaji Aizan (chapter 5) stated that 'they are a different race from common Japanese, and are a nomadic tribe and their descendants'. The folklorist Yanagita Kunio (chapter 12) once said 'they are a different race who were probably pastoralists'.[3] At the time, it was impossible to discuss the *burakumin* without mentioning race, and Kita was the historian who was most emphatic in denying the idea that they were an alien race.

In his 'Nippon minzoku no seiritsu', Kita first denied the theory that the sovereign and all his subjects shared the same ancestor. Although 'comprehensible as the product of the closed country period', this position was not suitable for the contemporary situation where a large number of different peoples had been incorporated within the empire. He noted that the theory of a mixed origin was the commonly accepted position in anthropology – 'the Japanese are a multi-national people that was originally constructed from various different tribes' – and regarded the alien peoples mentioned in the Kiki myths as Aborigines. He emphasised that Japan and Korea were once a unified region in which the same people lived, that, even after the two split, there were many records of migration to Japan, and that one-third of the Japanese clans mentioned in the *Shinsen shōjiroku* were of overseas origin. He also noted that the Empress Jingū and the Emperor Kanmu were the descendants of Koreans, and that the records that demonstrated that the Japanese and Koreans shared a common ancestor were destroyed during the reign of the Emperor Kanmu.

Thus far, Kita's ideas could be said to summarise the conclusions of all past writings on the mixed nation theory. Kita's own unique contribution was to unite this with his own views of the Emperor and theories of the *burakumin*.

According to Kita, the aboriginals of Japan, 'just like the aboriginals of Taiwan today', were 'in a terribly pitiful situation, disunited and constantly fighting each other'. It was into this situation that the Tenson nation led by the Imperial Family arrived. However, 'it was not the case that the native people were all killed by these newcomers and the population replaced' – rather, 'it was the sacred mission of the ancestors of the Imperial Household when they descended from Takamagahara to rule the natives peacefully and to make them, too, happy members of the Japanese nation'. Kita stated that the Tenson nation did not discriminate against the aboriginal peoples but actively intermarried with them to form a multi-national Japanese people.

Here we can see a world view different from the Meiji-era theories of a mixed nation, such as that developed by Bälz, who argued that the Japanese nation consisted of a Chōshū type, which was Korean or Chinese in origin, and a Satsuma type, which was Malay in origin, and that the two were still separate, with the former making up the upper class and the latter the lower class. In other words, Japan consisted of a ruling nation and a ruled nation. Japanese theorists such as Kita, however, did not warm to this view. According to Kita, the ruling Tenson nation did not discriminate against other peoples, but assimilated them through intermarriage.

The argument that, unlike the Europeans and Americans, the Japanese nation from ancient times had not discriminated against other nations but rather assimilated them, came to be widely diffused in the context of the theory of the superiority of the Japanese nation and the idealisation of assimilationist policies, especially after the Japanese annexation of Korea. The position that the Japanese nation was superior to Caucasians because it was a mixture and thus blessed with powers of adaptability and assimilation had already emerged. Kita extended this to argue that the Japanese nation was ethically superior to Caucasian nations, which were racist and hence shunned inter-racial marriage, because of the Japanese belief in the principle of *isshi dōjin* (universal brotherhood under the rule of the Emperor).

Kita's folklore and theory of the *burakumin* are developed from here. According to Kita, the ancestors of the *burakumin* were not an alien race but 'social outcasts', although, he admitted, 'naturally, many of these outcasts were originally the descendants of Aborigines, or of migrants to Japan, or of people who were at a disadvantage in surviving in society'. Through what process did these Aborigines and migrants come to be the targets of discrimination?

Of course, Kita could hardly attribute this to the unequal system of the imperial state. According to him, 'generally speaking, once a superior nation begins to live together with another nation that is inferior to it, the intelligent members of the inferior nation will quickly join the superior nation and be assimilated, but those who are not intelligent will fail to do so'. Those among the aboriginal peoples of the archipelago who were not assimilated were deprived of fertile fields and lived in the mountains far from settlements and cultivated land.

Among the Aborigines who fled to mountainous regions, 'those who later came to be known as wood men and mountain witches are the poor souls who remained to the last in the mountains'. According to Kita, as a result of their poverty, they stole from those who cultivated the land for a living, were feared because they kidnapped women, and in folk stories were described as demons or goblins. Some of these 'mountain people', however, served the Imperial Family with their special expertise: the Yasedōshi, who carried the sacred palanquin in imperial funerals, the Kuzu, who sang and danced in the Imperial Court, and the carpenters of Hida, who were said to be 'different from others in their language and appearance'. Kita stated that 'the aboriginals of Taiwan are a sort of mountain people, and hunt the heads of people who cultivate the land...they can be said to be a sort of demon'.

Assimilation into the Tenson nation meant to take up agriculture and become farmers. According to Kita, from ancient times in Japan, a farmer was the synonym for a subject. Some of the hunter-gatherer Aborigines 'persisted in their traditional life-style to the last and did not take up agriculture: these have long been discriminated against as mountain people. Moreover, among those who took up agriculture and mixed with village people, those who worked as butchers were called *Etori* or slaughterers, and came to be shunned'. Over time, *Etori* came to be widely used as the term for the victims of discrimination, and 'finally *Etori* or *Eta* became a broad term that encompassed beggars, cleaners, certain types of artisans and vagabonds' ('Eta' is still a highly offensive and discriminatory term for the *burakumin*).

The targets of discrimination took up various jobs that were normally despised, working as potters, makers of bamboo-ware, certain performers, tramps and wandering priests. Once a group of outcasts was formed, other outcasts and tramps who were not aboriginal peoples entered it. On the other hand, 'the descendants of the original Aborigines who became farmers all quickly became normal subjects'. Therefore, Kita explained, the racial make-up of the *burakumin* was not different to that of the general population.

Thus the cause of discrimination was not birth or race, but a failure to assimilate into the majority. This logic came to be applied to the alien peoples within the empire.

Today the *Ainu* live in Hokkaido. According to Kita, however, many *Ainu*, the indigenous people of the archipelago, used to live on the Japanese mainland, the Emishi in the Kiki myths were the *Ainu*, many place names, especially in the northeastern Tōhoku region of Japan, are derived from the *Ainu* language, and finally both those who started the Zenkunen (1051–62) and Gosannen (1083–87) battles against the imperial government and those who established the city of Hiraizumi in the northeastern Tōhoku region of Japan were the *Ainu*. Most were assimilated into the Japanese nation and became 'happy members' but 'those who remained deep in the mountains and who did not take up agriculture remained as mountain people, and those who lived in remote, secluded areas such as Hokkaido failed to gain the opportunity to join the Japanese nation and still remain as the *Ainu*'. In other words, those discriminated against as *Ainu* were not those with *Ainu* blood but those who failed to assimilate.

According to Kita, the *Ainu* were originally gifted in craftsmanship and martial valour. 'The chivalrous (*bushidō*) spirit and fine hand-craftsmanship of the Japanese owes much to the assimilation of the *Ainu*'. At the same time, today's *Ainu* are no longer 100 per cent full-blooded *Ainu*, but have Japanese blood in their veins. Therefore, 'the only difference between the two [the *Ainu* and the majority of the Japanese nation] is the degree to which their blood has been mixed', and 'many *Ainu*, once taught our customs and language, would be difficult to distinguish from the rest of the Japanese nation'.

Here, the racial difference between the *Ainu* and other members of the Japanese nation was reduced to one of 'degree'. It was therefore possible to argue that any differences would disappear if the *Ainu* adopted the same language and customs, and if intermarriage were promoted to fine-tune the 'degree' of difference.

Kita also stated that 'the descent from Takamagahara...in my opinion refers to the arrival through Korea'. Although he avoids saying so explicitly, this is the theory that the Imperial Family came from Korea. Kita did not delve any deeper into this issue, but continued that 'the majority of our ancestors came from Korea, or from further away [in the continent] through Korea'. The Koreans were therefore the same as the 'Japanese', and 'if a difference between the two were to be drawn, it would be in the different degrees of allocation of the various racial components. Such small differences can be seen in different regions of Japan'.

Here, too, the difference between the Japanese nation and Koreans was reduced to one of 'degree'. The argument that the difference between 'Japanese' and Koreans was smaller than that between individuals from different regions in Japan was propagated, as will be demonstrated in chapter 16, by the Government-General of Korea when it promoted a Japanisation policy. Furthermore, Kita argued that the myth of the Izumo cession of territory was an example of a peaceful assimilation by the ruling nation, and used this historical interpretation to criticise the March First Independence Movement in Korea. The Izumo region in Japan's southwest was the part of the archipelago closest to the Korean peninsula. As discussed in chapters 5 and 6, the Izumo people of the Kiki myths were frequently viewed as being a Korean tribe. The episode described in the Kiki myths where the Head of the Izumo voluntarily and peacefully ceded his territory to the Imperial Family was repeatedly cited as a precedent for an annexation of Korea based on peaceful agreement rather than military aggression. Kita viewed the independence movement in Korea, a movement that had erupted because of Japanese discrimination, as an expression of the anger of the Izumo God. He insisted that the annexation of Korea was a restoration and that an 'assimilation and fusion' should be implemented.

Assimilation as the Abolition of Discrimination

By thus explaining through a theory of nations and folklore the process by which a distinct group of victims of discrimination was formed, Kita clarified the path that the alien peoples inside the Great Japanese Empire needed to follow: to assimilate themselves into the Japanese nation as soon as possible, and to avoid following the example of those who had not done so and become the targets of discrimination.

Kita's ideal, however, was to implement 'assimilation' not only in the areas of language, customs and lineage, but also in those of status, treatment and rights. For Kita, these were inseparable, and it is clear that he had no intention of forcefully implementing any assimilation that did not involve equality. In this sense, his argument for assimilation was a conscientious one.

Kita is still highly esteemed today for having insisted that the *burakumin* were not an alien people and should be assimilated into Japanese society. From the contemporary viewpoint, however, his application of that theory to Korea and Taiwan seems incredibly strange. However, even the Zenkoku Suiheisha (The All-Japan Levellers Society) – a prewar movement that aimed to liberate the *burakumin* – had some members who accepted the theory that the *burakumin* were an alien people, called themselves the 'Eta nation', and advocated national self-determination for this people.[4] This attitude took the opposite tack to Kita's 'fusion and assimilation' line, but is the same in that it too searched for a common solution to the issues of Taiwan, Korea and the *burakumin*.

Even in Japan today, it is not unusual to mention in one breath the discrimination against the *burakumin*, the *Ainu*, and the *zainichi* Koreans as a problem caused by the Emperor System and the closed nature of Japanese society. However, if someone were to try to apply theories of self-determination, autonomous regions, or multiculturalism to the *burakumin*, it would be regarded as a mistake. It is now generally accepted that the issue of the *burakumin* is not one of ethnicity. That was not the case in Kita's times. Korea and Taiwan were not viewed as foreign countries but as a part of the Great Japanese Empire, and the *burakumin* were widely regarded as an alien nation.

Kita's theory of assimilation was based on good intentions and sympathy for the victims of discrimination. In 'Nippon minzoku no seiritsu' (The Formation of the Japanese Nation), where he described the Aborigines of Taiwan as mountain-dwelling demons, he does not forget to add the following. 'For them, stealing from settled areas, or taking the heads of those who worked the land, was a form of revenge against the oppression waged against them and, from their point of view, was perhaps seen as an exercise of their right of self-preservation'.

In the prospectus of the first issue of *Minzoku to rekishi* (Nation and History), Kita emphasised the importance, as a historian, of 'focussing on the standpoint of the losers and outcasts of history'. However, he also wrote, on the one hand, that the *burakumin* 'should be assimilated into the Japanese nation and treated completely equally', and, on the other hand, that 'my mission is to help the various nations that have recently joined the empire to assimilate completely into the Japanese nation and become loyal members of the nation' (Kita Sadakichi 1919a: 6–7).

Kita enjoyed interchanges with both the *burakumin* and the *Ainu*, and had a clear understanding of the severity of discrimination in Japanese society. He once tried to help a group of *Ainu* who had been swindled by a showman, and gave lectures in an active fight against discrimination. Although he personally worshipped the Emperor, he valued highly the contents of *Tokushu buraku issennenshi* (A Thousand Years of the *Burakumin*) by Takahashi Sadaki (see chapter 9), a socialist, even after it was banned from circulation, and despite differences in beliefs. Like Tsuboi Shōgorō, one of the few scholars who actively worked for the *Ainu* in the mid-Meiji Period, few intellectuals of the time directly tackled the problem of the *burakumin* to the extent that Kita did. The more his good intentions were emphasised, however, the more he advocated the assimilation of Koreans, Taiwanese and the *Ainu*.

Kita's criticism was therefore aimed against both the majority which was responsible for discrimination and the minority which was attempting to secede from the majority. At the time of the Japanese annexation of Korea, a marriage of convenience took place between a prince of the Korean Iy Dynasty and a princess of the Japanese Imperial Family. In an article published in 1919 to celebrate the marriage, Kita wrote that, in ancient times, Japan and Korea used to be one country, and continued as follows:[5]

> After more than 1,200 years, a tendency has emerged in Korea to shun Japan as a foreign country. In Japan, too, Korea is seen as a completely different country. Because of the influence of the closed-country policy of the Tokugawa Period and as a result of a boom in classical studies, there has been a rise in xenophobia, with some in Japan coming to believe that we Japanese are the only descendants of the gods,

and viewing foreigners without reason as vile and ignoble. Out of patriotism, many Japanese regard the theory that the ancestors of the Japanese nation came from abroad as a heretical doctrine, and insist that Takamagahara, the homeland of the Tenson nation, is located in the Yamato region [of the central archipelago]...Some are still enmeshed in the old ways of thinking. In Korea, I have often heard, there are even those who plot to become independent from Japan, with no regard to the current situation where many Koreans have been made happy by the annexation. In Japan, on the other hand, it is rumoured that there are some who despise the Koreans and are trying to hinder the mutual assimilation between Japan and Korea, or who, from a misconceived feeling of patriotism, harbour ill feelings about the marriage, even though they say nothing in public.

As Kita notes, it can be easily imagined that there was some resistance to this marriage of convenience which would result in the influx of Korean blood into the Imperial Family. From Kita's point of view, the Korean independence movement was as bad as Japanese discrimination and xenophobia, and he saw it as a Korean version of the pure blood theory. He mentioned the origin of the Empress Jingū and the Emperor Kanmu, and ended the article: 'here, I provide materials to help people with a misconceived sense of patriotism to realise their mistakes and celebrate the glorious future of a united Japan and Korea against the tide of national self-determination'.

'The People of the Oceans on All Sides are All Brothers'

Kita's ideas were not 'esoteric' ones limited to intellectuals. He actively delivered lectures to the public and, in 1928, wrote the first volume in a project entitled *Nippon jidō bunko* (Books For Japanese Children). Kita's work dealt with ancient Japanese history. The author of the second volume was Hiraizumi Kiyoshi, known as a representative theorist of the Imperial View of History.

This reference book for children noted that the Japanese nation was multi-national and that the Emperor Kanmu and Empress Jingū were the descendants of migrants, and argued that many nations had been assimilated into, and become loyal subjects of, the nation under the Emperor. This line of argument reflected Kita's usual position. He emphasised the fact that there was no reason to discriminate against the *burakumin*, and stressed that the *Ainu* revolts such as the eleventh century Zenkunen and Gosannen battles were caused by discrimination.[6]

At the same time, throughout this reference work, Kita advised children to respect the Imperial Family and to be conscious of themselves as his majesty's subjects. In the context of current views of the Emperor System, this may seem to be a contradiction, but Kita understood imperial subjects to include minorities, and believed that the Emperor was sent from the Heavens to create a peaceful and non-discriminatory state. In terms of Kita's sense of values, the more aware children became of their status as his majesty's subjects, the less they would discriminate against other imperial subjects, such as the *burakumin*, the *Ainu* and Koreans. Discrimination was due to 'wrong-minded people' who lacked this awareness. Kita's basic understanding was that the Imperial Family and the Japanese nation differed from foreign states based on conquest and that throughout history they had treated other nations equally and assimilated them into the nation.

It would be meaningless to ask Kita whether this argument was a means to fight discrimination, or merely an excuse to persuade minorities to become loyal imperial subjects. In his own mind, the abolition of discrimination meant equality within the empire and was a synonym for becoming loyal imperial subjects.

To reform the empire – that is, to change the regime of the Great Japanese Empire and abolish rule by the Emperor – was beyond Kita's powers of imagination. In this children's book, he wrote that the medieval Heian Period (794–1192), which produced many victims of discrimination, was a lawless and politically chaotic state, but also noted that 'we can live in safety today thanks to well-organised laws and the never-ending protection of the police'.[7] For Kita, it was anarchy that undermined unity and that was the root of collapses in social status and poverty producing the social outcasts who became the victims of discrimination. Though he says little about revolution, he perhaps thought that revolution was inseparable from chaos and should be avoided, and that social problems should be solved in a unified state under the rule of the Emperor.

Kita published a book *Kankoku no heigō to kokushi* (The Annexation of Korea and the History of Japan) at the same time to celebrate the annexation of Korea. In it, he stated that the Korea of the Iy Dynasty before the annexation was in a state of anarchy, with people driven into apathy when robbed of their wealth and exploited by the bureaucracy. The situation was as bad as during the Heian Period in Japan. Claiming that the anarchy of the Heian Period was solved by the twelfth century Kamakura Bakufu (1185–1333), he argued that annexation meant the salvation of the Korean people. He mentioned the Aborigines of the archipelago, the Korean blood in the Imperial Family, and the northeastern *Ainu*, and described the annexation as a restoration, like a younger brother of a branch family who had experienced hardships returning to his warm, comfortable head family.[8]

For Kita, the Heian Period was a time when xenophobia raised its head and many works on the theory of the common origin of the 'Japanese' and Koreans were destroyed, when the rebellion of the northeastern *Ainu* broke out in response to discrimination, and when many people became outcasts and victims of discrimination as a result of poverty and anarchy. From his historical point of view, the archipelago before the descent of the Tenson nation, the Japan of the Heian Period, and the Korea of the Iy Dynasty were all in a state of anarchy, and in each case the Emperor and his army restored order, with mutual antagonism and discrimination replaced by unification and assimilation. After seeing villages in Korea stricken by poverty, Kita wrote in a travelogue of his Korean trip in 1920, 'they remind me of people who fell into poverty and became victims of discrimination because of the tyrannical government of the Heian Period'.[9] He feared that the people of Korea might repeat the failure of the *burakumin* if they did not grasp the opportunity offered by the restoration of order that the annexation had made possible and assimilate into the Japanese nation.

What did Korean people think of Kita's theory of assimilation? In his Korean travelogue, it is recorded that he gave a lecture in Korea entitled 'the assimilation (*dōka*) of the nation'. This lecture explained that 'those who are quickly assimilated will become upstanding subjects, while those who are not will become outcasts and eventually form a caste that will be discriminated against'. Afterwards, when a Korean graduate from Kyoto Imperial University whom he had taught learned about the lecture, he told Kita, '*dōka* (assimilation) has the nuance that something small is absorbed into something bigger. The content is all right as it is, but I would have preferred a different title, like "*yūgō*" (melting together) or "*yūwa*" (fusion)'. This remark is very mild, perhaps because he was talking to an old teacher, but, for Koreans, although

Kita's criticism of discrimination was possibly valued, any one-sided annexation was, it must be thought, totally unacceptable.

Kita's idea of 'assimilation and fusion' was clearly one-sided. The metaphor he liked to use was the grafting of citrus fruits. Just as mandarin oranges can be successfully grafted on to other trees such as citrons, bitter oranges, or trifoliate oranges to produce mandarin oranges, so too could the Tenson be successfully grafted on to different nations. Although the Japanese nation was multinational, 'the mixture does not mean a mixture where several nations come together and create a new nation, but rather one where other nations are assimilated and fused into the Tenson nation which remains unchanged'. He also insisted that 'the people of Korea and Taiwan will also became a single Japanese nation by the same process'.[10]

Kita was opposed to any ideology based on a belief in pure blood. He criticised those who treated the alien peoples within the empire as despised 'step children' (*mamako*), insisting that the Japanese language was mixed with the language of the *Ainu* and of migrants from the continent and the south. Like Tsuboi, Ebina and Taguchi, Kita, too, compared Japan to America or Britain in the sense that all were mixed nations.[11] A strange impression is given that Kita, despite taking this line of argument, despite his own experience of suffering from discrimination and being fired by the Ministry of Education as a result of an attack by chauvinistic nationalists, still insisted on a one-sided assimilation. His argument that any nation could be successfully assimilated into the Japanese nation can be interpreted as something he thought necessary if he was to insist that, even given differences in 'degree', all were brothers. For him, the Japanese nation was multinational. Once the *Ainu* and Koreans joined the mixture with the Japanese, they too would cease to be pure blooded *Ainu* and Koreans but become mixed nations, or, in other words, Japanese. Any alien nation could become a member of the Japanese nation once it abandoned the idea of pure blood, took part in the mixture and was assimilated into it.

For Kita, to enlist with others in the Emperor's army and fight shoulder to shoulder for the Great Japanese Empire was the ultimate form of equality within the empire. According to him, those who formed the core of the Emperor's army during the Heian Period were the assimilated *Ainu* soldiers who had not been poisoned by the depravity and effeminacy of the aristocrats of the

Imperial Court.[12] He naturally mentioned the activities of generals of migrant stock, such as Sakanoue-no-Tamuramaro. In his later years, Kita was afflicted with cancer, but continued to give lectures and carry out research despite his sickness, and carried on writing even in bed. The Ministry of Education provided him with a grant to research 'the historical facts of the composition of, and changes in, the Japanese nation'. His theory of the nation was thus publicly approved by the empire. The year before his death, in an article published in 1938 during the Sino-Japanese War, 'Nippon minzoku no kōsei' (The Composition of the Japanese Nation), he yet again urged his theory of the mixed nation, ending with these words:[13]

> Today Japan's national glory has reached out overseas. Japan annexed Taiwan and Korea, and recently has enjoyed a fraternal relationship with Manchuria. His Majesty, the Meiji Emperor, deigned to say that 'the people of the oceans on all sides are all brethren. Why should we be in discord?' With these words in mind, the Japanese nation fought the Sino-Japanese and Russo-Japanese Wars in order to achieve peace in the Orient and bring about the happiness of our brothers. The people of the oceans on all sides are all brothers. The nations of the Far East are all elements of the Japanese nation and are particularly closely related brothers. Nevertheless, we are now fighting with China, one of these close brothers. This was necessary to defend ourselves against the infamous resist-the-Japanese, oppose-the-Japanese, despise-the-Japanese policies of China. We must wait for them to awaken from their madness and join with us to work for peace in the Far East and happiness for all humanity.
>
> The ancient history of the development of the Japanese state contains many examples of appeals to violence and the suppression of enemies...this, however, saved people from the abyss of their previous state where they lacked unity, drew borders between themselves, and were continually fighting one another. Moreover, the Japanese state gained many courageous loyal subjects by assimilation, secured peace on the frontiers, and developed its national strength.

'The people of the oceans on all sides are all brothers'. Inoue Tetsujirō had once said 'we are surrounded by enemies' in opposing mixed residence in the interior. Nothing could be more opposed to these words. Kita's lifelong aim was to prove that the victims of discrimination within the empire were 'all brothers', to solve the situation where 'borders were drawn to separate rather than unite people', and to save the victims of discrimination from 'the abyss'. But this is where he ended!

For Kita, research was not an activity aimed at acquiring knowledge for its own sake, but was a means to realise the social aim of overcoming discrimination. Kita was to criticise an article authored by Shinmura Izuru (1876–1947), a famous linguist who later became known as the editor of the prestigious Kōjien Dictionary. Shinmura demonstrated through meticulous research that there were mistakes in the theory that many place names in Japan had *Ainu* origins. Kita praised this cautious academic attitude, but also criticised him, saying 'this is too circuitous for our short lives'. Even with some slight mistakes, 'I still stick to my old amateurish theory'.[14]

Kita consistently believed that knowledge was necessary for the good of society, and particularly necessary in his own time for those suffering from discrimination. He also thought that it would be meaningless to discover the truth after people had died. To tackle current problems was imperative, even if it meant making some mistakes. Kita came to grips with the problems he encountered and fought to solve them until the day he died. However, in retrospect, whether he only made 'some' mistakes, and whether what he did was right or wrong is – unfortunately – quite another issue.

8 The Reformation of the National Polity Theory

'What is urgently required is to develop a National Polity theory based on the facts of today's National Polity, which has come to encompass various peoples, both inside and outside Japan, as nationals of the one country'.[1]

If Hozumi Yatsuka, Katō Hiroyuki and Inoue Tetsujirō are defined as first generation national polity theorists, the author of these words, which clearly show the situation that the national polity theory was placed in following the annexation of Korea, could be regarded as a member of the second generation. These younger theorists understood clearly that the status of the national polity theory as the dominant ideology of the Great Japanese Empire would be threatened unless it managed to evolve in harmony with the realities of a Japan that had developed into a multi-national empire.

To deal with this situation, from the Taishō Period (1911–25) to the early Shōwa Period (1925–89), national polity theorists successfully reformed the national polity theory by incorporating the mixed nation theory. From this point, the national polity theorists abandoned the image of an homogeneous and pure blooded Japan, and began to respond to the needs of an expanding empire.

Disorder in the National Polity Theory

The fact that hardly a single national polity theorist made an appearance in the national media at the time of the annexation of Korea was symbolic of the fact that the older national polity theory was increasingly losing relevance in the new multi-national empire. Those national polity theorists who tenaciously held fast to the image of an homogeneous and pure blooded Japan were unable to respond to the new realities.

For example, as late as 1915, Katō Hiroyuki (see chapter 3) attempted to gloss over these realities by obstinately insisting that 'although in recent times Taiwan has become the territory of our empire, and Korea has been annexed, the lineage of the Emperor, the quintessential patriarch of the nation, still wields supreme power in the empire, as it has throughout the ages, and so I still believe that it is natural for the Emperor to rule as a patriarch over Japan'.[2] Katō's life of 80 years ended the next year.

Kakei Katsuhiko, a professor of Tokyo Imperial University, in *Kanagara no michi* (The Path of the Gods), which recorded a lecture given in the presence of the Empress in 1926, wrote as follows.

> Whether we reach the conclusion that any part of the Japanese nation, or all of it, has always inhabited these islands, or that it migrated from the continent...that migration cannot be as recent as is frequently thought. It is so old that we should view the nation as having always lived on this land...Judging from its age and the path followed by migration, it should be said that the Japanese nation actually emerged from within Japan.[3]

This is indeed a very weak web of evasion. Although he was aware of the established theories of anthropology and history, Kakei obscured the reality with the conclusion that the nation 'actually emerged from within Japan'.

In his *Kokutai shinron* (A New National Polity Theory) published in 1919, Mozume Takami (1847–1928) argued that of all countries on earth, 'Japan and only Japan founded a state with one single race'. According to him, multi-national states like China required artificial concepts about how the state should be run, but Japan did not, because she was an homogeneous nation-state where the sovereign and his subjects were joined by the national emotions that existed between kin. Therefore 'many of the political parties raising the banners of democracy or communism are the products of multi-national countries, but this type of partisanship is unheard of among an homogeneous people'. According to Mozume, the Tsuchigumo and the Emishi of the Kiki myths 'for some reason died out', and 'the number of the descendants of those who migrated [to Japan] from overseas is...very small'.[4]

This position, however, could not account for the existence of Korea and Taiwan. If the concept of a pure blooded Japanese nation was adhered to, one option may have been to move towards the position of Takayama Chogyū (see chapter 3), and agree that ruling over alien nations required a power relationship. National polity theorists, however, obstinately insisted that rule by the Emperor was based on natural emotions between sovereign and subject, and not on an artificial power relationship. This was a point on which many of these theorists were unable to make any concessions.

This was also the case with Mozume, who argued that Japan was an homogeneous nation-state. He took the trouble to attach an appendix entitled 'Korea' to his *Kokutai shinron* and stated that 'just like the Japanese, Koreans are also the descendants of the gods and are compatriots'. According to Mozume, Japan and Korea enjoyed a close intercourse from ancient times and were almost completely the same in terms of race, culture and language. Therefore, even after annexing Korea, the Great Japanese Empire was still 'a single group consisting of the same race', joined under the Emperor by the emotions of kinship. This appendix was probably added in the context of the independence movement, which erupted in Korea on the eve of the publication of the book.

This is a typical example of the use of the common ancestor theory as 'the Great Japanese Empire version of the theory of the homogeneous nation'. To call Koreans 'the descendants of the gods' and 'compatriots', while at the same time denying in the same book the lineage of migrants who settled in Japan, is worse than duplicity. Moreover, even if this evasion could be applied to Korea, how did Mozume intend to deal with Taiwan? Finally, with this logic, the more the territory of the empire grew, the larger the range of 'the descendants of the gods' must become.

Incorporating the Theory of the Mixed Nation

The arguments of many other national polity theorists, however, were not as crude. They were fully aware of the necessity of reforming the national polity theory so as to be able to explain the mixed nation theory and the existence of alien peoples within the empire.

Hozumi Yatsuka (see chapter 3), who was attacked in the Meiji Period as a leading figure of the theory that the sovereign and his subjects shared the same ancestor, was one such theorist. He felt a sense of crisis about the mixed nation theory, saying 'if later generations of Japanese delve into anthropology and come to believe that we Japanese are not the same people...it would not only no longer be possible to expound the cardinal principles of the National Polity and the various structures of the civil law, but it would also be impossible to advocate folkways and daily customs'.[5] It is interesting to note that in the section on nations contained in a book published three months after the annexation of Korea, his efforts to counteract the mixed nation theory can be seen. Here Hozumi stated that a state is based on a nation, but also that 'one state does not always consist of one limited nation'. He continued in these terms:[6]

> ...The difference between nations is not absolute...Great nations often increase in size by mixing with peoples of other races and assimilating their descendants. The idea of a nation emerges from an awareness of a shared ancestor. This awareness is the product of history. Historically, people of the same race without this awareness have failed to form a nation, while people of different races with this awareness have succeeded in doing so.

A nation is the product of 'an awareness of a shared ancestor' and that awareness is historically created. This meant that the basis of his theory of the Family State had changed from the conception of a concrete blood relationship to the concept of a ficticious – and consciously ficticious at that – blood relationship. The argument that the essence of a nation lay not in being members of the same race, but in the views of each and every member about identity, seems at first to be open-minded, and to bear a close resemblance to contemporary definitions of ethnicity (and modern nations) which are based on a rejection of racial discrimination. Conversely, however, it meant that any alien people could be converted into 'Japanese' by beating a Japanese self-identity into them. Shortly after this, Hozumi was asked for his opinion while the Korean Education Law was being drafted, and suggested transplanting Emperor worship to Korea.

Hozumi himself died of illness in 1912. His arguments were taken up by Uesugi Shinkichi (1878–1929) who, as his direct disciple, took charge of Hozumi's course at Tokyo Imperial University. Uesugi was a national polity theorist who enjoyed close relationships with right-wing organisations and the military, but even he argued that the nation is the product of the subjective self-identification of its members, stating 'it has nothing to do with a shared race, language or religion...but is based on the beliefs of all members that they are all brothers and compatriots and belong to the same nation'. He continued that in ancient Japan 'the Tenson nation, the Izumo nation, and other indigenous nations existed, with some related to the Imperial Family, others to the native peoples, and yet others to the migrants, but they formed the sentiment, the sense and the conviction that they were just like a single family, all brothers and compatriots, making up a single, inseparable group', and the superior nation 'used a melting pot to fuse the other nations into one great nation'.[7]

Inoue Tetsujirō, who converted into a mixed nation theorist immediately after the annexation of Korea (see chapter 6), adopted a similar line of argument. In *Kokumin dōtoku gairon* (An Introduction to National Morals) published in 1912, he advocated an assimilation based on the mixed nation theory, while denying 'the simple idea that the sovereign and all his subjects share the same ancestor' because of the reality that 'today's Japan has various alien nations within its borders'. Citing the anthropological theories of Torii Ryūzō and Koganei Yoshikiyo, he stated that the 'Japanese are a mixed nation'. In the ancient archipelago, the *Ainu*, a southern people, Koreans, Negroids and the migrants who accounted for fully one-third of the names in the *Shinsen shōjiroku* all existed and 'were all united...and assimilated by the Tenson into a single unit'. He also mentioned the Koreans, the Han race, the *Ainu*, the Aborigines of Taiwan and the various indigenous peoples of Sakhalin, which had been ceded to Japan after the Russo-Japanese War, as different nations within the empire, and concluded that 'these should all be assimilated into the Japanese nation through education'.[8] This book was what could be called an authorised work of the Ministry of Education: it recorded the lectures given to secondary school teachers at the request of the Minister of Education.

This line of argument was not limited to Uesugi and Inoue. In a book written in 1912, Katō Genchi (1873–1965), another national polity theorist and professor at the Military Staff College, praised the Japanese 'powers of assimilation', giving as examples the assimilation in ancient times of the migrants to Japan and the *Ainu*, while noting the existence of Korea and Taiwan. Tatebe Tongo (1871–1945), a professor of Tokyo Imperial University and a nationalistic sociologist, stated in the second Japanese sociology conference held in 1914 that Japan required an extensive territory and 'one billion Japanese' in order to become a world power, and noted that 'it is unavoidable that some of the one billion Japanese will have mixed blood'. In a book published in the same period, he insisted that there were many loyal subjects who were originally from other lands.[9]

Furthermore, Tanaka Chigaku also supported the mixed nation theory. Tanaka had organised the Kokuchūkai (National Pillar Society), a nationalist group of the Nichiren sect – a Buddhist sect created by the thirteenth century priest, Nichiren (1222–1282). The Kokuchūkai was an organization that could be described as a fundamentalist Buddhist sect. Members advocated the creation of an ideal state based on Buddhism and world salvation, and argued for solving the problem of rural poverty in Japan and for building an Eden in the Chinese continent. This organization gained support in military circles during the recessions of the 1920s and 1930s. It is said that Tanaka was revered by military figures including Lieutenant-General Ishiwara (or Ishihara) Kanji (1889–1949), who planned the Manchurian Incident of 1931. As a mixed nation theorist, Tanaka praised the Japanese nation as 'the greatest nation in the world', one that had been entrusted with the mission to unite and assimilate 'all the nations in the world', based on the fact that the Tenson nation had successfully assimilated many 'aboriginal peoples' and migrants.[10] By about 1920, the mixed nation theory was thus already being utilised by national polity theorists.

Alien Nations as 'Adopted Children'

However much the ability to assimilate was emphasised from the point of view of the mixed nation theory, the fact remained that the empire still included alien nations, and would continue to do so until their assimilation was completed. How should these alien peoples be viewed in the Family State? This problem had to be solved if the national polity theory was to become the leading ideology of a multi-national empire.

There were roughly three answers to this question. The first was to rule the alien peoples by force. One example of this is seen in a lecture, 'Kokutai no shuyō mondai' (The Main Problems of the National Polity), given by Kanokogi Kazunobu in 1918 (Kanokogi later became a managing director and the secretary-general of the Genron Hōkokukai, an official organization of Japanese intellectuals during the Pacific War). Citing authors such as Georg Jellinek (1851–1911), Kanokogi asserted that *realpolitik* was power relations, and that 'invasion and conquest is in fact the sublime duty of a people in founding a state'. Furthermore, he advocated 'militarism' and 'imperialism', saying the creation of an empire that would rule all Asian nations was the 'realisation of Japanism'. According to Kanokogi, 'the talent of Japan lies in fighting, and the mission of Japan is to rule'. Therefore 'we must take our talent in commanding and ruling to meet the outside world. The result will be rule over alien nations, or in other words what I call imperialism'.[11]

However, hardly any other national polity theorist was cold enough or self-aware enough to use words like imperialism and militarism openly, or to advocate a power-based rule over alien nations. To repeat, the foundation of the national polity theory was the strong belief that rule by the Emperor was not rule by power. Most people are neither strong enough nor determined enough to be able consciously to do the wrong thing. Only when they are obsessed with the subjective idea that they are doing good can people become completely inconsiderate of the pain of others. A softer view of the alien peoples within the empire was therefore necessary.

The second answer was to make the national polity a universal ethic, not something unique to Japan. A representative example was Satomi Kishio (1897–1974), a son of Tanaka Chigaku and a heretical national polity theorist who published works such as *Tennō to puroretaria* (The Emperor and the Proletariat) and argued for the relief of workers and farmers through the ideology of a single sovereign and all his subjects (*ikkun banminshugi*). This was an ideology that emerged in Meiji Japan and was popularised during the recession of the 1920s. It argued in favour of redressing the differences between the rich and the poor under the Emperor, and stressed that all were equal under the Emperor. Satomi criticised other national polity theorists for not coming to grips with social realities such as poverty, and published *Kokutai ni taisuru giwaku* (Suspicions about the National Polity) in 1928.[12] This work took the form of posing and then answering 50 hypothetical questions about the national polity theory, such as 'Why is the Emperor sacred?' and 'Is it not simply idolatry to salute His Majesty's portrait?' One of the questions asked whether the fact that the empire included other nations would affect the national polity or not, to which Satomi gave the following answer.

> It is not the case that it is unnecessary or impossible to rule a people related by blood. Even if the nation are all blood kin,

they will not be able to carry out the will of Heaven if they do not understand the cardinal principles of the National Polity and if they are interested only in their own petty interests. What is most important, whether someone has always been a member of the Japanese nation or has just become a member, is to understand the Japanese National Polity and obey it. The foundation of Japan is not maintained merely by simple blood relationships between fathers and children, but by the sacred unification of the Emperor and his subjects. There is therefore no reason to exclude those who have just joined the nation.

Satomi used the ideology of a single sovereign and all his subjects to advocate the relief of poverty and the promotion of international peace. From his point of view, the national polity was synonymous with peace and equality. He believed that the assimilation of other nations in ancient Japan was proof of a lack of discrimination, and compared this to racial discrimination in Europe. He also argued that 'the Japanese National Polity is a universal and valid principle of life', and 'should be vigorously explained to Koreans, Chinese and Westerners. Justice has no borders'. For him, what was important was whether people believed in the ideal of the national polity, and the race and state they belonged to were secondary issues.

An extreme example of this type of thinking is seen in a lecture 'Kokutai no kenkyū' (Research of the National Polity) by an army officer, Satō Tetsutarō in 1918.[13] Satō praised 'the capacity of the Japanese' as a mixed nation, and predicted that the entire world would eventually come to admire the peaceful and harmonious Japanese national polity. He stated that Koreans, Taiwanese and Manchurians would become 'outstanding Japanese nationals if they came to value the Japanese National Polity and joined the Japanese nation. In that case, the difference in ancestors or race would no longer be issues'. For Satō, the Great Japanese Empire was merely a tool to propagate the national polity throughout the world and 'it does not matter if the Japanese state were to be destroyed in carrying out this purpose, so long as we can have our sacred Emperor and carry out the will of Heaven'.

While all used the term 'national polity', it was thus used differently. Some advocated militarism, imperialism and the rule of alien nations through power, while others advocated non-discrimination and harmony. This strange contrast within national polity circles was perhaps due to the ambiguity of the concept: national polity theorists could interpret it as they liked. The concepts of non-discrimination and pacifism used by Satomi and Satō were based completely on the premise of loyalty to the Emperor and the national polity, so cannot be accepted literally. In *Kokutai ni taisuru giwaku*, Satomi forcefully argued that Japan was not a militaristic country. This should be understood as a reluctance to accept the realities of the Japan of his day. He insisted that the annexation of Korea was not 'a militaristic invasion' but the salvation of the Koreans.[14]

However, just as most national polity theorists could not be as cold-hearted as Kanokogi, neither could they be as boldly universalistic as Satomi. To argue that the national polity theory was as universal as the various philosophies of the West and East meant competing with these philosophies on equal terms, but the national polity theory, of course, lacked the content required to compete. With the wall of the so-called unique character of the Japanese nation to hide behind, however, even a theory that lacked any content could still be viewed as an unparalleled masterpiece. On the other hand, it was clear that the national polity theorists had to break through this wall, at least to a certain extent, and broaden its base in order to keep up with the realities of an empire that was incorporating alien nations.

The third answer, adopted by many national polity theorists, was to maintain the concept of uniqueness but at the same time pursue a superficial universalism, with the idea of a Family State that included alien nations. How was this possible?

In 1918, *Tōa no hikari* (The Light of East Asia), a journal centred around Inoue Tetsujirō, brought together the leading national polity theorists of the time and published a series of lectures on the national polity theory over more than ten issues. This was a time when the First World War was drawing to an end and the ideal of national self-determination was being advocated by President Wilson. The following year, influenced by this ideal, the March First Independence Movement erupted in Korea. Kita Sadakichi's journal *Minzoku to rekishi* (Nation and History) was founded at about this time, and the problem of the various nations within the empire became one of the main themes in this series, which included the lectures by Kanokogi and Satō discussed above.

In these serialised lectures, the individual who advocated an interpretation of the alien nations within the empire most suitable for the national polity theory was Ōshima Masanori, in his 'Yo no kokutaikan to kokka jinkakuron' (My View of the National Polity and the Character of the State). Ōshima became a director of the Imperial Committee of Education after working as an associate professor at Tokyo Imperial University.[15] He first reaffirmed the basis of the national polity theory, saying that 'the Japanese Emperor and his majesty's subjects are united by national emotions of kinship'. The theory that the 'Japanese' and Koreans shared a common ancestor could not be relied on: 'some say the Koreans are the same as the Japanese nation, but this argument was too hurriedly produced'. Furthermore, he denied the idea of rule through power, saying 'of course, in one sense it might be necessary to use power to rule people, but it is more important to rule through morality, which is the traditional feature of Japan's Imperial Family, and to adopt a long-term policy of assimilating alien nations into the Japanese nation'.

How, then, were the alien nations within the empire explained, after the denial both of the theory that the 'Japanese' and Koreans shared a common ancestor and of rule through power, and after it had been decided to pursue assimilation but before assimilation was completed?

> Of course, it cannot be said that the Koreans are the same nation as the Japanese, but to accept them as adopted children, or foster children, or foundlings, and to treat them like real family members, seeing them spiritually as family, will enlarge our National Polity.

'Adopted children' are family members who are not blood relations. This is the logic that it was decided would 'enlarge our National Polity', maintain the idea of a Family State, and at the same time include alien nations.

Of course, the expression 'step-children' was used by Kita Sadakichi and Tsuboi Shōgorō and was not a newly invented idea. For the national polity theorists, however, who had seemingly been placed in a situation where they were forced to chose either blood relationships or imperial expansion, this rhetoric was highly convenient in accepting the realities of a multi-national empire. Even if the empire included alien nations, there would be no contradiction with the ideology of a Family State if these were regarded as adopted children.

This may seem to be mere sophism. However, an essential problem in the theory of the Family State can be seen here. In reality, the theory did not entail a real blood relationship even within the Japanese nation itself. For example, although the 'Japanese' were all said to be the descendants of the Emperors, it was certainly not the case that everyone in Japan could claim the right to succession to the throne or the right of inheritance. In the family system of China and Korea, kinship meant exclusively paternal kinship. For commoners to call themselves the children of the Emperor would be regarded as claiming that the relatives of the Emperor were illegitimate, and would be an act of disrespect. Furthermore, the family systems of China and Korea adhered to the principle of '*isei fuyō*', which prohibited adopting anyone with a different surname as a member of the family, so it was impossible in principle to adopt alien nations as family members. This issue will be discussed in further detail in the conclusion.

The Family State consists not only of kith and kin but also pseudo-blood relations such as adopted children. This logic was consciously developed in order to explain the alien nations within the empire, and was quickly taken up by the national polity theorists. Yoshida Kumaji (1874–1964), a professor of Tokyo Imperial University, a scholar in the field of education, and a representative member of the second generation of national polity theorists, stated in his lecture in *Tōa no hikari* that the Family State was a subjective one, and 'even if, in a historical or anthropological sense, various people with different lineages have become Japanese…[that would not matter so long as the subjects of the Great Japanese Empire could] gradually come to accept the notion that all Japanese nations were in effect members of a single nation and a single family'. In 1928, Yoshida wrote that historically the *Ainu*, the Kumaso and the foreign migrants were 'just like adopted children who have become members of their adoptive families and are not discriminated against…ideologically speaking, the Japanese are a single people united around the Imperial Household'.[16]

It is easy to ask whether alien peoples were really 'not discriminated against', but Yoshida would perhaps say in reply that the Japanese history of mixing with many nations proved beyond doubt that discrimination did not exist. If asked how the discrimination against the alien nations of his day should be interpreted, his answer would be that this was lamentable, that the small number of misdirected people responsible for discrimination needed to be told to mend their ways, and that assimilation and mixing blood needed to be prompted under the principle of *isshi dōjin* (universal brotherhood under the Emperor). It was not until the final formulation of an ideology that made it impossible to realise that rule was rule that the empire was able to mobilise people to rule.

'An Open Blood-Family Organisation'

It was Watari Shōzaburō, a professor of the Tokyo Higher Normal School, who was most systematic in reforming the national polity theory. His book, *Kokumin dōtoku honron* (An Essay on National Morals), published in 1928, was a complete survey of his past studies. He openly and actively mentioned the mixed nation theory of anthropology and history, and the fact that foreign migrants made up one-third of the clan names listed in the *Shinsen shōjiroku*. However, he also noted that the theories of the Family State and the common ancestry of the sovereign and all his subjects held true even with the entry of alien nations (Watari 1928a: 47–8).

> Once any individual, whether male or female, marries into another family, although their lineage ancestor is that of their birth family, structurally speaking they should regard the ancestors of their new family as their own ancestors...An extreme example of the difference between an ancestor by blood lineage and an ancestor by structure is when a married couple both join another family as adopted children, and both regard the ancestor of their foster family as their real family ancestor despite the fact that they are not related by blood...
> ...Therefore, the ancestors of these alien nations are different from us in terms of blood, but as members of the Japanese nation their ancestors are the ancient Japanese people who organised this empire, beginning with the Imperial Ancestors...In this sense, despite the large numbers of various alien nations our country has embraced since ancient times, it is still clearly the case that the sovereign and all his subjects share the same ancestor. We are all one family.

Alien nations are the same as adopted children and brides in that they are assimilated into the Japanese *ie* (family) they have joined under a new set of ancestors. Here the understanding is established that what counts in the Japanese *ie* is not blood, but structure. Though this is sophistry, it was a huge improvement on the national polity theorists of the Meiji era who were at a loss to cope with the mixed nation theory.

Furthermore, Watari argued that the Japanese nation from ancient times had treated alien nations equally and assimilated them. According to him, 'to rule large numbers of the conquered who have been made slaves or something similar frequently requires force, and turns the country which practises it into a conquest state or power state'. Needless to say, 'all European countries began as conquest states'. Japan, however, had mixed with alien nations on equal terms from ancient times. Much poetry in the *Man'yōshū*, a collection of Japanese poetry (c. 770), was authored by descendants of foreign migrants who were permitted 'to adopt Japanese names' (Watari 1928a: 57–9, 65). Here he changed the mixed nation theory into proof of non-discrimination and further developed it into a feeling of superiority to the West.

Watari also adopted Kita Sadakichi's historiography.[17] He emphasised that indigenous peoples and foreign migrants formed a part of the Emperor's army, and listed the loyal exploits of the Saekibe, an *Ainu* unit, and Sakanoue-no-Tamuramaro, the migrant general. He also noted that the culture of foreign migrants played a role in developing Japanese culture, and that migrants were even appointed as Shintō priests (Watari 1928a: 532–40). Finally, he criticised the Japanese nativist (*kokugaku*) scholars of the Meiji Period, saying that 'even in the Meiji Period, some of those who adhered to the tradition of the exclusion of foreigners advocated a xenophobic idea of blood and tried to interpret history to argue that there were only a few examples of foreigners coming to Japan' (Watari 1928a: 392).

Watari aimed at arguing that 'only those who enjoy a superior unity can embrace and assimilate a large number of outsiders'. Of course, this centred on 'the excellent powers of unification of the Imperial Family'. That is, 'whenever any antipathy or conflict between the original residents of Japan and those from outside occurred, the Imperial Family used an authority that transcended both parties to moderate the situation'. Watari claimed that there must have been some friction between this mixture of multiple races, and therefore there must have been some authority to mediate between conflicting parties. By emphasising the multi-national aspect of Japan, he was conversely able to stress Japan's 'strength of unity'. Although emphasising the frequent rebellions of the indigenous peoples and foreign migrants, he concluded: 'to have been able to overcome these difficulties and complete the assimilation proves the superiority of the unity of our country' (Watari 1928a: 531–41).

According to Watari, a blood-family organisation is not always closed, and 'our country is a blood-family body rich in the ability to embrace others' (Watari 1928a: 391–2). Moreover, 'the annexation of Taiwan and Korea' was 'exactly the same in theory...as the assimilation of the Hayato in the southwest and the Emishi in the northeast' (Watari 1928a: 66–7). The migrants who made up one-third of the names listed in the *Shinsen shōjiroku* corresponded to the number of Koreans and Taiwanese in the Great Japanese Empire at the time. Japan, he claimed, had experience in assimilating such a large number of alien peoples.

Furthermore, Watari was actually an insider. In February 1928, the Ministry of Education gathered people involved in education from all over Japan and held a lecture series that aimed to promote a heightened awareness of the national polity in order to combat the increasing influence of socialism. Watari took part as one of 20 national polity lecturers. Here, he again presented his ideas, mentioning the indigenous peoples and the foreign migrants listed in the *Shinsen shōjiroku*, and argued that 'there was no need to be pessimistic in viewing the problem of Korea and Taiwan'. Moreover, he even stated that the Empress Jingū was related to the ancient Korean kingdom of Silla and 'the mother of the Emperor Kanmu was Korean'. These lectures were published by the Ministry of Education to 'inform the nation widely'. This meant that the national polity theory which had incorporated the theory of the mixed nation had now gained official recognition.[18]

There is one more point that deserves notice. This regards the phrase 'homogeneous nation'.

Kiyohara Sadao, a professor of Hiroshima Bunrika University, was also one of the speakers in this series of lectures on the national polity, and wrote in a book published in 1930 that 'the people of our empire are not a purely homogeneous nation', mentioning the mixed origin of the Japanese nation and the influx of Korean blood into the Imperial Family.[19] He noted that the Family State was an ideological structure and real blood relationships did not matter if assimilation was completely carried out. To the best of my knowledge, there is no example of the phrase 'homogeneous nation' being used in the Meiji Period theory that the sovereign and all his subjects shared the same ancestor. This is perhaps the earliest example of the use of the term, and it was used negatively by a national polity theorist.

Thus the national polity theory was completely reformed. It had successfully encompassed the mixed nation theory and could proceed to expand indefinitely without worrying about the existence of alien nations within the empire. To note the historical existence of alien nations was now not only useless as a criticism of the national polity theory but actually served to re-enforce its logic. A month after the lectures by Watari and others were delivered, the empire used the Peace Preservation Law (see introduction, endnote 9) to make wholesale arrests of members of the Japanese Communist Party, and prepared for the Fifteen Years War (1931–45). The mixed nation theory had been incorporated fully into the logic of the empire and lay there until the time when it would be able to contribute to Japanese aggression.

9 National Self-Determination and National Borders

In March 1919, the March First Independence Movement erupted in Korea. Koreans held peaceful demonstrations all over the peninsula that were forcefully subdued by Japan. By May, it is said that about 7,500 people had been killed and more than 40,000 arrested.[1]

The 'Japanese' were greatly shocked by this movement. After the annexation, Korea had all but disappeared from the public discourse, except for a few scholars such as the leading theorist of democracy in prewar Japan, Yoshino Sakuzō (1878–1933), and the right-wing journalist, politician and activist, Nakano Seigō (1886–1943), both of whom were critical of Japanese rule in Korea. The March First Independence Movement, however, triggered an interest in Korea both inside Japan and overseas. On this occasion, the theory that the 'Japanese' and Koreans shared a common ancestor was again trotted out along with the mixed nation theory to justify the annexation.

The Neutralisation of the Theory of National Self-Determination

During the March First Independence Movement, not only Koreans throughout the peninsula but also those in the archipelago published a large number of declarations of independence. What these Koreans relied on spiritually was a belief that they were a unique nation with 4,000 years of history. The common ancestor theory therefore became one of the targets of their criticism.

To take one example, the declaration of independence issued by the Representative of Korean Labourers in Osaka noted that 'the Japanese people emphasise that the Koreans are the same race as the Japanese or share the same ancestors', but argued that 'we Koreans have 4,300 years of noble history, while Japanese history begins well over one thousand years later, which clearly demonstrates that the

Korean and the Yamato nations have nothing in common'. In a petition submitted to the Government-General of Korea and issued by the signatories to a letter of independence in Seoul, the differences between Japan and Korea were listed, with a claim that assimilationist policies were impossible. According to this petition, 'Koreans are continental, while the Japanese are insular'; 'Korea is a Confucian country, while Japan is Buddhist'; 'from the historical point of view, Korea has 5,000 years of history, while Japan has only half this'; and 'from the linguistic point of view, phonemic changes are rich in one but poor in the other, and from the alphabetic point of view, there is a huge gulf in the range of vocabulary. In short, Korean is a language with a world capacity, while the Japanese language is a regional dialect that is poor and weak'.[2]

The Japanese theories of the common ancestor and the mixed nation adopted a position contrary to this, with both claiming that Japan and Korea had shared a close relationship historically and had the same etymological and racial source.

In 1916, Komatsu Midori, a high-ranking bureaucrat in the Government-General of Korea, in response to Yoshino Sakuzō's criticism of the Japanese rule of Korea, had already argued that assimilation was possible because the '*Nissenjin*' (Japanese and Koreans) were the 'same race' as could be seen in the 'fact of the royal Korean blood of the Empress Jingū and even the Emperor Kanmu as is clearly written in Japanese historical records'.[3] This statement can be regarded as confirmation that the common ancestor theory, including the idea of Korean blood in the Imperial Family, had been accepted within the Government-General of Korea.

As already mentioned, Kita Sadakichi founded a magazine at around the time of the March First Independence Movement and developed a thesis about the fusion of Koreans and Japanese based on the mixed nation theory. In the field of anthropology, Torii Ryūzō gave a lecture, 'Nissenjin wa "dōgen" nari' (The Japanese and Koreans are of the 'Same Origin'), which appeared in the first issue of *Dōgen* (The Same Origin), a magazine published in Korea and supported by the Government-General to propagate the common ancestor theory.[4] In the third number of the magazine, Kita Sadakichi published an article that became the prototype of 'the theory of a common origin'. Torii Ryūzō argued against Yoshino Sakuzō, who had shown sympathy for the March First Independence Movement, stating:

The Korean people are not a different race from the Japanese, but the same nation that ought to be included in the same family-group. This is an indisputable fact racially and etymologically. Almost all Western scholars of ethnology, linguistics and history agree that the Japanese and Koreans are the same race...It is strange that scholars in Japan such as Mr. Yoshino actually deny this.

Some people cry that the Korean people should secede from the Japanese and become independent because of the importance of 'national self-determination', but this is completely wrong. The Japanese and the Koreans are the same nation. What is the rationale for separating one nation into two independent countries?...In the case of the *Nissenjin*, since they are a single nation, the right thing to do is to merge and unify the two. Only then will the aims of 'national self-determination' be fully realised.

Furthermore, Torii stated that 'both Japanese and Koreans enjoy close and friendly family relations' and insisted: 'I wish that people dealing with Korea – the policy-makers in the Government-General of Korea, politicians in Japan and other people – would keep this in mind from now on. There is no need for us to listen to the mistaken views of ignorant scholars and politicians'. At the end of this lecture, he proposed that 'a research institute be established within the Government-General to prove that the Japanese and Koreans share the same origins, racially, linguistically, and historically'. This would make the 'common origin of the Japanese and Koreans much clearer and extinguish suspicion on both sides'.

Following Tsuboi's sudden death in 1913, Torii became the leading Japanese authority in anthropology. As such, his words naturally carried weight, but, as with Kita Sadakichi, he seemed to have wanted to fight discrimination between Japanese and Koreans through mutual assimilation. Both thought that discrimination could be combated by proving that the Japanese and Koreans sprang from the same parental source, and perhaps believed that this was a conscientious position. However, their arguments led more and more people to deny Korean independence.

A similar logic can be seen in *Kokka kaizōan genri taikō* (A Plan for the Reorganisation of the State) by Kita Ikki (see chapter 3), a work published in August 1919 that is said to have influenced the army officers who led an attempted coup in 1936 (the so-called 26

February Incident).⁵ Here Kita emphasised the historical and racial links between Korea and Japan.

> The national differences between Koreans and Japanese only exist in parts of the language and customs. On the level of thought, which is the basis of people's lives, both Japan and Korea belong completely to the same genealogy. This is because, since the beginning of her history, Japan's cultural exchange with the continent has always been by way of Korea. It is clear anthropologically that the Japanese nation is a chemical crystallisation of the Koreans, Chinese, people of the South Seas, and aboriginal peoples, a fact which demonstrates to what degree Korean blood flows through Japanese veins. In particular, those who enjoyed close cultural interactions with Korea had a lot of pure Korean blood in their veins, and became aristocrats in the Monarchical Age. This is why many of the court nobles and the peerage today have long yam-like faces, which are proof of their Korean blood. Since the peerage had a great deal of Korean blood, it flowed from this privileged class into the Imperial Household. In this sense, there was an intercourse between the Emperors of Japan and Koreans. The marriage today between a Korean Prince and a Japanese Princess is therefore not the first trial of a union between the two.

According to Kita, the only difference between Korea and Japan lay in certain aspects of language and customs, and thus all that was needed to make assimilation complete was to change these. The opinion that the annexation of Korea could be justified from the position of national self-determination because the 'Japanese' and Koreans were members of the same national family could be seen in newspaper editorials at the time of the March First Independence Movement. The subtitle of one such editorial read 'The Japanese and Koreans are the Same Nation with a Common Ancestor – The Unification of the Two is Demanded by the Principle of National Self-Determination', and concluded 'those who oppose assimilation can be regarded as individuals who oppose the latest thinking on national self-determination'.⁶

This logic sounds like very odd sophistry. However, let us take Okinawa or North Italy as an example. If an independence movement based on national self-determination occurred in Okinawa (or North Italy), a debate about whether Okinawa and the

Yamato nation (or the peoples of North Italy and the rest of Italy) were the same people would become the focus of attention. In this sense, it was highly significant for specialists of history and anthropology like Torii and Kita Sadakichi to insist that Japan and Korea were of the same parental source. As I noted in my *'Nihonjin' no kyōkai* (The Boundaries of the 'Japanese'), Nakano Seigō and others argued at the time that Korea should be viewed as a Scotland or a Wales rather than as an Ireland hungry for independence (Oguma 1998). In other words, such authors recognised that the 'Japanese' and Koreans were different ethnic groups, but also believed that the two could coexist peacefully in a single country.

Later, when Nazi Germany annexed the Sudeten district of Czechoslovakia, it was argued that the annexation was the realisation of national self-determination since many of the Sudeten residents were Germans. When a nation is scattered across borders and resides in several countries, the logic of national self-determination can be used to justify aggression. However, in the case of Sudeten, those who had suffered invasion believed that they too were of German origin. By contrast, the theory that the 'Japanese' and Koreans shared a common ancestor was the sole creation of Japan.

Torii Ryūzō's Theory of the Origin of the Japanese Nation

A typical example of a theory of the origin of the Japanese nation of this period is that of Torii Ryūzō. Torii's *Yūshi izen no Nippon* (Pre-historical Japan) was a best-selling work in the 1920s, and was so influential that he could boast that 'today, nobody doubts my position'. His theory of the origin of the Japanese nation can be summarised as basically accepting that the Japanese were a mixture of the *Ainu*, a southern people and a continental people.[7]

According to the established ideas of the time, the archipelago had not experienced a Palaeolithic age. In the Neolithic age, the *Ainu* migrated to an uninhabited archipelago and were distributed over almost the whole of Japan from Hokkaido to Okinawa. What Torii called '*Ainu* pottery' – that is, Jōmon pottery – was the product of the *Ainu*. What was then commonly called the Tenson nation, a conquering nation, next migrated to the archipelago. Torii named this group the 'Japanese Proper'. They came to the archipelago from the continent via the Korean peninsula, and produced the Yayoi pottery. According to Torii, archaeological finds similar to Yayoi pottery had been unearthed in the Korean peninsula and Tsushima (an island located mid-way between the peninsula and the archipelago). 'In ancient times, the Japanese archipelago and the Korean peninsula were linked racially'. This was the foundation of his theory that the 'Japanese' and Koreans shared a common ancestor.

The 'Japanese Proper' first established themselves in the Kinki and Chūgoku regions in the central western part of the archipelago, after which there was a large-scale migration, which was described in the Kiki myths as the descent to the earth of the Tenson. Furthermore, according to Torii, in addition to the *Ainu* and the 'Japanese Proper', there also resided in the archipelago a southern people, the Indonesians, who had the blood of curly-haired negroids in their veins, and an Indochinese nation which was related to the small-statured Miyao nation in southern China and which left behind the bronzeware known as *dōtaku*. Thus, the Japanese nation was formed from a mixture of the 'Japanese Proper', the hirsute *Ainu*, southern Indonesians, the short Indochinese, and continental migrants. This was the reason there were 'Japanese' with continental faces and others with southern features, some who were hairy and others with curly hair, large people and short people.

In this way, Torii argued that the 'Japanese' and Koreans shared a common ancestor, based on his thesis about the origins of the Japanese nation. His theory was built on the premise that the conquering nation came from the Korean peninsula. This was why, in 1920, in an article published in *Tōhō jiron* (Contemporary Opinion of the East), a magazine edited by Nakano Seigō, Torii again denied the independence of Korea on the grounds that the 'Japanese' and Koreans shared a common ancestor, and stated that since a nation which came from the peninsula conquered the archipelago, 'Japan was what could be called a [Korean] colony'.[8] Although not emphasised, it is self-evident that Torii believed that the Imperial Family came from the peninsula.

Since Torii's theory included this sort of assumption, some members of minorities in Japan such as Ifa Fuyū, who was from Okinawa and is known as the founder of Okinawan studies, were sympathetic to his ideas.

Okinawa had originally been a kingdom known as the Ryūkyū Kingdom, but was annexed by Japan in 1879 and renamed Okinawa.

The residents of Okinawa Prefecture were granted Japanese nationality, and assimilationist policies centred on Emperor worship and Japanese language (*hyōjungo*) education were implemented. In general, majority Japanese discrimination against Okinawans was as bad as that against Koreans. By the late nineteenth century, the Okinawan movement to secede from Japan had almost completely disappeared, and the people of Okinawa began to actively assimilate in order to escape from discrimination. Unlike Korea and Taiwan, the residents of Okinawa were enfranchised, albeit 30 years later than the people of the rest of Japan Proper (see the conclusion).

The fact that Okinawa had in effect become a part of Japan was frequently cited as a precedent that demonstrated that Japan would be able to assimilate Korea. As noted in chapter 5, the linguist Kanazawa Shōzaburō argued that the Korean language was a dialect of Japanese just like Okinawan was.

Ifa established the theory that the 'Japanese' and Okinawans shared a common ancestor, basing it on Torii's theory that the *Ainu* had once resided in Okinawa, and on the linguistic ideas of Kanazawa Shōzaburō. According to Ifa, the nation which came to the archipelago from the Korean peninsula split into two groups, one of which travelled east while the other moved south. Those who moved east became the ancestors of the Japanese nation after the Eastern Expedition of the Emperor Jinmu, while those who moved south arrived in Okinawa. Both groups conquered the indigenous *Ainu* and a southern people, and both became mixed nations formed of the same elements.[9] Ifa developed this thesis in an attempt to abolish discrimination against Okinawans (see Oguma 1998).

As the established theory of the day, Torii's ideas were accepted by theorists affiliated with the Japanese Communist Party and wielded a large influence on the views that they developed of ancient Japan.

According to *Tokushu buraku issennenshi* (A Thousand Year History of the *Burakumin*) by Takahashi Sadaki (see chapter 7), an individual who was involved in the Suiheisha movement in Japan (this was a movement that aimed to liberate the *burakumin*), served in the Comintern in Moscow as an interpreter, and later died in prison in Japan, three different indigenous peoples – the *Ainu*, the Indonesians, and the *dōtaku* nation – had lived in the ancient archipelago, and a Mongolian 'Proto-Japanese (Japanese Proper)' people later migrated to the archipelago. In an article published in

1931, Watanabe Yoshimichi, a Marxist ancient historian, listed the *Ainu*, the Indonesians and the Tungus as 'the peoples living in the ancient Japanese islands'. In addition, Sano Manabu, who served as the head of the Japanese Communist Party, stated in *Proretaria Nippon rekishi* (A Proletariat History of Japan) published in 1933, that there used to be six nations in the ancient archipelago: the *Ainu* who were called the Emishi or Tsuchigumo, the Tungus 'Japanese Proper', the Indochinese, the Indonesians who were called the Hayato, curly-haired negroids, and migrant Han. Furthermore, in *Nippon kokuminsei no kenkyū* (Studies of the Japanese Character) edited by Sano in 1922, Torii and Kume Kunitake (see chapter 5) contributed chapters, and the social democrat and prolific commentator Hasegawa Nyozekan (1875–1969) argued that the Japanese nation was a mixed one.[10]

Generally speaking, the Marxist ancient historians of the time combined Torii's theory with a Marxist view of history that argued that an ancient, primitive communistic society was destroyed by the formation of the state and the emergence of slavery. It was stressed that the migrant nation conquered and enslaved the indigenous peoples, as can be typically seen in Takahashi's words: 'all states originate in conquest'.[11] This makes a stark contrast with Kita Sadakichi's insistence on a non-discriminatory assimilation of the indigenous peoples, and with the ideas (to be discussed in chapter 11) of the anarchist and feminist, Takamure Ituse.

What is interesting is that, even at this time, the mixed nation theory was taken up so enthusiastically that taboos were broken. Examples of this are 'before we start from the simple idea of the Japanese' (Takahashi) and 'an individual called Kurokawa Mayori once said that although Westerners may have evolved from monkeys, the Japanese are the descendants of the gods' (Sano).[12] It must be said that their understanding of the ideology of the Great Japanese Empire was limited to the level of Kurokawa in the mid-Meiji Period. By this time, the mixed nation theory had been accepted by the national polity theorists and publicly approved by the Ministry of Education.

Not only Torii, but all theorists of the time, beginning with Kita Sadakichi, believed that the change from Jōmon culture to Yayoi culture meant the replacement of one people by another. The only difference between the various theorists was which nation was thought to be responsible for which culture (Kita, for example, argued that Yayoi pottery was created by the Hayato).[13] Torii followed the trends of the time in bringing the mixed nation theory of prewar anthropology to completion. As a result, as will be seen in part 3, his theories later became the target of criticism by scholars who advocated the theory of the homogeneous nation.

The Changes in Japanese Textbooks

How were the origin of the Japanese nation and the existence of alien nations within the empire described in primary school textbooks compiled by the state?

The most marked transition can be seen in geography textbooks.[14] State textbooks were first published in 1903, and in geography textbooks of this first period (which lasted until 1909), the only remarks about the constituents of the empire were that 'the number of people living here [within the empire] amount to about 50 million. Led by the unbroken line of Emperors, they all live happily'. Nothing was said about the national make-up of the population. In the section on the Okinawa Prefecture, however, it was noted that 'the language and customs of the residents of Okinawa are strikingly different from the residents of other parts of Japan...Recently, however, public transport has been greatly developed and Okinawa will soon become just like other parts of Japan'. The section on Hokkaido is noteworthy. There is an illustration titled 'An *Ainu* Chief in His Best Dress and His Home', and the text stated that 'the *Ainu* used to live on the mainland a long time ago, but today the number of *Ainu* throughout Hokkaido is fewer than 20,000'.

This description changed slightly in the second period, after textbooks were revised and published in 1910. The 1910 edition geography textbook (which remained unchanged until 1918) consisted of two volumes, an introduction to geography (volume 1) and special geography (volume 2). Regarding the composition of the people within the empire, volume 1 noted that 'the inhabitants are generally members of the Yamato nation and the population is about 68 million. Led by the unbroken line of Emperors, the population is rich in loyalty and patriotism'. Here the phrase 'generally members of the Yamato nation' has been added, which clearly shows that the existence of the alien nations within the empire could no longer be ignored. Furthermore, in volume 2, Taiwan was explained as having 'a population of about 3 million, most of whom are the descendants of migrants from China'. It was stated that there were 'also several native tribes' which had long lived in Taiwan, and an illustration of the indigenous people was inserted. In the section on 'Sakhalin (Karafuto)', there appeared a reference to 'several tribes including the *Ainu*' with a statement that 'the Hokkaido region has traditionally been inhabited by the *Ainu*'. The ethnicity and customs of Korea were not discussed, but it was noted that 13 million people, or 20 per cent of the population of the empire, lived in Korea.

In the third period, when a revised edition was issued in 1918, the description changed greatly. Differences in the description of the constituents of the empire are especially striking.

> The majority of the nationals (*kokumin*) [within the empire] are the Yamato nation, with a population of more than 54 million. In addition, in Korea there are about 16 million Koreans, and in Taiwan, more than 100,000 natives and more than 3 million Chinese who migrated to Taiwan from China. In Hokkaido, there are the *Ainu*, and in Sakhalin the *Ainu* and some other native tribes. Although they are of different races, they are all equally loyal imperial subjects.

The state textbook openly described Japan as a multi-national empire, and provided a chart that mapped her ethnic make-up. The reason that the words 'nationals' and 'subjects' were both used here reflected the fact that Japan at the time was called the Great Japanese Empire but was, in a sense, something more than a nation-state but less than an empire (see the conclusion). The Meiji Constitution that defined sovereignty as residing with the Emperor used the word 'subjects', but the general populace, including politicians, frequently used the term 'nationals'.

In volume 2, it was clearly stated that 'the population of the Korean region is about 17 million, the majority of whom are Koreans', that 'in the Sakhalin region, there are indigenous tribes such as the *Ainu* and the Gilyaks', and that 'the Hokkaido region is traditionally mainly inhabited by the *Ainu*'. There was also an illustration of the indigenous Taiwanese.

In the fourth revised edition, issued from 1935 to 1936, the constituents of the empire were described in further detail.

> The entire population [of the empire] amounts to over 90 million nationals. Although the majority are members of the

Yamato nation, in Korea there are about 20 million Koreans, and in Taiwan about 4.3 million Chinese who migrated from China and more than 100,000 native Taiwanese. Moreover, in Hokkaido, there are a small number of *Ainu*, and in Sakhalin a small number of *Ainu* and other natives. About 600,000 members of the Yamato nation have migrated to foreign countries.

On the same page was added the illustration of 'Natives of Taiwan and Their Home' that had originally been printed in volume 2, together with illustrations of 'The *Ainu* and Their Home', and 'The Gilyaks and Their Home'. A pie chart entitled 'The Ethnic Diversity of [Japanese] Nationals and their Percentages' was added. This clearly showed the ratio of each ethnic group within the empire. On the other hand, the description of the various regions in the second volume was limited to geography, and descriptions of the ethnic make-up of the inhabitants of the empire were omitted except in the case of Sakhalin.

The fifth revised edition, published from 1938 to 1939 and used until the middle of the Pacific War, was almost exactly the same as the fourth edition, except that the illustrations in volume 1 were replaced by photographs of 'Native Taiwanese', 'Native People of Sakhalin' and 'Native People of the South Seas', and the national population figures were updated. The total population of the empire was said to be 100 million, which of course includes the non-Japanese subjects.

Where state history textbooks used in primary schools are concerned, no reference was made at the elementary level to archaeological theories about the origin of the Japanese nation.[15] However, since ancient history was described according to the Kiki myths, mention was made of the Emishi, Kumaso and foreign migrants in ancient Japan.

The first edition, issued in 1903, did not mention the goals of the Eastern Expedition by the Emperor Jinmu, but it did state that Yamato-Takeru-no-Mikoto put down a rebellion by the Kumaso in the south and the 'Emishi in the east'. The Emishi rebelled again during the Reformation of the Taika Era in the seventh century, and their rebellion was formidable enough to have the Emperor Kanmu appoint Sakanoue-no-Tamuramaro as the Barbarian-Conquering Generalissimo (*Seii Taishōgun*) in 797 to suppress them. Furthermore, it was noted that in the period of Empress Jingū, the Kumaso, supported by Silla, rebelled. There was also a detailed description of the foreign immigrants.

> After the subjugation of the Three Han Countries of Korea, our country [Japan] received various unusual presents from them, and Korean scholars and craftsmen migrated to our country. As a result, our country became increasingly civilised.
>
> In the reign of the Emperor Ōjin, the son of the Emperor Chūai, a scholar named Wani first brought books back from Pekche [in Korea], and the crown prince and other members of the Imperial Household studied them. As a result, academic studies began in our country. Next, an individual named Achi-no-omi visited our country with many others from China, and used his academic knowledge to serve the Imperial Court. Following this, the descendants of Wani and Achi-no-omi served as clerks of the Imperial Court for generation after generation. Weavers and tailors occasionally arrived from the three Han Countries and China, and various handcrafts developed in our country.[16]

The contribution made by migrant scholars and craftsmen was clearly recognised. However, where the annexation of Taiwan is concerned, the section on modern history made no mention of the fact that indigenous Taiwanese were incorporated into the empire.

The remarkable changes seen in the geography textbooks were not repeated to the same extent in the later history textbooks. In the second edition published in 1909–10, the description of foreign migrants was somewhat shortened, and the reference to the education of the imperial offspring was omitted, but virtually no other changes were made. As was also the case with Taiwan, there was no reference in the textbook to the native inhabitants of Korea, which had just been annexed. In the third edition, published from 1920 to 1921, the phrase, 'their visit was based on the glorious achievements of the Empress Jingū', was added to the section on foreign migrants, and details about the goals of the Eastern Expedition of the Emperor Jinmu were provided. In the section that introduced the annexation of Korea, it was noted that 'all the people of the peninsula became imperial subjects'. In the fourth (1934–35) and fifth (1940–41) editions, there were no remarkable changes in these areas.

In general, therefore, geography textbooks clearly adopted the view that Japan was a multi-national empire. Although there was no reference to the archaeological theory of the origin of the nation in history textbooks, mention was made of foreign migrants, the Emishi and the Kumaso. There was no description in either type of textbook of a pure blooded homogeneous Japanese nation.

What, then, was the case with the junior high school history textbooks that private companies edited and submitted to the Ministry of Education for approval (*kentei*)? To state my conclusions first, the description of the origin of the nation in these textbooks seems to have varied according to the company and author.

Many textbooks emphasised the idea of a mixture. Some noted that the history of the struggle against the 'persecution of different races, such as the Emishi and Kumaso' had made the Japanese nation an enterprising and valorous one. Some stressed that 'the Kumaso, Emishi and other tribes, together with newly arrived migrants from China and Korea, were all assimilated and became loyal Japanese nationals'. Some cited loyal retainers with migrant blood, such as Sakanoue-no-Tamuramaro, argued that 'though the migrants in ancient Japan were foreigners, they were moulded in the Japanese melting pot into loyal and brave nationals', and noted that 'Korean and Taiwanese people today will also become loyal and brave Japanese nationals in the future'. Others claimed that 'the Emishi are today's *Ainu* in Hokkaido. They used to live throughout eastern Japan' and provided an illustration of the *Ainu*.[17] Such textbooks existed throughout the period from the 1900s to the 1930s. Almost all argued that, although there was a racial mixture, rule by the Emperor did not entail a relationship of command and obedience as was the case with foreign countries, but rather that imperial subjects were united by a familial love.

An interesting example is *Kokushi kyōkasho* (Japanese History Textbook) published in 1902 for junior high school students, and written by Tsuda Sōkichi who will be discussed in chapter 14. He described the ancient era as one where 'there used to be several indigenous peoples in the various regions of Japan, and the entire east was occupied by the Emishi nation', emphasised the close relationship between Izumo in the Japan of the Kiki myths and Korea, and stated that in ancient times the Japanese nation occupied only the western half of the archipelago. He wrote that 'those foreigners who were conquered and those who were naturalised were all completely absorbed without trace into the

Japanese blood-family, which proves our nation's powers of assimilation as well as the dignity of our National Polity'.[18] Tsuda later became the leading homogeneous nation theorist, but at this stage he adopted the mixed nation standpoint.

On the other hand, a number of junior high school textbooks made no mention of the alien nations that had historically existed in Japan.[19] Although all textbooks mentioned the Emperor Jinmu's Eastern Expedition and the conquest of the Kumaso and the Emishi, some did not describe these incidents as an interaction with alien nations. However, even textbooks which emphasised the mixed origin of the Japanese were approved by the government. The state thus accepted textbooks for elementary and secondary students that described the realities of a multi-national empire and the mixed origin of the Japanese nation.

'All Korean Names should be Changed into Japanese Ones'

This chapter will conclude with a discussion of an issue regarding the Japanese nation that the empire thought as important as the discourse about Korea – the debate about the anti-Japanese movement in America.

At the time, Japanese migrants were prohibited from being naturalised as Americans or from obtaining citizenship on account of their race, and in 1920 a bill banning Japanese migrants from leasing or buying real estate was passed in California. In 1919, Japan proposed in vain that a clause forbidding racial discrimination be included in the Covenant of the League of Nations that was being discussed at the Peace Conference in Paris. In 1924, the revised US Federal Immigration Law completely closed the door to Japanese immigrants.

This problem was the focus of strong interest in Japan as symbolic of the anti-Japanese racial discrimination of the Western Powers. National meetings were held to criticise the USA, and one individual committed suicide to protest against America. Tokutomi Sohō advocated military expansion to wreak revenge on the USA, Uchimura Kanzō argued in favour of breaking off relations with the USA, and Nitobe Inazō publicly declared that he would not again set foot on American soil unless the USA revised its immigration laws (all three were prominent Christian intellectuals: see chapters 3 and 5).[20] The folklorist Yanagita Kunio, who was close to Nitobe and who will be discussed in chapter 12, and who was to be hugely influential in the formation of Japanese self-identity, was one of those influenced by this trend.

In this situation, the discourse on the Japanese nation split into two groups. One argued that 'the 60 million Japanese are an almost completely pure and homogeneous nation', comparing this with America, which 'is merely a multi-racial nation'.[21] This argument emphasised the homogeneity of the 'Japanese' out of a sense of crisis about the West. The figure of 60 million of course did not include the populations of Korea and Taiwan.

The other argument reflected the mixed nation theory. Many mixed nation theorists thought multi-racial Japan was similar to the USA. For example, a Japanese-American missionary wrote in his *Beikoku to jinshu sabetsu no kenkyū* (A Study of America and Racial Discrimination), published in 1919, that 'Japan is the melting pot of the East' and that 'the union of the Americans, created though a mixture of all Western nations and civilisations, with the Japanese, created through a mixture of all Eastern nations and civilisations, would surely contribute greatly to the happiness of people all over the world'. He thus argued that the USA should accept Japanese immigrants.[22]

After the complete exclusion of Japanese immigrants, however, such arguments changed into one-sided praise of Japan. In an anonymous leading article, 'Nippon minzoku no kosei to sono shimei' (The Uniqueness and Mission of the Japanese Nation), published in 1929 in an extra issue titled 'Sekai shinshutsu gō' (Advancing into the World)' of *Nippon oyobi Nipponjin* (Japan and the Japanese), which had become known as a right-wing magazine, it was stated:[23]

> According to the theory of one scholar, no other nation's blood is as complicated as that of the Japanese. Few nations are a mixture of as many different peoples as the Japanese nation. In fact, from ancient times, Japan has accepted and embraced a large number of alien nations. Some came from the South Seas, some from China, some from Mongolia, some from Manchuria, some from Korea, and some from Siberia. Japan has witnessed the migration of many alien races. In this sense, Japan is just like the USA. However, unlike America, the Japanese nation has never discriminated against or rejected any of these migrants, nor has there ever been the sort of tenacious anti-immigrant movement seen in America.

This article claimed that the fact that under the leadership of the Imperial Family 'the most complicated and mixed nation formed the most united and unified state, which is just like a great family' was 'proof above all of our nation's capacity for synthesis, which cannot be seen in the history of any other nation'. Here the theory of Japanese superiority was advocated, with Japan, which had proposed racial equality at the Peace Conference in Paris, a melting pot of more races than the USA.

An article written by Nakayama Satoru which appeared in *Nippon oyobi Nipponjin* in 1924, when the complete exclusion of Japanese immigrants was decided, is an extreme example of this line of argument.[24] This article began: 'The mission of the Japanese nation is to become the leader of Asia, and restore the rule over Asia which has been usurped by the white race, and to teach the white race the essence of the justice and humanity they constantly talk about by putting these principles into practice'. Following this, however, he asked whether 'Japan is also guilty of racial discrimination' and whether 'Japan is truly qualified to advocate justice and humanity, together with the abolition of racial discrimination, without first solving the problem of Korea'. This was a conscientious position compared to Kita Ikki's obstinate insistence in his *Kokka kaizōan genri taikō* that the 'Korean problem is not a problem of racial discrimination, since we belong to the same race'.

After claiming that Japan could not relinquish Korea, Nakayama argued for assimilation as a means of abolishing discrimination, saying that 'the synthesis of the Japanese people, contrary to the anatomical tendency of Western people, is the psychological base of today's Japan'. This argument, like many others, was based on the claim that 'from the ethnographic viewpoint, the Japanese are a racially mixed nation, and mainly a mixture of four races, the Koreans, Chinese, *Ainu* and Malays. Nevertheless, there is no racial strife in Japan, which proves the great powers of assimilation and generosity of our nation'. He proposed the following 'policy' for assimilating Korea.

> This policy is to change the names of all Koreans by law into Japanese names, to transfer the domicile of origin (*genseki*) of all Koreans to Japan, and to treat their residence in Korea as a domicile of choice. In addition, all proof of their Korean identity should be destroyed.

At the time of the Great Kantō Earthquake last year, it was not possible to distinguish Koreans from Japanese by their facial features [i.e. the only means to distinguish them was to get them to speak]. There is no difference in the facial or physical features of the Japanese and Koreans. If Korean names were all changed into Japanese names, it would be impossible to tell whether anyone was Korean or not. The contempt that Japanese feel on learning that someone is Korean would no longer have an opportunity to emerge.

In the Great Kantō Earthquake of 1923, roughly 100,000 people died in and around Tokyo. In the panic that followed, Koreans (together with some Chinese and two Japanese anarchists) were lynched, and about 3,000 Koreans were killed (although the exact number is still not known). At the time, Koreans were identified by their pronunciation. Nakayama stated that Koreans would be eager to become 'Japanese who are culturally far superior', and continued in the following vein:

At the same time as their names are changed into Japanese names, the Korean language must be completely abolished. A 30 year plan is needed which will have as its goal the destruction of the Korean language and the extinction of all remnants of Korean identity. We should be eager to see the new Japanese, who will speak Japanese and have Japanese names, appointed as bureaucrats, commended publicly when they deserve it, and literally becoming united with the Japanese through intermarriage. They should also be enlisted in the army. There must be no discrimination whatsoever.

For Nakayama, the fight against discrimination thus meant recognition of military conscription. However, he insisted that this assimilation should be applied 'only to the people of Korea, but not those of China, India or the Philippines'. The reason was that 'the facial features of the Chinese, Indians and Filipinos immediately betray their origin, and accordingly any change of names would be useless'. Unlike the Western Powers, which had advanced into regions populated by alien nations, the Great Japanese Empire had advanced into regions populated by the 'same race'. He argued that the change of names should be applied only to people of the same race. The title of his article was 'Chōsenjin no na o zenbu Nipponmei ni subeshi' (All Korean Names Should be Changed into Japanese Names).

If all differences were destroyed, discrimination too would disappear. This suggestion may have been subjectively well-intentioned. It was a consequence of the well-meaning mixed nation theory and the argument for the abolition of discrimination as developed by individuals such as Kita Sadakichi, and the theory of a Japanese melting pot superior to that of the West. As will be seen in chapter 16, the Government-General of Korea implemented a change of Korean names into Japanese ones 16 years later in 1940, several years before the introduction of conscription for Koreans.

10 The 'Japanese' as Caucasians

The 'Japanese' are in fact Caucasian. This strange theory of the origin of the Japanese nation first appeared early this century, and traces of its influence can still be seen today.

Suffering from an immense inferiority complex where the West was concerned, Meiji Japan responded with a variety of different theories about the Japanese nation. As already shown, some accepted the mixed nation theory, seeing this position as the product of Western scientific civilisation, and reconstructing it into a logic of imperialistic expansion and assimilationist policy. Others expounded the idea of the pure blood and unity of the Japanese nation as a way of resisting the Western menace. These were the two main responses, but others embraced entirely different options.

One was to remodel the Japanese nation itself into a 'superior Caucasian nation' by mixing the blood of the 'Japanese' with that of Westerners as much as possible. An example of this is Takahashi Yoshio's *Nippon jinshu kairyōron* (On Improving the Japanese Race), published in 1884 with a preface by Fukuzawa Yukichi (see chapters 2 and 3). This book created a sensation at the time, and many writers, including the national polity theorist Katō Hiroyuki (see chapter 3), vigorously criticised it.[1] Another option was to argue that the Japanese nation was originally 'Caucasian'.

In a word, this was a version of the story of a wandering prince rewritten on an enormous scale. Just like the descendants of a royal family who had fallen on hard times and become commoners, the ancestors of the 'Japanese' were a superior Caucasian nation that had wandered East in ancient times, and the present 'Japanese' had long since forgotten their illustrious past. The border area between the East and the West – places such as Judea, Babylon and Assyria which were supposed to be the birthplace of civilisation and which featured in the Bible – together with the Hittites, were favoured as possible origins of the Japanese nation in terms of geography and people. Like many stories of a wandering prince, this was an illusion created by those who were crushed by a strong inferiority complex and feelings of desperation.

The Japanese Nation as 'Descendants of a Noble Family'

As was the case with the mixed nation theory in anthropology, the notion that the Japanese nation was of Caucasian origin also originated from imported ideas, and was in fact a far older idea than the 'scientific' mixed nation theory.

As early as 1621, the *Historia y relacion de lo sucedido en los Reinos de Japon y China* written by Pedro Morejon (1562–1634?), a Spaniard, had already noted that the Chinese and 'Japanese' were nations formed from a mixture of migrants from Palestine, the Holy Land, and indigenous Eastern peoples. A German naturalist Engelbert Kömpfer (1651–1716), who arrived in Japan in 1690, advanced the theory that Babylon was the origin of the Japanese nation. According to him, the divergence of all national languages originated in the collapse of the tower of Babel, and since Japanese was different from Chinese, the Japanese nation could not be a Chinese splinter group, but must, rather, have migrated directly from Babylon. In the Meiji era, in 1878, a Scotsman named Macleod advanced the theory that the Japanese nation was a mixture of the descendants of the ten lost Judean tribes, the *Ainu*, and a Malay people. Although all these theories originated in biblical interpretations of the world, they were not completely unrelated to anthropological theories about the origin of the Japanese. For instance, as noted in chapter 1, Bälz suggested that the Chōshū type might have been related to the Akkadians.[2]

Among the writers who supported this theory of the origin of the Japanese nation, Taguchi Ukichi enjoyed the greatest public response. In the Meiji Period, he was known, together with Fukuzawa Yukichi, as the leading supporter of enlightenment, and the fact that a figure of his stature began to argue that 'the Japanese race was an Aryan race' had a great impact on the people of the time.

As noted in chapter 2, Taguchi argued in his *Kyōryūchi seido to naichi zakkyo* (Foreign Concessions and Mixed Residence in the Interior), published in 1893, that 'the Japanese race' had 'no reason to fear the Aryan race'. Comparing the superiority of the Japanese and Aryan races was a theme already covered quite extensively by Miyake Setsurei's *Shin zen bi Nipponjin* (The Truth, Virtue and Beauty of the Japanese), which had been published in 1891. Miyake Setsurei (1860–1945) was a representative nationalist (*kokusuishugisha*) known for his criticisms of government despotism and Westernism. *Shin zen bi Nipponjin* is a classic text in the *Nihonjinron* (theories of the Japanese) discourse. Although the superiority of the Japanese and Aryan races was discussed in Miyake's work, the premise that the 'Japanese' were a Mongolian race was not doubted. On the other hand, Taguchi argued in his 'Nippon jinshuron' (On the Japanese Race), published in 1895 immediately after the Sino-Japanese War, that it was a mistake to view the Japanese as belonging to the same 'yellow' race as the Chinese.[3] The contempt for the Chinese seen in the dispute over mixed residence thus re-emerged during the Sino-Japanese War, and led Taguchi to reject the idea that the 'Japanese' were the same 'yellow' race as the Chinese.

According to this article, the Japanese language was very different from Chinese and it was obvious that 'the intellect of the Japanese race is far superior to that of the Chinese race'. The reason 'some Japanese have a coarse appearance and an inferior intellect' is that they had mixed their blood with that of the indigenous Emishi. However, those who maintained their pure Tenson blood have 'skin even fairer and smoother than...that of the Aryan race'. Based on an interpretation of the Kiki myths and a linguistic analysis, he asserted that the Japanese ancestors were the Hsiung-Nu (in other words, the Huns) and that, in modern times, the Hungarians and Turks were the 'compatriots' of the 'Japanese'.

It was in a lecture, 'Kokugo jō yori kansatsu shitaru jinshu no shodai' (A Linguistic Approach to Identifying the Founder of Ethnic Groups), published in 1901, that Taguchi unveiled a full-scale theory that the Japanese were an Aryan race.[4] According to Taguchi, 'the Aryan race' belonged to the Indo-European family of languages that descended from Sanskrit. However, contemporary European languages had descended from German, and it was the languages of Turkey, Hungary, Tibet, Japan and Korea that were closest to Sanskrit. In other words, it was the Japanese nation 'which was the true descendant of the Aryan race', and for Europeans to call themselves Aryan was nothing less than 'to steal our ancestors, and demote us to the status of a branch family of the Aryan race'.

This speech is said to have ended 'amidst a storm of applause', but his complete denial of the idea of the family of Indo-European languages, an idea that was the basic concept of the linguistics of the time, triggered a storm of criticism from linguists. Above all,

Shinmura Izuru (see chapter 7), then a young, rising scholar, was especially harsh: Taguchi's theory had 'no scientific value whatsoever', and he was 'totally ignorant of the Indo-European family of languages at least'.[5] What Shinmura seems to have feared was that the opinion of academic linguistics might be placed on the same level as the views of laymen like Taguchi. This type of singular theory later came to be ignored in academic circles. However, since this was the dawn of Japanese linguistics and anthropology, and since Taguchi was a prominent scholar who had published in an authoritative journal, Shinmura could not remain silent.

Bitter words passed between Shinmura and Taguchi in two exchanges. However, Taguchi became increasingly obstinate in adhering to his views, Shinmura gave up trying to argue with him, and the dispute ended without the two coming to grips with one another. The famous novelist and army doctor, Mori Ōgai (1862–1922), who had once held Taguchi in high regard, could not hide his perplexity at Taguchi's views on nationality, but Taguchi merely continued as before.

In 1904, the year the Russo-Japanese War broke out, Taguchi published a work entitled *Ha ōka ron* (Destroy the Theory of a Yellow Peril) with the subtitle 'Nippon jinshu no shinsō' (The Truth of the Japanese Race).[6] This work criticised the discourse on the Yellow Peril that had emerged in Europe in response to Japan's victories in the Russo-Japanese War, and insisted instead that the 'Japanese' were not a 'yellow' race. According to Taguchi, the 'Tenson race' was Caucasian. Japanese skin had turned 'yellow' through intermarriage with the Emishi and Hayato, but if the Japanese dressed well in Western clothes and endeavoured to be diligent and healthy, 'this would be enough to banish the ill repute of the Japanese as a yellow race'.

Furthermore, in 'Nippon jinshu no kenkyū' (Research on the Japanese Race), which was published in the following year, Taguchi argued that Japan had modernised successfully, moving from feudalism to modern civilisation in a very brief time and, because the Japanese nation was superior, 'despite being a small island nation, defeated the huge Chinese Empire, and is continuing to win victories even in battles with a first-class Power like Russia'. Moreover, this superiority derived from the fact that the 'Japanese' were Caucasian. Four years previously, Taguchi had stated that the Korean language was also close to the Aryan language, but now he claimed that the ancient Korean Silla was a 'colony' founded by Susano-O, and concluded his speech by stating that the 'Japanese people need not admit that they are a yellow race...but should not hesitate to explain that, in fact, the Japanese are the descendants of a noble family'.[7] This same year, Taguchi died at the age of 50.

Of course, the victories in the Sino-Japanese and the Russo-Japanese Wars help to explain Taguchi's strange position, as did an inferiority complex towards the West. He was not satisfied with a mere 'Leave Asia and Join the West' (*datsu-A nyū-Ō*) policy, a popular Meiji Period slogan, but wanted the world to acknowledge that the Japanese people were a Caucasian race. In a series of papers that discussed race, Taguchi urged the 'Japanese' to wear Western clothes, and viewed the fact that Japan, unlike other 'yellow' Asian countries, had made rapid progress towards establishing a Western constitutional government as proof of the racial superiority of the Japanese nation. Since he still used concepts such as constitutional government as a yardstick to measure progress, it could be said that he retained the characteristics of a member of the Japanese enlightenment. However, his obsession with the importance of skin colour and his description of the Japanese nation as 'descendants of a noble family' went beyond mere praise of the West. The anthropologist, Tsuboi Shōgorō, who had asserted that 'skin colour means absolutely nothing', did not hide his contempt for Taguchi (although he did not mention him by name), saying that those who obstinately insisted that the 'Japanese' were Caucasian obviously 'believed that being white was good'.[8]

The next theorist to follow Taguchi and advocate the same position on the origin of the Japanese nation was Kimura Takatarō, who had attacked Christianity in the magazine *Nippon shugi* (Japanism). As noted in chapter 3, *Nippon shugi* was a magazine that rejected Western culture and advocated the idea of a supreme Japanism. It had published an article by Tsuboi that stated that the 'yellow race' was not inferior, and welcomed a piece of research by an American scholar that claimed that the brain size of the 'Japanese' was large. In 1911, the year following the Japanese annexation of Korea, Kimura published *Sekaiteki kenkyū ni motozukeru Nippon taikoshi* (Ancient Japanese History Based on Global Research).[9] The following sentence, printed as part of the preface, is an eloquent testimony to both the contents of the work and the writer's motives.

Although there was a scholar long ago who fanned the flames of controversy by stating that the Emperor Jinmu was a descendant of the Chief of the Wu, most scholars at universities today are even worse. They rant that the origin of the Japanese nation lies with the natives of the South Seas, or rave that it lies with the primitive barbarians of Manchuria and Mongolia, or cry that it lies with Korean migrants. Nevertheless, they receive no punishment whatsoever for their theories of an inferior origin for the Japanese race.

Kimura thus argued that the Japanese nation was not of 'inferior origin', and therefore not related to the people of Asia or the South Seas. He also stated that 'the imperial universities are a "cesspool" of "imbecile scholars" and "theorists who argue that the Japanese race is of inferior origin"'. On the other hand, he praised some 'Western views of the Japanese race', which 'agree that the Japanese are an Aryan race and are superior'.

According to Kimura, there were similarities between the Bible and Greek myths on the one hand and the Kiki myths on the other, and also between the Greek and Japanese languages. Based on these similarities, he argued that a Graeco-Latin race had travelled to the East and settled in Japan. Izanagi's visit to the land of Yomi (the land of the dead) was the story of Alpheus in Greek mythology, and the character 'na' in the Katakana script was equivalent to the Chinese character for 'ten' the Roman numeral 'X', the Buddhist swastika and the Christian cross. Moreover, the ideology of Judaism and Christianity was plagiarised from Japan. He also insisted that 'Takamagahara is Armenia', that Ōkuninushi was Joseph in the Old Testament, and that the land conquered by the Empress Jingū was not the Korean but the Italian peninsula!

According to Kimura, 'the Japanese nation was shut up in the tiny islands of the Far East for so long' that its 'ideology and aspirations' had become 'subservient'. Even after victories in the Sino-Japanese and Russo-Japanese Wars, 'although the Japanese have become to some extent aware of their own abilities, they are not yet fully aware of them'. Because of this, he tried to show 'the ancient history of the Japanese nation is really the ancient, central history of the world'.

Before the publication of this work, Kimura had translated works by Plato and Byron and this perhaps triggered his liking for Greece. Many theorists at this time, such as Inoue Tetsujirō, overcame their inferiority complex towards the West through the growth of the empire, while others who still had an inferiority complex developed these strange views, perhaps due to their exhilaration at the increase in national prestige following the victories in the Sino-Japanese and the Russo-Japanese Wars.

A Volunteer

In the Meiji Period that came to an end in 1911, however, this type of theory was not particularly unusual. Takegoshi Yosaburō noted in his *Nisen gohyakunenshi* (2,500 Years of Japanese Civilisation) that the two large civilisations of 'the Semitic race' (represented by Phoenicia), and 'the Hermitic race' (represented by India) had entered Japan. Kume Kunitake, who interacted with Taguchi, noted the similarity between the Egyptian script and the cuneiform characters of 'Akkad', the old capital of Sumer' on the one hand, and ancient Chinese characters on the other (for Takegoshi and Kume, see chapter 5). Although these did not necessarily argue in favour of a communality of race, at the same time it was not unusual for a close cultural relationship with Central Asia to be advocated. Beginning with the well-known racial thinker, Arthur de Gobineau (1816–1882), there seems to have been a tendency among European racial thinkers to share these strange views: after all, to accept that the Japanese nation which had defeated Russia was Caucasian was appropriate in maintaining a belief in Caucasian superiority.[10]

In the Taishō Period which began in 1911, however, the idea of a cultural relationship turned into the belief that Japan had assimilated Hellenistic civilisation through the Silk Road, and the theory of a racial link disappeared from the mainstream of public discourse. This was partly due to the development of anthropological and historical studies, but mainly to the confidence that the Japanese had regained, which meant that they were no longer as interested as before in the idea of a Caucasian origin. These theories came to be regarded as completely ephemeral, although they did not disappear totally. In fact, there is no end to the list of strange theories – such as that of a Sumer origin supported by Mishima Atsuo, or an Egyptian origin by Tokumasa Kingo, or a Judean origin by Sakai Katsugun.

Well-known writers propounding arguments of this sort include Deguchi Onisaburō, a leader of the Ōmoto religion (a Shintō splinter-group that had a different interpretation of the Kiki myths from the official one, and is known for having been suppressed by the government), and the anarchist, Ishikawa Sanshirō (1876–1956). In his work, *Reikai monogatari* (The Story of the Spirit World), Deguchi set the stage in Central Asia, and developed a story in which the characters are a mixture of those from the Bible and the Kiki myths. Ishikawa, known for having worked with another anarchist, Kōtoku Shūsui (1871–1911), an individual executed for his involvement in a plot to assassinate the Meiji Emperor, Sakai Toshihiko (1870–1933) and others to found the *Heimin shinbun* (Commoner's Newspaper), read, and was deeply impressed by, *Kojiki* while in prison. Following his release, he became interested in Mesopotamian history during his travels in England and France. In 1921, after returning to Japan, he published *Kojiki shinwa no shin kenkyū* (New Research of the *Kojiki* Myths) and argued for the Hittite origin of the Japanese people. According to this work, ancient Japan was a matriarchy. This is said to have influenced Takamure Itsue (see chapter 11) who, like Ishikawa, was also an anarchist and a devoted reader of *Kojiki*.[11]

Tanaka Chigaku, who organised the Kokuchūkai (National Pillar Society), a nationalistic organisation with links to Nichiren Buddhism, listed countries such as Greece and Italy as possible sites for Takamagahara. As mentioned in chapter 8, Tanaka advanced the mixture of nations and the assimilative abilities of the 'Japanese' as grounds for the racial superiority of the Japanese, whose 'holy mission was to unite the world'. He viewed the West and other foreign countries as caught up in a vortex of individualism, rule through power, self-interest, an over-emphasis on rights, and conflict. On the other hand, Japan was a country that had overcome the limits of an emphasis on 'self', and that assimilated ancient migrants and alien peoples without discrimination and enjoyed a natural harmony. Tanaka argued that the realisation of *hakkō ichiu* (bringing all corners of the world under a single roof under the Emperor), or the unification of the world, was the ultimate form of pacifism. It was a contradiction for him to say that Europe was the home of the Tenson nation, but here perhaps we can see the internal state of mind that lay beneath the surface of his public assertions. The famous author of children's literature, Miyazawa Kenji (1896–1933), who was then a passionate Kokuchūkai activist, said in a letter of 1920 to a close friend that 'you, like me, must be confused about the home of the Tenson race. However, we once swore to follow the absolute truth, didn't we?' in order to dispel his own doubts. It is important to note that Tanaka insisted that there had been equality between the sexes in ancient Japan and that an army of female warriors had existed. He also emphasised that Amaterasu was a goddess. This point is important in understanding Takamure Itsue's interest in the Kiki myths.[12]

Even today in Japan a large number of books are published that argue for various origins of the Japanese nation, such as Babylon. These are often linked with anti-Semitism. It is argued that the Jewish nation moved west from ancient Palestine, while the Japanese nation moved east, and that a central story in world history is the confrontation between Jewish capital which rules the USA and Europe, and the Japanese nation which represents Asia. Both the Pacific War and the postwar economic friction between the USA and Japan are explained as part of this confrontation.

Many of these books compare Jewish capital (which, it is claimed, pursues self-interest and destroys nature) with the Japanese nation (which has abandoned selfishness and is in harmony with nature). The Jews who appear in these works represent a 'West' that is contrasted with Japan. There are also a number of *Nihonjinron* (theories of the Japanese) which compare the Japanese nation and the Jews. Watsuji Tetsurō, who will be examined in chapter 15, and the 1970s best-seller, *The Japanese and the Jews*, which will be mentioned in chapter 17, are examples of this.

The framework of this discourse had thus been established by the 1920s. It was in this environment that Oyabe Zen'ichirō (1868–1941) published his *Nippon oyobi Nippon kokumin no kigen* (The Origin of Japan and the Japanese People) in 1929. It is worth taking notice of the circumstances in which he came to dedicate himself to the *Ainu* rather than to his charitable activities themselves.

Oyabe was born in 1868 into the family of a judge. He travelled to America by himself and obtained a Ph.D. from Yale University. Like Uchimura Kanzō (see chapter 4), Oyabe was profoundly moved during his stay in America by the education system for native peoples on both the American mainland and in Hawaii, and he appealed for an improvement of 'the education provided to the Aborigines of Hokkaido and Taiwan' to the then Japanese Minister to Hawaii, Shimamura Hisashi, and to the Japanese Minister to America, Hoshi Tōru (1850–1901). This petition was received favourably and, it seems, had an influence on the formation of the Hokkaido Former Aborigines Protection Act of 1899.[13]

After Oyabe returned to Japan, he became a major promoter of the Former Aborigines of Hokkaido Education Society which Tsuboi Shōgorō had publicised (see chapter 4). Dissatisfied with just giving lectures in Tokyo like Tsuboi, however, he moved to Hokkaido with his family. In 1906, a linguist who specialised in the *Ainu* language, Kindaichi Kyōsuke, visited Oyabe to research the *Ainu* language, and later wrote as follows.[14]

> At the time, Doctor Oyabe, who had received his degree in America and returned to Japan, was dedicated with his whole household to the education of *Ainu* children. An unaffected, generous and amiable person, Doctor Oyabe treated me as an old friend. He showed me all his samples and documents, and made available to me his whole stock of knowledge. I was overwhelmed by this. I was even more impressed by the brave and pure determination of Mrs. Oyabe who, as soon as she graduated from the Miyagi Girls School, devoted her life to the work of her husband on Japan's remote frontier.

Oyabe was then 38 years old. Kindaichi, a young student, saw Oyabe's devoted work as a volunteer at first hand, heard the story about how Oyabe wrote a book in America to scrape together his school fees and eventually obtain his Ph.D., and 'felt that I was seeing the hero of a success story with my own eyes and was overwhelmed with emotion'. Kindaichi visited the *Ainu* educational institution founded by Oyabe, where he saw Oyabe's muddy children, and said with a smile 'playing with *Ainu* children, your children seem to be exactly the same as them'.

Obtaining a Ph.D. from a Western University guaranteed social success in the Japan of the day, and Hokkaido was then an unimaginably remote, out-of-the-way place. This indicates that Oyabe's enthusiasm for the *Ainu* was real. Very few people at that time would have let their own children play with *Ainu* children.

However, Kindaichi had already seen some indications of Oyabe's future path. Oyabe told Kindaichi that after he named his daughter 'Isa', he discovered that 'Isa' meant 'woman' in Hebrew which (he believed) in turn meant that 'Hebrew words are contained in the Japanese language we speak every day'. A specialist in linguistics, Kindaichi did not know what to say to Oyabe, whom he respected very much, and he later described this as the result of 'the purity...of a hero who was a religious figure, an idealist, and a romantic...all of which made it easy for him to believe in the mysterious'.

These words appear in an essay Kindaichi published 19 years later in 1925 about Oyabe's *Jingisu-kan wa Minamoto-no-Yoshitsune nari* (Genghis Khan is Minamoto-no-Yoshitsune). Minamoto-no-Yoshitsune (1159–1189) was the younger brother of the Shōgun Minamoto-no-Yoritomo (1147–1199), the founder of the Kamakura Bakufu. Yoshitsune was a skilled warrior but, feared by his brother as a potential rival, was killed. He has remained a very popular tragic hero in Japan ever since. According to Kindaichi, it had been a popular idea since the Edo Period that Yoshitsune had not in fact been killed, but instead had escaped to Hokkaido, from where he crossed safely to the Asian continent. Among those who shared and transformed this legend were the *Ainu*. They believed in an ancestral god, Okikurumi, who was said not to have died but to have left for a foreign country. Kindaichi conjectured that people from mainland Japan heard this myth and told the *Ainu* that Okikurumi was in fact Yoshitsune, and the *Ainu* eventually came to say that the Japanese name for Okikurumi was 'Hōgansama', which means Yoshitsune.

From the *Ainu* point of view, one (albeit humiliating) way to encourage the 'Japanese' to accept their own god was to claim that this god was a hero respected by the 'Japanese'. A similar phenomenon where a conquered people came to mix their native beliefs with those of their conquerors is also seen in the case of the brown-skinned Guadeloupe Maria, 'Our Lady of Guadeloupe', a Virgin Mary worshipped by the indigenous Central Americans in Mexico. There are several variations of the Yoshitsune legend: Yoshitsune was adopted by the family of an *Ainu* leader, and in the Edo Period, the *Ainu* leader Shakushain who fought in 1669 against the Japanese feudal domain that ruled Hokkaido, the Matsumae domain, was Yoshitsune's illegitimate child. The idea that Yoshitsune had crossed to the Asian continent was so widespread that Philipp von Siebold gave an account of this story in his *Nippon* in the late Edo Period. The view that Yoshitsune was Genghis Khan was another version of the story.

After Oyabe heard the *Ainu* legend where the *Ainu* 'even today worship Yoshitsune as Honkansama', Oyabe preached the immortality of this hero in his work, *Jingisukan wa Minamoto-no-Yoshitsune nari*. At that time, Oyabe had been decorated for his work in *Ainu* education and had left Hokkaido. However, his activity as a volunteer was not totally divorced from this strange theory. The book became a huge contemporary best-seller. Oyabe presented a copy to the Imperial Court and was highly honoured when members of the Imperial Family inspected it. Among those who praised Oyabe to the skies were Amakasu Masahiko (1891–1945), an army officer who played a part in establishing a puppet regime in Manchuria in 1932 following the Manchurian Incident of 1931, and Ōkawa Shūmei, a Pan-Asian propagandist who was tried as a war criminal after the Second World War (see chapter 16). As was the case with the migration of Susano-O to the Korean peninsula, the legend of Genghis Khan as Yoshitsune was suitable for Japan's push into Asia.[15]

In 1929, Oyabe published *Nippon oyobi Nipponjin no kigen* (The Origin of Japan and the Japanese) which included the results of his fieldwork in Asia.[16] With a preface by Takegoshi Yosaburō (see chapter 5) and the lettering of the title by the leading right-wing figure Tōyama Mitsuru (1855–1944), the book claimed that the Japanese nation needed to look to the Hebrews to explain its origins. Oyabe argued that Takamagahara was *Hara*, the capital of 'the state of Tagaurm' in 'Armenia', and denied the view that the Japanese nation originated in 'the savages of the South Seas' or 'the Tungus', saying 'Great Japan is the land of the gods'. This of course was also the position adopted by Kimura.

However, the main characteristic of this book is the way the *Ainu*, as well as the Tenson nation, are described. Originally, Oyabe explained, the 'Esau tribe' lived in Palestine and Eso (Ezo) was a corrupted form of Esau (Esau was Jacob's older brother in the Old Testament). According to Oyabe, 'almost all the place names in the archipelago originate from the Ezo language'. Oyabe noted that the Ezo (or the Emishi) were driven north by the Tenson nation, saying 'I am overwhelmed by sympathy, thinking of their series of tragedies, and lack the courage to continue writing'. In the frontispiece of this book, photographs of *Ainu* leaders are compared with photographs of Tolstoy, Brahms, Marx and Darwin, and Oyabe emphasised the similarities between them. He thus attempted to demonstrate that the *Ainu*, together with the 'Japanese', were 'Caucasians' originating in Palestine.

Kindaichi, who had by this time become the leading expert in *Ainu* studies, also stated that 'the *Ainu* are certainly not an inferior race' and argued that they were Caucasian. Fundamentally, Kindaichi's views of the Japanese nation and *Ainu* policies were the same as those of Kita Sadakichi. Although it was true that the *Ainu* appeared in Japanese history as the Ezo or Emishi and the Abe clan of the northeast (this clan fought against the Imperial Family in the Zenkunen and Gosannen battles of the eleventh century), Kindaichi and Kita both urged the necessity of a 'solution through development', or in other words a solution through speedy assimilation into the Japanese nation. Kindaichi, however, wanted to research the *Ainu* culture before it disappeared.

The promotion of assimilation was, for Kindaichi, a drive towards the eradication of discrimination. In speaking to those who viewed themselves as 'Japanese', he urged the view that the *Ainu* were not an inferior race, and insisted that mixing blood with them would not lead to the deterioration of the Japanese nation. He claimed that, compared to the racially discriminatory West, Japan had adopted 'the most humanitarian way to deal with minorities' by the decision to mix with them and assimilate them under the principle of 'universal brotherhood'.[17] At this time, Japan had overcome its inferiority complex towards the West by means of the mixed nation theory, and the goal of salvation through the theory of a Caucasian origin was transferred to the *Ainu*, the ruled within the empire, rather than the 'Japanese', who had become a nation of rulers.

Referring to Oyabe's work, Kindaichi said that legends, however illogical, were a form of consolation created by people in order to be able to keep on living and 'we require legends so that we can live through the stern realities of life'. He thus stated his sympathy for Oyabe who had once been his hero.[18] The story of a wandering prince produced by Meiji Japan to ease its sense of inferiority towards the West eventually became the demented idea of a single individual who had devoted half his life to the welfare of the indigenous peoples of the north. This was just one episode in the history of the Great Japanese Empire which continued to expand, devouring the ideas of countless individuals as it did so.

11 'The Return to Blood'

Takamure Itsue (1894–1964) is known as an anarchist, a poet, and as a path-breaking feminist historian. In her 'Nisen roppyakunen o kotohogite' (Celebrating 2,600 Years of Imperial Rule), written during the government campaign in 1940 to mark the 2,600th anniversary of the mythological accession of the Emperor Jinmu, Takamure quoted the words of Japanese nativist (*kokugaku*) scholars, stating 'the land of the Emperors (*kōkoku*) respects motherhood: it is Chinese thought which respects men and despises women' (Takamure Itsue [1940] 1979).

The research of a large number of scholars in Japan has made it clear that Takamure published material that glorified war during the so-called 15 Year War from the Manchurian Incident of 1931 to the end of the Second World War in 1945, and especially from about 1940.[1] However, this has not detracted from the high esteem her research into the ancient Japanese matriarchy has received. This research is viewed as having undermined the foundations of the Japanese patriarchy.

This chapter will analyse Takamure as the individual in the Great Japanese Empire who developed the most detailed logic of national assimilation based on the mixed nation theory. I would like to make it clear that Takamure's aim was to demonstrate the existence of a matriarchial system in order to improve the status of women, and the production of a justification for ethnic assimilation was a mere side-effect of this. However, she suffered the same tragic fate as the Christian intellectuals and anthropologists had in the past, when a logic that had been developed to defend minorities eventually turned into a justification of overseas aggression.

From Poetry to Ancient History

Takamure was born in 1894, the year the Sino-Japanese War of 1894–95 started. After graduating from a girls' school in her home town Kumamoto in Kyūshū, she worked in a variety of areas, such as a labourer in a textile factory and as a substitute primary school teacher, before moving to Tokyo. At this time, women were not able to enter university, no matter how intelligent they might be. This was the case with Takamure, too: the path to becoming an academic was closed to her.

Takamure's debut work was a collection of poems, published in 1921 when she was twenty-seven. Although she continued to publish poems, in due course, Takamure came to be known as an anarchist disputant in the so-called *'ana-boru'* debates, the anarchist and bolshevist debates in Japan. As a poet, she had sung the praises of the ideals of liberty and love, and so it was perhaps natural that she should feel an incompatibility both with the good-wife wise-mother (*ryōsai kenbo*) morality of Japan at that time, and with dogmatic communism, and should join the anarchists. However, in 1931, at the age of thirty-seven, she moved away from the maelstrom of debate and the movement. Takamure shut herself up with her husband in their house, which they had named Home in the Woods (*Mori no ie*), on the outskirts of Tokyo, where she researched ancient history, refusing to see anyone, never leaving the house, and spending ten hours every day studying.

It is a puzzle why this anarchist poet should have taken up research in ancient history. However, in general, when people are tired and despair of their own age, they look for hope in either the past or the future. In doing so, they find that the past and future are inseparable, because in order to forecast the future, it is necessary to understand how the present was formed, or in other words to understand the past. Future reform frequently takes the form of a restoration of a golden age that is believed to have actually existed in the past. Thus the Jacobins of the French Revolution dreamed of a restoration of the ancient republic, the Meiji Restoration was effected under the slogan of the re-establishment of the imperial regime, all modern nation states were founded with claims of legitimacy from ancient times, and even the communists assumed the existence of a primitive communistic society. Takamure, too, discovered her ideal of a women's liberation unrestricted by artificial morals in the history of ancient Japan.

She began her research into ancient history by reading Motoori Norinaga's *Kojiki-den*.[2] Although the *Kojiki* (together with *Nihon shoki* one of the two texts from which the Kiki myths were derived) certainly is a historical source that must be read when researching ancient Japanese history, the decision to opt for Motoori's work as a first step – Motoori was the founder of the Edo Period *kokugaku* – cannot be said to have been necessary. A short article that was written at the time, 'Shintō to jiyū ren'ai' (Shintō and Free Love), sheds some light on her feelings.[3]

In this paper, Takamure stated that Shintō is 'in other words something like "primitive" or "natural", and as modern people were able to draw suggestions for social reform from their research into prehistoric society, in our country too, people are able to turn for help to Shintō each time their age reaches a deadlock'. Her orientation towards nature can be seen in the name of her house, Home in the Woods, which was taken from the title of the book by the American philosopher, Henry David Thoreau (1817–1862), *Walden: or Life in the Woods* (1854). For her, nature meant a state of liberation from the fetters of artificial morality.

Moreover, she continued, 'the followers of Shintō, including Hiraga Gennai [(1729–1779)] and Motoori Norinaga, are liberals, and view artificial morality as being a desecration of the path of the gods'. The theory of love of the Edo Period nativist scholars was 'one that is comparable to the most progressive love of today, that talks about the evils of an artificial marriage system, and advocates the righteousness of natural love' and 'that states that equality between the sexes is the right path for Japan, the land of the gods'. According to Takamure, her ideals – a liberation from artificial fetters, the praise of nature, and equality between the sexes – could be seen in the *kokugaku* views of ancient history. Her conclusion was that 'we do not need to thoughtlessly admire the West. Studying Japan itself is frequently enough to find the path to liberty and liberation'.

Takamure opposed native Japanese oppressions, beginning with the good-wife wise-mother morality. How could she so easily return to Japan? The answer lies in an understanding of nativism.

The tradition of nativism since the time of Motoori had been to denounce foreign thought and view Japan as a peerless land of the gods. However, although this is not always understood correctly, the foreign thought that Motoori and others opposed was not Western thought, but mainly Chinese thought and the ideology of the feudalistic system of the time, Confucianism. That is the reason why nativism could become an anti-establishment thought directed against the Bakufu during the Meiji Restoration period, and why feudalistic morality had a hostile relationship with it.

For Japan, from ancient times until the Edo Period, Chinese civilisation was absolutely central. Even if Japan tried to compete with China, this was impossible as far as civilisation was concerned. One way to cope with this dilemma was to import as much advanced civilisation from China as possible. This was the route chosen by some Japanese Confucian scholars. However, nativist scholars such as Motoori chose a different route. They rejected Chinese thought as artificial, described by words such as '*sakashira*' (slick) and '*karagokoro*' (foreign minded), and advocated a return to the 'pure, clear heart' of ancient Japan, describing ancient Japan as a nature without peer that had not been corrupted by the poison of civilisation. Thinkers such as Motoori viewed the influence of foreign Chinese thought as the cause of Japan's decline from the golden age of ancient times.

Concepts such as 'primitive' and 'nature' have no real existence, but are invented afresh when people become civilised and realise how stifling civilisation is. As in the relationship between past and present, these concepts were produced as comparisons that allowed present circumstances to be interpreted. If nature is defined as the state that existed before civilisation, then this 'nature' would have to be universal, and would not privilege any single ethnic group or state. To define oneself as belonging to nature in comparison with a corrupt civilisation is not uncommon, and was seen on the peripheries of European civilisation, such as Germany, Russia and America, as it is today in the third world. Thoreau, whose works Takamure read avidly, is just one example of such a thinker. Motoori's works continued to be read in a Japan troubled by a self-identity formed from feelings of being located on the periphery first of Chinese and then of Western civilisation.

Takamure inherited this tradition of the nativist (*kokugaku*) school of thought. She came to believe that the oppression of women in modern Japan was due to the influence of foreign ideologies, beginning with Chinese thought, and that these ideologies could be overcome through a return to ancient Japan. This was not a highly unusual line to take: many thinkers today stress the oppression of modern society to such a degree that they give the impression that they believe that a return to an earlier age would be a panacea for all problems. Takamure thus focused on 'the Japanese matriarchy as opposed to the Chinese patriarchy' and claimed that, even in wartime, 'the fact that Japanese men's views of women bear no resemblance at all to the Japanese spirit is in fact due to the influence of medieval thought that developed under the influence of Chinese thought', and criticised the 'so-called good-wife wise-mother education which seems to have adopted much from Confucian thought'.[4]

Where the main topic of this work, theories of the nation, was concerned, in 1934, as work was progressing on her research into the matrilineal system, Takamure wrote in an essay, 'Nippon seishin ni tsuite' (On the Japanese Spirit), that 'there are two types of nationalism', and continued as follows:[5]

> Interestingly enough, both of these nationalisms are based on a sort of feeling of superiority. On the one hand there are the German Nazis, for instance, who believe that white Aryan blood is superior, and reject the lineage of Blacks and Mongoloids.
>
> On the other hand, from the standpoint of people such as Blacks and Mongoloids, it is not only believed that there is there no superiority and inferiority between nations, but also that all nations, which are today separated into different groups, will one day come together and be united, and the time when the world will become a single family is looked forward to. Members of this second group look to their own nation to realise this historical mission, and to provide the opportunity for this process to be furthered.

She continued as follows. 'Although the phrase the Japanese Spirit has been described by a number of authors in questionable ways or in ways that suit their own theories, it can be viewed as being representative of the second of these two types of nationalism. Whether consciously or unconsciously, at no time has the idea of Japan leading a World Restoration been as strongly felt as today'. Criticising the colonisation of Asia and Africa by the Western Powers, she stated that Japan 'has been unexpectedly entrusted with the mission of acting as the embodiment of Global Justice'. In a paper written at the same time, she compared the patriarchy of the 'Semitic race' with Japan, and thus did not limit the focus of her criticism to China.

The Japanese Spirit was thus seen as embodying the ideals of the 'mingling and union' of mankind and the 'bringing of the world together as a single family'. Takamure concluded this paper: 'in short; the Japanese national spirit must be founded upon a love for all peoples of the world, and must deny all the world's evils'. The content of this 'love' was shown through her research into marriage and matriarchy.

Matriarchy and the Assimilation of Alien Nations

In 1938, after the eruption of the Sino-Japanese War of 1937–45, Takamure's research into the ancient matriarchy, *Dai Nippon joseishi* or a History of Women in Great Japan, was published (a new edition retitled *Bokeisei no kenkyū*, Research on Matriarchy, was issued after the Second World War).[6] This was a substantial work of about 640 pages. A large part of it was devoted to the attempt to prove the existence of a matriarchy in ancient Japan by following the family tree of the clans recorded in the *Shinsen shōjiroku*.

Two points need to be made when examining this work. Firstly, the *Shinsen shōjiroku* that Takamure used as historical material was, as I have already made clear, a source that was constantly cited by those who wanted to show that a large number of different nations had historically mixed and assimilated in Japan. As was the case with most intellectuals of the time, Takamure, too, believed that the Japanese archipelago of ancient times had seen the coexistence of a number of different nations. This belief is illustrated by her words that 'the powerful rural clans consisted of a number of races, including the Saeki, the Hayato, the Emishi, the Kunitsukami, and migrants, among others' (Takamure 1938a: 102).

The second point is that she was an avid reader of Kita Sadakichi, maintained a correspondence with him, and even went so far as to say that he was 'the first teacher (*onshi*) I adopted as a student of history'.[7] The issue of an ancient matriarchy had been mentioned by a number of scholars, including Nishimura Shinji (see chapter 16), as well as Kita. At the time of the Great Kantō Earthquake, Takamure revealed in her diary a deep sympathy for the Koreans and called those 'Japanese' who regarded Koreans with contempt 'narrow-minded xenophobes', so she may have been in sympathy with this aspect of Kita's thought as well.

Against this background, Takamure undertook her research into the ancient matriarchy. According to her, this research was 'a theory, if I was to express it in a word, that is multi-ancestorial' (Takamure 1938a: 634). Multi-ancestorial describes a situation where a single ancestor does not branch out and form a large number of clans, but rather where a group of people with a number of different ancestors are brought together into a single clan. To state the conclusion first, Takamure developed a theory about an arrangement by which different peoples with different ancestors were brought together, or 'united into one by blood', under one clan, the Imperial Family.

In her introduction to *Dai Nippon joseishi*, Takamure examined the legend of the 'making of the country', that is, the founding of the nation (Takamure 1938a: 28). This is the legend in which Ōkuninushi married women of various clans from a variety of areas, from Kyūshū in the south of the archipelago to Hokuetsu in the centre-north, and fathered 181 children. In other words, a leader of a centralised power, by marrying women from powerful local clans (according to her, these were different people 'racially'), was able to unite these 181 clans under his control. Although this method of assimilation through mixing blood had been advocated by many scholars, including Kita, Takamure examined it in greater detail.

As we have seen, the core of the national polity position was the view that rule by the Emperor did not mean rule by power, but rather a family-type union based on a paternalistic compassion. The line taken by Kita and the reorganised national polity theory was that different nations were assimilated peacefully, and that armed force was exercised only when necessary.

However, no matter how actively blood is mixed, for two different nations to completely mix their blood, a long time, perhaps hundreds or even thousands of years, is necessary. If these different nations were hostile to each other, the process would take longer. If there were a large number of different nations in the archipelago at the time of the founding of the nation, would it have been possible for them to mingle in only 2,600 years? Again, could the visitors to Japan, who constituted one-third of the population in the early Heian Period in the ninth century when the *Shinsen shōjiroku* was compiled, have all intermarried in the several hundred years until the Edo Period, when it was no longer possible to identify alien nations within the archipelago? If a central government had enforced a policy of intermarriage, then a contraction of the time-span could perhaps be explained. To take this position, however, would be a suicidal act for national polity thinkers. This point had the potential to become the Achilles' heel of the assimilationist ideology of the mixed nation theory. Takamure, however, by introducing the explanatory factor of matriarchy, was able to by-pass the problem.

According to Takamure, if the activities of Ōkuninushi in marrying were undertaken within the framework of polygamy, then no matter how superhuman these activities were, they would not have played a positive role in uniting the state. Even if the 181 children were Ōkuninushi's own, their status within their own clans would be only that of an outsider's child and they would have no influence, unless these clans had, from the outset, been under the jurisdiction of Ōkuninushi's authority.

This is, however, only true if these children were seen as the offspring of the 'outsider', that is, the 'father'. If the ancient clans viewed children as the progeny of the mother rather than the father – that is, if the ancient clans were matriarchal – then this no longer holds. Children born of Ōkuninushi and the powerful women of the regional clans would succeed along the matrilineal line within the clan and thus become the leaders of their clans no matter who the father was. At the same time, if these children were to turn to their forefathers along the patrilineal line, then the 181 clans would be gathered under their father, Ōkuninushi-no-Mikoto.

Compared to the primitive theory of the mixed nation that assumed an inter-marriage between all members of each people, this was a revolutionary idea. The different peoples of various regions believed in a matrilineal lineage and thought that they were linked by blood to a clan leader produced in a matriarchal system. These clan leaders, however, saw themselves as linked along the paternal line to the central government. Through this combination of patriarchy and matriarchy, it was possible to construct a family state that encompassed many different races in a short time and through only a limited number of marriages.

Of course, this kind of 'nation-founding manoeuvre is only possible in societies where the actual clan system is matrilineal, and where a patrilineal system is consciously being formed'. However, according to Takamure, 'the society of ancient Japan was just such a case, and therefore the unification of the state took place smoothly' (Takamure 1938a: 28). In ancient Japan, 'the more renowned a clan was, the more actively it married different peoples', and 'desiring an expansion of the sphere of the clan, they attempted to unite all alien races and alien peoples under their own ancestors...Thus, those clans that succeeded at this became large and powerful, whereas those that did not declined to small families, or disappeared altogether' (Takamure 1938a: 29, 291). It hardly needs to be said that the largest and most powerful clan was the Imperial Family.

As a result of this 'it is normal that after a long time people forget who is whose descendant', and so people's consciousness of belonging to a different nation than the Imperial Family disappears (Takamure 1938a: 109). The next step was for people to 'change their family names and realign themselves as members of the Imperial Clan' (Takamure 1938a: 108).

As she researched the *Shinsen shōjiroku*, Takamure discovered a large number of examples where those of Emishi and migrant stock had entered clans associated with the Tenson (descendants of the gods). According to previous academic doctrine, this was seen as a forgery of surnames. Takamure, however, viewed this as a vestige of the matriarchy. That is, if the state was united as described above, there would be many cases where, even if the maternal line was Emishi, the paternal line would be Tenson. These people would eventually 'change their names to the paternal line' (Takamure 1938a: 136). Moreover, after the Taika Reforms (a series of political reforms that began in June 645 or Taika 1 and aimed to build a centralised state centred on the Emperor), the 'bestowing of surnames' system, in which the Imperial Family 'bestowed Japanese (*kōkoku*) surnames' on clans of different stock, was vigorously implemented (Takamure 1938a: 459). Thus 'it was quite natural that even people of different races, or those descended from servants on the maternal line, could be honoured with the grant of a Japanese surname if their paternal line was of Japanese blood. In this fashion, almost all the various races and those of humble origin were assimilated into the most honourable and cultured nation (*bunka shuzoku*)' (Takamure 1938a: 532).

According to Takamure, 'there is no word in ancient Japanese corresponding to conquest' (Takamure 1938a: 617). That is, the 'Japanese' did not enslave different ethnic groups through conquest as was the case in many Western and other overseas countries, and as Marxists had insisted was the case in ancient Japan. Instead, 'in Japan, rather than creating a pure system of slavery, clans or families became a people of low and humble status, but later had Japanese surnames bestowed on them' (Takamure 1938a: 619). Japan's policy towards alien peoples since ancient times consisted of 'firstly, pacification, and secondly, assimilation of family lineages through marriage' (Takamure 1938a: 619).

Thus people of different nationalities first became 'people of low and humble birth as families' through 'pacification', then assimilation was advanced through marriage, and finally they 'were granted Japanese surnames'. This very rough pigeonholing corresponds to her description of the unification of the state in ancient Japan. As described in chapter 8, Koreans and others were described by the reorganised national polity thinkers as 'foster children' and in 1940, a policy to Japanise the names of Koreans was implemented.

In Takamure's own words, 'although the word Blood-Kin State has hitherto been narrowly interpreted to mean only blood, or mixed blood, it must be approached from the viewpoint of genealogical assimilation'.[8] The phrase 'genealogical assimilation' meant that even if each individual member was not of mixed blood, they would be included within the genealogy of native clans that was headed by the Imperial Family through the marriage of their clan leader or through having a family name bestowed upon them. This notion can be said to be the same as that of the reorganised national polity theory: even an alien nation with no actual blood relationship could share the same ancestor as a member of the Japanese *ie* (family or household) (see the conclusion).

To repeat, this schema was the result of an attempt to prove the existence of a matriarchy, and Takamure's aim was not to develop a logic that would justify the assimilation of alien nations. The *Shinsen shōjiroku* was originally edited by the government of the day to show that a large number of clans had been united under the Imperial Family, and any analysis of this material will inevitably show a return to the Imperial Family. As a result, some historians today claim that it cannot be used as an objective historical material.

However, as if captivated by the schema that she had produced, Takamure became negative in her evaluation of the matriarchy. According to her, 'the *yome-iri* system where a woman [leaves her own clan and] enters another [i.e. her husband's] clan...is conditional on it being a period when clannish xenophobia has vanished', and therefore matriarchy was a product of the times of 'clannish xenophobia' (Takamure 1938a: 628). In her conclusion titled 'The Return to Blood', she argued as follows (Takamure 1938a: 637).

> Everything in this world is according to reason. The transition from matriarchy to patriarchy was a natural development. Matriarchy is a conservative, xenophobic blood-clan group, whereas patriarchy is a progressive, all-inclusive marriage group. All social transitions will move in this direction.
> We find boundless joy in the progressive nature of the great Japanese patriarchy, a patriarchy that is positive towards

marrying into all alien nations and barbarian peoples and uniting them totally under its own lineage, and that created the state, the clan and the family, or was forced to do so by heaven-sent circumstances. The reason that we feel this joy is that the lineage and blood of alien nations and barbarians was returned to that of a civilised race, and slavery was replaced by the clan as a result of the progressive nature of this system. Foreign civilisations, which are consciously based on slavery and oppression, are undoubtedly inferior to Japanese civilisation, which is consciously based on harmony within the clan.

Here, too, the mixture of nations is transformed into a sense of superiority to the West. At the same time, however, Takamure emphasised the contribution of the matriarchy to the state, noting 'when thinking along these lines, one cannot but recall the sacrifice and support of the ancient matriarchy' (Takamure 1938a: 637). According to Takamure, the matriarchy disappeared after a transition to a patriarchy, but during the period of transition, it cooperated with the patriarchy and played an essential role in national unification. Her argument was that if it was assumed that the ancient mixture and assimilation was carried out peacefully, then the existence of the matriarchy would have to be accepted.

As a well-known anarchist, Takamure was subjected to interference while writing *Dai Nippon joseishi* from the Special Police Division (this division was mainly concerned with keeping a check on socialists). She had Tokutomi Sohō (see chapter 5), who had become the most important mouthpiece for the government of the day, contribute a preface in order to avoid having the book suppressed (Tokutomi was from the same prefecture, Kumamoto, as Takamure). Stressing their contribution to the state had been the option taken in the past by some Christian intellectuals, and perhaps was the price minorities paid in order to have their positions and existence accepted. Whatever the reason, however, a logic, once created, takes on a life of its own, and eventually binds the individual who created it. Takamure was no exception.

'Turning the World into One Family'

From this time until the end of the war, the path that Takamure was to follow can be described in a single word as tragic, especially considering that she herself was so serious about it. As the war intensified, having gained recognition as a feminist historian for *Dai Nippon joseishi*, she was asked by major newspapers and by *Nippon fujin*, the bulletin of the Dai Nippon Fujinkai (The Japanese Women's Association, an official organization in which all adult women were enrolled from 1942), to contribute articles that praised the Great Japanese Empire from her position as a woman. She responded to these requests. This might have been a manifestation of her patriotism, or it may have been due to the upsurge of emotions that sometimes is seen when an unaffiliated researcher suddenly achieves public recognition after a long period of obscurity.

In her *Josei nisenroppyakunen* (A 2,600 Year History of Japanese Women), which was published in 1940 to coincide with the mythological 2,600th anniversary of the founding of the imperial dynasty, Takamure celebrated the 'founding and women' of this dynasty, one that 'dissolved alien nations through a fusion of blood under the lineage of the Sun Goddess' (Takamure 1940: 17). Takamure was probably hoping that her readers would recall the words of Hiratsuka Raiteu (1886–1971), a pioneering Japanese feminist thinker she respected, 'women were originally the sun', by noting that Amaterasu was a woman.

Josei nisenroppyakunen emphasised that, under this female goddess, Japan embraced alien nations and expanded, while equality between the sexes existed in ancient times. According to Takamure, 'with women of ancient times, there were no differences at all in status between men and women...and as a co-operating half, their interests were entire and positive. Therefore, they were full of patriotism and the spirit of love for the homeland' (Takamure 1940: 39). However, later on, 'China's androcracy' was introduced to Japan, and this, together with Chinese feudalistic morality, 'suppressed women's positive intellect to an extreme extent, and so the spirit of service to the state and feelings of social responsibility could not be expected of women'. In addition, 'Confucianism forced women into the narrow, confined space of the home, and closed off their interest in national government'. The only positive development was that '*kokugaku*, which arose as a backlash against Confucianism, rejected the polarised view (*in'yōkan*) of men and women [as seen in Chinese thought], and often corrected the prevailing view of women' (Takamure 1940: 93, 101, 144).

For women to cooperate in the war effort was, for Takamure, equivalent to overthrowing feudalistic morals, leaving the home, regaining their relationship with society, and returning to the utopian conditions of ancient times. Actions against state control, such as hoarding, were actions of women who had been poisoned by 'imported thought', such as Chinese feudalistic morality and Western individualism, and who as a result had lost their social nature and thus could no longer think beyond their own households (Takamure 1940: 145).

Furthermore, the schema of 'conservative' versus 'progressive' which had been applied to matriarchism and patriarchism was used to describe the characteristics of men and women. Stating that Chinese characters (*kanji*) were the alphabet that men used to imbibe the civilisation of the continent, whereas the native script (*hiragana*) was a unique Japanese alphabet developed by women, Takamure claimed that 'Japanese men have always had the characteristic of being able to adopt other cultures, and thus enrich their own culture. Japanese women, on the other hand, have the ability to conserve tradition, and to utilise it in new circumstances'.[9] She also wrote: 'I believe that, looking back over our past history, the special quality of Japanese women is, in a word, a healthy conservatism and a moderate character' (Takamure 1940: 65, 150). It hardly needs to be said that this corresponded to her view of a patriarchy which interbred with alien nations and the role of the matriarchy in maintaining the internal unity of the clan.

Takamure argued that because men and women were equal in ancient times, women became soldiers like the men. In an essay, 'Gunji to josei' (The Military and Women), published in *Nippon fujin* in November 1943, Takamure mentioned the participation of women in the military in ancient times, stated that 'it is said that the Ryūkū Islands [Okinawa] especially maintain the ancient customs of Japan', and introduced a section of the Ryūkyū epic poem 'Omoro' as translated by Ifa Fuyū (see chapter 9) which described a 'holy army' led by a 'female hero'. During the battle of Okinawa in 1945, Takamure wrote an article titled 'Dentō no gojishin' (Defending Tradition) where she wrote: 'when I heard that enemy sources said that the women of Ryūkū had fought their way into the enemy's position, I thought that they were true Japanese women, and true Ryūkyū women, and could not help but feel a sympathy of blood' (Takamure Itsue 1945). In the spring of 1945, the US Army made a forced landing on the beaches of Okinawa and, in battles that lasted roughly three months, about 150,000 Okinawan noncombatants – men, women and children – died, or about one-third of the total population of the main island of Okinawa.

In 'Jingū Kōgō' (Her Majesty the Empress Jingū), published in August 1943 in *Nippon fujin*, a union between Takamure's view of China and her view of the Family State is sketched out. This paper contains phrases such as 'Japan is the same race (*dōshu*) as the three Han states of Korea' and 'the tale of East Asian unity', and described the invasion of Korea by the Empress Jingū as the same as the 'present holy war' – that is as a battle to establish order in a divided East Asia. The article contains the following section.

[The ancient archipelago before the descent of the Tenson can be described as follows]...A wide variety of clans created a narrow circle of blood relatives, under various family deities, and not a single day passed without struggle and the shedding of blood, and the so-called 'Shikomeki-no-kuni' (abyss) was realised. The Sun Goddess appeared and descended to earth in order to save mankind from this situation [and to bestow Shintō on human beings].

There were two ways of replacing this barbarian state with an ordered world. One was to respect and value the lineage of one central tribe, and to regard the lineage of all other tribes as ignoble, and thus to order the world along class lines. This method is exemplified by China's concept of the Chinese as opposed to the Barbarians (*kai*). The other was to respect the lineage of all tribes equally, and having done so, to extend this further still, until a more distant, larger common ancestor is reached, and to recognise the fact that all are fellow compatriots under this common ancestor. This latter is the position of Shintō, and Shintō is probably the only great ideal and method for humanity's salvation, full of love and wisdom, that has been seen so far in the history of the world.

When god's descendants (the Tenson) descended from Heaven to earth, where they alighted at the peak of Takachiho ...no matter what the race, once other people are deified [in the Shintō system] they immediately become fellow compatriots...Thus the process of creating the family within Japan proceeded smoothly and brightly.

...In this way, if we go forward, we will join the nations of Greater East Asia, and move from there to the so-called world family – but only when the feeling of blood affinity is gradually expanded world-wide will mankind find salvation. I believe that the Japanese spirit of founding the state was in fact established with this desirable future in mind, and, though I tremble at my boldness in saying so, that the phrase of the Emperor Jinmu 'the whole world under one roof' (in other words, the conversion of the whole world into one family), the imperial edict of the Emperor Takakura [(1161–81)], 'all seas under one roof', and the poem by His Majesty the Meiji Emperor that said that 'the peoples of the four seas are all siblings', are all manifestations of this spirit.

The Family State, for Takamure, was not one that shunned alien ethnic groups or stifled women, and was thus different to a state based on the lines of 'China's concept of the Chinese as opposed to the Barbarians'. Rather, the Family State was a country of the feminine soul, a country of 'graceful maidens' (*taoyame*), which was able to embrace alien nations with boundless love and marriage. In a short article, 'Taoyame', that was published in *Nippon fujin* in November 1944, Takamure wrote:

Japanese 'Taoyame' believe that the family spirit is life, and constantly wish to unite the whole world as a single family. Since this holy war is being fought against the obstacles to the conversion of the world to a single family, the war can be positively said to be a woman's war. The female will which encourages our children, our husbands, our brothers to fight and win lies here.

With a daily existence that was becoming more and more grim, Takamure projected her ideals – women's liberation, a nature unrestricted by artificial morals, open freedom and love – on to ancient Japan, and deluded herself that the war meant the revival of these ideals. As a result, although as an unintended consequence, Takamure produced the most sophisticated theorisation of the assimilation of alien nations within the empire. However, the reality of the Great Japanese Empire did not bear the slightest resemblance to her idealisation. It is said that her husband, Hashimoto Kenzō, who had supported her in all respects, including supporting her economically, doing the housework, and collecting materials for her research, when asked about her thinking during the wartime years, answered only that 'after all, there was not enough information'.[10]

Takamure wrote constantly about 'motherhood', but she never gave birth herself. After her death in 1964, her husband, Kenzō, edited the Complete Works of Takamure Itsue. This contains not a single piece of work from the wartime years.

Part Three
The Thought of an 'Island Nation'

12 The Birth of an Island Nation's Folklore

On Christmas Eve, 1919, the year the March First Independence Movement erupted in Korea, a high ranking bureaucrat resigned. His last government post was Chief Secretary of the House of Peers, but his original area of speciality was agricultural administration. He had also been decorated for his achievements at the time of the Korean annexation. This individual was Yanagita Kunio (1875–1962), who was then 44 years old.

There is an enormous amount of research on Yanagita, the founder of Japanese folklore studies.[1] However, most of the studies to date have focused solely on Yanagita, and there is little research that satisfactorily locates his thought within the context of the entire Japanese discourse on ethnicity of his period.

The aim of this book is not to examine the thought of individual theorists such as Yanagita, but to shed light on and analyse the national consciousness of Japan as a whole. Yanagita was one of the few writers who moved, contrary to the general tendency in the empire of the period, from the mixed nation theory to the theory of the homogeneous nation. An analysis of Yanagita thus constitutes a valuable case study for understanding the character of the myth of ethnic homogeneity. At the same time, he provides a model case that sheds light on how the 'Japanese' portrayed themselves against a background where Japan was caught between Asia and Europe.

The 'Mountain People' as an Indigenous Nation

Yanagita Kunio was born in 1875, the sixth son of the Matsuoka family in a farming village in Hyōgo Prefecture. It appears that his father originally practised folk medicine, but with eight children to feed, of whom three died early, the family was poor. Yanagita later called his home 'the smallest house in Japan'.

Yanagita – his surname was still Matsuoka at this stage – admired Western literature and, while proceeding from the elite First High

School to the Faculty of Law at the Tokyo Imperial University, published several love poems in literary magazines. Although these were well received, he devoted himself to the study of agricultural administration, and entered the Agriculture and Commerce Ministry in 1900, giving as his reason for entering the ministry his experience of rural famine in his youth. A friend, the novelist Tayama Katai (1871–1930), wrote a novel with a character modelled on Yanagita – still Matsuoka – who criticised his own poems as mere dilettantism. After entering the ministry, Yanagita was adopted by the Yanagita family as the husband of one of their daughters. This family had relations scattered across the justice system, the military and academic circles, and Yanagita made smooth progress as a high functionary, working for the Agriculture and Commerce Ministry for a little less than two years, while serving close to the Imperial Family as a clerk of the Imperial Household Ministry, and finally working as Chief Secretary of the House of Peers.

Tōno monogatari (Tales from Tōno), a work that collected folktales from Tōno, a mountain village in northeastern Japan, was effectively both the debut work of Yanagita folklore and of Japanese folklore studies. It was published in 1910, the year he took part in the annexation of Korea as a bureaucrat. Although Yanagita authored a large number of works and memoirs, he maintained a complete silence about his connection with Korea: exactly what role he played in the annexation is still not known.

The central concept of Yanagita folklore from *Tōno monogatari* until the end of the 1910s was that of the 'mountain people'. He entered the Japanese Anthropological Society in 1910, submitted a paper on the customs of the *Ainu* to the *Jinruigaku zasshi* (Journal for the Anthropological Society of Nippon) and was soon singled out by Kita Sadakichi who made it possible for him to present a conference paper on the mountain people (Yanagita 1962–71: vol. 4, 172). This chapter will begin by discussing Yanagita's theory of the mountain people as revealed in the papers written during this period.

Yanagita noted that his position was based on the premise that 'the notion that the contemporary Japanese nation is a mixture of many races...has become the established paradigm', claiming that 'the mountain people are the descendants of the indigenous people who long ago flourished in this island empire' (Yanagita 1962–71: vol. 4, 172, 449). He argued that Tōno was a place name derived from the *Ainu* language, and claimed that the conquest and assimilation of alien nations that began with 'the Eastern Expedition and Western Conquest were finally completed in the age of the Zenkunen and Gosannen battles' of the twelfth century. He continued: 'junior high school history textbooks claim that the indigenous people of Japan were completely driven away to the north...but the six Ōu prefectures of northeast Japan were inhabited by wild tribesmen at least until the age of Yoritomo [a twelfth century Shōgun]. More than half of the place names still derive from the *Ainu* language' (Yanagita 1962–71: vol. 4, 11, 174, 420–1) (For the Zenkunen and Gosannen battles, see chapter 7; for Yoritomo, see chapter 10).

As can be seen from these comments, Yanagita's mountain people were the indigenous people, including the *Ainu*, whose existence was accepted by the contemporary mixed nation theory.[2] As noted in chapter 5, Kume Kunitake had already advanced the theory that an indigenous people was defeated by the ruling nation and driven to the mountains where they became an alien people. Yanagita's theory of the mountain people was therefore based on the anthropological and historical research of that period, rather than being the vague poetic image it has sometimes been depicted as in Yanagita studies in Japan.

However, the distinguishing characteristic of Yanagita's theory of the mountain people is his statement that 'even today in the Meiji Period, people who have nothing whatsoever to do with the Japanese still live in the mountains of various regions of Japan', and his consideration of this point in relation to Japanese folk tales. According to Yanagita, after their military defeat, most of the indigenous people entered 'the villages and mingled with the common people, while the rest moved into the mountains, where they remained and eventually came to be called the mountain people', demons, mountain men, mountain witches and long-nosed goblins. The phenomenon popularly known as 'being spirited away' (*kamikakushi*) referred to the custom of the indigenous people in the mountains who, lacking spouses, kidnapped village women from the plains. The small shrines located all over Japan are 'a sort of sign erected between Japanese colonies and savage places' (Yanagita 1962–71: vol. 4, 177, 420, 502). It can be seen that Kita Sadakichi's folklore introduced in chapter 7 was used to develop Yanagita's theory of the mountain people.

Furthermore, Yanagita listed 'rice cultivation' as the defining characteristic of 'our ancestors, the newcomers' (Yanagita 1962–

71: vol. 4, 499). He described rice as the favourite food of the mountain people and claimed that they interacted with the people of the plains in order to obtain rice, hiring themselves out in return for rice balls and rice cakes, with the result that they were eventually assimilated. 'The power of rice' that Yanagita was later to describe as the fountainhead of Japanese culture was thus first described as the power to assimilate indigenous nations.

However, in 1919, from about the time of the March First Independence Movement, a time when Kita Sadakichi was beginning to tie the theory of the mixed nation and his research of folklore in with assimilationist policies, Yanagita was abandoning his theory of the mountain people. He also began to criticise Kume's theory. This was a persistent criticism that continued intermittently through to the postwar era. In Yanagita's last systematic work on the mountain people, *Yama no jinsei* (Life in the Mountains), published in 1926, the idea of an indigenous people hardly emerges at all. Following this work, he gradually came to ignore social outsiders such as the mountain people, goblins and mountain gipsies, and concentrated instead on describing the majority people of the plains, 'the common people' (*jōmin*), and on his theory of the South Islands.

Much research in Japan criticises Yanagita's abandonment of the theory of the mountain people as a renunciation of his interest in minorities. However, such criticism is one-sided: to mention indigenous peoples at that time meant to justify aggression and assimilation. Having an interest in minorities meant not only to sympathise with them, but also to subjugate them. When describing the mountain people, Yanagita stated that 'they truly are a pitiful people', but at the same time said: 'I intend to face their past...while maintaining my dignity as a descendant of the glorious and everlasting conquerors' (Yanagita 1962–71: vol. 4, 449). Here it is impossible to ignore the fact that his theory of the mountain people was a view of history as described by an elite bureaucrat who was a self-described descendant of the conquerors, and who glorified the Tenson nation.

Yanagita also said he would like to come to grips with the mountain people in the same frame of mind as 'the famous Tacitus when he described the German people' (Yanagita 1962–71: vol. 4, 449). In fact, 'the works of Tacitus and Caesar' are what Hozumi Yatsuka, who was mentioned in chapter 3, relied on in arguing in his 'Minpō idete chūkō horobu' (The Civil Laws Will Mean an End to Loyalty and Filial Duty) that the pre-Christian ancient German society was based on the same ancestral worship seen in Japan.[3]

In his *Germania*, the Roman author Publius Tacitus (c.55–120) described the Germans, who were viewed by the Romans as a northern barbarian race, as a sturdy natural people, in contrast with the Romans who had reached the apex of their urban civilisation and were in decline. Yanagita's theory of the mountain people was influenced not only by Tacitus but also by Heinrich Heine (1797–1856), whose work *Götter Im Exil* described the gods of ancient Greece driven away by Christianity and forced to live in reduced circumstances in the mountains, and by Anatole France (1844–1924) whose *Sur la Pierre Blanche* included a criticism of modern Christian civilisation and the emergence of the Yellow Peril.

When European intellectuals such as Heine and France criticised Christian civilisation, it was the pre-Christian societies, the 'Orient' and the 'South Sea islands', that were frequently idealised in contrast. These were all societies that were depicted as free from hypocritical formal morals and full of a natural vitality, and that were often described as fated to be destroyed by a powerful universal civilisation.

However, when Japanese intellectuals, who themselves were part of the 'Orient', read these works, they sometimes succumbed to the illusion that they had been charged with the mission to fight Christianity and modern civilisation. Hozumi's 'Minpō idete chūkō horobu' was, from his point of view, an expression of a sense of crisis that the Western civilisation, symbolised by Christianity and French civil law, would destroy a 'traditional and harmonious' Oriental society.

Of course, Hozumi and Yanagita were different. Hozumi feared that the Japanese nation would suffer the same fate as the ancient Germans whose customs had been destroyed, while the early Yanagita feared that the mountain people, a minority people within the Great Japanese Empire, would suffer this fate. However, this may have merely reflected a difference in the general Japanese self-consciousness: Hozumi was active before the Sino-Japanese War of 1894–95 when Japan was a small, weak country exposed to the threat posed by the West, while Yanagita was active after the annexation of Korea when Japan had developed into a multi-national empire.

Although there may appear to be an enormous gulf between seeing any group as backward and irrational savages, or as a mystical and natural people free from the poison of civilisation, in reality the only difference can sometimes be whether the viewers want to portray the people as savages so that they can affirm themselves as civilised people, or as a natural people so that they can criticise civilisation. Although Yanagita was sympathetic, his theory of the mountain people might be called an internalised Orientalism. Although he sympathised with the mountain people and criticised the majority, calling on the mountain people to come out and strike terror in the hearts of the people of the plains, at the same time he called himself 'a descendant of the glorious and everlasting conquerors'.

If he had wished, Yanagita could have become at least as important an ideologue of the mixed nation theory as Kita Sadakichi. However, he did not combine the theory of the mountain people with the discourse on assimilationist policies. The reason is not clear but, as a realist who had been involved in concrete policy making, Yanagita was perhaps tired of the chorus of mixed nation theorists who believed they were able to determine the policy of the day by debating the issue of the origins of the Japanese nation. In 1934, when talking about national language policy, he stated that the Stone Age had nothing to do with the present and asked 'why on earth do people bother delving into origins?' (Yanagita 1962–71: vol. 29, 165). In later years, his feelings about Kita became complicated and he came to ridicule the man who had helped him to enter academic circles (Yanagita 1962–71: vol. 2, 99).

After discarding the theory of the mountain people, Yanagita increasingly became interested in the South Islands. He was (or pretended to be) from first to last indifferent to Korea and Taiwan. As a result, he travelled in the opposite direction to many theorists of the time. As this work has shown, many of his contemporaries converted to the mixed nation theory and moved away from a self-image of Japan as an island nation because of their interest in Korea and Taiwan.

From a 'Mountain Country' to an 'Island Nation'

While developing his theory of the mountain people, Yanagita argued that 'Japan is far more mountainous than either Japanese or foreigners imagine it to be'. It was a country 'where there are still many places where man has never set foot, where the borders between the old feudal domains and prefectures are mostly located deep in the mountains', and in whose mountains an indigenous people, different from the people of the plains, lived (Yanagita 1962–71: vol. 4, 418, 420).

However in his preface to *Shima no jinsei* (Island Life), a work published after the Second World War, he noted that '*shima* (island) in Japanese' is a synonym for a village society where intimate 'family and friends' lived together in peace, adding that 'if a so-called indigenous people had resided in this archipelago, it would not have been possible to call both islands and villages *shima*, whether the village people lived in peace with the indigenous peoples, or fought against them' (Yanagita 1962–71: vol. 1, 384).

This dramatic change of emphasis from a mountainous country which included alien peoples to a peaceful island nation consisting of an homogeneous people symbolised the transition in Yanagita's view of Japan. How did this change come about?

From 1909 to 1910, a time when he almost certainly worked as a bureaucrat preparing for the annexation of Korea, Yanagita serialised a paper entitled 'Shimajima no monogatari' (A Tale of the Islands). According to this paper, 'in a word, mountains and islands are very similar'. Both are difficult to access, both tend to be isolated, are of little value and are frequently ignored. The reason that the islands and mountains of Japan had not been researched was because of 'the tendency of the empire to expand' into the plains of the Chinese continent (Yanagita 1962–71: vol. 1, 454, 446). Yanagita described islands and mountains as peripheries that had been left behind by the centre. In the poetry he wrote at school, Yanagita had already described islands and mountains as symbols of romantic and exotic places remote from the cities.

At that time, Yanagita had a greater interest in mountains. However, from about the end of the 1910s when he resigned his government position, he became interested in the history of southern islands such as New Guinea, and in 1921 had two decisive experiences. One was a trip to the islands of Okinawa, and the other was his trip to Geneva, Switzerland, as a committee member of the League of Nations Mandates Commission, where he participated in the decision-making process that determined the form of rule adopted for the South Sea islands (Micronesia). Japan had been an ally of Great Britain since 1902 when the Anglo-Japanese Alliance was signed, and so fought against Germany in the First World War. As a member of the victorious nations in this war, Japan was granted various German territories in the East Pacific after the war as mandated territories from the League of Nations.

Since much has been written in Japan about the relationship between Okinawa and Yanagita's writings on the South Islands, the focus here will be on the influence of Yanagita's Genevan experience.[4] According to his memoirs, he was persuaded to undertake the trip to Switzerland even though he had already resigned from his government position, but was so nervous and reluctant to travel to Europe that, on seeing a child innocently playing on a railway platform, 'thought how lucky that child is not to have to go to the West' (Yanagita 1962–71: bekkan 3, 332). This from the Yanagita who loved Western literature, thoroughly enjoyed taking trips in Japan, and travelled to Korea, Taiwan and Manchuria – he does not write much about this trip either – in 1917![5]

After entering the ministry, Yanagita had always travelled as a person of high status. While working as a public official, he was able to make long trips with all expenses paid to the places he wanted to visit by claiming that they were 'inspection tours'. As an elite bureaucrat, he received VIP treatment during these trips. Yanagita interacted with the people he met during his travels first as an elite member of the central government and then, following his retirement, as a member of the central cultural elite in his new position as an editorial writer for the *Asahi shinbun* newspaper.

However, this was no longer the case in Geneva, where 'Britain and France odiously lorded it over everyone else' (Yanagita 1962–71: bekkan 3, 392). Here, 'I understood, for the first time, the true meaning of *yamadashi* (someone fresh from the country [mountains in the Japanese], or country [mountain] bumpkin)' (Yanagita 1962–71: vol. 3, 307). Yanagita had previously enjoyed the status of a civilised man who, as a descendant of the conquerors, was able to talk in Japanese with sympathy to the mountain people. In Geneva, however, a place ruled by the English and French languages, the roles were reversed: it was now his turn to play the role of 'country bumpkin'.

Japan had been able to modernise without being colonised. As a result, education in Japan, including university education, was conducted in Japanese. Although some intellectuals of the early Meiji Period were taught by foreign missionaries and *Oyatoi*, and so were fluent in English, later intellects were not fluent in foreign languages, especially in conversation, a situation that has continued until today. Yanagita was no exception. Not only did he lack any prior knowledge of the issue of the mandated territories, but even when he managed to locate materials on it, his pace in reading texts written in the European languages was slow, and he was not able to argue his position satisfactorily. In the end, 'I keenly felt that I was completely out of my depth when I saw a delegate of fine appearance and respectable age from Persia or somewhere making a speech in French at the general assembly. Its content was not particularly funny, but his accent was so thick that the whole audience was giggling' (Yanagita 1962–71: vol. 3, 311). At the Paris Peace Conference held in Versailles in 1919, when the Japanese delegate made a speech with a Japanese accent, it is said that the French delegate, Georges Clemenceau (1841–1929), asked in a loud voice, audible to all, 'what on earth is that pigmy saying?' This episode says much about the atmosphere of the international conferences of that age when severe racial discrimination was still common. A similar state of affairs must have held in Geneva.

For Yanagita, a proud man who enjoyed a reputation for his extraordinary ability to excel simultaneously in folklore research and bureaucratic work, this must have been extremely painful, and he came to associate only with other 'Japanese'. In the diary that recorded his visit to Switzerland, he wrote mainly about his intercourse with other 'Japanese'. Expressions such as 'I did not see any Japanese this morning' or 'I did not see a single Japanese face the whole day' often appear, and demonstrate to what degree he longed for a space where he could communicate in his native tongue (Yanagita 1962–71: vol. 3, 257, 291). In this situation, he was too occupied with his own concerns and his strong desire to speak Japanese to be able to speak sentimentally about the mountain people with whom he could not communicate in Japanese.

Yanagita later wrote that what he learned from his work as a committee member on the mandated territories commission was 'the significance of islands in cultural history'. In the South Seas region, which was the object of mandatory administration, there were about 700 inhabited islands, 'each of which has a different history and to a certain extent different life-styles [and traditional folklore cultures]. This cannot be understood by continental peoples who are connected to each other by land' (Yanagita 1962–71: vol. 3, 310). According to Yanagita, European continental civilisation in its universalism had ignored the cultural and historical identity of the islands.

In 1924, immediately after his return from Switzerland, Yanagita wrote a short essay, 'Shima no jinsei' (Island Life), where he mentioned an epidemic that had broken out in Tahiti and Samoa in 1919, during which numerous islanders died, while civilised Westerners innocently dreamed about the world of palm trees depicted in Gauguin's paintings. While 'the spiritual border that divides our brethren [the Japanese] and Westerners is difficult to cross', 'it seems that, if only we can talk with the islanders without any reserve, we can open our hearts to these peoples with whom we have had hardly any contact, learn what is on each other's minds, and fully understand one another' (Yanagita 1962–71: vol. 1, 462–3).

This attitude of dreaming about a remote and isolated foreign place from a central position of power was exactly the same as that displayed by Yanagita towards the mountain people. Now, however, he viewed himself not as one who saw (standing alongside 'Westerners' and 'residents of a continent'), but as one who was seen (a South Islander). According to Yanagita, the reason that he sympathised with the South Islanders was because they shared with Japan 'the solitude and the distinctive ordeal that can only be experienced by islanders'. Furthermore, he mentioned that he had once explained to an Okinawan youth who suffered from economic recession and from discrimination by other 'Japanese' that the essence of the pain suffered by Okinawa was what he called an 'isolated island ordeal', and had continued as follows (Yanagita 1962–71: vol. 1, 464).

> What you [Okinawans] call the 'centre' [Tokyo] is not the true centre even of this small globe. The Peace Conference was held in Versailles, and the League of Nations is located in Geneva. To despatch delegates to Geneva, Japan must equip them in advance for two months of travel, sending delegates who cannot develop their arguments satisfactorily a long distance overseas...This is the agony of today's Japan, and at the same time is very similar to Okinawa's 'isolated island ordeal'.

Yanagita here described Japan as an 'island', like those of the South Seas and Okinawa, alienated from the centre of the world, the 'continental' states of the West. In the past, Yanagita had laid greater stress on mountains as the periphery than on islands, and had regarded Japan and himself as the centre. However, through his experience in Geneva, he came to portray Japan not as an empire that included 'mountains' within her borders, but as a tiny 'island' oppressed by the West. This corresponded to the change in his own status from a high-ranking bureaucrat who interacted with the regions ('mountains') from a central position of power, to a 'country bumpkin' mocked by European culture.

At the time he was propounding his theory of the mountain people, Yanagita thought of the 'Japanese' as a diverse mixed nation, stating: 'some fellow Japanese are so revolting that one shudders merely on seeing them. God only knows, but such people may have somehow inherited the blood of the mountain people' (Yanagita 1962–71: vol. 4, 449). However, in Geneva, his increased awareness of the bonds between 'fellow Japanese' was elevated to the level where he was no longer so selective about whom he associated with. The change in Yanagita's position was directly reflected in his views of the position of Japan and may be related to this heightened sense of affiliation.

The representation of 'self' is determined by the representation of 'Other'. Those who had once represented themselves solely as Germans and Latins, or Catholics and Protestants, began to identify themselves as 'Europeans' and 'Caucasians' when they met in Africa and Asia. Likewise, members of the Satsuma and Mito feudal domains in Japan discovered themselves to be fellow 'Japanese' as a result of the impact of the American 'Black Ships'. Yanagita, too, began to view the 'Japanese' as an homogeneous nation following his confrontation with the West.

The notion that Japan was an 'island' was also generated from a comparison. Perhaps none of those who lived in the four main Japanese islands of Hokkaido, Honshū, Kyūshū and Shikoku had ever really thought of themselves as living on an island. Unlike the islands of the South Seas around which one can walk in several hours or days, Honshū, for instance, is too large to be perceived as an island. The idea that Japan consisted of islands was gained through foreign maps and globes in much the same way as was the idea that the earth is round. In reality, the Japanese archipelago covers an area larger than united Germany, and Japan is not at all a 'tiny island nation'.

The self-image of Japan as a 'tiny island nation' was invented by the dispirited inhabitants of the archipelago when they were faced with the external threat posed by the West. Dealing with the West from a position of weakness was not unique to the residents of 'islands', but was also experienced, for instance, by the inhabitants of the Korean peninsula and the African continent. It is doubtful whether the people of Japanese Micronesia (this became Japanese mandated territory following the First World War) or Okinawa, both of which were then ruled by Japan, felt any sympathy with Yanagita's suggestion that their agony was the same as that of those in the central government of Tokyo.

There is no doubt that his trip to Okinawa in 1921 converted Yanagita to the theory of the South Islands, but another important factor may have been the fact that he could not prove the existence of the mountain people. A further factor was his relationship with the botanist, microbiologist and pioneer in folklore studies, Minakata Kumakusu (1867–1941), who did not accept the existence of the mountain people. However, his experience in Geneva clearly seems to have determined the direction of Yanagita's theory of the South Islands. Since he had received the order to go to Geneva on his return from Okinawa and had left for Europe immediately, he may have seen the two experiences as one, and most of his papers on Okinawa were published after his trip to Geneva.

As mentioned above, Yanagita's interest in the South Islands strengthened from about the 1910s. The anti-Japanese movement in America which strained American-Japanese relations from about this time may have been as influential as his Genevan experience. For several years after he returned from Switzerland, Yanagita wrote editorials as a leader writer for the *Asahi shinbun* newspaper, and repeatedly took up the issue of Japanese migrants. In the 1920s, when the threat of being colonised by the West had receded, this issue impressed on Japan her inferior position in the world and awakened her to the issue of Western discrimination. Yanagita could not but take up the theme of Japanese migrants who had been excluded from the 'continents' ruled by Caucasians.

As mentioned in chapter 9, at the Paris Peace Conference in 1919, the Japanese government proposed that a clause forbidding racial discrimination be included in the Covenant of the League of Nations (a proposal made with the issue of Japanese migrants in mind), but this was rejected because of the opposition of the Western Powers. In 1920, Yanagita wrote a long draft of a lecture, 'Junbi naki gaikō' (Diplomacy Without Preparation), that discussed this proposal for racial equality. Believing that the peoples of the Western continents were the perpetuators of racial discrimination, while the residents of island countries (the South Sea islanders) were the victims of discrimination, Yanagita emphasised that 'the bitter experience of a people who live on islands is something with which the Japanese are very familiar' – or, in other words, that Japan, too, was a victim. Moreover, Yanagita argued that 'rice has been the staple food of the Japanese since long, long ago, and is a product of the tropics' (in other words, not a product of the Asian continent, but of the South Seas) (Yanagita 1962–71: vol. 29, 505–6). He was already describing Japan at this time as an 'island' that cultivated rice. This self-image was created in order to face the threat posed by the West. As will be noted below, he gradually came to argue that the rice which came from the south lay at the core of Japanese culture.

The Great Japanese Empire had expanded into a multi-national Power and was often compared to the USA and Great Britain. For Yanagita, however, the USA that rejected Japanese migrants and the Great Britain that objected to the proposal for racial equality could not be considered to be the same as Japan. In his 'Junbi naki gaikō', he criticised with contempt the theory that the Japanese nation was Caucasian and, after emphasising the pain of an island people, argued that Britain was not an island but a fragment of the European continent, saying that 'Japan is sometimes called the Britain of the East, and we are inclined to agree. However, careful thought shows that this is not at all true. The real history of Britain demonstrates that Britain is a sort of annex for the northern Europeans, and a continental *daimyō* (feudal lord) came across the sea to Britain and founded an independent state' (Yanagita 1962–71: vol. 29, 505). After the Second World War, he argued until his death against Egami Namio's theory of the migration of a horse-riding people (see chapter 17). This theory claimed that the Imperial Family was 'a continental *daimyō*' which migrated to the Japanese archipelago from abroad and that 'ancient Japan was a United Kingdom' of the Imperial Family and the powerful clans.[6]

Conscious of the threat posed by the West, Yanagita described the 'Japanese' as a weak nation similar to the inhabitants of the South Islands who were a dying race, and insisted on their homogeneity. This sounds very similar to the arguments of another theorist – our old friend, Inoue Tetsujirō – at the time of the debate over mixed residence in the interior (Yanagita actually met Inoue in Switzerland: see Yanagita 1962–71: vol. 3, 264). One theorist who argued that Japan should aim to become the Great Britain of the East rather than the South Sea islands, and that the mountain residents were impairing the openness of the island nation, was

Kume Kunitake (see chapter 5), a theorist who was criticised by Yanagita. Of course, Yanagita and Inoue differ in thought and character but, in a sense, Yanagita's shift from the theory of the mountain people to one of the South Islands is easy to understand if it is seen as the opposite of Inoue's shift. In contrast with Inoue, who converted from a southern theory (islands) to a northern theory (continent), and advocated going out into the world, Yanagita became the leading theorist of the position that the 'Japanese' came from the south.

Inoue had once argued that the 'Japanese' needed to unify under the Emperor in order to resist the threat of colonisation. Yanagita, too, in 'Shima no jinsei' stated that the lack of internal unity in the South Islands had been exploited by the Western Powers and was one of the factors behind their sad plight (Yanagita 1962–71: vol. 1, 465).

When ships from the West, manned by explorers of limited knowledge who could not distinguish demons from pagans, arrived in the South Islands, the inhabitants of many of the islands were still fighting one another. The battles were small-scale – limited, for instance, to beating each other with sticks – but they ended in the face of the iron and gunpowder of the Europeans. The islanders were forced to recognise that it would be beneficial to stop the constant fighting, and so allowed themselves to be subjugated. The products of European civilisation, beginning with Christianity and trade goods, flowed in. With innocent laughter and song, the women of the islands bore the half-breed children of their conquerors. The result is the South Islands of today.

Lacking unity and overpowered by iron and gunpowder, the islands were invaded by an alien civilisation and religion, lost their own culture, and produced a large number of children of mixed parentage. Although this state of affairs was feared by Inoue and every conquered person, it was exactly what Japan was forcing on the *Ainu* and Koreans at the time Yanagita wrote this.

Yanagita was intelligent enough to realise this. In 'Junbi naki gaikō', he remarked: 'it is only Japan that is qualified to insist that without the hundreds of years of deeply mistaken interference, the coloured people of the islands, who are not treated as human beings today, could have built a finer country, albeit a bit later than the West. Nevertheless it is regrettable, even if it had not been for the last humiliation [the rejection of the proposal of racial equality], that Japan is imitating the bad old habits of Western colonial policies, and has belatedly begun to practise racial discrimination'. He thus criticised a Japan that 'has closed her eyes to her own blemishes such as the ill-treatment of the Koreans and *Ainu*' (Yanagita 1962–71: vol. 29, 509, 499). This is one of the few sentences where Yanagita mentions the situation in Korea, and we can catch a glimpse here of his feelings immediately after the March First Independence Movement and his retirement from public service. However, he did not publish this draft, perhaps because of the political prudence that he had acquired from his life as a bureaucrat, and he eventually came to refrain from emphasising this type of argument.[7]

Yanagita was thus aware of the minorities within the Great Japanese Empire – the Koreans, *Ainu* and the mountain people – but decided not to pursue his interest in them. After this period, he described the common people (*jōmin*) of the island nation, Japan, who were exposed to the threat from the West, as a minority in the world, and fought to defend and unite the unique native culture of Japan.

Folklore as a Means of Integrating the Nation

'Those who advocate the urgent necessity of national solidarity in order to realise a far-sighted plan for the state should not be ignorant'.

In 1925 after returning to Japan, Yanagita gave a lecture 'Nantō kenkyū no genjō' (Contemporary Studies of the South Islands) which he concluded with the words above (Yanagita 1962–71: vol. 25, 181).

After developing his theory of the South Islands, Yanagita argued for the urgent necessity of national unity in the same way as Inoue, but differed from him in his methods. While Inoue preached unification from above, Yanagita attempted to realise unity by generating an awareness from below that all people living in the archipelago were a single nation sharing a common culture.

Yanagita began this lecture by recounting an episode he had experienced in London after he had left Geneva, when he heard the news of the Great Kantō Earthquake of 1923.[8] All the 'Japanese' in London without exception were distressed by the enormous disaster that had hit their homeland. At that time, one old member of the Japanese Diet proclaimed that the earthquake was a divine punishment because the younger generations had abandoned themselves to luxurious and frivolous lives. In reply to this,

Yanagita vigorously argued that those who had died were the impoverished people of Yokohama and downtown Tokyo who had nothing whatsoever to do with high living, and so there was no reason for them to have been punished (Yanagita 1962–71: vol. 25, 159). Having already decided to resign from his post as a member of the mandated territories committee, he took the opportunity to quit Europe and return to Japan to take part in the efforts to rebuild his motherland.

In the past, Yanagita had viewed the people of the plains of Japan as the conquering majority, whose blood should curdle on meeting the mountain people. However, he now turned his back on the mountain people, regarded the people of the plains in Tokyo as 'fellow Japanese' and victims, and tried to associate himself with them.

This lecture referred to the example of Okinawa and argued that islands are fated to suffer economically. They are limited in land and resources, which means that production is restricted, while consumption is ruled by fads imported from overseas. Merchants from overseas and the 'shrewd people' of the cities who welcome them use 'a superior talent and greater capital than that of the common people' to encourage the common people to consume more imports than the island's domestic production. As a result, an excess of imports over exports becomes the normal state of affairs. According to Yanagita, the fate both of Okinawa, which was in the middle of a depression, and of Japan, which was then suffering from a chronic trade deficit, were determined by this principle (Yanagita 1962–71: vol. 25, 161–2).

Furthermore, he stated that the paupers who were burned to death in the Great Kantō Earthquake, and the people who enjoyed gaudy and prosperous urban lives in the well-heeled areas of Tokyo such as Ginza, 'normally live in two totally different worlds'. Although both groups were Japanese nationals, one led lives of dissipation in the imported Western culture of the cities, while the other was forced to work in grinding poverty. Against this background, the island nation was reduced to economic hardship and was losing its unique culture. Historically speaking, during the age of rival warlords, the various factions had imported the products of foreign civilisations in order to compete with each other, and this was one of the causes of 'the national psychology of imitating foreign culture seen in the residents of the islands'. The lack of unity within the islands was both the cause and the effect of the invasion of imported culture (Yanagita 1962–71: vol. 25, 160, 168).

How could this situation be overcome? The following passage, in which Yanagita compared the ancient civilisations of foreign countries such as Egypt and Greece with Japan, is noteworthy (Yanagita 1962–71: vol. 25, 165).

> [In foreign countries] slaves and the downtrodden are all the descendants of alien nations, war prisoners, or those who were bought and sold. By contrast, in Japanese society, those who were forced to work their fingers to the bone were without a doubt fellow members of the same blood-family. That is, they were people who shared the same language and gods, and were fellow members of the original Japanese nation.

The notion that ancient Japan began with the conquest and enslavement of the indigenous peoples appeared in the theories of contemporary Marxists such as Takahashi Sadaki (see chapter 9). Yanagita himself had previously argued that an indigenous people with different gods and language once existed in Japan. However, there is no longer any hint of such a people in this description of the archipelago. At the same time, his view of Japan differed from that of the national polity theorists who insisted that Japan was a warm-hearted country that had never abused slaves. According to Yanagita, Japan enslaved 'fellow members of the...Japanese nation' instead of alien peoples.

The common people who produce but are then deprived of the fruits of their production are the modern slaves exploited by the 'shrewd people' of the cities who enjoy imported Western culture. Yanagita differed from various other chauvinists in that he faced up to the reality of the differences in wealth in Japan. However, if the archipelago consisted of a collection of several different nations and if, as Bälz had argued, different nations formed different classes, it would be difficult to realise national unification from below. In such a situation, there would only be chaos and conflict, and rule through power and revolution, which could easily be exploited by outside powers. However, if the nation were homogeneous, it should be possible to end class conflict and unite the whole nation by searching for the original national characteristics of the Japanese untainted by imported culture, and by generating an awareness that all were 'fellow members of the [same] Japanese nation'.

The original national characteristics would be found only among the illiterate common people who had no contact with books. Yanagita's definition of the common people is not very clear, but in his English report on the mandated territories submitted in Geneva in 1923, he gave a clear image of concepts such as the 'common people' and 'common body'. These concepts referred to the original inhabitants of the islands, excluding the European colonists and their half-breed offspring, their interpreters, the privileged social strata who had received a Western education, and finally the individuals involved in local administration.[9]

In short, the 'common people' were all native people, a group from which the outside invaders, children of mixed parentage, and the 'shrewd people' who had allied themselves with the invaders were excluded. Illiterate people have the least ability to make contact with imported culture, and are therefore least likely to be poisoned by it. According to Yanagita, there used to be 'something that may be called the Japanese way of thinking that the Japanese originally possessed', which had existed before the influx of imported knowledge, beginning with Confucianism and Buddhism. 'To learn about the Japanese point of view and way of thinking...we have to examine the people in the city and villages who have little to do with education'.

For Yanagita, urban culture and written texts were close to imported culture and had nothing to do with the common people. In his 'Nantō kenkyū no genjō', he claimed: 'we know little about the history of the ordinary people who live at the far ends of the seas and deep in the mountains...because books are the products of urban areas and because it is thought that the whole of academic knowledge consists solely of book knowledge. This is the bitter fruit of the so-called centralised culture. Thus the culture of this whole country is today being judged by standards set by the American lifestyle represented by cafes and department stores' (Yanagita 1962–71: vol. 25, 166). What he developed instead was the folklore of the common people which was not recorded in books, and his research into the South Islands.

According to Yanagita, the 'main aim [of Western folklore was originally] to search for the religious state before Christianity' (Yanagita 1962–71: vol. 10, 175). He did not approve of using books to investigate history, and saw the folklore of Okinawa as a living history. According to him, the Japanese nation did not come from the continent to the north but from the islands to the south through the Okinawan islands, and therefore the ancient Japanese language and religion were preserved in Okinawa. The basis of his argument that the Japanese nation came from the south was the fact that the nucleus of Japanese culture was rice, which was a southern crop. In his 'Nantō kenkyū no genjō', Yanagita said that without the folklore scattered throughout the South Islands, beginning with Okinawa, 'which has preserved culture like stuffed specimens...we would be forced to depict the national character and national religion in vague terms from the literature of a handful of loquacious, privileged individuals living in the capital, together with that of the aristocracy and Buddhist priests'. This folklore was what the 'Japanese scattered throughout the archipelago' shared in common, and would make them realise that they were all 'fellow Japanese' (Yanagita 1962–71: vol. 25, 180). This hypothesis that Japanese folklore arrived from the south came to fruition in the postwar *Kaijō no michi* (The Ocean Road), a work published in 1951, which is famous for an episode where a coconut reaches Japan from an island in the south riding ocean currents.

The record of his trip to Okinawa in 1921, *Kainan shōki* (A Short Account of the South Seas), was published in 1925, and began with a preface that noted: 'I felt lonely during that winter in Geneva'. In this preface, Yanagita also expressed his hopes for a future 'bright world of racial equality', and wrote: 'I could not but feel contrition for my past romantic dilettantism' (Yanagita 1962–71: vol. 1, 219, 221). Yanagita gave up his school-boy interest in poetry as dilettantism, and concentrated instead on agricultural administration in an effort to save the poverty-stricken farmers. He only immersed himself in his work on the mountain people after the government rejected a proposal for agricultural policy that he had submitted. After Geneva, he abandoned his interest in the mountain people as another form of dilettantism, and embraced the concept of the common people. However his theory of a mountain people is viewed, he himself would not deny that it had virtually nothing to do with the salvation of the common people.

Of course, Yanagita was also deeply interested in the regional culture of the north of the archipelago as well as the South Islands. However, in the preface to one of his representative works, *Yukiguni no haru* (Spring in the Snow Country), published in 1928, which discussed the folklore of the north of the archipelago, he wrote that he hoped *Yukiguni no haru* would be read by the people of the south of the Japanese archipelago who knew nothing about the snow country of northern Japan, and explained his motives in writing the book, saying that if each region remained indifferent to the others, national unification would be 'mechanical' rather than organic. Yanagita thus hoped that the 'Japanese' would turn away from their fascination with the West and instead develop an interest in other regions of Japan (Yanagita 1962–71: vol. 2, 3).[10] In this book, too, he said that 'this nation which has continually moved northwards cannot feel at ease without cultivating rice', and that 'rice is a plant of the Asian tropics, our motherland, and its importance is amply demonstrated by the rice offered to the gods and used in festivals' (Yanagita 1962–71: vol. 2, 36).

For Yanagita, who in Geneva 'wanted to speak Japanese to my heart's content, even if only to myself', the issue of language was of great interest (Yanagita 1962–71: bekkan 3, 393). At one time, he placed his hope in the Esperanto Movement as a common global language, saying that Japan should devote her energy to spreading Esperanto, but his enthusiasm eventually wore off. In 1927, he insisted that even compared to the colonies of the Western Powers, there was no country in the world that had been invaded by foreign words (*gairaigo*) to the same extent as Japan, and that none treated their own national languages as badly. He came to argue in favour of 'limiting the necessity of foreign languages to the absolute minimum', saying that to 'despise our own language is the first step in submitting ourselves to Western tastes' (Yanagita 1962–71: vol. 29, 228–9).

Yanagita identified Japan with the South Islands that had lost their own unique culture after being invaded by Western civilisation. For him, the protection of the Japanese language was essential. This could only be realised through the integration and unification of Japan – that is, through the spread of a standard Japanese language (*hyōjungo*).

To advocate the spread of a standard Japanese meant to deny local dialects. Where the Okinawa that he loved so much was concerned, he stated in *Kainan shōki* that it was natural for the Okinawan people, subjected as they were to an assimilationist policy that was enforcing a shift to standard Japanese, to remain attached to the Okinawan language. At the same time, however, he also warned that the attempt to preserve it 'would come to nothing'. According to Yanagita, 'the reason is quite simple: the push to unite the Okinawan language has not yet been completed' (Yanagita 1962–71: vol. 1, 268). Since the Okinawan language was fragmented into several local dialects such as the Miyako, Yaeyama and Shuri dialects – Shuri was the capital of the Ryūkyū Kingdom before this kingdom was annexed by Japan and became Okinawa – it was impossible to resist outside pressure. In his opinion, to conserve the Okinawan language, the Shuri dialect would have to be made the standard Okinawan language, but this dialect itself was undergoing such rapid change in the process of modernisation and assimilation that any attempt to preserve it would fail.

In his report on the mandated territories submitted in Geneva, Yanagita noted that it was because of the failure to establish a standard language based on indigenous languages that indigenous peoples were forced to be educated in European languages.[11] In the Meiji era, the differences in the local dialects within Japan were so large that Nitobe Inazō and Uchimura Kanzō (see chapter 3), who could not understand the Tokyo dialect when they first moved to Tokyo, found it easier as young men to read and write in English than in Japanese, because they had been educated in English by missionaries. In his report, Yanagita noted that in the South Sea islands and Africa, the elite who had been educated in European languages identified with European culture, and looked with contempt on their own culture and their 'compatriots' which were both seen as 'backward'. The elite allied themselves with the suzerain state and played a role in ruling the native peoples who were split into several tribes. The after-effects still linger on today: in many third world countries, it is impossible to communicate across various regions within the same country without relying on the European suzerain language.

In order to interact with people from other regions without relying on a standard language or an European language, it would be necessary to master each and every one of the local dialects, but the reality in the Okinawan islands where there were dozens of local dialects, some limited to a single village, was beyond the capacity of Yanagita to understand, although he had experience of the local dialects within the archipelago. According to Yanagita, unless unification was quickly realised, the Japanese language and culture would suffer the same fate as the Okinawan languages, which were destined to perish because they were divided.

'A Whole that does not Exist'

However, for Yanagita, who disliked written language because he saw it as linked with the central government and close to imported culture, the standard language had to be an oral, not a written, language. According to Yanagita, 'it is the local dialects that are laughed at and corrected', but in Geneva he had witnessed a 'speech in French...the content of which was not particularly funny' being laughed at because of the way the words were pronounced (Yanagita 1962–71: vol. 2, 68). In *Yukiguni no haru*, he claimed that correcting local dialects by means of a standard written language was not an effective way of correcting pronunciation and accent, describing the results as 'similar to foreigners who learned Japanese only from books' (Yanagita 1962–71: vol. 3, 311). To attempt to unite a spoken language by teaching children the correct pronunciation through the use of records in reading classes was not going to work if other teachers continued to use heavily accented local dialects (Yanagita 1962–71: vol. 18, 590). Yanagita seems to have believed that Japan's prestige would be damaged in the eyes of the West if it did not have a united national language.

However, he did not deny that the local languages might remain as local dialects even after the propagation of the standard language and, in *Yukiguni no haru*, said that he would like to see some of the vocabulary of the Sendai dialect – Sendai was (and remains) the largest city of northeastern Japan, and the Sendai dialect is in a sense the standard language of northeastern Japan – incorporated into the Tokyo dialect (Yanagita 1962–71: vol. 2, 69). In 1941, however, he said that 'to establish a new standard language for the whole country, we will have to forsake all the divided local standard languages', and he criticised the 'nonchalant' residents of Tokyo who made no attempt to use the standard language (*hyōjungo*), but instead used their own native dialects their whole lives (Yanagita 1962–71: vol. 18, 513).

Yanagita, however, faced an essential contradiction in that the standard language that he argued should be a spoken language could only be firmly established through writing. Since the written form of language is stable, it can clearly establish the correct form of a standard language. By contrast, the spoken language changes rapidly and is also dominated by 'ways of speaking' that differ from individual to individual (Yanagita 1962–71: vol. 25, 487). With a spoken language, the standards required to unify the language could never be established. Yanagita went so far as to assert that 'those who do not wish the state to ensure that all Japanese will be able to communicate in a single pure national language [throughout Japan] could be called non-Japanese'. Nevertheless, he was at the same time critical of the central leadership which did not perceive that 'the standard language is today an ideal and the beautiful dream of the nation', and which 'was trying to force a whole that does not exist' on the common people, brandishing fragmented standard words, including Chinese compound words, based on a written language (Yanagita 1962–71: vol. 18, 591).

In the first place, for Yanagita, who 'saw with my own eyes Japan being treated in a discriminatory fashion at the League of Nations, but felt from the bottom of my heart that if only the barriers imposed by languages could be overcome, most problems would be solved' (Yanagita 1962–71: bekkan 3, 393), the ideal was a standard language that would give every local person the ability to communicate freely, and he opposed the imposition of a central language that would generate tension among the common people and silence them. Such a central language perhaps reminded him of his own experience of being silenced in a space ruled by English and French. However, Yanagita did not have any concrete answers to the question of what sort of standard language should be established.

In the same way, Yanagita fell into a similar contradiction with regard to the relationship between urban culture and regional culture. He criticised the central urban culture, and praised local practices as embodying native Japanese culture. However, praise of the various local cultures would not by itself lead to national unification. In 1941, in a lecture on cultural policy, he repeated opinions such as 'the more one appreciates local culture, the more one has to be aware of the importance of what is not limited to a single area, but is common to all of Japan', and 'we must not rely on the intelligentsia of city culture to do the research and define the magnificent common culture that unites the whole country or the Japanese life- style that can be seen throughout history, and we must also avoid focussing solely on individual regions' (Yanagita 1962–71: vol. 24, 488, 499).

The unification of a state is normally achieved when the centre crushes local areas, the written language of textbooks oppresses local spoken languages, and the modernised overwhelms the 'backward'. Though Yanagita wanted to protect Japan's cultural originality, he also realised that it was clear that Japan would be overpowered by the West unless she modernised. Thus Yanagita's attitude to modernisation was complex.[12] Since he did not reject the situation where the common people were adopting Western clothes and foreign words on their own initiative, and since he also supported the universal suffrage which would enable the voice of the common people to be reflected in national politics, his thinking was not a mere reactionary conservatism or a yearning for olden times.[13]

However, since he could not find the original Japanese identity in the urban centres where modernisation in the form of an acceptance of imported culture had occurred, he was forced to look to the folklore of the local regions of Japan to provide the bonds needed to unify the archipelago. He looked to the culture of the common people and the standard language to provide the contradictory ideal of a localised but uniform spoken language that would also bring people together. However, unless local cultures and languages were already homogeneous, this ideal remained unattainable.

Yanagita himself came to argue that the fundamental condition of this contradictory ideal, an homogeneous whole, was a 'whole that does not exist', and nothing but 'a beautiful dream'. Although he wanted to close the door of the islands of Japan to the outside world, he also needed to open the doors of each region to one another in order to unify the country internally. He focused on the common people's native culture (folklore) in order to fight against imported culture. However, native culture is reduced to a mere shell and loses its vitality as soon as a 'correct' form is firmly established. Yanagita failed to realise that the native culture, which he attempted to use as the basis of a new definition of the 'Japanese', was fluid, would continue to differ from region to region, and would be useless in unifying an 'island nation' that had a larger population than any Western country. In a small village or island where everyone knows everyone else, a native, homogeneous culture is possible, but the real Japan was much larger than his hypothetical South Islands.

Facing up to this contradiction, Yanagita increasingly concentrated on the only regional factor that was common throughout the archipelago – rice. When he was advancing his theory of the mountain people, and even though he defined rice cultivation as the culture of the Tenson race, he still claimed that 'the people of yesteryear would not have refused to establish a village in an area unsuitable for cultivating rice', and 'in the mountain countries, many people ate rice for the first time when they enlisted in the army' (Yanagita 1962–71: vol. 4, 494). Now, however, rice was seen as the only folklore that he could rely on to unite the whole country from below. To whatever degree local cultures and languages might differ, as long as rice remained the staple crop of Japan, he could use this as the folklore common throughout the archipelago. Therefore, the notion of the 'Japanese' without rice was to be rejected, as was the notion of rice as an imported culture. The 'Japanese' were not invaders of the archipelago, but a people who came from the South Islands with rice and settled in the archipelago, which was a place without an indigenous people. If these conditions were not met, it was clear that the idea of uniting the whole nation under an homogeneous folklore would come to nothing.

However, the anthropology of that age was dominated by theorists, Torii among them, who argued for the existence of an indigenous people, the *Ainu*, and the migration of a conquering people from the continent. At the time of the theory of the mountain people, Yanagita, swimming with the tide, submitted a paper on the *Ainu* to the *Jinruigaku zasshi* (The Anthropological Society Magazine), in which he said he hoped his research would contribute to 'providing new materials for anthropology' (Yanagita 1962–71: vol. 4, 186). However, when Yanagita came to swim against the main current of anthropology, the basis for his theory that the Japanese nation arrived from the south was too weak to compete with the anthropological excavation of ruins and human bones.

It was perhaps not just because of this, but Yanagita gradually came to keep anthropology at arm's length from his folklore. In his own words, the Japanese anthropology of the day had a bias towards the excavation of human bones, and was 'amateurish and extremely fastidious about what issues to tackle'. Accordingly, although folklore was waiting for the appearance of a useful anthropological theory, 'a reliable partner has yet to emerge' (Yanagita 1962–71: vol. 25, 350). One of the reasons that Yanagita, who disliked following 'in the footsteps of the white man' in his research, admired Sir James Frazer (1854–1941), was because Frazer was 'not particularly interested in the size of bones or the colour of eyes or hair, or in excavated stone tools and fossilised human bones, but was doing the sort of research that anthropologists in the Tokyo Imperial

University of today would never attempt to pursue' (Yanagita 1962–71: vol. 25, 234). Yanagita himself eventually became enthusiastic about the study of the origin of the Japanese nation, but he criticised 'the bias of physical anthropology towards ancient eras and the passion for the study of the origin of the nation' (Yanagita 1962–71: vol. 25, 350). On the other hand, as far as I am aware, Yanagita's theory of the origin of the Japanese nation was almost completely ignored by the anthropologists.

The first reason Yanagita kept anthropology at arm's length was that he needed to establish the independence of the new academic discipline of folklore from closely related academic disciplines. It is also possible that he was opposed to the methodology of Western cultural anthropology that investigated the customs of colonised regions from the standpoint of the civilised conqueror.[14] As a result, his theory of a southern origin was safe as long as he restricted himself to his own field of folklore. If, however, he had challenged the anthropologists to a debate, he would not have emerged unscathed.

Although Yanagita argued for 'the necessity of assimilating foreign elements' in cultural policy, he did not include Korea in this (Yanagita 1962–71: vol. 24, 488). He regarded 'the policy of propagating the Japanese language in the Korean peninsula' as unsuitable. According to him, the situation in Korea was totally different from that of Okinawa, but identical policies of propagating the standard Japanese language were being implemented in both areas. He clearly did not include the two in the same category (Yanagita 1962–71: vol. 18, 535). Although he criticised the written standard language, when speaking about teaching Japanese as a foreign language to alien nations, he encouraged teaching a form of Japanese close to 'the written form' (Yanagita 1962–71: vol. 18, 542). In his English report submitted in Geneva as a member of the mandated territories committee, a report that was not likely to be read by Japanese, he argued against an assimilationist policy.[15] Yanagita had no opinon of the suzerain state's policy of forcing the indigenous peoples to learn European languages, and so the Japanese policy of assimilation was something he could not glorify, even if he avoided criticising it directly in public.

In the first place, Korea was not an island. As long as the Great Japanese Empire included Korea, it could not be an island nation. Since Yanagita viewed Japan as an island nation, and advocated an homogeneous folklore, continental Korea lay outside his research interests, and from his point of view perhaps was seen as an obstacle to uniting the 'Japanese' through a native culture. However, precisely for this reason, he did not glorify assimilationist policies, nor take part in the argument that the 'Japanese' and Koreans shared a common ancestor.[16] For Yanagita, the position that the Japanese nation was of the same race and had the same parental source as a continental nation could not be tolerated.

Another problem with Yanagita's thought was his view of the Emperor. Although Yanagita was sensitive to the issue of Western cultural imperialism, he was not as aware of the issue of the power of the Emperor. One reason was because the Imperial Family did not have a history of collaborating with the West, unlike the case in many colonised regions of Asia and Africa. Moreover, the Japanese Emperor is also a Shintō shaman, and even today performs rites to celebrate the rice harvest. The form of these rituals has influenced the form of the prayers for bountiful harvests of the general populace, and the culture of rice cultivation in Japan has deep links with the Emperor. In a symposium held in the postwar era, Yanagita stated that 'it is with deep respect that I say that the common people also include the Imperial Family'.[17] Given his definition of the common people, if it was assumed that the Imperial Family preserved Japanese folklore, then the notion that the Emperor was also a commoner was not (for him) a contradiction. The Emperor from the Meiji Period on was actually an individual who wore a Western-style military uniform, but Yanagita did not mention this fact.

After the Great Japanese Empire was defeated in the Second World War, the prewar regime where sovereignty resided with the Emperor was abolished, and sovereignty was granted to the people. Many postwar theorists have therefore noted critically that what Yanagita called the common people was intertwined through rice with the rituals of the Imperial Family. However, among the various theories of uniting the nation developed by the intelligentsia of the Great Japanese Empire, Yanagita's line of argument was one in which the Emperor featured least. This is because, unlike Inoue and others, Yanagita attempted to unify the nation from below, and whether the Emperor was related to this unification or not could not be determined unconditionally by the system of folklore studies itself. Accordingly, in both the prewar and postwar eras, some members of the Japanese left-wing have looked to folklore to provide both the original prototype of the people untainted by bourgeois culture, and a logic of unity from below.

However, unification from below through an homogeneous folklore was a path closed to a people which consisted of a plurality of nations with a variety of folklores. In the postwar era, Yanagita's theory of a common people moved into the limelight when 'Japanese nationals (*kokumin*)', the majority, believed they needed to unite as victims of state power, but the theory of the mountain people was praised at times when the 'Japanese' regarded themselves critically as the assailants of the third world or minorities. This postwar phenomenon emerged in the 1970s after Japan came to be called an economic superpower, and it sheds light on the character of Yanagita's thought. Many prewar contemporary theorists approved of the inclusion of alien nations within the Great Japanese Empire provided the authority of the Emperor was recognised, but Yanagita's theory of a common people had no room for alien nations. Conversely, however, it was precisely because of this that his folklore, unlike Kita Sadakichi's ideas, could never become a ruling ideology of the multi-national empire.

In a sense, Yanagita's thought was a mixture of exclusivism and a type of pacifism. The Japan he depicted was a narrow world without alien peoples, where all were unified by an homogeneous culture, where a self-sufficient agriculture was practised, and where, as a result, there were no 'difficulties', no struggle, no invasion and no inter-cultural friction. This illusion of a homeland – as expressed by his concepts of village (*mura*) and island (*shima*) – was generated by a heart in search of peace that had been alienated by his experience overseas. Yanagita's theory that the 'Japanese' came from the south was not highly influential, and he did not deny the mixed nature of the Japanese nation even after he discarded his theory of the mountain people.[18] However, the schema of an island nation with an homogeneous folklore based on rice cultivation had a decisive influence on the later self-images of Japan. This duality of exclusivism and peace was to become a fundamental characteristic of the postwar myth of the homogeneous nation.

13 Japanisation versus Eugenics

Although a policy of assimilation, justified at least in part by the mixed nation theory, was the basic line followed in the Japanese rule of Korea and Taiwan, some voices were raised against it within the Great Japanese Empire. A small minority criticised assimilationist policies from a humanitarian point of view. These included Yoshino Sakuzō, an advocate of Taishō Democracy, and Yanagi Muneyoshi (1889–1961), who played an active role in pioneering the Japanese folk art movement.

However, among the critics was a singular group that differed from the humanitarians. This was the group that espoused eugenics and a racial ideology.

Previously published research has argued that the racial thought that emerged from France was used by Japanese scholars of colonial policy such as the prestigious academic Yanaihara Tadao (1893–1961) and Nitobe Inazō in their criticism of assimilation.[1] This research diverges from the main theme of this book, the theory of the Japanese nation, so it will not be discussed here in detail, but one of the biggest issues was the discussion of the advantages and disadvantages of mixed blood.

An assimilationist discourse basically approves of inter-racial marriage and mixed blood. This was especially true in the case of the Japanese discourse that was based on the mixed nation theory, and where an important element was the obliteration of conquered nations through the promotion of inter-racial marriage. However, for the supporters of racial thinking and eugenics, it was unforgivable to permit the blood of the superior ruling nation to be contaminated by mixing it with the blood of inferior ruled nations. It was also believed to be the height of folly, as well as futile, to attempt to force an inferior race to acquire the civilisation of a superior race and assimilate. Inferior races, it was said, should be segregated to prevent them from mixing their blood with that of the superior race, should be left alone to live according to the traditional customs that suited their inferior genetic abilities, and should be exploited indirectly.

This criticism of assimilationist policies on the grounds of a racial ideology was firmly established in Japanese research on Western colonial policies by the beginning of the twentieth century. In Japan, another criticism of assimilationist policies also emerged from the eugenics school, which prepared the ground for a unique theory of the homogeneous nation – one that was more 'scientific' than that of the national polity theorists – in arguing against the mixed nation theory that underpinned the policy of assimilation.

An Island Nation of Pure Blood

Following the Japanese annexation of Korea, two currents of thought were put forward by the adherents of eugenics and racial ideology with regard to proposals for dealing with alien nations, and especially to the issue of mixed blood.

One was represented by Unno Kōtoku, a professor of Ryūkoku University. One of the pioneers of Japanese eugenics, he published an article, 'Chōsen jinshu to Nippon jinshu no zakkon ni tsuite' (On Mixed Marriages Between the Korean and Japanese Races), in *Taiyō* immediately after the annexation of Korea.[2]

His argument can be summarised as follows. It is important to maintain the pure blood of a superior race, but consanguineous marriage alone will cause a deterioration in inherited physical character and a degeneration in powers of adaptability. Therefore, 'mixed marriages' with alien peoples are necessary within appropriate limits. However, since inter-racial marriages between two very different races, such as whites and blacks, have disastrous results, intermarriage between similar races is preferable. Thus 'it is obvious that mixed marriages between the Japanese and Korean races are highly promising'. Furthermore, since 'the inherited physical character of the superior race will overwhelm that of the inferior', the Koreans would be absorbed by the 'Japanese' through inter-racial marriages.

This point of view was based on the application of the concept of heterosis to the improvement of crops and domestic animals, and will be referred to here as the theory of heterosis.

The theory was eminently suitable as a justification for assimilationist policies, and existed for many years within the eugenics school of thought in Japan, though without ever occupying the mainstream of Japanese eugenics. Furthermore, I have never seen this line of argument in the Government-General of Korea discourse that glorified assimilationist policies. Instead, it was limited to the endorsement of the policy of assimilation by individual proponents of racial thought such as Unno.

In contrast, the theory that gradually gained greater influence year by year, and that was eventually reflected in government policy, vigorously rejected the idea of mixed blood and was opposed to assimilationist policies.

An early example of the rejection of the notion of intermarriage with Koreans from a racial standpoint was Kawakami Hajime (1879–1946) in 1915.[3] This may be surprising, given his image as a Marxist economist and socialist, but at that time he was an adherent of racial thinking. Later, when he became an ardent Marxist, Kawakami moved away from that position, but in a short paper in a book published in 1915, 'Nippon minzoku no chi to te' (The Blood and Hands of the Japanese Nation), he argued that 'there are reasons for believing that the Japanese are an exceedingly superior nation with few equals in the world', and attempted to substantiate this opinion on the basis of racial thinking.

Basing his argument on the ideas of Chamberlain, a contemporary racial thinker, Kawakami claimed in the paper that 'in order to create a superior race it is necessary first of all to have a race of good stock that mixes its blood with others, and then, having once done so, stringently segregates itself from other races and maintains the purity of its blood'. Chamberlain claimed that the English were the superior European race, because after the Celts and Teutons had mingled, they maintained the purity of their blood in the island-country of Britain. Kawakami stated that the origin of the Japanese nation was exactly the same. Though accepting the paradigm of the day that 'a long time ago, during what is called the Age of the Gods, a large-scale mixture of blood took place', he went on to say:

> However, after this large-scale mixture of blood took place, our ancestors fortunately confined themselves to these isolated islands for a long time, and quickly established the Japanese state...since then, more than 2,000 years have passed, and the Japanese have maintained their pure blood until the present time. What has made us what we are today is the fact that the Japanese have maintained the purity of

their blood for so long. It is not an empty boast to claim that we have been presided over by an unbroken line of Emperors for 2,500 years.

In an economics reading circle in 1915, Kawakami gave a report entitled 'Jinshu mondai' (The Problem of Race) that followed the same lines as his paper. In the debate that followed, he argued as follows:

> Regarding the problem of mixing blood, we must distinguish between domestic animals and peoples. Pairing a good horse with a bad horse will produce an intermediate horse, something with which we are frequently satisfied. However, the intermediate race that would be produced by mixing the blood of Japanese and Koreans is not something that we could tolerate.

Kawakami argued that any mixture of blood with Koreans should be avoided because it would ruin the superiority of the 'good horse', the 'Japanese' nation. This view was based on a racial ideology that assumed the Japanese nation was a superior one. At the same time, however, it clashed head-on with the intermarriage between Japanese and Koreans that the Government-General of Korea was promoting as part of its assimilationist policy.

Tōgō Makoto, a high-ranking bureaucrat in the Government-General of Taiwan, criticised assimilationist policies based on a racial ideology in a more systematic way than Kawakami. He enjoyed some connections with Nitobe and Yanaihara, but his criticisms put him in a difficult position within the Government-General, and he resigned his post in 1925 to become a member of the House of Representatives.

In a work published the year he resigned, Tōgō declared: 'I believe it is extremely irrational for an intermarriage policy to exist that is intended to destroy one race completely and assimilate it into another nation through mixed marriages'.[4] Instead, he advocated a 'segregation policy' that would separate the 'Japanese' from indigenous peoples in schools and other places, as an alternative to implementing assimilationist policies in Korea and Taiwan. Once the races were separated, a mixture of blood would not occur. This amounted to a Japanese version of apartheid.

In this context, the mixed nation theory was a problem for Tōgō. Although he agreed that the Japanese nation had mixed with indigenous alien nations in ancient times, like Kawakami he claimed that 'for a long period of about 2,000 years following this, the Japanese were isolated in their remote islands, maintained national purity...and became the superior Japanese nation'. Hence, if the Great Japanese Empire 'maintains the present policies of promoting assimilation and mixed marriages everywhere, the precious character of the Japanese nation, which was only gained through 2,000 years of protecting its purity, will gradually deteriorate through a mixture with these alien nations', and Japan would eventually suffer the same fate as the Roman Empire. As noted in chapter 3, Takayama Chogyū and Hozumi Yatsuka had already referred to the collapse of the Roman Empire as an example of the fate of a multi-national empire. The theory that accepted the established paradigm that a mixture had occurred in ancient times, but insisted that pure blood was maintained for the following 2,000 years, became the common position in the criticism of assimilationist policies as developed by eugenic theorists.

However, most eugenicists were not originally passionately involved in the issue of inter-racial marriage. The representative academic journals of eugenics at the time were *Yūseigaku* (Eugenics), first issued in 1924 by the Nippon Yūseigakkai (The Japanese Eugenics Association), and *Minzoku eisei* (Racial Hygiene), founded in 1931 by the Nippon Minzoku Eiseigakkai (The Japanese Racial Hygiene Association).[5] However, until about 1937, the problem of inter-racial marriage was rarely discussed, and the main interest of these journals was health control, population growth, hereditary diseases among the 'Japanese', and the establishment of a sterilisation law for mentally handicapped people and those with hereditary diseases.

Although the reasons for this emphasis are not clear, two conjectures might be made. Firstly, the Western racial thought they admired so much might have been suitable for 'whites' to discriminate against 'blacks' or 'yellow people', but not so suitable for one 'yellow people' to discriminate against another 'yellow people'. In any case, it would have seemed odd to Western racial thinkers for Japan, a country of 'yellow people' whom they viewed as inferior, to itself adopt a racial ideology. If Japan wanted to discriminate against Koreans or Taiwanese for racist reasons, a clear difference that separated them from the Japanese nation would have to be demonstrated. However, the main current of Japanese anthropology of the time held that the 'Japanese' and

Koreans shared a common ancestor, and embraced the mixed nation theory.

Secondly, the issue of mixing blood was taboo. Many eugenicists, especially after the mid-1930s, responded positively to Nazi racial policies. From this point of view, inter-racial marriage and mixing blood was to be shunned, but to argue this openly would have meant to criticise the empire's assimilationist policies. As it happened, there was no need to face this contradiction and risk criticising imperial policy in the 1920s because the issue of intermarriage was not yet a pressing one: as late as 1925, the number of marriages between Japanese and Korean couples in Korea was still a mere 404 per year.

However, this situation had changed by the late 1930s. At about the time the Sino-Japanese War erupted in 1937, the Japanisation (*Kōminka*) policy, which culminated in a push from 1940 onwards to change Korean names into Japanese ones, was into its stride. Minami Jirō (1874–1955), who took up his post as Governor-General in 1936 (he served until 1942), was, at least on the surface, especially enthusiastic about intermarriage. He proclaimed that Korea and Japan 'should become as one in shape, mind, blood and flesh', and mentioned three items – common names, intermarriage, and matrimonial alliances – as 'concrete means of unifying Japan and Korea within the legal system'. Encouraged by a policy of active support (at least in terms of propaganda), marriages between Japanese and Koreans continued to increase, and their number in Korea broke the 1,200 barrier in 1937. In March 1941, 137 inter-racial couples who had married the previous year in Korea were officially commended and presented with hanging scrolls penned by Minami himself.

After 1937, in order to make up for the lack of labour in the Japanese archipelago (*naichi*) as Japanese males were called up and sent to the battle-fields of China, a large number of Korean labourers were shipped to the Japanese mainland, many by force. The number of Korean residents in the archipelago was 130,000 in 1925, but increased to 1.19 million in 1940, and to over 2 million in 1945. An unintended consequence of this was that the number of marriages between Korean men and 'Japanese' women increased in Japan Proper (*naichi*) as well. The advocacy of 'Japan and Korea as One' and the promotion of intermarriage by the government accelerated this trend.[6] Naturally, this became an issue that the eugenic school could not ignore any longer.

The Mixed Nation Theory in support of the Policy of Japanisation

Published works issued by the Government-General of Korea during the period of the Japanisation policies drew heavily on the mixed nation theory.

For example, *Kodai no Naisen kankei* (Ancient Japanese-Korean Relations), published in 1937 by the Government-General's Bureau of Education, stated that 'long ago there were many different races in Japan' – it listed the Tenson, Izumo, Emishi and Kumaso – and claimed that 'these four great nations combined to form today's Japanese nation'. Furthermore, Japan and Korea were now united under the Emperor, 'and only when these two nations are completely unified and merged will the true Great Japanese Nation be formed and embark on great ventures on the world stage'.[7]

In June 1941, *Naisen ittai no rinen oyobi sono gugen hōsaku yōkō* (The Ideal of the Amalgamation of Japan and Korea and Policies for its Realisation) was published with the approval of the Government-General. This work stressed that historically 'a large number of Koreans had migrated to Japan' and had been assimilated. Moreover, since 'social structure in the West is generally based on the nation', national self-determination movements and the break-up of states tend to occur, but in the East 'the philosophy of racial harmony' exists, and in Japan under the Imperial Family, 'several nations combined to form the single Japanese nation of today'.[8]

After this work was published, a large number of lectures and publications followed its line of argument and glorified the Japanisation policy. It is important to note that this homage to the slogan of Japanisation included not only the mixed nation theory but also a criticism of the Nazis. It may seem surprising that the Government-General of Korea should have criticised them but, as this work has already stated, the Nazi Jewish policies strictly prohibited inter-racial marriages and excluded Jews even from military service. To introduce such policies in Korea would be to deny the inter-racial marriages that the Government-General was encouraging and make it impossible to continue to conscript Koreans into the Imperial Army.

Facing shortages of man-power during the Sino-Japanese War, the Imperial Army introduced a system of voluntary enlistment for

Koreans in 1938, and had already examined the idea of introducing conscription (the decision to do so was made in 1942 and conscription was enforced from 1944). Those appointed Governor-General of Korea had to be army officers – Minami Jirō was a General – and the Government-General therefore went along with the idea.

Of course, this does not mean that the Government-General intended to treat Koreans equally. Although Korean enlistment in the Japanese army was depicted by Government-General propaganda as an honour, both *Naisen ittai no rinen oyobi sono gugen hōsaku yōkō* cited above, and those discussed below who lauded Japanisation, stressed that the slogan 'Japan and Korea as One' did not mean equality in terms of rights or duties.[9] It did not mean granting the Koreans suffrage, nor did the Japanisation of Korean names mean a transfer to Japan Proper of the *honseki* or Family Register.[10] The Government-General tried to destroy the national identity of Korea and mobilise the Koreans, at the same time as it maintained discrimination. This was even worse than Kita Sadakichi's 'conscientious' theory of assimilation. Even so, however, the Government-General still rejected the notion of applying a Nazi pure blood policy directly to Korea.

In 1941, for example, Furukawa Kanehide, the head of the Public Peace Section of the Bureau of Police Affairs of the Government-General of Korea, criticised the emergence of the Nazi-influenced 'argument about the contamination and purity of blood'.[11] According to Furukawa, this argument meant 'in a word, that the policy of assimilation is a mistake because it will lead to the contamination of the pure blood of the Yamato nation. Many chauvinists with a mania for Germany seem to be arguing for this position. Even among those in important positions who form the nucleus of the bureaucracy in Japan Proper, there are some who share these opinions. However, at least as far as the relationship between Korea and Japan is concerned, I wish to demonstrate that the argument is fallacious'.

As will be shown later, the pure blood policy was examined in detail within the Ministry of Health and Welfare in the central government in Japan, where the eugenics school of thought was highly influential. Furukawa stated that 'it would be a disaster if the government were to adopt and institutionalise the pure blood policy'. If it were to be adopted and if those who were not members of the Japanese nation were to be denied recognition as

'Japanese', Koreans 'would not only be prohibited from marrying Japanese but would no longer be regarded as imperial subjects', and both the Japanisation policy and the enlistment of Koreans would no longer be possible. Furthermore, 'it must be said that opposing the exchange of blood means to treat the Koreans as Jews. Needless to say, this view is mistaken. It is a crude position that ignores both the fact that the Yamato nation itself is the most mixed of all Asian nations, and the fact of the annexation [of Korea]'.

In a lecture of the same year, Odaka Tomoo, a legal scholar and professor of Keijō (today's Seoul) Imperial University, also criticised the Nazis.[12] According to Odaka, the Nazis 'will not permit a Germanisation of the alien nations within Germany...the official position is that Germanisation is impossible and should not be attempted. As is well known, this exclusivist racial policy was established especially with regard to the Jewish people'. He criticised 'those who believe that the amalgamation of Japan and Korea will contaminate the purity of the Yamato nation' as 'individuals who are aping the racial supremacy of Nazi Germany'.

According to Odaka, 'in Japan, the state exists because the Emperor reigns, and the nation exists because of the state, and so the nation does not have an absolute meaning'. He stated that during the period depicted in the Kiki myths, there existed people 'with a different lineage from that of the Tenson nation', and that 'with regard to the philosophy of a sovereign and all his subjects (*ikkun banmin*), even foreign peoples were able eventually to become true imperial subjects, and what is called the Yamato nation was formed...on this point, there is a clear-cut difference between the official position of Nazi Germany and the cardinal principle of the National Polity of Japan'. Moreover, 'the same history is being repeated today on a larger scale than ever before on the Korean peninsula'.

Tsuda Tsuyoshi who was the president of what was in effect an extra-governmental body of the Government-General, the Green Flag (*Ryokuki*) League that advocated the promotion of the slogan of 'Japan and Korea as One', stated that 'originally in ancient Japan the Tenson lived in Hyūga, the Izumo in Izumo, the Emishi in the north, and the Kumaso and Hayato in Kyūshū', and that the Emishi were 'the *Ainu*' and the Hayato were 'clearly Malay'. This 'chaotic society', he continued, with its complicated mixture of alien nations, was peacefully unified by the Tenson nation.

Tsuda also argued that assimilation would be easy since 'anthropologically speaking, the difference in physique between the people of the peninsula and those of the Kansai region [of mid-west Japan] is smaller than that between Japanese from Kansai and Japanese from Tōhoku [northeast Japan]'. This was the theory put forward by Ueda Jōkichi, an anthropologist and professor of medicine at Keijō Imperial University, and might be seen as an extreme form of the theory that the 'Japanese' and Koreans shared a common ancestor. Ueda developed Torii Ryūzō's position that the conquering nation that migrated from the peninsula established a firm foothold in the Kinki region in Kansai (see chapter 9), formulating his theory on the basis of statistics of physical measurements taken from various regions of the peninsula and the archipelago. Torii himself published an article from an anthropological viewpoint in a Government-General organ in 1939 where he repeated the theory that the 'Japanese' and Koreans were 'the same race', and argued that 'it would be more appropriate to give Korea the geological name "northern Japan"'.[13]

Kurashima Itaru, the head of the Information Section of the Government-General of Korea, wrote as follows in a chapter entitled 'Ketsueki no kon'yū' (The Mixture of Blood) in 1942.[14]

> Physical anthropological research in Japan has reported that the people of central Korea are in all respects very similar to the Japanese of the Kinki region, and that the difference between the two is much smaller than regional differences within the archipelago...Among the 1,182 names recorded in the *Shinsen shōjiroku*, the number of naturalised people was about one-third of the total, at 326...It must be concluded that to oppose inter-racial marriage as a corruption of the pure blood of the Japanese nation or a degradation of the Japanese spirit is a reflection of a narrow-minded, intolerant and insular spirit in people familiar only with the Japan of the Meiji Period which was limited to Hokkaido and 46 prefectures.

Minami Jirō, the Governor-General of Korea, made the following statement in a lecture at the time the Pacific War broke out.[15]

> Furthermore, looking back over the 3,000 years of Japanese history, it is clear that our ancestors who formed the Yamato nation of today were not limited only to the homogeneous

Yamato nation, but also included countless peoples who had migrated from various regions, among them...the Kumaso, the Emishi, the Chinese, the South Sea islanders and the Koreans from the three Hans...who all became naturalised as Japanese...

...According to the *Shinsen shōjiroku* and other sources it can be easily imagined that about one-third of the Japanese population centred on the Kinki region then consisted of naturalised Korean migrants.

The lineage of the Emperor was also not taboo. The literary critic Yasuda Yojūrō (1910–1981), a member of the Japanese Romantic school, wrote in a Korean travelogue published in 1938 that 'the mother of the Emperor Kanmu' was 'of Royal Pekche stock', and noted that he believed the legend that the Japanese Imperial Family and the Korean Royal Family had a blood relationship. I Kuangsu, a pro-Japanese Korean intellectual, obtained the permission of the Government-General of Korea in 1941 to write about the birth of the Empress Jingū and the Emperor Kanmu, and argued for the notion of 'Japan and Korea as One', saying that Japan and Korea enjoyed a blood relationship from the lowest to the highest classes.[16]

It was natural that there should be opposition from the pure blood theorists to a Japanisation policy promoted on the basis of this line of argument. Although the opposition had difficulty emerging into the open because of war-time restrictions on speech, one individual, Furuya Eiichi, did print a handbill that protested to the Government-General of Korea about the change of names, and also submitted a petition to the President of the House of Peers.

In a handbill printed in 1939 entitled *Chōsen dōhō ni Nippon denrai no myōji o rankyo subeki ka* (Should We Thoughtlessly Permit our Korean Compatriots to Use Traditional Japanese Family Names?), which aimed at 'urging the Ministry of Overseas Affairs and the Government-General of Korea to reconsider their position', Furuya claimed that 90 per cent of 'all Japanese family names' were those of 'imperial descendants', directly related to the Imperial Family.[17] He also wrote that to give Koreans traditional Japanese family names was a 'great invasion of the family lines of the Japanese nation' and would create 'a hothouse of decadent thought even more deadly to the National Polity than communism'. It would make the lineage of the ancestors of the

Japanese nation unclear, and 'decrease the percentage of names that can be traced back to the Imperial Family'. If a name change was absolutely necessary, he continued, 'we should make Koreans use Japanese-style names that are not used in Japan', so that, for example, a Korean named Kim with the Chinese character for 'gold' could be re-named 'Kanedera, Kanemizu, or Kanezuki', all of which also include the same character, and a Korean named Rim – 'trees' – could be renamed 'Hayashikura...or Hayashimoto' which again incorporate the character for 'trees'.[18]

Furuya's motivation boiled down to a fear that if Japanese and Koreans could not be identified by their family names, discrimination would no longer be possible. In reality, the name change policy was based on the premise that even if family names were changed into Japanese ones, Family Registers (*koseki*) could still be used to look up details of an individual's birth, so that it would not be impossible to discriminate on the basis of birth as Furuya feared. In other words, it was not possible to transfer Family Registers to Japan Proper from Korea. When Nakayama Satoru, who was discussed in chapter 9, proposed a change into Japanese names, he argued that all evidence of Korean birth should be deleted from the Family Registers. The name change policy that was actually introduced clearly differed from this.

To repeat, the Government-General of Korea emphasised the point that the idea of 'Japan and Korea as One' did not entail equality in rights and duties. The argument was for erasing the nation rather than for ending discrimination, and there was little hesitation in calling Koreans an alien nation and discriminating against them. In a Privy Council Conference which Koreans were not aware of, Minami, the Governor-General who strongly advocated the unity of Japan and Korea (*naisen ittai*), stated that Koreans could not be treated equally since they were an alien nation.[19] Even so, the Japanisation policy infuriated the pure blood theorists.

In order to deal with Furuya's petition, the Government-General of Korea drew up an internal document, *'Seigansho' ni arawaretaru gobyū* (Mistakes in the 'Petition'). As will be noted later, Furuya was a contributor to *Yūseigaku* (Eugenics), and it is likely that the Government-General was conscious of the eugenics school and of the Ministry of Health and Welfare bureaucrats who were backing Furuya.

This internal document also noted that the Family Register could be used to identify birth, and claimed that Furuya misunderstood the name change policy. Moreover, it was noted that Furuya's 'claim that 90 per cent of Japanese family names could be traced back to the Imperial Family' was 'a statistically baseless position' and that the Korean migrants listed in *Shinsen shōjiroku* made up over 20 per cent of the total. Finally, the document clearly stated that 'our ancestors who formed today's Yamato nation were not always an homogeneous Yamato nation'. In an internal document prepared by the Legal Affairs Bureau of the Government-General of Korea in January 1940, *Sōshi kaimei ni kansuru hōan no gimon gitō* (Questions and Answers about the Name Change Act), the existence of foreign migrants was stressed in reply to the question whether '90 per cent of Japanese family names descend from the Imperial Family', and an excerpt from the *Shinsen shōjiroku* was added.[20]

This line of argument was not limited to the Government-General of Korea. *Ronsetsu bunrei kaiseimei dokuhon* (The Name Change Reader), published in 1943 in Taiwan, noted that 'as is well known, the Yamato nation was not originally a single, pure blood family…it included a large number of naturalised foreign migrants', and urged that names be Japanified to suit 'the harmonious single Yamato nation'. In a pamphlet published in 1939, the Manshū Teikoku Kyōwakai (Manchurian Empire Concordia Association) noted the ethnic mixture in the ancient archipelago and justified the Japanese leadership in the Manchurian Empire, stating that the Japanese nation historically 'possessed the spirit of racial harmony in its blood'.[21]

Kita Noriaki, an official who was the *de facto* head of the Aboriginal Office of the Social Section of the Hokkaido Agency, stated that 'when Japan was founded, there were many races in the country'. He noted that the *Ainu* were responsible for the medieval Zenkunen and Gosannnen battles and the city of Hiraizumi, and urged their assimilation into the mixed Yamato nation. Furthermore, Shimomura Hiroshi (1875–1957), a manager of the Chūō Kyōwakai (Central Concordia Association) that advocated the assimilation of Korean migrants living in Japan Proper, said in 1941 in a lecture, 'Dai tōa kyōeiken' (The Greater East Asia Co-prosperity Sphere), that 'nations from all over the world – from Siberia to Tartary, Korea, China, the Ryūkyū islands, Taiwan and the South Sea islands – had assembled in the Japanese islands…to form today's harmonious Yamato nation', and argued that these regions should be 'harmoniously united' under Japanese leadership.[22]

However, this line of argument did not mention the issue of the location of the birthplace of the 'Tenson nation', Takamagahara, and confined itself to emphasising the historical achievements of assimilation and mixture. The taboo was extended to cover not only the foreign origin of the Imperial Family but also the location of Takamagahara.

The Ministry of Health and Welfare and the Eugenics School of Thought

'I look all over the world to find a great statesman who will resolutely enforce eugenic policies, and find only one – Adolf Hitler. Heil Hitler!'

The Japanese Racial Hygiene Association, a body that advocated social reform based on eugenics, was established in 1930. It was called an Association (*gakkai*), although it was in fact an interest group, because it had failed to gain legal recognition as a foundation (*zaidan hōjin*). Five years later, it was renamed the Japanese Racial Hygiene Committee (*kyōkai*). The aims of the organisation were the sterilisation of 'inferior individuals' and those with hereditary diseases, the promotion of 'eugenic marriages' through the diagnosis of eugenicists, opposition to birth control, and an increase in the population of the Japanese nation. At the time of its establishment, the Board of Trustees included individuals such as Yoshida Shigeru and the postwar Prime Minister and professional politician Hatoyama Ichirō (1883–1959). The words quoted above were written in 1936 by Nagai Hisomu, the managing director of the committee and a professor of the Faculty of Medicine at the Tokyo Imperial University, in a preface to *Minzoku eisei* (Racial Hygiene) in which he praised the Nazi sterilisation law. He was a perfect example of what the Government-General of Korea called someone with a 'German mania'.[23]

As noted above, the association's journal *Minzoku eisei* originally did not display much interest in the issue of mixed blood. However, at the Second Conference of the Japanese Racial Hygiene Association held in 1932, Nagai gave a lecture, 'Minzoku no konketsu ni tsuite' (On the Mixed Blood of the Nation), where he argued that 'from the standpoint of a superior nation, we should keep our blood pure and avoid the mixture of blood as much as possible'.[24] The Roman Empire was again presented as an example of an imperial power that collapsed because it mixed its blood with alien nations. At that time, the mixed nation theory was the accepted theory, and Nagai admitted that 'at the beginning of the world, several nations intermarried and mixed their blood with each other to form our superior ancestors'. However, he also noted that, after this, 'due to the happy geographical conditions of the island empire, pure blood has been preserved until today, a situation which is perhaps unparalleled in the world'. Although he chose his words carefully so as not to criticise the assimilationist policies in Korea and Taiwan, his real intention was clear.

The individual who played an important role in having the Japanese Racial Hygiene Committee movement reflected in policy was the vice-president, Furuya Yoshio, a professor of the Kanazawa Medical University, who was sympathetic to Nazi racial policies, and who, in 1939, entered the recently established Ministry of Health and Welfare. Subsequently, he held various posts, including Head of the National Physical Strength Department in the Scientific Health and Welfare Research Centre, Head of the Department of Scientific Health and Welfare in the Research Centre of the Ministry of Health and Welfare and, after the war, Head of the Public Health Bureau.

Policies brought into effect by the Ministry of Health and Welfare with the cooperation of the eugenic school include the National Eugenics Act, the predecessor of the postwar Eugenic Protection Act, which legalised the sterilisation of individuals with hereditary diseases, and the National Physical Strength Act, which aimed to promote an increase in physical strength through state health care (both were enacted in 1940).[25] Besides drafting these acts, Furuya Yoshio seems also to have been deeply involved in drawing up the Cabinet Planning Board's 'Manifesto for Establishing a Population Policy' which was determined in 1941, and included arguments similar to those of Furuya and the eugenics school, such as the propagation of eugenic thinking, the prohibition and prevention of contraception and abortion in order to increase the population, and the maintenance of the rural population.[26] Furuya especially felt a sense of crisis that the urban population, which was effeminate and easily infected by dangerous ideas, was increasing year by year, while the rural population that had been responsible for many of the births in the Japanese nation was decreasing.

Furuya emphasised in a lecture submitted to *Yūseigaku* (Eugenics) the year he entered the ministry that 'we should not permit the mixture of blood – no one can say that Japan in the future will be free from a peril like that of the Jews in Germany'. While admitting that an ancient mixture had occurred in the Japanese nation, he criticised the prevalent 'argument that claims that national assimilation through a marriage policy would be acceptable', an argument based on the mixed nation theory. According to him, Korea and Taiwan should not be incorporated through a 'racial assimilation' based on a mixture of blood, but rather Japanese settlers should be sent there, 'large numbers of Japanese farm villages should be established', and the countries 'should be reoccupied by Japanese farmers'.[27]

Furthermore, in his work of 1941, *Kokudo·jinkō·ketsueki* (National Land, Population and Blood), Furuya argued against the position of the Government-General of Korea.[28] He stated that criticism of the pure blood theory could be divided into three main groups. The first held that since the empire was destined to include many nations, 'to utter the word "race" vainly would be a great obstacle in establishing the Greater East Asian New Order'. According to Furuya, the National (*kokumin*) Eugenics Act, which legalised sterilisation, had originally been called the Racial (*minzoku*) Eugenics Act when it was a bill, but the name was apparently changed because the use of the word *minzoku* was thought to be inappropriate. The second group held that 'today's fad for nationalism is inherited from Nazi Germany'. The third group propagated the 'notion that infests Japan, which claims our nation was originally a mixed nation, and so denies that there is any reason to fear mixture'. He rejected the first criticism out of hand as excessive sensitivity, and handled the second criticism by defending the Nazis.

Where the third criticism was concerned, Furuya argued that he could 'not agree at all' with the idea of national assimilation based on the mixed nation theory. According to him, bringing together two nations which differed in the 'degree of culture' and in the 'power of propagation' would trigger an 'intensification of racial competition'. The high population growth of the Koreans was a source of concern not only for Furuya but also for the eugenic school of thought. He opposed the shipment of Koreans to Japan as a source of labour, saying that 'the general notion of Japan and Korea as One is certainly not bad, but an unnatural and over-hasty introduction of peninsular Japanese [Koreans] into Japan Proper is not a sensible policy'.[29] Whatever the justification, he said, the influx of alien nations was not desirable. Furthermore, he emphasised the problem of children of mixed parentage, saying that 'a policy to encourage marriage between the two nations is all very well, but what will become of the education of the children born to such parents?', and insisted that 'mixing blood with the Chinese will be even more problematic'. Because of his status as a bureaucrat, he could not criticise Japanisation openly in an official publication and so expressed himself carefully, but the attitude underlying these words is clear.

The deepening relationship between the Japanese Racial Hygiene Committee and the Ministry of Health and Welfare can be clearly seen in the contents of the academic conferences held by the committee. From the ninth to the eleventh conferences, held from 1940 to 1942, papers given by individuals linked to the Ministry of Health and Welfare made up over 30 per cent of all the reports, including an explanation of ministry policy by the Head of the Eugenic Section and reports by researchers from research institutions affiliated with the ministry. The conferences used to be held at universities, but the twelfth conference of 1943 was held in the Research Centre of the Ministry of Health and Welfare.

Parallel with this movement, research into the issue of the mixture of blood increased. In these conferences, papers were given on inter-racial marriages between Japanese and the *Ainu*, Chinese, South Sea islanders, Westerners and Indians, along with other conference papers on the rate of the population increase in Korea and the fertility of Korean women. In the Committee's journal, *Minzoku eisei*, expressions such as 'from the viewpoint of the state, mixing blood should be avoided completely' began to appear.[30]

At the same time, explanations of policy authored by individuals linked with the Ministry of Health and Welfare were also published in almost every edition of *Yūseigaku* (Eugenics). Indeed, some editions were filled with ministry papers, and the journal became a *de facto* public relations bulletin of the ministry. In 1942, it published a survey of the physical constitution and intelligence of the children of Japanese-Korean couples. Furuya Eiichi, who had campaigned against the name change, had contributed to *Yūseigaku* from as early as the 1920s, and in 1940 serialised an article in *Yūseigaku* that argued against the name change and for the proposition that the Japanese state was populated by descendants of the Imperial Family, and that criticised the name change as a 'scandalous event' that ran counter to the propagation of the national polity (*kokutai meichō*).[31]

The Contradiction Between Pure Blood and General Mobilisation

In 1943, on the orders of the Minister of Health and Welfare, the Population and Nation Department section of the Ministry Research Centre put together a work of over 3,000 pages, *Yamato minzoku o chūkaku to suru sekai seisaku no kentō* (An Examination of Global Policy Centred on the Yamato Nation). Its material was secret, and only 100 copies were printed and distributed within the government. Judging from the fact that elite technocrats from the ministry together with the Head of the Department of Population Policies in the Population and Nation Department gave papers to Japanese Racial Hygiene Association conferences, and that the Research Centre provided a conference venue to the committee, there were close links between the Research Centre and the Association.[32] In this work, the ethnic policy of the eugenics school can be seen more clearly than in the more careful expressions used in the public media.

First of all, the importance of preventing the mixture of blood was repeatedly emphasised. At this time, roughly 6 million 'Japanese' – or 8 per cent of the population of the archipelago – resided in colonies and occupied territories outside Japan Proper. Mixing blood with the nations of the areas into which the 'Japanese' had marched lacked 'eugenic consideration', and as a result, 'under the name of assimilationist policies, will actually destroy the unification of the Yamato nation and drag our cultural standards down to their level, and will lead to a rejection of the consciousness and power of leadership'. In order to prevent the mixing of blood, it was suggested that those moving overseas should be compelled to take their spouses with them. It was also suggested that 'Japanese' born overseas should be obliged to study in Japan Proper for a set period of time in order to instil patriotism in them.

According to this work, many 'mixed marriages' (*zakkon*) were based on the sexual drive, and 'mixed-marriage couples are inferior in social status and intelligence compared to average members of their respective races'. Moreover, such marriages led to the destruction of the family system as the couples often married despite the opposition of their parents. Children of mixed parentage were deficient in adaptability and resistance to diseases and, as generations passed, would grow increasingly distant from the ruling Japanese nation and become instead closer to the indigenous peoples or turn into a different ethnic group. Furthermore, it was emphasised that 'their characters have a tendency to rely on others, to flunkeyism and irresponsibility; they have weak wills, and are nihilistic and self-destructive'.[33]

Moreover, warning bells were rung about the increasing number of marriages between Japanese women and Korean men, whose numbers had rapidly increased in Japan Proper as a result of the decision to recruit them as forced labour and ship them to the archipelago. Not only was mixing blood to be avoided, but what made matters worse was that 'the fundamental principle of a relationship based on domination is that the males of the ruling or conquering nation marry females of the ruled or conquered nation, but this has been reversed in Japan Proper'. In fact, almost 80 per cent of the inter-racial couples in Korea decorated by the Government-General of Korea were matches between Korean men and Japanese women. More than 1,500 marriages that consisted of Japanese women and Korean men residing in Japan Proper were investigated by the Population Research Institute of the Ministry of Health and Welfare (this later became the Department of Population and Nation Studies), and it was determined that the children of these couples 'lacked any sense of shame and patriotism'. There were many cases where Japanese females 'mistook Korean males for Japanese' and married them, and this was explained as a 'tragic aspect of an extreme unification of Japan and Korea and of the name change'.[34]

Since many of the Koreans forcefully brought to Japan were young males, it was to be expected that matches between Korean males and Japanese females would increase. It was also natural that Koreans forced to adopt Japanese names and learn the Japanese language should be mistaken for Japanese. Japanisation and the general mobilisation thus contained the seeds of the destruction of the pure blood ideology.

In the Nazi Germany of the same period, the mixing of blood between Germans and foreign labourers who had been forcibly mobilised was seen as a serious problem. It was therefore decided that the numbers of male and female labourers brought from the Soviet Union and Poland should be about the same, and the German Government established brothels staffed by foreign women for the sole use of foreign labourers. In cases where sexual intercourse with German females was discovered, the male was executed.[35] In Japan, however, although it has been demonstrated that brothels staffed by Korean 'comfort women' for male Korean labourers were established in several working places, intermarriage between Koreans and Japanese was encouraged by the government – at least officially. This situation must have been intolerable for the researchers who staffed the research institutes of the Ministry of Health and Welfare.

How, then, did they intend to deal with the issue of Korea and Taiwan? The question was answered in a section entitled 'The Enforced Migration of Taiwanese and Koreans' in the chapter 'East Asian National Population Policies'. Here, it was noted that despite the fact that 'Korea and Taiwan play important roles as bases for military supplies', both Koreans and Taiwanese 'have high birth rates, and still have not been assimilated'. In order 'to prevent Korea and Taiwan from causing harm to the empire, despite all the favours bestowed on them', the following five proposals were put forward.[36]

1. Koreans living in Japan Proper should not be allowed to take up permanent residence, but should be sent back to Korea after the war in order to make them understand their status in Japan Proper as non-permanent migrant workers.
2. Koreans living in northern Korea and on the eastern border of Manchuria should be relocated: care must be taken not to inflame relations with the Soviet Union in doing so. Majority Japanese (*naichijin*) should be moved there *en masse* to replace the Koreans.
3. Koreans should be sent to settle infertile areas such as New Guinea in order to open up new land.
4. The number of majority Japanese in Korea and Taiwan should amount to at least 10 per cent of the total population.
5. The colonial policy represented in the extreme form of 'Japan and Korea as One' should be corrected, as it had resulted in majority Japanese being oppressed by Koreans.

These proposals can be seen as a more concrete version of the argument by Furuya Yoshio and others to remove the indigenous peoples of Korea and Taiwan and replace them with Japanese farmers.

The fifth proposal – to correct the 'Japan and Korea as One' policy – listed policy issues that required re-examination, including the 'problem of the name change' and the 'problem of intermarriage'. Mention was also made of troubles caused by the influx of labourers due to national mobilisation, such as 'the problem of disputes between Japanese and Koreans', 'the problem with economic and labour conditions', and 'the problem of public morals'. Furthermore, 'the problem of co-education with Japanese and Koreans in the same class room' was added to the list, and can be seen as a proposal for the policy of segregation previously urged by Tōgō.

It is important to note that the 'issue of conscription' was included as an item for re-examination. It had already been decided at this stage to extend conscription to include Koreans, so the suggestion for a re-examination seems to have been aimed at removing Koreans from the military. To have large numbers of Koreans trained in the use of firearms was not only dangerous for the Japanese colonial rulers, but the contamination by Koreans of the pure blood of the 'honourable Imperial Army' was also unacceptable for many 'Japanese' of the time. If Koreans received military decorations, it would be difficult to look down on them with contempt, and 'Japanese' would have to obey Korean officers. In fact, there were already many Korean officers in the Japanese army who had not waited for conscription but volunteered for service, including one individual who eventually became a Lieutenant-General.[37]

However, none of this implied a refusal to use Koreans and Taiwanese as a human resource. In fact, another section mentioned 'the compulsory requisition of Taiwanese and Koreans as labourers'. Of course, it would have been thought desirable to strictly segregate those requisitioned and send them back to Taiwan and Korea when no longer needed, unless they were working in their own countries or the occupied South Seas. Where military mobilisation was concerned, it was proposed that 'an army of the nations of the Greater East Asia Co-prosperity Sphere, a foreign legion, be formed and utilised' in preference to enlisting Koreans and Taiwanese in the Japanese military.[38] To form Korean and Chinese military units segregated from Japanese units and staffed with Japanese officers would be one way to mobilise alien peoples without ruining the pure blood of the Japanese military. If conscripted and included in the Japanese military, those who rendered remarkable services would have to be promoted, but would not have to be promoted in the Japanese military if enlisted in a separate foreign legion (this policy was not implemented: see the conclusion).

Yamato minzoku o chūkaku to suru sekai seisaku no kentō also demonstrated a deep interest in the origin of the Japanese nation, with a chapter devoted to the issue. Although it accepted the established position of the day, it suggested that a mixture took place centred around the 'proto-Japanese', and that this was followed by a long period during which pure blood was maintained, so that the modern Japanese nation was a 'uniquely pure race'. It was also noted that the German nation, though identical with the Japanese in that it, too, had a history of mixing blood in ancient times, not only had 'not reached the conclusion of some Japanese intellectuals that the mixture of blood is to be welcomed', but actually advocated a pure blood policy instead.[39]

In fact, 'taking the steps necessary to maintain the purity of the Yamato nation, such as having Japanese settlers take their families with them' was also urged in 'Dai tōa kensetsu kihon kōryō' (Fundamental Policies for Constructing Greater East Asia), a report on population and national policy submitted by the Council for Establishing Greater East Asia in July 1942. The council was headed by the Army General and, from October 1941, Prime Minister, Tōjō Hideki (1884–1948), and included a large number of intellectuals. However, in reality, control was exercised by bureaucrats of the Cabinet Planning Board, which was in charge of managing the council (the Planning Board subsequently became the postwar Economic Planning Agency). The records of the council's deliberations are not available, but in *Dai tōa kensetsu no kihon kōryō* (A Basic Program for Establishing Greater East Asia), published in February 1943 by a research group of the Planning Board, the population growth of the Japanese nation, the maintenance of farm village populations, the joint movement overseas of the spouses of settlers, study in Japan Proper by Japanese children born abroad, and the thorough propagation of eugenic thought were all advocated.[40] Although the book did not list the names of the authors, its arguments resemble those of the eugenic theorists. The Planning Board cooperated with the Ministry of Welfare in drawing up the population policy that Furuya Yoshio had also had a hand in, and the two institutes exchanged personnel.

It may have been because of these developments that the Government-General of Korea criticised the pure blood policy advocated 'by those in Japan Proper who form the nucleus of the bureaucracy' with a 'German mania'. A pro-Japanese Korean intellectual who enjoyed a close relationship with the Government-General wrote that 'the outcry for pure blood' influenced by Nazi thought could be seen in 'Ministry of Health and Welfare and

Planning Board circles'. He noted that 'the philosophy that "it is detestable" to mix Korean blood with Japanese blood or that "Koreans must be stopped from coming to Japan Proper"' had spread and was proving to be an obstacle to the Japanisation policy.[41]

Of course, neither the Government-General of Korea nor the eugenics school of thought was monolithic. Some members of the former argued against marriages between Japanese and Koreans and, as already noted, some of the latter were in favour of the theory of heterosis. It is perhaps also true that the 'Japan and Korea as One' position of the Government-General was only superficial. However, it is difficult to believe that the name change, marriages between Japanese and Koreans, and the shipping of Korean labour to Japan were all products of a merely superficial position. Needless to say, the eugenics school of thought did not intend to protect Koreans or Taiwanese from assimilationist policies, nor did the Government-General argue in favour of equality. While one tried to destroy national identity and promoted mobilisation, the other attempted to prevent the influx of other nations into Japan and was afraid that the basis of discrimination, the differences between nations, would disappear.

As long as the pure blood of the Yamato nation remained the focus of debate, the origin of the nation was an issue that neither side could ignore. While the Government-General utilised the theory of the mixed nation as a powerful weapon, eugenic pure blood theorists regarded the theory as a stumbling block. Even so, the eugenic school included some anthropologists.

The Rise of an Anthropological Theory of the Homogeneous Nation

The major trends in Japanese anthropology from the 1920s to the 1930s included the movement towards physical anthropology and the emergence of cultural anthropology. Since this book is not a history of academic theories, I will not explain each theory in detail, but will note that a movement towards specialisation emerged from the hotchpotch of the Meiji Period. In 1924, in an event symbolic of a generational change, Torii Ryūzō resigned from Tokyo Imperial University following a dispute over the assessment of a Ph.D. thesis that dealt with physical anthropology. At that time, only Tokyo Imperial University offered a specialised anthropology course, and enthusiastic scholars from other faculties played a major role in anthropological research. The trend towards physical anthropology was advantageous for medical scholars who had a good understanding of the human body, and the Japanese Racial Hygiene Association, which had been established by individuals such as the medical doctors Nagai and Furuya Yoshio, contained several anthropologists with medical backgrounds.

One such was the association's regional director Furuhata Tanemoto, a professor at Kanazawa Medical University and later at Tokyo Imperial University. His speciality was medical jurisprudence and blood types, and he triggered the postwar boom in the latter, writing a book aimed at a general readership. Blood types became the focus of attention for the eugenic theorists of that period in both Japan and Europe. An examination of the issues of *Minzoku eisei* (Racial Hygiene) and *Yūseigaku* (Eugenics) published in the first half of the 1930s shows that a great deal of research was carried out on the connection between intelligence and physical abilities on the one hand, and blood type on the other. There were papers on the relationship between temperament and blood type, such as those that argued that individuals with blood type A are delicate, while those with blood type O are bold. The origin of the contemporary theory of blood types which is so popular in Japan today can be seen here.[42]

Within the eugenic school, some argued that each race and nation had a specific distribution ratio of blood types, which was an index of the nation's temperament and of its superiority or inferiority. Furuhata's position was that the Japanese nation had a unique distribution ratio of blood types different from that of neighbouring nations, and that, to whatever degree mixture had taken place in ancient times, 'the Japanese nation is a superior, great family nation created in the Japanese islands and presided over by the unbroken line of Emperors, and the only homeland of the Japanese nation is the Japanese islands'.[43]

Another individual who joined the Board of Trustees of the Japanese Racial Hygiene Association from the start was Kiyono Kenji (1885–1955), a professor of the Faculty of Medicine of Kyoto Imperial University, and Hasebe Kotondo (1882–1969), a professor of the Faculty of Medicine at Tōhoku Imperial University. From the 1920s onwards, Kiyono contributed articles on the origin of the Japanese nation to *Yūseigaku*, and advocated 'choosing spouses according to eugenics'.[44] Kiyono was a pathologist, and a mentor of Lieutenant-General Ishii Shirō (1892–1959), who was in charge of the infamous 731 Unit which carried out experiments on Chinese while developing bacteriological weapons. Furuhata influenced only a small group of people interested in blood type research, but Kiyono and Hasebe created the established theories of postwar anthropology, and played a crucial role in the formation of the myth of the homogeneous nation.

What characterises the research of Kiyono and Hasebe is that, unlike previous theories that tended to rely on interpretations of the Kiki myths, it emphasised a statistical analysis of physical measurements, a methodology which at first glance looks scientific. From the early 1920s, Kiyono and Hasebe rejected previous interpretations of the Kiki myths in which the Emishi and others were seen as alien peoples. Kiyono based his arguments on human bones unearthed from archaeological sites, while Hasebe based his on a survey of physical measurements from various regions of the modern archipelago. It is said that Kiyono's grasp of an enormous amount of statistical data in particular stunned contemporary academic circles. Their position during the 1920s can be summarised as a denial of the contemporary paradigm as developed by Torii and others that the Stone Age people of the archipelago were the Emishi, who in turn were the *Ainu*. In their view, the Stone Age people were not an indigenous nation but the direct ancestors of the Japanese nation, and there was no replacement of nations by conquest.[45]

According to Hasebe, the archipelago could be roughly divided into two regions – prefectures with high average heights and prefectures with low average heights – and this was a vestige of a pre-historic mixture between a tall and a short nation. At that time, height was thought to be almost completely determined by genes. Based on a comparison of the heights of the people of northeastern Japan where the Emishi were said to have lived and the *Ainu*, he argued that the Emishi were not the *Ainu*, and claimed that the people of the Stone Age should be associated with the 'Japanese' not the *Ainu*.

Kiyono's article demonstrated a firm command of statistical data and is far from easy to read, but his argument is quite simple. If the *Ainu* were indeed an indigenous people, the bones of the Stone Age people should have similar characteristics to theirs. However, according to his research, human bones from the Stone Age resembled neither those of the modern Japanese nation nor those of the modern *Ainu*. He therefore argued that the people of the Stone Age were not the ancestors of the *Ainu*, but the direct ancestors of the modern Japanese nation. Following later evolution and intermarriage with neighbouring ethnic groups of the south and north, Stone Age man split into two groups, some becoming the *Ainu* and others the modern 'Japanese'.

The year after it was established, the Japanese Racial Hygiene Association appointed Torii, then the leading anthropological authority, as a director, and had him give a special lecture in its second conference of 1932. In this conference, the chief director, Nagai Hisomu, delivered the paper criticising mixed blood that was discussed earlier. By contrast, Torii did not mention the origin of the Japanese nation, merely giving a perfunctory lecture entitled 'Genshijin no seikatsu' (The Life of Primitive Man), and neither listened to nor gave conference papers in the years following. Having lost Torii, the association instead asked Kiyono to give a lecture on the Stone Age 'Japanese' at the third conference of 1934.[46] It is not clear how favourably Kiyono's position with its strong mathematical bias was received. However, since the association asked him to fill in as a substitute lecturer even though he was not as famous an authority as Torii, and even though he actually argued against Torii's ideas, his position must have been well received by the association.

A more precise account of their position would be that, until about this time, Kiyono and Hasebe denied the theory of a conquest of indigenous peoples but did not necessarily deny the theory of a mixed origin, something which would have fallen outside the bounds of commonsense of contemporary anthropology. Their acceptance of a mixed origin lasted until the early to mid-1930s, a time during which eugenic theorists felt no sense of crisis about the problem of mixed blood. However, the pair's research undoubtedly posed a threat to the existing theories that supported assimilationist policies, even if few scholars could openly oppose research that demonstrated such a firm grasp of an abundance of measurements and statistical analysis.

Among those who did argue against their position, the strongest line of attack was developed by Ueda Jōkichi, the professor of Keijō (Seoul) Imperial University mentioned above, whose theory was adopted in the 'Japan and Korea as One' position of the Government-General of Korea. In an extension of Torii's theory that the indigenous *Ainu* had been conquered by Koreans who had migrated to the Kinki region of central-west Japan, he claimed that the physical differences between Koreans from central Korea and Kinki Japanese were smaller than regional differences among the Japanese themselves. According to Ueda, the people of the eastern and northern Hokuriku, Kantō and Tōhoku regions had a large amount of *Ainu* blood in their veins, while the people of the centre-west regions (Chūgoku and Kinki) were similar to Koreans. This position obviously ran counter to the ideas of Kiyono and Hasebe.

Ueda was originally an anatomist, and was experienced in body measurement. He was also one of the few anthropologists of the era who was well versed in statistics, and so was able to argue against Kiyono and Hasebe on an equal footing. He claimed that Kiyono had made a mistake in his statistical analysis and threatened to make this mistake public unless Kiyono corrected it.[47] According to Ueda, the differences noted by Kiyono between the bones of the Stone Age people and the modern *Ainu* merely reflected the results of the mixture of the blood of the Stone Age *Ainu* with that of a conquering nation. This threat seems not to have been an empty one: Kiyono was forced to publish a corrected article under the name of one of his students in 1934. This backlash against their ideas perhaps helps to explain Kiyono's and Hasebe's approval of the notion of a mixed origin at the time.

'We Should Take Steps to Deal With Mixed Blood'

However, from about 1938, when a full-scale Japanisation policy was implemented, their line of argument began to change. Two years earlier, the professor of anthropological studies at Tokyo Imperial University, then the only university with a chair in anthropology, suddenly died and, partly as a result of a campaign by Kiyono, Hasebe was elected to the post in 1936. Hasebe lobbied Nagayo Matarō, a medical doctor and then President of the University as well as a member of the Board of Trustees of the Japanese Racial Hygiene Association, saying that the national situation required research into the peoples of Asia. Anthropology was raised to the status of a department in 1939 and Hasebe became the founding professor of the first anthropology department in Japan.[48] In late 1939, he gave a radio lecture titled 'Taiko no Nipponjin' (The Prehistoric Japanese), in which he abandoned his previous position, completely denying the concept of a past mixture and adopting a pure blood position instead.

According to this lecture, which began with a celebration of 'the 2,600th anniversary of the accession of the Emperor Jinmu', the Tsuchigumo, Kumaso and Emishi were in fact all members of the Japanese nation, and were regional power-centres led by 'evil elements who resisted the Imperial Army'. However, since differences in customs were exaggerated, later historians misinterpreted them as alien nations. Not only were the people of the Stone Age not the *Ainu*, but 'mixing blood with alien nations' was an exceptional occurrence. Rice was already cultivated in the archipelago during the Stone Age, and a cultural continuity existed between the Stone Age and modern Japan in all the basic essentials of life – food, clothing, and housing. As for the 'theory that the Japanese migrated from the continent or the south', Hasebe said: 'there is no evidence of this. It is a figment of peoples' imagination. I believe that soon after the birth of mankind, the ancestors of today's Japanese occupied this island. So, leaving aside the birthplace of mankind, there is no homeland for the Japanese but Japan'.

Hasebe recognised neither a foreign migration nor any mixture. This was a position that was to be described by a scholar of ancient history in later years as 'a theory that brings to mind the Nazi theory of the superior pure German race'. On the other hand, in a postwar paper, Hasebe insisted that 'popular wartime theories such as the idea that the Japanese and Koreans are the same race' were wrong, and that the differences between Japan and Korea were obvious. At the same time, he criticised the mixed nation theory as lacking any foundation. Hasebe's theory meant the complete denial of the theory that the 'Japanese' and Koreans shared a common ancestor as well as of the theory of the mixed nation – both of which were officially approved by the empire. Given this fact, and perhaps fearing a backlash, he published the lectures only in an obscure technical journal, 'omitting' the section in his broadcast lecture where he denied the notion of migration.[49]

However, Hasebe made his views clear in an unpublished paper. In April 1942, five months after the outbreak of the Pacific War, and on the eve of the submission of a report by the Greater East Asia Construction Committee that advocated the maintenance of the pure blood of the Yamato nation, he presented to the vice-president of the Planning Board a written opinion entitled 'Dai tōa kensetsu ni kanshi jinruigaku kenkyūsha to shite no iken' (An

Opinion as an Anthropologist about the Construction of Greater East Asia).⁵⁰ This began as follows.

1 To construct Greater East Asia, the Japanese should first know themselves.

I believe that the Japanese have lived in Japan since remote prehistoric times. There is no way of knowing today where Takamagahara is located. However, to assert that it is located overseas is to make the baseless assumption that it is not located in Japan. The Japanese climate was already fit for human habitation in the late diluvian epoch. This is clear from the various animals that existed in [the archipelago of] that period. Therefore, the Japanese must have lived in Japan from this time, although evidence of human existence remains to be discovered.

This is not an academic theory, but rather a religious belief. In the diluvian (Pleistocene) epoch, a land bridge still existed between what was not yet an archipelago and the continent! As will be mentioned in chapter 17, Hasebe found his 'evidence' for human habitation in a model of human bones located in the anthropology department of Tokyo University after the war, and advocated the famous theory of Akashi Man.

His written opinion went on to insist that the 'people of the Stone Age [who lived in the archipelago] were in fact Japanese' and that their culture from that age was 'highly unique', and 'superior' to that of the 'modern *Ainu*, or the Dayaks of Borneo'. He continued in these terms:

[Despite these facts,] several theories have been used to substantiate the opinion that the people of the Stone Age were not Japanese, but rather an indigenous people. These include the argument that traces of an *Ainu* inhabitation of Japan exist; that the Emishi of history are identical with the modern Ezo, in other words the *Ainu*; the theory that totally ignores the uniqueness of Japanese culture and tries to explain everything as due to a Chinese influence; and the theory that the Japanese and Chinese or the Japanese and Koreans are the same race...It is obvious that the *Ainu*, Koreans, Oroke, Gilyaks, Mongolians, Indochinese, peninsular Malays, the people of the East Indies, and the people of Japanese

231

Micronesia and other Pacific islands are totally different from the Japanese.

Both the theory that the 'Japanese' and Koreans shared a common ancestor and the theory of the existence of an indigenous nation were thus persistently and completely denied, and emphasis was placed on the uniqueness of the 'Japanese', who differed from all neighbouring nations, beginning with the Koreans. Hasebe recognised only an affinity between the 'Japanese' and Chinese, and this became the basis for his postwar theory that human beings had already migrated to the archipelago when a land-bridge still existed between the archipelago and the Chinese continent. He stressed that 'the view that the Japanese are a mixed nation is completely wrong and will have a harmful effect on the policy of creating Greater East Asia', and noted that the 'Japanese inherently possess a noble distinctiveness in Greater East Asia'.

The second section was titled 'Jinkō zōshoku ni tomonau shidōryoku no kyōka' (Strengthening Leadership Through Population Growth), and began: 'Population growth is not only crucial to the survival and rise of the empire, but also essential to the construction of Greater East Asia'. According to Hasebe, the newly-born 'Japanese' could be divided into three types: 'good', 'ordinary' and 'bad'. Those designated as 'ordinary' could be improved through education and instruction, while those designated as 'bad' needed be 'removed according to the sterilisation act of the criminal law'. The third section began as follows.

3 We should take steps to deal with the issue of mixed blood.
Since the annexation of Korea, a great number of Koreans have been brought to Japan Proper to replenish the labour force. As a result, a large number of half-breed children have already been born. It is an indisputable fact that Koreans are very different from Japanese in constitution and disposition...I have deep misgivings that the increase of mixed-breed children with a Korean parent will increase the ratio of 'ordinary' people in various meanings of the word. One of the most important issues in the construction of Greater East Asia is prudently to research policies to address the issue of mixing blood with Koreans.

This written opinion continued with sections on the 'Japanese' ability to adapt to the tropics, the propagation of the Japanese language, and the necessity of anthropological surveys of the areas into which the Japanese nation had marched, but further examination is perhaps not necessary here. This 'specialist opinion' from a professor of Tokyo Imperial University, the supreme authority in Japanese anthropology, was perhaps one of the causes behind the move of the Planning Board and the Greater East Asia Construction Committee to place greater emphasis on the maintenance of pure blood. Hasebe was also included as the only anthropologist on the board of the Special Committee for Ethnic Scientific Research established in 1939 as part of the Japan Society for the Promotion of Science (Furuya Yoshio was also a member of the managing board of this Special Committee). In a report published by the Special Committee in 1943, a strong argument was put forward in favour of the prevention of mixed blood.[51]

On the other hand, Kiyono noted in a chapter included in *Jinruigaku·senshigaku kōza* (Lectures on Anthropology and Prehistory), a book he co-authored with Hasebe, Furuhata and Furuya Yoshio:[52]

> When human beings migrated to Japan for the first time, they formed the people of the Japanese Stone Age...As time went by, various people migrated to Japan, some from the continent, others from the South Seas, and mixed [with the Japanese Stone Age man]. However, this mixture did not suddenly cause a change in the physical constitution of the Japanese Stone Age people.
>
> In this sense, the Japanese islands have been the homeland of the Japanese since the birth of mankind. The genesis of the Japanese occurred in Japan. The Japanese were not a people who occupied the motherland of the *Ainu*. The motherland of the Japanese race, the homeland of the Japanese, has been Japan since mankind first lived in Japan.

Kiyono recognised a greater mixture of blood than Hasebe, but denied any large physical change. His original theory was that the people of the Stone Age were different from both the modern *Ainu* and the modern Japanese nation, and developed into two nations as a consequence of intermarriage with neighbouring races and evolution. In 1936, two years previously, he had emphasised the change brought about by intermarriage, and had stated that the Stone Age people could not be called 'Japanese'.[53] Here, however, he manipulated subtle expressions to minimise the importance of any mixture of blood, and described the 'Japanese' as if they had lived in 'Japan' since the Stone Age. Moreover, according to this article, the Eastern Expedition of the Emperor Jinmu was not 'a battle between races', but rather the 'Imperial Household was Japan's Imperial Household since the Age of the Gods'.

In 1938, Kiyono – an avid collector of historical materials – was arrested for stealing precious ancient texts, lost his post at Kyoto Imperial University, and went on to live in seclusion, spending his time copying out manuscripts. In 1941, however, a state policy body, the Taiheiyō Kyōkai (Pacific Committee), asked him to carry out an investigation in the south. For Kiyono, who had been effectively consigned to social oblivion, this was salvation. He accepted the offer, saying, 'I wanted to study the half-breed children of the Japanese and other races', and travelled to Tokyo to become a member (*shokutaku*) of the committee. Subsequently, he published a series of books on ethnic studies that advocated the construction of the Greater East Asia Co-prosperity Sphere, stating that he 'desired that anthropology should prove helpful in constructing the south'.[54]

In a book published during this period, Kiyono made compromises with the contemporary line of argument, saying that 'it is inevitable that we concede that...mixture with the southern races has taken place to a certain extent', and that this 'would greatly enhance Japanese adaptability to the tropics'. However, like Hasebe, he denied the existence of ethnic groups in ancient Japan, claiming that the different nations that appeared in the Kiki myths 'are certainly not alien races, but only rebellious elements within the same race'. According to Kiyono, the theory that an indigenous people was conquered was the product of Japanese scholars who had uncritically accepted the ideas of Western scholars who inferred that migrants conquered the natives because that had been the case in American history. He praised Kurokawa Mayori (mentioned in chapter 1) as a Japanese theorist who resisted this point of view.[55]

Moreover, Kiyono stated that 'judging from the political and eugenic standpoint, the Japanese must multiply their own numbers and lead the Co-prosperity Sphere'. He argued that the Japanese should avoid mixing blood and 'endeavour to form the Greater East Asia Co-prosperity Sphere, maintaining the pure blood of the Japanese race while increasing their numbers'. He also claimed that second generation individuals born overseas were 'on the whole distinctive for their weak patriotism, lack of fortitude, and unhealthy thinking (with a shallow and strong individualism)', and thus insisted that they should be brought to Japan and 'receive a suitable education as imperial subjects'.[56] This line of argument coincided completely with that of the Research Centre of the Ministry of Health and Welfare.

Furthermore, during the war Kiyono wrote a book for a general readership, *Nippon minzoku seiseiron* (On the Genesis of the Japanese Nation), which was unlike his previous difficult and therefore little read works. In the 'national crisis' of wartime Japan, the person who strongly urged Kiyono to write this book in order to 'make the nation believe in their national lineage' was the prolific author and politician Tsurumi Yūsuke (1885–1973). In the book, Kiyono developed his position using 'mathematical theory' to prove the 'value of the Land of the Emperors' and the 'unique breeding of the Japanese nation', and stated that his 'intention was to help the Japanese people become more aware of their status as Japanese'. He based the book on the work he had done while at Kyoto Imperial University, but here the issue of mixed-blood was downplayed to an even greater degree. Instead, increased emphasis was placed on the absence of an indigenous people and on the idea that 'the homeland of the Japanese is Japan'.[57]

How was the theory of the origin of the Japanese nation as developed by Hasebe and Kiyono received? Hasebe did not argue for his ideas in the general media, while Kiyono's works were difficult to read without expert knowledge and, as a result of the American air raids, the publication of his introductory work, *Nippon minzoku seiseiron*, was delayed until after the war. However, a few people did read their works, including even their highly technical articles. Watsuji Tesurō, who will be discussed in chapter 15, was one such individual, as (unexpectedly) were the Marxist historians who occupied the mainstream in postwar Japan.

The earliest example is Nezu Masashi's introduction of Kiyono's theory in *Rekishigaku kenkyū* (The Journal of Historical Studies) in 1936.[58] Here, Nezu said that 'with the exception of Dr. Kiyono, [theories of the origin of the Japanese nation to date] do not consist of reliable arguments based on measurements of skeletal anthropology and statistical analysis', and claimed that the reason Kiyono's scientific theory had not been widely accepted was because of the 'feudal spirit which still persists in academic circles'.

However, it was not only for his 'scientific' attitude that Nezu praised Kiyono. He wrote that his theory 'shattered the fanciful theory that argued that the users of Jōmon pottery were the *Ainu*, and the Japanese Proper (the users of Yayoi pottery and the builders of the *kofun* or large tumuluses) drove them out and occupied the archipelago'. This 'fanciful theory' was the 'traditional interpretation of the Emperor Jinmu's Eastern Expedition'. Nezu thus welcomed Kiyono's theory as shattering the conventional interpretation of the Kiki myths.

Although it is true that Kiyono and Hasebe departed from conventional interpretations of the Kiki myths, their political position was ignored in evaluations of their work. In the same year, Hayakawa Jirō wrote in *Minzokuron* (On the Nation), one in a series of books on materialism, that 'Hasebe Kotondo and Kiyono Kenjirō have completed scientific research [into the origin of the Japanese nation] that is as scientific as the limitations of the bourgeoisie allow'. This reflected the acceptance of their theories among Marxist historians.[59]

In the Meiji era, the denial of the mixed nation theory was ridiculed in the name of science. Now, however, the situation had begun to reverse. After defeat in the Second World War, when the empire was cut down to its original size of 'the Meiji Japan which consisted only of Hokkaido and 46 prefectures', and when both the theory that the 'Japanese' and Koreans shared a common ancestor and the theory of the mixed nation lost their influence, the ideas of these two anthropologists on the origin of the Japanese nation came to be accepted as the new paradigm despite the fact that the environment which had generated it was gone forever.

14 The Revival of the Kiki Myths

Following the annexation of Korea, the theory of the homogeneous nation which argued that the Japanese nation was pure and homogeneous seemed to have been relegated to the sidelines of the Japanese press. However, it had not disappeared, and was already being formed in the Taishō Period (1911–26) by historians who were one step ahead of the anthropologists. Here, Shiratori Kurakichi (1865–1942) and Tsuda Sōkichi (1873–1961) will be discussed as representative theorists.

Together with Naitō Konan, Shiratori founded the academic study of Oriental (East Asian) history in Japan, and also produced a large amount of research in the field of linguistics. Tsuda was Shiratori's favourite pupil, and studied ancient Japanese history through the Kiki myths. Tsuda was attacked by the right-wing and brought to trial after commenting that the Kiki myths did not impart historical facts but rather were fictitious stories. Because of this, he is viewed today as symbolic of the conscientious historian oppressed by the Great Japanese Empire, and became highly valued in postwar historical circles and deeply influential in the postwar study of ancient Japanese history. At the same time, together with Watsuji Tetsurō (see chapter 15), Tsuda has become the focus of recent attention in Japan as a figure who prepared the intellectual foundations for the postwar Symbolic Emperor System (see chapter 17).[1]

The significance of their theories of the Japanese nation in the context of the Great Japanese Empire, however, has received little attention. In a word, their position embodied the major antithesis to the mainstream discourse in the press of the empire of the day – the mixed nation theory – and their theories played a large role in the formation of the postwar myth of the homogeneous nation.

The Disunity of the Continent and the Unity of the Island Nation

Shiratori Kurakichi was a little younger than Inoue Tetsujirō and

Hozumi Yatsuka, and belonged to the first generation of historians who majored in modern historiography from the Department of History at Tokyo Imperial University (then known as Bunka Daigaku). Immediately after his graduation, at the age of 25, Shiratori became a professor at Gakushūin University and then, after studying in Europe, a professor at Tokyo Imperial University, where he taught Oriental history. (This 'Oriental history' was a study not of the history of Japan, but mainly of China and Korea, and was structured on the European model of Oriental Studies).

In a lecture given in 1905, Shiratori explained why he had decided to research Oriental history. 'In order to identify the origins of the Japanese...it is necessary to identify the origins of the nations around Japan. This is why I am studying both Korean and Chinese history' (Shiratori 1969–71: vol. 2, 350). In the Meiji era, when the Great Japanese Empire was still a developing country of Asia, the elite who received the most advanced education in areas outside the practical sciences frequently attempted to form a national identity for Japan. Shiratori was one such individual.

Shiratori began to explicitly deny the mixed nation theory immediately after his return from studying in Europe, when he published 'Waga kuni no kyōsei narishi shiteki gen'in ni tsuite' (On the Historical Causes of the Strength of Japan) during the Russo-Japanese War in 1904. According to Shiratori, compared to continental countries such as China and Russia, 'the peoples of island nations always unite easily. This island nation [Japan] was especially blessed in regard to social union, because the only alien race was the *Ainu*, the vast majority were the Yamato nation, and there were only small differences in language and customs' (Shiratori 1969–71: vol. 9, 166). He explained the Russo-Japanese War as a battle to defend Japan's northern bulwark, saying this had historically consisted of the Liaotung Peninsula, Korea and Manchuria.

At the time of the Russo-Japanese War, Shiratori was not the only individual to insist that the 'Japanese' were easily united because of a simple national make-up. What is special about him, however, is that while the national polity theorists were forced either into silence or into abandoning their position in the face of the mixed nation theory, Shiratori moved to form an academic theory of the homogeneous nation.

In *Kanshi gaisetsu* (A General History of Korea) published three years later, Shiratori opposed the position that viewed the Kumaso and others as alien nations and that argued that the 'Tenson race' later migrated to Japan. According to Shiratori, the Izumo and the Kumaso could not be considered alien nations. Many of the contemporary theories of the origin of the Japanese nation followed the chronology of the emperors as given in the Kiki myths, and assumed that the migration of the 'Tenson nation' had occurred 2,600 years previously, and that this was after the development of a culture that used metal tools, since the Kiki myths contained descriptions of mirrors and swords. Shiratori, however, argued that 'this oral tradition was born much later, and the ancestors of the Japanese came to the Japanese islands through the Korean peninsula long before' (Shiratori 1969–71: vol. 9, 290).

Here he is claiming that the myths were created in a later period by a more advanced civilisation or, in other words, that the formation of the Kiki myths was not contemporaneous with the origin of the Japanese nation. This was an idea that touched on a blind spot in the common sense of that time that assumed the Japanese nation and the myths of the foundation of the nation were inseparable. Here lies the important characteristic of the academic theories of Shiratori and Tsuda.

Though Shiratori argued in this article that the Japanese nation arrived through the Korean peninsula, he denied the theory that the 'Japanese' and Koreans shared a common ancestor: 'there is a huge gulf between...the Japanese and Koreans'. According to Shiratori, the two nations 'belong to different family trees', and 'the relationship between them is nothing like that between the Japanese and the people of Ryūkyū [Okinawa]' (Shiratori 1969–71: vol. 9, 290). This contrasts with Kanazawa Shōzaburō (see chapter 5), who argued that the relationship between the Japanese and Korean languages was the same as that between the Japanese and Ryūkyū languages. Shiratori had claimed in an article a decade prior to this that the Japanese language and the Korean language enjoyed a close relationship,[2] but his view changed after his experience of study in Europe and of the Russo-Japanese War. At that time, of all the leading linguists and historians, Shiratori was the only one to deny explicitly the theory that the 'Japanese' and Koreans shared a common ancestor.

What is still valued today as Shiratori's major achievement in linguistics is 'Nichi·Kan·Ainu sankokugo no sūshi ni tsuite' (On the Numerals in the Japanese, Korean and *Ainu* Languages) published two years later in 1909, on the eve of the annexation of

Korea. Here he argued that numerals in the Japanese language had no affinity whatsoever with those of either the *Ainu* or the Korean languages, and this fact alone 'shows that at least until the time when the ancestors of the Japanese reached the cultural standard that possessed numerals, there was no interaction between these two nations [i.e., between the Japanese and the Koreans]' (Shiratori 1969–71: vol. 2, 453). Shinmura Izuru later argued against this research, saying that there was a way of counting in ancient Koryo similar to the Japanese language – a notion heartily welcomed by Kita Sadakichi who used it to substantiate his theory that the 'Japanese' and Koreans shared a common ancestor.[3] Shiratori himself, however, continued to advocate this lack of affinity as proof that 'the ancestors of the Japanese' separated from the continent in time immemorial.

At the time of the annexation of Korea, Shiratori wrote critiques for magazines such as *Chūō kōron*. He welcomed the annexation, saying that securing Korea as a buffer zone was important in realising 'peace in the Orient'. On the other hand, he insisted that the rule of the peninsula by Susano-O was a myth and that, in spite of popular beliefs, the archipelago had never completely ruled the peninsula historically. The annexation thus had no historical precedent, and people should not relax because of the statements in the Kiki myths, but remain alert. What he emphasised instead was the 'lesson' he claimed to have learned from Oriental history: 'if we are defeated in Korea by a power that moves down from the north, we will inevitably be driven from the continent'.[4] Needless to say, the northern power he was thinking of here was Russia.

The theory that the 'Japanese' and Koreans shared a common ancestor and the theory of the mixed nation were usually developed to extol assimilation without openly arguing for a naked rule through power. From an early stage, however, Shiratori argued for a rule based on power, asserting that 'since Japan and Korea have been mutually antagonistic from ancient times, it is totally futile to attempt to lead Korea with friendship and virtue' (Shiratori 1969–71: vol. 9, 276). From the first, Shiratori viewed Korea only as a base for Japan's advance into the continent and as a bulwark for Japan's national defence, or in other words as a mere geopolitical piece of land, and hardly discussed the issue of how to deal with the people living there, something in which he seemed to have little interest.

The Kiki Myths Are Not Historical Facts

Before the annexation of Korea, Shiratori had written that the Yamato nation migrated to Japan through the peninsula, and did not deny the notion that both the Japanese and the Korean languages belonged to the Ural-Altaic family. However, in 1913, three years after the annexation, he argued that 'not only does the Asian continent not have a language like that of Japan, but no other continent has either', and began to advocate the idea that the migration of the Japanese nation occurred 'tens of thousands of years' ago, and 'the Yamato nation was [virtually] born in these islands'.[5]

According to Shiratori, the Japanese language did not belong to the Ural-Altaic family, making the point that 'it is quite natural for Japanese who know only Chinese or English to feel on learning an illogical language like Korean that it is similar to Japanese, but those Japanese would probably feel the same way if they learned Mongolian, Turkish or Tamil' (Shiratori 1969–71: vol. 3, 377). Taguchi Ukichi's idea that the Japanese and Turkish languages were similar had been ridiculed (see chapter 10), and Shiratori insisted that the common ancestor theory was an equally nonsensical idea.

Furthermore, in 'Nippon jinshuron ni taisuru hihyō' (A Criticism of Theories of the Japanese Race) published in 1915, Shiratori completely rejected the view that Takamagahara was located in a foreign country. Shiratori's theory of the Japanese nation was completed about this time, and underwent no great changes until his death in 1942.

According to this article, neither the northern lands of the 'Gilyak' (Nivkhi) and the Tungus, nor southern Malaya and Indochina, nor the Korean peninsula could be considered as the location of Takamagahara as all were either 'savage countries' or 'even if not inferior certainly not superior to Japan'. Moreover, although China was culturally advanced, the names and thoughts of the gods in the Kiki myths were very Japanese, so 'to regard China as Takamagahara is to miss the mark completely' (Shiratori 1969–71: vol. 9, 191–2). Eventually, the only conclusion that remained was that the Japanese nation was 'born in these islands'. He explained the alien nations in the Kiki myths in the following way (Shiratori 1969–71: vol. 9, 197):

> Yamato, Izumo and Kumaso are the names of three political groups, not three nations, of ancient Japan. In ancient times,

apart from the *Ainu,* no nation was living in Japan other than the Japanese. The Izumo and the Kumaso were pure Japanese. In the records of the gods (*shinten*) [such as the *Kojiki*], these two were therefore regarded as relatives of the Imperial Household, but the same was not true of the *Ainu.* Not only did this sort of story [of links with the Imperial Household] not exist in the case of the *Ainu,* but they were actually compared to a large, evil snake. From this example, we can see to what degree our ancestors shunned foreign nations.

Shiratori's view of history as described here contrasts with that of authors such as Kita Sadakichi. Mixed nation theorists stressed that the Tenson, unlike Western nations, did not discriminate against alien peoples, but assimilated them warm-heartedly and without prejudice (*isshi dōjin*). Shiratori, however, argued that the Izumo and Kumaso were the same nation, and that the one alien people, the *Ainu*, were completely ostracised. In later years, Shiratori began to argue that the *Ainu* invaded the archipelago after the Tenson had arrived, and 'our aboriginal ancestors' fought against them in defence of the archipelago (Shiratori 1969–71: vol. 9, 246).

In this article, Shiratori also insisted strongly that the most valid means to classify nations was not through an examination of archaeological remains or human bones, but through language (Shiratori 1969–71: vol. 9, 197). At the time, the mixed nation theory completely dominated anthropology, and there was almost no basis for the theory of the homogeneous nation except his linguistics theory. Shiratori later explained the reason he put a greater emphasis on language than physical features in these terms (Shiratori 1969–71: vol. 9, 238–9):

> Let us imagine a Korean is here. He was born in Korea, migrated to Japan, learned the Japanese language and speaks it fluently, wears Japanese cloths, and behaves completely like a Japanese. Who could tell he is Korean? It is a natural consequence that he looks no different from a Japanese...such being the case, it must be said that we are a long way from being able to distinguish races by their physique.

Physical anthropology was rejected because Koreans who had internalised the Japanese language and manners could not be distinguished from 'Japanese'. Shiratori tried to find a way to distinguish and exclude even those Koreans who were idealised by the policy of Japanisation. It was self-contradictory for him to say that language was crucial in distinguishing between nationalities while postulating the example of a Korean who had mastered the Japanese language. However, he insisted that whatever the physical features may be, since the Japanese language was the most unique language in the world, the homeland of the Japanese nation was the archipelago.

There was one more counter-argument he had to deal with. If the migration of the Japanese nation took place 'tens of thousands of years' ago, the Kiki myths that claimed that the descent of the Tenson nation occurred 2,600 years ago would have to be nonsense. If the Japanese nation had migrated before the descent, his position would be that a Japanese nation had existed without the Emperor. This was a hurdle that might have proved dangerous if not properly handled.

According to Shiratori, arguments such as the existence of 'the Tenson nation, the Yamato nation, the Izumo nation and the Kumaso nation', or that Takamagahara was located overseas, originated in the assumption that the Kiki myths were historical facts. However, it 'totally misses the mark to seek the origin of the Japanese race in the Kiki myths' (Shiratori 1969–71: vol. 9, 197). He described the Kiki myths as follows (Shiratori 1969–71: vol. 9, 192):

> If you ask me what the records of the gods are, I would reply that these works are great stories that beautifully and poetically describe the beliefs, systems, politics, manners and customs of ancient Japan.

Shiratori claimed that the Kiki myths were not historical facts but 'stories'. If that were the case, it would not be a contradiction to argue that the Japanese nation migrated to the archipelago in 'time immemorial', not 2,600 years ago. In other words, however, this was effectively to insist that the Kiki myths were fairy tales. This was an expression that fell only slightly short of blasphemy at the time, but was a step that had to be taken if the theory of the homogeneous nation were to be advocated. It was Tsuda Sōkichi who further pushed this line of argument and actually committed what was seen as blasphemy.

The Kiki Myths as an Argument for the Homogeneous Nation

In 1908, Shiratori talked to Baron (later Viscount and finally Count) Gotō Shinpei (1857–1929), who moved from working as the head of the civil administration under the Government-General of Taiwan to become the first president of the South Manchuria Railway Company – a company modelled on the British East India Company – about the need to investigate the Manchurian and Korean regions. He persuaded him to establish a research section of Manchurian and Korean history and geography in the Tokyo branch office of the Company, and this subsequently began to research these areas. Gotō was one of the statesmen of great calibre who was sceptical of assimilationist policies. A pioneer in the eugenics school, Tōgō Makoto, was a subordinate of Gotō in the Government-General of Taiwan, and Tsurumi Yūsuke, who urged Kiyono Kenji to write a book on the Japanese nation, was both Gotō's biographer and son-in-law. Tsuda Sōkichi was one of those chosen by Shiratori to work as a researcher in the research section of Manchurian and Korean history and geography.

Shiratori's junior by 8 years, Tsuda was born in the mountains of the mid-western Gifu Prefecture in 1873 in a *samurai* household that had supported the Shogunate. He worked as a teacher in Kyoto after graduating from the Tokyo College (Tōkyō Senmon Gakkō, today's Waseda University), but moved to Tokyo in 1895 at the age of 21, and became dependent on Shiratori in both his studies and his life. He taught history in junior high schools in the Kantō region, but disliked his life as a teacher and moved from school to school. Meanwhile Shiratori was the only person he could turn to for advice. Tsuda was 34 when he became a researcher in the research section of Manchurian and Korean history and geography, where he took charge of studying the history of Manchuria and Korea, but his interest lay in research into ancient Japan through a decoding of the Kiki myths.

As mentioned in chapter 9, Tsuda adopted the mixed nation theory in a history textbook he edited in 1902, and showed pride in the 'assimilative power of the nation'. However, like Shiratori, he converted to the homogeneous nation theory following the Russo-Japanese War and the annexation of Korea.

In the preface to his first work, *Kamiyoshi no atarashii kenkyū* (New Research into the History of the Age of the Gods), Tsuda noted that he started writing the book the day after hearing a lecture in which Shiratori had stated that he viewed the Kiki myths as 'invented stories'. In the main body of the work, Tsuda used detailed textual analysis to argue that the Kiki myths were far from being historical facts, but rather were 'fictitious stories'. Moreover, in the conclusion, he explained the emergence of the belief that the Imperial Family and imperial subjects were related in these terms: 'our nation in fact is an homogeneous nation which shares the same race, language, customs and history, and therefore the Imperial Household and the common people are bound together by feelings of love' (Tsuda 1986–89: bekkan 1, 5, 14, 124).

There is no need to dwell upon this for very long. *Kamiyoshi no atarashii kenkyū* is even today a highly valued work, as it objectively analysed the Kiki myths – the sacred and inviolable myths of the Great Japanese Empire – and proved them to be 'fictitious stories'. It was, however, in line with Shiratori's strategy for Tsuda to argue for the theory of the homogeneous nation by refusing to treat the Kiki myths as historical facts.

This strategy became even clearer in *Kojiki oyobi Nihon shoki no shinkenkyū* (New Research in *Kojiki* and *Nihon shoki*) published in 1919. In the introduction, Tsuda first made the preliminary remark that 'it is still thought today that the homeland of the Japanese nation, Takamagahara, is located somewhere overseas...based on this idea, even the term *Tenson nation* was created, as was the opposing *Izumo nation*'. However, he denied these popular views, saying 'there is no such description in the texts themselves, and this is not written down anywhere'. He claimed that these views emerged from failure to read the Kiki texts closely (Tsuda 1986–89: bekkan 1, 194).

Furthermore, Tsuda said that if, in addition to the interpretations of the Kiki myths, 'an academic knowledge of race and nations' proved that ancient Japan was a multi-national land, it would be possible to research 'the description in the Kiki myths as a record of the actions of different races and alien nations'. However, looking at language alone, for example, it was clear that 'this would be virtually impossible' (Tsuda 1986–89: bekkan 1, 202). Most of the mixed nation theories of the day consisted of a combination of interpretations of the Kiki myths and anthropology. To separate the two was identical with the methodology of Kiyono and Hasebe in later years (see chapter 13).

The book consisted of six chapters of analysis of the Kiki myths. The first three chapters examined 'the story of the subjugation of

Silla', 'the story of the subjugation of the Kumaso', and 'the story of the eastern countries and the Emishi'. If the section 'on the Tsuchigumo' were included, it could be argued that the whole book is constructed around a criticism of those sections in the Kiki myths that dealt with interaction with alien nations. The detailed textual analysis undertaken by Tsuda will not be discussed here, but his conclusion, as was clearly stated in his previous work *Kamiyoshi no atarashii kenkyū*, was that 'Emperor Jinmu's Eastern Expedition', 'Yamato-Takeru-no-Mikoto's subjugation of the east and west', and 'Empress Jingū's subjugation of Silla' were 'all wild fantasies'. Moreover, Susano-O's trip to Silla was said to be a later addition, and the migration of Ame-no-hiboko, a Silla prince who was supposed to be an ancestor of the Empress Jingū, 'contained not a single fact' (Tsuda 1986–89: bekkan 1, 17, 287–8). In this way, the theory that the 'Japanese' and Koreans shared a common ancestor and the claim that there was an influx of Korean blood into the Imperial Family were automatically denied.

According to the contemporary school textbooks compiled by the state, the Empress Jingū's conquest of the peninsula was an event that triggered an active interaction between the peoples of the archipelago and the peninsula, and led to the migration of many from the peninsula to the archipelago. Having shattered the premise underlying this position, Tsuda argued in a later article, 'Banbetsu no ie no keifu ni tsuite' (On the Genealogy of the *Banbetsu* Families), that many surnames listed in the *Shinsen shōjiroku* said to be of migrant stock were 'actually pure Japanese whose ancestors were nevertheless said to be Chinese or Korean'. He also said in this article that the descriptions in the 'classic' texts which provided the grounds for the argument that many migrants arrived were 'difficult to believe as historical facts'. He also stated that Sakanoue-no-Tamuramaro was not the descendent of a migrant (Tsuda 1986–89: vol. 3, 492–3, 500).

By defining the descriptions of alien nations in the Kiki myths as wild fantasies, Tsuda dismantled the foundations of the mixed nation theory. Moreover, he noted in the conclusion of *Kojiki oyobi Nihon shoki no shinkenkyū* that 'it is one of the proofs that the state always consisted of a single nation (or at least of what at the time was seen as a single nation)…that there was not a single trace in the Kiki story of the concept of racial competition within the state'. He also noted that there was no evidence that the alien nations used a different language, and there was 'nothing to show that powerful alien nations were antagonistic to one another' (Tsuda 1986–89: bekkan 1, 495–6). He did indicate that the Emishi were the *Ainu* but, like Shiratori, resolved this matter by claiming that the *Ainu* were later arrivals.

I do not intend to judge the validity (or otherwise) of academic theories, so here will note only that Tsuda's interpretation of the Kiki myths which claimed there was no description of ethnic controversy between alien peoples was then highly unusual, and difficult to justify unless all sections that seemed to describe conflict were explained away as fiction. If, for the sake of argument, the validity of Tsuda's ideas is accepted, how then should Kita Sadakichi's position that assimilation occurred peacefully through the impartial policies of the Imperial Family, and that conflict was the exception, be dealt with? Kita's position could explain the absence of records of violent racial conflict in the Kiki myths and the absence of evidence of different languages. Tsuda replied to this in the following terms (Tsuda 1986–89: bekkan 1, 497):

> It is possible for the language of one nation to be assimilated into that of another nation. However, that can only happen when there is an enormous gulf between the two nations in terms of culture or political power, when the two coexist or inter-marry, and when the two are interlinked in daily life to such an extent that the inferior nation has no choice but to use the language of the superior nation. Moreover, even when these conditions are met, the process would still take a very long time...It is thus illogical to think that there were local political powers that consisted of alien nations.

The assimilation of nations can only take place under the rule of an overwhelmingly superior political power, and a peaceful assimilation is not possible. Therefore, if there were alien nations in the ancient Japanese archipelago, a history of conflict would have been seen. Tsuda's perception was thus similar to that of Takayama Chogyū (see chapter 3), who had insisted that peaceful coexistence with alien nations was impossible, and there could only be conflict and rule through power.

China as an Example of Rule through Power

Whatever their intentions, Shiratori and Tsuda eventually formed the academic foundation of the theory of the homogeneous nation

– Shiratori through his work on Oriental history and linguistics, and Tsuda through his research into the Kiki myths.

Tsuda was not, however, a loyal follower of Shiratori. In his preface to Tsuda's *Kamiyoshi no atarashii kenkyū*, Shiratori stated that there were 'not a few disagreements between us' and that there was 'no prospect of compromise', however much they debated one another (in Tsuda 1986–89: bekkan 1, 3). It is not known for sure what they disagreed about, but the greatest difference between the two may have lain in their views of China and the Japanese nation.

Shiratori's view of Oriental history was the same as that of Kume Kunitake (see chapter 5), with the idea of a struggle between a northern and a southern nation running through it. According to Shiratori, northern nations such as the Tungus and the Mongolians, although inferior in culture, were a martial people, and were constantly pushing southward. On the other hand, the Chinese, the representative southern nation, were 'weak at war', but 'a race that loved peace and thoroughly respected culture'. The Japanese nation was a superior nation that had inherited the merits of both, and was well versed in the arts of both peace and war (Shiratori 1969–71: vol. 9, 211–2). It was because of this view of history that he considered the Korean peninsula and Manchuria to be the defensive bulwark of Japan. His argument that the safety of the archipelago required a defensive strongpoint on the continent, and that the thirteenth century invasion of Japan by the Mongolians during the Kamakura Period was an example of a northern nation breaking through this bulwark and advancing onto the archipelago, also emerged from this view of history (Shiratori 1969–71: vol. 9, 264).

Moreover, according to Shiratori, 'the special character of the progress of Japanese civilisation lies in its ability to assimilate the merits of outside cultures'. Japan first absorbed the culture and thought of China (Korea was a mere intermediary), adopted Buddhism from India, and thus 'collected the essence of Oriental culture'. By the Meiji Period there was nothing left to learn from the East so Japan next began to absorb and assimilate Western civilisation, and became 'the place of contact of both Eastern and Western civilisations'. Even so, since Japan rejected that which did not match her national polity, Japanese originality was maintained (Shiratori 1969–71: vol. 9, 180–8).

The notion that Japan absorbed and assimilated the best of Eastern and Western civilisations, or synthesised the merits of various nations, was not original to Shiratori. As we have seen, such ideas were widespread at the time. In advocating the theory of the homogeneous nation, Shiratori adopted an eclectic line of argument, using the rhetoric of the mixed nation theory to sing the praises of the superiority of the Japanese nation.

Tsuda's views of China and the Japanese nation, on the other hand, provide a distinctive contrast to those of Shiratori. In his *Kamiyoshi no atarashii kenkyū*, Tsuda emphasised that 'the Imperial Household does not rule over the people from the outside, but lies within the people, and is the centre of ethnic unity and the core of national unification. The relationship between the Imperial Household and the people is the close one of a family joined by kinship, not a relationship of oppression and obedience based on power'. In contrast to Japan, China was described in the following terms (Tsuda 1986–89: bekkan 1, 123):

> This is completely different from Chinese thought, where the difference between the Emperor and the people is that between heaven and earth. To view heaven as the symbol of the Emperor's power, and the Emperor as ruling over the people on earth as the delegate of heaven, is to define the Emperor and the people as opposites between whom there is a huge gulf, and their relationship as that between the ruler and ruled, in which they are united only by an outside force. This is why the people [in China] are always ready to cut the string that ties them to the Emperor. This is why revolutions actually take place so frequently. Since relations are like this, the political thought of the Chinese is in one sense very democratic, but at the same time the power of the Emperor is very despotic. The word 'heaven' already has a despotic meaning. The history of the political thought of the Japanese Age of the Gods is completely different... The Imperial Household and the people were originally one, and do not stand in remote opposition to one another. The relationship between them is like that between the core and the flesh of fruit: it is internal, and therefore cannot and should not be cut. Thus an unbroken line of Emperors has been maintained.

Here Tsuda described the China that Shiratori viewed as 'a race that respects culture' as a representative example of a despotic society in which the people and the ruler were divided. The ruler was merely the governor with power. Only two choices existed – despotism or democracy – and this generated the idea of revolution. On the other hand, Japan was a country where the people and the Emperor were an homogeneous unified nation. There was no need to rule through power, and therefore no need for the idea of revolution. This is, needless to say, a typical example of the national polity theory before it was reformed to respond to the existence of alien nations within the empire.

Tsuda's view of the Japanese nation as expressed in *Kamiyoshi no atarashii kenkyū* is summarised as follows (Tsuda 1986–89: bekkan 1, 144–5):

> Since the ancient Japanese were a people of remote islands isolated from the continent, and since they were a farming people living in a mild climate with easy lives, they experienced hardly any interaction with neighbouring alien nations, and therefore there was no national movement against foreign countries. Within Japan, since the nation was homogeneous, there was no ethnic conflict, and therefore almost no war. In daily life also, because the Japanese were an agricultural people, they did not live urban and crowded lives, and therefore did not undertake small-scale public activities...such being the case, the Japanese naturally have neither national legends nor national epics.

This image of the Japanese nation clearly differed from that of other theorists, including Shiratori, who claimed the Japanese nation was superior in the arts of both peace and war, was courageous, and excelled in fighting. The mixed nation theorists lauded Japan's expansion overseas, using the logic that the Japanese nation had a rich experience since prehistoric times of ruling other nations. However, the Japanese nation as described by Tsuda was a peaceful farming people with no experience of war or foreign interaction, and lacked the political or cultural abilities involved in understanding public activities or writing national epics. Yanagita also saw the Japanese nation as a farming people with an homogeneous folklore who inhabited an island nation, but Tsuda's view was an extreme version of this.

This position, however, was not unique to Tsuda. As was seen in chapter 8, Mozume Takami wrote that revolutionary thought was the product of multi-national states such as China, and was alien to the homogeneous nation-state, Japan. The historian and

Tokyo Imperial University professor, Kuroita Katsumi (1874–1946), also said in his *Kokutai shinron* (A New Theory of the National Polity) that the Japanese nation was a pure and 'naive' one that knew nothing about power politics, while minimising the degree to which it had been mixed.[6] According to the Edo Period nativist scholar, Motoori Norinaga, since all was anarchy in China and the monarch was a despot, Confucianism emerged to gild over power politics. A rhetoric frequently used by nativist scholars since Motoori to conceal their sense of cultural inferiority to China was to argue that Japan had achieved peace under the Emperors from time immemorial, and therefore had no need to develop scholarship and culture.

Roughly speaking, Tsuda's thought was an expanded version of that part of the national polity theory that argued that imperial rule was not rule through power, but a union created by the natural affection that joined the Emperor and people. This is not to argue that Tsuda was a national polity theorist or that he was influenced by the national polity theory. The simple fact is that people are the product of their times, and cannot escape from the influence of contemporary mainstream thought.

Many national polity theorists tried to extend to Korea and Taiwan the logic that imperial rule was not rule through power but family affection, and adopted the mixed nation theory to argue that the nations governed by the empire were relatives of the Japanese nation. However, Tsuda thought there could be no union of natural affection with alien nations, but only antagonism or power relations. According to his view of the world, there was a choice between a turbulent multi-national state characterised by either tyranny or revolution, or a peaceful homogeneous nation-state where the monarch and the people were as one.

Tsuda rejected the use of history to justify aggression, and asserted that 'the annexation of Korea...is something that became necessary (necessary for Japan of course) for the first time in the modern era, and has nothing to do with the past' (Tsuda 1986–89: vol. 27, 195). He also claimed to have determined, through his research into the Kiki myths, that the rule over the peninsula in the ancient era was on a much smaller scale than the popular view suggested, and that it had failed because it was solely an undertaking of the government and did not develop into a national enterprise (Tsuda 1986–89: bekkan 1, 145). Of course, as can be seen in the words 'necessary for Japan', he regarded the annexation as an established fact. However, it also seems clear that he was so unenthusiastic about the annexation that he claimed that overseas expansion had nothing to do with the nation, but was the doing of government power. Annexation was an act more becoming to China where power and the people were divided than to the peaceful ancient archipelago where the sovereign and all his subjects were one. This is why he could calmly deny the theory that the 'Japanese' and Koreans shared a common ancestor.

Tsuda mentioned Koreans and Chinese in his diary with contempt (Tsuda 1986–89: vol. 26, 480, 482). They were formidable enemies to fight against or to rule over but, unlike Kita Sadakichi, Tsuda did not view them as the objects of compassion or assimilation. For Tsuda, as long as Japan remained a multi-national empire, the ideal of a peaceful and non-authoritarian homogeneous nation-state would remain unrealised. Therefore, he probably thought it a nuisance that Korea and Japan had enjoyed close relations both in the past and in the present. Unlike Shiratori, Tsuda would have welcomed the idea of Korea cutting its ties with Japan, either by separating and again becoming independent or through other means, as he had little interest in national security and national glory.

An Imperial State Without Power

Kita Sadakichi and Watari Shōzaburō (discussed in chapter 8) highlighted the authority of the Emperor by arguing that there must have been a unifying power in the ancient archipelago that mediated ethnic conflicts. However, Tsuda had a strong dislike for the idea of any state power (even one that unified the various ethnic groups), and his position was that the Japanese Emperors could not have been involved in it.

Tsuda was a nativist who rejected nationalism (*kokkashugi*). As can be seen in the relationship between WASP nativism and national integration in the USA, nationalism and nativism contradict one another in multi-national states. Ebina Danjō (see chapter 3) was a nationalist who rejected nativism, and endeavoured to erase the nativism of both Japan and Korea which he saw as obstacles to unification. For Tsuda, Japan was an homogeneous nation-state and therefore the Japanese nation (*minzoku*) and Japanese nationals (*kokumin*) were one and the same. However, he explicitly differentiated between the state and the nation. He wrote that the Kiki myths recorded the origin of the state and the Imperial Family, and therefore were of no use in tracing the origins of the nation (Tsuda 1986–89: bekkan 1, 498).

The argument that the Kiki myths recorded the history of the state and not the nation had two implications. The first is that it made it possible to insist that the origin of the Japanese nation lay far back in time immemorial. Even if the history of the state dated back only 2,600 years, the nation had existed in the archipelago for a very long time before that. The second is that it strengthened the idea of the existence of a peaceful Japanese nation and the absence of alien nations. In other words, the reason for the existence of myths of conquest, such as the Eastern Expedition of the Emperor Jinmu, in a Japan populated by an homogeneous and peaceful nation, was that the Kiki myths were stories created by the state. Moreover, descriptions in the Kiki myths were greatly influenced by the Chinese thought adopted by the government of the ancient archipelago.

Tsuda had an extreme dislike of naked state power such as the high-handedness of bureaucrats and the tyranny of the police. He was a moderate with a passion for pot plants. His memory of the mountain farm village where he grew up was of a harmonious and peaceful autonomous community, where conflict was resolved through mutual agreement reached in village meetings, where public enterprises such as cleaning the roads were jointly undertaken by all, and where finance was managed by a fund sponsored by the villagers (Tsuda 1986–89: vol. 24, 53–4). Unsolvable conflicts such as class struggle or ethnic conflict did not exist in such farm villages or 'mountain villages', which were thus societies where the state power or revolution required to mediate such conflicts was unnecessary. The ancient archipelago he described was a very similar world. For him, the state meant power, and his ideal of the nation (synonymous with nationals, synonymous with the people) was peaceful and autonomous.

In reality, however, Tsuda lamented the fact that the people of modern Japan had become accustomed to despotic rule and lacked this sort of autonomous spirit and public virtue (Tsuda 1986–89: vol. 27, 102–3). A people atomised like sand, and without the public virtues that made mutual help possible, could only maintain order through despotic rule or the formal morality of Confucianism. According to his view of the world, both means were Chinese, so that, when he criticised domestic Japanese politics, he used phrases such as the 'Chinese-like arrogance and double-dealing of the

Katsura cabinet' – Katsura Tarō (1847–1913) was Prime Minister three times between 1901 and 1913 – and called police violence 'Chinese manners' (Tsuda 1986–89: vol. 26, 479–80). Tsuda regarded the Koreans as a nation that had lost its vitality and been destroyed by the conventions of Confucianist morality and formalism. Moreover, as we can see from statements like 'the so-called Chinese cuisine was developed as the food of the gourmet class, the bureaucrats and the bourgeoisie', Tsuda's ideal was a nation (synonymous with people) devoid of Chinese elements who, like Yanagita's common people, were healthy producers (Tsuda 1986–89: vol. 27, 56, 279). Tsuda attempted to contrast power rule and formal morals with the autonomous society and the overflowing natural vitality of the Japanese nation (people).

In the sense that he opposed state power, Tsuda could be called a liberal thinker. It was precisely because of this that he turned a cold shoulder to Marxism. A liberal like Tsuda could not possibly agree with ideas such as the nationalisation of industry. On the other hand, he showed some sympathy towards Kōtoku Shūsui (see chapter 10), a socialist, but an anarchist socialist rather than a Marxist.[7] It is, of course, not rare in the history of ideas for liberals and anarchists to have a high opinion of one another, since both opposed Marxism, and both shared a desire to minimise state power.

The reason that anarchists such as Takamure Itsue (see chapter 11) and Ishikawa Sanshirō (see chapter 10) so ardently admired *Kojiki* (and thus the Kiki myths) and the national polity theory was because the ideology of the national polity was to a certain degree anti-authoritarian. Moreover, like Takamure, Tsuda advocated 'a philosophy of vitalism' that loved nature, affirmed the passion of love and resistance, and was antagonistic to the formal morality of Confucianism. Of course, the national polity theory was the state ideology, and phrases such as impartiality or unity through non-authoritarian love were merely rhetoric concealing discrimination and power rule. However, the enlargement of parts of this rhetoric eventually led to a criticism of the *status quo*. Just as Kita Sadakichi expanded the concept of impartiality and criticised discrimination to the extent that he became unorthodox, to focus attention on and develop the notion of anti-authoritarianism was to move away from the orthodoxy.

As an individual who hated power, what were Tsuda's feelings about the Emperor? For him, the Emperor and the nation (Japanese nationals, the people) were inseparable. As early as 1916, he called the Emperor 'the living symbol of the national spirit' (Tsuda 1986–89: bekkan 2, 9). The idea that those with whom the Emperor interacted in the political sphere were the heads of the clans and not the people appeared consistently in his arguments from *Kamiyoshi no atarashii kenkyū* onwards (Tsuda 1986–89: bekkan 1, 122). This meant that the political function of the Emperor was to mediate between the various clans. The head of each clan was responsible for ruling the general populace, and the Emperor did not participate directly in this rule. Imperial mediation did not lead to conflict because the various clans and the Emperor were members of the one nation, bound by natural affection. When the use of military force became absolutely necessary, it was exercised through the clans. The authority of the Emperor was generated from his position at the highest pinnacle of culture and not through military force. According to Tsuda, since Japan was an homogeneous nation, and alien cultures did not exist, the idea of a cultural authority was possible.

In his view, ancient Japan was originally a peaceful and autonomous collection of agricultural communities, and almost all problems were dealt with autonomously within farming villages. At most what was necessary was to adjust the interests of the communities. In addition, foreign wars and diplomacy with alien nations hardly existed, and therefore government power was all the more unnecessary.

The Emperor as depicted by Tsuda was not a powerful ruler who used military force to conquer alien nations, but rather was like a village elder respected by all the villagers. Tsuda recalled that in the mountain village where he grew up, delegates from each family (the patriarchs) assembled at village meetings and his father and grandmother both played the role of mediators. Tsuda was shy and deeply attached to his grandmother, and fondly recollected her listening to the opinions of the villagers in these meetings. His image of the Emperor was close to this. He also lamented the circumstances where a bureaucratic office, the bridgehead of government power, was established in his village following the Meiji Restoration – as noted above, Tsuda was born in a *samurai* family that had supported the Bakufu – and the idyllic small cosmos was replaced by the exaltation of the official above private life (Tsuda 1986–89: vol. 24, 53, 74).

The Emperor was thus described as the 'symbol' of the unity of an autonomous nation (people) and contrasted with rule through power. According to Tsuda's world view, if the unity of the community of the nation (people) collapsed, and people were atomised and lost their public virtue, there would only be one option left: a Chinese-style order consisting of power rule and a formal morality. Thus, while showing sympathy for anarchism, he attributed its origin to the government preventing the Emperor and the people from forming close ties, and abusing power in the name of the Emperor. In his words, the cause was 'the government's refusal to work to increase the affinity between the Imperial Household and the people but rather to attempt to divide them, and its presentation of the Imperial Household as an authority rather than making it feel close to the people'.[8]

Tsuda's research focused on proving that his ideal vision of Japan was historically justified. According to this view of history, times such as the Edo Period when the Emperor did not directly rule but instead delegated rule to the *samurai* and others were the historical norm, and this state of affairs occupied the greater part of Japanese history. Direct rule by the Emperor – which was assumed at the time to be the correct state of affairs – such as that of the Kenmu administration under the Emperor Godaigo (1288–1339) and the period following the Meiji Restoration were exceptions and deviations.

In his lifework and masterpiece, *Bungaku ni arawaretaru waga kokumin shisō no kenkyū* (Research into the Thought of Japanese Nationals as Seen in Literature), Tsuda argued that the influence of Chinese culture in Japan was limited only to some of those in positions of power and some of the intellectuals, while the nation or 'people' enjoyed a unique Japanese culture separately. This argument was possible because he distinguished in the book between the culture of the nation and that of the authorities. According to Tsuda, the temples and Buddhist statues of Nara and Kyoto created by the authorities in imitation of China were, as far as the general populace was concerned, alien and oppressive (Tsuda 1986–89: bekkan 2, 63–4).

In *Shina shisō to Nippon* (Chinese Thought and Japan), a work that will be mentioned again in chapter 16, Tsuda was soon to go so far as to argue for the abolition of classes in the Chinese classics and Chinese literature, saying that Chinese thought existed in the Chinese characters (*kanji*). Tsuda was to advocate using as few *kanji* as possible in writing Japanese and came to sign his name in *hiragana* rather than *kanji* (for the relationship between *hiragana* and *kanji*, see chapter 1, endnote 7).

In 'Shina saiken no shidō seishin ni tsuite' (The Spirit of Leadership in the Rebuilding of China), written in answer to a request from the East Asian Research Center during the Sino-Japanese War (1937–45), Tsuda argued that since the Japanese and Chinese were totally different nations, 'it is futile to try to force the unique Japanese customs on the Chinese', while also stating: 'the Chinese will never obey those who lack power and authority...it is necessary to make them constantly aware that the Japanese possess a mighty power'.[9] The combination of a criticism of assimilationist policies and rule through power can be seen here.

Despite this strong and consistent dislike of China, Tsuda was very generous about the influence of the West. Since he claimed that Japan was not a part of the East that was influenced by China, but a part of the world that was greatly influenced by the West, he seems to have welcomed Western culture as something that would neutralise Chinese culture.

Such perceptions of China and the West were sharply opposed to the trend of the Great Japanese Empire of the time. As the 15 Year War (1931–45) proceeded, Western culture and Western languages were increasingly rejected. However, although China was also an enemy nation, voices in favour of rejecting Chinese culture and characters (*kanji*) did not surface. This was because the official government position was that the Great Japanese Empire was fighting against the Western Caucasian Powers in order to liberate Asia, that China was Japan's sibling with a common race and culture, and that the Sino-Japanese War was an act of love to correct the ill-conceived anti-Japanese thought of the younger brother, China. The theory of the mixed nation that became widespread during the war argued from first to last that the Japanese nation was a mixture of the various Asian nations. Caucasians, on the other hand, were supposed to be a completely alien race and savage brutes.

Tsuda's position, however, was the exact opposite of this. After the Manchurian Incident, even Shiratori criticised as 'a mistaken opinion' the argument that it was natural for Japan, Korea and Manchuria to unite because they were siblings belonging to the same Tungus race and the Ural-Altaic family of languages (Shiratori 1969–71: vol. 9, 237). Even so, Shiratori was able to avoid a collision by approving the rule through power of Korea and Manchuria as a defensive bulwark for Japan, and insisted that the Japanese nation excelled at fighting. He did not wholly deny the cultural links between Japan and China, nor did he regard the invasion of Korea by the Empress Jingū as a complete fiction. Tsuda, however, called even the Shōgun Hideyoshi's attack on Korea in the sixteenth century – something that was praised at the time – 'an unjustifiable foreign invasion' (Tsuda 1986–89: bekkan 4, 65). However, both Tsuda and Shiratori regarded themselves as true patriots, and certainly never dreamed that their arguments implied any criticism of the Emperor System.

The reason that Tsuda called the Kiki myths fictitious stories was not only because it was necessary to do so if he was to argue for the theory of the homogeneous nation, but also because it was, in his opinion, the best way to truly respect the texts. According to Tsuda, the Edo Period Confucian scholar Arai Hakuseki who regarded the Kiki myths as fables of historical facts, and the nativist scholar Motoori Norinaga who insisted that the Kiki myths described the miracles of the Age of the Gods, were both contaminated by the 'shallow Chinese rationalism' that claimed that the myths were 'worthless unless true' (Tsuda 1986–89: bekkan 1, 195). Kume Kunitake (see chapter 5) whom Tsuda probably assumed to be an adversary was, for Tsuda, the modern equivalent of Arai Hakuseki. For Kume, on the other hand, someone from a mountain village like Tsuda was probably seen as a ringleader of Japan's closed mind.

Tsuda himself took the position that it was meaningless to use 'Chinese rationalism' to interpret the beautiful myths produced by the ancient people. In the conclusion of *Kojiki oyobi Nihon shoki no shinkenkyū*, he summarised his 'basic philosophy' as the idea that 'the ancient Kiki stories are poetry rather than history. And poetry tells us more about the inner life of the nation than history does' (Tsuda 1986–89: bekkan 1, 499). The myths could only become symbols of the sacred national spirit when protected by a firewall from the shallow rationality of the human world. To undercut the sacred status of the Kiki myths was far from his intention.

However, Tsuda's contemporaries did not understand this. As will be noted in chapter 16, his freedom of expression was curtailed by the Great Japanese Empire. Both supporters and opponents viewed his research as a rational criticism of the Kiki myths. It is true that it was highly detailed and rational, but Tsuda's aim was to revive the Kiki myths as myths that could not be touched by reason because he believed that the mixed nation theory had damaged them, and thought it impossible to view the myths as historical facts if they were interpreted rationally. This may have been a methodology he learned from Shiratori's study of the Chinese classics. Originally, however, the idea that the Japanese myths contained the truth of the gods precisely because they seemed irrational to human understanding, while Chinese literature was a man-made product that could be rationally interpreted, was put forward by Motoori Norinaga.[10] Although Tsuda criticised Motoori, he shared the methodology that sanctified the myths as being beyond human rationality after a close critical reading of the texts. This aspect of Tsuda's thought remained unnoticed.

The historians of postwar Japan – a time when Marxism dominated academe in Japan – especially lionised Tsuda as a scientific critic who had fought against the ideology of the Emperor System. Since Tsuda distinguished the history of the nation from the history of the state, and also distinguished the culture of the people from the culture of the authorities, he was viewed as the founder of a history that focused on the people. His argument in favour of limiting the use of Chinese characters (*kanji*) also seems to have been understood in postwar Japan in the context of the postwar democratic standpoint that attempted to simplify the Japanese language and make it more accessible to the Japanese people. The fact that Tsuda did not agree with the rejection of Western culture, that he showed sympathy to an anarchist, Kōtoku Shūsui, that he opposed state power, and especially that his freedom of expression was suppressed by the Great Japanese Empire – all this was in harmony with the postwar progressive sense of values. On the other hand, postwar historians were perplexed by, and felt antagonistic to, Tsuda's stance in favour of the Emperor and against communism. Nevertheless, his research into the Kiki myths was accepted whole-heartedly as the orthodox way to interpret ancient history.

15 From 'Blood' to 'Climate'

'Professor Watsuji often said that "the Japanese national polity means that the folk (*minzoku*) and the nation (*kokumin*) coincide completely"'.

This is the recollection of a scholar of ethics, Katsube Mitake, who studied under Watsuji Tetsurō (1889–1960) from his college days and enjoyed a close relationship with him.[1] Needless to say, the correspondence of the folk with the nation (which in turn was synonymous with nationals) meant that Japan was an homogeneous nation-state. This recollection was published in 1967, a time when the criticism of the myth of the homogeneous nation was yet to emerge, and Katsube called the ethics of Watsuji 'the ethics of an homogeneous society', using the phrase in a positive sense.

Watsuji Tetsurō was a giant in the field of Japanese ethical studies, and also wielded an enormous influence on the discourse of Japanese culture, authoring works such as *Fūdo* (Climate) and *Koji junrei* (A Pilgrimage to Ancient Temples). In this chapter, I will locate Watsuji's theory of the Japanese nation within the context of the entire discourse of his time. Together with Yanagita and Tsuda, his influence on the postwar theory of Japanese culture was enormous. At the same time, his writings on the Japanese nation are also important in understanding the nature of the theory of the Symbolic Emperor System which will be discussed in chapter 17.

The Synthesis of the Northern and Southern Races

The son of a doctor in a farming village in Hyōgo Prefecture (in centre-west Japan), Watsuji was born in 1889. In his memoirs, the village was described as an egalitarian and peaceful community, linked by ties of emotion, and his father seems to have been respected by all the village people for his integrity.

After graduating from a local junior high school, Watsuji proceeded to the First High School in Tokyo, and then on to Tokyo Imperial University. He originally felt inferior in face of the culture of Tokyo, but in the course of time struck up an acquaintance with Tanizaki Jun'ichirō (1886–1965), who was to become famous as a aesthetic novelist, and became deeply involved in theatre activities. He studied philosophy, his major, under Inoue Tetsujirō, with whom he seems to have been completely incompatible. Watsuji became the focus of attention as a young researcher of European philosophy, publishing a study of Nietzsche in 1913 at the age of 24, and another on Kierkegaard two years later. It was from about 1916 that Watsuji began to show an interest in ancient Japanese history and the theory of the Japanese nation, an interest triggered by his admiration for the culture of Buddhism and the Buddhist temples of the ancient Asuka (592–645) and Nara Periods (710–784) (Watsuji 1920: i).

The earliest work among Watsuji's writings on the Japanese nation is an article, 'Kodai Nipponjin no konketsu jōtai' (The Mixed Blood of the Ancient Japanese), published in 1917, which began as follows (Watsuji 1989–92: vol. 21, 192):

> The sophisticated culture of ancient Japan was the product of a nation with mixed blood. Today's concept of the 'Japanese' does not directly mean the nation that produced the Hōryūji Temple. For me, this fact was an astonishing and deeply interesting discovery.

Watsuji here stated that the Japanese nation was of mixed blood, and that it was a shock for him to learn the modern 'Japanese' were not directly related to the nation that produced the Hōryūji Temple. Since the mixed nation theory no longer requires explanation, I will here give a rough summary of the contemporary discourse on the Buddhist temple culture of Japan.

The first edition of the history textbook compiled by the state and published in 1903 noted that the Regent Shōtoku Taishi (574–622) imported Buddhism and built the Hōryūji Temple during the Suiko Period (592–628). In the third edition of the 1920s, the words 'the main buildings [in Hōryūji] are said to be exactly the same as when first built, and are the oldest buildings in Japan' were added.[2] The Hōryūji Temple was thus one of the symbols of national cultural identity in the Great Japanese Empire, and the Meiji government began to support repair work for selected temples from as early as the late nineteenth century.

However, there were two problems with the Hōryūji Temple. One was whether the buildings were the originals, as the government textbook claimed, or whether they had been rebuilt after 670, when *Nihon shoki* suggested that a fire destroyed some of the temple buildings. This was called the Rebuilding of Hōryūji Debate (*Hōryūji saiken ronsō*); and Kita Sadakichi was the leading proponent of those who insisted some of the buildings had been rebuilt.

The second issue was exactly who built the temple. The fact that it had been built under the influence of imported Buddhist culture could not be denied. The problem was to what degree Japanese originality had been added to the imported culture, and whether the architects were foreign migrants or 'Japanese'. The existing literature sheds much light on the first issue.[3] The latter was closely related to the theory of the Japanese nation.

This issue of who built the temple was of interest to the theorists examined in this work. A former Prime Minister, Ōkuma Shigenobu (see chapter 5), argued that the Hōryūji Temple was built by Korean migrants. The same position was taken by the Governor-General of Korea, Minami Jirō (see chapter 13), in 1941. On the other hand, the Sinologist, Naitō Konan severely criticised the Golden Hall of the Hōryūji Temple in 1919 as being inferior even to the 'miniaturised versions of Chinese architecture [built in Japan and elsewhere] at that time', saying that ancient Japanese artwork was a localised or degenerate version of Chinese culture. An anthropologist influenced by eugenicism, Kiyono Kenji, described the Nara Period as a time when Japan was invaded by migrants and foreign culture.[4] As mentioned in chapter 14, Tsuda Sōkichi claimed that the temples of Nara and Kyoto were the products of imported Chinese culture, and were lionised only by the aristocracy, having nothing to do with the common people.

Watsuji's admiration for the ancient Japanese temples was absolute. Although he had a high opinion of Tsuda's research into the Kiki myths, Watsuji stated 'I cannot but say "no" to each page' of Tsuda's theory of culture (Watsuji 1989–92: vol. 21, 218). However, Watsuji was rational enough to recognise that the ancient temples were built with the help of foreign migrants. As he confronted this question, he began little by little to form a theory of ethnic homogeneity that differed from that of Tsuda.

In 'Kodai Nipponjin no konketsu jōtai', Watsuji stated that, in his 'opinion', 'the refinement of the ancient Japanese nation' was one that 'felt an affinity with Indian culture' and was 'stimulated by a mixture with the Chinese race' (Watsuji 1989–92: vol. 21, 192). The argument that the two great cultures of the East, those of India and China, were synthesised in Japan was at the time frequently seen under the phrase 'Asia is One'. Watsuji also adopted this position in his argument about the origin of the Japanese nation.

According to this article, the Japanese nation was formed when 'a southern race', a conquering nation that 'came riding on the Kuroshio (Black) Current', conquered and mixed with 'a northern race', a Tungus people which had migrated from the continent but were 'a different nation from the Han Chinese'. The 'descent of the Tenson is the tale of washing ashore from the south', and the northern race was distributed in 'Izumo and South Korea' (Watsuji 1989–92: vol. 21, 195–7). The idea of a mixture of the northern and southern races was one often seen in Meiji era theories of the Japanese nation such as those of Yamaji Aizan and Kume Kunitake. In fact, when Watsuji began to study the history of ancient Japan, it seems that he first read *Nippon kodaishi* (The History of Ancient Japan) by Kume Kunitake, a work discussed in chapter 5 (Watsuji 1939: i).

However, the distinctive feature of Watsuji is that he excluded the Chinese Han nation from both the northern and the southern races. Many contemporary theorists claimed the northern race was a Mongolian or Tungus people, while the southern race was Chinese. Even Shiratori Kurakichi, who argued for the theory of the homogeneous nation, insisted that the Japanese nation was a superior nation that possessed both the cultural refinement of the southern (the Chinese Han) and the military ability of the northern (the Mongolian) races. A large number of theorists also assumed the southern race to be Malay, but Watsuji did not discuss his view of the origin of the southern race in this article. However, in a cutting from the journal which carried this article discovered in the Watsuji household, the words 'if I was able to take the position that the birthplace of the southern race was India, it would be all the more convenient for my argument' had been added (Watsuji 1962: vol. 20, 311).

The theory that the birthplace of the southern race could be traced back as far as India had been advanced by Kume Kunitake in *Nippon kodaishi* (Ancient Japanese History). However, Kume developed his position into strange theories such as that there were archaeological sites in Japan similar to those in Babylon or that Caucasians had migrated to Japan, but had withdrawn these ideas by the time Watsuji published his article.[5] That is, the theory that the birthplace of the southern race was India was beginning to be seen as an heretical view. What, then, was 'convenient' about this theory for Watsuji?

What is important here is his view of the northern race. In the second half of the article, Watsuji tackled the issue of the arrival in the Japanese archipelago of the 'Chinese Han nation' and of 'Koreans' who brought with them an advanced culture that included Buddhism. Here he accepted the influx of a large number of migrants, but stated that by the reign of the Emperor Yūryaku in the late fifth century, 'although they were called naturalised peoples', they were regarded as 'Japanese of mixed breed'. He continued to state that the Emperor Yūryaku who used these 'Japanese of mixed breed' was 'a very ingenuous, sturdy and passionate "natural child"'...we must not overlook the fact that the central dynamism of ancient culture lies here'. He also argued that the northerners, the indigenous people of the archipelago, were primitive, but artless with a 'very intuitional' sense (Watsuji 1989–92: vol. 21: 199, 206–7).

According to Watsuji, those who assimilated the advanced culture of the Chinese Han nation were the Japanese nation, an intuitional and emotive people who were a mixture of the northern and southern races, and who were 'ingenuous, sturdy and passionate "natural children"'. Claiming that the Northern Wei of ancient China was a mixed country where a northern Tungus race had conquered the Chinese Han nation and actively adopted the advanced culture of the Chinese, Watsuji wrote as follows (Watsuji 1989–92: vol. 21, 200–1):

> This race [the northern race] showed a far greater ability than the Chinese Han nation in adopting the culture of India. The stance shown by the Northern Wei unmistakeably resembles that of the [Japanese] Suiko Dynasty...By mixing with the Chinese nation, both artless and sturdy nations were intellectually awakened, and emotionally inspired by

Indian culture...what enabled them to eagerly absorb one aspect of the culture of India (especially the aesthetic aspect) was the blood of the Tungus. What made it possible for the glorious Buddhist culture to blossom in China was mainly the hot dynamism of this blood.

The ideas that the culture of India was 'emotional' and 'aesthetic', that the Chinese Han nation was 'intellectual' but lacking in 'emotion' and 'aestheticism', and that the northern race felt an affinity with Indian culture, were treated as given facts without any attempt to substantiate them. In the Japan of the Suiko Dynasty when the Hōryūji Temple was built, as well as in China, while the intellectuality of the Han nation was an important element, the dynamism that produced the glorious Buddhist art was actually the 'blood' of the Tungus and the 'emotion' of Indian culture. Such being the case, if the intellectuality of Chinese migrants was absorbed into a Japanese nation that had been formed from a mixture of Indian southerners and an artless and sturdy northern race that felt close to the culture of India, the most idealistic form of Buddhist art would be produced.

This schema was transformed and developed in Watsuji's *Fūdo*, but first *Nippon kodai bunka* (Ancient Japanese Culture), a mid-period work published in 1920, will be examined.

The World of the Natural Children

Nippon kodai bunka was Watsuji's favourite work. His enthusiasm for it can be seen in the fact that he continued to work on it and published three revised editions. A quick glance at the footnotes is enough to demonstrate that Watsuji absorbed a broad knowledge from contemporary anthropology and history, beginning with the work of Torii, Hasebe, Tsuda and Shiratori.

In the first (1920) edition of the work, Watsuji claimed that 'all would agree' that the Japanese were a mixed nation. However, relying on the research of Hasebe, he criticised the idea represented by the theory of Torii that the *Ainu* were an indigenous people who created the Jōmon pottery and that the conquering Korean 'Japanese Proper' who arrived later were responsible for the Yayoi pottery. Instead, he argued for the mixture of two groups, a 'pan-*Ainu*' that differed from the modern *Ainu*, and a Korean people.[6]

According to Watsuji, the origin of the 'pan-*Ainu* race' could be traced back to India and 'seems to be related to the Indo-European race'. The Koreans were 'south Tungus'. However, both races coexisted on the archipelago, and their relationship was not that of an indigenous people and a conquering people. Clearly guided by the work of Tsuda, Watsuji insisted that the mixture of the two dated much further back than the time when the Kiki myths were written. By then, the Japanese had already 'completely formed one mixed nation' which had 'one Japanese language', and that there was 'no proof that one race with a unique language was opposed to other races' (Watsuji 1920: 1–11).

Two characteristics emerge here. First, the schema of a mixture of an Indian and a Tungus race was maintained. Secondly, however, the works of Hasebe and Tsuda were used to criticise the theory of Torii, and it was argued that there was no conquest of an indigenous nation but that both races had combined to form one single nation by the time the Kiki myths were written.

The art, religion, character, and social organisation of this Japanese nation were said to be very plain and artless, and the Kiki myths to describe 'the deification of the natural child'. In ancient Japan, acts triggered by natural human emotions were forgiven, including even the impiety to parents and adultery that the morality of both Confucianism and Buddhism condemned. Watsuji described – and praised – this as a situation 'beyond Good and Evil' (Watsuji 1920: 431). However, the influx of 'Chinese customs which oppressed natural love with rules' gradually led to the 'decline' of the 'great innocent "childishness" of the natural child' (Watsuji 1920: 370, 377).

Moreover, Watsuji insisted that until an established family system emerged in Japan, there existed equal rights for both sexes and a matriarchy (Watsuji 1920: 47). These notions are very similar to Takamure Itsue's views of ancient Japan (see chapter 11). In fact, when Watsuji first started to study the history of ancient Japan, he too 'read *Kojiki-den* (The Legend of *Kojiki*) by Motoori Norinaga, was impressed by the beauty of *Kojiki*, and realised the greatness of the true scholars of Japan' (Watsuji 1939: ii). In 1917, Watsuji cited Kume Kunitake, while criticising Motoori and praising Tō Teikan who had insisted that the Emperor Jinmu was a descendant of the Chief of the Wu Dynasty

(Watsuji 1989–92: vol. 21, 214). However, in the first (1920) edition of *Nippon kodai bunka*, he described the debate between Motoori and Confucian thinkers as 'a conflict between "beyond Good and Evil", and "a universal morality"', and took the side of Motoori (Watsuji 1920: 440).

Watsuji's reversion to Japan is said to have occurred from about the time of the First World War, and resulted in works such as *Koji junrei* (A Pilgrimage to Ancient Temples) published in 1919. It is not known what happened between 1917 and 1920, when Watsuji's evaluation of Motoori changed completely. One reason for the change might have been the shock of the First World War, when so many were killed with the help of modern science, and the resulting awareness of the limits of Western civilisation and modern rationality that emerged in the European intelligentsia. Another reason may have been the anti-Japanese movement and the rejection of Japan's proposal for racial equality that also occurred around 1919. Anatole France's *Sur la Pierre Blanche*, a work that criticised the rise of the Yellow Peril in Europe, was recommended to Watsuji by Yanagita.[7] Influenced by this book, Watsuji wrote that 'in the whole world, it is only Japan which can resist' the Caucasians who were colonising and ruling coloured peoples, and 'Japan must save the larger part of humanity by arguing for racial equality' (Watsuji 1989–92: vol. 22, 193).

That Watsuji was influenced by Motoori, however, does not necessarily mean that he converted to the chauvinism of the time. His view of the ancient Japanese as a natural people overlapped with Nietzsche's concept of 'beyond Good and Evil' (needless to say, Nietzsche was a thinker Watsuji admired). This was also a form of opposition to Inoue Tetsujirō, the teacher Watsuji disliked, who had used the Kiki myths to argue for a national morality. If the Kiki myths were regarded as beyond Good and Evil, it would be impossible to extract a morality from them.[8] Moreover, Inoue was a specialist not only in Western philosophy, but also in Confucianism. As has already been seen, nativism (*kokugaku*) and Confucianism were opposed to one another. Since Watsuji interpreted ancient Japan as a time when Japan was free from an artificial and Confucian morality and when the Emperor and the people were linked by natural affection, he was highly critical of extracting a Confucian-like feudal morality from the Kiki myths and imposing it by force on the Japanese people.

Watsuji expressed the confrontation between Motoori and the Confucian scholars as that between '"beyond Good and Evil" and "a universal morality"', and seems to have reached the same position as Tsuda who was looking for a Japan free from the influence of Chinese civilisation, and Yanagita who believed the unique Japanese identity was being threatened by the modern universalism of the West. Like Watsuji, Yanagita and Tsuda also praised the native culture and natural life of the community as opposed to a formal morality and universalism. The only difference was that Yanagita saw the symbol of universalism as the West (the continent), while Tsuda saw the symbol of a formal morality as China. Watsuji found these in both the West and China.

Unlike Motoori and Takamure, however, Watsuji did not adopt the view that ancient Japan was corrupted by the influence of Chinese philosophy. If he had, the Buddhist temples of Nara and Kyoto constructed under the influence of Chinese culture would have been seen – as Tsuda saw them – as a collection of decadent architecture.

According to Watsuji, even after the influx of Buddhism (synonymous with intelligence and morality), 'the natural people of Japan' did not lose their original innocent childishness and achieved 'a unique development of Buddhism' (Watsuji 1939: 378). That is, 'there was contact between the Japanese who were then especially intuitive, and the Chinese who were then especially abstract, and a youthful new energy emerged to assimilate an already decadent and weak intelligence'. The culture produced from this was one that 'certainly would never have been possible without the stimulation of the Chinese', but still was 'a unique Japanese culture that differed from that of China' (Watsuji 1939: 171).

By the time of 'the Nara Period, naturalised migrants had already become completely Japanese', and the 'Japanisation of Chinese characters (*kanji*) – a representative example of the assimilation of imported culture – was achieved by the Japanese, whether naturalised migrants or Japanese proper' (Watsuji 1920: 143, 196). The literature has noted that in his *Koji junrei*, Watsuji emphasised that the ancient temples were built by 'Japanese' and that he also tended to minimise the importance of the influence of China and Korea on ancient Japanese temples, while stressing that of Hellenism and India.[9]

Watsuji had abandoned the schema of the conquest of an indigenous people, arguing instead that it was self-evident that 'the Japanese are mild-natured and lack any passionate desire to conquer others'. The ancient 'Japanese' were a 'mass' that was not divided into individuals. They were united by natural affection, created small countries, and had no need for artificial systems or power from above. This was because 'equal individuals unite naturally without the necessity of an external force. Moreover, they do not demand a unification larger than their natural unity' (Watsuji 1939: 46). What is important in relation to Watsuji's later theory of a Symbolic Emperor is his description of the status of the monarchs of these small countries (Watsuji 1939: 46).

> Both monarch and the people are mere puppets of the public will which emerges as the will of the gods. The will of the gods, or in other words the will of the group, is symbolised by the monarch.

This monarch was not a tyrant who oppressed the people with an iron fist, but the 'symbol' of the general will which was the 'will of the gods'. In the world of a natural people beyond Good and Evil, divisions such as those between the interior and exterior, emotions and morals, religious festivals and politics, and the individual and the whole, were yet to emerge, and therefore the power required to unite them by force was unnecessary. This view of the monarch looks like the world of the natural people as depicted by Rousseau, and to resemble a type of anarchism and communitarianism, but it also has much in common with the theory of the national polity.

According to an article published in 1919, Watsuji argued that the examples of oppressive rule seen in Japanese history were the responsibility of the Shōgun or ministers who did not represent the will of the people, and had nothing to do with the Emperors. Giving as an example the story in the Kiki myths where the Sun Goddess Amaterasu 'followed the general consensus instead of stating her own opinion' at a meeting attended by 8 million gods (Shintō believed that gods dwelled in all objects in the natural world: 8 million was a symbolic figure that represented all gods), Watsuji stated that 'the history of the Japanese Imperial Household has consistently demonstrated this democratic spirit. This is what has made the unbroken line of Emperors possible'.

This was not a contradiction because Watsuji understood democracy (*minponshugi*) to mean conducting the affairs of state according to the will of the people, and believed the Emperor symbolised the general will. In the context of this logic, Watsuji criticised the contemporary national polity theorists who were attacking democracy in the name of the national polity, claiming that they misunderstood the nature of both Japanese democracy and the national polity (Watsuji 1989–92: vol. 22, 149, 162). Like Tsuda, Watsuji stressed that the Emperors were as one with the people, and at the same time rejected the idea of an iron-fisted rule in the name of the Emperor.

Watsuji's view of the Japanese nation and the Japanese state as expressed in the articles above can be summarised as follows.

First of all, the Japanese nation emerged through a mixture of an Indian and a Tungus people. Both excelled in the areas of emotion and intuition, and formed the character of the Japanese nation as a natural people. The relationship between the two peoples was originally described as that of an indigenous people and a conquering people, but by 1920 Watsuji had revised this and argued instead that they mixed without conflict to form a single nation, and were a peaceful group led by a symbolic monarch. In the land of this natural people who were 'beyond Good and Evil', an intellectualism that included Buddhism flowed in from China, and a unique Buddhist culture flowered. Originally, it was because of the blood of the Tungus who excelled in emotion, not the Chinese Han nation, that Buddhist art was produced in China. Moreover, all migrants to the archipelago were naturalised and became completely 'Japanese', and the assimilation of the Chinese alphabet (*kanji*) and Buddhism were accomplished by the 'Japanese'.

It is easy to imagine that Watsuji, who had studied Nietzsche and Hegel, had a positive view of ancient Japan, regarding it as 'beyond Good and Evil', and as a dialectic higher step that had synthesised intelligence (China) and emotion (India and the Tungus). To place emotion and intuition above a universal rationalism was a trend that could be seen among the philosophers of this period, where it was claimed that the Western modern rationalism had reached an impasse. Moreover, the approach coincided with Motoori's argument against Confucianism. As a young man, Watsuji had been introverted, but also had a passionate love for plays and art, and described himself as 'a born rebel'. Both his admiration for Nietzsche, who praised Greek tragedy and rejected Christian morality, and his inability to get along with Inoue who preached the importance of a national morality, were expressions of his character.

According to Nietzsche, the best Greek tragedies consisted of a harmonious coexistence of two principles, represented by the chaotic vitality of Dionysus and the reason and order of Apollo. The Bacchanalia which celebrated Dionysus were said to have originated in Asia Minor and Babylon, both of which were close to India. Nietzsche argued, however, that this harmony was destroyed by the ascendancy of reason. Here Apollo was the god of the principle of individualisation, and ancient Greece was described as a society in which there was no division between artistic (or religious) festivals and political community.[10] This was identical with Watsuji's view of ancient Japan where the individual and the whole were not separate, and the will of the community as general consensus was symbolised by the monarch. Watsuji in fact originally wrote in his research into Nietzsche published in 1913 that 'I believe there is something in the blood of the true Japanese that corresponds with Nietzsche' (Watsuji 1989–92: vol. 1, 9).

At the same time, this view of ancient Japan and the Emperor was also very similar to that of Tsuda. However, Tsuda thought that the 'Japanese' were a nation of farmers, who lived on the periphery of civilisation and lacked both culture and military ability, and that the ancient temples were infected by Chinese culture. Watsuji, however, could not deny the cultural abilities of the 'Japanese', whatever he thought of their military abilities. Moreover, since he praised the ancient temples as the sublimation of Indian and Chinese culture, or the harmony of rationalism and emotion, he was not able to exclude the notion of complexity. The Chinese influence could be explained away as something that affected Japan after the formation of an homogeneous nation, but where the Indian element was concerned, the only card he had to play was an explanation that relied on the influx and mixture of the nation's 'blood'.

In other words, Watsuji could only explain the complexity of Japanese culture by using the idea of a national mixture that rested on the weak theory that the Japanese nation originated in India. On this point, Watsuji adopted the same stance as the contemporary mixed nation theorists who regarded the southern and northern elements in Japanese culture as automatic proof of the migration of southern and northern nations.

In the late 1920s, however, Watsuji was dealt another card. This provided powerful support to the postwar theory of the homogeneous nation in that it could explain the complexity of Japanese culture without mentioning the issue of ethnicity. This was his concept of '*fūdo*' (climate).

A Complex Homogeneous Climate

Watsuji left for Europe in 1927 as an overseas researcher for the Ministry of Education, sailing for Germany via the Indian Ocean and Suez Canal, and stopping on the way at ports in India, Egypt and Greece. At the time, teachers of European culture and philosophy in imperial universities were required to study overseas when they were promoted. Watsuji's trip to Germany was a duty, and not one that he relished. He felt even more uncomfortable than Yanagita overseas. As with many Japanese intellectuals at the time, Watsuji was able to read European languages but was weak in conversation. Apart from his German tutor and his landlady, he spoke to hardly anyone, failed to attend classes, and eventually returned to Japan a nervous wreck six months sooner than planned.

Based on his experience of the trip, Watsuji began to write a series of articles which were later published in a single volume, *Fūdo* (Climate). Here he argued that culture was closely related to climate, and divided the world's civilisations into three types: the 'monsoon' type represented by India, the 'desert' type represented by the world of the Old Testament, including Arabia and Judea, and the 'pastoral' type represented by ancient Greece and Europe. This work became a classic in Japan and was to exercise great influence on the discourse on Japanese culture.

In 1917, Watsuji had argued in 'Kodai Nippon no konketsu jōtai' that the 'blood' of a nation was a decisive element in its 'spiritual culture' (Watsuji 1989–92: vol. 21, 192). This was why he had to tie (what he thought to be) Indian elements in Japanese culture to the idea that the Japanese nation originated in India. In *Fūdo*, however, he discussed cultures from Japan and around the world, but hardly mentioned the issue of ethnic origins. Here culture was explained from the viewpoint of climate rather than blood.

An analysis of these three types of civilisation will be helpful in understanding the theory of Japan that was developed in *Fūdo*.

First of all, the characteristic of the 'monsoon' type is the powerlessness of human beings in the face of the tyranny of nature, as exemplified in the heat and humidity about which humans can do nothing. This climate makes humans receptive and submissive, and dulls the human will. Moreover, in the south, because changes in the four seasons are not experienced, people have monotonous natures and lack any sense of hisory. In India, however, unlike the South Sea islands, an acute aesthetic susceptibility and overflowing emotion exist. Unlike Greek philosophy, which depicted a world in conflict with humans, Indian philosophy praised the power of nature which produced life. From the Western viewpoint, it might seem disorderly, but it is a philosophy in which a rich variety of things are accepted and brought together.

The 'desert' type is a world ruled by dryness and bleakness. Here, it is impossible to live as an individual, and humans are forced to live in groups, which require clear organisation and rule through power. It is a world based on antagonistic human relationships, and obedient and aggressive human beings who are able to obey orders and fight over wells. In the desert, only man-made things prove that life exists. Nature has no value, and artificial geometry is regarded as the essence of beauty. Specific examples of this world are the religious fraternity of Judea with its stern monotheistic god and the commandments, and the geometrical beauty of the pyramids produced by power and obedience.

Climatically speaking, the 'pastoral' type is characterised by a synthesis of humidity and dryness. Its greatest characteristic, however, is the fact that grass can be used even if left without care. What this amounts to is the supremacy of human beings over nature. Here nature is obedient and humans are the masters. Mankind is freed from the constraints of nature, and at the same time, unlike in the desert, competition and division between individuals are accepted. As typically seen in ancient Greece, human are divided into citizens (the masters) and cattle-like slaves. The system of slavery which was later established in the USA was only a copy of this. When citizens and slaves are divided, citizens exercise their reason and intelligence, and observe without using their hands. When Rome built a multi-national empire and prevented the unique features of each nation's culture from developing, a hollow universalism began to flourish. The division between the conquering masters and the conquered slaves was a reflection of the conquest of nature by human reason. (Here, we can see the influence of Hegel.)

It is, of course, easy to refute this schema. Slavery also existed in Africa and Central and South America. Moreover, recent research has shown that the vegetation of the ancient Mediterranean differed from that of the modern age. However, what is important here is that the 'emotion' that had been given an Indian origin in the theory of the Japanese nation was now attributed to the 'monsoon' type, Chinese intelligence and Tungus aggressiveness were now attributed to the 'desert' type, and the ancient Greek and European 'pastoral' type was described as an example of the synthesis of the two.

How then did Watsuji view China and Japan? After presenting his three types, he argued that both were special forms of the monsoon type. The theory of Japan which will be examined below constituted the second half of an article, 'Kokumin dōtokuron' (On the Morals of the Japanese Nation), written in 1931. In this article, Watsuji is said to have fleshed out the ethical content of his Symbolic Emperor System.[11] His theory of China was written in 1929 and rewritten in 1943 during the Pacific War.

First of all, Watsuji stated that the Chinese lived in a land that instilled 'rarely changing, hazy and monotonous feelings' because of the vast panorama of the Yangtze valley, and the 'Chinese people can be especially characterised by their apathy'. However, the Yellow River links desert and monsoon areas, and so the Chinese have the aggressiveness of the desert type, but not the characteristic spirit of absolute obedience, and have an apathetic 'disobedient-submissive' character that shows a false obedience to those in power. This was, of course, Watsuji's reaction against the China which refused to submit to Japan and continued to resist in the Sino-Japanese War (1937–45).

The Chinese, who relied solely on themselves and their relatives to live apathetic and calculating money-making lives, were a disorderly people who lacked the concept of the state or public spirit. The superior artwork of ancient China was the product of the culture of the northern Yellow River area. In the present China, however, there was only an indifferent, insensitive and meaninglessly gigantic culture. This hollow gigantism of

Chinese culture was also characteristic of the Chinese Empire, which only had size in its favour. The superior culture of ancient China, such as that of the Tang Period, had travelled to Japan where it received the addition of the sensitivity of the 'Japanese', and where it was better preserved than in China itself.

Watsuji had previously argued that the artworks of China were not the product of the Chinese Han nation. What was different was that his explanation now focused on the 'climate' of the northern Yellow River, rather than the 'blood' of the northern Tungus. China was deprived even of its status of intelligence by the 'desert', and was relegated to the status of a calculating, apathetic and disorderly existence.

In a draft of 'Kokumin dōtokuron', Watsuji strongly criticised the 'mercenary spirit' which 'viewed money-making as the most important end and regarded morality as a means', and wrote that 'utilitarian individualism must be destroyed, and the authority of the whole must be re-established' (Watsuji 1989–92: bekkan 1, 443). (In 1931, when Watsuji wrote this, Japan invaded Manchuria, the world depression hit Japan and economic disparities in wealth and the collapse in morals became topical issues.) For Watsuji, 'the Chinese are a practical nation which has no understanding of turning life into an art form, while the Japanese are an impractical nation which is far too eager to pursue art in life. On this point, the Chinese are more Jewish than the Jews, while, by contrast, the Japanese are more Greek than the Greeks...A Chinese victory would be a backward step for humanity' (Watsuji 1989–92: vol. 4, 255).

What then about Japan? According to Watsuji, Japan enjoyed a rich nature in the humid monsoon zone, and therefore the 'Japanese' were receptive and submissive. However, unlike the South Seas, Japan was blessed with clear changes in the four seasons. Moreover, there were seasonal winds with a 'dialectic character' – the 'seasonal but sudden' typhoons. Japan also had heavy snowfalls, which were non-existent in the tropics. In other words, Japan had the 'twin character of the tropics and the arctic regions'. The character of the Japanese was neither the overflowing monotonous emotion of the tropics nor the monotonous endurance of the arctic regions, but rather was composed of a stable foundation combined with an ever-changing surface. Further, a monsoon submissiveness was blended with a typhoon suddenness to create a sudden submissiveness, as seen in aggressive but resigned 'recklessness' (*yake*) and 'candid forgetfulness'.

This was an attempt to explain the complexity of Japanese culture by focusing on the idea of the homogeneous but complex climate of the archipelago, instead of the migration of the Tungus (northern) and Indian (southern) peoples. It also fitted in easily with the schema of an assimilation of imported culture at the same time as the original identity was maintained.

The notion that all 'Japanese' shared the same 'Japanese' disposition produced by a unique climate was, of course, fiction. Typhoons only affect south-western Japan and the side of the archipelago that faces the Pacific Ocean, while heavy snowfall is found only in northeastern Japan and on the side that faces the Japan Sea. There are no typhoons in Hokkaido and no snowfall in Okinawa. If Japan were divided into East and West Japan, with two separate states established on the lines of Germany, the theory of the importance of climate would collapse. Even if the archipelago had enjoyed a uniform climate, Watsuji would still not have been able to explain the existence of alien nations with different cultures, such as the *Ainu*. In his climate theory, it should not have been possible for different peoples with different cultures to live in regions with the same climate. According to Watsuji, Japan was a synthesis of the tropics and the arctic region, of northern and southern peoples, and of submissiveness and aggressiveness.

Among those countries that had experienced this sort of synthesis, how did Watsuji see the difference between Japan and Greece or Europe? In Japan, people 'did not try to conquer nature nor were they hostile to it'. Furthermore, in the pastoral culture, conquering males took conquered females to form families, in the same way as civilisation conquered nature, so the family had little significance and ancestor worship was weak. The Japanese family, on the other hand, was characterised by 'a gentle love that aimed at unification without distinctions'. This love, however, was passionate as well as gentle, and the 'Japanese' did not hesitate to sacrifice their lives for the honour of the family. Therefore, the Japanese family was a realisation of the 'Japanese "relationship" (*aidagara*)' which was gentle, but also aggressive and candid.

Moreover, in Japan, 'the "*ie*" (family) means the totality of the family. It is represented by the patriarch, but it is the totality that makes him the patriarch rather than the patriarch that makes the totality'. Like the monarch of ancient Japan, the patriarch symbolised the whole, and the totality of the family including its ancestors stood above the individual patriarch. From first to last, 'the totality of the family comes before the individual members', and 'the division between individuals perishes' inside the family. In ancient Japan, people were firmly united by religious festivals, and lived in 'communities of love and harmony which did not require awareness as individuals'.

In 'Kodai Nipponjin no konketsu jōtai' published in 1917, Watsuji had argued that the males of the conquering nation mixed with the females of the indigenous nation (Watsuji 1989–92: vol. 21, 198). Now, however, that type of relationship was contrasted with that of Japan. Moreover, Watsuji described the status of the gods of ancient Japan in the following terms:

> What is most characteristic about Japanese myths in comparison with Greek and Indian myths is that, despite the traces of various primitive beliefs, they are powerfully unified by a single festival. The only equivalents are the myths of the Old Testament. In these myths, however, a clear line is drawn between god and mankind. The Japanese gods, on the other hand, are very close to, and seen as relatives of, mankind. The god of the Old Testament rules over people with a stern, even wilful, authority, while the Japanese gods do not give wilful commands, but rule consistently over people with a mild, even affectionate, mercy. The description of Amaterasu clearly shows this. This proves that human relationships as a religious fraternity [in Japan] were characterised by 'unification without any distinctions' and 'gentle affection'. The Greek gods were similar in that they, too, were close to mankind, but they already reflected intellectual and republican human relationships. This demonstrates that the Greek nation was not united by a single festival.

Here we can see a schema that synthesised in Japan the merits of the three types: an Indian (monsoon) naturalness, the Old Testament (desert) unity, and the Greek (pastoral) humanity. Unlike the Greek experience where the harmony of intelligence and emotion, of festival and political community, was destroyed by 'intellectual and republican human relationships', people were united by a single festival in Japan. In other words, a society superior to the society idealised by Hegel and Nietzsche had been realised in Japan.

The fact that the word *'matsurigoto'* (festival) is used in Japan in both a political and religious sense was claimed in postwar criticisms of the Emperor System to show that Japan was a divine theocratic state where the modern, secular division between church (religion) and state (politics) had not yet occurred. However, according to Watsuji, the views of Amaterasu and the ancient Emperors coincided with the general consensus, and they were not despotic individuals detached from the whole. The Emperors, let alone their subjects, were not individuals, but 'puppets' of the community. Watsuji was opposed to the ultra-nationalism that emerged in the 1930s and promoted the idea of direct rule by the Emperor. For Watsuji, this would open the door to individual despotism in the name of the Emperor, and was a deviation from the essential nature of the Emperors that had been the norm since ancient times.

Thus Watsuji was able to discard the mixed nation theory and explain the complexity of Japanese culture in terms of the complexity of the Japanese climate. It was now possible for the image of the 'Japanese' as a peaceful, natural community, which enjoyed an homogeneous but complex culture, to free itself from the shackles imposed by the theory of the mixed nation and move on to centre stage.

An Emperor System Limited by National Borders

In 1939, Watsuji published a new and greatly revised edition of *Nippon kodai bunka*.[12] It began with a long citation of over two pages from Kiyono Kenji's *Jinruigaku·senshigaku kōza* (Lectures on Anthropology and Prehistory) which had been published the previous year, and which argued that 'the Japanese certainly did not occupy the motherland of the *Ainu*. The motherland of the Japanese race, the homeland of the Japanese, has been Japan since man first began to live in Japan'. Moreover, Watsuji stated, 'this conclusion of anthropology proves that there were never any racial wars in Japan. This has enormous significance since it shows that the unique character of the Japanese nation already existed in the Stone Age'.

In the past, Watsuji had used Tsuda's theory to argue that a peaceful and homogeneous Japanese nation which had conquered no one was formed by the time depicted in the Kiki myths. However, he now used Kiyono's theory to trace it back to the Stone Age. In this new edition, he cited Shiratori's study of linguistics to emphasise the uniqueness of the Japanese language when compared with the languages of neighbouring peoples.

According to Watsuji, this 'single nation', unlike those of Europe, consisted of a 'mild' and 'peaceful' people who had 'frank wills and only temporarily passionate emotions, and who were not violent' because of their diet of fish and vegetables rather than meat. This made a 'distinctive contrast with both the ancient Chinese, who were characterised by the burning lust for conquest of their tyrannical kings and their gaudy hedonism and debauchery, and with the violent barbarians who seemed to enjoy running about the bleak plains of the continent'. In discussing aesthetics, he praised the peaceful curved lines of Japan in contrast to the 'accurate geometrical lines so beloved of continental peoples', calling on his readers to 'compare the soft outlines of the stoneware' of the archipelago with 'the tremendous sharpness of continental weapons'.

One reason that Watsuji's theory of the homogeneous nation survived until the postwar years, which were characterised by a backlash against the militarism of the imperial era, is doubtlessly because it included an orientation towards peace. His theory, however, was not just a description of the Japanese nation as a peaceful people who had never invaded or mixed with alien nations. His view of the state can be seen from an analysis of the second volume of his *Rinrigaku* (Ethics) published in 1942.[13]

At the time, Watsuji followed the Hegelian view that the state was the supreme stage in human morals (*geist*), and took the position that it was the supreme form of the human community. All the same, he described the nation as a 'cultural community defined by shared blood and soil', and stated that 'the essence of the nation lies in a shared culture and not in a unity of blood'. His shift in emphasis from 'blood' to 'climate' can be seen here.

Watsuji criticised the multi-national state, giving as an example the Roman Empire, which had been described as embodying an empty universalism in *Fūdo*.

...In the blink of an eye, Alexander the Great created a situation where one state that included many nations emerged from a situation where one nation was scattered across many states. The Roman Empire inherited this situation. In these circumstances, it is natural that the totality of the state and the totality of the nation were not identical. Alexander the Great formed an empire by military force. So did Caesar. The power of such states is not sacred.

According to Watsuji, an ideal monarch becomes the sovereign of the state as the symbol of the totality of the nation, which is a cultural community. In a draft of the outline of 'Kokumin dōtokuron', he wrote: 'when the state and nation are identical, law and morals are identical. This was the case with Greece, but not with Rome' (Watsuji 1989–92: bekkan 1, 416). As with Immanuel Kant, a central issue in ethics was how to reconcile a universal law with individual morals. Watsuji tried to find a solution by locating the *volk* (cultural community) as a mediator between the state and the individual.

However, in a multi-national state, where the totality of the nation is not identical with that of the state, this solution fails. In this type of state, artificial power rules the whole, and 'once such a system of rule is firmly established, not only alien nations but also one's own nation will begin to be "ruled". The monarch will no longer be an expression of the totality of the state, but becomes a "private" individual, who monopolises state power'.

Thus when a monarchy is transformed into the despotism of an individual, the people wrest power away by revolutions and establish democratic states. However, since no one among the people can express the totality of the state, under the fiction of an artificial 'whole people', the 'majority of the total number of private individuals' grasp power and the tyranny of the majority emerges. In such cases, the totality that includes minorities is not expressed in the state.

The choice between tyranny and democracy, or the 'issue of the difference between the sovereignty of the monarch and the sovereignty of the people only occurs in a state that has discarded the sacredness of the sovereign, and is degraded to a system of rule. This has never happened and will never happen in a state that maintains its original absolute totality through the living totality of the nation'. An homogeneous nation-state is the 'genuine state', whereas in a multi-national state, 'a division between state and nation' and 'a separation between the cultural community and the state' occurs, and the state is degraded to a mere organisation to enforce rule through power.

An homogeneous state might be criticised as having the defect of narrow mindedness. Watsuji replied to this criticism as follows:

> It is precisely those who claim that they hate the narrow mindedness of a nation, and assume that they themselves have adopted the standpoint of mankind, who are usually responsible for the most extreme expressions of ethnic egotism. This is because they view the characteristics of their own nation as absolutes, refuse to recognise the special characteristics of other nations, and thus try to encompass the whole of mankind within the characteristics of a single nation. This is what they call the standpoint of mankind! The god of a certain specific nation becomes the god of all mankind. The language of a certain specific nation becomes the world language. Some people might claim that this means the destruction of the narrow mindedness of the nation. In reality, however, the strongest form of narrow mindedness is established instead. This is because closed mindedness is hardened through competition with alien nations, and therefore becomes so strong that it is not easily broken even if alien nations are included within the nation. On the other hand, respect for the uniqueness of the cultural community and the identity of the nation leads to the true common ideal of mankind. For this viewpoint does not see the characteristics of one's own nation as absolute, and therefore accepts and respects the identity and status of all alien nations. The ideal of a universal brotherhood of mankind is realised not by denying the individuality of the nation, but by embracing it and allowing it to blossom.

Watsuji's theory of the homogeneous nation was thus based on a sort of international pluralism, and supported by the idea that each homogeneous nation throughout the world would create a political organisation based on the culture of each nation. The culture and independence of each nation was respected, and multi-national empires that ruled over a plurality of nations were the objects of criticism. According to his theory of climate, as long as regions which enjoyed the same climate became independent, they would include no alien nations with alien cultures, and the problem of racial discrimination and cultural conflict would be solved.

Given this logic, it was inevitable that Watsuji should oppose assimilationist policies. In the draft of 'Kokumin dōtokuron', which he started writing immediately after his return from Europe, he stated that 'the Greek attitude to slaves is the Caucasian attitude to coloured peoples. The Caucasian advance into the East was carried out in this spirit', and argued that it was 'Japan's duty' to 'liberate the peoples of the East, and unite the cultures of the East and the West' (Watsuji 1989–92: bekkan 1, 412, 440). His criticism of the multi-national state was a criticism of the West which had established colonial empires and had described English and French as 'world languages' and Christianity as the 'universal religion'. At the same time, this position was the expression of a secret resistance to the Japanese ultra-nationalists whom he opposed. Although Watsuji formed his philosophy to overthrow the universal modern thought of the West and to protect the identity of Japan, it was a double-edged sword in the sense that the universalism urged by some Christian intellectuals in the Meiji was utilised as a justification for overseas aggression.

To respect Japanese originality, the assimilationist policies that deprived other nations of their national originality needed to be criticised. Although Watsuji supported the Pacific War, this was because he regarded it as a fight to liberate Asian nations from Western colonial rule. It was a slogan of the Greater East Asia Co-prosperity Sphere to make it possible for Asian nations to 'respect their own identity and status'. In reality, it was merely a justification for a class-based order where the Japanese nation (defined as leaders) led the 'inferior' Asian nations (defined as followers). However, when Watsuji used the phrase, he placed the emphasis on respect for ethnic identity.

In April 1942, Watsuji presented a written opinion to the vice-director of the Cabinet Planning Board in which he argued in favour of 'not interfering in religion or customs, but respecting the traditions' of the nations in the areas into which Japan had advanced. However, even in this written opinion, Watsuji stated that since the war was a fight to settle (*aufheben*) the problem of

Western colonial rule and modernism, 'we should not flinch from using the peoples of East Asia as labourers for the sake of the Greater East Asia War, and even sacrifice these nations for the war'. In a lecture sponsored by the Naval Ministry the following month, he asserted that 'the construction of Greater East Asia is driven above all by force, by power'.[14] Watsuji's limits lay in the fact that this did not contradict the arguments of the eugenic school. On the other hand, however, it shows that he was fully aware that an Emperor who did not actualise power was only valid within the Japanese nation, and that the notions of impartial love and harmonious assimilation based on the theory of the mixed nation could not be applied to alien nations.

Therefore, Watsuji's idea of a Symbolic Emperor based on this philosophy was, in a sense, a criticism of the Japan which had grown into a multi-national empire. In 1928, he had already excluded the Koreans, Taiwanese and emigrants from Japan from the focus of his analysis of the national character of the 'Japanese' (Watsuji 1989–92: bekkan 1, 377). Immediately after the end of the war, he recollected that his ideas were 'criticised for not including Koreans and Taiwanese as Japanese nationals at a time when Korea and Taiwan were part of Japan', and stated that 'the divinity of the Emperor is a notion that emerged from the foundations of the Japanese national community, and should not be forced on to alien nations'. Moreover, he criticised as 'insane' the notion of world rule by the Emperor that had been advocated by the Edo Period nativist scholar, Hirata Astutane (1776–1843) and his school, and then by the ultra-nationalists who adopted Hirata's views during the Second World War. Instead, he stated that 'the attempt to apply this to the modern world and regard it as the governing principle of Greater East Asia makes me, as a fellow Japanese, blush with shame' (Watsuji 1989–92: vol. 14, 328, 337). These are postwar words, but Watsuji probably already entertained such thoughts in the war years.

Watsuji's theory of the homogeneous nation was thus formed before the war ended and included elements of peace and culture that were warmly embraced in postwar Japan. Moreover, his theory of climate, which excluded the ethnic element from previous theories of Japanese culture that tended to attribute the complexity of Japanese culture to the migration of alien peoples, came to be as influential as the ideas of Yanagita in creating the postwar image of Japan. Together with Tsuda, Watsuji was to become one of the leading figures who supported the postwar Symbolic Emperor System.

16 The Collapse of Empire

During the period from the Manchurian Incident (1931) and the Sino-Japanese War (1937–45) until the first half of the Pacific War (1941–45), a large number of mixed nation theorists were active in the press. Since the Japanese puppet state in Manchuria, 'Manchukuo', was officially portrayed as an independent state based on the idea of harmony between the five nations of Japan, Korea, Manchuria, China (the Han Chinese) and Mongolia, the public discourse on this state did not emphasise the assimilation of other nations by the Japanese nation from the mixed nation point of view to the same extent that discussions on Korea and Taiwan, which were parts of the Great Japanese Empire, did. However, as already noted, the mixed nation theory in Korea peddled the Japanese Government-General line.[1]

The Wartime Mixed Nation Theory

There were a large number of mixed nation theorists during this period, even apart from the theorists already mentioned in this work.

One figure who is representative in that he enjoyed a strong public following was Tokutomi Sohō (see chapter 5). As early as 1925, Sohō had written in his *Kokumin shōkun* (Admonishing the Nation) that 'the present Yamato nation is not necessarily a single race, but a mixture and fusion of all nations', and praised the Japanese as being 'a type of alloy'. Following the outbreak of war with China, he began writing educational works, beginning with *Shōwa kokumin dokuhon* (The Shōwa National Reader) in 1939, which was recommended by the Ministry of Education, and continued at a pace of one book almost every year with *Kōdō Nippon no sekaika* (Imperial Japan as a Global Power), *Manshū kenkoku dokuhon* (The Foundation of Manchuria Reader), and *Sensen no taishō* (The Imperial Proclamation of War). All these works glorified the expansion of the Japanese empire, adopted the mixed nation theory, and praised the assimilative ability of the Japanese nation and the ability of the 'Japanese' to adapt to, and hence march into, both tropical and arctic regions. During the Pacific War he published a newspaper article that took a similar line which was bitterly criticised by Kiyono Kenji.[2]

The Pan-Asianist, Ōkawa Shūmei, wrote in *Nippon nisen-roppyakunenshi* (2,600 Years of Japanese History), a best-selling work of 1939 that sold 500,000 copies, that the *Ainu* were the indigenous people of the archipelago and that the Yamato nation had migrated from the south. Ōkawa claimed that 'the descendants of the indigenous people, as well as the descendants of nationalised migrants, were all assimilated without exception by the Yamato nation which was based on the Jinmu clan'. In 1943, he argued in a paper on the Greater East Asian Co-prosperity Sphere that the experience of assimilating the Emishi should be utilised. As was also the case with Kume, Ōkawa accepted a historical view of the Orient that was based on the concept of a struggle between southern and northern races.

Ishiwara Kanji, a staff officer of the Kwantung (Guandong) Army and later Head of the Operations Division at the General Staff Office, also argued in 1941 that the Japanese nation was a mixture of both southern and northern races, and possessed the strengths of both. Yet another Pan-Asianist, Tachibana Shiraki (1881–1945), who contributed to the founding of 'Manchukuo', advocated an ethnic national policy based on the mixed nation theory that aimed to destroy Japanese insularity (*shimaguni konjō*) in order to bring all corners of the world under one roof (*hakkō ichiu*), and to realise universal brotherhood under the Emperor (*isshi dōjin*).[3]

The Kyoto School philosopher and professor at Kyoto Imperial University, Nishida Kitarō (1870–1945), also wrote in a wartime paper that 'neither struggle nor conquest between races or nations can be seen in the history of the formation of the Japanese state. Rather, different races and nation were united and merged into a single nation under the Tenson'. From this history of overcoming the contradiction of confrontation between individual entities, he argued that 'an internal unity could be seen in the Japanese National Polity that existed nowhere else'. He added that this could be used to usher in the ideals of 'the principle of the formation of an East Asian-type world', 'bringing all corners of the world under one roof'.

The sociologist and economist, Takata Yasuma (1883–1972), who became the Director of the National Ethnic Research Centre, wrote in 1942 that 'blood from almost all the East Asian peoples' runs in the veins of the 'Japanese', and praised the Japanese advance into Asia, the ancient 'homeland' of the Japanese nation, as a 'return to the nation's home'.[4] The Head of the General Affairs Department of this Research Centre, Oka Masao, and a research fellow, Egami Namio, were to advocate the 'migration of a horse riding people theory' in the postwar era (see chapter 17).

Furthermore, Nishimura Shinji (1878–1943), an anthropologist and folklorist who is known for his research on the origins of the Japanese nation and on ancient ships, argued in 1941 that the Japanese nation had from ancient times been a sea-faring nation which had advanced overseas in boats. According to Nishimura, the Japanese nation was a mixture of seven different Asian nations in addition to Jews and Romans. He also claimed that the Japanese nation's homeland covered all areas of Asia, and argued for the 'superiority of the Yamato nation', taking the position that 'the blood of the Yellow Race, the White Race, and even a little of the Black Race has been mixed together and...only the best of each has been passed down to today'. Moreover, Japan was a society 'centred on maternity' where adopting a man into a family as the husband for a daughter was widely practised. This, however, 'could not be classed with' Western 'feminism'. Japan was a Family State in which matriarchy had been merged with a patriarchal system and was thus 'regulated by a maternity-centred patriarchy'. In 1943, he emphasised in an educational book for children that the Japanese nation was superior because it was a mixture of different ethnic groups.[5]

At this time, individuals such as Yanagita and the folklorist Orikuchi Shinobu (1887–1953) also gave lectures in which they described the relationship between the Japanese nation and the south. In a lecture entitled 'Kaijō bunka' (A Seafaring Culture), Yanagita spoke in 1940 on his long-cherished theory that the Japanese nation had migrated from the south, and emphasised the importance of ships in Japanese culture. Yanagita's pet opinion was that 'the Japanese people were not great seamen', but it seems that he had been encouraged by the Japanese push to the south in the early years of the Pacific War. In a round-table talk in 1943 on 'Building a Greater East Asian Folklore Studies', he stated that 'since I originally came from the political world, I have a strong desire to see my research put to actual social use, and believe that folklore should be rejected unless it contributes to the unification of Greater East Asia' and 'as long as one is a little patient, politicians will utilise [the results of one's research], so the best methodology, I think, is to tell the truth correctly. Since I am a politician myself – albeit an unsuccessful one – the politician in me influences my ideas about my research'. In 'Kodai Nippon bungaku ni okeru Nanpōteki yōso' (Southern Elements in Ancient Japanese Literature) published in 1943, Orikuchi argued that the Japanese nation and peoples of the south shared a common ancestor, and claimed that the Japanese nation was superior: 'the history of this great nation of the north which rules the Co-prosperity Sphere will be talked about among the peoples of the south'.[6]

At this time, there were a great number of theories of ethnicity (both those that discussed the Japanese nation and those that examined the issue of 'ethnic policy' in the areas ruled by Japan), and although the majority did not discuss the issue of origins, the minority that did almost without exception adopted the above line of argument. From 1939 alone, the following authors published books in praise of assimilationist policies and overseas aggression from the standpoint of the mixed nation theory: the national polity theorist, Nagai Tōru (see chapter 8), a member of the House of Peers, Shimomura Hiroshi (Kainan), the heterosis theorist, Taniguchi Konen, Kita Sadakichi's friend, Uchida Ginzō (this was published after his death), the Japanese historian, Akiyama Kenzō, and Shirayanagi Shūko.[7]

Among these works, the phrase 'homogeneous nation' is worthy of attention. It was not widely used at the time and, as noted at the beginning of this work, when used was almost always used in a negative sense such as 'the Japanese nation did not originally form as an homogeneous nation' or 'the Great Japanese Empire is not an homogeneous nation-state, nor is it a country of nationalism (*minzokushugi*)'.[8] The status of the phrase at this time can be gathered from the fact that the above citations are from works published by the Japanese Ministry of Education. The argument that Japan was not a country of nationalism – in other words, was not a country where ethnic identity was emphasised – meant that, as the Government-General of Korea had insisted, Japan was not a country that followed the Nazi ideology of an exclusive nationalism (*minzokushugi*), but rather one that believed in an assimilation of nations centred around the Emperor. At the time, Tokutomi Sohō published a newspaper article titled 'Kōshitsu chūshin to minzoku chūshin' (The Centrality of the Imperial

Household and the Centrality of the Nation) and stated that Japan was not a country that emphasised the centrality of the nation.

The Rise of a Pure Blood Theory

At the same time, however, there was also a backlash against the mixed nation theory. As with the eugenics school of thought, one cause of the backlash was a growing anxiety about intermarriage and the mixing of blood as a result of the increasing emphasis on Japanisation policies.

In 1938, for instance, Shiratori Kiyoshi, a professor at Gakushūin University, noted in a report of the Committee of the Promotion of Studies in Japan (published by the Bureau of Educational Affairs at the Ministry of Education) that despite the national emergency, a variety of theories about the origins of the Japanese nation were floating about, and listed those scholars who should be criticised.[9] In this report, various theories such as the migration of a Malay people and the migration of a Tungus people received critical mention, while Shiratori Kurakichi's linguistic research and Furuhata Tanemoto's blood-type research were praised.

At the same time, the 'notion that the Japanese nation is the same nation as the Koreans' was included as a target for criticism. Moreover, the scholar who topped this list was the author of *Nissen dōsoron* (The Theory that the Japanese and Koreans Share a Common Ancestor), Kanazawa Shōzaburō (see chapter 5). The other scholars that Shiratori listed as targets of criticism included Torii Ryūzō, Inoue Tetsujirō, Taguchi Ukichi and Nishimura Shinji. Shiratori Kiyoshi's argument was one that undermined the position of the Great Japanese Empire, which was using the mixed nation theory to pursue overseas aggression and assimilation.

This was not a contradiction limited just to Shiratori. In May 1942, Abe Yoshishige (1883–1966), Tanigawa Tetsuzō (1895–1989) and Watsuji Tetsurō expressed the following views at a secret round-table talk on philosophy sponsored by the Ministry of the Navy:[10]

Tanigawa: Although the notion that the Japanese are the same race with the same origin as the peoples of the south has been propagated in today's occupied territories, it is very problematic.

Abe: We must also be very careful about marriages between Koreans and Japanese, and we should not promote

> marriages between Japanese and the people of the south based on the belief that we are a single race with the same ancestors. It may be that intermarriage with Koreans should also be forbidden...
>
> Watsuji: No nation that has permitted intermarriage has ever been successful.
>
> Tanigawa: Just as the progeny of marriages between men and native women return to the level of the natives, this latest report from the Japan Society for the Promotion of Society claims that it is unpardonable to claim that the Japanese people are the same race with the same roots as the southern nations.

These last words refer to the above mentioned lecture by Shiratori Kiyoshi.

There was a backlash not only against mixing blood but also against the conscription of Koreans and Taiwanese into the Japanese military. In a political research group meeting, also sponsored by the Ministry of the Navy and also held in May 1942, the following argument was put forward against the idea that Japan might 'recognise the mixed blood of Japanese and superior southern nations...and use these people as a buffer zone': there is 'the risk that Japan might suffer the fate of Rome and also disappear. The lesson of the Roman Empire shows that the Japanese move to conscript Koreans into the Imperial Army will be the first step towards the collapse of Japan. The disappearance of a Roman Army of Romans was the cause of the collapse of Rome'. It was thus feared that the Japanese military might cease to be one made up of the Japanese nation and become one composed of Koreans and Taiwanese.

The Imperial Japanese Army set a standard which stated that the number of Koreans in combat units should not exceed twenty per cent of the total number of soldiers, and Koreans were sent to man PoW camp units and Quartermaster Corps, among others. As a result, a large number of Koreans were tried after the war as B and C class war criminals for mistreating PoW (the Japanese Government still refuses to pay these Koreans compensation). Despite this, the influx of Koreans into the Imperial Army was seen as a threat. It was even reported at the time that Korean soldiers who had died in combat had been buried in the Yasukuni Shrine, a place that was thought to be sacred and pure.[11]

The common ancestor theory and the mixed nation theory were useful in justifying aggression, in implementing assimilationist policies, and in conscription and mobilisation. However, an inevitable by-product of these theories was the birth of people of mixed blood. To renounce the mixed nation theory in an effort to prevent the mixing of blood would be to confess that Japan's invasion of Asia was not based on the solidarity of Asian blood or a union of compassion, but simply on dominance through power. It may have been possible previously to view the mixed nation theory as an abstract argument and nothing more, but once mixed marriages produced offspring with mixed blood, the contradictions of the theory came to pose an unavoidable dilemma.

A Double-Bind

The confusion within the empire at this juncture was symbolised by a charge of infringing the publication law that was laid against Tsuda Sōkichi on the grounds of suspected blasphemy against the Imperial Household. The case began when Tsuda published a book, *Shina shisō to Nippon* (Chinese Thought and Japan), during the Sino-Japanese War in 1938. In this work, he argued strongly, as he had consistently done in the past, that Chinese thought had had only a superficial influence on Japan.

According to this work, because Confucianism developed particularly as the morality of China's ruling class, it almost completely lacked universality, and 'viewed the common people as no better than beasts'. As a result, 'Chinese politics and Chinese society have not improved even a little, and the happiness of the Chinese people has not improved even slightly'. On the other hand, the influence of Chinese thought in Japan was felt by only one part of the Japanese ruling class. Moreover the Japan-as-Centre thinking of the Edo Period nativist scholars, Motoori Norinaga and Hirata Atsutane, together with the attempt to derive the morality of the gods from the *Kojiki*, was the result of the influence of the 'ideology of China as the Central Kingdom' in which China saw itself as located at the centre of the world, with the Chinese Emperor enjoying a higher status than the kings of all other regions, and of the Chinese method of expounding a formal morality drawn from books. Since Japanese culture was a distinct product of the Japanese nation and totally different from Chinese culture, there was no such thing as an 'Orient' encompassing both countries.

At the time, the Sino-Japanese War had broken out and ties of friendship between Japan and China were emphasised in an attempt to undermine Chinese resistance. It was thus stressed in Japan that China was a fellow Oriental country sharing the same race and the same culture, and related by kinship. However, according to Tsuda, since China believed itself to be the fountainhead of Oriental culture, if Japan were to continue to proclaim the existence of a common culture, 'this would give the impression that Japanese culture was subordinate to Chinese culture, and would if anything lead them to despise the Japanese people'. Furthermore, not only was this related to the stubborn anti-Japanese movement in China, but 'an important aspect of the Chinese character is that, once they have decided that someone is weak, there is nothing they would not do to that person'.

To overcome this state of affairs, it was necessary to look to Western culture for help in heightening Japan's culture. The first step was to do away with Chinese characters (*kanji*). The *kanji* 'alphabet itself contains Chinese thought', and Tsuda thought that literary Chinese (*kanbun*) classes where students were taught to read Chinese literature and the Chinese classics in the original 'should be abolished as soon as possible'. He thus criticised the 'United Orient' point of view as 'something that did not have a firm belief in the uniqueness of Japan's past culture, but proclaimed it to be subordinate to Chinese culture by calling it an Oriental culture'.[12]

Tsuda's rejection of the Orient was based on a resolute dislike of China and a belief in Japan's uniquness. However, it was precisely because of this that he was criticised by the right-wing.

The criticism of Tsuda was spearheaded by Minoda Kyōki (1894–1946), a member of the right-wing organisation, Genri Nipponsha, which supported the propagation of the national polity (*kokutai meichō*), and which denounced the speech and conduct of scholars it deemed to be anti-Japanese. However, when Minoda first took up the issue of *Shina shisō to Nippon* in 1939, he spoke highly of Tsuda. According to him, Tsuda had declared his faith in Japan's uniqueness, and he praised him for:

> noting and warning that the 'disdainful anti-Japanese' thought and actions of China that are the root causes of this incident [the Sino-Japanese War] were caused by the general academic traditions and trends of thought that have hitherto

been prevalent in Japan – that is, the academic fallacy of the intelligentsia in becoming uncritical sycophants where Chinese thought, Oriental culture and Western culture are concerned.[13]

However, another member of the Genri Nipponsha was later to begin to criticise Tsuda. After reading Tsuda's *Shina shisō to Nippon*, he stated that he had a 'slightly different view [of the book] than Mr. Minoda'. He believed that Tsuda's arguments called for an 'obliteration of the Orient' in that they spoke against the solidarity of Greater East Asia centred on Japan, and his rejection of the Orient was supported by an acceptance of Western culture. Moreover, he claimed that 'Mr. Tsuda states that Japan's unique culture "lacks a global universalism"'.[14] It was only after this that Minoda and others switched to an all-out attack on Tsuda.

In a sense, Minoda was someone who embodied the contradictions of the Great Japanese Empire. At first, he praised Tsuda for proving Japan's distinctiveness, but then criticised him for stating that Japan lacked universality. It is said that Tsuda once remarked to Maruyama Masao (1914–1996), with whom he had taken refuge in a Western restaurant (it was typical of Tsuda that this was not a Chinese restaurant) after being surrounded and castigated by right-wing students during a lecture at Tokyo Imperial University, that 'it is when people like that thrive that the Japanese Imperial Household is really threatened'.[15]

As a result of the campaign waged against him by Minoda and others, Tsuda was forced to appear in court where he was accused of blasphemy against the Imperial Family because he had suggested that the Kiki myths were 'made-up stories'. During his trial, Tsuda made the following statement in court:

> If it is true that the Tenson nation migrated [to the archipelago] from overseas and conquered the Izumo nation, and if this historical event did take place during the time of the gods, then that would mean that Japan is a conquest state. It would mean that the Imperial Household subjugated the people of this country by armed force, and that it was this subjugation that made the foundation of the state possible. This views the Imperial Household and the commoners as being of totally different origins, and joined only by armed force and power. I

firmly believe that this way of thinking is damaging to the spirit of Japan's national polity.

In fact, the power of the Chinese Emperor consists in just this, and therefore the relationship between the Chinese Emperor and the people is merely one between the strong and the weak, like that between a conqueror and the conquered ...This way of thinking is totally alien to the Japanese national polity because, in Japan, the Imperial Household and the people have from the first been united in one body, as we can see in [the phrase] the 'Emperor and His Subjects Are One' (*kunmin ittai*).

Tsuda believed that if the Kiki myths were seen as historical facts, then the idea that the Tenson nation arrived from overseas would also have to be accepted. Only by viewing them as made-up stories 'can the writings in both the *Kojiki* and the *Nihon shoki* really come alive as narratives'. Furthermore, Tsuda argued, 'if these myths are viewed as records of historical events, it will destroy and kill the contents of the *Kojiki*'. 'I believe that the research of scholars to date has served to kill the classics'. 'What I have done is not to destroy the classics, nor to kill them, but to bring them back to life, or, in a word, to resurrect them'.[16]

It is not known what the judges thought of this defence. However, Watsuji, who appeared in court as a defence witness, understood Tsuda's intentions correctly, and made the following statement in court.[17]

If it is accepted that the Tenson nation came to Japan from overseas, then nothing sacred emerges from that fact. If the ancestors of our Imperial Household are the Tenson nation which came from overseas, then the very fact that they arrived from overseas means that the God Incarnate [the Emperor] is not sacred.

In my opinion, what Mr. Tsuda most wanted to say was that he was concerned that people generally accept such a distorted view [of the Kiki myths].

Although the publication of his research was prohibited, Tsuda was found innocent on almost all charges, perhaps as a result of this defence, and on the one count where he was found guilty, only received a suspended sentence. He appealed against this finding, and submitted a long written statement, but this ended without a clear conclusion. Tsuda criticised the theory of the conquest of an indigenous people in this statement, too, and declared that this theory had been shown to be false by 'the knowledge of today's archaeology, which has recently become clearer'.[18] Watsuji had probably informed him about the existence of Kiyono's theory. In 1944, Watsuji, too, was to be attacked by Minoda and others, and as a result the republication of his *Nippon kodai bunka* (Ancient Japanese Culture) was suspended.

In 1944, Ōkawa Shūmei criticised the position that rejected the Orient, citing Tsuda by name. According to him, Japan had used its unity and capacity for tolerance to integrate the two great cultures of the Orient, those of India and China, and was fighting to liberate the Orient. One of Ōkawa's works, *Nippon nisenroppyakunenshi*, was attacked by Minoda and criticised in the National Diet in 1940, and an expression that referred to the *Ainu* as the archipelago's indigenous people was amended. This amendment, however, came about as a result of over-reaction on Ōkawa's part. The criticism of Minoda and the Diet was directed solely at other aspects of Ōkawa's view of history, and his remark that the *Ainu* were an indigenous people was not censured.[19] If remarks like that were also to become the subject of censure, then too many works would have to be pulped. On the other hand, it is also true that an atmosphere had emerged in which Ōkawa felt he had no choice but to amend his work.

The Tsuda trial was an event in which the theory of the homogeneous nation led to a rejection of the Orient and was shown to be of no help to Japan's external aggression, and so was suppressed. Ōkawa's amendment indicates that an atmosphere had emerged in which the mixed nation theory was also denounced for denying the concept of pure blood. At this stage, the discourse on the Japanese nation within the Great Japanese Empire fell into a complete double-bind. Writers were attacked if they argued that it was pure and homogeneous, and were also attacked if they argued that it was mixed.

The result of this double-bind was a *de facto* state of silence. In the wartime years, although there were a large number of remarks about the nation, the number that addressed the issue of the origins of the Japanese nation in concrete terms, apart from those affiliated with the Government-General of Korea or the Research Centre of the Ministry of Health and Welfare, were a far smaller percentage than when Korea was annexed. As can be seen in the Ministry of

Education publication mentioned above, even when the issue of origin was mentioned, some writers claimed that Japan was not an 'homogeneous nation', while others in the same work rejected the mixed nation theory, and it seems that there was no set policy on the issue. The general trend appears to have been that mixed nation theorists did not mention the place of origin of the Tenson nation and the Imperial Family, while the pure blood theorists did not mention any specific origin, but talked in abstract terms of the Japanese nation being pure. In this way, a compromise emerged in which neither side discussed those areas where conflict could easily arise.

Even so, until about 1942, when the tide of war was favouring Japan, the mixed nation theory appeared to a certain extent in major magazines and books in the form of an argument for the adaptability of the Japanese nation, in that it was able to move into areas that the Imperial Army had occupied or in pursuit of policies of assimilation. The mixed nation theory discussed in the first half of this chapter was a product of this era. However, in about 1944, when the tide of war had obviously turned against Japan, the mixed nation theory almost completely disappeared from the pages of the major magazines. Even Tokutomi Sohō in his work of 1944, *Hisshō kokumin dokuhon* (The National Victory Reader), recognised that Japan was 'fighting against very heavy odds' and called for the unity of the Japanese people. At the same time, he was not only silent about his long-held views on the Japanese nation as an alloy, but in a comment on current events stated that 'America is a complete racial mix' and that racial confrontation would occur within the USA if the war were drawn out, claiming that a war of attrition would favour Japan because Japan enjoyed a superior national unity. Tokutomi thus used the mixed nation theory to argue for overseas expansion and assimilation at a time when the areas under Japanese occupation were expanding, but emphasised homogeneity and advocated union once Japan was driven on to the defensive.[20] Perhaps reflecting this general trend, the sixth edition of the state-compiled geography textbook of 1944 no longer contained a description of the variety to be found in the ethnic composition of the empire.[21]

It is not, however, true to say that the homogeneous nation theory came to the fore during the later years of the war, at least as far as the contents of the major magazines are concerned. This academic theory was not widely known, and, what is more, at a time when the tide of war was running against Japan and it was becoming increasingly a matter of urgency to conscript and mobilise Koreans and Taiwanese, it was not possible to deny concepts such as the theory that the 'Japanese' and Koreans shared a common ancestor, or the slogan of 'Japan and Korea as One'. The theories of the Japanese nation during the later part of the war eventually became only abstract slogans that did not touch upon the issue of origins, and then, due to the shortage of paper, the printed media itself disappeared. For the general populace, the only impression left was probably that the word 'nation' was used profusely. Apart from this, all that remained was a logical impasse and a lack of any medium in which to continue the debate. If nothing else, as far as the theory of the Japanese nation is concerned, the Great Japanese Empire had already collapsed internally before its military defeat.

17 The Myth Takes Root

In August 1945, Japan surrendered unconditionally: about 3 million people or 4 per cent of the population of Japan Proper had died, and large sections of major Japanese cities had been destroyed. Following this defeat, Japan was driven from the areas she had advanced into. The loss of Korea and Taiwan, especially, meant that the numbers of non-Japanese who had constituted one third of the empire's population suddenly plummeted.

As a result of the defeat, Japanese intellectuals could no longer call upon the logic of the past, such as the theory of assimilation or the Family State, and lost the framework with which they could discuss alien ethnic groups within Japan. Most of these intellectuals found it impossible to talk about coexistence with alien peoples except in step with the expansion of empire.

Everything that had previously been thought to be correct was, of necessity, turned upside down, and the logical framework of each and every position had to be re-examined. However, there were almost no attempts to formulate a vision of a new Japan as a multi-national state. The alien ethnic groups within Japan were now tiny minorities, and there were numerous other issues that needed to be addressed. If anything, since alien nations had been incorporated into Japan as a result of imperial expansion, the concept of multi-nationalism itself was rejected by some postwar intellectuals.

Where the Koreans, Taiwanese and others left behind in Japan were concerned, there was a tendency to believe that it would be better to help them return to their newly independent countries as quickly as possible, rather than to formulate a new vision of coexistence within Japan. This tendency, it need hardly be said, did not lend itself to a conception of Japan as a multi-national state. With very few exceptions, the *Ainu* (who had no country of their own) were almost completely overlooked, while occupied Okinawa was separated from the rest of Japan and was not returned until 1972.

It was in this environment that a number of theorists emerged, who argued for a peace-loving homogeneous state to replace the prewar militaristic multi-national empire. The self-image of Japan as an island nation that contained no aliens and was therefore peaceful and tranquil, proved to be very attractive to a people tired of war. In this discourse, the Emperor came to symbolise the unity of this peaceful island nation.

The World of an Agricultural People

Immediately after Japan's defeat, the magazine *Sekai* (World), founded in 1946 in an attempt to revive a social-democratic press, asked Tsuda Sōkichi (see chapter 14) to contribute a paper. Tsuda's article, 'Nihon rekishi no kenkyū ni okeru kagakuteki taido' (The Scientific Attitude in Researching Japanese History), was published in the March edition of 1946. In it, Tsuda was already criticising the theory of the migration of the Tenson nation. He went on to publish an article in the April edition that defended the Emperor – 'Kenkoku no jijō to banse ikkei no shisō' (The Situation at the Time of the Founding of Japan and the Thought of the Unbroken Line of Emperors).[1]

In a departure from normal practice, this second paper was published together with a long letter from the editorial board, which had been surprised by the manuscript and had written to Tsuda asking him to rethink his position. Since Tsuda had made no changes to the general line of his argument, the letter was published by an editorial board which had not expected this sort of pro-Emperor manuscript from a historian who had been oppressed by the empire. At the time, the prewar political regime that had inflicted the horrors of war on Japan and Asia was being subjected to vigorous criticism, one aspect of which was the proposal from the JCP (Japanese Communist Party) and others to abolish the Emperor System. The editorial board had looked to Tsuda to criticise the prewar Imperial View of History (*kōkoku shikan*) which had provided a justification for the Emperor System and propagated the idea that the Kiki myths were historical facts, and thus to criticise the Emperor System itself.

Tsuda's second paper did indeed begin by noting that, following the defeat, the necessity to break free from the Imperial View of History had been recognised. However, he went on to say that he intended to provide a 'personal explanation' of ancient Japanese history – this 'personal explanation' being nothing less than the homogeneous nation view of history and the Symbolic Emperor System.

The arguments developed in the paper were a continuation of Tsuda's prewar thinking, and contain little that is new. According to Tsuda, 'the Japanese state was formed by a single nation that can be called the Japanese nation, and no related nations lived close at hand', and 'since the Japanese nation has lived from a long time ago as a single nation, it was not formed by a mingling of many nations'. This homogeneous nation was a peaceful agricultural people that lived in an isolated island nation, lacked any experience of interacting with alien peoples, and was united in a peaceful manner under the Emperor through the ties of compassion natural to an homogeneous nation. Finally, the fellow-feeling natural to an homogeneous nation, the absence of wars with alien nations, and a government system where the Emperor did not directly rule but reigned by means of cultural and religious authority rather than military force, meant that the idea of an unbroken line of Emperors, and the idea that the people and the Emperor would be as one for as long as the world existed, emerged naturally.

What was new in Tsuda's argument was his heart-searching reflections on the war, and his response to the emerging concept of the Emperor's responsibility for it (something that was seen on the left especially in the postwar era). According to Tsuda, following the Meiji Restoration, the clan-dominated (*hanbatsu*) government accepted an ideology from China and Europe that was 'based on the philosophy that the monarch and the people are opposed to one another, and that believed that the way to consolidate the status of the Imperial Household was to strengthen the power of the Emperor over the people, and to limit the political influence of the people as far as possible'. In this way, the Meiji government established a bureaucratic system and a military organisation based on Prussian models, and 'rather than harbouring feelings of affection for the Imperial Household, the people were compelled to obey its power and majesty'. As a result, even though the proper form of imperial government was for the Emperor to reign without ruling, the army and bureaucrats, in the name of rule by the Emperor, turned the Emperor System into a despotic monarchy, and misappropriated his name to prosecute the war.

Tsuda's conclusion was that 'the *raison d'etre* of the Imperial Household was to be the centre of national unity and the living symbol of the national spirit' in the homogeneous nation-state that was Japan, that if democracy was a system where the people became the masters of the state, then it was only natural that 'our Emperor' – the symbol of the Japanese nation (which was equivalent to the Japanese people and Japanese nationals) – should also become the symbol of the state, and finally that 'the people love the Imperial Household, and it is in this love that a thoroughgoing democracy can be seen'.

The Symbol of National Unity

In March 1946, at almost the same time that Tsuda's article was published, the Japanese government unveiled a draft for a new Constitution that was based on an earlier version drawn up by the GHQ (General Headquarters of the Supreme Commander for the Allied Powers) of the occupation authorities. This new Constitution extolled the ideals of democratisation, the abolition of the military, and a shift of sovereignty from the Emperor to the 'people' (a word translated in the Constitution as *kokumin* to exclude foreigners). Article 1 of the new Constitution stripped the Emperor of all real political power and defined him as the symbol of national unity. Although the JCP, among others, driven by their belief in the Emperor's responsibility for the war, argued that the Emperor System should be abolished, the majority of the Diet voted in favour of this Constitution, which was promulgated in November 1946. Unlike the Emperor of the Great Japanese Empire, this new Constitution defined the Emperor as a symbol, and the postwar system is therefore known as the Symbolic Emperor System.

The other intellectual active in defending the Symbolic Emperor System with Tsuda was Watsuji Tetsurō (see chapter 15). In 1948, Watsuji published a book, *Kokumin tōgō no shōchō* (The Symbol of National Unity), which was based on a number of papers he had written immediately after the defeat.[2] Here, he introduced a criticism of a short piece that he had written in late 1945 in which he had defended the Emperor System and stated that if the Emperor manifested the general will of the people, then 'the fact that sovereignty resides with the people and the fact that the Emperor is the sovereign become one and the same thing'. Under the heading 'A Grave Distortion of Japanese History; A Rehashing of a Fanatical Theory; The Emperor System and Watsuji Philosophy', a regional newspaper had criticised his argument, saying that 'the imperial clan conquered many native nations, and the Emperor is not the ancestor of the majority of the Japanese people'. In response, Watsuji said that the criticism 'is too puerile, and it is disrespectful to Dr. Tsuda Sōkichi, who even fought in court for the freedom to criticise the original Kiki texts'. He dismissed the article, stating that 'the idea that the Tenson nation was a conquering one is a relic from the mid-Meiji Period, and is only a hypothesis of no academic value derived from a belief that the myths are historical facts' (Watsuji 1989–92: vol. 14, 329, 332–3).

Watsuji's arguments in this book were also basically further developments of his prewar position. According to Watsuji, 'nations (*kokumin*) are cultural communities which share the same language, customs, history and beliefs', and in ancient Japan, 'the general will of the people' was expressed in the person of the Emperor through gatherings of the people (festivals), a method completely different to merely piling up individual wills together through a people's conference (Watsuji 1989–92: vol. 14, 337–8). Furthermore, the unification accomplished through the Emperor was due not to military might but religious authority, and the descriptions in the Kiki myths that seemed to depict a conquering state were merely the result of the influence of Chinese culture (Watsuji 1989–92: vol. 14, 343). Finally, Watsuji emphasised the fact that although the Emperor had from time immemorial reigned but not ruled, and in principle had no real political power, the people still thought of the Emperor as the symbol of their totality.

As with Tsuda, what was newly added to Watsuji's arguments was a criticism of the military and a response to the discussion of responsibility for the war. Watsuji started by criticising the wartime debate on loyalty to the Emperor. According to him, the Confucian concept of loyalty was originally merely the morality of the individual relationship of allegiance between feudal lords and their retainers, and had no relation to the general will of the people. 'Feudalistic lords oppressed and ruled the people through brute force, and had absolutely nothing which could act as a symbol of the people's unity'. Compared to this, in Japan from time immemorial, 'the words people used to express "sincerity" to the Emperor were pure-heartedness, straight-forwardness and devotion, and not fidelity or loyalty'. In his notes for the outline of 'Kokumin dōtokuron' (On the Morals of the Japanese Nation) written in about 1930, Watsuji had already drawn a line between these feelings for the Emperor and the feudalistic ideology of loyalty to the ruler, calling the former 'reverence for the Emperor', and further developed the idea in *Sonnō shisō to sono dentō* (The Philosophy and Tradition of 'Respect the Emperor') published in 1943. Watsuji argued that the prewar ideology of loyalty to the ruler was in fact 'an enforced linking of the Confucianist lord-vassal relationship of order and obedience with the "symbol of the unity of the Japanese people", the Emperor, and a substitution of the feudalistic ideology of loyalty to one's lord with reverence for the Emperor, which is a self-awareness of national unity' (Watsuji 1989–92: 322, 367–8).

At this time, Japan's imperialism and the Emperor System were often understood to be a product of feudalism, and the slogan 'anti-feudalism' was frequently used. Watsuji probably agreed with this slogan. After all, from his point of view, feudalism was a product of Chinese thought, and it was only after feudalism was dismantled that the essence of the Emperor as a symbol of the Japanese people's unity could be restored. Simultaneously to advocate anti-feudalism and the overthrow of the Emperor system almost certainly seemed to Watsuji to be a repetition of the mistakes of the prewar ultra-nationalists, who did not distinguish between the Confucian ethic of loyalty and Japanese feelings for the Emperor.

The state had backed Shintō from the Meiji Period, using the education system, for instance, to propagate the Kiki myths. State support became particularly notable during the 15 Year War when visiting shrines to pray for victory was effectively enforced on the populace. To visit Shintō shrines was also to express loyalty to the Emperor, who was (believed to be) the direct descendant of the most important Shintō deity, Amaterasu. As part of the Japanisation polity, large shrines were erected in Korea and Taiwan, and Koreans and Taiwanese were forced to pray there. Shrines were also established in other occupied areas, such as in China and Singapore. This situation came to be called 'State Shintōism' in the postwar era and has remained the object of criticism ever since. However, Watsuji also stated that there was no relationship between State Shintōism and overseas aggression, on the one hand, and the Emperor on the other.

The notion that Japan was a country whose national religion was Shintō – a religion centred around the Emperor – and that this needed to be propagated overseas was also seen in the Edo Period nativist (*kokugaku*) scholars. However, according to Watsuji, Shintō doctrine had actually been formulated a long time after the first reign of an Emperor, and the consolidation of Shintō doctrine

– originally a religion similar to a natural animism – into a state religion was due to an attempt to compete with Buddhism and with the influence of Confucianism. Although nativist thinkers such as Motoori Norinaga and Hirata Atsutane had advocated the rejection of Chinese thought, their belief that Japan as a state lay at the centre of the world was in fact a reflection of this thought. The views of Motoori and Hirata were similar to those of Tsuda. Therefore, the attempt to apply Shintōism to the world was a grave mistake and a deviation from the original essence of Japan and the Emperor. As a result, the mistaken 'impression' that 'imperial aggression was of necessity linked to the tradition of rule by the Emperor' was given (Watsuji 1989–92: vol. 14, 325–8).

Furthermore, Watsuji argued that elections were inappropriate as a reflection of the Japanese totality, because Japan had a history where elected politicians repeatedly abused their offices and eventually succumbed to the military. The only alternatives were either a directly elected President or the Emperor. The former, if applied to Japan, he claimed, would produce the same result as the dictatorships of South America. Needless to say, to manifest the totality of the Japanese people in the person of the Emperor was completely different to direct rule by the Emperor as an individual dictator. Thus Watsuji welcomed the fact that the new Constitution had stipulated that the Emperor was 'the symbol of national unity', and argued that it was desirable that 'each individual Japanese national participate to a far greater extent in the determination of the general will [as manifested in the person of the Emperor]', or in other words that it was desirable that the Emperor as a symbol and democracy be welded together (Watsuji 1989–92: vol. 14, 340, 350, 353).

Recent research has noted that the decision to define the Emperor as a symbol in the draft of the new Constitution was not necessarily forced on Japan by the USA, but that it was advocated by a movement within Japan, and that it is possible that this not only influenced GHQ policy but also helps to explain the Japanese acceptance of the idea of the Emperor as a symbol. Watsuji's arguments influenced the concept of a Cultural State that the then Minister of Education, Amano Teiyū, developed in his 'Kokumin jissen yōryō' (A Practical Outline for the People of Japan) in 1951. They also influenced the famous novelist, Mishima Yukio (1925–1970), and Nakasone Yasuhiro (1918–), a politician who was to become Prime Minister (these two will be discussed below). In

1945 and 1946, the draft proposals for a new constitution as developed by the Constitutional Research Association, the JSP (Japan Socialist Party) and the Constitution Round Table, all advocated the separation of the Emperor and politics, using phrases such as 'national community' (JSP) and 'joint rule by the sovereign and people' (Constitution Round Table). The arguments of Tsuda and Watsuji were thus developed in an environment where a widespread discourse and common ground existed. Leaving aside the issue of the degree to which the arguments of Tsuda and Watsuji influenced the political process and popular opinion, there is no doubt that they embodied in summary form the postwar logic of the Symbolic Emperor System.

In a sense, it can also be said that the prewar Japan, a multinational empire, had the ultimate means – military force – to deal with any alien cultures and alien peoples within Japan which rejected assimilation. Postwar Japan lost this means. However, while military force can easily overcome ethnic barriers, cultural authority cannot. Therefore, in order to depict reverance for the Emperor as founded on culture rather than military power, as Tsuda and Watsuji did, the existence of alien peoples within Japan had to be denied. Their thinking emerged against a background in which they either resisted or ended up resisting the prewar discourse that attempted to make the Emperor a powerful sovereign ruling over a multitude of alien nations. On the other hand, while their thinking contained elements that acted as a brake on the assimilationist policies and the expansion of the empire, it could not recognise the existence of alien peoples within Japan.

The Theory of Akashi Man

In 1948, when Tsuda and Watsuji were arguing for the Symbolic Emperor System, Hasebe Kotondo (see chapter 13), a professor of Tokyo University and the supreme Japanese authority in anthropology, published a paper on 'Akashi Man' (*Akashi genjin* or *Nipponanthropus Akashiensis*), which argued that Palaeolithic man had existed in the archipelago. This came at a time when Japan had been liberated from the prewar national polity discourse on the nation, and there was a strong demand for a new position on the origin of the Japanese nation.

The human bones Hasebe used as the basis for his stance had been unearthed in 1931 by another scholar, Naora Shinobu, who announced them to be those of Palaeolithic man. At that time, however, the dominant belief was that there had not been a Palaeolithic era in the archipelago. Since the circumstances behind the excavation were uncertain, and no other human bones were excavated from the same layer, Naora's position was quickly dismissed. The original bones were destroyed in the air raids of 1945, but a plaster cast remained unnoticed in a classroom corner in Tokyo University, to be rediscovered almost 20 years later by Hasebe. Hasebe's argument about the origin of the Japanese nation, including this theory of Akashi Man, was summarised in an article, 'Nihon minzoku no seiritsu' (The Birth of the Japanese Nation), published in 1949.[3]

In the article, Hasebe also restated his wartime position, denying 'the idea that the Japanese are a mixed or a mixed-blooded nation', and arguing that the *Ainu* were not the indigenous people of the archipelago. Instead, he urged 'the theory that the Japanese are the original inhabitants of Japan'. According to Hasebe, the mixed nation theory was a mere result of 'an uncritical acceptance of the ideas of foreigners' in the Meiji era. He emphasised the necessity for a theory of the origin of the Japanese nation based on the natural sciences, and criticised the interpretation of the Kiki myths that assumed the *Ainu* were the Emishi.

According to Hasebe, Akashi Man (*Nipponanthropus Akashiensis*) existed in the archipelago of the diluvian epoch, after which a Stone Age people migrated to Japan from south China, which was then connected to Japan by land. The physical differences between this Stone Age people and modern Japanese resulted from evolution, not a mixture of blood. Even if there were some physical variety among modern 'Japanese', this emerged only from the process of evolution as physical differences which had already existed among the people of the Stone Age were accentuated.

In addition to the denial of mixed blood, Hasebe's argument had two major characteristics. One is that he completely denied any relationship with Korea, and instead argued that the Japanese nation directly descended from China, the centre of Asian culture. According to Hasebe, it was clear that 'those who resemble either the *Ainu* or Koreans cannot easily be found among the people of the Japanese nation', and the people of the Kinki region who had been thought close to the Koreans were in fact closer to the people of south China. He criticised the 'theory that the Japanese and Koreans shared a common ancestor' (*Nikkan dōsoron*) and the 'overestimation' of the number of migrants, and stated that 'it was highly unlikely that the Japanese would have readily accepted migrants...from Manchuria and Korea, poor areas on the periphery of Asia, as compared with China, the centre of Asian culture'. He also stated that the language and culture of the people of ancient Japan was 'exactly as it was handed down from our remote ancestors in south China', and that it was impossible to think that Korea was the route by which culture was imported into Japan.

This first characteristic contrasts with Tsuda's dislike of China, but the second characteristic has a great deal in common with both Tsuda and Watsuji. Hasebe depicted the archipelago as an isolated and peaceful utopia which was blessed by nature.

First of all, Hasebe criticised the idea that the Jōmon people were a conquered indigenous people, the *Ainu*, in the following terms:

> No matter how superior the culture of the conquering nation may have been, it would have been impossible for this nation to come to Japan and immediately overpower the flourishing people of the late Jōmon period, and wrest power away from them. During several overseas military expeditions, the Imperial Japanese Army learnt not to underestimate guerrilla warfare, and experienced difficulties in gaining supplies of clothing and food when a long way away from their home soil. This was as true in the past as it is today.

Mixed nation theorists had once argued that invasion and assimilation in the present would be easy because of the history of the Tenson in successfully pursuing invasion and assimilation in the past. Hasebe, however, claimed that a past migration of a conquering nation to Japan would have been impossible, giving as an example the troubles experienced by the Japanese military with guerrilla warfare and the defeat in the Asian continent and in the south during the Second World War.

According to Hasebe, shortly after a Stone Age people arrived from southern China, which was then connected to the archipelago by land, 'this land bridge sank beneath the ocean, interaction with the continent was cut off, and Japan was isolated. The descendants of this people multiplied in the peaceful utopia, Japan, which was blessed with the products of the mountains and seas. This situation lasted until the present, and produced the Japanese'. It can be easily imagined that such a theory appealed to his contemporaries who were returning home from remote foreign countries, tired of war and craving for peace.

On the other hand, following the collapse of the Taiheiyō Kyōkai with the end of war, Kiyono Kenji (see chapter 13) was appointed in 1948 to head the Health and Welfare Research Centre, and wrote a large number of books for both academic and general readers on the origin of the Japanese nation. He, too, criticised the discourse on the origin of the nation as full of 'conjecture and bunkum' and emphasised the scientific nature of his own theory. His argument was the same as during the war: 'since this land was first inhabited, the Japanese race has lived and developed here, and the homeland of the Japanese race is Japan'; 'the Imperial Household has been the Japanese Imperial Household since the Age of the Gods'; and 'the rapid cultural progress of the Japanese nation has always been centred around the Imperial Household'.[4]

On the other hand, Naora Shinobu, who had excavated the human bones Hasebe used as the basis for his argument on Akashi Man, succeeded after the war in excavating more Palaeolithic human bones. This added immensely to the credibility of Hasebe's theory. Since then, the theories of Kiyono and Hasebe have become the two major established anthropological theories on the origin of the Japanese nation. Ironically, the first to accept their theories were the progressive historians who had already started to adopt them before the end of the war (at the time, 'progressive' was synonymous with Marxist in the world of Japanese historiography).

The Postwar Historiography which Leaned Towards the Theory of an Homogeneous Nation

Although the JCP was not successful in electoral politics in postwar Japan, it was influential among the intelligentsia, especially in the field of history. Many prewar historians had committed themselves to the Imperial View of History and so lost all credibility in the postwar era. The Marxist historians, however, had opposed this position, and as a consequence their reputation in postwar Japan was enhanced.

Marxist historians of the time criticised the prewar Imperial View of History as 'unscientific', defining their own position as 'scientific history' or 'progressive history'. In the Japan immediately following the Second World War, the shock of defeat triggered a backlash against Japanese culture and a rush to Westernisation or modernisation. In this environment, both 'science' and 'progress' were popularly acclaimed.

In 1946, before Hasebe announced his theory of the Akashi Man, the first issue of *Nihon rekishi*, the journal of the Japanese Historical Society which aimed to rebuild Japanese historiography from the ashes of defeat, published a number of articles on ancient history aimed at destroying the Imperial View of History. In this issue, Nezu Masashi (see chapter 13) and Koshiro Shūichi introduced Kiyono's theory as the most up-to-date and scientific one.[5]

According to Koshiro's article, 'it has been a widely accepted idea that the Japanese nation is not an homogeneous nation in a simple sense, but emerged from a mixture of racial elements with different origins', but 'these theories...were mostly limited to mere conjecture'. He claimed that Kiyono's theory was based on a scientific analysis, and proved both that 'the homeland of the Japanese has been Japan since mankind first began to reside on the Japanese islands...it is not the case that the motherland of the *Ainu* was invaded and occupied', and that 'the influence of the mixture of blood was not powerful enough to change the physical constitution of Stone Age man'. Moreover, according to Koshiro, this theory was 'winning broader direct and indirect support'.

Even if Kiyono's conclusions derived from the measurement of excavated bones are accepted, as has already been seen in chapter 13, all that follows from his conclusions is that the people of the Stone Age were unlike both the modern Japanese nation and the modern *Ainu*. Kiyono argued from his results that the people of the Stone Age became the Japanese nation and the *Ainu* by the process of mixing blood with the northern and southern races and through evolution. However, as we see in the criticism of Ueda Jōkichi, who advanced the theory that the 'Japanese' and Koreans shared a common ancestor, the people of the Stone Age might have changed into the *Ainu*, and another conquering nation might have migrated separately to the ancient archipelago. Or, as Hasebe argued, the people of the Stone Age might have evolved directly into the Japanese nation. Nobody could prove which of these positions was correct. Moreover, from the war years Kiyono had manipulated his language to underestimate the mixture of blood. Koshiro's introduction of Kiyono's theory, which argued that mixed blood did not essentially transform the people of the Stone Age, was a result of his being led astray by Kiyono's expressions.

On the other hand, Nezu introduced Kiyono's theory as an argument that the people of the Stone Age had evolved into the *Ainu* and the Japanese nation through the mixture of blood. Nezu's position towards the Emperor was a long way from the homage shown by Tsuda and Kiyono: 'the Emperor is not a god, but a powerful landlord, militarist, and invader'. At the same time, however, he also denied the existence of an indigenous people, stating that the 'Emperor State' sprang from 'a conquest of the one nation'. Moreover, he argued that the history of the Imperial Family was, at about 1,600 years, much shorter than 2,600 years, while the Japanese nation had lived in the archipelago for 4,000 years and had created a 'primitive communistic society' before the appearance of the Emperor.

The historical view that the Japanese nation had existed on the archipelago before the arrival of the Imperial Family also appeared in an article by Inoue Kiyoshi published in the same year.[6] According to Inoue, 'it has been argued that Takamagahara is the mythologised homeland of the Japanese nation, and that the descent of the Tenson is a story about a national migration. However, since the research of Tsuda, every conscientious scholar has agreed that these interpretations are all far-fetched distortions'. He stated that 'long before the emergence of the Emperor, that is, at least from 4,000 or 5,000 years ago, the Japanese enjoyed a peaceful, liberal and completely democratic society on these islands'.

In the past mixed nation theory, the Japanese nation and the Emperor were seen as inseparable. It was beyond imagination that a group within the Japanese nation could rebel against the Imperial Family. It was therefore argued that the Japanese nation migrated from Takamagahara together with the Imperial Family 2,600 years previously (the descent of the Tenson), and those who rebelled against the Imperial Household were all alien peoples. Tsuda's theory of the homogeneous nation destroyed this belief. He argued that the history of the Japanese nation was older than that of the state, and that the different peoples depicted in the Kiki myths were not alien nations. Nezu's and Inoue's view of the Emperor differed from Tsuda's, but they were quick to agree with him that the Japanese nation had lived in the archipelago long before the Emperor, and had created a peaceful, primitive communistic society.

Although Tsuda was not a Marxist, he was held in the highest esteem by postwar progressive historians because he had described the Kiki myths as fiction and had been silenced by the state. Indeed, in 1946, it was said that 'the way one values the achievements of Professor Tsuda is a barometer of the correctness of one's scholarly spirit'.[7] Bewilderment spread when Tsuda began to write a large number of comments on current affairs that defended the Emperor and denounced communism. Nonetheless, Tsuda's prewar research into the Kiki myths maintained its high reputation.

The same was true of Kiyono. In 1948, a work of his was reviewed in *Rekishi hyōron*, issued by the Society of Democratic Scientists (an organization effectively run by the JCP). This review described the homage of the Emperor by Kiyono, an anthropologist who was supposed to be scientific, as 'very strange' and stated that 'it is most regrettable that an author who has shed a great deal of light on the history of the primitive age from the viewpoint of natural science trots out nothing more than the orthodoxy of conservative reaction when it comes to writing about history. This reminds us of the recent series of articles by Professor Tsuda'. However, Kiyono's academic theory was seen as something separate and remained highly valued.[8]

The Imperial View of History was re-examined on the basis of the theories developed by Tsuda and Kiyono, among others. Jinmu's Eastern Expedition, the conquest of the Kumaso, and the invasion of Korea by the Empress Jingū were no longer regarded as historical facts, and the theory that the 'Japanese' and Koreans shared a common ancestor disappeared from academic circles. The idea that the *Shinsen shōjiroku* could not be used as a historical material became widely accepted by historians. The different peoples depicted in the Kiki myths were explained away as resulting from the fact that 'those who shared blood but not customs were regarded as alien nations'.[9]

Thus an environment emerged in Japanese historiography in which 'if you ask whether or not there existed any indigenous peoples in Japan...the reply would be..."Are you still thinking about that? Almost all academics today agree that there were no such people"' (Gotō Morikazu 1946). Once Hasebe's theory of Akashi Man was added, the victory of this mindset was secured. Ideas such as the following began to spread. 'Our ancestors lived on the Japanese archipelago from the remote past and archaeology is now gradually making it clear that there was no indigenous nation' (Tōma Seita 1951); 'racially, the Japanese are the descendants of the Neolithic Japanese Proper and there has been no remarkable racial change since then. Some people such as Torii Ryūzō still adhere to their position that an indigenous nation existed, but this position is not tenable' (Fujitani Toshio 1952); and 'the Japanese nation was created from an almost completely homogeneous race...This homogeneous Japanese race has lived together in the same place for 2,000 years' (Inoue Kiyoshi 1957).[10]

The mixed nation theory did not immediately disappear completely, but it was now regarded as old-fashioned in the field of historical studies. This trend naturally influenced public discourse, and the voice of those who argued for the prewar mixed nation theory was almost completely drowned out. Although Tokutomi Sohō, the most popular mixed nation theorist, wrote in 1953 that 'our ancestors were not homogeneous but complex', this argument was treated as a remnant of the old school of thought.[11]

The Theory of the Migration of a Horse-Riding People which was not Accepted

In these circumstances, a great stir was created in Japan by the theory of the migration of a horse-riding people, which was published in 1949 in the form of a talk by the historian Egami Namio (1906–) and others. This theory argued that a conquering horse-riding nation had migrated to the ancient Japanese archipelago from Mongolia, and that the Imperial Family descended from this people. In the prewar mixed nation theory, even when the mixture of nations was discussed, the issue of the location of the homeland of the Imperial Family was taboo. The theory of the migration of a horse-riding people was in a sense an extension of the mixed nation theory, but was new in that it brought the migration of the Imperial Family to the fore.

However, this theory failed to establish itself in academic circles, for several reasons. First of all, it was published in the form of a talk, and was not re-written as an academic article until a long time later. Another reason may be that the arguments relied partly on the Kiki myths rather than on the measurement of human bones which was easier to accept as scientific (Tsuda's position that the Kiki myths could not be used as historical material was in fact criticised in this talk). Moreover, Egami was not a scholar in ancient Japanese history, nor a physical anthropologist, nor a Marxist. Finally, Yanagita and Hasebe, the giants of Japanese ethnology and physical anthropology, also criticised this theory.

Furthermore, the theory of the migration of a horse-riding people was too similar to the mixed nation theory that was considered out of date. Egami praised Kita Sadakichi's 'Nissen ryōminzoku dōgenron' (The Common Origin of the Japanese and Korean Nations), stating that 'on the main points, my own ideas coincide with Kita's' and that 'such being the case, my research can be called a modern version of Kita's theory'. Egami may not have been aware of the political context of Kita's 'Nissen ryōminzoku dōgenron', but he was criticised by historians for having supported the theory that the 'Japanese' and Koreans shared a common ancestor.[12]

It was also disadvantageous for the theory of the migration of a horse-riding people that the Marxist theory of stages of endogenous development was popular at the time. The prewar Marxist notion that the indigenous peoples of Japan had been enslaved lost its influence after the prewar conversion (*tenkō*) of Takahashi Sadaki and Sano Manabu in the 1930s (chapter 9). After being oppressed, these two had renounced communism in favour of the Emperor System, and disappeared from view once the argument for the existence of an indigenous nation was rejected by Japanese anthropologists.

As an example of Marxist thinking, Shiga Yoshio, a member of the JCP Central Committee, stated in his 1949 work *Kokkaron* (On the State) that 'the state developed from the emergence of classes from within the primitive communistic society of the clan system. Some people, however, do not recognise that this basic internal element is fundamental, and claim instead that the state was formed through the conquest and rule by one tribe, nation or race of others'. He rejected this as an old-fashioned idea, and at the same time noted that 'we Japanese have lived in this island-country since Neolithic times'. Another progressive historian of ancient Japan, Tōma Seita, stated in 1951 that there were two routes to developing standards of living – the 'development of productivity' and 'exploitation through conquest'. He argued that the ancient 'Japanese chose the former route and rejected the latter'. In discussing the formation of rice cultivation in ancient Japan, Ishimoda Shō (1912–1986), a progressive historian of medieval Japan, emphasised endogenous independence within the archipelago rather than any external influence, and stated that the Japanese language had been unique since the Jōmon era.[13]

The argument that the state was formed through a struggle between nations or through conquest, as well as the idea that the rise and fall of heroes and great warriors moves history, might strike the amateur at first glance as interesting and pleasing, but it tended to be regarded as ignorant of the scientific rules of history – namely, the development of productivity and the class struggle. Together with Hasebe and Yanagita, Tōma was one of the main theorists who opposed the theory of the migration of a horse-riding people. Egami was aware of this, and so wrote that he would follow a 'historicism' that stressed external influences instead of the 'evolutionism' that viewed the endogenous development of the 'homogeneous nation' in the archipelago as the driving force of history.[14] This stance itself demonstrated that the theory of the migration of a horse-riding people was opposed to the Marxist school of history.

It has been briefly noted at times that this trend of Marxist historicism was responsible for a neglect of external forces in Japanese history, such as the migration of a horse-riding people. Much later, in 1975, the Okinawan novelist Shimota Seiji wrote: 'the reason why Marxist historians have not really bothered to take notice of, for example, the fact that Yayoi culture was introduced as a cultural compound along with the importation of rice, or the issue of migrants who contributed to establishing the ancient Japanese state, is mainly because of their dogmatic understanding of the historical stages of endogenous development', an opinion shared by Kim Talsu, a *zainichi* Korean Marxist novelist known for his research into ancient migration. In the same year, Suzuki Takeki, a researcher in German literature, noted that when he supported the theory of the migration of a horse-riding people, a historian affiliated with the JCP replied that 'what matters are the laws of development and the means to overcome the contradictions unique to Japanese society: the origin of the Imperial Family has nothing to do with history'.[15]

This view of history was also seen in textbooks. In the one and only postwar social studies textbook compiled by the state and published in 1948 – all later textbooks were published by private firms and then vetted by the government – the process of the development of productivity from the Stone Age through to the Metal Age and then on to agriculture was explained without any reference either to overseas migration into Japan or to conquest.[16] On the other hand, the conquest of alien peoples as described in the Kiki myths that the prewar government textbooks had mentioned gradually disappeared from postwar history textbooks.

At the time, the phrase 'multi-national state' did not necessarily enjoy the positive image that it does today in Japan. The answer to the issue of ethnicity was not seen to be the coexistence of a number of ethnic groups, but national self-determination. The deep regret felt about the fact that prewar Japanese governments had denied Korean claims to national self-determination strengthened this tendency. The idea of national self-determination easily misled people into believing that a state formed as a result of self-determination would be homogeneous. From this point of view, the multi-national state was viewed as one where the principle of national self-determination had not been fully realised, and where a ruling nation was preventing the ruled nations from achieving independence.

For example, in 1951, the above-mentioned Tōma Seita described ancient Japan's invasion of Korea as 'a transformation of an homogeneous nation-state into a world empire that ruled over many nations'. In other words, the term 'multi-national state' was synonymous with 'world empire'. In 1952, yet another progressive historian, Fujitani Toshio, stated that 'countries that first formed homogeneous nation-states, such as England, France and Italy, became multi-national states or colonial states, by acquiring the territories of other nations, and thus ceased to be nation-states', and that 'the rulers of Japan took possession of Taiwan and Korea, acquired leased territories in China, and formed a multi-national state or colonial state, thus closing the door to becoming a democratic nation-state'.[17] Here, the multi-national state was a synonym of a colonial state, with the opposing concepts being an 'homogeneous nation-state' or a 'state of a single nation'.

As is the case today, the USA was then also frequently cited by Japanese intellectuals as an example of a multi-national state. At that time, however, the USA was not necessarily viewed by progressive Japanese intellectuals in a positive light. It was 'American Imperialism' – a country responsible for the Korean War – that had built military bases all over Japan and discriminated against African-Americans at home. In face of the USA of the 1950s with its rampant racial discrimination, it was only natural that hardly anyone in Japan saw a multi-national state as an ideal. It was only after the 1970s, when minorities within the USA gained a certain degree of equality through the civil rights movement, that the phrase 'multi-national state' began to acquire a positive value in Japan, and that the USA began to be thought of in positive terms as a model.

Needless to say, progressive historians propagated neither the theory of the homogeneous nation nor the Symbolic Emperor

System. They were opposed to the reactionary moves of the Japanese government and to any defence of the Emperor, including that of Tsuda. At that time, however, Japan was not the world power it is today, and the most urgent issues were to rebuild the economy and overcome the problem of feeding the people. No one imagined that foreign workers would migrate to such a country. It was often thought that the ideal solution to the issue of the *zainichi* Koreans would be to apologise for past wrongs and encourage them to return home. Dealing with the issue of ethnicity was believed to be far less important than taking steps to prevent Japan from re-arming and once again becoming a multi-national empire. In these circumstances, to advocate the homogeneous nation theory was not thought to be wrong.[18]

The Forgotten Mixed Nation Theory

After the rise in anthropology and historiography of the homogeneous nation theory and the collapse of the prewar mixed nation theory, there was nothing left to prevent the myth of ethnic homogeneity from taking root. Japan came to be viewed as an isolated, remote and peaceful island nation, in which an homogeneous nation had lived from time immemorial, while the 'Japanese' were viewed as children of nature, an agricultural people with no experience of interacting with alien nations and lacking in skills of both war and diplomacy. Leaving aside the issue of whether the 'Japanese' were led from the beginning by the Emperor-as-symbol, or whether Japan formed a democratic primitive communist society, this self-portrait fitted the mood of a postwar Japan which had lost all confidence in international relations.

Immediately after the war, it was argued that the ideal Japan should aim for was to become the 'Switzerland of the East'. Switzerland was imagined to be an agricultural country located in a remote region, isolated by mountains from the struggles of the outside world, and which remained at peace by means of an eternal neutrality. The other aspect of Switzerland as a multi-national state with a plurality of official languages was overlooked.

In this environment, the phrase 'an homogeneous nation' which had formerly been used in a negative sense began to take on a positive meaning. To the best of my knowledge, it was in the 1960s, when Japanese economic growth took off, that the phrase began to appear frequently in the press.

There were, roughly speaking, two ways by which the myth of an homogeneous nation was established. One was through a conservative discourse that argued for the unity of the nation with the state and the Emperor. For example, according to an article on Japan published in 1961 by Koizumi Shinzō (1888–1966), an economist who was close to the Imperial Family, the archipelago had been inhabited by the 'Japanese' since time immemorial and, unlike Europe, India, Russia or China, all of which consisted of 'incalculable' nations and languages, 'the Japanese people is fortunately homogeneous and this has been a great strength'.[19]

In 1968, the novelist and later politician Ishihara Shintarō (1932–) stressed that 'almost no other example can be found of a people which is almost completely an homogeneous nation that speaks an homogeneous language which is totally different from the languages of other states, and which has formed a totally unique culture over such a long period of time'.[20]

Mishima Yukio's 'Bunka bōeiron' (Defending Culture) published in 1968 is a typical example of a conservative homogeneous nation theory. Citing Tsuda's and Watsuji's theories of a cultural community and the Symbolic Emperor System, he argued that 'Japan is an homogeneous nation with an homogeneous language, something rarely found in the world. Our nation has language and cultural traditions in common, and has maintained a political unity since time immemorial. The continuity of our culture is chiefly due to the fact that the nation is identical with the state'. According to Mishima, 'the Japan which was pushed back within her present territory through the defeat [in 1945] is almost completely free of the domestic issue of alien peoples', and 'the issue of the *zainichi* Koreans may be an international problem or a refugee problem, but is not a domestic Japanese one'. He advocated 'restoring the Emperor as a cultural idea' that 'represented the cultural totality' by encouraging 'Japan to awaken to her original self, in which the purpose of the nation and the purpose of the state were enveloped by a cultural concept centred on the Emperor and were as one'.[21]

On the other hand, the homogeneous nation theory was also used by critics of Japan. According to them, the problematic aspects of Japan, especially the lack of an international sense, originated because Japan was a unique homogeneous nation-state.

One representative example is the best-selling *Tate shakai no ningen kankei* (Human Relations in a Vertical Society, translated as *Japanese Society*) by the anthropologist Nakane Chie published in 1967. According to this work, the 'Japanese' were homogeneous and refused to mix with other nations. The 'Japanese' have 'a rustic tendency in every field' and 'show an excessive lack of any international sense'. Nakane argued that 'going as far back as the present academic standards allow us, the Japanese archipelago was occupied by an overwhelming majority of an homogeneous nation, and it is clear that they shared a basic culture'. She developed her theory of the vertical society as the essence of the Japanese social group that was unique to Japan because of a degree of homogeneity rarely seen elsewhere in the world. She called this theory 'the logic of an homogeneous society'.[22]

Junsui bunka no jōken (The Conditions of Pure Culture) by Masuda Yoshio, a researcher into South American history – his field was the impact of European imperialism on the indigenous peoples of South America – was also published in 1967 and included similar critical elements. According to this book, Japan was formed under 'the extremely unusual conditions of pure cultivation where a nation since prehistoric times has remained homogeneous and has maintained an homogeneous culture'. This is why the 'Japanese are good-natured, headstrong, naive and idealistic'. 'European culture is a slick hybrid culture which was born from the mixture of numerous bloods and cultures. On the other hand, Japanese culture is the purest of pure cultures, that of a pure blood nation which has calmly defended an homogeneous culture without any friction or conflict with other nations'. Moreover, 'the Japanese are not skilled at dealing with alien nations', and he criticised both Hideyoshi's invasion of Korea in the sixteenth century and the Pacific War. He attributed the cause of these conflicts to lack of experience in interacting with alien nations, stating that 'the Japanese are not slick like the West Europeans or the Russians because the Japanese have never experienced hard times'.[23]

The conservative and the critical homogeneous nation theories were sometimes used and blended together to suit the interests of individual theorists. An example of this can be seen in an article written by Maeda Hajime, managing director of the Japan Association of Employers Federation, in 1964. While stressing that 'the Japanese nation is not a group of alien nations and is not the product of mixed blood, and the unity of this nation forms the basis for the belief in the centrality of the Emperor', Maeda stated that the Japanese economy was a 'flower that bloomed in a greenhouse' and was ignorant of the hardships of the outside world. Moreover, the 'Japanese' are blessed with an obedience produced by a harsh climate, a sensibility created by the changes in the four seasons, a diligence produced by the natural products of the oceans and mountains, and an exclusive complacency that was a consequence of the fact that Japan was an island-country. His conclusion was that the 'Japanese' should utilise the virtues of diligence and obedience to increase productivity, and maintain pressure on wages in order 'to make the Japanese nation reflect on its conceits, and modestly nourish its abilities'.[24]

Although 'the change from an insular closed economy to a global open economy' was seen as a crisis in Maeda's article, from the second half of the 1960s, the international status of the Japanese economy was gradually enhanced. By this time, the older generation of Japanese culture theorists, including Tsuda, Watsuji and Yanagita, had passed away one after the other.

In the 1970s, trade friction and the high yen (*endaka*) forced the 'Japanese' to recognise Japan's position in the international economy. As Japan's status in international society rose, a self-consciousness about how the 'Japanese' were viewed overseas increased, and there was an unprecedented boom in theories about the Japanese (*Nihonjinron*).[25] Many examples of such theories – including the best selling works *Nihonjin to Yudayajin* (The Japanese and the Jews) by Yamamoto Shichihei (under the pen-name of Isaiah BenDasan) published in 1970, and *Amae no kōzō* (Anatomy of Dependence) by Doi Takeo published in 1971 – stressed that the 'Japanese' did not understand the harsh realities of international society, thought that water and security were free because they lived in an island-country blessed by nature, and were spoilt within an homogeneous nation. According to these authors, international society was a world ruled by the law of the survival of the fittest, with the Americans and the Jews often described as the opposites of the 'Japanese'. Much of the *Nihonjinron* discourse stressed in concert the extent to which the 'Japanese' were unique and had been homogeneous since time immemorial, whether this was intended to praise 'Japanese' diligence, unity, naturalness and artlessness, or to criticise the lack of a public spirit and the Japanese closed mind.

Kamishima Jirō, a political scientist, made the following observation in a lecture published in 1982:[26]

> In prewar Japan, everyone said that the Yamato nation was a mongrel (*zasshu*) nation, a mixed nation. People argued in this way even while they were advocating Japanism. However, after the war, something very strange happened. People, including the progressive intelligentsia, began to insist that the Japanese are an homogeneous nation. There is absolutely no foundation for the claim, but this baseless theory is rampant.

These were words that expressed the experience of a man who had lived in both the prewar and postwar eras. However, Kamishima's point was almost completely ignored, even in the criticisms of the homogeneous nation myth of the latter half of 1970s, let alone by the homogeneous nation theorists.

Conclusion

This book has attempted to shed light on the transitions in the discourse on the Japanese nation from the era of the Great Japanese Empire through to the postwar years. A sociological analysis will allow us to pigeonhole the prewar mixed nation theory and the postwar homogeneous nation theory. The argument developed by mixed nation theorists can be summarised as follows.

1. The empire has gained Korea and Taiwan, and the original inhabitants of these regions have come to be accepted as imperial subjects. The idea that the 'Japanese' should be limited only to pure blood members of the Japanese nation is an impediment both to imperial expansion and to the incorporation of other peoples into the empire. It therefore should be rejected.
2. In time immemorial, Japan successfully assimilated a large number of alien peoples and immigrants. The blood of immigrants flows even in the veins of the Imperial Family. Therefore, the Japanese nation excels at ruling and assimilating alien peoples, and this experience should be used to carry out Japanese policies of expansion and assimilation.
3. The Japanese nation is a mixture of the various peoples of North and South Asia, and the peoples of these areas are blood relations of the Japanese. It should therefore be easy to assimilate them. Moreover, the Japanese advance into Asia is a return to the Japanese homeland, and the Japanese have physical constitutions that will enable them to adapt to life in both the north and the south.
4. From ancient times, Japan has mixed with and assimilated various peoples under the policy of universal brotherhood. Therefore, the concept of racial discrimination is totally alien to the Japanese nation. On this issue, Japan is ethically superior to the West.
5. The annexation of alien peoples does not conflict with the fact that Japan is a Family State, so long as these peoples are treated as foster-children.

6 In time immemorial, the Imperial Family crossed to the Japanese archipelago from the Korean peninsula. Since the Emperor was the King of that land, it is natural that it should once again be reclaimed as the territory of the Imperial Family.

Of the above arguments, the sixth was taboo, but the others were all widely disseminated.

On the other hand, the myth of ethnic homogeneity became generally accepted after the Second World War when the numbers of non-Japanese in Japan suddenly plummeted. The arguments of this myth can be summarised as follows.

1 From ancient times, Japan has been occupied by a single homogeneous nation, and was a peaceful, agricultural state with no experience of conflict with alien nations.
2 The Imperial Family were not conquerors who came from overseas. Rather, it symbolised the unity of the cultural community of this peaceful nation.
3 From time immemorial, the Japanese nation has lived on a remote island-country and has had little contact with alien peoples. As a result, the Japanese lack ability both as diplomats and as warriors.
4 Because Japan is an homogeneous nation-state, historically it has been peaceful, and remains so today.

The line of this argument contrasts with the views of the Emperor and Japanese nation expressed in the prewar mixed nation theory which argued that the Emperor was 'a powerful monarch who conquered the aboriginal inhabitants of the ancient Japanese archipelago, and today rules over a multi-national empire', and that the Japanese were 'a people who, from time immemorial, have had a rich experience of ruling and assimilating many alien peoples'. Needless to say, the myth of ethnic homogeneity dovetailed with the postwar Symbolic Emperor System, the loss of confidence in international relations produced by the defeat in 1945, and the psychology of the isolationist 'one-state pacifism' where the Japanese, tired of war, came to say that they did not want to become involved in any international disputes. (One-state pacifism involved a rejection of any troublesome event outside Japan in an attempt to maintain domestic peace and stability.)

In summary, the transitions in the discourse on the 'Japanese' constituted a movement to use the theory of ethnic homogeneity for protection when Japan was weak, and to use the mixed nation theory to interact with the outside world when she was strong. How are these two theories to be situated sociologically?

On the Concept of 'Japanese'

As mentioned in the introduction, Fukuoka Yasunori uses a typology framework to analyse the concept of the 'Japanese'.

Types	1	2	3	4	5	6	7	8
Lineage	+	+	+	−	+	−	−	−
Culture	+	+	−	+	−	+	−	−
Nationality	+	−	+	+	−	−	+	−

From Fukuoka (1993: 5; 2000: xxx)

This framework uses 3 categories, lineage (Fukuoka emphasises that lineage is a concept and not a reality), culture, and nationality, and gives a plus (+) sign for 'Japanese' and a minus (−) sign for non-Japanese. So, according to Fukuoka, Type 1 is a 'pure Japanese' who is 'Japanese' in lineage, culture, and nationality, while Type 8 is the opposite, a 'pure non-Japanese'. Type 2 covers first-generation Nikkei (Japanese emigrants) who have 'Japanese' lineage and culture but not nationality (the so-called issei). Type 3 covers those 'Japanese' educated overseas, such as the returnee children (*kikoku shijo*); Type 4 are those who have become 'Japanese' by naturalisation; Type 5 are third-generation Nikkei and the Chinese war orphans; Type 6 are young *zainichi* Koreans not educated in Korean schools in Japan; and Type 7 are the *Ainu*.

According to Fukuoka, the concept of a 'Japanese' in Japan generally tends to be limited to Type 1 and, of the three elements, lineage, culture, and nationality, '"lineage" is clearly the dominant one'.[1] If the concept of 'Japanese' was broadened to include other elements besides 'lineage', the idea that those with different 'lineage' should also enjoy rights would spread. However, this is prevented by the narrowness of the concept. If this understanding is correct, then the main culprit behind the oppression of minorities in Japan is the myth of the homogeneous nation, which claims that the 'Japanese' are constituted from a Japanese nation that has a single and pure origin, and the way to end this oppression is to destroy the idea that the nation shares pure blood. It is for this reason that Fukuoka writes that the Japanese nation is a mixture of various Asian peoples, and mentions the migrants who came to Japan as noted in the *Shinsen shōjiroku*.

However, as has been argued in this book, the mixed nation theory dominated the prewar discourse and justified assimilationist policies. Was the prewar mixed nation theory, then, better than the myth of the homogeneous nation which used lineage to limit the concept of the 'Japanese'?

I believe not. Although the mixed nation theory differed in *form* to the postwar myth of the homogeneous nation, in some aspects at least it was similar in *function*. The Great Japanese Empire was in reality a multi-national empire, and this reality did not allow the myth of ethnic homogeneity to form. In this situation, there were only three options.

The first was to abandon all regions inhabited by alien peoples and to recreate the reality of Japan into (what could be thought of as) an homogeneous nation state. Postwar Japan followed this path, although not of her own volition. However, giving up territory was not seen as an option in prewar Japan.

The second option was to treat the alien peoples within the empire as being a different entity to the Japanese nation, and to refuse to accept them as 'Japanese'. This would make it possible to adhere to the belief that the Japanese nation was pure blooded, but the price would be to neglect the Emperor's non-Japanese subjects and allow them to remain alien nations. If, as was the case in postwar Japan, the numbers of non-Japanese were small, it might have been possible to ignore and neglect them. However, in the Great Japanese Empire, where one-third of the total population consisted of non-Japanese subjects, people were forced to recognise the existence of an Other that was clearly different.

Once the existence of a different Other is recognised – and only then – two new options open. One is to discriminate against and exclude the Other. The second is to pursue a universal value that is larger than the differences between the self and the Other. Leaving aside the question of whether there is a problem with this universal value, ideals such as universal equality and rights that are larger than the confines of nationality only emerge after it is decided to pursue it

However, the logic of the third option, the prewar mixed nation theory, was neither of these. The peoples within Japan and territories into which Japan had expanded were depicted as blood relations of the Japanese who had been, in time immemorial, elements of the Japanese nation. This logic allowed the difference between Fukuoka's Type 1 and Type 4 to be eroded, and the difference between Type 1 and Type 7 to be whittled away to the extent that it became possible to bridge the gaps. All that was then required was to use force do away with the differences that could be rectified, such as the inability to speak Japanese. This was an underhand way of erasing the Otherness of alien peoples and turning them into 'defective Japanese'.

The prewar mixed nation theory did not deny the role of lineage in determining nationality. The myth of the homogeneous nation had two elements: the notion that the Japanese nation had pure and homogeneous origins, and the notion that only those with the same lineage as other members would be accepted as 'Japanese'. When the empire expanded to include alien nations, these two elements could no longer be reconciled. Theorists were forced to choose one. A comparatively small minority chose the first, rejected the second, and criticised assimilationist policies from a pure blood position. The majority, however, adopted the mixed nation theory and abandoned the first in favour of the second, arguing for assimilationist policies such as intermarriage.

The mixed nation theory functioned in the same way as the postwar theory of the homogeneous nation. Neither allowed for the emergence of the concepts of nationality or human rights independent of a belief in 'lineage' or 'blood'. The concept of human rights will not emerge independently of lineage in a relationship with an Other whose differences are rejected.

Late-Developing Imperialism

How can Japan's mixed nation theory be characterised in comparison with other countries?

To define one's nation as the product of a mixture of many nations, to adopt such a definition as a cornerstone of national identity, and to use it to promote the assimilation of alien peoples within one's borders is not a phenomenon limited to the Great Japanese Empire. The Melting Pot of the USA is another well-known example. As noted in the introduction, Milton Gordon distinguishes between three types of assimilation in the USA: Anglo-Conformity, the Melting Pot, and Cultural Pluralism. Anglo-Conformity is where minorities abandon their own culture in favour of Anglo-Saxon culture, and the Melting Pot is where all ethnic groups are mixed together to produce a new culture and nation.[2]

The USA Melting Pot discourse, however, locates its ideal in the future, as an unknown aim that has to be realised through the mixture and assimilation of various nations. On the other hand, Japanese mixed nation theorists took as their ideal the *status quo* of the Japanese nation in the past. In the sense that it promoted a unilateral assimilation into the pre-existing ruling nation, the mixed nation theory pursued what could be called Japanese-Conformity. However, Anglo-Conformity did not view the Anglo-Saxons as a mixed nation. In other words, the mixed nation theory was created by combining the characteristics of both theories.

The way the modern Japanese state was formed helps to explain why the mixed nation theory was able to emerge.[3]

The first characteristic was the fact that the Meiji government embarked on the process of creating a modern state as a way of escaping the risk of being colonised by the Western Powers. The pace both of modernisation and of the creation of a nationalism centred on the Emperor was a forced one. Moreover, the Meiji government argued that it was necessary to secure defensive positions in the areas surrounding Japan to prevent them being used as beachheads for any future attack on the archipelago.

The areas surrounding the Japan of the day – Hokkaido, Okinawa, Taiwan and Korea – were not rich in natural resources. Even then, doubts were expressed within Japan about whether the economic benefits to be derived from exploiting these areas would outweigh the costs of colonial rule. However, it was decided that the military benefits outweighed the economic costs. As a result, these regions were annexed and became part of Japan. The residents were 'granted' Japanese nationality, and assimilationist policies centred on Japanese language education and Emperor worship were implemented.

The British and French advisers employed by the Japanese government argued against these policies. Using Great Britain's contemporary colonial policy as an example, they argued instead in favour of a form of indirect rule that would use native power structures and preserve native customs. This would help to minimise any anti-Japanese backlash, as well as helping to cut the costs of colonial rule.

However, many Japanese involved in the policy-making process and most intellectuals argued instead for assimilation. The major reason given was that indirect rule could not guarantee that, if any of these regions were to be invaded by a Western Power, the residents would remain loyal to Japan. Therefore, it was said, it was necessary to turn the residents of these areas into 'Japanese' who would be loyal to the Emperor.

Thus, one of the reasons that these regions were incorporated into Japan was to limit the risk of any Western Power claiming them. In 1905, Korea became a Japanese protectorate modelled on the French rule over Tunisia, and was annexed in 1910. The first Resident-General of the protectorate, Itō Hirobumi, was opposed to the annexation because of the costs, but preference was given to securing territory. The Western residents of both Taiwan and Korea lost their special privileges as soon as these areas formally became part of Japan, and were placed under Japanese jurisdiction instead.

As noted in this work, the decision to grant Japanese nationality to the peoples of Taiwan and Korea was one over which they had no say. In the case of Taiwan, it was announced that all those who had not left Taiwan within two years would become Japanese subjects. Koreans were not given even this period of grace. Furthermore, in Korea there were no legal provisions to enable Koreans to renounce Japanese nationality. These were steps taken to bring all residents of Korea – including those active in the anti-Japanese movement – under the jurisdiction of Japan. The decision to 'grant' these people Japanese nationality was a means to an end – to secure territory.

Unlike the various Western Powers, modern Japan did not possess a universal civilisation that would prove attractive outside Japanese borders. Since Japan herself had imported modern civilisation from the West, it was difficult to justify colonial rule as bringing the fruits of civilisation. Moreover, the mindset of the peoples of East Asia, and especially the Confucian worldview, saw both Korea and China as superior to Japan in terms of East Asian civilisation. As a result, Japan was forced to emphasise the standard Japanese language (*hyōjungo*) and the Emperor as the basis for Japan's superiority to the people of her colonies. In other words, the only form of rule available to Japan was to use the Emperor and the Japanese language as tools in pursuing national unification in her territories. In the 1930s, when territorial expansion was no longer internationally acceptable, Japan advanced into Manchuria and Southeast Asia, but did not annex these territories, nor grant Japanese nationality to the their peoples.

Even here, however, the emphasis on Japanese language education and Emperor worship remained unchanged.

The Japanese government could not look to the claim that it was spreading a universal civilisation to justify any grab for territory. Since this territory was located in regions surrounding Japan, the government instead turned to the argument that the Japanese nation was related to the peoples of these regions.

In 1879, when the Japanese Meiji government debated the future of Okinawa with the Chinese Qing government, Japan argued that Okinawans were racially and linguistically a part of the Japanese nation. The written documents prepared by the Japanese government for these negotiations drew on Western anthropology and linguistics to substantiate these claims (this was five years before the first anthropological research association was opened in Tokyo). The Pan-Asianism of later years which argued that all Asian nations were related to the Japanese and that Japan's mission was to liberate these peoples from Western rule was an extension of this position vis-à-vis the Okinawans.

As noted in chapter 5, at the time of the annexation of Korea, Ōkuma Shigenobu noted that whereas Europe had expanded into 'countries of alien races, alien nations, and alien religions', Japan was expanding into regions populated by the 'same race and the same nation'. One characteristic of Japanese expansion was indeed that the Other existed in neighbouring regions, a characteristic that was a necessary consequence of Japan's late-developing imperialism and the inability to invade territories in remote regions. The peoples of Korea and Taiwan were thus 'racially' close to the Japanese nation, and all existed within a broad cultural sphere centred on China.

Japanese rule over neighbouring regions was thus not a clear colonial rule but rather an extension of domestic policies implemented during the process of national unification characteristic of a modern state. As a result, it was necessary to view Koreans and Taiwanese as 'Japanese'. As with many modern states, when ancient history and theories of national origins were constructed in Japan as a means of national unification, these political necessities were reflected in accounts of ancient history. Just as the theory that the sovereign and all his subjects shared the same ancestor was argued to the majority Japanese, the theory that the 'Japanese' and Koreans shared a common ancestor was argued to the Koreans.

Conclusion

However, although Koreans and Taiwanese were granted Japanese nationality, discrimination still existed, not only in people's minds but also structurally. Members of the House of Representatives were not elected from Korea and Taiwan, and it was not possible to move one's permanent domicile in the Family Register (*koseki*) system from Korea or Taiwan to Japan Proper. Although a change into 'Japanese' was enforced in the area of loyalty and cultural assimilation, exclusion from 'Japanese' was pursued in the area of rights. Koreans and Taiwanese were not organised into armies for fear of any uprising. After the Pacific War broke out, conscription was introduced because of shortages in human resources, but no Korean, Taiwanese, *Ainu*, or Okinawan units were organised, again because of a fear of armed revolts. Instead, where combat troops were concerned, small numbers were incorporated into units where 'Japanese' formed the majority.

To grant minority peoples Japanese nationality and recognise them as fellow 'Japanese subjects', but not grant them equal rights, may seem contradictory. However, the Great Japanese Empire had not achieved equality in political rights for its majority subjects, something that is said to be a condition of a modern nation state. The Imperial Diet was first convened in 1890, but universal male suffrage was not introduced until 1925, and from the 1930s onwards the military ruled politics. Sovereignty did not reside with the people but rather with the 'divine' Emperor.

It is interesting to note that individuals such as Yanagita Kunio, Tsuda Sōkichi and Watsuji Tetsurō, who prepared the groundwork for the myth of ethnic homogeneity, all took a negative line to military expansion and the assimilationist policies of the Great Japanese Empire, and emphasised the rights of the people of Japan Proper, agreeing with universal suffrage but paying no attention to the issue of suffrage in Korea and Taiwan. In constructing a Symbolic Emperor System that enjoyed popular support, they were attempting to democratise the Emperor System.

These thinkers could be said to have aimed for an homogenisation of the Great Japanese Empire in two senses – an ethnic homogenisation that excluded alien nations, and an homogenisation of rights, beginning with political rights. Instead of the 'nationalism from above' created by the Meiji government, they attempted to create a 'nationalism from below' that would homogenise Japan as a nation-state.

The discourse on the nation and the Pan-Asianism of Japan was closer to Germany and Imperial Russia than to the colonial rule of Great Britain and France. For instance, following the First World War when Germany and Poland struggled over possession of Silesia, the issue of whether the ancient residents of the region had been Germans or Slavs became a point of contention. In this case, the country that could prove that its own ancestors were also the common ancestors of this region would be able to justify possession. As argued in chapter 9, when Nazi Germany annexed Austria and part of Czechoslovakia, it was emphasised that the residents of these regions were German.

In Russia in the late nineteenth century, Russianisation policies were urged for neighbouring regions such as the Baltic states, Ukraine and Poland. As relations with Germany worsened, questions about the loyalty of German residents of the Baltic states were raised. As a result, Russian was made the official language, pressure was placed on people to convert to the Russian Orthodox Church, and Russian history and culture were taught in the education system.

In his *Imagined Communities*, Benedict Anderson proposes the concept of 'official nationalism', giving Russia as one of his examples.[4] This concept can be viewed as resulting from a forced compromise between the realities of a multi-national empire and the principle of a nation-state, at a time when a multi-national empire under a royal family was attempting to adopt policies of modernisation.

To pursue the principle of the modern nation-state without compromise would mean to abolish the empire under the rule of the monarchy, to separate all ethnic groups into independent entities, and turn them into small homogeneous states (in terms of both ethnicity and rights). However, when Czarist Russia embarked on its push for modernisation, the size of its imperial territory and the number of ethnic groups remained unchanged and the Czar remained in charge. Instead, an homogenisation of all ethnic groups was promoted through policies of assimilation.

It was the nationalism of the minority ethnic groups which desired independence, and the Pan-Slavism of the Russian nation, that stood in opposition to this official nationalism. Some Pan-Slavists argued for a pure Russian culture rather than imperial expansion, criticised attempts to Westernise Russia, and praised the uniqueness of Russian culture. Moreover, they viewed the upper classes which aped the West with disdain, and instead praised the common people as having preserved traditional Russian culture. As a result, their works were frequently banned and they were oppressed by the government. A comparison between Slav ideology and the thinking of a Yanagita Kunio or a Tsuda Sōkichi, or between Pan-Slavism and Pan-Asianism, would prove a fruitful research project.

The imperial expansion and discourse on nationality in the Great Japanese Empire can be seen as a case study of late developing imperialism. Moreover, a characteristic of the mixed nation theory was to add the notion of a national unification of a number of ethnic groups, something seen in the Melting Pot discourse of the USA.

It can be said that the political status of modern Japan – a nation that was located in Asia but managed to avoid being colonised and became a late-developing imperial power – was reflected to a great degree in the Japanese discourse on nationality. Immediately following the Second World War, Japan was homogenised to a greater extent than the Great Japanese Empire in two ways. First, as a result of losing Korea and Taiwan, Japan was ethnically homogenised. Secondly, because the new Japanese Constitution defined sovereignty as residing with the people rather than the Emperor, Japan was homogenised in the area of political rights. In postwar Japan, and especially from the 1960s when high economic growth produced a further homogenisation of life-styles, the myth of the homogeneous nation became firmly established.

Coloured Imperialism

There was, however, an important difference between the Great Japanese Empire on the one hand and the Western Powers on the other – Japan was clearly a 'coloured' state.

When facing the West, the people of modern Japan felt inferior, perceiving themselves as a 'coloured' people threatened by the Western Powers. When facing the peoples of their own colonies, however, they saw themselves as superior members of an Imperial Power. The dichotomy that dominated the discourse of the day contrasted the 'West' (synonymous with 'white', 'civilised', and 'rulers') with the 'East' (synonymous with 'coloured', 'barbaric', and 'ruled'), and the national identity that emerged from this discourse was understandably a complex one.

Two positions emerged in Japan. The first defined the 'Japanese' as an entity close to the 'West' (white rulers) and is known by the

Meiji Period slogan 'Leave Asia and Join the West' (*datsu-A nyū-Ō*), while the second, 'Pan-Asianism', claimed that the 'Japanese' were the leaders of the 'East' (coloured victims).

Needless to say, the residents of the Japanese archipelago had not perceived themselves as 'coloured' before they encountered the West. With the exception of the theory that the Japanese nation was itself Caucasian (discussed in chapter 10), the majority of theories of the Japanese nation began with an acceptance of the notion that the 'Japanese' were 'coloured'.

At the same time, the theory that the Japanese nation was a mixed one entered Japan. As noted in chapter 1, this theory was originally developed by Western academics who had travelled to Japan. As a result, the Japanese discourse on the nation was forced to begin with an acceptance of the premises that the 'Japanese' were 'coloured' and 'mongrel'.

The premises forced on Japan by the West were, however, actively reconstructed as a new national identity was forged. The mongrel, coloured Japanese nation, it was argued, was the victim of Western racism but at the same time enjoyed superior adaptability and powers of assimilation, and possessed a natural vitality unblemished by the poison of civilisation.

This reconstruction of a self-image that had originally been imposed by the West was frequently accomplished by theorists who had themselves adopted Western criticisms of Western civilisation. Nishida Kitarō, the philosopher mentioned in chapter 16, argued that the 'mongrel' Japanese nation had overcome the limits of the dualism of the individual and the whole that was the *aporia* or impasse of Western philosophy. Hozumi Yatsuka claimed that Japan did not have to face the dilemma between order and freedom that troubled political thinkers in the West, because Japan was a Family State where the ruler and people were as one.

This narrative linked up with Pan-Asianism, which saw Japan as the leader of an oppressed East that needed to confront the West. Moreover, it was argued that the Japanese rule over Korea and Taiwan aimed to assimilate the residents of these regions as 'Japanese' and was therefore different to Western colonial rule and Western racism.

In order to maintain the self-image of the 'Japanese' as victims of Western racism, Japanese intellectuals and politicians had to avoid participation in any Western-style racist discourse. As I have argued here, one of the main concerns of Japanese anthropologists was to combat the Western racist thinking that claimed that Caucasians were a superior race. Even those theorists influenced by eugenicism, such as Kiyono Kenji, discussed in chapter 13, denied any *a priori* racial superiority or inferiority. Although allied with Nazi Germany from 1940, many intellectuals in Japan rejected Hitler's racism as something that advocated the superiority of Caucasians.

What emerged and took root instead was the position that the Japanese nation had transcended racism (and had done so from time immemorial in terms of its historical origins) and was thus superior to the West. In this way, ethnocentrism was advocated and overseas aggression and discrimination justified.

The reason that the mixed nation theory as developed by minorities within the Great Japanese Empire such as Christians and women was transformed into a political justification of overseas aggression can now be understood. The logic developed to argue for the rights of 'domestic minorities' was used to argue to the West for the rights of the 'minority of international society', the Great Japanese Empire.

This use of the history of the nation can be viewed as a type of renaissance discourse. The promotion of modernisation and the construction of a national identity were both necessary in the effort to build a modern state but, in a late-developing country that modernised by importing Western civilisation, the two were in contradiction to each another. In this situation, a renaissance discourse emerged that claimed that modernisation was not merely Westernisation but a restoration of something that had existed in the nation's past.

The Meiji Restoration overthrew the feudalism of the Edo Period and began the process of constructing a centralised modern state. This process was accomplished under the slogan of restoring the ancient system of direct rule by the Emperor. Japan's overseas aggression was argued to be a return to the ancient motherland of the Japanese nation. As noted in this work, Watsuji Tetsurō argued that democracy under the Emperor was a return to ancient traditions, and Takamure Itsue made the same argument about sexual equality.

Reconstruction of self-images imposed by the West and the renaissance strategy can both be seen in third-world countries today. In Japan, however, the expression 'coloured' given by the West was used to justify overseas aggression and produced what could be called 'coloured imperialism'.

It is not unusual today to see countries justify aggression while claiming a history of victimisation by the West. However, in the late nineteenth and early twentieth centuries, Japan was the only country in Asia capable of pursuing a modern imperialism. In this sense, the discourse that appeared in Japan during this period can be seen as an early example of the various discourses that emerged from the 1950s in newly independent countries in Asia and Africa to justify authoritarian regimes and participation in international conflicts. The Great Japanese Empire was the last example of imperialism by an advanced nation, and at the same time was the first example of imperialism by a third-world nation.

A Reflection of the Family System

In addition to the comparison with how the British and French interacted with the peoples of their colonies, another characteristic of Japan can be seen from a comparison with China and Korea, both of them neighbouring countries within East Asia. This characteristic is the family system, an examination of which will also shed light on the concept of 'blood'.

It is not commonly recognised that the Japanese family system differs from the systems of China, Taiwan and Korea, which are based on paternal lineage. In China and Korea, the surname indicates lineage on the father's side and remains unchanged for life. Thus, for instance, if a Mr. Kim marries a Miss Kan, her surname, received from her father, will remain unchanged, while all children of the marriage will adopt their father's surname. This is a system that clearly identifies paternal lineage. In both China and Korea, there can also be seen the principle of not marrying someone with the same surname or adopting a child with a different surname (those with the same surname are able to marry if their paternal ancestors hail from different regions).[5]

In modern Japan, however, people were quite happy to change their surnames. When a couple marries, they adopt a single surname, usually that of the husband, but sometimes that of the wife. Yanagita, for instance, took his wife's surname. Those adopted, whether male or female, take the surname of their new *ie* (family). In other words, the surname in Japan differs from the surname in China and Korea in that it does not necessarily indicate paternal lineage, but rather the *ie* one belongs to. During the debate on mixed residence in the interior, Inoue Tetsujirō wrote that his surname had changed three times. This would be unthinkable in a country like Korea, and explains why the Korean resistance to the 1940 name change policy was so strong.

This Japanese family system certainly has its strengths. In the merchant houses of the Edo Period, it was possible to utilise men of talent through adoption even if they were not kin. Unlike cultures where kinship is clearly limited by paternal lineage, individuals without lineage could become 'relatives' and members of the family business in Japan. Although different from the universal meritocracy of the West, this system also differed from the closed family systems of China and Korea. It was an open organisation that allowed for the acceptance of outsiders, and, as such, has been described as the '*ie* society as civilisation' by academics who in the 1970s praised the so-called system of 'Japanese management'.[6]

However, this openness also had an oppressive character. This is because although anyone can in principle be adopted into the Japanese family system, once adopted, individuals are forced to forget their origins, to change their names, and to adopt totally the traditions of the new *ie*.

What influence does this family system have on international relations? First, it must be noted that the relations that we can actually experience are limited to the dimensions of our daily human relations. The relationship between large groups such as states and nations are frequently not understood as such, but anthropomorphised, and people tend (sometimes without realising it) to search for solutions within the framework of their experience of human relations.

According to Emmanuel Todd, European family systems can be divided into four groups, determined by whether the parents are authoritarian or liberal, and whether any estate is divided between the (male) children in an equal or an unequal fashion.[7] He argued that politics developed according to the family system. Thus even within the same socialist regimes, in Northern France where the family system was liberal and egalitarian, socialism was anarchistic; in authoritarian and egalitarian Russia, it became a party-led communist system; in frequently liberal and unegalitarian England, socialism was moderate; and in authoritarian and unegalitarian Germany, it developed into a social democracy centred on the state and other organisations.

Leaving aside the issue whether the family system really does determine society to this extent, there is no doubt that the assimilationist discourse seen in the Family State paradigm reflected the Japanese family system. Beginning with Kita Sadakichi and Watari Shōzaburō, it was very common at the time to describe the status of Korea and Taiwan in the Family State as that of 'foster children'.

People brought up in the Japanese family system believed that it was natural for foster children to try to forget their origins, to change their names, and to assimilate into their new families. On the other hand, Japanese migrants identified themselves as foster children when they attempted to assimilate into their host countries. However, this logic was undoubtedly beyond the comprehension of Koreans, who believed in the principle of not adopting anyone with a different surname.

In the Japanese family system, on the other hand, it was often the case that the maintenance and prosperity of the *ie* group was given preference over lineage. In the *samurai* families, it was customary for the oldest son to be the sole heir and become the head of the *ie*. However, when there was no kin relation as the heir, or only an incapable blood relation, rather than allowing the *ie* to come to an end or fall into decline, the continuation of lineage was abandoned and a capable foster child was adopted as heir.

Moreover, in this case, even where ties of lineage did not exist, members of the *ie* could share an ancestor. As seen in chapter 8, Watari Shōzaburō argued that the Japanese *ie* had two groups of ancestors – those determined by lineage and those by the *ie* system – and that since the Koreans had been adopted by the Family State, in addition to their ancestors by lineage, they also had a new ancestor by structure in the Emperor. If this logic was extended far enough, it would eventually encompass all the peoples of the world in a single *ie*, as described in the slogan 'all corners of the world under a single roof'.

A national polity theorist who lived in Korea wrote in 1925 as follows.[8]

> What needs to be noted here is that the family is a gathering of different people – the husband and wife – who form its basis. Therefore, the family begins when people not related, or only remotely related, by blood come together. The essence of the Family State does not reside in sharing the same blood. Different people must first be welcomed and made as one [that is, assimilated]. If anything, the word

family-like means to make as one...If this principle were extended and applied to distant people as well as to neighbours, it would be possible to realise universal brotherhood. When assimilation is thoroughly pursued, the entire world will eventually be embraced within a single *ie*.

Needless to say, this position could not emerge from the family systems of China and Korea, where the surnames of married couples were not identical, and where relatives were defined by paternal lineage.

Moreover, in the Great Japanese Empire, the ancestor of Japanese subjects was said to be the Emperor, but these subjects did not claim to be eligible to inherit the throne: the heir to the throne is determined by paternal lineage, and no foster child has ever become Emperor. Imperial subjects understood that although they were said to be the 'Emperor's children', this was unrelated to lineage. Because of the Japanese concept of the family, it was possible to extend the theory of the Family State beyond the borders of Japan.

The reason that many Japanese theorists accepted the mixed nation theory was perhaps related to the ambiguity about lineage in the Japanese family system. In this system, as long as the ancestors of the *ie* are linked to the current membership, 'blood' is of secondary importance. With the exception of the Imperial Family, it was not considered a dishonour, even in famous families boasting long pedigrees, for foster children to have entered the family line and be included among the *ie*'s ancestors. The standard used to judge ancestors was not lineage, but the degree of the contribution made to the *ie*. What was seen as important was how long the *ie* had lasted, the success in maintaining it, and the degree to which it had prospered, not the fact that the 'blood' of aliens had not entered the family blood-line, and that the paternal lineage had been protected.

As noted above, the theory of the Family State based on the *ie* system created an order without drawing a clear distinction between the self and the Other. In order firmly to situate the ruled in a situation where they are not treated equally as individuals the same as self, nor clearly distinguished as the Other, it is necessary to perceive them as neither self nor Other. What came into play here was the concept of the family, which is neither self nor Other. Moreover, the *ie* had a 'natural' hierarchy – the head of the family, followed by the elder brother and then the younger brother.

Even today, discrimination against Koreans and Chinese in Japan is not called 'racial discrimination' but rather 'national (*minzoku*) discrimination'. If racism is a discrimination based on a biological discourse, then equal treatment is called for when the victims of discrimination can be shown to be the same race biologically. In this sense, racism easily emerges in a society where a consciousness of equality within the same race has been established to a certain extent. This is one of the reasons why this type of racism is a phenomenon seen in the modern era and mainly in advanced countries. In societies dominated by a worldview that assumes a hierarchical social order among members of the same race, it is not always necessary to discriminate through racism.

In the family system of the Great Japanese Empire, the head of the family was enormously powerful, and the oldest son was the sole heir. The discourse of the Great Japanese Empire identified the nations ruled by Japan as 'brothers' belonging to the same race. However, while the word 'brother' in English does not distinguish between older and younger brothers, the Japanese word '*kyōdai*' (brother) does, and thus implies a hierarchical order. The anthropology, linguistics and historiography of the Great Japanese Empire were able to incorporate the ruled nations within the theory of the Family State, with the Emperor as the family head and the Japanese nation as the elder brother, by 'proving' that the ruled nations were the brothers of the Japanese. The 'younger brothers' were viewed as foster children and forced to assimilate into their adoptive families, and their lower status vis-à-vis the 'elder brother', the Japanese, was fixed for eternity. This was a method of disguising the realities of rule through power and forcing the ruled nations into a 'natural' hierarchy.

In 1942, the Korean Governor-General, Minami Jirō, gave a speech to a Korean audience where he put forward the theory that the 'Japanese' and Koreans shared a common ancestor, and urged Koreans to cooperate in the war effort. At the time, Koreans expected that they would be enfranchised in return for their cooperation. However, Minami stated that 'before selfishly demanding rights, Koreans must first thoroughly master the essence of being loyal imperial subjects', and continued in these terms:[9]

> Generally speaking, the essence of imperial subjects is fundamentally different from the Western belief that one should 'start' by demanding one's rights. All imperial

subjects are part of a great family that consists of a single sovereign and all his people (*ikkun banmin*), where the relationship is that between liege and lord but where the emotional ties are those of a father and his children. In interacting with the family head, family members do not talk in terms of rights and obligations. Rather, the elder brother acts as befits an elder brother, while the younger brother acts as befits a younger brother. It is natural and fundamental that all should cooperate in harmony to help the family flourish and move up in the world.

In any family, parents look forward to their children growing up and, when they are old enough, they take all the steps that are needed to ensure that they are educated. This is a consequence of the parents' feelings and love. It is not the custom in Japanese families for children to start ranting about their right to an education simply because they are old enough to attend school. Those who shamelessly practise what is not the custom in Japanese families are delinquents, and it must be said that this in and of itself disqualifies them from becoming imperial subjects.

These expressions are premised on a family system where the oldest son only inherits the headship of the family. In China, the family estate was divided equally between all brothers, and so the Chinese would not have understood the implications of 'the elder brother acts as befits an elder brother, while the younger brother acts as befits a younger brother'.

It can be said that the Great Japanese Empire as depicted in the theory of the Family State was an ever-expanding *ie*, centred around the 'family head', the unbroken lines of Emperors, where the 'elder brothers' accepted and assimilated the 'younger brothers' and 'newcomers', and where all were given specific roles to play within the *ie*. When verbalised, this was expressed as 'the world is a single family, mankind are all brothers', a phrase that at first seems attractive. However, it included no awareness of discrimination. No matter what degree of inequality existed in reality, it would not contradict this attractive slogan.

Although it is not a mistake to say, as Fukuoka does, that lineage is viewed as important in Japan, it is not clear what is meant by 'lineage'. In modern Japan, the notion of 'lineage' consisted of a mixture of three elements: a biological pure blood consciousness, the paternal 'lineage', and the genealogy of the *ie* group. This consciousness of lineage is reflected in the discourse on the nation. In a multi-national state it is said that the world view of a narrow community is destroyed to give way to a universally valid ideal that transcends the nation. In the Great Japanese Empire, however, the pseudo-universalism of the mixed nation theory and the *ie* system acted as substitutes for this ideal. Jeffrey Herf has developed the concept of reactionary modernism through his analysis of conservative German thought, an analysis that attempted to answer the question of why the Nazis, who believed in an irrational racism, were able to make use of rational modern science.[10] When faced with the need to effect a change to universalism, society will first create a pseudo-universalism from within the framework of existing culture.

However, this is a problem of the world view, and must be distinguished from the constitutive elements of actual society. Emmanuel Todd developed his arguments on the premise that the family system has not changed over the last 500 years. The discourse in Japan on the *ie* society and on theories of the Japanese (*Nihonjinron*) is also based on this premise. However, at least as far as the legal system is concerned, the establishment of the Japanese family system is a recent development. It was the Civil Law of 1898 that unified the surnames of couples: before this time, it was not unusual for couples to have separate surnames.[11] Although the custom by which the foster child took on the name of the foster family can be traced back further, it is not clear where its origin lies.

Family systems differed according to region and class before the centralisation brought about by the Civil Law, and therefore no single phenomenon can be identified as *the* 'Japanese family system'. This system was not a cultural destiny that had held the 'Japanese' spellbound from time immemorial, nor did it constitute the 'essence of Japan', but rather, was to a large extent a product of the legal system. The Japanese family system was created in modern times. But even if the family system does not determine the shape of society, an examination of the direction of the family system will still be of use, I believe, in shedding light on the assimilationist discourse of the theory of the Family State.

Moreover, the characteristics of this *ie* system were not unknown in other regions of the world. For instance, under the *Compadrio* system of Latin America, economically and politically powerful individuals acted as surrogate parents to children to whom they were not related, and in doing so were able to bring the birth families of these children under their control as well. The surrogate child and the birth parents were helped economically by the surrogate parents, in finding work and at ceremonial occasions such as marriage. In return, they served the surrogate parents, forming a patron-client relationship. The more powerful the individual, the more surrogate children he had. The great plantations of Brazil, for instance, flourished as plantation owners acted as surrogate parents to their agricultural workers.[12]

The problem of the consciousness of 'lineage' and the concept of the *ie* in Japan, together with the character of the theory of the Family State, have been the focus of much research and debate: what has been discussed in this work provides only hints from the perspective of theories of assimilation and nation.[13] However, an analysis of the discourse of the *ie* which combined with the mixed nation theory sheds a great deal of light on the slogan 'all corners of the world under a single roof'. It also helps explain why the Chinese and Koreans found it impossible to understand.

The Conservative Critique of the Theory of the Homogeneous Nation

In the myth of ethnic homogeneity that took root after the war, minorities such as the *zainichi* Koreans and the *Ainu* were treated as a source of trouble to be avoided as much as possible.

In the immediate postwar period, the USA-led occupation authorities introduced policies of democratisation in an attempt to ensure that Japan would never again become a military power. However, with the advent of first the Cold War and then, in 1950, the Korean War, the USA adopted a new set of policies designed to develop Japan as a member of the anti-communist world. In 1952, the San Francisco Treaty came into effect, and the occupation was brought to an end. It was at this time that the Koreans and Taiwanese within Japan's borders were stripped of their Japanese nationality.

Although many of the Koreans who remained in Japan after 1952 were allowed to apply for Japanese nationality, this entailed some onerous obligations, such as the provision of a list of personal property together with a written declaration of loyalty to the Japanese state. When they took Japanese nationality, pressure was frequently placed on individuals to adopt Japanese names. Koreans who remained in Japan and decided not to apply for Japanese nationality lost their rights as Japanese nationals.

The *Ainu*, on the other hand, were never stripped of their Japanese nationality. However, their rights were limited by the Hokkaido Former Aborigines Protection Act which was not repealed until 1997. Okinawa remained under the control of the American military authorities until 1972, and 41 per cent of the usable land (the plains) of the main island of Okinawa was set aside for American military bases. Even today, 75 per cent of the land mass of all American military bases in Japan is in Okinawa.

Japan's postwar Constitution ensured that Japan demilitarised. Although the Self-Defence Forces – effectively a military force – were established as a result of the USA shift in policy, the size of these forces has been kept in check by the Japanese peace movement. Japanese security in the postwar era has been maintained by the American military bases in Okinawa and the Japan-US Security Treaty. As a result, Japan has remained dependent on the USA for her security, and has been able to avoid being caught up in any postwar military confrontations, from the Korean and Vietnam Wars right through to the Gulf War. Moreover, in the case of the wars in Korea and Vietnam, Japan prospered by selling various materials to the military forces doing the actual fighting. This diplomatic stance of remaining well out of harm's way has been criticised in Japan as 'one-state pacifism'.

The right of the *zainichi* Koreans, the *Ainu*, and the Okinawans to have their children taught their own culture and language in the public education system has not been recognised. In 2001, Japan's policies towards her minorities were criticised as unjust by the UN Committee on the Elimination of Racial Discrimination.

In his analysis of postwar Japanese policies towards *zainichi* Koreans, Fukuoka Yasunori identifies four possible types: 'expulsion', 'assimilation', 'respect for human rights', and 'subjugation'.[14] Fukuoka argues that 'subjugation' best describes the postwar *zainichi* Korean policies, with 'expulsion' and 'assimilation' merely playing subordinate roles.

As noted above, when the San Fransisco Peace Treaty came into effect in 1952, the Japanese government unilaterally stripped *zainichi* Koreans of their Japanese nationality. According to Fukuoka, however, if the Japanese government had intended to pursue the logic of 'expulsion' consistently – that is, if it had wanted all Koreans to leave Japan as quickly as possible – it would have provided financial aid to Korean schools in Japan and encouraged second-generation *zainichi* Koreans born in Japan to learn the Korean language and return home. On the other hand, if the Japanese government had intended to pursue 'assimilation' vigorously, it would certainly not have stripped *zainichi* Koreans of their nationality but would rather have encouraged them to naturalise by establishing a quick-track system for naturalisation: policies of this sort firmly fix the subordinate status of minorities, without trying either to accept them into society, or to exclude them clearly from it.

In Japan today, there is a belief that this treatment of minorities is due to the existence of the Emperor – the last vestige of a system that determines rank by birth – and to the xenophobic myth of the homogeneous nation. Many of those who take this position also believe that the myth must have been dominant in Japan before defeat in 1945.

The destruction of the myth of ethnic homogeneity may prove useful in any criticism of the postwar Symbolic Emperor System. However, what will then emerge remains an unknown: either the often idealised egalitarian multi-national state, or the prewar multi-national empire. Moreover, the postwar myth of the homogeneous nation and the Symbolic Emperor System coincided in a sense with the postwar 'one-state pacifism'. Japan today is not the small, weak country it was when Tsuda and Watsuji drew up their blueprints for the Symbolic Emperor System immediately following the defeat. The reason that 'internationalisation' is advocated by people of all political positions in Japan today is because the former closed nature of Japan no longer suits her international status.

As already noted, from the debate on mixed residence in the interior to the postwar era, Japan oscillated between the theory of the homogeneous nation to protect herself when she was weak, and the theory of a mixed nation to interact actively with the outside world when she was strong. It is therefore possible that as the international presence of the economic super-power that Japan has become increases, the theory of the homogeneous nation as a reflection of a consciousness of purity of blood will gradually go into decline, and the mixed nation theory will once again rise.

In fact, a conservative criticism of the homogeneous nation theory and an argument for the mixed nation theory can already be seen. For example, individuals such as Hayashi Fusao, who is known for his work *Dai tōa sensō kōteiron* (An Affirmation of the Greater East Asia War), and the critic Kase Hideaki have argued for the prewar mixed nation theory from a position of support for the Emperor System, stating that 'it must be said that it was a miracle accomplished by the Imperial Family to have successfully united many alien nations and to have created a unified state'. A Shintōist thinker, Ashizu Uzuhiko, insisted that 'it would be quite natural for Japan to accept 5 million or 10 million foreign migrants, which would be a similar percentage to other advanced nations' and stated that Japan 'must not oppose the ideal of "all corners of the world under a single roof"'.[15]

Moreover, according to Kim Talsu, Hashimoto Tomisaburō, a former Chief Secretary of the Liberal Democratic Party, stated that '90 per cent of the basis of ancient Japanese history can be attributed to the Korean peninsula and 10 per cent to native peoples'. Kim noted: 'I remember that somebody, perhaps Ikeda Hayato [a Prime Minister of Japan in the early 1960s], stated that the problem of relations with Korea originated in the age of Susano-O'. This is proof that both the mixed nation theory and the theory that the 'Japanese' and Koreans shared a common ancestor are still alive among conservative politicians in Japan.[16]

Among the conservative criticisms of the homogeneous nation theory, that of the philosopher, Umehara Takeshi, is of particular interest. Umehara is the individual who, as the head of the International Research Centre for Japanese Studies founded by Nakasone Yasuhiro (a conservative politician who was Prime Minister in the 1980s) to establish the identity of Japanese culture, was entrusted by the Japanese government with the task of drawing the self-portrait of the 'Japanese'. In a symposium 'Minzoku no kigen o motomete' (Searching for the Origins of the Nation) held in 1979, Umehara made the following statement:[17]

> These days I have ceased to believe that the Japanese nation is an homogeneous nation. Rather, it is a composite, or more precisely a mixed nation, which was formed when the nation responsible for Yayoi culture conquered the aboriginal residents.
>
> I think that a principle of assimilation is at work in Japanese culture. That is, there lies at the base of Japanese culture an excellent device that assimilates people of various racial origins.

According to Umehara, the indigenous inhabitants of the archipelago in the Jōmon era were the *Ainu*, and a conquering nation migrated from the Korean peninsula in the Yayoi era, and 'among the Japanese [today] the northeastern Japanese are close to the *Ainu*, while the Kinki region Japanese are close to Koreans'. For Umehara, therefore, the *Ainu* had preserved the language and culture of ancient Japan and possessed this 'principle of assimilation'. He criticised discrimination against the *Ainu*, but his argument was that the origin of discrimination was the belief that the *Ainu* were an alien people. Instead, he expressed the view that the language and race of the *Ainu* were the same as the language and race of the 'Japanese'. Needless to say, this position is very similar to that of Kita Sadakichi.

Furthermore, Egami Namio, the anthropologist who advanced the theory of the migration of a horse-riding people, claimed in a talk with Umehara in 1979 that there were two kinds of people in Japan: an indigenous long-headed agricultural nation and a conquering short-headed pastoral nation. 'It is usually these people [the pastoral nation] who are interested in business, war and territorial expansion, and who even today distinguish themselves by their extraordinary achievements in the global economic war, earning the description "economic animals"'. Egami's theory of the migration of a horse-riding people had a structure that allowed it to merge with nationalism and elitism. Egami was decorated with the Order of Cultural Merit in 1991 – a sign that his theory had received the official approval of the state (readers may be interested to note that Ozawa Ichirō, another conservative politician, was once described by his supporters as a member of a horse-riding nation because he, too, had destroyed the political '*ancien régime*').[18]

What about Nakasone Yasuhiro who established the International Research Centre for Japanese Culture headed initially by Umehara? In 1978, Nakasone criticised the prewar 'rampant militarism and ultra-nationalism' and, insisting that 'I support the symbolic Emperor who is detached from power', used the Kiki myths to argue that 'our ancestors, the ancient Japanese...were, it seems, placid natural children'. Here the influence of Watsuji can clearly be seen. Nakasone supported the theory of a migration from the south as the explanation for the origin of the Japanese nation. However, in 1986, when he began to argue for internationalisation as Prime Minister, he stated that 'the Japanese nation was formed from the indigenous people who, over a long history of residence in the Japanese archipelago, mixed and became one with the southern and northern peoples and with the various peoples in the continent'.[19]

In his joint work with the Malaysian Prime Minister, Mahathir bin Mohamad (1925–), *NO to ieru Ajia* (The Asia That Can Say No), Ishihara Shintarō wrote in 1994 that 'it is absurd that some people argue that Japan is a unique homogeneous country', stating instead that 'the Japanese are a mixture of all Asian nations'. Ishihara is a novelist turned politician. A conservative, he is at present the Governor of Tokyo, and is well-known for his anti-American comments and his rejection of foreign workers. *NO to ieru Ajia* followed on from the *NO to ieru Nihon* (The Japan That Can Say No) by Ishihara and the then Head of Sony, the late Morita Akio (1921–1999), which argued that Japan should say 'no' to American demands that Japan open her markets. According to Ishihara, his father looked exactly like an Indian and his mother like a Chinese, Asian nations are all the siblings of Japan, and 'there is no equivalent of the Western disease in the Asian Co-prosperity Sphere'.[20] As noted in chapter 17, he insisted in 1968 that Japan was an homogeneous nation-state that had no parallel anywhere in the world. However, with a change in international affairs, he converted to the mixed nation theory. Thus, an emphasis on a common Asian identity emerges together with an awareness of a rivalry with the Other that is the USA.

It is inevitable that Japan will exert an influence in the outside world, absorb labour from all over the world, and become a multi-national state. The problem to be faced then is to distinguish what should cross national boundaries and what should not, and to determine exactly what sort of multi-national state Japan should create. The Great Japanese Empire expanded across international borders, the mixed nation theory occupied the mainstream, and Japan was a multi-national empire. The idea that the shortcomings of the Emperor System and Japanese society will be overcome only if Japan is internationalised, the consciousness of pure blood is destroyed, and Japan becomes a multi-national state, is based on a misunderstanding of the Great Japanese Empire. This idea is not only wrong, but dangerous.

Breaking Away from the Myth

The search for the identity of a nation almost always emerges as a reaction to a challenge to the assumptions and preconceptions (*ninshiki chitsujo*) caused by an encounter with an alien existence. At such times, the history of the nation is invented as a storehouse of knowledge from which the inventor as a member of the nation can draw guides to behaviour. The origin of the nation especially is a convenient object for this creative activity because conclusive historical material from that period is extremely rare compared to other historical times, so the inventor has no option but to rely on conjecture.

This creativity is not necessarily an intentional distortion of history. It is, so to speak, a form of the Rorschach test in psychology. In a Rorschach test, the person being tested is shown a meaningless stain of ink on a sheet of paper and is asked what it represents. Various answers will be given – it might look like an urn, or the face of a demon, or a person kneeling in front of god – but the answer is, of course, a mere projection of the subject's state of mind. The subject is not deliberately trying to see the face of a demon in the stain, but believes that it does in fact look like one.

The theory of the origin of the Japanese nation contains no accepted set of beliefs. Just like constellations formed by drawing lines between stars, different individuals form different theories by combining scraps of historical materials. As argued in this book, however, the theory of the Japanese nation oscillated whenever Japanese relations with the outside world changed. Many theorists merely verbalised their own *Weltanshaung* or sub-consciousness in talking about the history of the Japanese nation.

For mankind, nothing is more attractive than the ability to talk freely about one's past. One might be the descendant of a pure and unstained nation, or the direct descendant of a valiant horse-riding group which conquered an indigenous people, or the child of a Caucasian nation depicted in the Bible, or of a farming nation that migrated from the south islands carrying rice, or the descendant of a natural people not bound by formal morals. The Japanese nation may have experienced a peaceful assimilation of other nations, or perhaps lived in a matriarchal world where women were treated equally. The reason why the theory of the origin of the Japanese nation has been and remains so popular in Japan is that it is the best way for people to live their dreams.

Even today, many people discuss the character of the 'Japanese', and develop arguments on modern Japanese society, based on their ideas of the origin of the nation. What sort of relationship, however, is there between a time thousands or tens of thousands of years ago when, it is assumed, the nation originated, and the politics and society of today? The only link between the two is the tacit premise that the inhabitants of the archipelago thousands of years ago were already 'Japanese', and that their character has remained unchanged ever since.

Even if today's Japan is relatively homogeneous compared to other countries, the main reason for this lies in the international conditions of the past century that allowed Japan to avoid being colonised and divided, without allowing Japan to become advanced enough to establish a large-scale empire. Unlike many third-world countries, Japan did not experience a colonial rule under which borders were drawn up despite traditional ethnic boundaries, or a policy of rule through division that exasperated differences between ethnic groups, nor were large numbers of alien peoples introduced to provide labour. Also, unlike many other imperial powers, Japan did not advance into remote regions or rule her colonies long enough to establish a close relationship that would allow for large-scale migration even after her former colonies became independent. Many island nations such as Great Britain and Indonesia are classified as multi-national states today. If Japan had been divided and ruled in the nineteenth century, 'Japanese' living in the south of Japan might have been classified as a different ethnic group with a different language from those living in the north, and there might have been an established anthropological theory supporting the differences between the two.

Not only Japan but almost all nation-states have created myths about their origins. Unlike the heroism of many myths, however, what lies behind the mindset that searches for myths is the desire to escape from present realities.

The essence of mythologising the past is to escape from the trouble and fear involved in facing up to the Other, and to project on to the past categories that people wish to apply to the present. Many of the views of Korea, Taiwan, China, the South Seas, the *Ainu*, the 'West' and the 'Japanese' discussed in this book are stereotypical and were justified as views of history. Of course, stereotypes are to some degree necessary for human life. However, to avoid directly confronting the Other, and gradually to create stereotypes, to escape into myths, and to attempt to explain the entire world with a single story because we are not able to endure the shock of even a small-scale interaction, is to negate and oppress the Other. Here lies the origin of all myths.

Conclusion

The conclusion of this book, therefore, is very simple. It is not sufficient to fight against myths by destroying one myth and replacing it with another, as in, for example, criticising the myth of the homogeneous nation by replacing it with the myth of the mixed nation. What is required is to liberate ourselves from all myths – something which will require some work. As one becomes older and more experienced, human knowledge is accumulated and beliefs are deepened, while on the other hand the physical strength to interact sincerely with the Other on an individual basis decreases. It is this gap between overconfidence and physical weakness that allows myths to emerge. However, I want to believe that we can all at least become aware of this and escape from being captured by myths. Myths are not necessary to coexist with Others. What is required is a little strength and wisdom.

Notes

Introduction

1 Murofushi Takanobu (1942: 18). Monbushō shakaikyōikukyoku (1942: 15). Yun Koncha (1994) cites the second of these works and suggests that the theory of the homogeneous nation was not advocated in Japan in the prewar period.
2 The Japanese term *minzoku* can be translated into English as race (racial), nation (national), people and ethnic group (ethnicity). *Minzoku* has mainly been translated here as 'nation', but other words have been used according to the context. The phrase *Nihonjin* can mean Japanese national, a member or members of the Japanese nation, the Japanese race and the residents of the Japanese archipelago before a state had formed. This work will examine the process by which this phrase emerged, especially after Koreans and Taiwanese were granted Japanese nationality and treated as 'Japanese'. (It should be noted that Japanese nationality was forced on all those who had not left Taiwan within two years after it was ceded to Japan, and was forced on all Koreans immediately after Korea was annexed so as to enable Japan to use domestic Japanese law to clamp down on the Korean independence movement. In 1952, Koreans and Taiwanese living within Japan's borders were stripped of their Japanese nationality.) By using quotation marks for the 'Japanese', I will attempt to make it clear that the term can mean both 'holders of Japanese nationality' and members of the 'Japanese nation'.
3 Ōnuma Yasuaki (1986: 340–1).
4 The so-called *Chūgoku zanryū koji*: Japanese babies and children who were separated from their parents in the chaos following the end of the Second World War and adopted by Chinese parents. The Chinese war orphans began to return to Japan from 1981.

5 The *Ainu* are the indigenous people of Japan. There are currently about 30,000 living in Japan, mainly in Hokkaido (although this number varies depending on how those with some *Ainu* lineage are defined). After initiating modernisation policies, the Meiji government attempted to assimilate the *Ainu*, referring to American policies for the native American Indians. An *Ainu* movement in Japan has strengthened from the 1980s, stimulated by indigenous movements from around the world, such as North America and Australia.

The *zainichi* Koreans (or Koreans living in Japan) are those Koreans who moved to Japan after Korea was annexed and their descendants who still reside in Japan. It is said that roughly 600,000 to 1 million *zainichi* Koreans live in Japan today, although this figure varies, depending on the definition of '*zainichi* Korean'. According to official statistics published in June 2001, there are 630,000 individuals in Japan with Korean (North or South) nationality. This, however, includes new and recent arrivals from South Korea. There are no official data on the numbers of *zainichi* Koreans with Japanese nationality or on the number of children of Korean-Japanese couples.

6 Fukuoka Yasunori (1993: 2–16). Also see Fukuoka (2000).
7 Amino Yoshihiko (1982: 11–21). For a criticism of the myth of the homogeneous nation by another historian, see Ubukata Naokichi (1979). Yoshino Makoto (1993) examines the relationship between the discourse on the nation and the rule of alien nations, focussing on the theory of Kita Sadakichi and others that the 'Japanese' and Koreans shared a common ancestor (see chapter 7). Yamamuro Shin'ichi (1990) examines the period (the 1890s) that saw a transition from the debate on nationalism to the birth of the theory of the nation-state.
8 See Oguma Eiji (1998).
9 Milton M. Gordon (1964).
10 The *kokutai* (national polity) is a concept that emerged in Japan during the Edo Period in the works of nativist scholars and members of the Mito School (which fused Confucianism, nativism and Shintō thought together) and indicated a state centred on the Emperor. In the Meiji Period, it was for a time used as a translation of 'constitution' in the sense of the constitution of a state, as in a republic or monarchy, in

comparisons between the Japanese state and Western states. From the late nineteenth century, however, it lost its neutral meaning and once again became synonymous with the Japanese constitution – a monarchy centred on the Emperor. In the Peace Preservation Law (*chian iji hō*) of 1925, the Emperor System was defined as the Japanese *kokutai*, and any activity that protested against the Emperor System became punishable as an attack on the national polity. The discourse in Japan that lauded the monarchy centred on the Emperor as the Japanese national polity will be called 'the theory of the national polity' (*kokutairon*) in this work.

11 Following Japan's move to a centralised state in 1868, a custom was established by which each era was named after the reigning Emperor. Thus the Meiji Period is named after the Meiji Emperor, who reigned from 1868 to 1911. In the same way, the Taishō Period lasted from 1911 to 1925, and the Shōwa Period from 1925 to 1989. Note that the eras overlap.

12 Mita Minesuke (1971). Yamanaka Hayato (1982–83). It is perhaps important here to discuss briefly the way in which the Western social sciences have been accepted in Japan. In the modern era, it was frequently the case that when Western ideas were imported into Japan, an attempt was made to 'invent' a corresponding idea in Japanese history. Taguchi Ukichi, who will be discussed in chapter 2, studied Herbert Spencer's theory of social evolution and wrote *Nippon kaika shōshi* (A Short History of Japanese Modernisation, a title that could perhaps be translated as A History of the Evolution of Japanese Society) as the Japanese version of this philosophy. Mita Minesuke's *risshin-shusse shugi* attempts to identify the spiritual foundations of Japanese capitalism in Japan, and is the Japanese version of Weber's research of the Protestant ethic. Japanese Marxists have long been ardently searching for the equivalents in Japanese history of the European Absolute Monarchy and the French Revolution.

When Edward Said's *Orientalism* (Said 1978) was translated and published in Japanese in 1986, a similar phenomenom was seen. 'Orientalism' was accepted as an authoritative academic paradigm of the West, and as a new, universal discourse. A number of scholars in Japan started to search for and identify Japanese versions of Orientalism in the words used by modern

Japanese intellectuals when referring to Chinese and Koreans. On the other hand, however, there was very little research on how Japan was portrayed by the West as part of the 'Orient'.

There are two reasons for this. The first is the deep sense of responsibility and regret that many Japanese researchers feel about Japan's invasion of Taiwan, China and Korea. The second is the fact that, from the Meiji Period on, Japanese right-wing thinkers have so frequently emphasised Western discrimination against Japan that many researchers are very reluctant to use the same language. Ironically, however, the more researchers emphasise the fact that an Orientalism existed in modern Japan just as it did in the West, the more they 'prove' that Japan had accomplished a modernisation that could be compared to that experienced by Western nations.

Although this work analyses written language in a somewhat similar fashion to *Orientalism*, there are a large number of differences in approach. Said focuses on the representation of the Other. In this work, however, I will examine the construction of the Japanese self-image that emerged from an academic reconstruction of ancient myths.

Another difference between this work and *Orientalism* is that Said emphasises the descriptions of the Orient mainly by the nationals of Great Britain, France and the USA, or in other words, representations of the Other by individuals who had no superiors. Said does not examine the situation in late-developing imperial states such as Russia, Germany and Japan that expanded while suffering from a sense of inferiority to the West. My work, on the other hand, analyses the process by which Japanese self-images were developed in an environment where Japan expanded into other regions of Asia while suffering a sense of crisis about the threat of the West.

13 Kano Masanao (1988).
14 It hardly needs to be said that the 'West' and 'Asia' only exist as concepts. It was not uncommon for there to be rivalry between the different areas of the 'West', and large differences exist within these areas. However, the 'West' and 'Asia' did exist within the consciousness of the individuals examined in this work, and these concepts were a premise of their arguments and actions. In this sense, both actually exist, and will be used in this work.

Part One: The Thought of an 'Open Country'

1 The Birth of Theories of the Japanese Nation

1 On Western anthropology, theories of nationality in the Edo Period, and the activities of figures such as Tsuboi Shōgorō discussed in this chapter, see Terada Kazuo (1975: 5–43, 72–3) and Kudō Masaki (1979: 1–81). Also see Ōta Yūzō (1988), Ayabe Tsuneo ed. (1988), Yoshioka Ikuo (1987) and Murakami Yōichirō (1980). In 'Kokumin no tanjō to "Nihonjinshu"' (The Birth of the Japanese People and the 'Japanese Race'), Tomiyama Ichirō (1994) examines the role of anthropology in the formation of the Japanese nation-state through an examination of the view that early Japanese anthropology took towards the *Ainu* and Ryūkyū islanders. For a comprehensive critical appraisal of prewar anthropology and archaeology in Japan, see Tode Hiroshi (1986).
2 Tokyo Imperial University was established in 1877 as Tokyo University, the first modern institution of higher education in Japan. In 1886 it was named the Imperial University, and then in 1897 Tokyo Imperial University to distinguish it from the second institution of higher education to be established in Japan, Kyoto Imperial University. It was renamed Tokyo University in 1947. In the interests of simplicity, if not historical accuracy, the prewar institution will be consistently referred to here as Tokyo Imperial University.
3 Existing on the periphery of Chinese civilisation, Japan has always been influenced by China. Buddhism and Chinese legal thought were imported from China from the eighth century and added to an animistic religion native to Japan, Shintō (literally, the Path of the Gods). From the fourteenth century, the Emperor was deprived of any real power, and the *samurai* ruled. During the feudalistic Edo Period, Confucianism was imported from China and became the official academic study of the Edo Bakufu. Thus Japan saw the coexistence of Shintō, Buddhism and Confucianism.

From the second half of the Edo Period, Japanese Confucian scholars viewed China as an advanced nation, and actively imported Chinese civilisation in an attempt to maintain the feudalistic system. In a backlash to this view, a type of Shintō fundamentalism called *kokugaku* (Japanese nativism) emerged which rejected Chinese civilisation and saw the essence of Japan's cultural originality as embodied in Shintō. Nativist thinkers provided the Meiji Restoration with a philosophical backbone by arguing against the Western Powers and the Edo Bakufu. Following the Restoration, the Meiji statesmen faced the realities of international politics, shifted to an acceptance of Western technology, and promoted policies of importing Western civilisation. Nativist (*kokugaku*) scholars, however, remained active.

Arai Hakuseki was a representative Confucian scholar of the seventeenth century, and was a high-ranking bureaucrat in the Edo Bakufu. Confucian scholars who wrote about ancient Japan accepted the notion of an influx of people and culture from China and Korea, and tended to adopt a rational interpretation of the ancient Shintō myths. On the other hand, nativist scholars denied the influence of China and Korea on ancient Japan and tended to view the ancient myths as sacred texts that transcended human rationality. If Arai Hakuseki is a representative Confucian scholar, then Motoori Norinaga (1730–1801) is a representative nativist scholar. Both were frequently depicted by the scholars of modern Japan discussed in this work as pioneers of possible responses to overseas culture.

4   The ancient Japanese myths are not only sacred Shintō texts, but also describe the origins and history of the Imperial Household (Shintō is a polytheistic religion that worships nature). In the early eighth century, the ancestors of the present Imperial Household had two sacred texts edited – the *Kojiki* and the *Nihon shoki* – that claimed that the ancestor of the Imperial Household was the Sun Goddess. The two texts are commonly referred to as the Kiki myths (both end with ki). Since Japan did not have an alphabet at the time, the Chinese alphabet was used to edit these works.

According to the Kiki myths, ancient Japan emerged as follows.

First Izanagi, the Land God, and Izanami married and gave birth to the Japanese archipelago. The Yamato Dynasty, centred on the Sun Goddess, Amaterasu (literally 'shining from the Heavens'), or in other words the ancestors of the Imperial Household, descended to the archipelago from Takamagahara (the 'Plain of High Heaven'). This is known as the Descent of the Tenson. As this work will demonstrate, the Japanese frequently referred to themselves as the 'Tenson', or (literally) the 'descendants of the gods'. The first Emperor, Jinmu, advanced eastwards from the area where the Tenson alighted. This push is known as the Jinmu Eastern Expedition, and during this expedition various local peoples – the Emishi, Tsuchigumo and Kumaso – were conquered.

Since the Meiji government actively used this mythology in primary education in an effort to promote nationalism, the myths became the source of a common vocabulary shared by all Japanese. As will be argued in this work, these myths were used to justify Japanese actions so that, for instance, the story of how Ōkuninushi (literally 'Lord of the Great Land'), a prominent leader of the Izumo nation that was said to have resisted the Imperial Family, peacefully ceded his territory to the Yamato Court was used to justify the Japanese annexation of Korea.

5   Jules Verne ([1873] 1990: 154). Bruno Taut, diary entry, 30 January 1934, in Taut (1975: 69).
6   During the Edo Period, Japan closed her doors to most of the West, retaining trading relations only with Holland. As a result, the study of Western science and technology in Japan was limited to books written in Dutch, and thus came to be known as *rangaku* or Dutch Studies.
7   'Jinruigaku no Tomo' was written in the *hiragana* script, a custom that was the latest trend of the time. In East Asia, the written Chinese language – *kanbun* – that used ideographic characters – *kanji* – was the equivalent of the Latin of Europe. Until the Edo Period, public documents in Japan, together with upper-class literature, were written either in Chinese or in a form of Chinese that had been reorganised on Japanese lines.

The authors of the Kiki texts, lacking an alphabet of their own, used *kanji* (Chinese characters). *Hiragana* were developed in about the tenth century by simplifying specific *kanji*, and was a phonetic alphabet suitable for the Japanese language. Until the Edo era, it was mainly women and the lower classes who used *hiragana*, while the upper-class politicians and intellectuals mainly used *kanji*.

Just as Latin declined in the West, *kanbun* also declined in Japan after the Meiji Restoration. There was a push to abolish *kanji* in favour of the simpler *hiragana* in Meiji Japan in order to increase literacy rates and combat the influence of Chinese culture. However, *kanji* proved their worth in translating the abstract Western concepts necessary for modernisation. As a result, *kanji* were not abolished in Japan and the modern Japanese language uses a mixture of both *kanji* and *hiragana*.

Although the Meiji push to abolish *kanji* failed, others such as Tsuda Sōkichi (1873–1961, see chapter 14) advocated the abolition of *kanji* as a means of combating the Chinese influence. Following the Second World War, there was another push from the left-wing of Japanese politics centred around the Japanese Communist Part (JCP) to make a greater use of *hiragana* in order to make academic knowledge more readily accessible to the Japanese populace. The motives differed, but there was agreement on the desirability of excluding Chinese culture. This helps to explain why Tsuda's theories of ancient Japanese history were accepted so readily by the postwar left-wing intelligentsia despite his open admiration for the Emperor.

8 The later three titles, Jinruigaku Kenkūkai, Tōkyō Jinruigakkai and Nippon Jinruigakkai were written in Chinese characters. Notice that Japan came to be called Nippon even in English as the Japanese became more confident of themselves and their culture.

9 Ono Azusa (1936: vol. 2, 211). Yokoyama's quotation is cited in Ono (1936: vol. 2, 216).

10 Kurokawa Mayori ([1892] 1911). The quotation is from Kurokawa ([1892] 1911: 225). Other works by Kurokawa on ancient Japan include 'Kekkyo kō' (On Cave Dwellers) and 'Jōdai sekki kō' (On Ancient Stone Tools). See Kurokawa ([1881] 1911, [n.a.] 1911).

11 Naitō Chisō ([1888] 1933). Quotations from Naitō ([1888] 1933: 325, 358).

12 Kurokawa Mayori ([1880] 1911). The quotation is from Kurokawa ([1880] 1911: 19).

13 Ono Azusa ([1879] 1936).

14 Western-style dance parties (formal balls) were held at the Rokumeikan, where Western residents of Japan were invited to socialise with leading Japanese figures. The ultimate aim was to revise the unequal treaties. Domestic criticism was fierce and, in the 1890s, the Rokumeikan was no longer able

to function as a forum for diplomacy. It is a word still used in Japan today to symbolise a policy of following the lead of the West in areas such as foreign relations and culture.

2 The Debate on Mixed Residence in the Interior

1 The debate on mixed residence in the interior is mentioned in Inoue Kiyoshi (1955). Ino Tentarō (1976) covers the outline of the debate. Also see Ino ed. (1992). Yamawaki Keizō (1993) mentions the debate on mixed residence and makes it clear that Koreans were already permitted to live in Meiji Japan. Unoura Hiroshi (1988) notes the racial inferiority complex towards Westerners that can be seen in the arguments against mixed residence developed by Inoue Tetsujirō and Katō Hiroyuki. For a sociological approach to this topic, see Takita Yukiko (1992). Takita argues that Inoue's opposition to mixed residence is one of the sources of today's discrimination against minorities and the ostracism of foreigners that is based on the myth of ethnic homogeneity. The debate about mixed residence is broad and diverse, and that between Taguchi and Inoue is only one of many examples. The aim of this chapter is not to evaluate the character of the entire debate on mixed residence, but to show that the prototype of the rhetoric of the later theories of the mixed and the homogeneous nation had already formed by this period.
2 During the Edo Period, trade was controlled by the Bakufu, and links with foreign nations were limited by what is known as the 'closed country' policy. After the arrival of the 'Black Ships' in 1853, Japan adopted a friendly stance to the Western Powers in an 'open country' policy. Following the adoption of this latter policy, treaties were concluded between Japan and the Western Powers. These were typical of the unequal treaties forced on Asian countries at the time: Japan was not allowed to set tariffs, and the Japanese government was not allowed to try nationals of the Powers with which she had concluded treaties. Instead, trials were run in the extraterritorial concessions. In return, foreigners were allowed to reside only within the concessions.

In the late Edo Period, a position known as 'expel the barbarians' (*jōi*) was advocated. This rejected the idea of opening the country, and established links with nativist (*kokugaku*) scholars. Arguing that Japan was a Shintō 'Land of the Gods', it resisted the Bakufu which had established relations with the Western Powers, and instead supported the Emperor as Head of State. Hence their major slogan, '*sonnō jōi*' (Respect the Emperor and Expel the Barbarians). Although this position was the starting point of the Meiji Restoration, the Meiji government quickly switched to a realistic policy of building a modern state on Western lines, with the Emperor defined as a Western monarch. The greatest diplomatic issue for the Meiji government was to rewrite the unequal treaties, a task that was understood as being identical with gaining Western recognition of Japan as a civilised equal. The Meiji government also signed a treaty with China in which Chinese extraterritoriality in Japan was recognised, so there were also Chinese residents in the extraterritorial concessions.

Following the Plaza Accord of 1985, the number of foreign workers in Japan dramatically increased, and there was vigorous debate about whether they should be accepted. At the same time, economic friction with the USA erupted. Japan was criticised for her protectionist policies and for having a closed domestic market, especially in agricultural produce, and great pressure was brought to bear on Japan to liberalise rice imports.

At this time, the historical metaphors 'closed country' and 'open country' were frequently used in the domestic debate about both foreign workers and rice. The demands, mainly from the USA, to open Japanese markets to rice and other agricultural produce were described as a new wave of 'Black Ships'. In the debate on foreign workers, the experience of Germany with Turkish workers was frequently used in discussing how Japan should cope with the influx of workers from Asian countries such as China and the Philippines. The positions in favour of market liberalisation for either rice or labour were labelled 'open country' policies, while those who argued against liberalisation were labelled 'closed country' theorists.

3 Yokoyama Gennosuke (1954: 16).
4 As noted above, the second half of the 1870s saw what is know as the 'Liberty and People's Rights Movement' (*jiyū-minken undō*). In order to combat the radical Western ideas

that were flowing into the country, the government had the Emperor issue the Imperial Rescript on Education that advocated morals centred on Confucian concepts such as 'loyalty' and 'filial duty', and ensured that all children memorise the Rescript in the compulsory education system (compulsory education was introduced in Japan in 1872).

This policy aimed to restore an order disrupted by imported Western thought through an ideological Confucian education. It is perhaps ironic, and certainly an interesting example of modernism in Asia, that this Confucian Rescript was distributed through a Western-style compulsory education system and in state textbooks published with Western printing technology, and that those who drafted it and the author of the official commentary studied Western thought and used it to justify an 'Eastern' moral education.

5 Taguchi Ukichi ([1879] 1927–29: 80–3). Taguchi (1927–29: vol. 5) also contains Taguchi ([1889] 1927–29), quotations from Taguchi ([1889] 1927–29: 46–8); Taguchi ([1893] 1927–29), quotations from Taguchi ([1893] 1927–29: 60–1, 65, 70, 73); and Taguchi ([1899] 1927–29), quotation from Taguchi ([1899] 1927–29: 437).
6 It is said that Chinese and Koreans migrated to the ancient Japanese archipelago, a fact that was frequently mentioned in the debate in Japan in the 1980s on the issue of foreign workers. Even during the so-called 'closed country' of the Edo Period, the Bakufu allowed Holland to maintain trade relations with Japan (a trade the Bakufu monopolised), so there were Dutch residents in a few limited port cities of Japan.
7 Taguchi Ukichi (1884: 306).
8 Taguchi Ukichi (1889a: 38–9).
9 Taguchi Ukichi (1889b: 72–3).
10 The following is from Inoue Tetsujirō (1889).
11 The migration of Japanese to the USA began to increase from the late nineteenth century, and from about 1906–07, Japanese migrants in California were prohibited from owning land and their children were excluded from schools. The Japanese government protested about this discrimination and, as a result of diplomatic negotiations, resolved the issue by agreeing to 'voluntarily' limit the number of migrants. However, the anti-Japanese discrimination continued. In

1922, it was determined that first generation Japanese migrants would not be allowed to take American citizenship and, in 1924, immigration law was revised to totally exclude Japanese migration. As will be discussed in chapter 9, this revised immigration law was depicted in the Japanese media as symbolic of American racial discrimination.

12 With the Meiji Restoration, the feudalistic domain system of the Edo Period and the division of society into four main classes – the *samurai*, the farmers, the artisans, and the merchants – was abolished. Many of the domains had fallen into financial difficulties by the end of the Edo Period. The living standards of the feudal lords were guaranteed by the Meiji government in return for an agreement to have the feudal domains abolished in 1871. A peerage based on the Western model was created as a part of the Westernisation and modernisation process undertaken by Japan, and the feudal lords were made peers. Japan's new peers were appointed to the House of Peers.

13 Inoue Tetsujirō (1891a). The quotations are from Inoue (1891a: 18–21, 57). The quotation on the narrative on origins from the appendix is from the first appendix of this work, Inoue (1891a: 9–10).

14 From the Edo until the early Meiji Periods, it was common in Japan for boys and young men to be adopted into families whose surname they also adopted. For the Japanese family system, see the conclusion.

15 Taguchi (1891). The quotations are from Taguchi (1891: 707–9). Although the author of this article was anonymous, the index of volume 5 of Taguchi's Complete Works gives him as the author.

16 Both Silla and Pekche were ancient kingdoms of the Korean Peninsula.

17 Anon. (1893).

3 The Theory of the National Polity and Japanese Christianity

1 Christianity was first propagated in Japan in the sixteenth century when Portuguese and Spanish missionaries brought Catholicism to south Japan. Southern *daimyō* (feudal lords) were at first favourable to Christianity because of their interest

in the benefits of trade with the West, but later came to view the growing influence of Christianity with alarm. The Edo Bakufu eventually imposed a complete ban on Christianity. Diplomatic relations with Portugal and Spain were cut, and limited ties maintained with Holland on condition that Christianity was not propagated.

The Meiji government accepted Christianity in order to re-establish relations with the West, but remained wary of the religion, and banned religious education, asserting the importance of secularism and the separation of religion and politics (or church and state). Meanwhile, the official government position was that Shintō was a 'traditional culture' of Japan and not a religion, and therefore to teach the ancient myths in the compulsory education system did not constitute an infringement of the principle of secularism.

Many of the Christian intellectuals of Meiji Japan were either from the south or were *samurai* who had been allied with the old Bakufu and were not given opportunities in the new Meiji government, and many were active in the introduction of Western human rights and in the Liberty and People's Rights Movement. As a result, the pro-government national polity theorists criticised them as pawns of the West who had lost their sense of patriotism.

2 The concept of the modern national polity is said to have been influenced by Confucianism. Since the land and people of a feudal domain were seen as the property of the feudal lord, the feudal 'state' was the same as the 'family' of the lord. Confucianism thus contains the notion of ruling the state by ruling the family. Needless to say, in feudalistic times, this was the philosophy of feudal lords.

Japanese *kokugaku* (nativism) emerged as a backlash against the Confucianism imported from China. It focused on the ancient mythology of Japan, and viewed all residents of Japan – including the lowest strata of society – as having descended from the Emperors. This concept had the potential to be intertwined with the Confucian belief in the state as identical with the family, and in the late Edo Period was influenced by anxieties generated by the arrival of the Western Powers. The result was the '*sonnō jōi*' (Respect the Emperor and Expel the Barbarians) position. However, in the Edo Period, this position, which placed greater emphasis on the Emperor than on the Shōgun, was never publicly approved by the Bakufu. It was only after the Meiji Restoration and the introduction of the concept of the nation-state and a modern system of Western education that all Japanese were taught that the 'state' was identical with the 'family'. In other words, the national polity theory was formed from a mixture of Confucianism, *kokugaku*, and a modern nationalism.

There were some contradictions in this mixture. In Chinese Confucianism, 'filial duty' to parents and 'loyalty' to the sovereign were seen as independent moral principles, and clashes between the two – an order from one's parents and a contradictory order from one's sovereign – were seen as moral issues. However, it was argued that there was no contradiction between the two in the national polity theory of Japan because the sovereign was viewed as the 'father' of his subjects, and therefore loyalty to the sovereign was a filial duty (this was also said to be a characteristic unique to Japanese morality). This idea was reflected in the nationalism of Japanese authors who wanted to distinguish Japan from China.

3 Inoue Tetsujirō (1891b: i–v).
4 Inoue Tetsujirō (1899: vol. 2, 165).
5 The Hokkaido Former Aborigines Protection Act aimed to turn the *Ainu*, the indigenous people of Japan, into farmers and assimilate them into Japan. However, it included clauses that limited their ability to sell the land the government had allocated them and ordered them to till, and that enforced an education where their children were segregated from those of the majority 'Japanese'. This Act is said to have been influenced by the Dawes Act (the General Allotment Law of 1887) of the USA, a law that purported to protect native Americans. The Hokkaido Former Aborigines Protection Act continued to exist until 1997, when it was abolished as a result of an *Ainu* movement.
6 In Hozumi Shigetaka ed. (1943). The quotations are from Hozumi ed. (1943: 223, 225). The quotation on Hozumi Yatsuka's views of international relations is from Hozumi ed. (1943: 913). For a detailed examination of Hozumi Yatsuka and his theory of the national polity, see, for instance, Matsumoto Sannosuke (1969) and Nagao Ryūichi (1981).
7 Hozumi Yatsuka (1897: 4–5, 14, 21–2).

8 Fukuzawa Yukichi (1969–71: vol. 15, 269, 355).
9 For a detailed description of this debate, see Seki Kōsaku ed. ([1893] 1988). For the example of colonisation in Latin America and elsewhere, see, for instance, Seki ed. ([1893] 1988: 99–101) in the *Seihen* edition and Seki ed. ([1893] 1988: 376–8) in the *Shūketsu* edition.
10 Watase Tsunekichi (1897). The quotations are from Watase (1897: 41–2). For Watase, see, among others, Han Sokki (1988), Iinuma Jirō (1973) and Matsuo Takayoshi (1968).
11 Ōnishi Hajime (1897). The quotation is from Ōnishi (1897: 47). The commentary is anonymous, but in Matsumoto Sannosuke ed. (1977) it is reprinted with the author given as Ōnishi. For works that focus on this debate see, for instance, Suzuki Masayuki ([1981] 1986) and Komagome Takeshi (1993).
12 Takayama Chogyū ([1897] 1925–33). The quotations are from Takayama ([1897] 1925–33: 363–73). Hashikawa Bunzō (1962) claims that Takayama noted the limits of Japanism in this paper.
13 Takayama Chogyū ([1899] 1925–33b). The quotation is from Takayama ([1899] 1925–33b: 388).
14 Kimura Takatarō (1897: 110). Yumoto Takehiko (1897: 23–4). The citation is from Takayama Chogyū ([1897] 1925–33: 365).
15 Takayama Chogyū ([1899] 1925–33a). In this paper, Takayama cited the legend of how Susano-O colonised Izumo from the south and argued in favour of establishing colonies throughout the world.
16 Kita Ikki ([1906] 1959–72). The quotation is from Kita ([1906] 1959–72: 264–6).
17 A mythical figure, the Empress Jingū was said to have led an ancient Japanese army that invaded the Korean peninsula. Sakanoue-no-Tamuramaro was a general in the early ninth century who conquered the Emishi in northeastern Japan on the Emperor's orders. Both were heroes of Imperial Japan and depicted in government textbooks used in schools attended by all 'Japanese'. As Taguchi Ukichi noted (see chapter 2), at the time it was argued that the Empress Jingū and the ninth century Emperor Kanmu were descendants of Korean migrants, while Sakanoue-no-Tamuramaro was a descendant of Chinese stock.
18 Katō Hiroyuki (1907: 21, 44, 86). For Katō's ideas on mixed residency, see Unoura (1988). For the exchange between Katō

and Ebina Danjō, on one hand, and between Katō and Ukita Kazutami on the other, see Yoshida Kōji (1976) and Tahata Shinobu (1959).
19 In Ebina Danjō (1907). The quotation is from Ebina (1907: 61–2).
20 Ukita Kazutami (1908: 32). Mamiya Kunio (1990) mentions Ukita's views of race, but does not touch on Ukita's theory of expansionism that was based on his ideas of the origin of the Japanese nation.
21 Uchimura Kanzō (1980–84: vol. 16, 44). For his discussion of heroes, see Uchimura (1980–84: vol. 3, 256).
22 Katō Hiroyuki (1911: 96–8, 277).
23 Izawa Shūji (1897: 9). For Mochiji Mutsusaburō's comments, see Yoshino Hidekimi (1927: 146). I would like to express my gratitude to Chen Peifeng who provided useful hints and historical materials related to this topic.

4 The Anthropologists

1 The Japanese government was aware that the customs of the peoples of the colonies of Great Britain and France were being surveyed. Moreover, a number of officials of the Governments-General were in favour of indirect rule, and as a result customs were surveyed in both Taiwan and Korea, although this work was hardly reflected in policy at all. These surveys were undertaken by legal scholars rather than anthropologists. Legal scholars in Japan had imported jurisprudence from the West – mainly from France and Germany – and created a modern legal system. Since they were forced to reconcile Japanese customs and Western legal concepts, they had experience in surveying customs within Japan Proper (*naichi*). See Oguma (1998).
2 See Terada (1975).
3 Katō Hiroyuki (1900: 158–9).
4 Katō Hiroyuki (1904: 81).
5 Inoue Tetsujirō (1905). The quotation is from Inoue (1905: no. 283, 178–9).
6 Tsuboi Shōgorō (1905). The quotations from this paper are from Tsuboi (1905: no. 232, 439–40, 442–3).
7 In *Tōkyō jinruigakkai zasshi*, no. 171 (see Anon. 1900). For Tsuboi's philanthropic work with the *Ainu*, see Kaiho Yōko

(1992: chapter 6). In the fifth Domestic Industrial Exhibition held in March 1903 (this is also examined by Kaiho), Tsuboi organised an anthropological 'exhibition' of the *Ainu*, the Okinawan peoples, and indigenous Taiwanese. Kaiho's book does not mention this anthropological exhibition, but it was without question discriminatory. I will write about this incident at a later date (I have mentioned it in Oguma [1998: chapter 12]). In his 'Jinruigaku kenkyūjo to shite no wagakuni' (Japan as an Anthropological Research Labrotory), published five months before the Exhibition was opened, Tsuboi (1902) emphasised that 'no country is as advantageous a place as Japan for carrying out anthropological research' because Japan was a multi-national state. From this, it could be concluded that Tsuboi saw no contradiction in his perception of Japan as a multi-national state and his organisation of an anthropological 'exhibition'.

8   Tsuboi (1906). The quotation is from Tsuboi (1906: 432–3).
9   Koganei Yoshikiyo (1928: 511, 513).
10 Tsuboi (1903: 270).
11 Uchimura Kanzō ([1895] 1980–84). The quotations are from Uchimura ([1895] 1980–84: 97, 100–1).
12 For a discussion and citations of the *Ainu* soldiers, see Ogawa Masato (1993).
13 The Golden Kite appears in the Kiki myths, and was reputed to have saved the Emperor Jinmu.
14 Kitakaze Isokichi is not an *Ainu* name. It is a Japanised name, translatable as 'Northwind Beach', and perhaps given to this individual by a bureaucrat with his tongue firmly in his cheek. All *Ainu* were registered under Japanised names in the Family Register (*koseki*) system. For the Family Register system, see chapter 13, endnote 10.

5 The Theory that the Japanese and Koreans share a Common Ancestor

1   For the theory that the 'Japanese' and the Koreans share a common ancestor, see Ueda Masaaki (1973; 1978b), Hatada Takashi (1968; 1983), Kim Ilmyon (1984) and Nakatsuka Akira (1993). In general, these are not comprehensive examinations, and merely criticise representative theorists

such as Kita Sadakichi as 'self-evidently evil' without focusing on the duality of invasion and mixture. For an overview of Japanese historians, beginning with Kume, Takegoshi and Yamaji, I have relied on Nagahara Keiji and Kano Masanao eds (1976).

2 For a detailed examination of the academic theories of the Edo Period, together with the theories of the Japanese nation developed by Hoshino Hisashi and Kume Kunitake, see Kudō (1979). Kudō, however, does not focus on the dual nature of their arguments. For Kume, also see Ōkubo Toshikane ed. (1991). This work does not, however, focus on Kume's theory of the Japanese nation.

3 Hoshino Hisashi (1890). The quotations are from Hoshino (1890: 17–18, 28, 30, 36, 38, 40–2). For the attack on Hoshino, see Kano Masanao and Imai Osamu (1991: 267).

4 Kume Kunitake (1889).

5 The representative work of Yoshida Tōgo on the theory that the 'Japanese' and Koreans share a common ancestor is *Nikkan koshidan* (On Ancient Japanese-Korean History) (Yoshida Tōgo 1893). He acknowledged in his introduction that Kume had read his manuscript.

6 Kume Kunitake (1894). The citations are from Kume (1894: no. 223, 15–19, no. 224, 11, 13, no. 225, 12, 17, no. 226, 11, 14–15).

7 For the following, see Kume (1905).

8 See Ōno Susumu's remarks (*kaisetsu*) in Ikeda Jirō and Ōno Susumu eds (1973).

9 Kanazawa Shōzaburō (1910: i–ii).

10 For the following, see Takegoshi Yosaburō (1896).

11 Takegoshi (1910a).

12 Yamaji Aizan (1901). The citation on the 'Churanian' theory is from Yamaji (1966: 301). For Yamaji's theory of the Japanese nation, see Sakamoto Takao (1988) and Kudō (1979).

13 Yamaji (1910: 15).

14 Torii Ryūzō (1975–77: vol. 1, 410–24).

15 Tokutomi Sohō (1894: 2).

16 Ōkuma Shigenobu (1906: 67–8, 70–1).

17 Ōkuma Shigenobu ed. ([1907] 1970: 16–17). Ōkuma ([1910] 1913: 12).

6 The Japanese Annexation of Korea

1. For the tone of argument in Japanese newspapers and magazines at the time of the annexation of Korea, see the representative work, Kang Tongzin (1984), which surveys editorials and articles in the major newspapers and magazines of general opinion of the time. In addition, see Yoshioka Yoshinori (1967; 1968), Ui Keiko (1969), Yoshioka Masao (1969), Hirata Ken'ichi (1974) and Masubuchi Nobuo (1992). None of these focus on the theories of the Japanese nation. The total number of articles contained in magazines of general opinion will vary according to whether the short talks (*danwa*) contained in individual articles are themselves counted as separate articles. On this point, I have followed Kang (1984).
2. This is reprinted in Naitō Konan (1969–76: vol. 4). The quotation is from the 4 September 1910 number.
3. For editorials, see, for instance, Anon. (1910e) and Anon. (1910c), for articles, see Anon. (1910a).
4. Ukita Kazutami (1910a: 3). Ōkuma Shigenobu (1910: 6–7).
5. Takegoshi Yosaburō (1910b: 22). Tomizu Hirondo (1910: 26). Sawayanagi Masatarō (1910: 113).
6. Takegoshi (1910c: 52).
7. Ukita Kazutami (1910b: 2).
8. Ebina Danjō (1910: 117, 119, 121–2).
9. Shimamura Hōgetsu (1910: 131–4).
10. Inoue Tetsujirō (1910: 1, 6–7, 8, 12, 13, 16).
11. Editorials in *Yorozu chōhō* (Anon. 1910b) and *Tōkyō asahi shinbun* (Anon. 1910d). The Nitobe lecture is contained in Tanaka Shin'ichi (1980).

Part Two: The Thought of 'Empire'

7 History and the 'Abolition of Discrimination'

1. There are a number of works on Kita Sadakichi, including, on the one hand, Hatada (1968; 1983) and Kudō (1979), which emphasise Kita's common ancestor theory and, on the other, Ueda Masaaki (1978a) and Kano Masanao (1983), which, while recognising this 'pitfall', praise Kita as a critic of the pure blood theory. My own view is that Kita was a

typical theorist of the position that argued the 'Japanese' and Koreans shared a common ancestor, and that this theory itself contradicted the pure blood theory. For Kita's early life, see Ueda Masaaki (1978a) and Yamada Norio (1976).
2 Kita Sadakichi (1921a). The citations are from Kita (1921a: no. 2, 6, 11–14, no. 3, 5, 13, no. 4, 6, 8–10).
3 Yamaji (1966: 262). Yanagita Kunio ([1902] 1962–71: 318).
4 See Kim Chongmi (1989).
5 Kita Sadakichi (1919b: 52–4).
6 See Kita Sadakichi ([1928] 1981: 5–9, 130–1, 190–1, 220–3).
7 Kita Sadakichi ([1928] 1981: 193).
8 Kita Sadakichi (1910: 7–19, 38–9, 64–77).
9 Kita Sadakichi (1921b: 12). For the lecture and the response, see Kita (1921b: 44–5).
10 Kita Sadakichi (1979–82: vol. 8, 8, 51, 59).
11 Kita Sadakichi (1979–82: vol. 8, 17, 19–20, 37).
12 Kita Sadakichi (1979–82: vol. 8, 28–9).
13 Kita Sadakichi (1979–82: vol. 8, 75–6). For the grant provided by the Ministry of Education, see Ueda Masaaki (1978a: 114).
14 See the appendix in Shinmura Izuru (1920). Kita has added some comments to the end of Shinmura's article.

8 The Reformation of the Theory of the National Polity

1 Nagai Tōru (1928: 283). Research on the theory of the national polity largely focuses on the Meiji Period. For the Taishō Period, research is limited to works such as Suzuki Masayuki (1986) and Morikawa Terunori (1986). Both works argue that the national polity theory, which had been regarded as lacking in content and unworthy of serious study, was reformed to oppose Taishō Democracy. Morikawa focuses on an incident where the publication of Inoue Tetsujirō's *Waga kokutai to kokumin dōtoku* (The Japanese National Polity and National Morals), Kōbundo, 1925, was suspended after being attacked by the right-wing. This incident, however, has nothing directly to do with the debate on the Japanese nation, and accordingly I have omitted any reference to it here. Neither work focuses on the reformation of the national polity theory to deal with the alien nations within the empire or on the discourse on the Japanese nation.

2 Katō Hiroyuki (1915: 127–8).
3 Kakei Katsuhiko (1926: 6–7).
4 Mozume Takami (1919: 6–8, 22–3). The citation on Korea is from Mozume (1919: 524, 538).
5 Cited from Watari Shōzaburō (1928a: 46).
6 Hozumi Yatsuka (1910: vol. 1, 11). For Hozumi's participation in the Korean Education Law, see Ozawa Yūsaku (1966).
7 The following citations are from Uesugi Shinkichi (1921: 40–1; 1925a: 720; 1925b: 161). For Uesugi, see Nagao (1981).
8 Inoue Tetsujirō (1912: 62–73).
9 Katō Genchi (1912: 167–8). Tatebe's lecture, 'Teikoku no kokuze to sekai no senran' (The War-Torn World and the National Policy of the Empire), is contained in *Nippon shakaigakuin nenpō* (The Annual Report of the Japanese Social Academy) (see Tatebe Tongo 1914). For the foreign migrants (*banbetsu*), see Tatebe (1912: 993).
10 Tanaka Chigaku ([1920] 1942: 42).
11 Kanokogi Kazunobu (1918). The citations are from Kanokogi (1918: no. 6, 45, no. 7, 10).
12 Satomi Kishio (1928: 70, 113, 119–20, 133).
13 Satō Tetsutarō (1918). The cited sections are from Satō (1918: no. 4, 41–2).
14 Satomi (1928: 113–9).
15 Ōshima Masanori (1918: 14–15). However, Ōshima was not the first individual to use this concept. For example, according to Chen Peifeng, Nakagawa Yūjirō, the minister of the treasury of the Taiwanese Government-General, in 'Kokutai to dōka' (The National Polity and Assimilation), *Taiwan kyōikukai zasshi*, no. 103, 1910, had already tried to reform the theory of the Family State by advocating the position that the Taiwanese were adopted children.
16 Yoshida Kumaji (1918: 16). Yoshida (1928: 208–9).
17 However, Watari Shōzaburō was opposed to the idea that the Japanese nation was a mixed one. According to him, a nation was not a biological concept but an ideological one. Therefore, once a racial mixture or assimilation was completed, the nation would no longer be a mixed one. Watari (1928a: 65–6).
18 Watari (1928b: 60, 56). For the aim of the lectures and their publication, see the introduction.

19 Kiyohara Sadao (1930: 41). What is important here is the negative use of the phrase 'homogeneous nation' by a national polity theorist. This does not deny the possibility that this phrase had been used before this.

9 The Self-Determination and Boundaries of the Nation

1 There are a large number of accounts of the general Japanese discourse on the March First Independence Movement. See, for instance, Kang Tongzin (1984). There is no research, however, that focuses on theories of the nation.
2 Kang Toksang ed. (1967: 34, 54).
3 Komatsu Midori (1916: 53). This article is mentioned by Matsuo Takayoshi (1974) and by Kang (1984). However, neither of these authors focuses attention on the section cited here.
4 In Torii Ryūzō (1975–77: vol. 12, 538–9). In this work, I have cited a number of histories of Japanese anthropology; Torii is referred to in all these books as well as in other histories of Japanese anthropology. For biographies, see Hachiman Ichirō (1975), Suenari Michio (1988), Shiratori Yoshio (1992) and Nakazono Eisuke (1995). Only Kudō (1979) and Yoshino Makoto (1993) mention Torii's theory that the 'Japanese' and Koreans shared a common ancestor. Iesaka Kazuyuki ([1980] 1986: 38–9) regards Torii's remark cited here as an example of racially discriminatory imperialism.
5 Kita Ikki (1959–72: vol. 2, 260–1). Abe Hirozumi (1975: chapter 2, section 3), notes the similarity of Kita's theory of the nation and the ideas of Takata Yasuma and Tokutomi Sohō (these will be discussed in chapter 16). Takimura Ryūichi ([1973] 1987: chapter 5, section 5) also mentions Kita's theory of the nation.
6 Anon. (1919). For the example of the annexation of Sudeten, see Uemura Hideaki (1992: 105).
7 Contained in Torii Ryūzō (1975–77: vol. 1). The citations are from Torii (1975–77: vol. 1, 212, 189). However, Torii insisted that the Izumo were members of the 'Japanese Proper', and that migration occurred before the descent of the Tenson nation. This view of history was therefore accepted to some degree at this time.

8   Torii (1920: 106). This is not included in his Complete Works.
9   Ifa Fuyū ([1910] 1974–76).
10 Takahashi Sadaki (1992: 42–3). Watanabe Yoshimichi (1931: 44). Sano Manabu (1933: 21–5). Sano ed. (1922).
11 Takahashi (1992: 45).
12 Takahashi (1992: 23). Sano (1933: 17).
13 Kita Sadakichi (1979–82: vol. 8, 43).
14 Kaigo Muneomi ed. (1979: vol. 16). The citations are from Kaigo ed. (1979: vol. 16, 352, 383, 385) for the first edition; Kaigo ed. (1979: vol. 16, 394, 415, 417, 418) for the second edition; Kaigo ed. (1979: vol. 16, 430, 456, 458, 461, 462) for the third edition; Kaigo ed. (1979: vol. 16, 489) for the fourth edition; and Kaigo ed. (1979: vol. 16, 579) for the fifth edition.
15 The following are from Kaigo ed. (1979: vols. 19 and 20). The references to the first edition are from Kaigo ed. (1979: vol. 19, 441–4, 448, 450, 492). Other citations are from Kaigo ed. (1979: vol. 19, 628, 727). In the *Kōtō shōgaku shūshinsho* textbook (for third year students) published in March 1910 immediately before the annexation of Korea, there appear expressions such as 'our nation mostly shares the same ancestor' (Monbushō kyōgakukyoku 1910: 1), or 'our nation has hardly ever mixed with other nations, and all Japanese nationals believe that they are the same people. Although there were some foreign migrants, these were all assimilated into the nation in due course' (Monbushō kyōgakukyoku 1910: 4). Such expressions disappear from the 1913 edition. This was perhaps a result of the annexation of Korea, after which it could no longer be said that there were only a few members of 'other nations' in Japan. This does not mean, however, that the mixed nation theory was officially accepted. Since the textbooks for junior high schools differed from one another, it can be said that although the theory was 'officially approved' in education, it was not 'absolute'.
16 The Empress Jingū was the mother of the Emperor Ōjin and the wife of the Emperor Chūai.
17 The citations from junior high school textbooks that incorporated the mixed nation theory are from Inobe Shigeo (1934: 5), Shiba Kuzumori (1934: vol. 1, 2), Sanseidō editorial board ed. (1926: 4–5) and Saitō Hishō (1933: 11). Kinomiya Yasuhiko (1933), Fuzanbō editorial board ed. (1929), Ariga

Nagao (1913) and Sanseidō editorial board ed. (1934) all mention the idea of a mixed origin.
18 Tsuda Sōkichi (1902: 3, 7), reprinted (with slight differences) in Tsuda (1963–66: vol. 23).
19 Junior high school textbooks that did not mention the idea of a mixed origin include Kiyohara Sadao (1941), Uozumi Sōgorō (1933), Kurita Genji (1937) and Ōmori Kingorō (1933).
20 For the exclusion of Japanese immigrants, see Wakatsuki Yasuo (1972).
21 The citation is from Shibukawa Genji (1924: 33). Also see Yamagata Isoo (1924), who adopted the same line of argument.
22 Kobayashi Masasuke (1919: 102, 138).
23 Anon. (1929: 11).
24 Nakayama Satoru (1924). The citations are from Nakayama (1924: 37, 38, 40, 41). The citation from Kita Ikki is from Kita (1959–72: vol. 2, 260).

10 The Japanese as Caucasians

1 Takahashi Yoshio ([1884] 1961). For research that precedes that of this chapter, see Mimura Saburō (1984), which discusses the history of the theory of a Jewish origin. Also see Taga Kazufumi (1988) and Takeuchi Ken (1972). For Taguchi's theory of race, see Kudō (1979) and Inoue Shōichi (1994). For Oyabe, see Matsuyama Iwao (1993). Kamishima Jirō (1961) also mentions Oyabe. In this chapter, I will discuss not only the aspirations of a developing state, but also the inferiority complex towards the West, as the background to these theories.
2 For these theories developed by Western intellectuals, see Kudō (1979: 38–42, 78–9). Bälz' theory is introduced in Terada (1975: 27).
3 Taguchi Ukichi ([1895] 1927–29). The quotations are from Taguchi ([1895] 1927–29: 478, 479, 482). Suzuki Kentarō ([1891] 1927–38: 446–51) argued for the enlargement of Japanese power through overseas expansion and the promotion of the mixture of blood.
4 Taguchi (1901). The citations are from Taguchi (1901: 18, 26).
5 Shinmura Izuru ([1901] 1971–83: 104, 109). For Ōgai's reaction, see Mori Ōgai (1971–75: vol. 25, 530).

6   Taguchi ([1904] 1927–29). The citation is from Taguchi ([1904] 1927–29: 500).
7   Taguchi ([1905] 1927–29). The citations are from Taguchi ([1905] 1927–29: 501, 509, 514).
8   Tsuboi (1905). The citation is from Tsuboi (1905: no. 231, 391).
9   Kimura Takatarō (1911). The citations are from Kimura (1911: vol. 1, viii–ix, xiv, xxii).
10 Takegoshi (1896: 3–4). Kume (1905: 15–18). For the reaction to this theory in Europe, see J. Krainer (1988).
11 The reference to the matriarchal system can be seen in Ishikawa Sanshirō (1924: 290–3). For the influence on Takamure Itsue, see Kōno Nobuko (1990: 160).
12 Tanaka Chigaku ([1920] 1942: 257–8, 267–71, 276–93). Miyazawa Kenji (1973–77: vol. 13, 195). In addition to Greece and Italy, Tanaka mentions Japan as another possible location of Takamagahara. Hosaka Kanai, to whom Miyazawa sent this letter, rejected Miyazawa's invitation to join the Kokuchūkai and broke off his friendship with him. However, Miyazawa never lost his respect for his friend. See Sugawara Chieko (1994). Hosaka seems to have argued that the Japanese nation came from somewhere in Asia and was not a special race, rejecting Miyazawa's position, which was influenced by Tanaka's dogma, that the Japanese were a superior nation with a holy mission to unite the world.
13 For this petition, see Takakura Shin'ichirō (1942: 608–9). For the Hokkaido Former Aborigines Protection Act of 1899, see chapter 3, endnote 5.
14 Kindaichi Kyōsuke ([1925] 1992–93: 560–1, 562). For the Yoshitsune legend, see this article together with Kikuchi Isao (1982) and Matsuyama (1993: 285–6). Kindaichi stated that when questioned by Yamato Japanese, the *Ainu* initially answered that Okikurumi was 'Honkansama', but further questioning made it clear that Yoshitsune was not always an *Ainu*.
15 Oyabe Zen'ichirō (1924: 86). For the reaction of Amakasu and Ōkawa, see Matsuyama (1993: 294–5).
16 Oyabe (1929). The citations are from Oyabe (1929: 7, 77, 329).
17 Kindaichi Kyōsuke (1992–93: vol. 12, 447, 448, 449). However, Kindaichi insisted that although the *Ainu* were the

indigenous people of northeastern Japan, they were not the indigenous people of the entire archipelago.
18 Kindaichi (1992–93: vol. 12, 570).

11 'The Return to Blood'

1 General research on Takamure includes that by Akiyama Kiyoshi, Takara Rumiko, Kōno Nobuko, Murakami Nobuhiko, Ishikawa Junko, Nishikawa Yūko, Terada Misao and Yoshie Akiko. For works that especially focus on Takamure's wartime writings, see Kanō Mikiyo ([1979] 1987) and Kano Masanao and Horiba Kiyoko (1977). In Kano and Horiba, *Takamure Itsue* (1977), Kano defines Takamure's research on matriarchy as a 'new *kokugaku*'. Kurihara Hiroshi (1994) argues that in her research of the history of marriage, Takamure developed her ideas first, and deliberately arranged her historical materials to fit these after. As far as I am aware, the first author to emphasise that Takamure's research on the matriarchy dealt with inter-racial marriage was Yamashita Etsuko (1988). Yamashita (1988: 181) notes that 'leaving aside the question whether or not Takamure was aware of it, she did suggest that Japan was not an homogeneous nation-state, but a state based on conquest which was unified through the fusion of the blood of many different races'. In this chapter, it will be argued that (1) Takamure's research on the matriarchy fitted the contemporary paradigm that believed the Japanese state had been unified through an assimilation of many ethnic groups in ancient times and (2) Takamure's view of Chinese thought was influenced by the *kokugaku* philosophy. For Takamure's wartime writings, including those cited here, see Takamure Itsue ronshū henshū iinkai ed. (1979). The quotations from Takamure Itsue ([1940] 1979), 'Nisen roppyakunen o kotohogite' (Celebrating 2,600 Years of Imperial Rule), Takamure ([1931] 1979), 'Shintō to jiyū ren'ai' (Shintō and Free Love), Takamure ([1934] 1979), 'Nippon seishin ni tsuite' (On the Japanese Spirit), Takamure ([1943] 1979a), 'Gunji to josei' (The Military and Women), Takamure ([1943] 1979b), 'Jingū Kōgō (Her Majesty the Empress Jingū) and Takamure ([1944] 1979), 'Taoyame' (Graceful Maidens) are from Takamure Itsue ronshū henshū iinkai ed. (1979: 221, 192–3, 206–8, 240, 224–6, 262).

2. *Kojiki-den* is an annotated edition of *Kojiki* that consists of 4 volumes, and was written between 1764 and 1798.
3. Takamure ([1931] 1979).
4. Takamure (1965–67: vol. 10, 247). Takamure (1938b), also cited in Takamure Itsue ronshū henshū iinkai ed. (1979: 215). Takamure (1940: 151). For Takamure on 'Semu shuzoku' (The Semetic Race), see Kano and Horiba (1977: 181).
5. Takamure ([1934] 1979).
6. Takamure (1938a).
7. Takamure (1940: 262). For her impressions on the Great Kantō Earthquake, see Takamure (1965–67: vol. 10, 204).
8. Takamure (1939: 74).
9. Both *katakana* and *hiragana* are phonetic symbols (*moji*) created by simplifying specific *kanji*. Because *hiragana* were originally used by women who could not read Chinese *kanji*, this alphabet was not treated with great respect. It is sometimes said by Japanese nationalists that it is the women and lower classes who maintain and develop national culture in late-developing cultures where the male elite immerses itself in an advanced foreign culture. Also see chapter 1, endnote 7.
10. Kano and Horiba (1977: 247).

Part Three: The Thought of an 'Island Nation'

12 The Birth of the Folklore of an Island Nation

1. For research published between 1946 and 1975, see the 20 volume collection, Gotō Sōichirō ed. (1986–88). The major pre-1977 studies on Yanagita are summarised in a list attached to the end of Irokawa Daikichi (1978). For recent monographs, see research by Gotō Sōichirō, Iwamoto Yoshiteru, Kamishima Jirō, Okaya Kōji, Miyazaki Shūjirō, Shōji Kazuaki, Ōfuji Tokihiko, Wakamori Tarō, Miyata Noboru, Satō Kenji, Itō Mikiharu, Sakurai Tokutarō, Tsurumi Kazuko, Murakami Nobuhiko, Yoshida Kazuaki, Akasaka Norio, Funaki Hiroshi, Yamashita Kōichirō, Matsumoto Mikio, Fukuda Ajio, Osahama Isao, Uchida Ryūzō, Yoshimoto Takaaki, Tanigawa Ken'ichi, Suzuki Mitsuo, Chiba Tokuji, Kajiki Tsuyoshi and Makita Shigeru. In this chapter, I will argue (1) that Yanagita's theory of the mountain people followed the established theory

of the origin of the Japanese nation of the day, (2) that the impact of the West played a role in Yanagita's shift to his theory of the South Islands, and (3) that, following this shift, Yanagita's folklore came to include an element that aimed to unify the Japanese nation. For the third point, see Kawada Minoru (1985). Kitsukawa Toshitada (1983) adopts a similar point of view to my own. However, neither of the above two works focus on Yanagita's theory of ethnicity (*minzokuron*). For Yanagita's emphasis on spoken language, see Tanaka Katsuhiko (1978). For Yanagita and the issue of the colonies, see Murai Osamu ([1992] 1995), although it must be noted that this last work is full of conjectures and mistakes.

2 Although it has been argued in Japanese Yanagita studies that Yanagita called the mountain people the indigenous people as a result of his own hypothesis, or that he obtained the idea from the indigenous tribes in the mountains of Taiwan – for examples, see Irokawa (1978: 32) and Nakamura Akira ([1974] 1985: 25) – the notion that an indigenous people lived in the archipelago was in fact an 'established paradigm' so popular that it was included in junior high school textbooks, and Yanagita merely accepted it. Yanagita's submission to *Jinruigaku zasshi*, 'Ainu no ie no katachi' (The Shape of *Ainu* Houses), is reprinted in Yanagita Kunio (1962–71: vol. 31). For the circumstances behind Yanagita's criticism of Kume Kunitake, see Saeki Arikiyo (1988). Iwamoto Yoshiteru (1982a: 215, 216–7) notes the influence of Tsuboi and Koganei on Yanagita's theory of the mountain people and the fact that he used the phase 'the mountain people of the islands' in his school-day poetry. Kitsukawa (1983) notes that the mixed nation theory existed in prewar Japanese anthropology, and that it is possible that Yanagita based his arguments on this theory.

3 Hozumi Shigetaka ed. (1943: 224). For Publius Cornelius Tacitus, see Tacitus (1999). For the influence of Heine and France, see Nakamura ([1974] 1985: 13–14), Iwamoto ([1983] 1994: 167–72), and finally Ozawa Toshio (1975).

4 For research that focuses on Yanagita's experience in Geneva, see Iesaka ([1980] 1986: chapter 5) and Iwamoto (1982b: chapter 1; 1985: part 3). Sections of these works mention the influence of this experience on his views of the South Islands.

5   For Yanagita's trip to Taiwan, see Iwamoto (1990). For his 'Junibi naki gaikō', see Chiba Tokuji (1991). For Clemenceau's utterance, see Michel Braker (1976: ii).
6   See Egami Namio (1985: vol. 7, 40). In 1902, Yangita noted in 'Nōgyō seisakugaku' (Agricultural Policy Studies) that 'the ancestors of the Japanese in the main came from the south' (Yanagita [1902] 1962–71: 318) and seems to have believed in a southern origin from this time.
7   Later references to the situation in Korea are limited to Yanagita, 'Kokusai rōdō mondai no ichimen' (One Aspect of the International Labour Problem), published in 1924, where Yanagita briefly mentions the discrimination against Koreans by Japanese colonisers (Yanagita 1962–71: vol. 29, 125). For Yanagita's view of Korea, see Yang Yonghu (1980). Also see Iwamoto (1993).
8   The Great Kantō Eathquake struck the Kantō region on 1 September 1923. With a registered magnitude of 7.9, it caused extensive damage in Tokyo and Yokohama.
9   This report, *The Welfare and Development of the Natives in [the] Mandated Territories*, is contained in translation in an appendix in Iwamoto ([1983] 1994). Iwamoto discusses Yanagita's definition of the 'common people' in Iwamoto ([1983] 1994: 184–5 and 1982b: 79–80).
10 According to Momokawa Yoshito (1988), this section shows that Yanagita was interested in Japanese national unity. Together with the fact that Yanagita described his work on the mountain people as dilettantism in *Kainan shōki*, this demonstrates the emergence of 'an awakening nationalism' caused by Yanagita's experience in the West.
11 See Iwamoto ([1983] 1994: appendix, 227–8). For Nitobe and Uchimura, see Ōta Yūzō (1981: chapter 2).
12 In a discussion with Ienaga Saburō in 1949, Yanagita argued that modernisation was not a simple process, that the process of change in Japan was different from that in other countries, and that it had begun from below before Japan's interaction with the West. This indicates that he believed in a sort of endogenous development. See Yanagita et al. ([1949] 1964).
13 A Diet was opened in 1890, but the right to vote was limited to mature males who were paying a set amount of tax, which denied the majority the vote. It was not until 1925 that universal suffrage for males was recognised.

14 In a discussion with Hashikawa Bunzō, Kamishima Jirō lists Yanagita's criticism of the attitude shown to native peoples by Western ethnology as another reason to explain why he kept folklore separate from anthropology. See Hashikawa and Kamishima (1975).
15 See Iwamoto ([1983] 1994: appendix, 227). In this report, Yanagita expressed his surprise that in the South Sea islands, people thought of themselves as members of different ethnic groups even within the same island. It can be surmised that this reinforced his perception that the lack of a unified national consciousness was a cause of the lack of unification of the South Sea islands. In a lecture in 1926, he criticised the policies of assimilating the *Ainu*, and stated that the settlement of Hokkaido was a copy of Western 'coloured' policies. See Yanagita ([1926] 1980).
16 Yanagita was opposed to Kanazawa Shōzaburō's argument that the 'Japanese' shared a common ancestor with both Okinawans and Koreans (Yanagita 1962–71: bekkan 3, 416). In his unpublished 'Hikaku minzokugaku no mondai' (The Problems of Comparative Folklore), he wrote that 'the attempt to reconstruct the life of the people of the *Man'yōshū* from the ancient customs of the peninsula is a poetic practice, and does not even come close to being academic work' (Yanagita 1962–71: vol. 30, 70). It is interesting to note that he viewed poetry and research here as opposing concepts.
17 Yanagita et al. (1957). For Yanagita's statement on the 'Japanese way of thinking', see Yanagita et al. ([1949] 1964: 186). In *Yanagita Kunio no shisō* (The Thought of Yanagita Kunio), Kajiki Tsuyoshi (1989: chapter 4) argues that the 'common people' was 'a natural definition of a single nation' designed to provide a foothold to resist 'European universalism'.
18 In an analysis of beautiful women (*bijinron*) published in 1929, Yanagita stated that 'it is clear that the Japanese people were originally made up of more than one race' (Yanagita 1962–71: vol. 3, 338), and after the war criticised 'the position that the Japanese consist of a single nation' (Yanagita 1962–71: bekkan 3, 417). Although Yanagita's view of the Japanese nation tended towards a theory of homogeneity, he was always ambiguous about this point, perhaps because of his past work on the mountain people.

13 Japanisation versus Eugenics

1. Oguma Eiji ([1994] 1998). See this chapter for Tōgō Makoto.
2. Unno Kōtoku (1910). The citations are from Unno (1910: 101, 103).
3. The following citations are from Kawakami Hajime (1982: vol. 8, 47, 50, 51, 534).
4. Tōgō Makoto (1925: 236, 269–71).
5. Other magazines include the Nippon Yūsei Undō Kyōkai (The Japanese Eugenic Movement Society) journal, *Yūsei Undō* (The Eugenic Movement, founded in 1926), and the Nippon Yūsei Kekkon Fukyūkai (The Japanese Eugenic Marriage Propagation Society) journal, *Yūsei* (Eugenics, founded in 1936). This chapter, however, will focus only on the two representative magazines.
6. For the promotion of marriages between 'Japanese' and Koreans and data on the number of such marriages, see Suzuki Yūko (1992: 76–87, 101–14).
7. Chōsen sōtokufu gakumukyoku shakai kyōikuka (1937: 19–20). The various texts of the Government-General of Korea (apart from those authored by Torii Ryūzō and Minami Jirō), together with Furuya's handbill cited here, are contained in the Ōno Rokuichirō files, Kensei shiryōshitsu, National Diet Library of Japan. Although there is little research that directly examines the issue of the 'Japan and Korea as One' ideology of the Japanisation policy period, for works that are indirectly related, see Miyata Setsuko (1985) and Takasaki Sōji (1993). For Furuya's petition, see Miyata Setsuko, Kim Yongtal and Yang Teho (1992). This work, however, does not examine this petition from the viewpoint of the opposition between the idea of pure blood and the policy of Japanisation.
8. Kokumin sōryoku Chōsen renmei bōei shidōbu ed. (1941a: 3, 4).
9. See, for instance, Kokumin sōryoku Chōsen renmei bōei shidōbu ed. (1941a: 6).
10. The system of national registration introduced in modern Japan is known as the *koseki*, or Family Register, In addition to family relations and current address, the *koseki* also records the *honseki*, or original location of the household.

   Since the *honseki* in many cases made the original location of a family clear, it was possible to use the *koseki* to identify a person's background. Since Okinawans and the *burakumin* suffered from discrimination because of their place of origin, and since it was possible to transfer one's *honseki* on moving house, it was possible to escape from discrimination by transferring one's *honseki*. However, it was not possible to transfer *honseki* between Korea, Taiwan and Japan Proper, and so, unlike Okinawans and *burakumin*, this particular means of escaping from discrimination was not available to the Koreans and Taiwanese. See Oguma (1998).

11 Kokumin sōryoku Chōsen renmei bōei shidōbu ed. (1941b: 29, 31).
12 Odaka Tomoo (1941: 48, 50, 61–3).
13 Tsuda Tsuyoshi (1941: 34, 35, 49). For Ueda's theory, see Ueda Jōkichi (1935). Kohama Mototsugu adopted a position similar to Ueda's. Torii Ryūzō (1939: 38).
14 Kurashima Itaru (1942: 12).
15 Minami Jirō (1942: 13–14).
16 Yasuda Yojūrō (1985–89: vol. 16, 42, 47). However, in an article published in 1942, Yasuda criticised the theory that the Japanese migrated from overseas. Yasuda (1985–89: vol. 16, 374). Pak Chunil (1969) criticises this travelogue of Yasuda, but does not mention the section cited here. For I Kuangsu, see I Kangsu (1941). Kim Ilmyon (1984) mentions I Kuangsu's article, but argues that such a line of argument, before the period of the Japanisation policy, would have been viewed as *lèse-majesté*.
17 The Ministry of Overseas Affairs (Takumushō) was in effect a Ministry of Colonial Affairs. The official Japanese government position, however, was that Korea and Taiwan were part of 'Japan' and not colonies, and that this could explain and justify the policy of 'Japan and Korea as One' under which Korea was being assimilated. In 1929, the Department of Overseas Affairs in the Ministry of Internal Affairs was made independent and promoted to a Ministry (Hokkaido also came under its jurisdiction).
18 Furuya Eiichi (1939).
19 Miyata (1985: 166).
20 Chōsen sōtokufu hōmukyoku (n. p.; 1940: 37). Both are internal documents of the Legal Affairs Bureau of the Government-General of Korea. The first text has no page numbers.
21 Takeda Masuo, *Ronsetsu bunrei kaiseimei dokuhon* (The Name Change Reader), Nanpōdō, 1943, is cited in Uesugi

Mutsuhiko (1987: 122). Manshū Teikoku Kyōwakai Chūō Honbu ed. (1939: 41).
22 Kita Noriaki (1936: 80). For Shimomura Hiroshi (or Kainan), see Higuchi Yūichi ed. (1991: vol. 2, 81). For a detailed account of Kita Noriaki, see Takagi Hiroshi (1993).
23 Nagai Hisomu (1936). For the Japanese Racial Hygiene Association, see Suzuki Zenji (1983: 143–64). Suzuki, however, is mainly interested in the sterilisation act, and does not mention the issue of mixed-blood or Furuya Yoshio's activities. For the directors (*yakuin*) at the time of founding, see *Minzoku eisei* (Racial Hygiene), vol. 1, no. 1. The Yoshida Shigeru given here as a Trustee was probably the Yoshida Shigeru who became the Minister of Health and Welfare in the Yonai Cabinet after working as a bureaucrat in the Ministry of Home Affairs, and not the prewar diplomat and postwar Prime Minister of the same name.
24 Nagai Hisomu (1933). The citation is from Nagai (1933: 56).
25 The Eugenic Protection Act was abolished in 1996 and replaced with the Botai Hogo Hō (Mother's Body Protection Law).
26 For Furuya's personal history, see Ōkurashō ed. (1939–50) and for his activities, see Furuya Yoshio (1942: introduction). For the Manifesto for Establishing a Population Policy, see Ishikawa Junkichi (1976: 1103–5). For Furuya's ideas about population, see Furuya Yoshio (1935).
27 Furuya Yoshio (1939). The citations are from Furuya (1939: no. 189, 13 and no. 190, 2, 5).
28 Furuya Yoshio (1941: 175–83).
29 At the time, Koreans and Taiwanese were regarded as 'Japanese', and so were not called 'Koreans' or 'Taiwanese'. Instead, the public media used phrases such as 'peninsular Japanese' or 'people of the peninsula' and 'people of the main island [of Taiwan]' (*hontō*).
30 For the contents of the conferences, see *Minzoku eisei*, vol. 9, no. 1, vol. 10, nos. 3, 5, and vol. 12, no. 1. Research institutions affiliated with the Ministry of Health and Welfare included the Public Heath Board and the Population Issues Research Institute. The citation is from Ishihara Fusao and Satō Hifumi (1941: 164).
31 For editions of *Yūseigaku* (Eugenics) with a large number of Ministry of Health and Welfare papers, see, for instance, no.

209, July 1941. For an introduction of research into children of mixed Japanese and Korean parentage, see Mizushima Haruo (1942). Mizushima, however, takes a neutral stance to mixed blood. Furuya Eiichi (1940: no. 193, 9). Furuya's past contribution is Furuya Eiichi (1927–28).

32 Reprinted as Kōseishō kenkyūjo jinkō minzokubu (1981), *Minzoku jinkō seisaku kenkyū shiryō* (Materials on Ethnic and Population Policies Research). Of the 8 volumes of reports, the first two were published in December 1942 as *Sensō no jinkō ni oyobosu eikyō* (The Influence of the War on Population), and the remaining six as *Yamato minzoku o chūkaku to suru sekai seisaku no kentō* (An Examination of Global Policy Centred on the Yamato Nation) in July 1943. John W. Dower (1986) examines this work, but does not mention the contradiction with the policy of Japanisation. According to the *Shokuinroku* (List of Government Employees) of the Ministry of Finance, Tate Minoru was Head of the Population Policy Research Department of the Population and Nation Department in the Ministry of Health and Welfare Research Centre (see Ōkurashō ed. 1939–50). He gave a paper at the eleventh conference of the Japanese Racial Hygiene Association. Elite bureaucrats Aoki Nobuharu and Nishio Mutsuo, together with a researcher, Yokota Nen, gave papers at the tenth and eleventh conferences. For the Population Research Centre, see Takasawa Atsuo (1992).

33 Kōseishō kenkyūjo jinkō minzokubu (1943: 304–7, 2364).

34 Kōseishō kenkyūjo jinkō minzokubu (1943: 328–30). However, Suzuki Yūko (1992) gives a number of cases where Japanese parents agreed to their daughters marrying Korean men because of the state's promotion of intermarriage. The section of *Yamato minzoku o chūkaku to suru sekai seisaku no kentō* (Kōseishō kenkyūjo jinkō minzokubu 1943: 303–68) that examines the problem of mixed blood is almost exactly the same as Koyama Eizō (1944: 571–645). Moreover, Koyama's earlier *Minzoku to jinkō no riron* (A Theory of Nations and Population) (Koyama 1941: 23–8) is also very similar. Koyama was a professor at Rikkyō University and, as of 1942, was a researcher at both the Population Research Centre and the Planning Board. He later became Head of both the First and Fourth Departments of the Ministry of Education Ethnic Research Centre. From 1942 to 1943, the Population Research Centre was reorganised as the Population and Nation Depart-

ment in the Ministry of Health and Welfare Research Centre, and there is a high probability that this part was written by Koyama. However, in a book for the general public, those sections that may have been interpreted as criticisms of Japanisation were all removed.
35 Martin Kaneko (1994).
36 Kōseishō kenkyūjo jinkō minzokubu (1943: 2360–2). The fifth item also mentioned 'the problem of the franchise within Japan Proper'. These proposals were discussed in Oguma (1998: chapter 14). As regards education, the children of majority Japanese in Korea and Taiwan officially attended classes with local children. However, children were separated according to their ability in the Japanese language, and so a *de facto* segregation existed. In Japan Proper, the children of Korean residents went to school together with those of majority Japanese.
37 For the Korean officers in the Imperial Army, see Yamamoto Shichihei (1986). This work discusses the officer, Hon Saik, who became a Lieutenant-General and was executed in the Philippines as a war criminal after the Second World War. He had been despatched by the Korean government to Japan's Military Academy (*Rikugun Shikan Gakkō*) before the annexation of Korea, was trained in the modern military sciences, and was incorporated into the Japanese military following the annexation. This was why he was able to become a high-ranking officer even though Koreans were not incorporated into the Japanese military until 1938. As will be mentioned in chapter 16, during the Pacific War, Korean soldiers were only allocated to front-line units on a limited basis because of concerns about Koreans rebelling; instead, preference was given to allocating such soldiers to units behind the front lines, such as guards of PoW camps. Hon Saik was appointed as CO (*sōkan*) of units stationed behind the front lines in the south late in the war, and was deemed responsible for the mistreatment of PoW.
38 Kōseishō kenkyūjo jinkō minzokubu (1943: 2360).
39 For the chapter on the origin of the Japanese nation see Kōseishō kenkyūjo jinkō minzokubu (1943: 2200–93). The citation is from Kōseishō kenkyūjo jinkō minzokubu (1943: 310–2).
40 Ishikawa Junkichi (1976: 1300). For the pure blood policies of the Council for Establishing Greater East Asia, see Ishii

Hitoshi (1992). The Cabinet Planning Board's research group's publication was Kikakuin kenkyūkai ed. (1943).
41 For the citation of the pro-Japanese Korean intellectual, see Ueda Tatsuo (1942: 4–5). For the argument against intermarriage in the Government-General of Korea, see Miyata (1985: 168). For the theory of heterosis within the eugenics school, see Taniguchi Konen (1943).
42 See, for instance, Furukawa Takeji (1931). For Furukawa Takeji and Furuhata's work on blood types, see Matsuda Kaoru (1994).
43 Furuhata Tanemoto (1935: 101).
44 The citation is from Kiyono Kenji (1926: 23). The paper on the origin of the nation is Kiyono (1929). For the relationship with Ishii Shirō, see Matsuda Kaoru (1994: 145).
45 For their academic theories until the 1920s, see Hasebe Kotondo (1927). Kiyono Kenji and Miyamoto Hiroto (1926a; 1926b). While Kiyono and Hasebe are inevitably mentioned in works on the history of Japanese anthropology, the only research that is not merely an introduction to their theories is Sakano Tōru (1993), which examines Kiyono's wartime writings. Sakano mentions neither the relationship with the eugenics school nor the postwar influence.
46 Torii Ryūzō (1933). Kiyono (1934).
47 For this threat, see Terada (1975: 202).
48 For this series of events, see Terada (1975: 243–6).
49 Hasebe (1940: 28, 30, 34). The postwar citation is from Hasebe (1949a: 6). For the description of Hasebe's position as similar to that of the Nazis, see Mizuno Yū (1960: 341).
50 Reprinted in Doi Akira ed. (1991). The citation is from Doi ed. (1991: 33–5).
51 Furuya Yoshio ed. (1943). The members are listed in Furuya ed. (1943: ii).
52 The citations are from Kiyono (1938: 24). Kiyono (1944a: 158) and Kiyono (1946: 443) both make the same argument.
53 See Kiyono (1936: 44).
54 For this series of events and the citation, see Kiyono (1956: 244, 296). Kiyono (1944b: ii).
55 Kiyono (1944b: 557). Hirano Yoshitarō and Kiyono Kenji (1942: 296). Kiyono (1944a: 27, 52).
56 Kiyono (1944b: 575, 569; 1944a: 169).
57 The citations are from Kiyono (1946: i, iii, 441).

58 Nezu Masashi (1936: 80, 81, 89–90). *Rekishigaku kenkyū* is still well-known today in Japan as a left-wing historical journal.
59 Reprinted in Hayakawa Jirō ([1936] 1976). The citation is from Hayakawa ([1936] 1976: 20).

14 The Revival of the Kiki Myths

1 For Shiratori Kurakichi, see, among others, Shiratori Yoshio (1975) and Goi Naohiro (1976). For Tsuda Sōkichi, see Inenaga Saburō (1972), Ueda Masaaki ed. (1974) and Ōmuro Mikio (1983), in addition to the recent research by Koseki Motoaki and Imai Osamu. Research until 1985 has been listed in the *geppō* of Tsuda's second Complete Works (see Tsuda 1986–89). Egami Namio ed. (1992) contains one chapter on Shiratori and another on Tsuda. For research that focuses on the theory of the Symbolic Emperor System as developed by Tsuda and Watsuji, see, for instance, Akasaka Norio (1990). The only research to focus on the theory of the origin of the Japanese nation as developed by Shiratori and Tsuda is Kudō (1979). Although Kudō notes with approval that both rejected the theory that the 'Japanese' and Koreans shared a common ancestor, he does not pay attention to their theory of the homogeneous nation. Ishida Mikinosuke ([1942] 1969–71: 534) noted that Shiratori's theory of the origin of the Japanese nation and his view of the Kiki myths formed the prototype for those of Tsuda. Stefan Tanaka (1993) focuses on Shiratori in examining the views of the East and the nation seen in Oriental studies in Japan, but does not understand the confrontation with the theory of the mixed nation. This chapter will show that Shiratori's theory of the Japanese nation was a minority position: Tanaka's position therefore cannot be said to be an analysis of the entire range of theories of the Japanese nation and views of Asia of the day. Kawamura Minato (1987) emphasises Tsuda's criticism of Chinese thought. Inoue Tatsuo (1992), a philosopher of law, discusses Tsuda as an example of a thinker who combined participatory democracy and the Emperor. Saeki Arikiyo (1991) mentions the influence of Shiratori's view of the Kiki myths on Tsuda and Tsuda's opposition to Kume. I received advice on Tsuda from Kurosu Kiyotada.

2 Shiratori Kurakichi ([1897] 1969–71). Here Shiratori argued against Inoue Tetsujirō's theory of a migration from the south.
3 Kita Sadakichi (1919c).
4 Shiratori Kurakichi ([1910] 1969–71: 341). The only paper that I am aware of where Shiratori discussed Korean policies is 'Nippon wa hatashite Chōsen o dōka shiubeki ka' (Can Japan Really Assimilate Korea?) (Shiratori 1910), a paper not included in his Complete Works. Here, Shiratori argued for the assimilation of Koreans, but stated that the ancient Japanese rule of Korea was of only part of the peninsula and that 'it is a new experience for the Japanese nation to assimilate another' (Shiratori 1910: 10). This statement meant that Shiratori differed from the mixed nation theorists. At this time, he had not yet clearly discarded the position that the Japanese nation migrated from Korea and that Japanese belonged to the Ural-Altaic family of languages. After this, he stopped discussing Korean policies, and showed an increasing keenness for the theory of the homogeneous nation. He seems to have gradually become sceptical of assimilationist policies through his opposition to the praise of the assimilation policy based on the mixed nation theory, his interaction with Gotō Shinpei and others, and the state of affairs in Korea following the annexation.
5 Shiratori Kurakichi ([1913] 1969–71: 178–9).
6 Kuroita Katsumi (1925: 153).
7 Ienaga (1972: 185). It is, however, unclear to what degree Tsuda's appreciation of Kōtoku was based on an understanding of his thought.
8 Tsuda Sōkichi (1963–66: vol. 12, *geppō*, 3). Tsuda was however critical of the *samurai* morals because they were similar to Confucianism.
9 Tsuda Sōkichi (1986–89: hokan 2, 316–7). In 'Chingen tōgo' (Unpleasant Platitudes) contained in the same volume, Tsuda denied the theory that the 'Japanese' and Koreans shared a common ancestor. However, in a postwar work, he noted that 'unlike the European colonial policies, Japan introduced the same cultural infrastructure in Taiwan and Korea as existed in Japan Proper – the plan to propagate education is a good example – and this must be highly evaluated'. Thus he seems not to have been negative about the propagation of education, whatever his thoughts about the coercive introduction of Japanese culture. Tsuda (1986–89: vol. 20, 503).

10 For the idea that the methodology of not always accepting the classical texts as factual was due to the influence of Shiratori, see Ienaga (1972: 246). For Motoori's argument, see Motoori Norinaga (1795–1812).

15 From 'Blood' to 'Climate'

1 Katsube Mitake (1967: 389). For Watsuji Testurō's thought, see the research of Yuasa Yasuo, Katsube Mitake, Sakabe Megumi, Yoshizawa Densaburō, Ikematsu Keizō and Robert N. Bellah. For works that especially focus on Watsuji's view of the Emperor, see Akasaka (1990), Kuginuki Kazunori (1986), Sakai Naoki (1990), Minato Michitaka (1990), Yuasa Yasuo ([1981] 1995: chapter 8), Yamada Kō (1987), Yorisumi Mitsuko (1989) and Kaneko Tateo (1991). Also see Yonetani Masafumi's series of studies (see below). For the view of China developed in *Fūdo*, see Sakai (1992). Also see the various chapters in Yuasa ed. (1973). No research that I am aware of focuses on Watsuji's theory of the homogeneous nation. For Watsuji's childhood, see Yuasa ([1981] 1995). For his interaction with Tanizaki and his theatre activities, see Katsube ([1987] 1995). Yonetani Masafumi provided advice and materials on Watsuji. As the proofs of the Japanese edition of this book were being checked, Karube Naoshi (1995) was published.
2 Kaigo Muneomi ed. (1979: vol. 19, 446, 629).
3 Inoue Shōichi (1994).
4 Naitō Konan (1969–76: vol. 6, 298). Kiyono (1944a: 165).
5 Kume Kunitake (1906). Also see Inoue Shōichi (1994: 120–1).
6 The concept of a pan-*Ainu* race that could be traced back to India was the idea of an anthropologist active at the time, Matsumoto Hikoshichirō, who argued that a nation that migrated from Korea conquered and mixed with this indigenous pan-*Ainu* nation, and thus that the Japanese nation was a mixture of Asians and Europeans, and possessed the ability to fuse and assimilate Eastern and Western civilisations. See Matsumoto Hikoshichirō (1919).
7 Yanagita Kunio et al. (1964: 28). For the influence of France's book, see Yonetani Masafumi (1992).
8 Yonetani (1994a: 108). This article analyses in detail the transformation of the view of the Emperor system seen in the revised version of *Nippon kodai bunka*.

9   See Ōta Tetsuo (1987).
10 For Nietzsche's view of the Greek tragedies, see Friedrich Nietzsche (1965) and Mishima Ken'ichi (1987: 60–88).
11 Yonetani (1990: 48). The citations below which are not from Watsuji's Complete Works are, for Watsuji on China, Watsuji (1944: 203, 206, 214–22), and for Watsuji on Japan, Watsuji (1935: 224–9, 234–40, 249–50).
12 The citations below are from Watsuji (1939: 2–3, 7, 11–12, 13).
13 Apart from the draft of the outline of 'Kokumin dōtokuron', the citations below are from Watsuji (1942: 440–2, 481–3, 485). Hashimoto Mitsuru (1992) examines the theory of the nation as developed in *Rinrigaku*.
14 Doi ed. (1991: 17, 287).

16 The Collapse of Empire

1   When the Government-General of Korea began to advocate the idea of 'Japan and Korea as One' (*Nissen ittai*) in about 1940, it claimed that the Koreans were not a separate 'nation'. As a result, there was a clash between the government of Manchukuo, which counted the Koreans as one of the five nations, and the Government-General of Korea. Many of the bureaucrats who held office in the Manchukuo government were 'Japanese' despatched to Manchukuo by the Japanese government, and these, together with other 'Japanese' migrants who had settled in Manchukuo, were reluctant to give up their Japanese nationality and passports. As a result, there was a debate about whether the Manchukuo government should recognise dual nationality, and Manchukuo never managed to legislate a nationality law.
2   Tokutomi Sohō (1925: 47; 1938: 2; 1939: 71–5; 1940: 2–6; 1942a: 19–24). The newspaper article is Tokutomi (1942b). For Kiyono's criticism, see Kiyono (1944a: 164).
3   Ōkawa Shūmei (1961–74: vol. 1, 503–4, 506, vol. 2, 908). Ishiwara Kanji (1993: 75–9). Tachibana Shiraki (1966: vol. 3, 322–52). For Ōkawa's view of the Japanese nation and the *Ainu*, see Matsumoto Ken'ichi (1986) and Ōtsuka Takehiro (1990). Both Matsumoto and Ōtsuka view Ōkawa's mixed nation theory as a position unique to him. Matsumoto also adopts the position that Ōkawa's mixed nation theory was influenced by Takegoshi (see chapter 5). However, neither

Matsumoto nor Ōtsuka seem to realise that the mixed nation theory was the general line of argument of the day, and that it was certainly not unique to Ōkawa, nor the result of the influence of any one individual. Moreover, neither focuses on the fact that Ōkawa's mixed nation theory acted as a justification for assimilation.

4 Nishida Kitarō (1965–66: vol. 12, 416–9). Takata Yasuma (1942: 237–50).
5 Nishimura Shinji (1941: 7–14, 31, 44–8; 1943: iv–v, vii–ix).
6 Yanagita Kunio ([1940] 1962–71). For the statement on seamanship, see Yanagita (1962–71: vol. 29, 506). For the round-table talk, see Yanagita Kunio, Hashiura Yasuo, Okada Ken, Nakamura Akira and Kanaseki Takeo (1943: 7, 11). For Orikuchi, 'Kodai Nippon bungaku ni okeru Nanpōteki yōso' (Southern Elements in Ancient Japanese Literature), see Orikuchi Shinobu (1965: vol. 8, 68).
7 Nagai Tōru (1939: 133–6). Shimomura Hiroshi (Kainan) (1941: 149–67). Taniguchi Konen (1942: 90–106). Uchida Ginzō (1941: 48–71). Akiyama Kenzō (1943: 1–28). Shirayanagi Shūko (1940: 148). For the mixed nation theory seen in *Dai tōa kensetsuron* (On Building Greater East Asia), Daiichi shobō, 1943, by Murayama Michio, a Cabinet Planning Board secretary (*shokikan*), see Sakai Naoki (1994).
8 A professor at Nippon University, Kawai Hiromichi (1941: 134) stated that by mixing with various nations, Japan could 'create an homogeneous nation'. This usage differs from the negative depiction of the pure blood theory as homogeneity, but I am not aware of any other case where this expression was used in this fashion. Moreover, in the next lecture contained in the same book, Noda Yoshiharu (1941: 139), an individual attached to the Ministry of Foreign Affairs, stated 'as Professor Kawai has just noted, the Japanese nation is not necessarily an homogeneous nation in the strict sense of the word'.
9 Shiratori Kiyoshi (1938).
10 Doi ed. (1991: 269–70). The citation for the political research meeting is at Doi ed. (1991: 302). The 'Yabe' who spoke about conscription is almost certainly Yabe Teiji, a professor of political science at Tokyo Imperial University and a trusted advisor of Konoe Fumimaro.

11 The standard of twenty per cent is mentioned in Utsumi Aiko (1991: 50). For the reports on the enshrinement at the Yasukuni Shrine, see, for instance, Anon. (1942).
12 Tsuda Sōkichi (1938: v–xii, 5, 7, 16, 71–4).
13 Minoda Kyōki (1939: 62).
14 Matsuda Fukumatsu (1939: 24, 28).
15 Maruyama Masao (1974: 109).
16 Kakegawa Tomiko ed. (1965: 505, 535, 903).
17 Watsuji (1989–92: bekkan 2, 433).
18 Tsuda Sōkichi (1986–89: vol. 24, 364).
19 Ōkawa (1961–74: vol. 2, 979, 985). Minoda (1940). Ōtsuka (1990: 242–6).
20 Tokutomi (1944a; 1944b: 7).
21 Kaigo ed. (1979: vol. 17).

17 The Myth Takes Root

1 The following citations are from Tsuda Sōkichi (1946b: 30, 31, 50, 51, 53, 54). Tsuda (1986–89: vol. 3, 440, 441, 467, 468, 471, 473) contains almost exactly the same sentences. The criticism of the theory of the migration of the Tenson nation is in Tsuda (1946a: 19–20).
2 Watsuji ([1948] 1989–92). For the analysis seen in the arguments of Tsuda and Watsuji about the Symbolic Emperor System and for their influence, see Akasaka (1990) and Yonetani Masafumi (1990). However, note that neither of these works focuses on the fact that the theory of the homogeneous nation was a premise for these arguments. Yonetani (1994b) analyses Watsuji's view of the Emperor through an examination of *Sonnō shisō to sono dentō* (The Philosophy and Tradition of 'Respect the Emperor').
3 Hasebe Kotondo (1949b). The citations are from Hasebe (1949b: 16, 23, 56, 60, 72).
4 Kiyono Kenji (1947). The citations are from Kiyono (1947: ii, 238, 242).
5 Koshiro Shūichi (1946: 18, 21). Nezu Masashi (1946: 32, 33).
6 Inoue Kiyoshi (1974: 75, 76).
7 Hayashi Motoi (1946: 26).
8 Anon. (1948).
9 Higuchi Kiyoyuki (1947: 32).

10 Gotō Morikazu (1946: 43). Tōma Seita (1951b: 2). Fujitani Toshio (1952: 41). Inoue Kiyoshi (1957: 74).
11 Tokutomi Sohō (1953: 4).
12 Ishida Eiichirō ed. (1966: 15). For the criticism of Egami, see Nishikawa Hiroshi (1970).
13 The citations are from Shiga Yoshio ([1949] 1969: 146, 147). Tōma Seita (1951a: 35). Ishimoda Shō (1988–90: vol. 12, 260).
14 Ishida Eiichirō, Egami Namio, Oka Masao and Yawata Ichirō (1958: 229).
15 Shimota Seiji (1975: 12). Kim Talsu and Hisano Osamu (1975: 26). Suzuki Takeki and Sasaki Mamoru (1975: 165).
16 Kaigo Muneomi ed. (1979: vol. 17).
17 Tōma (1951b: 5; 1951a: 209). Fujitani (1952: 37, 39).
18 For an example of attempts to deal with *zainichi* Koreans in this fashion, see Fujishima Udai, Maruyama Kunio and Murakami Hyōe (1958). For the Japan Communist Party's position on *zainichi* Koreans, see Tamaki Hajime (1967).
19 Koizumi Shinzō ([1961] 1967–72: 540).
20 Ishihara Shintarō ([1968] 1969: 365).
21 Mishima Yukio (1968: 108, 109, 117).
22 Nakane Chie (1967: 53–4, 187–8).
23 Masuda Yoshio (1967: 44, 142).
24 Maeda Hajime (1964: 14, 16, 17).
25 According to the 'Sengo Nihonjinron nenpyō' (Chronological Table of Postwar *Nihonjinron*) included in Nomura sōgō kenkyūjo ed. (1978), the average number of books on *Nihonjinron* published in 1971–78 were three times those published in 1961–70.
26 Kamishima Jirō (1982: xvii–xviii). In his 'Nihon bunmeiron no ninshiki wakugumi' (A Cognitive Framework for Theories of Japanese Civilisation), Kamishima (1986) notes that, in the prewar Japan, it was necessary to advocate the theory of 'mixed blood and the mongrel nation' in order to assimilate the alien nations of Japan's colonies.

Conclusion

1 Fukuoka (1993: 14).
2 Gordon (1964).

3   For the following discussion of Japanese colonial rule, see Oguma (1998).
4   Benedict Anderson (1983).
5   For the Korean family system, see Miyata, Kim and Yang (1992: 46–50). For the family system and family registration system of Japan and East Asia, I am indebted to Sakamoto Shin'ichi.
6   Murakami Yasuaki, Kumon Shunpei, and Satō Seizaburō (1979).
7   Emmanuel Todd (1990). For the Japanese migrants' self-identification as adopted children, see Maeyama Takashi (1992: 46–7). For Korean views of adoption, see Chōsen sōtokufu (1913: 324–5).
8   Sasaki Yomoji (1925: 314–5).
9   Minami (1942: 20–1). Komagome (1993) notes that the Chinese would not be able to accept the Japanese view of the Family State because of differences in the Chinese family system.
10 Jeffrey Herf (1984).
11 See Hisatake Ayako (1988). In the Edo Period, the custom of *samurai* families was for the oldest son to become the sole heir or for a foster child to maintain the *ie*. *Samurai* families, however, followed the Chinese custom of having separate surnames for married couples. On the other hand, the rural population, the farmers who made up the vast majority of the population, did not have family surnames, and so the idea of separate surnames was alien to them. Following the Meiji Restoration, the entire population was registered and all were given surnames. Although the government was initially in favour of a system of separate surnames, the rural population refused to accept this, and a single surname became the norm. In the Civil Law of 1898, the *samurai* custom of a single heir was enacted into law, but the government abandoned its wish for separate surnames, and enacted a single surname system instead.
12 See Mita Chiyoko and Okayama Kyōko eds (1992: chapter 4).
13 There is much research on the theory of the Family State, but one representative view in history is that of Ishida Takeshi (1954), who argues that the theory of social organisation and a Confucianist family-ism merged (I have my doubts about

whether the family-system of Japan can be called 'Confucianist' without any qualifications). Also see Kano Masanao (1982). For an anthropological approach, see Nakane Chie (1970) and Itō Kanji (1982). For the direction of anthropological research, see Kiyomizu Akitoshi (1985) and Tamanoi Riko (1986).
14 Fukuoka (1993: 38–50; 2000: 12–20).
15 Hayashi Fusao (1974: 31). The citations are from Kase Hideaki (1985: 50) and Ashizu Uzuhiko (1989: 151, 157).
16 Kim and Hisano (1975: 26).
17 Umehara Takeshi (1982: 365). Umehara et al. (1984: 419, 416–7).
18 For Egami, see Umehara et al. (1984: 262). For the description of Ozawa, see Urao Teru (1994: 142).
19 For Nakasone's theory of Japan, see Bunka hyōron henshūbu ed. (1986: 442, 446). The statement on mixture is from a Standing Committee on the Budget debate, 107th Diet (House of Representatives), 4 November 1986.
20 Ishihara Shintarō and Mahathir Mohamad (1994: 205, 236).

References

Abe Hirozumi (1975), *Nihon fashizumu kenkyū josetsu* (An Introduction to Japanese Fascism), Miraisha.
Akasaka Norio (1990), *Shōchō Tennō to iu monogatari* (The Story of the Symbolic Emperor), Chikuma shobō.
Akiyama Kenzō (1943), *Nippon rekishi no naisei* (Reflections on Japanese History), Iwanami shoten.
Amino Yoshihiko (1982), *Higashi to nishi no kataru Nihonshi* (Japanese History seen from the East and West), Soshiete.
Anderson, Benedict (1983), *Imagined Communities: Reflections on the Origin and Spread of Nationalism*, London and New York: Verso.
Anon. (1893), 'Nippon kokumin no dōkaryoku' (The Assimilative Ability of the Japanese), *Kokumin no tomo*, no. 206.
·········· (1900), 'Zappō' (To Our Readers), *Tōkyō jinruigakkai zasshi*, no. 171.
·········· (1910a), 'Kanjin no rekishi' (The History of the Koreans), *Tōkyō nichinichi shinbun*, 28 August.
·········· (1910b), 'Kankoku heigō no nochi' (After the Annexation of Korea), editorial, *Yorozu chōhō*, 28 August.
·········· (1910c), 'Issenmannin no fukkatsu' (The Revival of 10 Million People), editorial, *Yomiuri shinbun*, 31 August.
·········· (1910d), 'Gappei to rekkoku' (The Annexation and the Powers), editorial, *Tōkyō asahi shinbun*, 7 September.
·········· (1910e), 'Chōsen no shūkyō' (The Religion of Korea), editorial, *Tōkyō mainichi shinbun*, 22 September.
·········· (1919), 'Nissen no yūgō – Nissen ryōmin wa dōso dōzoku nari, Nissen yūgō wa minzoku jiketsushugi no meizuru tokoro nari' (The Fusion of the Japanese and Koreans: The Japanese and Koreans are the Same Nation with a Common Ancestor – The Unification of the Two is Demanded by the Principle of National Self-Determination), *Tōkyō nichinichi shinbun*, 4 March.
·········· (1929), 'Nippon minzoku no kosei to sono shimei' (The

Uniqueness and Mission of the Japanese Nation), *Nippon oyobi Nipponjin*, 1 November.

.... (1942), 'Chōsen dōho no eiyo' (Honouring Our Korean Brothers), editorial, *Tōkyō nichinichi shinbun*, 10 May.

.... (1948), Book review, '*Nihon rekishi no akebono*' (The Dawn of Japanese History), *Rekishi hyōron*, vol. 3, no. 4.

Ariga Nagao (1913), *Chūtō kokushi kyōkasho* (Japanese History Textbook for Secondary Schools), for upper grades, Sanseidō, 1913 edition.

Ashizu Uzuhiko (1989), *Tennō* (The Emperors), Jinja shinpōsha.

Ayabe Tsuneo ed. (1988), *Bunka jinruigaku gunzō* (Figures in Cultural Anthropology), vol. 3, Akademia shuppankai.

Braker, Michel (1976), translated by Ikei Yū, *Nemawashi kakimawashi atomawashi* (Japan's International Negotiating Behaviour), Saimaru shuppankai.

Bunka hyōron henshūbu ed. (1986), *Sōtokushū Tennōsei o tou* (Questioning the Emperor System), Shin-Nihon shuppansha.

Chiba Tokuji (1991), *Yanagita Kunio o yomu* (Reading Yanagita Kunio), Kōseidō.

Chōsen sōtokufu (1913), *Kanshū chōsa hōkokusho* (Report of a Survey of Korean Customs), Chōsen sōtokufu.

Chōsen sōtokufu gakumukyoku shakai kyōikuka (1937), *Kodai no naisen kankei* (Ancient Japanese-Korean Relations), Chōsen sōtokufu gakumukyoku shakai kyōikuka.

Chōsen sōtokufu hōmukyoku (1940), *Sōshi kaimei ni kansuru hōan no gimon gitō* (Questions and Answers about the Name Change Act), internal document of the Legal Affairs Bureau of the Government-General of Korea.

.... (n.p.), '*Seigansho' ni arawaretaru gobyū* (Mistakes in the 'Petition'), internal document of the Legal Affairs Bureau of the Government-General of Korea.

Doi Akira ed. (1991), *Shōwa shakai keizai shiryō shūsei* (A Collection of Historical Materials on the Society and Economy of the Shōwa Period), Daitōbunkadaitōyō kenkyūjo, vol. 16.

Dower, John W. (1986), *War Without Mercy*, New York: Pantheon Books.

Ebina Danjō (1907), 'Katō Hakase no *Waga kokutai to Kirisutokyō* o yomu', (Reading Dr Katō's *The Japanese National Polity and Christianity*), *Taiyō*, vol. 13, no. 13, October.

.... (1910), 'Shokumin to Nipponjin seikakuron' (On the Character of the Japanese as Colonists), *Taiyō*, vol. 16, no. 15.

Egami Namio (1985), *Egami Namio chosakushū* (The Collected Works of Egami Namio), Heibonsha.

────── ed. (1992), *Tōyōgaku no genryū* (The Founders of Oriental Studies in Japan), Taishūkan shoten.

Fujishima Udai, Maruyama Kunio and Murakami Hyōe (1958), 'Zainichi Chōsenjin rokujūmannin no genjitsu' (The Realities of the 600,000 *Zainichi* Koreans), *Chūō kōron*, December.

Fujitani Toshio (1952), 'Minzoku·minzoku bunka to wa nani ka' (What is the Nation and National Culture?), *Nihonshi kenkyū*, no. 16.

Fukuoka Yasunori (1993), *Zainichi Kankoku·Chōsenjin (Zainichi Koreans)*, Chūkō shinsho.

────── (2000), *Lives of Young Koreans in Japan*, translated by Tom Gill, Melbourne: Trans Pacific Press.

Fukuzawa Yukichi (1969–71), *Fukuzawa Yukichi zenshū* (The Complete Works of Fukuzawa Yukichi), Koizumi Shinzō et al. eds, Iwanami shoten.

Furuhata Tanemoto (1935), 'Ketsuekigata yori mitaru Nipponjin' (The Japanese seen from Blood Types), in Tōkyō jinruigakkai ed. (1935).

Furukawa Takeji (1931), 'Ketsuekigata to seishin genshō' (The Spiritual Phenomenon of Blood Types), *Minzoku eisei*, vol. 1, no. 3.

Furuya Eiichi (1927–28), 'Ichi shizoku kokka to shite no Nippon' (Japan as a Single Clan State), *Yūseigaku*, December 1927, February, March and May 1928.

────── (1939), *Chōsen dōhō ni Nippon denrai no myōji o rankyo subeki ka* (Should We Thoughtlessly Permit our Korean Compatriots to Use Traditional Japanese Family Names?), handbill.

────── (1940), 'Seishi ni yoru kokutai meichō undo' (The Movement to Clarify the National Polity Through Family Names), *Yūseigaku*, nos. 193–94.

Furuya Yoshio (1935), *Minzoku mondai o megurite* (On the Problem of the Nation), Jinbun shoin.

────── (1939), 'Minzoku kokusaku no shomondai' (Various Problems in the Government Ethnic Policy), *Yūseigaku*, nos. 189–90.

────── (1941), *Kokudo·jinkō·ketsueki* (National Land, Population, and Blood), Asahi shinbunsha.

────── (1942), *Minzoku seisaku ronsō* (The Debate on Ethnic Policies), Nippon hōsō shuppan kyōkai.

.... ed. (1943), *Minzoku kagaku kenkyū daiisshū* (Scientific Research on the Nation, 1), Asakura shoten.

Fuzanbō editorial board ed. (1929), *Chūtō kokushi* (Japanese History for Secondary Schools), for upper grades, Fuzanbō.

Goi Naohiro (1976), *Kindai Nihon to tōyō shigaku* (Modern Japan and the Study of Oriental History), Aoki shoten.

Gordon, Milton M. (1964), *Assimilation in American Life*, New York: Oxford University Press.

Gotō Morikazu (1946), '"Nihonjin" no "furusa"' (The 'Age' of the 'Japanese'), *Nihon rekishi*, no. 4.

Gotō Sōichirō ed. (1986–88), *Yanagita Kunio kenkyū shiryō shūsei* (Yanagita Kunio Research: A Collection of Materials), Nihon tosho sentaa.

Hachiman Ichirō (1975), 'Torii Ryūzō', in Shiratori Yoshio and Hachiman Ichirō (1975).

Han Sokki (1988), *Nihon no Chōsen shihai to shūkyō seisaku* (Japan's Rule of Korea and Religious Policies), Miraisha.

Hasebe Kotondo (1927), *Senshigaku kenkyū* (Research in Prehistoric Studies), Ōokayama shoten.

.... (1940), 'Taiko no Nipponjin' (The Prehistoric Japanese), *Jinruigaku zasshi*, vol. 55, no. 1.

.... (1949a), 'Jinrui no shinka to Nihonjin no kengen' (The Evolution of Mankind and the Manifestation of the Japanese), *Minzokugaku kenkyū*, vol. 13, no. 3.

.... (1949b), 'Nihon minzoku no seiritsu' (The Birth of the Japanese Nation), in *Shin Nihonshi kōza* (New Lectures on Japanese History), Chūō kōronsha, 1949.

Hashikawa Bunzō (1962), 'Takayama Chogyū', in Asahi shinbunsha ed., *Nihon no shisōka I* (Japan's Thinkers, vol. 1), Asahi shinbunsha, 1962.

.... and Kamishima Jirō (1975), 'Mōretsunaru seishin' (A Rampant Spirit), *Gendai shisō*, vol. 3, no. 4.

Hashimoto Mitsuru (1992), 'Minzoku – Nihon kindai o tōgō suru chikara' (The Nation: The Power to Unite Modern Japan), in Senjika Nihon shakai kenkyūkai ed. (1992).

Hatada Takashi (1968), *Nihonjin no Chōsenkan* (Japanese Views of Korea), Keisō shobō.

.... (1983), *Nihonjin to Chōsenjin* (Japanese and Koreans), Keisō shobō.

Hayakawa Jirō ([1936] 1976), 'Nihon minzoku no keisei katei' (The Process of the Formation of the Japanese Nation), 1936, reprinted in Rekishi kagaku taikei vol. 15, *Minzoku no mondai* (The Problem of the Nation), Azekura shobō, 1976.

Hayashi Fusao (1974), *Tennō no kigen* (The Origin of the Emperor), Kabushiki kaisha roman.

Hayashi Motoi (1946), 'Nihon kodaishigaku no dentō' (The Tradition of Historical Studies of Ancient Japan), *Rekishi hyōron*, vol. 1, no. 3.

Herf, Jeffrey (1984), *Reactionary Modernism*, Cambridge and New York: Cambridge University Press.

Higuchi Kiyoyuki (1947), 'Jinmu Tennō setsuwa no izoku' (The Alien Peoples in the Story of the Emperor Jinmu), *Nihon rekishi*, vol. 2, no. 4.

Higuchi Yūichi ed. (1991), *Kyōwakai kankei shiryōshū* (A Collection of Materials on the Concordia Asociation), Ryokuin shobō.

Hirano Yoshitarō and Kiyono Kenji (1942), *Taiheiyō no minzoku = seijigaku* (The Nations and Politics of the Pacific), Nippon hyōronsha.

Hirata Ken'ichi (1974), '"Chōsen heigō" to Nihon no yoron' (The 'Annexation of Korea' and Japanese Public Opinion), *Shirin*, vol. 57, no. 3.

Hisatake Ayako (1988), *Uji to koseki no joseishi* (A Feminist History of Surnames and the Family Register System), Sekai shisōsha.

Hoshino Hisashi (1890), 'Honpō no jinshu gengo ni tsuite hikō o nobete yo no shinshin aikokusha ni tadasu' (Questions from an Old Man to the True Patriots Regarding the Race and Language of Japan), *Shigakkai zasshi*, no. 11.

Hozumi Shigetaka ed. (1943), *Hozumi Yatsuka hakase ronbunshū* (The Collected Articles of Dr. Hozumi Yatsuka), Yūhikaku.

Hozumi Yatsuka (1897), *Kokumin kyōiku aikokushin* (National Education: Patriotism), Yao shoten, Yūhikaku.

────── (1910), *Kenpō teiyō* (Elements of Constitutional Law), Yūhikaku.

I Kuangsu (1941), 'Shintaiseika no geijutsu no hōkō' (The Direction of Art under the New Regime), *Sanzenri*, January.

Ienaga Saburō (1972), *Tsuda Sōkichi no shisōshiteki kenkyū* (An Intellectual History of Tsuda Sōkichi), Iwanami shoten.

Iesaka Kazuyuki ([1980] 1986), *Nihonjin no jinshukan* (Japanese Views of Race), Kōbundō.

Ifa Fuyū ([1910] 1974–76), 'Ryūkyūjin no sosen ni tsuite' (On the Ancestors of the Okinawan People), 1910, reprinted in Hattori

Shirō et al. eds, *Ifa Fuyū zenshū* (The Complete Works of Ifa Fuyū), Heibonsha, 1974–76, vol. 1.

Iinuma Jirō (1973), '3·1 jiken to Nippon Kumiai Kyōkai' (The March First Incident and the Japanese Congregational Church), in Dōshisha jinbun kagaku kenkyūjo/Kirisutokyō shakai mondai kenkyūjo ed., *Nihon no kindaika to Kirisutokyō* (Japan and Modern Christianity), Shinkyō shuppansha, 1973.

Ikeda Jirō and Ōno Susumu eds (1973), *Nihon jinshuron gengogaku* (Theories of the Japanese Race: Linguistics), in *Ronshū Nihon bunka no kigen* (A Collection of Articles on the Origin of Japanese Culture), vol. 5, Heibonsha.

Ino Tentarō (1976), *Jōyaku kaiseiron no rekishiteki tenkai* (The Historical Development of the Debate on Treaty Revision), Komine shoten.

.... ed. (1992), *Naichi zakkyoron shiryō shūsei* (A Collection of Materials on the Debate on Mixed Residence in the Interior), Meiji hyakunen shiryō gyōsho, Hara shobō, 6 volumes.

Inobe Shigeo (1934), *Teikoku shōshi* (A Short History of the Empire), for upper grades, Chūbunkan shoten.

Inoue Hideo ed. (1969), *Seminaa Nitchō kankeishi I* (Seminar: The History of Japanese-Korean Relations I), Ōfūsha.

Inoue Kiyoshi (1955), *Jōyaku kaisei* (Treaty Revision), Iwanami shoten.

.... (1957), 'Marukusushugi ni yoru minzoku riron' (The Marxist Discourse on Ethnicity), Iwanami kōza, *Gendai shisō*, vol. 3.

.... (1974), 'Rekishika wa Tennōsei o dō miruka' (How Historians View the Emperor System), reprinted in Hisano Osamu and Kamishima Jirō eds, *'Tennōsei' ronshū* (Essays on the 'Emperor System'), San'ichi shobō, 1974.

Inoue Shōichi (1994), *Hōryūji e no seishinshi* (A Spiritual History of the Hōryūji Temple), Kōbundō.

Inoue Tatsuo (1992), *Kyōsei e no bōken* (The Adventure of Coexistence), Mainichi shinbunsha.

Inoue Tetsujirō (1889), *Naichi zakkyoron* (On Mixed Residence in the Interior), Tetsugaku shoin.

.... (1891a), *Naichi zakkyo zokuron* (Revisiting the Issue of Mixed Residence in the Interior), Tetsugaku shoin.

.... (1891b), *Chokugo engi* (On the Imperial Rescript), Keigyōsha, Tetsugansha.

.... (1899), *Zōtei chokugo engi* (On the Imperial Rescript, Revised Edition), Keigyōsha.

.... (1905), 'Bunmeishijō yori mitaru Nippon senshō no gen'in' (The Cause of Japan's Victory in the War seen from the History of Civilisations), *Tōyō gakugei zasshi*, nos. 282–85.

.... (1910), 'Nikkan heigō ni tsuite no shokan' (My Views of the Annexation of Korea), *Tōa no hikari*, vol. 5, no. 10, December.

.... (1912), *Kokumin dōtaku gairon* (An Introduction to National Morals), Sanseidō.

Irokawa Daikichi (1978), *Yanagita Kunio*, Nihon minzokugaku taikei 1, Kōdansha.

Ishida Eiichirō, Egami Namio, Oka Masao and Yawata Ichirō (1958), *Nihon minzoku no kigen* (The Origin of the Japanese Nation), Heibonsha.

Ishida Eiichirō ed. (1966), *Shinpojiumu Nihon kokka no kigen* (Symposium: The Origin of the Japanese State), Kadokawa shoten.

Ishida Mikinosuke ([1942] 1969–71), 'Shiratori Kurakichi Sensei shōden' (A Short Biography of Shiratori Kurakichi), 1942, reprinted in Shiratori Kurakichi (1969–71: vol. 10).

Ishida Takeshi (1954), *Meiji seiji shisōshi kenkyū* (Research on Meiji Intellectual History), Miraisha.

Ishihara Fusao and Satō Hifumi (1941), 'Nikka konketsu jidō no igakuteki chōsa' (A Medical Survey of Japanese-Chinese Half-Breed Children), *Minzoku eisei*, vol. 9, no. 3.

Ishihara Shintarō ([1968] 1969), 'Sokoku ni tsuite' (On My Motherland), 1968, reprinted in Yoshimoto Takaai ed. (1969).

.... and Mahathir Mohamad (1994), *NO to ieru Ajia* (The Asia That Can Say No), Kōbunsha. Translated as Mahathir Mohamad and Shintaro Ishihara, *The Voice of Asia: Two Leaders Discuss the Coming Century*, New York: Kodansha International, 1995.

Ishii Hitoshi (1992), 'Taiheiyō sensōka no tai-Nanpō kyōiku seisaku' (Educational Policies for the South during the Pacific War), *Kokuritsu kyōiku kenkyūjo kiyō*, no. 121.

Ishikawa Junkichi (1976), *Kokka sōdōin shi* (A History of National Mobilisation), Kokka sōdōinshi kankōkai, shiryōhen (4).

Ishikawa Sanshirō (1924), *Kojiki shinwa no shin kenkyū* (New Research of the *Kojiki* Myths), Hakuyōsha, 1924 edition.

Ishimoda Shō (1988–90), *Ishimoda Shō chosakushū* (The Collected Works of Ishimoda Shō), Aoki Kazuo et al. eds, Iwanami shoten.

Ishiwara Kanji (1993), *Saishū sensōron·Sensōshi taikan* (The War to End All Wars, and A General Survey of Military History), Chūkō bunko.

Itō Kanji (1982), *Kazoku kokkakan no jinruigaku* (The Anthropology of the Views of the Family State), Mineruva shobō.

Iwamoto Yoshiteru (1982a), *Yanagita Kunio*, Kashiwa shobō.

────── (1982b), *Zoku Yanagita Kunio* (More Yanagita Kunio), Kashiwa shobō.

────── ([1983] 1994), *Mō hitotsu no Tōno monogatari* (Another *Tōno monogatari*), Tōsui shobō.

────── (1985), *Ronsō suru Yanagita Kunio* (Yanagita Kunio in Debate), Ocha-no-mizu shobō.

────── (1990), *Yanagita Kunio o yomi naosu* (Rereading Yanagita Kunio), Sekai shisōsha.

────── (1993), 'Shokuminchi seisaku to Yanagita Kunio' (Colonial Policy and Yanagita Kunio), *Kokubungaku*, vol. 38, no. 8.

Izawa Shūji (1897), 'Taiwan no kōgakkō setchi ni kansuru iken' (On the Establishment of Public Schools in Taiwan), *Kyōiku kōhō*, no. 195.

Jinkō mondai kenkyūkai ed. (1941), *Jinkō·minzoku·kokudo* (Population, Nation, National Land), Tōkō shoin.

Kaigo Muneomi ed. (1979) *Nihon kyōkasho taikei* (Japanese Textbooks), Kōdansha.

Kaiho Yōko (1992), *Kindai hoppōshi* (A History of the Modern North), San'ichi shobō.

Kajiki Tsuyoshi (1989), *Yanagita Kunio no shisō* (The Thought of Yanagita Kunio), Keisō shobō.

Kakegawa Tomiko ed. (1965), *Gendaishi shiryō*, 42, *Shisō tōsei* (Modern Historical Materials, vol. 42, Thought Control), Misuzu shobō.

Kakei Katsuhiko (1926), *Kanagara no michi* (The Path of the Gods), Naimushō jinjakyoku.

Kamishima Jirō (1961), *Kindai Nihon no seishin kōzō* (The Spiritual Structure of Modern Japan), Iwanami shoten.

────── (1982), *Jiba no seijigaku* (The Politics of Tacit Pressure), Iwanami shoten.

────── (1986), 'Nihon bunmeiron no ninshiki wakugumi' (A Cognitive Framework for Theories of Japanese Civilisation), *Hikaku bunmei*, no. 2.

Kanazawa Shōzaburō (1910), *Nikkan ryōkokugo dōkeiron* (On the Common Genealogy of the Japanese and Korean Languages), Sanseidō shoten.

Kaneko, Martin (1994), 'Doitsu to Nihon no gaikokujin rōdōsha' (The Foreign Workers of Germany and Japan), *Yoseba*, no. 7.

Kaneko Tateo (1991), 'Watsuji Tetsurō to Tennōsei' (Watsuji Tetsurō and the Emperor System), *Shōnan kōka daigaku kiyō*, vol. 25, no. 1.

Kang Toksang ed. (1967), *Gendaishi shiryō*, 26, *Chōsen (2)* (Modern Historical Materials, vol. 26, Korea [2]), Misuzu shobō.

Kang Tongzin (1984), *Nihon genronkai to Chōsen 1910–1945* (The Japanese Media and Korea, 1910–45), Hōsei daigaku shuppankyoku.

Kano Masanao (1982), *Senzen 'ie' no shisō* (The Thought of the Prewar *Ie*), Sōbunsha.

.... (1983), *Kindai Nihon no minkangaku* (The Non-Establishment Scholarship of Modern Japan), Iwanami shinsho.

.... (1988), *'Torishima' wa haitteiru ka* (Where Do the Boundaries of Japan Lie?), Iwanami shoten.

.... and Horiba Kiyoko (1977), *Takamure Itsue*, Asahi shinbunsha.

.... and Imai Osamu (1991), 'Nihon kindai shisōshi no naka no Kume jiken' (The Kume Incident in the History of Modern Japanese Thought), in Ōkubo Toshikane ed. (1991).

Kanō Mikiyo ([1979] 1987), 'Takamure Itsue to Kōkokushikan' (Takamure Itsue and the Imperial View of History), in Takamure Itsue ronshū henshū iinkai ed. (1979), reprinted in Kanō Mikiyo, *Onna-tachi no 'jūgo'* (The 'Home Front' for Women), Chikuma shobō, 1987.

Kanokogi Kazunobu (1918), 'Kokutai no shuyō mondai' (The Main Problems of the National Polity), *Tōa no hikari*, vol. 13, nos. 6–7.

Karube Naoshi (1995), *Hikari no ryōkoku – Watsuji Tetsurō* (The Bright Land: Watsuji Tetsurō), Sōbunsha.

Kase Hideaki (1985), *Shinpi naru Tennō* (The Mysterious Emperor), Nihon kyōbunsha.

Katō Genchi (1912), *Waga kenkoku shisō no hongi* (The First Principles of the Thought of the Foundation of Japan), Meguro shoten.

Katō Hiroyuki (1900), 'Junkoku no setsugi' (Adhering to the Principle of Dying for One's Country), in *Katō Hiroyuki kōenshū dainisatsu* (The Lectures of Katō Hiroyuki, vol. 2), Maruzen.

.... (1904), *Shinkagaku yori kansatsu shitaru Nichi-Ro no unmei* (The Destiny of Japan and Russia Viewed from the Theory of Evolution), Hakubunkan.

.... (1907), *Waga kokutai to Kirisutokyō* (The Japanese National Polity and Christianity), Kinkōdō.

.... (1911), *Kirisutokyō no gaidoku* (The Peril of Christianity), Kinkōdō shoseki.

.... (1915), *Jinsei no shizen to wagakuni no zento* (Human Nature and the Future Path of Japan), Dai Nippon gakujutsu kyōkai.

Katsube Mitake (1967), 'Watsuji Tetsurō to *Rinrigaku*' (Watsuji Tetsurō and *Rinrigaku* [Ethics]), *Chūō kōron*, October.

.... ([1987] 1995), *Seishun no Watsuji Tetsurō* (The Young Watsuji Tetsurō), PHP bunko.

Kawada Minoru (1985), *Yanagita Kunio no shisōshiteki kenkyū* (An Intellectual History of Yanagita Kunio), Miraisha.

Kawai Hiromichi (1941), 'Kōdōshugi shokuminseisaku' (The Colonial Policy of Imperial Japan), in Jinkō mondai kenkyūkai ed. (1941).

Kawakami Hajime (1982), *Kawakami Hajime zenshū* (The Complete Works of Kawakami Hajime), Suekawa Hiroshi et al. eds, Iwanami shoten.

Kawamura Minato (1987), 'Tsuda Sōkichi', *Kikan bungei*, vol. 26, no. 3.

Kikakuin kenkyūkai ed. (1943), *Dai tōa kensetsu no kihon kōryō* (A Basic Program for Establishing Greater East Asia), Dōmei tsūshinsha.

Kikuchi Isao (1982), 'Yoshitsune "Ezo seibatsu" monogatari no seitan to kinō' (The Birth and Function of the Story of Yoshitsune as 'Conqueror of the Ezo'), *Shien*, vol. 42, no. 1.

Kim Chongmi (1989), 'Chōsen dokuritsu·han sabetsu·han Tennōsei' (Korean Independence, Anti-Discrimination, Anti-Emperor System), *Shisō*, no. 786.

Kim Ilmyon (1984), *Tennō to Chōsenjin to Sōtokufu* (The Emperor, the Koreans, and the Government-General), Tahata shoten.

Kim Talsu and Hisano Osamu (1975), 'Sōgo rikai no tame no teian' (A Proposal for Mutual Understanding), *Kikan sanzenri*, no. 4.

Kimura Takatarō (1897), 'Taiwan-tō dendō' (Propagating Shintō in Taiwan), *Nippon shugi*, no. 1.

.... (1911), *Sekaiteki kenkyū ni motozukeru Nippon taikoshi* (Ancient Japanese History Based on Global Research), Hakubunkan.

Kindaichi Kyōsuke ([1925] 1992–93), 'Eiyū fushi densetsu no kenchi kara' (From the Standpoint of the Legend of an Undying Hero), 1925, reprinted in Kindaichi Kyōsuke (1992–93: vol. 12).

.... (1992–93), *Kindaichi Kyōsuke zenshū* (The Complete Works of Kindaichi Kyōsuke), Kindaichi Kyōsuke zenshū henshū iinkai ed., Sanseidō.
Kinomiya Yasuhiko (1933), *Shin Nipponshi* (A New History of Japan), for third and fourth year students, Toyamabō.
Kita Ikki ([1906] 1959–72), *Kokutairon oyobi junsei shakaishugi* (The National Polity and Pure Socialism), 1906, reprinted in Kita Ikki (1959–72: vol. 1).
.... (1959–72), *Kita Ikki chosakushū* (The Collected Works of Kita Ikki), Misuzu shobō.
Kita Noriaki (1936), 'Kyūdojin hogo jigyō ni tsuite' (On the Effort to Protect the Ex-Aborigines), *Hokkaidō shakai jigyō*, no. 49.
Kita Sadakichi (1910), *Kankoku no heigō to kokushi* (The Annexation of Korea and the History of Japan), Sanseidō.
.... (1919a), '"Minzoku to rekishi" hakkan shuisho' (The Purpose of Launching *Minzoku to rekishi* [Nation and History]), *Minzoku to rekishi*, vol. 1, no. 1.
.... (1919b), 'Kōzoku go-konke no ichi shinrei ni tsuite' (A New Example of an Imperial Marriage), *Minzoku to rekishi*, vol. 1, no. 2.
.... (1919c), '"Nippon minzoku" to gengo' (The 'Japanese Nation' and Language), *Minzoku to rekishi*, vol. 1, no. 2.
.... (1921a), 'Nippon minzoku no seiritsu' (The Formation of the Japanese Nation), *Minzoku to rekishi*, vol. 5, nos. 2–4.
.... (1921b), 'Koshin Senman ryokō nisshi' (A Travel Diary to Korea and Manchuria), *Minzoku to rekishi*, vol. 6, no. 1.
.... ([1928] 1981), *Nippon rekishi monogatari* (The Story of Japanese History), vol. 1, Arususha, 1928, Fukkokuban kabushiki gaisha meicho fukyūkai, 1981.
.... (1979–82), *Kita Sadakichi chosakushū* (The Collected Works of Kita Sadakichi), Ueda Masaaki et al. eds, Heibonsha.
Kitsukawa Toshitada (1983), 'Yanagita Kunio ni okeru nashonarizumu no mondai' (The Issue of Nationalism in the Thought of Yanagita Kunio), *Kanagawa hōgaku*, vol. 19, no. 1.
Kiyohara Sadao (1930), *Nippon dōtokushi* (A History of Japanese Morals), Chūbunkan shoten.
.... (1941), *Chūgaku kokushi kaname* (Key Issues in Japanese History for Junior High School Students), for beginners, Shūbunkan.
Kiyomizu Akitoshi (1985), 'Nihon no ie' (The Japanese *Ie*), *Minzokugaku kenkyū*, vol. 50, no. 1.

Kiyono Kenji (1926), 'Nenrei no byōrigakuteki kōsatsu' (A Pathological Consideration of Age), *Yūseigaku*, vol. 3, no. 5.

.... (1929), 'Nippon ni jinrui ga kyojū shite kara Nipponjin ga arawaruru made' (From When Humanity Resided in Japan until the Japanese Emerged), *Yūseigaku*, vol. 6, no. 8.

.... (1934), 'Nippon kojūmin no taishitsu ni kansuru gentō' (Slides on the Physical Constitution of the Ancient Residents of Japan), *Minzoku eisei*, vol. 3, no. 6.

.... (1936), 'Nippon minzoku' (The Japanese Nation), in *Iwanami kōza Tōyō shichō* (Iwanami Lecture Series: Eastern Thought), Iwanami shoten, 1936.

.... (1938), 'Kofun jidai Nipponjin no jinruigakuteki kenkyū' (Anthropological Research of the Japanese of the Kofun Period), in Yūzankaku ed., *Jinruigaku·senshigaku kōza* (Lectures on Anthropology and Pre-history), vol. 2, Yūzankaku.

.... (1944a), *Nippon jinshuron hensenshi* (A History of the Changes in Theories of the Japanese Race), Koyama shoten.

.... (1944b), *Sumatora kenkyū* (Research of Sumatra), Taiheiyō kyōkai ed., Kawade shobō.

.... (1946), *Nippon minzoku seiseiron* (A Theory of the Genesis of the Japanese Nation), Nihon hyōronsha.

.... (1947), *Nihon rekishi no akebono* (The Dawn of Japanese History), Chōryūsha.

.... (1956), *Zuihitsu ikō* (Literary Jottings and Posthumous Works), Kiyono Kenji Sensei kinen ronbunshū kankōkai.

.... and Miyamoto Hiroto (1926a), 'Tsugumo sekki jidai wa Ainujin nari ya' (The Tsugumo Stone Age was not *Ainu*), *Kōkogaku zasshi*, vol. 16, no. 8.

.... and .... (1926b), 'Futatabi Tsugumo kaizuka sekki jidaijin no Ainujin ni arazaru riyū o ronzu' (Again on Why the Stone Age People of the Tsugumo Shell Mounds were not *Ainu*), *Kōkogaku zasshi*, vol. 16, no. 9.

Kobayashi Masasuke (1919), *Beikoku to jinshu sabetsu no kenkyū* (A Study of the USA and Racial Discrimination), Bunsendō.

Koganei Yoshikiyo (1928), *Jinruigaku kenkyū* (Anthropological Research), Ōokayama shoten.

Koizumi Shinzō ([1961] 1967–72), 'Nihon to Nihonjin' (Japan and the Japanese), 1961, reprinted in *Koizumi Shinzō zenshū* (The Complete Works of Koizumi Shinzō), Tomita Masafumi et al. eds, Bungei shunjūsha, 1967–72, vol. 17.

Kokumin sōryoku Chōsen renmei bōei shidōbu ed. (1941a), *Naisen ittai no rinen oyobi sono gugen hōsaku yōkō* (The Ideal of the Amalgamation of Japan and Korea and Policies for its Realisation), Kokumin sōryoku Chōsen renmei bōei shidōbu.

.... (1941b), *Naisen ittai no gugen* (Realising the Amalgamation of Japan and Korea), Kokumin sōryoku Chōsen renmei bōei shidōbu.

Komagome Takeshi (1993), 'Iminzoku shihai no "kyōgi"' (The 'Dogma' of Ruling Alien Nations), *Iwanami kōza kindai Nihon to shokuminchi* (Iwanami Lectures: Modern Japan and Japanese Colonies), Iwanami shoten, vol. 4, 1993.

Komatsu Midori (1916), 'Chōsen tōchi no shinsō' (The True State of the Japanese Rule of Korea), *Chūō kōron*, August.

Kōno Nobuko (1990), *Takamure Itsue*, Riburopōto.

Kōseishō kenkyūjo jinkō minzokubu (1943), *Yamato minzoku o chūkaku to suru sekai seisaku no kentō* (An Examination of Global Policy Centred on the Yamato Nation).

.... (1981), *Minzoku jinkō seisaku kenkyū shiryō* (Materials on Ethnic and Population Policies Research), Bunsei shoin.

Koshiro Shūichi (1946), 'Nihon minzoku no kōsei' (The Make-up of the Japanese Nation), *Nihon rekishi*, vol. 1, no. 1.

Koyama Eizō (1941), *Minzoku to jinkō no riron* (A Theory of Nations and Population), Hata shoten.

.... (1944), *Nanpō kensetsu to minzoku jinkō seisaku* (Constructing the South and National Population Policies), Dai Nippon shuppan.

Krainer, J. (1988), 'Yōroppa shisōshi ni okeru Nihonkan' (The View of Japan in European Intellectual History), *Minpaku tsūshin*, no. 42.

Kudō Masaki (1979), *Kenkyūshi Nihon jinshuron* (History of Research: Theories of the Japanese Race), Yoshikawa kōbunkan.

Kuginuki Kazunori (1986), 'Watsuji tetsugaku to Tennōsei ideorogii' (Watsuji's Philosophy and the Ideology of the Emperor System), *Bunka hyōron*, no. 302.

Kume Kunitake (1889), 'Nippon fukuin no enkaku' (The History of Japanese Territory), *Shigakkai zasshi*, nos. 1–3.

.... (1894), 'Shimabito konjō' (The Insular Spirit), *Kokumin no tomo*, nos. 223–26.

.... (1905), *Nippon kodaishi* (A History of Ancient Japan), Waseda daigaku shuppanbu.

.... (1906), 'Nippon minzoku no kokyō' (The Homeland of the Japanese Nation), *Rekishi chiri*, vol. 8, no. 11.

Kurashima Itaru (1942), *Zenshin suru Chōsen* (Korea on the Move), Chōsen sōtokufu jōhōka.

Kurihara Hiroshi (1994), *Takamure Itsue no kon'in joseishizō no kenkyū* (Research on Takamure Itsue's Representation of the History of Marriage and Women), Takashina shoten.

Kurita Genji (1937), *Shintai chūgaku sōgō kokushi* (A General Japanese History for Junior High School Students), for beginners, Chūbunkan shoten.

Kuroita Katsumi (1925), *Kokutai shinron* (A New Theory of the National Polity), Hakubundō.

Kurokawa Mayori ([1880] 1911), 'Kun-Shin setsu' (On the Relationship Between the Sovereign and His Subjects), 1880, reprinted in Kurokawa Mayori (1911: vol. 6).

……… ([1881] 1911), 'Kekkyo kō' (On Cave Dwellers), 1881, reprinted in Kurokawa Mayori (1911: vol. 5).

……… ([1892] 1911), 'Emishi jinshu ron' (On the Emishi Race), 1892, reprinted in Kurokawa Mayori (1911: vol. 4).

……… ([n.a.] 1911), 'Jōdai sekki kō' (On Ancient Stone Tools), reprinted in Kurokawa Mayori (1911: vol. 5).

……… (1911), *Kurokawa Mayori zenshū* (The Complete Works of Kurokawa Mayori), Kurokawa Mamichi ed., privately printed.

Maeda Hajime (1964), 'Antei seichō e no daiichi nendo taru ninshiki o' (A Call to Regard this Year as the First Year of Steady Growth), *Keieisha*, February.

Maeyama Takashi (1992), *Imin no Nihon kaiki undō* (The Awaking Identity as Japanese among Japanese Immigrants), Nihon hōsō shuppan kyōkai.

Mamiya Kunio (1990), 'Taishō demokuratto to jinshu mondai' (Taishō Democrats and the Issue of Race), *Jinbun shakai kagaku kenkyū*, vol. 30.

Manshū Teikoku Kyōwakai Chūō Honbu ed. (1939), *Minzoku kyōwa no Manshūkoku* (Manchukuo, Land of National Harmony), Manshū Teikoku Kyōwakai Chūō Honbu.

Maruyama Masao (1974), 'Aru hi no Tsuda Hakase to watashi' (Dr. Tsuda and Myself One Day), in Ueda Masaaki ed. (1974).

Masubuchi Nobuo (1992), *Nikkan kōshōshi* (A History of Korean-Japanese Interaction), Sairyūsha.

Masuda Yoshio (1967), *Junsui bunka no jōken* (The Conditions of Pure Culture), Kōdansha.

Matsuda Fukumatsu (1939), 'Tsuda Sōkichishi no tōyō massatsuron

hihan (jō)' (A Critique of Tsuda Sōkichi's Theory of Eradicating the Orient, part 1), *Genri Nippon*, March.
Matsuda Kaoru (1994), *'Ketsuekigata to seikaku' no shakashi* (A Social History of 'Blood Types and Character'), Kawade shobō shinsha, second revised edition.
Matsumoto Hikoshichirō (1919), 'Nippon senshi jinruiron' (On Prehistoric Man in Japan), *Rekishi to chiri*, vol. 3, no. 2.
Matsumoto Ken'ichi (1986), *Ōkawa Shūmei*, Sakuhinsha.
Matsumoto Sannosuke (1969), *Tennōsei kokka to seiji shisō* (The Emperor State and Political Thought), Miraisha.
……… ed. (1977) *Meiji shisōshū 2* (A Collection of Meiji Thought, vol. 2), Chikuma shobō.
Matsuo Takayoshi (1968), 'Nippon Kumiai Kirisuto Kyōkai no Chōsen dendō' (The Japanese Congregational Church and Propagation in Korea), *Shisō*, no. 529.
……… (1974), *Taishō demokurashii* (Taishō Democracy), Iwanami shoten.
Matsuyama Iwao (1993), *Uwasa no enkinhō* (The Law of Perspective of Gossip), Seidosha.
Mimura Saburō (1984), *Yudaya mondai to uragaeshite mita Nihon rekishi* (The Jewish Problem and Japanese History), Hachiman shoten.
Minami Jirō (1942), *Jikyoku to Naisen ittai* (The Present Situation and 'Japan and Korea as One'), Kokumin sōryoku Chōsen renmei.
Minato Michitaka (1990), 'Watsuji Tetsurō – kaiki no kiseki' (Watsuji Tetsurō: Following the Tracks of His Return), *Shisō*, no. 798.
Minoda Kyōki (1939), 'Chishiki kaikyū saikyōikuron' (Reeducating the Intellegentsia), *Genri Nippon*, January.
……… (1940), 'Ōkawa Shūmeishi no gakuteki ryōshin ni uttau' (An Appeal to Ōkawa Shūmei's Academic Conscience), *Genri Nippon*, March.
Mishima Ken'ichi (1987), *Niiche* (Nietzsche), Iwanami shinsho.
Mishima Yukio (1968), 'Bunka bōeiron' (Defending Culture), *Chūō kōron*, July.
Mita Chiyoko and Okayama Kyōko eds (1992), *Raten Amerika kazoku to shakai* (Families and Society of Latin America), Shinhyōron.
Mita Minesuke (1971), *Gendai Nihon no shinjō to ronri* (The Mind and Soul of Modern Japan), Chikuma shobo.

Miyata Setsuko (1985), *Chōsen minshū to 'Kōminka' seisaku* (The Korean People and the 'Japanisation' Policy), Miraisha.
.... , Kim Yongtal and Yang Teho (1992), *Sōshi kaimei* (The Name Change), Akashi shoten.
Miyazawa Kenji (1973–77), *Miyazawa Kenji zenshū* (The Complete Works of Miyazawa Kenji), Amasawa Taijirō and Irisawa Yasuo eds, Chikuma shobō.
Mizuno Yū (1960), *Nihon minzoku no genryū* (The Origin of the Japanese Nation), Yūzankaku.
Mizushima Haruo (1942), 'Nippon minzoku no kōsei to konketsu mondai' (The Make-up of the Japanese Nation and the Problem of Mixed Blood), *Yūseigaku*, nos. 220–21.
Momokawa Yoshito (1988), 'Ikai·kokugaku·Tennōsei' (The World of Spirits, Nativism, and the Emperor System), *GS*, no. 7.
Monbushō kyōgakukyoku (1910), *Kōtō shōgaku shūshinsho* (Ethics for Higher Elementary School Children), Monbushō.
Monbushō shakaikyōikukyoku (1942), *Kokumin dōwa e no michi* (The Road to National Unity), Dōwa hōkōkai.
Mori Ōgai (1971–75), *Mori Ōgai zenshū* (The Complete Works of Mori Ōgai), Iwanami shoten.
Morikawa Terunori (1986), 'Taishō-ki kokumin kyōikuron ni kansuru ichi kōsatsu' (An Examination of the Debate on National Education in the Taishō Period), *Nihon rekishi*, no. 463.
Motoori Norinaga (1795–1812), *Tamakatsuma* (The Jeweled Bamboo Basket: A Collection of Essays), vol. 14.
Mozume Takami (1919), *Kokutai shinron* (A New Theory of the National Polity), Kōbunko kankōkai.
Murai Osamu ([1992] 1995), *Nantō ideorogii no hassei* (The Birth of the Ideology of the South Islands), Fukutake shoten.
Murakami Yasuaki, Kumon Shunpei, and Satō Seizaburō (1979), *Bunmei to shite no ie shakai* (The *Ie* Society as Civilisation), Chūō kōronsha.
Murakami Yōichirō (1980), *Nihonjin to kindai kagaku* (The Japanese and Modern Science), Shin'yōsha.
Murofushi Takanobu (1942), 'Daitōa no saihensei' (The Reorganisation of Greater East Asia), *Nippon hyōron*, February.
Nagahara Keiji and Kano Masanao eds (1976), *Nihon no rekishika* (Japanese Historians), Nihon hyōronsha.
Nagai Hisomu (1933), 'Minzoku no konketsu ni tsuite' (On the Mixed Blood of the Nation), *Minzoku eisei*, vol. 2, no. 4.

References

.... (1936), 'Kantōgen' (Preface), *Minzoku eisei*, vol. 5, nos. 1–2.
Nagai Tōru (1928), *Nippon kokutairon* (On the Japanese National Polity), Nippon hyōronsha.
.... (1939), *Shin kokutairon* (A New National Polity Theory), Yūhikaku.
Nagao Ryūichi (1981), *Nihon hōshisōshi kenkyū* (Research into the History of Japanese Legal Thought), Sōbunsha.
Naitō Chisō ([1888] 1933), 'Kokutai hakki' (Manifesting the National Polity), 1888, reprinted in Takasu Yoshijirō ed., *Mitogaku zenshū* (The Complete Mito Studies), vol. 5, Nittō shoin, 1933.
Naitō Konan (1969–76), *Naitō Konan zenshū* (The Complete Works of Naitō Konan), Kanda Kiichirō and Naitō Kankichi eds, Chikuma shobō.
Nakamura Akira ([1974] 1985), *Shinpan Yanagita Kunio no shisō* (Yanagita Kunio's Thought: A New Edition), Hōsei daigaku shuppankyoku.
Nakane Chie (1967), *Tate shakai no ningen kankei* (Human Relations in a Vertical Society), Kōdansha. Published in English as *Japanese Society*, Berkeley: University of California Press, 1970; Harmondsworth: Penguin, 1973.
.... (1970), *Kazoku no kōzō* (The Structure of the Family), Tōkyō daigaku tōyō bunka kenkyūjo.
Nakatsuka Akira (1993), *Kindai Nihon no Chōsen ninshiki* (Modern Japan's Perceptions of Korea), Kenbun shuppan.
Nakayama Satoru (1924), 'Chōsenjin no na o zenbu Nipponmei ni henzubeshi' (All Korean Names Should be Changed into Japanese Names), *Nippon oyobi Nipponjin*, 15 September.
Nakazono Eisuke (1995), *Torii Ryūzō*, Iwanami shoten.
Nezu Masashi (1936), 'Genshi Nippon no jinrui to sono keifu' (Ancient Japanese Man and his Geneaology), *Rekishigaku kenkyū*, no. 37.
.... (1946), 'Nihon minzoku to Tennō kokka no kigen' (The Origin of the Japanese Nation and the Emperor State), *Nihon rekishi*, vol. 1, no. 1.
Nietzsche, Friedrich Wilhelm (1965), *Higeki no tanjō* (The Birth of Tragedy), translated by Akiyama Hideo, Iwanami bunko.
Nishida Kitarō (1965–66), *Nishida Kitarō zenshū* (The Complete Works of Nishida Kitarō), Abe Yoshishige et al. eds, Iwanami shoten.

Nishikawa Hiroshi (1970), 'Nihon teikokushugika ni okeru Chōsen kōkogaku no keisei' (The Formation of Korean Archaeology under Japanese Imperialism), *Chōsenshi kenkyūkai ronshū* (Papers by the Korean History Research Association), no. 7.

Nishimura Shinji (1941), *Nippon bunka ronkō* (A Study of Japanese Culture), Kōseikaku.

.... (1943), *Nipponjin wa doredake no koto o shite kita ka* (What Have the Japanese Accomplished to Date?), Kaitei Nippon shōkokumin bunko, Shinchōsha.

Noda Yoshiharu (1941), 'Sekai shintaisei to jinrui byōdō' (The New World System and Human Equality), in Jinkō mondai kenkyūkai ed. (1941).

Nomura sōgō kenkyūjo ed. (1978), *Nihonjinron kokusai kyōchō jidai ni sonaete* (*Nihonjinron*: Preparing for an Era of International Cooperation), Nomura sōgō kenkyūjo.

Odaka Tomoo (1941), *Kokutai no hongi to Naisen ittai* (The Cardinal Principle of the National Polity and 'Japan and Korea as One'), Kokumin sōryoku Chōsen renmei bōei shidōbu.

Ogawa Masato (1993), 'Chōhei·guntai to Ainu kyōiku' (Conscription, the Army, and *Ainu* Education), *Rekishigaku kenkyū*, no. 649.

Oguma Eiji ([1994] 1998), 'Sabetsu sunawachi byōdō – Nihon shokuminchi tōchi shisō e no Furansu jinshu shakaigaku no eikyō' (Discrimination as Equality: The Influence of French Racial Sociology on Japanese Ideas of Colonial Rule), *Rekishigaku kenkyū*, no. 662. Reprinted as Oguma (1998: chapter 7).

.... (1998), *'Nihonjin' no kyōkai – Okinawa·Ainu·Taiwan·Chōsen shokuminchi shihai kara fukki undō made* (The Boundaries of the 'Japanese': Okinawa, the *Ainu*, Taiwan and Korea. From Colonial Domination to the Return Movement), Shin'yōsha.

Ōkawa Shūmei (1961–74), *Ōkawa Shūmei zenshū* (The Complete Works of Ōkawa Shūmei), Ōkawa Shūmei zenshū kankōkai ed., Iwasaki shoten.

Ōkubo Toshikane ed. (1991), *Kume Kunitake no kenkyū* (Research of Kume Kunitake), Yoshikawa kōbunkan.

Ōkuma Shigenobu (1906), 'Tai-Kan iken' (On Korea), *Taiyō*, vol. 12, no. 5, April.

.... (1910), 'Nippon minzoku no bōchō ni tsuite' (On the Expansion of the Japanese Nation), *Taiyō*, vol. 16, no. 15, November (rinji zōkan).

.... ([1910] 1913), *Kaitei kokumin dokuhon* (The Revised National Reader), 1913, first edition 1910, pamphlet.
.... ed. ([1907] 1970), *Kaikoku gojūnenshi* (A Half-Century of the Open Country), Hara shobō, vol. 1.
Ōkurashō ed. (1939–50), *Shokuinroku* (List of Government Employees), Ōkurashō.
Ōmori Kingorō (1933), *Shintai kokushi kyōkasho* (Japanese History Textbook), Sanseidō, 1933 edition.
Ōmuro Mikio (1983), *Ajiantamu shō* (A Life Dedicated to Adiantums), Shin'yōsha.
Ōnishi Hajime (1897), 'Sosenkyō wa yoku sekyō no kiso taru bekika' (Can Ancestor Worship Become the Foundation for a World Religion?), *Rikugō zasshi*, vol. 201.
Ono Azusa ([1879] 1936), 'Tada Nippon ari' (Japan and Japan Alone), 1879, reprinted in Ono Azusa (1936: vol. 2).
.... (1936), *Ono Azusa zenshū* (The Complete Works of Ono Azusa), Nishimura Shinji ed., Fuzanbō.
Ōnuma Yasuaki (1986), *Tan'intsu minzoku shakai no shinwa o koete* (Moving Beyond the Myth of the Homogeneous Society), Tōshindō.
Orikuchi Shinobu (1965), *Orikuchi Shinobu zenshū* (The Complete Works of Orikuchi Shinobu), Orikuchi Hakase kinen kodai kenkyūjo ed., Chūō kōronsha.
Ōshima Masanori (1918), 'Yo no kokutaikan to kokka jinkakuron' (My View of the National Polity and the Character of the State), *Tōa no hikari*, vol. 13, no. 4.
Ōta Tetsuo (1987), 'Watsuji rinrigaku ni okeru *Koji junrei* no ichi' (*Koji junrei* in the Ethics of Watsuji), chapter 8, *Taishō Demokurashii no shisō suimyaku* (Chapters in the Thought of Taishō Democracy), Dōjidaisha.
Ōta Yūzō (1981), *Eigo to Nihonjin* (English and the Japanese), TBS Buritanika.
.... (1988), *E. S. Mōsu* (E. S. Morse), Riburopōto.
Ōtsuka Takehiro (1990), *Ōkawa Shūmei to kindai Nihon* (Ōkawa Shūmei and Modern Japan), Bokutakusha.
Oyabe Zen'ichirō (1924), *Jingisukan wa Yoshitsune nari* (Genghis Khan was Yoshitsune), Toyama shobō.
.... (1929), *Nippon oyobi Nippon kokumin no kigen* (The Origin of Japan and the Japanese), Kōseikaku.
Ozawa Toshio (1975), 'Haine ni okeru kodai no kamigami' (The Ancient Gods in the Thought of Heine), *Gendai shisō*, vol. 3, no. 4.

Ozawa Yūsaku (1966), 'Dōka kyōiku no rekishi' (The History of Assimilationist Education), *Chōsenshi kenkyū*, no. 56.

Pak Chunil (1969), *Kindai Nihon bungaku ni okeru Chōsenzō* (Views of Korea in Modern Japanese Literature), Miraisha.

Rekishigaku kenkyūkai ed. (1951), *Rekishi ni okeru minzoku no mondai* (The Problem of the Nation in History), Iwanami shoten.

Saeki Arikiyo (1988), *Yanagita Kunio to kodaishi* (Yanagita Kunio and Ancient Japanese History), Yoshikawa kōbunkan.

────── (1991), 'Kume Kunitake to Nihon kodaishi' (Kume Kunitake and Ancient Japanese History), in Ōkubo Toshikane ed. (1991).

Said, Edward W (1978), *Orientalism*, New York: Pantheon Books.

Saitō Hishō (1933), *Chūgaku kokushi* (Junior High-School Japanese History), for third year students, Dai Nippon tosho kabushiki gaisha.

Sakai Naoki (1990), 'Seiyō e no kaiki / Tōyō e no kaiki' (The Return to the West / The Return to the East), *Shisō*, no. 797.

────── (1992), 'Bunkateki sai no bunsekiron to Nihon to iu naibusei' (The Analysis of Cultural Difference and the Identity of Japan), *Jōkyō*, December.

────── (1994), '"Tōyō" no jiritsu to dai tōa kyōeiken' (The Independence of the 'Orient' and the Greater East Asia Co-prosperity Sphere), *Jōkyō*, December.

Sakamoto Takao (1988), *Yamaji Aizan*, Yoshikawa kōbunkan.

Sakano Tōru (1993), 'Kiyono Kenji no Nihonjinshuron' (Kiyono Kenji's Theory of the Japanese Race), *Kagakushi·kagaku tetsugaku*, no. 11.

Sano Manabu (1933), *Puroretaria Nippon rekishi* (A Proletariat History of Japan), Hakuyōsha.

────── ed. (1922), *Nippon kokuminsei no kenkyū* (Studies of the Japanese Character), Daitōkaku.

Sanseidō editorial board ed. (1926), *Nippon rekishi kyōkasho* (Japanese History Textbook), for upper grades, Sanseidō, fourth revised edition.

────── (1934), *Shinsei Nipponshi* (A New History of Japan), vol. 1, Saiseidō.

Sasaki Yomoji (1925), *Jinseiron yori mitaru Nippon kokutairon* (The Japanese National Polity seen from Theories about How to Live), Takeda hōshindō.

Satō Tetsutarō (1918), 'Kokutai no kenkyū' (Research of the

National Polity), *Tōa no hikari*, vol. 13, nos. 3–4.
Satomi Kishio (1928), *Kokutai ni taisuru giwaku* (Suspicions about the National Polity), Arususha.
Sawayanagi Masatarō (1910), 'Shokumin to shite no Nipponjin seikakuron' (On the Character of the Japanese as Colonists), *Taiyō*, vol. 16, no. 15.
Seki Kōsaku ed. ([1893] 1988), *Inoue hakase to Kirisuto kyōto* (Dr. Inoue and the Christians), Tetsugaku shoin, 1893, reprinted edition, Misuzu shobō, 1988.
Senjika Nihon shakai kenkyūkai ed. (1992), *Senjika no Nihon* (Wartime Japan), Kōronsha.
Shiba Kuzumori (1934), *Shinsei kokushi* (A New History of Japan), Meiji shoin.
Shibukawa Genji (1924), 'Nani o osoruru ka Nippon' (Japan Has Nothing to Fear), *Chūō kōron*, July.
Shiga Yoshio ([1949] 1969), *Kokkaron* (On the State), 1949, reprinted in Yoshimoto Takaaki ed. (1969).
Shimamura Hōgetsu (1910), 'Shokumin to Nippon bungei no shōrai' (Colonisation and the Future of Japanese Literature), *Taiyō*, vol. 16, no. 15.
Shimomura Hiroshi (Kainan) (1941), *Kurubeki Nippon* (The Future Japan), Daiichi shobō.
Shimota Seiji (1975), 'Nihon bunka no dentō to Chōsen' (The Tradition of Japanese Culture and Korea), *Kikan sanzenri*, no. 3.
Shinmura Izuru ([1901] 1971–83), 'Taguchi Hakase no gengo ni kansuru shoron o yomu' (Reading Dr. Taguchi on Linguistics), 1901, reprinted in *Shinmura Izuru zenshū* (The Complete Works of Shinmura Izuru), Kindaichi Kyōsuke et al. eds, Chikuma shobō, 1971–83, vol. 1.
.... (1920), 'Nippongo ka Ainugo ka' (The Japanese Language or the *Ainu* Language?), *Minzoku to rekishi*, vol. 4, no. 6.
Shiratori Kiyoshi (1938), 'Nippon minzoku no kigen' (The Origins of the Japanese Nation), Nippon shogaku shinkō iinkai kenkyū hōkoku, dai 4 hen (Research Report of the Committee of the Promotion of Studies in Japan, vol. 4), Monbushō kyōgakukyoku.
Shiratori Kurakichi ([1897] 1969–71), '*Nihon shoki* ni mietaru kango no kaishaku' (The Interpretation of the Korean Language Seen in *Nihon shoki*), 1897, reprinted in Shiratori Kurakichi (1969–71: vol. 4).

── (1910), 'Nippon wa hatashite Chōsen o dōka shiubeki ka' (Can Japan Really Assimilate Korea?), *Kyōiku jiron*, no. 915, 15 September.

── ([1910] 1969–71), 'Waga jōko ni okeru Kanhantō no seiryoku o ronzu' (A Discussion of the Ancient Japanese Foothold in the Korean Peninsula), 1910, reprinted in Shiratori Kurakichi (1969–71: vol. 9).

── ([1913] 1969–71), Tōyōshijō yori mitaru Nipponkoku' (Japan as Seen from Oriental History), 1913, reprinted in Shiratori Kurakichi (1969–71: vol. 9).

── (1969–71), *Shiratori Kurakichi zenshū* (The Complete Works of Shiratori Kurakichi), Ishida Mikinosuke et al. eds, Iwanami shoten.

Shiratori Yoshio (1975), 'Shiratori Kurakichi', in Shiratori Yoshio and Hachiman Ichirō (1975).

── (1992), 'Torii Ryūzō', in Egami Namio ed. (1992).

── and Hachiman Ichirō (1975), *Shiratori Kurakichi·Torii Ryūzō*, Nihon minzoku bunka taikei 9, Kōdansha.

Shirayanagi Shūko (1940), *Tōyō minzokuron* (On Oriental Nations), Chikura shobō.

Suenari Michio (1988), 'Torii Ryūzō', in Ayabe Tsuneo ed. (1988).

Sugawara Chieko (1994), *Miyazawa Kenji no seishun* (Miyazawa Kenji's Youth), Takarajimasha.

Suzuki Kentarō ([1891] 1927–33), 'Jinshu taiseiron' (The Relative Strengths of the Various Races), in *Shin zen bi Nipponjin* (The Truth, Virtue and Beauty of the Japanese), 1891, reprinted in Yoshino Sakuzō et al. eds, *Meiji bunka zenshū* (The Complete Collection of Meiji Culture), Nippon hyōronsha, 1927–38, vol. 23.

Suzuki Masayuki ([1981] 1986), 'Kindai Tennōsei no shihai genri ni kansuru ichishiron' (Thoughts on the Ruling Principles of the Modern Emperor System) in *Buraku mondai kenkyū*, no. 68, 1981, reprinted in Suzuki Masayuki, *Kindai Tennōsei no shihai chitsujo* (The Ruling Order of the Modern Emperor System), Azekura shobō, 1986.

── (1986), 'Taishō demokurashii to kokutai mondai' (Taishō Democracy and the Problem of the National Polity), *Nihonshi kenkyū*, no. 281.

Suzuki Takeki and Sasaki Mamoru (1975), 'Tennōzoku no shutsuji to gendai' (The Origin of the Imperial Clan and Modern Times), *Gendai no me*, December.

Suzuki Yūko (1992), *Jūgun ianfu·Naisen kekkon* (The Comfort Women and Japanese-Korean Marriages), Miraisha.
Suzuki Zenji (1983), *Nihon no yūseigaku* (Eugenics in Japan), Sankyō shuppan.
Tachibana Shiraki (1966), *Tachibana Shiraki chosakushū* (The Collected Works of Tachibana Shiraki), Tachibana Shiraki chosakushū kankōkai ed., Keisō shobō.
Tacitus, Publius Cornelius (1999), *Tacitus: Germania* (Clarendon Ancient History Series), translated and edited by J. B. Rives, Oxford: Clarendon Press.
Taga Kazufumi (1988), '"Nihon shinkokuron" no keifu' (The Genealogy of the 'Theory of Japan as Land of the Gods'), *GS*, no. 7.
Taguchi Ukichi ([1879] 1927–29), 'Naichi zakkyoron' (On Mixed Residence in the Interior), 1879, reprinted in Taguchi Ukichi (1927–29: vol. 5).
.... (1884), 'Naichi zakkyo o ronzu (dai 2)' (Debating the Issue of Mixed Residence, part 2), *Tōkyō keizai zasshi*, no. 205.
.... (1889a), 'Naichi zakkyo no kiyū' (Groundless Worries about Mixed Residence), *Tōkyō keizai zasshi*, no. 478.
.... (1889b), 'Nanzo gaijin no tochi kaiire o kobamu o enya' (Why Not Allow Foreigners to Purchase Land?), *Tōkyō keizai zasshi*, no. 479.
.... ([1889] 1927–29), *Jōyaku kaiseiron* (On the Revision of the Treaties), 1889, reprinted in Taguchi Ukichi (1927–29: vol. 5).
.... (1891), 'Inoue Tetsujirō ni tadasu' (Querying Inoue Tetsujirō), *Tōkyō keizai zasshi*, no. 573.
.... ([1893] 1927–29), *Kyoryūchi seido to naichi zakkyo* (Extraterritorial Settlements and Mixed Residence in the Interior), 1893, reprinted in Taguchi Ukichi (1927–29: vol. 5).
.... ([1895] 1927–29), 'Nippon jinshuron' (On the Japanese Race), 1895, reprinted in Taguchi Ukichi (1927–29: vol. 2).
.... ([1899] 1927–29), 'Kyoryūchi o shite sumiyaka ni dōka seshimu beshi' (The Extraterritorial Settlements should be Quickly Returned to Japan), 1899, reprinted in Taguchi Ukichi (1927–29: vol. 5).
.... (1901), 'Kokugo jō yori kansatsu shitaru jinshu no shodai' (A Linguistic Approach to Identifying the Founder of Ethnic Groups), *Shigaku zasshi*, no. 139.
.... ([1904] 1927–29) *Ha ōka ron – Nippon jinshu no shinsō*

(Destroy the Theory of a Yellow Peril: The Truth of the Japanese Race), 1904, reprinted in Taguchi (1927–29: vol. 2).

.... ([1905] 1927–29), 'Nippon jinshu no kenkyū' (Research on the Japanese Race), 1905, reprinted in Taguchi (1927–29: vol. 2).

.... (1927–29), *Teiken Taguchi Ukichi zenshū* (The Complete Works of Taguchi Ukichi), Teiken Taguchi Ukichi zenshū kankōkai.

Tahata Shinobu (1959), *Katō Hiroyuki*, Yoshikawa kōbunkan.

Takagi Hiroshi (1993), 'Fashizumuki, Ainu minzoku no dōkaron' (The Discourse on the Assimilation of the *Ainu* Nation in Fascist Japan), in Akasawa Fumiaki and Kitakawa Kenzō eds, *Bunka to fashizumu* (Culture and Fascism), Nihon keizai hyōronsha, 1993.

Takahashi Sadaki (1992), *Hisabetsu buraku issennenshi* (A Thousand Year History of the *Burakumin*, original title *Tokushu buraku issennenshi*), Iwanami bunko.

Takahashi Yoshio ([1884] 1961), *Nippon jinshu kairyōron* (On Improving the Japanese Race), 1884, reprinted in *Meiji bunka shiryō sōsho* (Meiji Cultural Materials), vol. 6, Kazama shobō, 1961.

Takakura Shin'ichirō (1942), *Ainu seisakushi* (A History of *Ainu* Policies), Nippon hyōronsha.

Takamure Itsue ([1931] 1979), 'Shintō to jiyū ren'ai' (Shintō and Free Love), *Fujo shinbun*, 6 December 1931, reprinted in Takamure Itsue ronshū henshū iinkai ed. (1979).

.... ([1934] 1979), 'Nippon seishin ni tsuite' (On the Japanese Spirit), *Fujin shinbun*, 12 August 1934, reprinted in Takamure Itsue ronshū henshū iinkai ed. (1979).

.... (1938a), *Dai Nippon joseishi* (A History of Women in Great Japan), Kōseikaku.

.... (1938b), 'Nippon seishin to josei kenkyū' (The Japanese Spirit and Womens' Studies), *Josei tenbō*, May.

.... (1939), 'Jōdai keifu ni okeru shizoku mata wa kazuko to shite no reimin' (Serfs as Clans and/or Families in Ancient Japan), *Rekishi kōron*, vol. 8, no. 1.

.... (1940), *Josei nisenroppyakunen* (A 2,600 Year History of Japanese Women), Kōseikaku.

.... ([1940] 1979), 'Nisen roppyakunen o kotohogite' (Celebrating 2,600 Years of Imperial Rule), *Kagayaku*, November 1940, reprinted in Takamure Itsue ronshū henshū iinkai ed. (1979).

.... ([1943] 1979a), 'Gunji to josei' (The Military and Women), 1943, reprinted in Takamure Itsue ronshū henshū iinkai ed. (1979).

.... ([1943] 1979b), 'Jingū Kōgō (Her Majesty the Empress Jingū), 1943, reprinted in Takamure Itsue ronshū henshū iinkai ed. (1979).

.... ([1944] 1979), 'Taoyame' (Graceful Maidens), 1944, reprinted in Takamure Itsue ronshū henshū iinkai ed. (1979).

.... (1945), 'Dentō no gojishin' (Defending Tradition), *Asahi shinbun*, 2 June.

.... (1965–67), *Takamure Itsue zenshū* (The Complete Works of Takamure Itsue), Hashimoto Kenzō ed., Rironsha.

Takamure Itsue ronshū henshū iinkai ed. (1979), *Takamure Itsue ronshū* (Papers on Takamure Itsue), JCA shuppan.

Takasaki Sōji (1993), 'Chōsen no shin-Nichiha' (Pro-Japanese Koreans), in *Iwanami kōza kindai Nihon to shokuminchi* (Iwanami Lectures: Modern Japan and Japanese Colonies), Ōe Shinobu et al. eds, Iwanami shoten, vol. 6, 1993.

Takasawa Atsuo (1992), 'Senjika Nihon ni okeru jinkō mondai kenkyūkai to jinkō mondai kenkyūjo' (The Population Problem Research Group and the Population Research Centre in Wartime Japan), in Senjika Nihon kenkyūkai ed. (1992).

Takata Yasuma (1942), *Minzoku taibō* (National Austerity), Kōu shoin.

Takayama Chogyū ([1897] 1925–33), 'Waga kokutai to shinhanto' (The Japanese National Polity and Our New Territories), *Taiyō*, November 1897, reprinted in Takayama Chogyū (1925–33: vol. 4).

.... ([1899] 1925–33a), 'Shokuminteki kokumin to shite no Nipponjin' (The Japanese as a Colonising People), 1899, reprinted in Takayama Chogyū (1925–33: vol. 4).

.... ([1899] 1925–33b), 'Teikokushugi to shokumin' (Imperialism and Colonisation), 1899, reprinted in Takayama Chogyū (1925–33: vol. 5).

.... (1925–33), *Kaitei chūshaku Chogyū zenshū* (The Complete Works of Chogyū), Anezaki Masaharu et al. eds, Hakubunkan.

Takegoshi Yosaburō (1896), *Nisen gohyakunenshi* (2,500 Years of Japanese Civilisation), Keiseisha.

.... (1910a), *Nangokuki* (An Account of the Lands of the South), Niseisha.

.... (1910b), 'Nanpō keiei to Nippon no shimei' (Managing the South and Japan's Mission), *Taiyō*, vol. 16, no. 15.

.... (1910c), 'Shokumin to shite no Nis-Shin-Ei-Futsu-Doku shokokumin no hikaku' (A Comparison of the Nationals of

Japan, China, Great Britain, France and Germany as Colonists), *Taiyō*, vol. 16, no. 15.
Takeuchi Ken (1972), 'Nihonteki kyōki no engen o saguru' (Weird and Wonderful Origin Theories in Japan), *Paidia*, no. 12.
Takimura Ryūichi ([1973] 1987), *Kita Ikki*, Keisō shobō.
Takita Yukiko (1992), '"Tan'itsu minzoku kokka" shinwa no datsu shinwaka' (Demythologising the Myth of the 'Homogeneous Nation-State'), in Kajita Masamichi ed., *Kokusai shakaigaku* (International Sociology), Nagoya daigaku shuppankai, 1992.
Tamaki Hajime (1967), 'Nihon kyōsantō no zainichi Chōsenjin shidō' (The Japanese Communist Party's Leadership of the *Zainichi* Koreans), chapter 5, *Minzokuteki sekinin no shisō* (The Philosophy of National Responsibility), Ocha-no-mizu shobō.
Tamanoi Riko (1986), 'Ōbei ni okeru "ie" no rikai' (The Understanding in the West of the *Ie*), *Minzokugaku kenkyū*, vol. 50, no. 4.
Tanaka Chigaku ([1920] 1942), *Nippon kokutai no kenkyū* (Research of the Japanese National Polity), Tengyō minpōsha.
Tanaka Katsuhiko (1978), 'Gengogaku to shite no Yanagitagaku' (A Linguistic Approach to Yanagita Studies), in Tanaka Katsuhiko, *Gengo kara mita minzoku kokka* (The Nation and State as seen through the Politics of Language), Iwanami shoten, 1978.
Tanaka Shin'ichi (1980), 'Nitobe Inazō to shokuminchi Chōsen' (Nitobe Inazō and the Korean Colony), *Hokudai hyakunenshi henshū nyūsu*, no. 11.
Tanaka, Stefan (1993), *Japan's Orient: Rendering Pasts into History*, Berkeley: University of California Press.
Taniguchi Konen (1942), *Tōyō minzoku to taishitsu* (Oriental Peoples and Physical Constitution), Yamagabō.
.... (1943), 'Konketsu mondai' (The Problem of Mixed Blood), *Yūseigaku*, no. 229.
Tatebe Tongo (1912), *Sekai rekkoku no taisei* (The General Trends of the World Powers), Dōbunkan.
.... (1914), 'Teikoku no kokuze to sekai no senran' (The War-Torn World and the National Policy of the Empire), in *Nippon shakaigakuin nenpō* (The Annual Report of the Japanese Social Academy), year 2, vols. 3–4.
Taut, Bruno (1975), *Nihon* (Japan), translated by Shinoda Hideo, Iwanami shoten.
Terada Kazuo (1975), *Nihon no jinruigaku* (Anthropology in Japan), Shisakusha.

Todd, Emmanuel (1990), *L'Invention de l'Europe*, Paris: Editions du Seuil.
Tode Hiroshi (1986), 'Nihon kōkogaku to shakai' (Japanese Anthropology and Society) in *Gendai to kōkogaku, Iwanami kōza Nihon kōkogaku* (Iwanami Lectures on Japanese Anthropology: Modern Anthropology), Iwanami shoten, vol. 7, 1986.
Tōgō Makoto (1925), *Shokumin seisaku to minzoku shinri* (Colonial Policies and the National Psychology), Iwanami shoten.
Tokutomi Sohō (1894), *Dai Nippon bōchōron* (The Expansion of Great Japan), Min'yūsha.
.... (1925), *Kokumin shōkun* (Admonishing the Nation), Min'yūsha.
.... (1938), *Kōdō Nippon no sekaika* (Imperial Japan as a Global Power), Min'yūsha.
.... (1939), *Shōwa kokumin dokuhon* (The Shōwa National Reader), Tōkyō nichinichi shinbunsha.
.... (1940), *Manshū kenkoku dokuhon* (The Foundation of Manchuria Reader), Nippon denpō tsūshinsha.
.... (1942a), *Sensen no taishō* (The Imperial Proclamation of War), Tōkyō nichinichi shinbunsha.
.... (1942b), 'Kōshitsu chūshin to minzoku chūshin' (The Centrality of the Imperial Household and Centrality of the Nation), *Tōkyō nichinichi shinbun*, 1 April.
.... (1944a), *Hisshō kokumin dokuhon* (The National Victory Reader), Mainichi shinbunsha.
.... (1944b), 'Jikyoku montō' (Questions and Answers on Current Affairs), *Kaizō*, vol. 26, no. 4, April.
.... (1953), *Kokushi yori mitaru Kōshitsu* (The Imperial Household seen from the History of Japan), Fujimaki sensei kiju shukugakai.
Tōkyō jinruigakkai ed. (1935), *Nippon minzoku* (The Japanese Nation), Iwanami shoten.
Tōma Seita (1951a), *Nihon minzoku no keisei* (The Formation of the Japanese Nation), Iwanami shoten.
.... (1951b), 'Kodai ni okeru minzoku' (The Nation in Ancient Times), in Rekishigaku kenkyūkai ed. (1951).
Tomiyama Ichirō (1994), 'Kokumin no tanjō to "Nihonjinshu"' (The Birth of the Japanese People and the 'Japanese Race'), *Shisō*, no. 845.
Tomizu Hirondo (1910), 'Nanpō ka, Hoppō ka' (The South or the North?), *Taiyō*, vol. 16, no. 15.

Torii Ryūzō (1920), 'Minzokujō yori mitaru sen, shi, shiberi' (Korea, China, and Siberia as seen from the Viewpoint of Ethnicity), *Tōhō jiron*, April.
────── (1933), 'Genshijin no seikatsu' (The Life of Primitive Man), *Minzoku eisei*, vol. 2, no. 4.
────── (1939), 'Watashi no miru Chōsen' (My Views of Korea), *Chōsen*, no. 284.
────── (1975–77), *Torii Ryūzō zenshū* (The Complete Works of Torii Ryūzō), Asahi shinbunsha.
Tsuboi Shōgorō (1902), 'Jinruigaku kenkyūjo to shite no wagakuni' (Japan as an Anthropological Research Labrotory), *Tōkyō jinruigakkai zasshi*, no. 199.
────── (1903), 'Jinshudan' (On Race), *Tōkyō jinruigakkai zasshi*, no. 205.
────── (1905), 'Jinruigakuteki chishiki no yō masumasu fukashi' (The Need for Anthropological Knowledge is Greater than Ever), *Tōkyō jinruigakkai zasshi*, nos. 231–33.
────── (1906), 'Hokkaidō kyūdojin kyūiki jigyō' (An Education Project for the Hokkaido Natives), *Tōkyō jinruigakkai zasshi*, no. 245.
Tsuda Sōkichi (1902), *Kokushi kyōkasho* (A Japanese History Textbook), Hōbunkan.
────── (1938), *Shina shisō to Nippon* (Chinese Thought and Japan), Iwanami shinsho.
────── (1946a), 'Nihon rekishi no kenkyū ni okeru kagakuteki taido' (The Scientific Attitude in Researching Japanese History), *Sekai*, no. 3.
────── (1946b), 'Kenkoku no jijō to banse ikkei no shisō' (The Situation at the Time of the Founding of Japan and the Idea of the Unbroken Line of Emperors), *Sekai*, no. 4.
────── (1963–66) *Tsuda Sōkichi zenshū* (The Complete Works of Tsuda Sōkichi), Iwanami shoten.
────── (1986–89), *Tsuda Sōkichi zenshū* (The Complete Works of Tsuda Sōkichi), Iwanami shoten.
Tsuda Tsuyoshi (1941), *Sekai no taisei to Naisen ittai* (International Affairs and 'Japan and Korea as One'), Kokumin sōryoku Chōsen renmei bōei shidōbu.
Ubukata Naokichi (1979), 'Tan'itsu minzoku kokka no shisō to kinō' (The Thought and Function of the Homogeneous Nation-State), *Shisō*, no. 656.
Uchida Ginzō (1941), *Nippon kokumin seikatsu no hattatsu* (The Development of the Life of the Japanese), Sōgensha.

Uchimura Kanzō ([1895] 1980–84), 'Amerika dojin no kyōiku' (The Education of Native Americans), 1895, reprinted in Uchimura Kanzō (1980–84: vol. 3).

.... (1980–84), *Uchimura Kanzō zenshū* (The Complete Works of Uchimura Kanzō), Suzuki Toshirō et al. eds, Iwanami shoten.

Ueda Jōkichi (1935), 'Chōsenjin to Nipponjin to no taishitsu hikaku' (A Comparison of the Physical Constitution of Koreans and Japanese), in Tōkyō jinruigakkai ed. (1935).

Ueda Masaaki (1973), 'Kodaishigaku to Chōsen' (The Study of Ancient History and Korea), *Sekai*, no. 330.

.... (1978a), *Kita Sadakichi*, Nihon minzoku bunka taikei 5, Kōdansha.

.... (1978b), '"Nissen dōsoron" no keifu' (The Genealogy of 'The Theory that the Japanese and the Koreans Share a Common Ancestor'), *Kikan sanzenri*, no. 14.

.... ed. (1974), *Hito to shisō – Tsuda Sōkichi* (Tsuda Sōkichi: The Man and His Thought), San'ichi shobō.

Ueda Tatsuo (1942), *Chōsen no mondai to sono kaiketsu* (The Problem of Korea and its Resolution), Keijō seigaku kenkyūjo.

Uemura Hideaki (1992), *Senjū minzoku* (Indigenous Nations), Kaihō shuppansha.

Uesugi Mutsuhiko (1987), 'Taiwan ni okeru Kōminka seisaku no tenkai' (The Development of the Japanisation Policy in Taiwan), *Takachiho ronsō*.

Uesugi Shinkichi (1921), *Kokka shinron* (A New Theory of the State), Keibunkan.

.... (1925a), *Kokutairon* (On the National Polity), Yūhikaku.

.... (1925b), *Kokkaron* (On the State), Yūhikaku.

Ui Keiko (1969), 'Heigō o meguru Nihon to gaikoku no shinbun ronchō' (The Line of Argument Taken in Japanese and Foreign Newspapers about the Japanese Annexation of Korea), in Inoue Hideo ed. (1969).

Ukita Kazutami (1908), 'Kokka to shūkyō' (The State and Religion), *Teiyū rinrikai kōenshū*, no. 67.

.... (1910a), 'Kankoku heigō no kōka ikan' (The Effect of the Annexation of Korea), *Taiyō*, vol. 16, no. 13, October.

.... (1910b), 'Nippon ni taisuru sekai no gokai (sono ni)' (The World's Misunderstandings about Japan, Part 2), *Taiyō*, vol. 16, no. 16, December.

Umehara Takeshi (1982), *Umehara Takeshi chosakushū* (The Collected Works of Umehara Takeshi), vol. 20, Shūeisha.

.... et al. (1984), *Kodai Nihon o kangaeru* (Thinking about Ancient Japan), in *Umehara Takeshi zentaiwa* (The Complete Conversations With Umehara Takeshi), vol. 2, Shūeisha, 1984.
Unno Kōtoku (1910), 'Chōsen jinshu to Nippon jinshu no zakkon ni tsuite' (On Mixed Marriages Between the Korean and Japanese Races), *Taiyō*, vol. 16, no. 16, December.
Unoura Hiroshi (1988), 'Shinkaron to naichi zakkyoron' (The Theory of Evolution and Mixed Residence in the Interior), *Kitazato daigaku kyōyōbu kiyō*, no. 22.
Uozumi Sōgorō (1933), *Shinshū Nipponshi* (Japanese History), for first year students, Hoshino shoten.
Urao Teru (1994), *Ozawa Ichirō shinjitsu no sakebi* (Ozawa Ichirō: The Call of Truth), Sanshindō shuppan.
Utsumi Aiko (1991), *Chosenjin 'Kōgun' heishitachi no sensō* (The War as Experienced by the Korean Soldiers in the 'Imperial Army'), Iwanami shoten.
Verne, Jules ([1873] 1990), *Around the World in Eighty Days*, Harmondsworth, Middlesex: Puffin.
Wakatsuki Yasuo (1972), *Hainichi no rekishi* (The History of Japanophobia), Chūkō shinsho.
Watanabe Yoshimichi (1931), 'Nippon genshi kyōsan shakai no seisan oyobi seisanryoku no hatten' (The Development of Production and Productivity in the Japanese Primitive Communistic Society), *Shisō*, no. 110.
Watari Shōzaburō (1928a), *Kokumin dōtoku honron* (On National Morals), Chūbunkan shoten.
.... (1928b), 'Kenkoku no hongi to kokumin dōtoku' (The First Principles of the Foundation of Japan and National Morals), in Monbushō futsū gakumukyoku ed., *Kokutai kōenroku* (Lectures on the National Polity), vol. 1, Hōbunkan.
Watase Tsunekichi (1897), 'Waga kokuze to shūkyōteki shinnen' (Japan's National Policy and Religious Belief), *Rikugō zasshi*, no. 199.
Watsuji Tetsurō (1920), *Nippon kodai bunka* (Ancient Japanese Culture), Iwanami shoten.
.... (1935), *Fūdo* (Climate), Iwanami shoten, 1935 (first) edition.
.... (1939), *Nippon kodai bunka* (Ancient Japanese Culture), revised edition, Iwanami shoten.
.... (1942), *Rinrigaku* (Ethics), Iwanami shoten, vol. 2.
.... (1944), *Fūdo* (Climate), Iwanami shoten, 1944 edition.

.... ([1948] 1989–92) *Kokumin tōgō no shōchō* (The Symbol of National Unity), 1948, reprinted in Watsuji Tetsurō (1989–92: vol. 14).

.... (1962), *Watsuji Tetsurō zenshū* (The Complete Works of Watsuji Tetsurō), Abe Yoshishige et al. eds, Iwanami shoten.

.... (1989–92), *Watsuji Tetsurō zenshū* (The Complete Works of Watsuji Tetsurō), Abe Yoshishige et al. eds, Iwanami shoten (third edition).

Yamada Kō (1987), *Watsuji Tetsurō ron* (On Watsuji Tetsurō), Kadensha.

Yamada Norio (1976), *Rekishika Kita Sadakichi* (The Historian, Kita Sadakichi), Hōbunkan.

Yamagata Isoo (1924), 'Beika haiseki yori Beika haiseki' (Rejected Americanisation Rather than American Dollars), *Taiyō*, vol. 30, no. 11, September.

Yamaji Aizan (1901), 'Nipponjin-shi no daiichi peiji' (The First Page of the History of the Japanese People), *Shinano mainichi shinbun*, 3 November.

.... (1910), 'Nippon jinshuron' (On the Japanese Race), *Dokuritsu hyōron*, no. 7.

.... (1966), *Kirisutokyō hyōron·Nippon jinminshi* (A Critique of Christianity and A History of the Japanese People), Iwanami bunko.

Yamamoto Shichihei (1986), *Hon Saik chūjō no shokei* (The Execution of Lieutenant-General Hon Saik), Bungei shunjū.

Yamamuro Shin'ichi (1990), 'Kokumin kokka·Nihon no hatsugen' (The Nation-State: Japan's Point of View), *Jinbun gakuhō*, LXVII.

Yamanaka Hayato (1982–83), 'Chōsen "dōka seisaku" to shakaigakuteki dōka' (Korean 'Assimilationist Policies' and Sociological Assimilation), Kansai gakuin daigaku, *Shakaigakubu kiyō*, nos. 45–46.

Yamashita Etsuko (1988), *Takamure Itsue ron* (On Takamure Itsue), Kawade shobō shinsha.

Yamawaki Keizō (1993), *Kindai Nihon no gaikokujin rōdōsha mondai* (Modern Japan and the Problem of Foreign Workers), Meiji gakuin kokusai heiwa kenkyūjo.

Yanagita Kunio ([1902] 1962–71), 'Nōgyō seisakugaku' (Agricultural Policy Studies), 1902, reprinted in Yanagita Kunio (1962–71: vol. 28).

.... ([1926] 1980), 'Ganzen no ijinshu mondai' (The Immediate

Problem of Alien Races), *Zaidan hōjin keimeikai dai jū hakkai kōenshū* (The Keimeikai Eighteenth Lecture Series), 1926, reprinted in Kōno Motomichi ed., *Ainushi shiryōshū* (Collected Materials on *Ainu* History), vol. 5, *Gengo fūzoku hen (2)* (Language and Mores, 2) vol. 7, Hokkaido shuppan kikaku sentaa, 1980.

.... ([1940] 1962–71), 'Kaijō bunka' (A Seafaring Culture), 1940, reprinted in Yanagita (1962–71: vol. 1).

.... (1962–71), *Teihon Yanagita Kunio shū* (The Collected Works of Yanagita Kunio), Teihon Yanagita Kunio henshū iinkai ed., Chikuma shobō.

.........., Hashiura Yasuo, Okada Ken, Nakamura Akira and Kanaseki Takeo (1943), 'Yanagita Kunio shi o kakomite – Dai tōa minzokugaku no kensetsu to *Minzoku Taiwan* no shimei' (A Talk with Yanagita Kunio: The Creation of a Greater East Asia Folklore Studies and the Mission of *Minzoku Taiwan* [Folklore in Taiwan]), *Minzoku Taiwan*, vol. 3, no. 12.

.... et al. ([1949] 1964), 'Nihon rekishi kandan' (A Rambling Conversation on Japanese History), *Kaizō*, vol. 30, no. 6, 1949, reprinted in Yanagita Kunio et al. (1964).

.... et al. (1957), 'Nihon bunka no dentō' (The Traditions of Japanese Culture), *Kindai bungaku*, vol. 12, nos. 1–2.

.... et al. (1964), *Yanagita Kunio taidanshū* (Collected Conversations with Yanagita Kunio), Chikuma shobō.

Yang Yonghu (1980), 'Yanagita Kunio to Chōsen minzoku' (Yanagita Kunio and Korean Folklore), *Kikan sanzenri*, no. 21.

Yasuda Yojūrō (1985–89), *Yasuda Yojūrō zenshū* (The Complete Works of Yasuda Yojūrō), Kōdansha.

Yokoyama Gennosuke (1954), *Naichi zakkyogo no Nippon* (Japan After Mixed Residence), in Yokoyama Gennosuke, *Naichi zakkyogo no Nippon ta ippen* (Japan After Mixed Residence and Another Work), Iwanami bunko.

Yonetani Masafumi (1990), 'Shōchō Tennōsei no shisōshiteki kōsatsu' (An Intellectual History of the Symbolic Emperor System), *Jōkyō*, December.

.... (1992), 'Watsuji rinrigaku to jūgonen sensōki no Nihon' (Watsuji Ethics and Japan During the 15 Year War), *Jōkyō*, September.

.... (1994a), 'Watsuji Tetsurō to Tennōsei no aratana shinwaka' (Watsuji Tetsurō and the New Mythologisation of the Emperor System), *Kokubungaku* (Japanese Literature), vol. 39, no. 6.

.... (1994b), 'Watsuji Tetsurō to ōken shinwa no saikaishaku' (Watsuji Tetsurō's Reinterpretation of the Myth of the Divine Right of the King), *Kokugo to kokubungaku*, November.
Yorisumi Mitsuko (1989), 'Watsuji rinrigaku to Tennōsei' (Watsuji's Ethics and the Emperor System), *Junshin gakuhō*, no. 6.
Yoshida Kōji (1976), *Katō Hiroyuki no kenkyū* (Research on Katō Hiroyuki), Shinseisha.
Yoshida Kumaji (1918), 'Waga kokutai no shakaiteki kiso' (The Social Foundations of the Japanese National Polity), *Tōa no hikari*, vol. 13, no. 8.
.... (1928), *Kokumin dōtoku to sono kyōyō* (National Morality and its Cultivation), Kōdōkan.
Yoshida Tōgo (1893), *Nikkan koshidan* (On Ancient Japanese-Korean History), Fuzanbō.
Yoshimoto Takaaki ed. (1969), *Kokka no shisō* (The Philosophy of the State), Sengo Nihon shisō taikei 5, Chikuma shobō.
Yoshino Hidekimi (1927), *Taiwan kyōikushi* (A History of Education in Taiwan), Taiwan nichinichi shinpōsha.
Yoshino Makoto (1993), 'Tan'itsu minzoku kokkakan to iminzoku shihai' (The View of the Homogeneous Nation-State and Rule of Alien Nations), in Rekishi kyōikusha kyōgikai ed., *Atarashii rekishi kyōiku* (A New Historical Education), vol. 2, 1993.
Yoshioka Ikuo (1987), *Nihon jinshu ronsō no makuake* (The Dawn of the Controversy over the Japanese Race), Kyōritsu shuppan.
Yoshioka Masao (1969), 'Heigō to Kirisutosha' (The Annexation and Christians), in Inoue Hideo ed. (1969).
Yoshioka Yoshinori (1967), '"Chōsen heigō" to Nihon no yoron' (The 'Annexation of Korea' and Japanese Public Opinion), *Chōsen kenkyū*, no. 65, no. 72.
.... (1968), 'Nihon kokunai shokaikyū no shisō jōkyō' (The State of Mind of the Various Classes Within Japan), in Watanabe Manabu ed., *Chōsen kindaishi* (Modern Korean History), Keisō shobō, 1968.
Yuasa Yasuo ([1981] 1995), *Watsuji Tetsurō*, Chikuma gakugei bunko.
.... ed. (1973), *Hito to shisō – Watsuji Tetsurō* (Watsuji Tetsurō: The Man and His Thought), San'ichi shobō.
Yumoto Takehiko (1897), 'Nippon shugi hakkan ni tsukite' (On the Founding of *Nippon shugi*), *Nippon shugi*, no. 1.
Yun Koncha (1994), *Minzoku gensō no satetsu* (The Failure of the Illusion that is the Nation), Iwanami shoten.

Index

Abe Yoshishige, 289–90
Ainu, xxiv, xxix, 4–9, 22, 47–9, 51, 53–63, 76–7, 85, 89, 91, 100–3, 105–7, 109, 114, 120, 122, 129, 130–5, 137, 140, 144, 151–5, 176–7, 188–9, 199, 211, 215, 219, 227–31, 233, 236, 238–40, 242, 247, 265–6, 276, 278, 286, 295, 298, 306–7, 309–10, 323, 329, 341–2, 345, 348, 351 endnote 5, 354 endnote 1, 363 endnote 5, 365–6 endnote 7, 374 endnote 14, 374–5 endnote 17, 379 endnote 15
Akamine Seichirō, 74
Akiyama Kenzō, 288
Amakasu Masahiko, 154
Amano Teiyū, 304
Amaterasu, Amaterasu Ōmikami, xvii, 8, 65, 67, 151, 167, 169, 269, 277–8, 303, 355–6 endnote 4
Ame-no-hiboko, 85, 246
Amino Yoshihiko, xxix–xxx
An Chung Ken, 89
Arai Hakuseki, 3–5, 65, 69–70, 73, 258, 354–5 endnote 3
Aston, William George, 74

Bālz, Erwin von, 6, 12, 79, 98, 144, 191

Chinese Learning, also see Confucianism, 66, 69

Christian, Christianity, xxiii, 22, 24, 32, 36–42, 46–51, 53, 56, 60–1, 63, 70, 77, 80, 87, 89, 92, 138, 147–8, 156, 166, 179, 188, 192, 271, 282, 333, 361–2 endnote 1
Civilisation and Enlightenment Movement, 10–11
Confucian, Confucianism, xix–xxi, 3, 31, 65–6, 126, 158–60, 167, 192, 251, 253–4, 258, 266–8, 291, 302–4, 327, 354–5 endnote 3, 359–60 endnote 4, 362–3 endnote 2, 393–4 endnote 13

Deguchi Onisaburō, 149–50
Denitz, W., 5
Doi Takeo, 319

Ebina Danjō, 48–51, 82, 89, 107, 252
Egami Namio, xxix, 187, 287, 312, 313, 314, 345
Emishi, xvii, 5, 9, 28, 69, 72, 76, 77, 79, 84, 100, 111, 123, 132, 135, 137, 138, 145, 146, 154, 155, 161, 164, 209, 211, 213, 227, 230, 231, 246–7, 286, 306
Ezo (also see *Ainu* and Emishi), 4, 22, 47, 59, 154–5, 231

Family State, 31, 35, 113, 115, 118–21, 123, 169–70, 287, 298, 321, 332, 336–41, 370 endnote 15, 393–4 endnote 13
France, Anatole, 179, 267
Franklin, Benjamin, xxxi–xxxii
Fujioka Katsuji, 90
Fujitani Toshio, 312, 315
Fukuoka Yasunori, xxix, 323, 325, 339, 342
Fukuzawa Yukichi, 16–17, 37–8, 143–4
Furuhata Tanemoto, 226–7, 233, 289
Furukawa Kanehide, 210–1
Furuya Eiichi, 213–5, 219
Furuya Yoshio, 217–9, 222, 224, 226, 233

Godaigo, Emperor, 256
Gordon, Milton, xxxiv, 325
Gotō Morikazu, 311
Gotō Shinpei, 244, 387 endnote 4
Government-General (Governor-General) of Korea, 40, 49, 54–5, 95, 101, 126–7, 142, 205–6, 208–16, 218, 221, 224–5, 228, 262, 285, 288, 295, 338, 365 endnote 1, 389 endnote 1
Government-General of Taiwan, 50–1, 54, 206, 244, 365 endnote 1

Hasebe Kotondo, 226–36, 245, 265–6, 305–9, 311–2, 314
Hasegawa Nyozekan, 132
Hatoyama Ichirō, 216

Hayakawa Jirō, 236
Hayashi Fusao, 243–4
Hayashi Hōmei, 24
Hayato, 77, 79, 83, 123, 132, 146, 161, 211
Hegel, 21, 270, 274, 278–9
Heine, Heinrich, 179
Hiraga Gennai, 158
Hiraizumi, 100, 215
Hiraizumi Kiyoshi, 104
Hirata Atsutane, 283, 291, 304
Hiratsuka Raiteu (Raichō), 167
Hokkaido Former Aborigines Protection Act, xvi, 35, 58, 151, 342, 363 endnote 5
Hōryūji Temple, 78, 261–2, 265
Hoshi Tōru, 151
Hoshino Hisashi, 66–9, 73–5, 80, 86
Hozumi Yatsuka, 33, 35–7, 39–40, 42, 47–48, 90, 110, 112–3, 178–9, 207, 238, 332

I Kuangsu, 213, 381 endnote 16
Ifa Fuyū, 130–1, 168
Iha Fuyū see Ifa Fuyū
Imperial Rescript on Education, xvi, xx–xxi, 17, 32–3, 35, 38, 359–60 endnote 4
Imperial View of History, xxxiii, 104, 299, 308–9, 311
Inoue Enryō, 21
Inoue Kakugorō, 24
Inoue Kiyoshi, 310, 312
Inoue Kowashi, 33
Inoue Mitsuru, 82
Inoue Tetsujirō, 17–18, 21–6, 29–30, 33–6, 38–9, 41,

45, 48, 50–1, 56–7, 63, 69, 71, 90–2, 108–10, 114, 118, 148, 187–9, 201, 237, 261, 267, 271, 289, 334–5, 369 endnote 1
Inukai Tsuyoshi, 96
Ishihara Kanji see Ishiwara Kanji
Ishihara Shintarō, 317, 346
Ishii Shirō, 227
Ishikawa Sanshirō, 150, 254
Ishimoda Shō, 313
Ishiwara Kanji, 115, 286
Itō Hirobumi, 89, 327
Iwakura Tomomi, 66
Izawa Shūji, 50–1
Izumo, region and nation, xvii, 67, 73, 76, 82, 87, 91, 101, 114, 137, 209, 211, 239, 241–3, 245, 263, 293, 355–6 endnote 4, 364 endnote 15, 371 endnote 7

Jellinek, Georg, 115
Jingū, Empress, xvii, 28, 47, 65, 67, 69–70, 73, 76, 82, 82–5, 97, 104, 123, 126, 135–6, 148, 169, 213, 246, 258, 311, 364 endnote 17, 372 endnote 16

Kakei Katsuhiko, 111
Kamishima Jirō, 319–20, 392 endnote 26
Kanazawa Shōzaburō, 74–5, 82, 84–6, 131, 239, 289
Kangaku see Chinese Learning
Kano Masanao, xxxvi
Kanmu, Emperor, 28, 47, 67, 76, 84, 97–8, 104, 123, 126, 135, 213, 364 endnote 17
Kanokogi Kazunobu, 115–6, 118
Katō Genchi, 114
Katō Hiroyuki, 15, 33, 47–51, 56, 77, 90, 110–1, 143
Katsube Mitake, 260
Katsura Tarō, 254
Kawakami Hajime, 205–7
Kiki Myths, xvii, xx–xxi, xxiii, 4, 28, 31, 53, 65–7, 70, 73, 75, 82, 97, 100–1, 111, 130, 135, 137, 145, 148, 150–1, 157, 211, 227, 234, 236–7, 239–41, 243–8, 251–4, 258–9, 262, 266–7, 269, 279, 293–4, 299, 302–3, 306, 310–2, 314, 345, 355–6 endnote 4, 366 endnote 13
Kim Talsu, 314, 344
Kimura Takatarō, 39, 44–5, 147–8, 154
Kindaichi Kyōsuke, 85, 152–5, 374 endnote 14
Kita Ikki, 46–7, 127–8, 140
Kita Noriaki, 215
Kita Sadakichi, 83, 86–7, 95–109, 118–9, 122, 126–7, 129, 132, 142, 155, 161–2, 176–8, 180, 202, 210, 240, 242, 247, 252, 254, 262, 288, 313, 336, 345, 351 endnote 7
Kiuchi Sekitei, 4
Kiyohara Sadao, 123
Kiyono Kenji, 226–9, 233–6, 244–5, 262, 278–9, 286, 295, 308–11, 333

Koganei Yoshikiyo, 8, 47, 55, 59, 75, 114
Koizumi Shinzō, 317
Kojiki, also see Kiki myths, xx, 4, 53, 72, 75, 150, 157, 242, 245–6, 254, 258, 266, 291, 294, 355–6 endnote 4
Kokugaku see Nativism
Kokutai, kokutairon see National Polity
Komatsu Midori, 126
Kōmpfer, Engelbert, 144
Koshiro Shūichi, 309
Kōtoku Shūsui, 150, 254, 259
Kumaso, xvii, 5, 65, 67, 120, 135, 137–8, 209, 211, 213, 230, 238–9, 241–3, 246, 311
Kume Kunitake, 66, 69–74, 77–80, 84, 86, 132, 149, 17–8, 188, 248, 258, 263–4, 266, 286
Kurashima Itaru, 212
Kuroita Katsumi, 251
Kurokawa Mayori, 8–9, 11–12, 14, 29, 132, 234
Kyōiku Chokugo, see Imperial Rescript on Education

Liaotung Peninsula, 54–5, 238
Liberty and People's Rights Movement, 10–11, 31, 78, 359–60 endnote 4, 361–2 endnote 1

Maeda Hajime, 318–9
Manchukuo see Manchuria
Manchuria, 13, 48–9, 54–5, 76, 108, 139, 148, 154, 182, 215, 222, 238, 244, 248, 257, 285–6, 307, 327, 389 endnote 1
Manchurian Incident, xvi, 115, 154, 156, 257, 285
March First Independence Movement, 86, 96, 101, 118, 125–8, 175, 178, 189
Maruyama Masao, 293
Masuda Yoshio, 318
Milne, John, 5
Mimana, 84
Minakata Kumakusu, 186
Minami Jirō, 208, 210, 212, 214, 262, 338
Minamoto-no-Yoritomo, 153, 177,
Minamoto-no-Yoshitsune, 153–4, 374 endnote 14
Minoda Kyōki, 292–3, 295
Mishima Atsuo, 149
Mishima Yukio, 304, 317
Mita Minesuke, xxxvi, 352–3 endnote 12
Miyake Setsurei, 24, 144–5
Miyake Yonekichi, 74
Miyazawa Kenji, 150–1, 374 endnote 12
Mochiji Mutsusaburō, 51
Mori Ōgai, 146
Morse, Edward S., 3–5, 8–9, 12–13, 15, 74
Motoori Norinaga, 65, 68–9, 157–9, 251, 258–9, 266–8, 270, 291, 304, 354–5 endnote 3
Mozume Takami, 111–2, 250

Nagai Hisomu, 216–7, 226, 228
Nagai Tōru, 110, 288
Nagayo Matarō, 229
Naitō Chisō, 9, 14, 18, 29

Naitō Konan, 83, 237, 262
Nakane Chie, 317–8
Nakano Seigō, 125, 129–30
Nakasone Yasuhiro, 304, 344–6
Nakayama Satoru, 140–2, 214
Naora Shinobu, 305–6, 308
National Learning see Nativism
National Polity (*kokutai*), National Polity Theory, xx, xxxiv–xxxv, 9, 15, 17, 25–6, 31–3, 35, 37–8, 40–2, 44–50, 53, 56, 63–4, 66, 68–9, 80, 90, 110–24, 132, 138, 143, 162, 165, 191, 204, 211, 213, 219, 238, 248, 250–1, 254, 260, 269–70, 286, 288, 292, 294, 305, 336, 351–2 endnote 10, 362–3 endnote 2, 369 endnote 1
Nativism, nativist, xix–xxi, 8–9, 14, 18, 33, 51, 65–6, 68–9, 73, 80, 122, 156, 158–9, 167, 251–2, 258, 267, 283, 291, 303–4, 351–2 endnote 10, 354–5 endnote 3, 358–9 endnote 2, 362–3 endnote 2, 375 endnote 1
Nezu Masashi, 253–6, 309–10
Nietzsche, F., 261, 267, 270–1, 278
Nihon shoki also see Kiki myths, xx, 4, 53, 66, 72, 75, 84, 157, 245–6, 258, 262, 294, 355–6 endnote 4
Nintoku, Emperor, 83
Nishida Kitarō, 286, 332
Nishimura Shinji, 161, 287, 289

Nitobe Inazō, 92, 138, 195, 203, 206
Nori Toshio, 82

Odaka Tomoo, 211
Ogino Yoshiyuki, 84
Oka Masao, 287
Ōkawa Shūmei, 154, 286, 295, 389–90 endnote 3
Ōkuma Shigenobu, 78–80, 83–4, 87–90, 262, 328
Ōkuninushi, xvii, 73, 148, 162–3, 355–6 endnote 4
Ōnishi Hajime, 40–1
Ono Azusa, 8, 14
Ōnuma Yasuaki, xxix
Orientalism, xix, xxxvi, 11, 180, 352–3 endnote 12
Orikuchi Shinobu, 287–8
Ōshima Masanori, 119
Ōya Tōru, 74
Oyabe Zen'ichirō, 151–5

Peace Preservation Law, 124, 351–2 endnote 10
Pekche, 28, 67, 136, 213, 361 endnote 17

Rousseau, Jean Jacques, 21, 269

Sakai Katsugun, 149
Sakai Toshihiko, 150
Sakanoue-no-Tamuramaro, 28, 47, 84, 108, 122, 135, 137, 246, 364 endnote 17
Sano Manabu, 132, 313
Sasagawa Shigerō, 87
Satō Tetsutarō, 117–8
Satomi Kishio, 116–8
Sawayanagi Masatarō, 88

Shiga Shigetaka, 24
Shiga Yoshio, 313
Shigeno Yasutsugu, 66
Shimamura Hisashi, 151
Shimamura Hōgetsu, 90
Shimomura Hiroshi (Kainan), 215, 288
Shimota Seiji, 314
Shinmura Izuru, 109, 146, 240
Shinsen Shōjiroku, xxix, 24, 83, 97, 114, 121, 123, 161–2, 164–5, 212–3, 215, 246, 311, 324
Shiratori Kiyoshi, 289–90
Shiratori Kurakichi, 87, 237–45, 247–50, 252, 257–9, 263, 265, 279, 289, 386 endnote 1, 387 endnote 2, 387 endnote 3
Shirayanagi Shūko, 288
Shōtoku Taishi, 261
Siebold, Heinrich Phillip von, 4, 8
Siebold, Phillip Franz von, 4–5, 8, 153
Silla, 28, 67–8, 73, 82, 85, 123, 136, 146, 246, 361 endnote 17
South Manchuria Railway Company, 244
Susano-O, Susano-O-no-Mikoto, xvii, 65, 67, 73, 83, 147, 154, 240, 246, 344, 365 endnote 15
Suzuki Takeki, 314

Tachibana Shiraki, 286
Tacitus, Publius Cornelius, 178–9
Taguchi Ukichi, 17–22, 24–30, 37, 51, 78, 107, 144–7, 149, 241, 289, 352–3 endnote 12, 364 endnote 17
Takahashi Jirō, 74
Takahashi Sadaki, 103, 131–2, 191, 313
Takahashi Yoshio, 143
Takamagahara, 4–5, 47, 51, 98, 101, 104, 148, 150, 154, 216, 231, 241, 243, 245, 310, 355–6 endnote 4, 374 endnote 12
Takamure Itsue, xxi, 76, 132, 150–1, 156–71, 254, 266, 268, 333, 375 endnote 1
Takata Yasuma, 286–7
Takayama Chogyū, 41–4, 46, 50, 111, 207, 247
Takegoshi Yosaburō, 47, 75–7, 80, 88, 91, 149, 154
Tanaka Chigaku, 115–6, 150–1, 374 endnote 12
Tani Tateki, 24
Tanigawa Tetsuzō, 289–90
Taniguchi Konen, 288
Tanizaki Jun'ichirō, 261, 388 endnote 1
Tatebe Tongo, 114–5
Taut, Bruno, 6
Tayama Katai, 176
Thoreau, Henry David, 158–9
Tō Teikan, 65, 68, 266
Tōgō Makoto, 206–7, 244
Tojō Hideki, 224
Tokumasa Kingo, 149
Tokutomi Sohō, 24, 28, 70, 75, 78, 80, 138, 166, 285, 288–9, 296, 312, 371 endnote 5
Tōma Seita, 311, 313, 315
Tomizu Hirondo, 84, 88
Torii Ryūzō, 8, 13, 54–5, 77, 85–6, 114, 126–7, 129–32,

199, 212, 225, 227–8, 265–6, 289, 311, 371 endnote 4, 371 endnote 7
Tōyama Mitsuru, 154
Toyotomi Hideyoshi, 49, 68
Tsuboi Shōgorō, 7–9, 12–5, 45–7, 52–63, 75, 80, 82, 85–6, 88, 103, 107, 119, 127, 147, 152, 365–6 endnote 7, 377 endnote 2
Tsuchigumo, xvii, 5, 72, 111, 132, 230, 246, 355–6 endnote 4
Tsuda Sōkichi, 72, 137–8, 237, 239, 243–60, 262–3, 265–6, 268, 270–1, 279, 284, 291–5, 299–302, 304–5, 307, 310–2, 316–7, 319, 329, 343, 356–7 endnote 7, 386 endnote 1, 387 endnote 7, 387 endnote 8, 387 endnote 9
Tsuda Tsuyoshi, 211–2
Tsurumi Yūsuke, 235, 244

Uchida Ginzō, 84, 288
Uchimura Kanzō, 38–9, 49–50, 60–1, 63, 138, 151, 195
Ueda Jōkichi, 212, 228–9, 309
Uesugi Shinkichi, 113–4
Ukita Kazutami, 49–50, 87–9, 364–5 endnote 18, 365 endnote 20
Umehara Takeshi, 344–5
Unno Kōtoku, 87, 204–5
Ural-Altaic family of languages, 241, 257, 387 endnote 4

Watanabe Yoshimichi, 132

Watari Shōzaburō, 121–4, 252, 336, 370 endnote 17
Watase Tsunekichi, 39–41, 48–50
Watsuji Tetsurō, xx, xxxv, 72, 151, 235, 237, 260–84, 289–90, 294–5, 301–5, 307, 317, 319, 329, 333, 343, 345, 386 endnote 1, 388 endnote 1, 391 endnote 2
Weber, Max, xxxi, xxxvi, 352–3 endnote 12

Yagi Shōzaburō, 46
Yamada Saburō, 85
Yamaji Aizan, 76–7, 80, 97, 263, 367 endnote 12
Yamamoto Shichihei, 319
Yamanaka Hayato, xxxvi
Yamato, region and people, xvii, xxvii, 44, 49, 51, 67, 77, 85, 104, 126, 129, 133–5, 210–3, 215, 220, 224–5, 230, 238, 241, 243, 285–7, 320
Yamato Takeru-no-Mikoto, 5, 135, 246,
Yanagi Muneyoshi, 203
Yanagita Kunio, xxii, xxxv, 72, 97, 138–9, 175–202, 250, 254, 260, 267–8, 272, 283, 287, 312, 314, 319, 329, 334, 376–7 endnote 1, 377–9
Yanaihara Tadao, 203, 206
Yasuda Yojūrō, 213, 381 endnote 16
Yokoyama Gennosuke, 16–7
Yokoyama Yoshikiyo, 8
Yoshida Kumaji, 120

Yoshida Tōgo, 69, 84, 86, 367
    endnote 5
Yoshino Sakuzō, 125–7, 203
Yumoto Takehiko, 44

Zenkunen and Gosannen
    Battles, 100, 105, 155,
    177, 215